WITHDRAWN
UTSA Libraries

Joint International Business Ventures

Joint International

Edited by

and

COLUMBIA UNIVERSITY PRESS

Business Ventures

WOLFGANG G. FRIEDMANN

GEORGE KALMANOFF

New York and London

Copyright © 1961, Columbia University Press, New York and London
Library of Congress Catalog Card Number: 61-7173
Printed in the United States of America
ISBN: 0-231-02465-7

9 8 7 6 5 4 3 2

Preface

THE PRESENT BOOK is the product of a four-year research project directed by the undersigned on behalf of Columbia University. Although conducted under the auspices of the Law School, as part of its International Legal Studies Program, it is essentially a study of a vital aspect of contemporary international relations. The problem of partnership between the developed and the less developed countries, in investment and other aspects of economic development, obviously involves an intricate mixture of political, economic, managerial, and legal problems. Hence, we have sought and obtained the cooperation of government officials, economists, businessmen, and lawyers. The project has been a sustained effort in collaboration between those concerned in the industrially developed countries and their counterparts in less developed countries. The direction of the project from an American university accounts in part for the preponderance of contacts with United States government departments and business enterprises. But we have had the active cooperation of public authorities and business enterprises in Great Britain, Italy, West Germany, and other countries.

The materials used and analyzed in the study derive largely from twelve individual country studies, mostly of economically less developed countries but also including some which are both recipients and exporters of industrial skill and capital. These studies, though not published as books, have been widely circulated among international agencies, government departments, business firms, lawyers, and universities. Under the general supervision of the editors of this book the studies have in most cases been prepared by nationals of the countries concerned. This method not only has insured a balance of approach between the sometimes divergent viewpoints of capital-exporting and capital-importing countries, it has also been a modest experiment in international collaboration and, it is hoped, has made a small contribution to better understanding between countries and persons of widely divergent background and experience.

The country studies were developed on the basis of information furnished by government agencies and business enterprises in the respective countries. In addition, invaluable assistance was received in discussions with United States and foreign government agencies, public international organizations, and investing companies in the capital-exporting countries. The agencies and firms that cooperated are far too numerous to mention individually, but this omission does not make their participation any less crucial to the final product. The specific organizations and firms mentioned throughout the book will indicate the vast extent of our indebtedness.

The importance of collaboration between the various groups and countries was symbolized by a three-day conference held at Arden House, Harriman, New York, in March, 1960. The conference was attended by some fifty senior business executives, public officials, and university professors, each closely acquainted with the project, and representing in approximately equal proportions governments and business enterprises of some of the most important capital-importing countries, leading United States and European firms engaged in joint ventures in less developed countries, United States and international public agencies, and institutions of higher learning. Drafts of most of the chapters of the present book were submitted and discussed in confidential sessions at the conference, and the editors greatly profited from the many constructive contributions made by the participants.

In the general organization and editing of the book, the editors have had the invaluable assistance of Professor Roy Blough, Professor of International Business, Columbia University. Apart from their individual written contributions, the following persons have also been actively associated with the project as a whole: Ervin O. Anderson, Financial Consultant, Washington, D.C.; Emile Benoit, Associate Professor of International Business, Columbia University; and Richard C. Pugh, member of the New York Bar.

The project was financed by a four-year grant from the Ford Foundation to Columbia University, and is evidence of the Foundation's abiding interest in problems of international economic development. I should like to express my particular gratitude to Mr. John B. Howard, Director, International Training and Research Program, and to Mr. H. C. L. Merillat, formerly of the Ford Foundation, for their help, both in the planning and in the execution of this project.

WOLFGANG G. FRIEDMANN
Professor of Law, and
Director, International Legal Research
Columbia University School of Law

New York
March, 1961

Contributors

ALTHOUGH THIS BOOK, like the project from which it results, has been a collaborative and collective effort, the authorship of the individual chapters in Part I should be credited as follows:

Chapter I	Wolfgang G. Friedmann
Chapter II	George Kalmanoff
Chapter III	George Kalmanoff
Chapter IV	George Kalmanoff
Chapter V	Emile Benoit
Chapter VI	George Kalmanoff
Chapter VII	Ervin O. Anderson (Governmental Policies) Richard C. Pugh (Private Law and Tax Factors) Wolfgang G. Friedmann (Anti-Trust Law) [1]
Chapter VIII	Wolfgang G. Friedmann

The authors of the preliminary country studies were as follows:

"Joint International Business Ventures in Colombia" (November, 1957) and Supplement (March, 1959):
George Kalmanoff, Economic Consultant

"Joint International Business Ventures in Cuba" (July, 1958):
Philip C. Newman, Economic Consultant

"Joint International Business Ventures in The Philippines" (September, 1958):

The following members of the Social Economy Association of The Philippines:

[1] In substance this section corresponds to an article published in *The Columbia Law Review*, LX (June, 1960), 780–91, by agreement among the author, the publisher, and the Columbia Law Review Association, Inc.

Joachim Ahrensdorf
Quirico Camus, Jr.
Amado Castro
Armand Fabella
Benito Legarda, Jr.
Thomas R. McHale
Sixto K. Roxas

and the following accountants:

Arturo Monzón
Juan Díaz, Jr.
Francisco de Guzmán, Jr.
Generoso Villanueva, Jr.

"Joint International Business Ventures in the Union of Burma" (February, 1959):

Tun Thin, Alternate Executive Director, International Monetary Fund; formerly Director of Research and Chairman, Department of Economics, University of Rangoon
William Paw, Chairman, Department of Commerce and Administrative Studies, University of Rangoon,

assisted by the following members of the Department:

U Kin Maung Kyi
U Tin Nyunt
U Tin Lwin
U Sein Maung
U Maung Maung
U Sa

and

U Than Aung, Advocate
U Tin Htut, Head, Department of Commerce, University of Mandalay

"Joint International Business Ventures in Mexico" (February, 1959):

George Kalmanoff, Economic Consultant
Benjamín K. Retchkiman, Subdirector General de Comercio de la Secretaría de Industria y Comercio, Federal Government of Mexico

"Japan's Foreign Investments and Joint Ventures Abroad" (April, 1959):

Ervin O. Anderson, Financial Consultant

"Joint International Business Ventures in India" (May, 1959):

M. V. Pylee, Reader in Economic Administration, The Delhi School of Economics, University of Delhi

assisted by:

A. V. Alex
S. S. Moorthy
Suresh Kumar
Kashmir Singh

M. V. George
P. K. Kuriakose
J. I. Levinson, Attorney
S. P. Sinha

"Joint International Business Ventures in Turkey" (July, 1959):

Vakur Versan, Director, Institute of International Law and International Affairs, Istanbul University

assisted by:

Feridun Özgür, Acting Director of the Institute of Business Administration, University of Istanbul

Nezih Neyzi, Assistant Director, Institute of Business Administration, University of Istanbul

Ervin O. Anderson, Financial Consultant

"German Capital Exports and Joint Ventures in the Less Developed Countries" (July, 1959):

B. Orwin Ahlers

"Joint International Business Ventures in Pakistan" (September, 1959):

I. A. Mukhtar, Deputy Director, Institute of Public and Business Administration, University of Karachi

"Joint International Business Ventures in Brazil" (September, 1959):

José Garrido Torres, member of the National Economic Council of Brazil and editor of "Conjuntura Econômica"

Denio Nogueira, Director of the Finance Division of the National Economic Council of Brazil and assistant editor of "Conjuntura Econômica"

"Joint International Business Ventures with Italian Participation" (November, 1959):

Roberto Zaneletti, Research Office of the Confederazione Generale dell' Industria Italiana

Contents

Part I. General Analysis

Part II. Case Studies

PART I. *General Analysis*

I. Introduction: General Objectives and Scope

JOINT INTERNATIONAL business ventures in the less developed countries have become an important phenomenon of the postwar period. In these countries the attainment of political independence, or the desire to develop a purely agricultural or single commodity economy into a more diversified and potentially richer economic system, has, almost everywhere, led to ambitious plans for industrialization. The motives are in part economic: Rapidly rising populations will overcrowd the countryside in increasingly desperate conditions unless a substantial part of the population can be diverted to industrial employment. They are in part political: The ability to manufacture at least consumer goods and, to an increasing extent, basic industrial commodities such as steel, tractors, or chemical fertilizers, is seen as a hallmark of maturity, as well as a means of lessening economic—and, thereby, political and military—dependence on other countries. The extent of these programs varies with the resources and ambitions of the different economically underdeveloped countries, but the desire to develop the communications system, the basic utilities, at least some industrial goods and some weapons, is almost universal.

At the same time, ambition has often had the better of sober planning. Scarce foreign exchange has been expended for the importation of modern machinery, which has remained unused or has rapidly worn out because of lack of sufficiently trained personnel or the absence of a domestic market. Gradually, an increasing number of the industrially underdeveloped countries have come to modify—though certainly not to abandon—their goals or at least the methods by which to reach these goals. They have come to see that cooperation with industrially developed countries for the use of their capital, their resources, and their skill and experience is a more economic, and ultimately a quicker way of achieving industrialization than to "go it alone." On the other hand, these countries have not abandoned the basic ambition to attain national sovereignty, not only political but also economic. This implies keeping control, or at least general direction, over basic industries and, if possible, over the entire field of foreign investment. The result of these divergent desires and problems has been an increasing interest in some form of partnership association which permits the foreign investor to invest his capital, his know-how, and his managerial and technical skills, in a local enterprise, in association with national—public or private—interests.

There has been a corresponding evolution—more often by necessity than by desire—in the capital-exporting and industrially developed countries. Reluctantly in most cases, willingly in some, governments and entrepreneurs have come to realize that the days are gone or are rapidly passing when a United States or British or French corporation could direct its foreign operations (for example, in manufacturing abroad) without regard to the desires and interests of the host country. It is increasingly recognized that operating through local branches or even wholly owned subsidiaries does not give sufficient play for the development of true partnership. Every year brings more examples of enterprises, originally wholly owned by American, British, or French interests, converting to joint ownership with national interests. At the same time, many new enterprises being established in economically underdeveloped countries are, from the beginning, jointly owned.

The desirability of joint international business ventures in the less developed countries is recognized. What then are the objectives of this study? There is, of course, the general objective of conveying information. The joint international business venture is a significant social institution which needs to be better understood as part of our understanding of the world and the way it works.

The need to study joint international business ventures is not, however, limited to the scholarly interest in information. It is a need that is specific and urgent. A very great interest is evidenced by members of the various groups concerned. Joint ventures raise many questions, the answers to which will have a bearing on the attitudes, policies, and practices of the interested parties. These may be business enterprises in the industrially advanced or capital-exporting countries, governments of the host countries, investors and business interests in the host countries, and governments of the capital-exporting countries. Each of the parties has special legitimate interests and a particular point of view. Cooperation is needed if joint international business ventures are to be possible. The international flow of capital is dependent upon at least acquiescence by both the capital-exporting and the host governments.

The basic problems of joint ventures arise from a mixture of harmonies and conflicts of interest. Today it is generally recognized that there is basic harmony among the various parties in their desire to promote the development of the less developed countries and to increase the productivity of their peoples. On the other hand, basic conflicts are inevitable, as they are in economic relations everywhere, with respect to the division of the increased output. Real conflicts may also arise with respect to the control of the business and the policies of its operation.

Joint international business ventures have emerged as a possible technique for reducing conflicts and promoting harmony. It is too much to hope that any single technique will eliminate conflicts altogether; the central question is rather whether the joint international business venture shows promise of lessening the conflicts and producing a greater degree of cooperation than can be anticipated from available or conceivable alternatives.

Definition of "Joint Ventures"

The central concept in the joint international business venture is that of partnership. Partnership has two sides—technical and emotional. On the technical side, it is a joining of contributions; on the emotional side, it is a feeling of united or cooperative effort. In either sense of the word, it is possible to achieve some degree of international partnership in any form of enterprise, however owned or controlled. The creation of local sources of supply, the training and employment of local labor and managerial staff, and the stimulation of "demonstration effects" on the business community at large are a few examples of the possible ways of achieving partnership.

It stands to reason that some forms of organization and relationship will work better than others in promoting partnership. This study deals only with certain forms which are designated as "joint international business ventures." In the widest sense, the "joint venture" comprises any form of association which implies collaboration for more than a very transitory period. It excludes pure trading operations. Associations that do imply a degree of partnership may range from a long-term construction job, in which the industrialized country supplies the machinery, the leading personnel, technical assistance, and, in some cases, long-term loans (often backed by government guarantees), and the recipient country supplies the land, the labor, some of the materials, and the administrative conditions for the development of the enterprise, to equity partnerships in the narrower sense. Such partnerships show a great variety of patterns. There may be "50-50" partnerships, in which the local investor—public or private—holds one-half of the shares, and the foreign investor, the other half. There may be equity associations in which one partner holds a majority (though often only 51 percent of the shares) and the other partner the minority. An existing enterprise may be transformed into a joint venture with the foreign investor retaining a controlling interest, while the minority shares are held by the local government or a government-controlled development corporation, a small group of local capitalists, or the public. National investment laws or policies, especially in the field of basic raw materials, public utilities, and basic industries sometimes will hold the foreign investor to a minority participation. All these alternatives and their pros and cons in various circumstances are dealt with in this study.

Legal Aspects

Joint ventures, especially in the less developed countries, are beset with three major legal problems. There is, first, the question of what form of organization to choose for a joint venture in a specific country. Even within the common law world, there are certain important differences (such as the institution of the private company in the countries of the British Commonwealth, not paralleled in the United States). As between the common law and the civil law world, there are also substantial differences.

There are multitudes of special investment laws and regulations which may limit the participation of foreigners in certain industries deemed to be of vital national interest.

There are many kinds of regulations that affect foreign investment directly or indirectly. Hardly any of the economically underdeveloped countries is in a position to afford free transfer of currencies or to leave imports from abroad entirely unregulated. On the other hand, a joint venture designed to start a vital manufacture, for example, of Diesel tractors or trucks, may lead to special privileges granted in the form of concessions, instruments of approval, or written agreements. Such special conditions may, either through a general regulation or through a special arrangement, confer tax privileges, preferential rates for the exchange of local for foreign currency, import privileges, and the like.

These various legal aspects are so important and so complex that they have formed the subject of a special volume issued in conjunction with the present project.[1] In this symposium, forty country studies and a comparative analysis survey the relevant corporation and investment laws of a like number of individual countries. While reference must be made to that volume for detailed information and analysis of these aspects of joint ventures a brief survey of the different possible forms of corporate organization is given in the present volume, with special emphasis on the problems of legal control. It has also been found necessary to devote a special section here to the tax aspects of joint ventures, which often are a crucial factor in the investment decision. How far do tax considerations, at home and abroad, affect the form, the control, and the financing of a joint venture? Another aspect of special interest, although predominantly to the United States investor, is the impact of anti-trust laws, to which a short special section is also devoted.

[1] *Legal Aspects of Foreign Investment,* Wolfgang Friedmann, R. C. Pugh (editors), Boston: Little, Brown & Co., 1959.

Management and Labor Problems

A discussion of only the legal and organizational aspects of joint ventures would leave out essential elements. Joint international business ventures are experiments not only in financial partnership, but also, perhaps even more importantly, in technical and human cooperation between countries and people often separated by deep divergencies of tradition, training, and outlook. Hence our case studies have devoted considerable attention to the managerial and human aspects of cooperation: the relations between foreign managerial and technical executives and local labor; the relationship established between foreign private investors and local public authorities; the adaptability of local personnel to new methods and processes, and the wider aspects of the training in skills and responsibilities of this personnel, which in many cases will eventually replace all foreign personnel, even at the top level. This leads to the crucially important question of the extent to which joint ventures with foreign firms are looked upon by both the government and the private entrepreneurs of the economically underdeveloped country and the foreign entrepreneur as a transitory or intermediate stage between the formerly completely foreign control of finance and industry and the stage at which foreign participation, on the financial as well as the managerial and technical levels, may become altogether redundant.

The Role of Government

Joint manufacturing ventures between industrially developed countries, such as the United States and the Netherlands, Britain and Italy, West Germany and France, Sweden and Canada, can be, and overwhelmingly are, conducted between private entrepreneurs, since all these countries have comparable levels, methods, and experience in the field of private enterprise. They need no government participation, except insofar as currency regulations, labor laws, and other matters of public and social concern are subject to government control. It is far different in the great majority of economically underdeveloped countries. The government of necessity plays a major role. This is partly inherent in the strongly political character of industrial development plans. It is also often dictated by the initial poverty of local private venture capital, or the unreliability and the speculative character of such capital as is available. This may well be a transitory phenomenon, but the period of transition in which we live is assuredly long and important enough to require a consideration of the role of government. It is not a question of which economic system we prefer, but of a sober appraisal of realities. Any study professing to examine the whole joint ventures problem would be seriously deficient if it did not include joint public-private ventures.

The direct participation of governments or government-controlled institutions in partnership with foreign investors, while significant, is not the most important part played in joint ventures by the governments of the countries of investment. Of far greater impact are the policy-directing functions of governments, which express themselves in basic policies toward foreign investment and joint ventures—whether or not laid down in formal laws. Such policies find many expressions, through allocations of raw materials, import quotas, currency regulations, negotiations on the purchase of land for factory sites, remission of earnings for foreign personnel to their home country, labor permits and a multitude of other legal and administrative measures.

Hardly less important is the attitude of governments in capital-exporting countries. As a purely commercial proposition, many of the economically underdeveloped countries are attractive to the private investor from the industrialized country, in inverse proportion to their need and, in many cases, to the political importance of such investments. For the American investor, for example, the prospects of investment and joint ventures in such countries as Canada, Mexico, or those of Western Europe are generally more attractive than investments in India or Indonesia or in some of the Latin-American countries. In order to stimulate investment in such countries, without undue risk to the investor, various governments have developed guarantee schemes, such as those of the United States and, more recently, of West Germany. The schemes deserve some consideration insofar as they may produce or promote joint ventures.

The public element also comes in through the important part played more and more by public international agencies such as the World Bank and the International Finance Corporation, to which the newly established Inter-American Development Bank and International Development Association are being added. These are supplemented by public national credit institutions such as the Export-Import Banks of the United States and Japan or the Development Loan Fund of the United States, the British Colonial Development Corporation, and others.

For all these reasons, special consideration is given in our study to the principles and impacts of governmental policies, in both capital-importing and capital-exporting countries, as well as to the role of public international institutions in joint ventures.

Plan of the Study

The foregoing brief introductory observations indicate the pattern of this book. The present volume is the final product of a four-year study. Its interim products, supplying the bulk of the material analyzed in this volume, have been twelve country studies, varying in length from 100 to 200 pages each and, in the great majority of cases, prepared by a small group of nationals, under the plan prepared by the director and revised by the "headquarters" group.[2] The studies covered a number of countries in different parts of the world in various stages of development. All of them can be described as economically underdeveloped, except Italy, Japan, and West Germany, highly industrialized and scientifically advanced countries, which, after the Second World War, found themselves in a position different from that of the majority of the Western countries, and had to reorganize their foreign trade and investment policy. The country studies generally follow the pattern of first

[2] The countries dealt with in the twelve special studies are: Brazil, Burma, Colombia, Cuba, India, Italy, Japan, Mexico, Pakistan, the Philippines, Turkey, and West Germany. The study of Cuba was completed before the advent of the revolutionary regime at the beginning of 1959, and has been rendered largely obsolete by subsequent events there.

giving the general background, the historical, economic, and legal conditions for foreign investment, and then a specific study of joint ventures. The greatest amount of effort went into the selective case studies of specific joint ventures. The most detailed and important of these are collected in the present volume. They are selected to illustrate not only differences in the experiences, problems, and prospects of joint ventures as they arise between one country and another, but also different patterns of ownership and distribution of equities as they vary for specific types of industries. The problem of a joint venture is, for example, a vastly different one in the case of a mass-manufactured standard product and a heavy engineering project. Again, legal and administrative conditions often differ for a joint venture in a basic industry such as steel, and a consumer product such as margarine or pharmaceuticals. The cases reproduced in Part II include a number of significant joint ventures between public authorities and private investors. They also include some cases of multinational joint ventures, a form that is likely to increase in significance as the present attempts to coordinate and pool the resources of the major Western industrial countries in regard to foreign investment progress come to be consolidated.

After an assessment of the global economic significance of direct foreign investments, and of joint ventures as a special aspect of foreign investment the central part of the study gives a comparative analysis of the existence, types, and operations of joint international business ventures. This includes in a separate chapter a survey of joint ventures by countries and different types of industries and products. A succeeding chapter analyzes types of joint ventures by various characteristics: the nature of the parties associating; majority versus minority holdings by the foreign investor; non-equity types of joint ventures; and public agencies as partners in joint ventures.

Another chapter is devoted to a study of the attitudes toward joint ventures of participants or potential participants, especially those from the capital-exporting countries. This is a field in which definite conclusions are particularly difficult, since so much depends on personal inclinations and on accidental factors. However, the materials gathered from hundreds of cases as well as from numerous interviews with executives in charge of these operations permit some conclusions on the attitudes and motivations underlying joint venture decisions.

Another chapter is concerned with the internal operation of joint ventures, including the problems of direction, management, technical control, and the whole field of relationships between foreigners and nationals in such enterprises, as well as operations with governments as partners. This is followed by a study of the more specifically legal factors affecting joint ventures. In the field of public law this includes a study of the legal and administrative attitudes of governments and international public agencies, as well as of tax and antitrust law aspects. In the private law field, the study concentrates on a survey of the legal forms available for joint venture investment.

The final chapter attempts a frank and objective evaluation of both the achievements and the failures of joint venture experiments in international business relations and of the prospects of this form of international partnership as a major factor in the transformation of these relations in the foreseeable future. Although the many materials and cases assembled in the course of our studies do not claim to be exhaustive, they appear to be sufficiently representative of the different types and problems of joint ventures to permit certain conclusions. These, it is hoped, will be of help to international credit institutions, to governments both of capital-exporting and capital-importing countries, and to private enterprises.

II. Quantitative Importance

AS AN INTRODUCTION to the findings reported in subsequent chapters on the nature and manner of operation of joint international business ventures in the less developed countries, some global quantitative data are presented here to indicate the importance these ventures have assumed in the total of foreign investments. These indications are not statistically complete because of the difficulties inherent in the gathering of comprehensive data on international capital movements and foreign investments.[1] But they do permit some appreciation of the extent to which this form of foreign investment has taken hold in the less developed countries.

Joint ventures in the form of joint equity investments in enterprises in the less developed countries by nationals or companies from the industrialized or capital-exporting countries together with nationals or companies from the capital-receiving countries themselves are given the main emphasis in our study. The quantitative data presented in this chapter concentrate on this type of joint venture, although some consideration is also given to the extent to which our investigations uncovered instances of non-equity joint ventures in the less developed countries. As background for these findings, consideration is given first to the general nature of international long-term capital movements in the postwar period and the extent to

[1] These difficulties are amply illustrated in various recent studies by international agencies: United Nations, Department of Economic and Social Affairs, *The International Flow of Private Capital 1956–1958*, New York: 1959; and International Bank for Reconstruction and Development, Economic Staff, Dragoslav Avramovic, *Debt Servicing Capacity & Postwar Growth in International Indebtedness*, Baltimore: The Johns Hopkins Press, 1958.

which the less developed countries have been the recipients of capital from abroad.

International Long-Term Capital Movements

International long-term capital movements during the decade 1946–55 were marked by certain well-defined tendencies.[2] During the first half of the period, the movements were very large and were dominated by the massive United States public aid for the reconstruction of war-devastated Europe. As this program tapered off, the total of the capital movements also declined and their direction shifted. Public grants and loans to the less developed countries, which had been extended during the first half of the decade, accelerated during the second half, and by the end of the period non-European countries were the major recipients of the public funds. Private capital exports proceeded, mainly in the form of direct investments, although they constituted a minor part of the total compared to the movement of public funds. The private capital exports started at a low level, but tended to rise during the decade. They were directed to extractive industries, such as petroleum and plantation agriculture, and manufacturing, and the principal recipient countries were Canada, petroleum areas in the Middle East, and some of the larger countries of Latin America.

During the first half of the decade, 1946–50, the gross long-term international capital flow on public account amounted to a total of $43.8 billion, or an annual average of $8.8 billion. Of this amount, $30.8 billion, or an annual average of $6.2 billion, went to Western Europe.[3] United States private capital exports, which constituted the bulk of all private capital exports, covering new capital issues, net direct investment (including reinvestment by subsidiaries), and net transactions in outstanding securities and in medium-term and long-term banking and commercial loans, amounted to a total of only $6.9 billion during the five years. Direct investments alone

[2] Cf. Avramovic, *Debt Servicing Capacity*.

[3] Austria, Belgium and Luxemburg, Denmark, Finland, France, West Germany, Greece, Iceland, Ireland, Italy, Netherlands, Norway, Portugal, Spain, Sweden, Switzerland, Turkey, United Kingdom, Yugoslavia.

accounted for $5.2 billion of the United States private capital exports.

The international flow of capital on public account declined to a total of $25.3 billion during the second half of the decade (1951–55), as aid to Western Europe fell to $11.1 billion. The annual average aid to Western Europe of $6.2 billion observed during the first half of the decade had fallen to only $1.4 billion by 1955.

At the same time, the public aid to areas outside of Europe and North America [4] increased from a total of $8.5 billion to $12.1 billion—about 50 percent. The annual average aid received by these countries of $1.7 billion in 1946–50 had risen to $2.9 billion by 1955 (out of a world total of $4.6 billion, and compared to the $1.4 billion for Western Europe).

United States private capital exports increased from $6.9 billion in 1946–50 to $9.1 billion in 1951–55.[5] Furthermore, during the second half of the decade private capital exports were effected in some appreciable magnitude by countries of Western Europe, principally the United Kingdom, Switzerland, France, Belgium and Luxembourg, the Netherlands, and, during the last few years of the period, West Germany. The total of private capital exports from these countries in 1951–55 amounted to $4.9 billion.[6]

Thus, international capital movements during the first postwar decade were dominated by loans and grants from and to public agencies. The figures cited for gross flows on public account come to a total of about $69 billion for the 10-year period, while those for private capital exports reached only some $21 billion.[7]

[4] Latin American Republics, the independent sterling area countries, European dependent territories in Africa and elsewhere, and Egypt, Iran, Israel, Lebanon, Syria, Sudan, Saudi Arabia, Ethiopia, Liberia, Thailand, Philippines, Indonesia, Japan, Korea, and China (Taiwan).

[5] These consisted mostly of direct investments ($7.3 billion).

[6] This sum should be taken as merely an indication of the general order of magnitude; the items making up the capital exports are not completely comparable; cf. Avramovic, *Debt Servicing Capacity*, pp. 10–11.

[7] The figures involve some double counting but not to the extent of changing the relative importance of financing from public and private sources. The "public account" figures, compiled from recipient government sources by staff of the International Bank for Reconstruction and Development, include $4.7 billion of governmental financial receipts from the private capital market,

Flows on public account to the less developed countries were also more important than private capital exports, but the disparity between the two was not as great as in the total of world capital movements. Based on the figures cited, the total of flows on public account to these countries amounted to about $21 billion during the decade. Of the total private capital exports to all countries, also amounting to an estimated $21 billion, perhaps half went to developed areas such as Canada, other countries of the British Commonwealth, and Western Europe. Thus, about $10–11 billion of the private capital exports went to the less developed countries. There is considerable difference in this respect within the less developed regions themselves, a point to which we return when we consider the nature of capital movements during more recent years: Private capital is much more important than public capital in Latin America and the Middle East, while the reverse is true in the less developed countries of Asia. This is a reflection of a number of factors: the attraction of private capital to the development of petroleum and other primary products resources; the investment of private capital in manufacturing industries where an economic base for further development already exists; and the concentration of public capital in areas closer to the frontiers of the cold war.

Since 1955 international capital movements have entered a new phase in response to the structural changes in the world economy.[8] The process of reconstruction of national economies prostrated by the war has been completed, and there is a greater concentration on the direction of capital to the less developed countries, at the same time that the sources of capital for these countries are widening. Western Europe in particular (a decade ago the largest recipient of foreign public capital), and countries such as Canada, Australia, and Japan are rapidly increasing their own ability to invest abroad. Private capital exports are gaining in importance relative to the flow of funds from public sources.

The flow of private capital from the main capital-exporting countries has averaged some $4 billion per year since 1955—twice

---

which in turn are also included in the private capital export figures, taken from sources in the capital-exporting countries.

[8] Cf. United Nations, *International Flow of Private Capital.*

the annual average maintained during the first postwar decade. This flow reached a peak of $5.7 billion in 1957. These figures include the retained profits of branches and subsidiaries abroad. About half the total, or some $2 billion per year including reinvested profits, has gone to the less developed countries, mostly as direct investments. The stepping up of private capital exports to the less developed countries (about twice the annual average of some $1 billion during the first postwar decade) has brought them to the point of being about equal to the volume of public aid to those countries.

The almost equal amount of private and public capital going to the less developed countries is an average that conceals the disparities among various groups of those countries. In fact, little private capital has been moving to the lowest-income countries in such areas as Africa, Asia, and the Far East, where the opportunities for internal development have been hampered by difficult economic and political conditions and where the possibilities of exploitation of natural resources are relatively limited; and the deficiencies of private capital arising from the very nature of these regions and their problems have had to be made up by public funds. Latin America, on the other hand, is the region in the less developed group that has been most favored by private investors, attracted by the existing evidence of development, profitable opportunities in extractive industries, and generally less disturbed political conditions. In 1957 the net inflow of long-term private capital into Latin America was slightly under $1.5 billion, compared to net receipts of long-term official capital of only about $130 million; in the same year, ten low-income countries of Asia [9] received less than $100 million of private long-term capital, while their net receipts of official funds, in both loans and grants, amounted to somewhat more than $600 million.

Joint Equity Ventures in United States Investments Abroad

It has been indicated that direct investments have constituted the bulk of postwar foreign investments of private capital. This is cer-

[9] Burma, Ceylon, Republic of China, Indonesia, India, Iraq, Pakistan, Philippines, Thailand, and the Republic of Viet-Nam.

tainly the case as far as investments in the less developed countries are concerned. Portfolio investments by private capital, so characteristic of the international capital movements during the 1920s, have once again assumed some importance, but these have not been investments, for the most part, in the less developed countries.[10]

The latest census of direct foreign investments of the United States covers the year 1957. Certain data compiled for the census, which are reproduced in Table 1, are useful in judging the extent to which joint ventures figure among direct investments. These data break down the total of United States direct investments on the basis of the percentage of United States ownership. The data do not necessarily relate only to joint ventures in the sense in which they are considered in our study, since some of the non-United States ownership may be by nationals of countries other than the country of investment. It is safe to assume that at least a substantial portion of the non-United States ownership is by nationals of the country of investment, and, therefore, that the data are significant in connection with our study.

Direct investments are defined by the United States government as those in which equity ownership by United States nationals is at least 25 percent. The figures to be quoted therefore exclude investments where the United States equity ownership is less than 25 percent. The excluded investments would not appreciably change the significance of the results.

The total value of United States direct foreign investments in all areas, according to the census of 1957, was $25.3 billion. More than half of this was in Canada, Europe, and other industrialized areas that are excluded from the scope of our study. About 40 percent, or some $10 billion, was in areas that might be considered less developed—the Latin American Republics, Western Hemisphere dependencies, Asia, and Africa.

About a fourth of the total investments in all areas involved less

[10] Cf. United Nations, *International Flow of Private Capital,* Chapter III. United States purchases of foreign securities amounted to almost $1 billion in 1958, involving mainly securities of Canada, Western Europe, and international institutions. The securities of international institutions, of course, indirectly affect the economically less developed countries.

than 95 percent United States ownership; this figure may be taken as an indication of the extent of joint ventures in United States direct foreign investments. Most of this joint investment (20 percent, out of the total of 25 percent) was in the category of 50–95 percent United States ownership. Minority positions for the United States investors (in effect from 25 percent to 50 percent ownership) are represented only to a small extent. The category of "95 percent or more ownership," which accounts for three-fourths of the total, may be taken to represent wholly United States-owned investments.

The figures show that United States investors engage in joint ventures to a greater extent in industrialized countries than in less developed countries. Thus, in comparison with the average representation of joint ventures in all areas of 25 percent, it is 31 percent for the industrialized countries and 17 percent for the less developed countries. Nevertheless, the minority of close to one-fifth for joint ventures in the total of United States direct investments in the less developed countries is an appreciable one.

In addition to the $25.3 billion of United States direct foreign investments in 1957, there was a total of $228 million of United States investments in "associated foreign enterprises," defined as those in which the United States participation is in the range of 10–25 percent. This figure is, of course, to be added to the total of United States joint ventures. However, it is small relative to the total of direct investments, amounting to less than one percent, and so does not change the order of magnitude.

Thus, an appreciable minority of United States direct foreign investments in 1957, in the order of some 25 percent for all areas and some 17 percent for the less developed areas, may be considered to have consisted of joint ventures. Although it is not possible to make an exact comparison, certain data from the previous census of United States direct foreign investments relating to the year 1950 indicate that joint ventures have become more important relative to the total in the postwar period.

In 1950, the total of United States direct investments was $11.8 billion, of which $8.5 billion was invested in companies incorporated abroad, and $3.3 billion was in foreign branches of United States

TABLE 1. UNITED STATES DIRECT FOREIGN INVESTMENTS, BY PERCENT OF UNITED STATES OWNERSHIP AND AREA, 1957 (*Values in Millions of Dollars*)

	(1) Total		(2) 50–95% Ownership		(3) Less than 50% Ownership		(4) Less than 95% Ownership (2) plus (3)		(5) 95% or More Ownership	
	Value	%	*Value*	%	*Value*	%	*Value*	%	*Value*	%
All Areas	25,262	100.0	5,041	20.0	1,313	5.2	6,354	25.2	18,908	74.8
Latin American Republics	7,434	100.0	884	11.9	201	2.7	1,085	14.6	6,349	85.4
Western Hemisphere Dependencies	618	100.0	105	17.0	1	0.2	106	17.2	512	82.8
Asia	2,019	100.0	399	19.8	69	3.4	468	23.2	1,551	76.8
Africa	664	100.0	146	22.0	35	5.3	181	27.3	483	72.7
Sub-Total	10,735	100.0	1,534	14.3	306	2.9	1,840	17.2	8,895	82.8
Canada	8,637	100.0	2,505	29.0	770	8.9	3,275	37.9	5,362	62.1
Europe	4,151	100.0	859	20.7	119	2.9	978	23.6	3,173	76.4
Other	1,739	100.0	143	8.2	118	6.8	261	15.0	1,478	85.0
Sub-Total	14,527	100.0	3,507	24.1	1,007	6.9	4,514	31.0	10,013	69.0

Source: United States Department of Commerce, Office of Business Economics.

companies. The branches, of course, by their very nature are wholly United States–owned investments, and can be eliminated from the consideration of the extent of joint ventures. They predominate for the most part in extractive industries, such as petroleum, mining, and plantation agriculture.

In connection with the $8.5 billion invested in companies incorporated abroad, there was also a foreign investment in securities of the companies involved amounting to $2.3 billion. This investment does not necessarily relate exclusively to native capital of the respective countries of the investment, but also includes capital from countries other than that of the investment. It seems reasonable to assume that at least a large part of it is native capital.

The total United States and foreign investment in these foreign corporations amounted to $10.8 billion, of which $8.5 billion was United States capital, and $2.3 billion (22 percent of the total) was foreign capital. If this amount of foreign capital is related to the figure of $14.1 billion (the sum of the $10.8 billion plus the $3.3 billion in United States branches), the proportion of foreign capital declines from 22 percent to 17 percent, as indicated in Table 2. The average for all areas of 17 percent is a composite of 22 percent for the industrialized countries and 11 percent for the less developed countries.

Joint ventures appear to have increased significantly in the total of United States direct foreign investments between the census of 1950 and 1957 (from some 11 percent to 17 percent in the less developed countries, from 22 percent to 31 percent for the industrialized countries, and from 17 percent to 25 percent for all areas combined). The increase in joint ventures relative to total investments in the less developed countries (+55 percent) has been greater than that in the case of the industrialized countries (+41 percent).

Other Indications of Joint Equity Ventures

For the countries studied in detail for this project there are also some indications of the extent of joint equity ventures in the total of foreign investments. A few of these countries—West Germany,

TABLE 2. UNITED STATES DIRECT INVESTMENTS ABROAD IN BRANCH ORGANIZATIONS AND UNITED STATES AND FOREIGN INVESTMENTS IN UNITED STATES-CONTROLLED FOREIGN CORPORATIONS, 1950

(*Values in Millions of Dollars*)

	(1) *Total of (2) and (3)*	(2) *U.S. Investments in Branch Organizations*	(3) *Total U.S. and Foreign Investments in U.S.-Controlled Foreign Corporations* [a]	(4) *Foreign Investments in Securities of U.S.-Controlled Foreign Corporations*	(5) *(4) as % of (3)*	(6) *(4) as % of (1)*
All Areas	14,136	3,314	10,822	2,349	21.7	16.6
Latin-American Republics	5,039	2,109	2,930	303	10.3	6.0
Western Hemisphere Dependencies	101	16	85	1	1.2	1.0
Asia	1,155	525	630	338	53.7	29.3
Africa	469	61	408	124	30.4	26.4
Sub-Total	6,764	2,711	4,053	766	18.9	11.3
Canada	4,591	421	4,170	1,011	24.2	22.0
Europe	2,169	120	2,049	449	21.9	20.7
Other	612	62	550	123	22.4	20.1
Sub-Total	7,372	603	6,769	1,583	23.4	21.5

[a] in which 25 percent or more of the voting stock is United States-owned.

Source: United States Department of Commerce, *Direct Private Foreign Investments of the United States, Census of 1950*, Supplement to *Survey of Current Business, 1953*.

Japan, and Italy—are capital exporters.[11] To supplement the data given on the United States, data on these countries are presented first.

WEST GERMANY, JAPAN, AND ITALY

In the case of West Germany, the primary emphasis in the country's postwar foreign economic policy has been on the gradual rebuilding of its external economic and financial position, and especially on the reconstruction of its foreign trade. There has been much emphasis on foreign investments in the form of export credits and export credit insurance; this conscious policy was supplemented by the involuntary accumulation of claims on other countries of Europe under the European Payments Union, as West Germany's industry and ability to export rapidly strengthened during the postwar period. Furthermore, much of the overseas capital movements out of West Germany in the postwar period have necessarily taken the form of payments on foreign debt and of reparations and indemnification for war damages. Accordingly, it is only in recent years that direct foreign investments have begun to assume some importance.

From the elimination of restrictions on capital exports in early 1952 through 1958, Germany's direct foreign investments amounted to a total of about $520 million. The amount of direct investments has increased somewhat in recent years to an annual average of about 490 million marks or close to $120 million in the years 1956–58.

These magnitudes for direct investments may be compared with the following figures for some of the other types of more important, foreign capital movements: Payments on foreign debt amounted to an estimated $750 million in the period 1953–58; payments on reparations and indemnification for war damages amounted to an estimated $1.03 billion in the period 1952–57; export credit insurance for credits to less developed countries was outstanding in mid-1958 in the amount of about $1.2 billion; West German claims under the European Payments Union amounted to somewhat over $1

[11] Italy is actually a capital importer on a net basis, but is a significant capital exporter vis-à-vis the less developed countries.

billion when the EPU was officially discontinued as of December 27, 1958; and, during the year 1958, the West German Government committed assistance to the governments of India, Turkey, Egypt, Iceland, and Greece in the amount of 2,049,400,000 marks or close to $490 million. Direct foreign investments by West Germany have constituted a minor aspect of its overseas capital movements during the postwar period.

Of the approximately $520 million that has moved out into direct foreign investments, the greater part has been in sales and service organizations abroad, which generally do not take the form of joint ventures. It is especially in manufacturing investments that West German companies associate with local capital in the country of the investment. In these cases, the companies welcome local capital in order to avoid having to invest cash; they bring in machinery, know-how, and other assets, and tend to rely on the local partners for required cash investments. This type of investment, however, has constituted to date only a minor part of the relatively small West German direct foreign investments.

Total foreign equity investments for Japan since the end of the Second World War have been even less important than those of Germany, amounting at the end of 1959 to $157 million. As in the case of Germany, other forms of foreign investment, especially through the granting of commercial credits and medium-term loans, have been much more important than direct foreign investments. Strenuous efforts were made to promote exports in order to finance the imports of raw materials on which the country is so heavily dependent. The annual flow of Japanese commercial credits and medium-term loans during the past several years has exceeded $300 million.

The rate of foreign direct investment by Japan has increased sharply in recent years, especially since 1955. The increase in such investment amounted to only some $3 million in 1951 and $9 million in 1955, but in 1957 it was $23 million, and in 1959 it was $41 million. Most of Japanese foreign equity investment has been in joint ventures in association with local capital.

Italy, with a dual-structured economy in need of foreign capital but capable of exporting not only capital but also technical know-how in many fields, has been both on the receiving and giving ends. On a net basis it has been a capital importer during the postwar period. From 1948 through 1957, foreign investments in Italian equities amounted to $245 million, and an estimated additional $170 million flowed into the country in the form of loans, purchases of bonds, and purchases of government securities.[12] Italian holdings of stocks of foreign corporations amounted to $132 million as of December 31, 1957. An appreciable part of both types of equity investments (foreign investments in Italy and Italian investments abroad) represent recent activity. Thus, of the $245 million of foreign investments in Italian stocks, over 50 percent was made in the two years 1956–57 ($72 million in 1956, and $60 million in 1957). The Italian holdings of stocks of foreign corporations, which amounted to $99 million at the end of 1956, increased by $33 million or about one-third in 1957. The latter increase was equivalent to 55 percent of the amount of foreign equity investment in Italy during the same year.

Joint ventures have been represented in an important way in the flows in both directions. Many of the foreign direct investments in the country are in association with local capital and enterprise, and Italian enterprises frequently enter into patents and technical process agreements with foreign firms even where no capital participation by the latter is sought. Italian legislation is generally quite liberal with respect to the investment of foreign capital in the country, but it is even more liberal in certain respects when the investment is in the form of joint ventures.[13]

Italian investments abroad generally involve the export of machinery, patents, manufacturing rights, and technical assistance rather than the investment of cash, because of the chronic shortage

[12] The loan commitments of the International Bank for Reconstruction and Development to the Cassa del Mezzogiorno (the government agency charged with the development of the economically less developed South of the country) alone amounted to $240 million as of June 30, 1958.

[13] Thus, wholly foreign-owned enterprises may contract debts and float bonds in Italy only up to 50 percent of the capital introduced into the country, while there is no limitation at all in the case of joint ventures with no more than 30 percent foreign participation; where the foreign participation is more than 30 percent, the 50 percent debt limit may be exceeded, but the amount of internal debt exceeding this limit must then be matched by credits obtained abroad.

of capital in Italy. Government approval of Italian investments abroad is required, but there is the most liberal treatment of applications involving the transfer of assets other than cash. This circumstance tends to favor foreign investments in the form of joint ventures, in which cash requirements are supplied by the local partners. Some investments of this type have been made in recent years, especially in Latin America, by important Italian enterprises such as Snia Viscosa in the synthetic textiles field and Fiat in automotive equipment, both of which, incidentally, have much experience in cooperative business arrangements with foreign firms in connection with their own domestic activities in Italy.

LATIN AMERICA

Data revealed by the studies of the Latin American area (Brazil, Mexico, Colombia, and Cuba) bearing on the extent of joint ventures indicated that they had been growing in importance as a form of foreign investment, but that they were still quantitatively in the minority.

In Brazil, a compilation as of October, 1958 of enterprises with both foreign and domestic capital, compared to an estimate of the value of all direct foreign investments in the economy, permits the judgment that joint equity ventures account for about one-fifth of the total. Foreign investment in the joint ventures amounted to an estimated $650 million, and total direct foreign investment to somewhat more than $3 billion.

During the entire postwar period, Brazil has relied heavily on foreign loan capital to help finance its development, but in the most recent years the inflow of foreign capital for direct investment has increased substantially. At the end of 1958, total medium- and long-term foreign debt outstanding amounted to $2.2 billion, made up of credits from such diverse sources as the International Bank for Reconstruction and Development, the Export-Import Bank of Washington, the International Monetary Fund, private exporters, and private banks; the majority of the debt represented development loans and suppliers' credits, but balance of payments loans made up as much as one-third of the total. Since 1955, particularly as a result of the adoption of a foreign exchange regulation that favored the inflow of foreign capital for direct investment, direct investment has become much more important; the inflow on this account, which amounted to less than $10 million in 1954, has risen steadily as follows: to $31 million in 1955, $56 million in 1956, $108 million in 1957, and $278 million in 1958. Since the administrative procedure for application of the 1955 exchange regulation discourages its use by new, wholly foreign-owned enterprises, it is felt that much of the stepped-up flow of direct investments has gone into joint ventures. The International Finance Corporation, which engaged in its first operation anywhere with an enterprise in Brazil,[14] has granted investment commitments to five enterprises in the country, and three are joint ventures.[15]

In recent years there has been a large inflow of foreign capital for direct investment in Mexico. The value of United States investment in the country at the end of 1957 was estimated by the Banco de México, the country's central bank, to be $1.2 billion. It has not been possible to determine how much of this is in joint ventures, but the Banco de México, which regularly compiles data on foreign direct investments, made a special investigation, in cooperation with this project, of the extent of joint ventures among new enterprises formed with foreign investment in the years 1950–57. The investigation revealed that the total foreign investment in new enterprises amounted to 5,555,000,000 pesos, and that 595,000,000 pesos, or 11 percent of the total, consisted of foreign investment in new joint equity ventures. These joint equity ventures were mostly in the fields of manufacturing (43 percent) and trade (32 percent), with the balance distributed among other activities such as mining, construction, agriculture, petroleum, and transportation. Most of the foreign investment in the new joint ventures (86 percent of the total) was in enterprises where 75 percent or more of the capital was foreign-owned. The special investigation of the Banco de México showed that foreign investment in new

[14] In June 1957, with Siemens do Brasil, Companhia de Eletricidade—a German-Brazilian venture manufacturing electrical machinery and electronic equipment.

[15] Siemens, and the following two: Willys Overland do Brasil S.A., Indústria e Comércio (a United States-French-Brazilian venture manufacturing automotive vehicles); and Companhia Mineira de Cimento Portland S.A. (a joint Israeli-French-Brazilian enterprise to manufacture cement).

enterprises has gone into joint ventures only to a minor extent, and even then overwhelmingly into enterprises with a firm majority of foreign capital. Nevertheless, the direct investigation of the approximately 65 significant joint venture situations that constituted the major part of the work for the Mexico study performed under our project justifies some qualification of the impressions left by this global quantitative investigation. The direct investigation suggests that joint ventures are much more important in the Mexican economy than implied by the global figures cited; they dominate in such principal fields of activity as the manufacture of iron and steel, synthetic textile fibers, machinery, refractories, tires, and electrical equipment, and the provision of aviation services. There appears to be more of minority foreign participation, or at least of smaller foreign majorities, than indicated by the global quantitative data. The reason for these disparities may be differences in the coverage of the two sets of data; many of the enterprises covered in the direct investigations were in existence in one form or another prior to 1950. In any case, there has been a particularly pronounced trend in Mexico toward joint ventures in the postwar period, both in the transformation of existing enterprises and in the formation of new ones.

In Colombia, as in Brazil and Mexico, numerous important joint ventures were encountered, but there are indications that they must be in the minority in total foreign direct investments. Approximately 40 significant joint venture situations were investigated in Colombia, representing a wide variety of important economic activities with a notable trend toward the formation of joint ventures in the postwar period. The interest in joint ventures in recent years has been sufficiently great to result in the formation of an investment company by prominent Colombian banking and financial interests to promote such enterprises in particular.[16]

There are no estimates available of the total value of all foreign direct investments in Colombia, but foreign corporations operating in the country through branches had a capital assigned to their

[16] Originally constituted at the end of 1956 as the Sociedad Coordinadora de Inversiones Nacionales y Extranjeras, S.A. (Coordinating Company for Domestic and Foreign Investments).

local branches of 1,060,000,000 pesos, or approximately $180 million,[17] at the end of 1957, according to registration figures maintained by the Office of Superintendent of Corporations. This amount may be compared with the value of United States direct investments in Colombia for the same date—$297 million.[18] United States investments constitute the bulk of total foreign direct investments in Colombia, and if the United States figure is arbitrarily taken to represent the total, the amount for foreign branches is equal to some 61 percent of the total. Thus, more than half of the foreign investment in the country may be estimated to be in the form of branch operations, which preclude the joint venture form. It is obvious that joint ventures can constitute only a minority of direct foreign investments in the economy.

Before the revolution of 1959 in Cuba, 35 out of a sample of 56 leading United States-owned companies operating in the country were organized under United States law. The branch form predominated, and joint ventures probably represented only a minor part of total direct foreign investments. A trend toward joint ventures had set in since 1950, and this trend was gaining ground up to the point when the future of any foreign investments in that country was jeopardized by the radical turn taken by the revolutionary regime.

FAR EAST AND MIDDLE EAST

The remaining less developed countries studied are the Philippines, India, Pakistan, and Burma in the Far East, and Turkey in the Middle East.

The most comprehensive statistical data on direct foreign investments and joint ventures in this area were found for the Philippines. An economic census of 1948 conducted in the Philippines showed that total assets for seven industries (forestry, transportation, mining, electricity, fisheries, commerce, and manufacturing) amounted to $1.25 billion, of which Filipino citizens owned 52 percent, while both resident (mainly Chinese) and non-resident citizens of foreign countries held 48 percent. The largest single group of

[17] At the free rate of exchange then prevailing of about six pesos to the dollar.

[18] United States Department of Commerce, *Survey of Current Business*, September, 1958.

foreigners was the Americans, who held assets worth $218.5 million or 36 percent of total foreign holdings. These holdings, important enough on a total basis since they accounted for almost half of the assets in the seven industries, were of even greater importance in certain key sectors of the economy: Foreigners, mostly American, owned some 82 percent of total investments in electricity; in mining, Americans held 38 percent and foreign investments as a whole amounted to 58 percent of total assets; foreign holdings accounted for 54 percent of total investments in commerce; and in manufacturing, foreigners accounted for 51 percent.

The value of foreign holdings thus calculated to amount to $600 million in these seven branches of economic activity in 1948 apparently increased substantially in later years of the postwar period. Private long-term foreign investment is estimated to have increased by $230 million from 1950 to 1956, mostly out of reinvested earnings. Domestic investments appear to have increased to an even greater extent than foreign investments, and the ratio of foreign investments to total assets probably declined from the 1948 level. Data compiled at the Philippine Securities and Exchange Commission, the Bureau of Commerce, and the Central Bank show that domestic (Filipino) investment accounted for two-thirds of total investments in newly registered businesses (sole proprietorships, partnerships, and corporations) in the period 1949–56, while foreign investment (about 80 percent of which was Chinese, or resident foreign capital) accounted for only one-third.

There are no comprehensive statistical data on the importance of joint ventures in the total stock of foreign investment, but some data are available on their extent among newly registered partnerships and corporations, based on the records of the local Securities and Exchange Commission. There were foreign investments with a value of $44 million in 1,898 newly registered partnerships and corporations in the period 1953–56; of these, 50 percent of the number of cases and 33 percent of the value of the foreign investments involved some degree of joint investment with local capital. There was majority foreign control of 51 percent or more in 16 percent of the number of cases and 19 percent of the value of the foreign investments; 50 percent foreign participation in 3 percent of the total, in both numbers and value; and minority foreign participation in 31 percent of the number of cases, representing 11 percent of the value of the foreign investments. Most of the cases of majority foreign control involved a control of 95 percent or more, so that they were joint ventures more of form than substance. This leaves a relatively small minority that might be considered genuine joint ventures.

It has become quite difficult for foreign investors to obtain official approval in the Philippines for wholly foreign-owned subsidiary projects. Approval is required to obtain guarantees of exchange for remittances of profits or dividends, and some form of local equity participation has become almost a prerequisite to obtain the approval.

In India, foreign-held business investment is estimated to have amounted to $1.01 billion at the end of 1955. Between 1948 and 1955 the United Kingdom, the United States, West Germany, and Switzerland increased their investments by about $368 million. Statistical data on the extent of joint equity ventures among these investments are not available, but Indian policy since its independence has been geared to the promotion of foreign investment in this form. The government has the ultimate sanction with respect to foreign investment, and directs them to the areas it considers appropriate for development, and at the same time dictates the terms under which it is to operate. Certain economic fields and industries are reserved for state enterprise; in some cases foreign participation has been sought and obtained, but not on an equity basis. For example, Russian, West German, and British participation has been obtained for three new steel plants (Bhilai, Rourkela, and Durgapur, respectively), but their participation is limited to technical service agreements for the designing, construction, and placing in operation of the plants, and the provision of equipment and credits—the plants are owned and operated by a statutory government corporation, Hindustan Steel Ltd. Because of the policy of state ownership in basic industrial fields, foreign direct investment, especially from the United States, has been inhibited to a considerable extent.

Data are not avalable on the value of foreign direct investments or on the extent of joint equity ventures among them in Pakistan.

This nation, newly created in 1957 by partition from India, has received foreign investments mostly in the form of public grants and loans. Grants, mostly from the United States, amounted to some $1.2 billion by 1958; loans, mostly from the United States and from the International Bank for Reconstruction and Development, amounted to close to $300 million. With respect to direct investments, the data available indicate that close to half the number of enterprises in the country with foreign participation (289 out of a total of 591) are branches of foreign firms incorporated abroad, thus excluding for this segment the possibility of their being joint ventures. However, as is true for India, Pakistan places great emphasis on the joint venture form of foreign investment.

In Burma, which also attained independence at the end of the Second World War, virtually all the direct foreign investments in the country were British. These investments are estimated to have amounts to £47 million (about $190 million) in 1941. After the war, the major British investments, which were in the extractive industries, were rehabilitated as joint ventures on a partnership basis with the government of Burma, and almost all the other British enterprises were nationalized (in shipping, timber, electric power, cement, and sugar). These joint ventures, together with a British-Burmese venture in soaps and a small Japanese-Burmese venture in fishing, constitute the only important remaining foreign direct investments in Burma. Their capital amounts to about £21 million ($59 million).

Burma has received much more in the way of foreign public loans and grants during the postwar period (about $260 million by 1958) than direct private investment. However, the direct private foreign investment that there is in the country is almost entirely on a joint venture basis, and it dominates the important sectors of the economy in which it operates.

Turkey, in the Middle East, represents a pattern similar to that found for most of the countries in the Far East: a large amount of foreign public assistance in the postwar period through grants and loans relative to foreign direct investment; a small amount of foreign direct investment in absolute terms; and a marked trend toward joint ventures among the direct investments that have been made.

Through the end of 1958, United States aid to Turkey beginning with the Marshall Plan totaled $766 million; International Bank loans to Turkey amounted to $60 million; and substantial additional aid had been received from the Organization for European Economic Cooperation countries. Actual private foreign direct investments effected during the postwar period, on the other hand, totaled only an estimated $20 million by early 1959. The trend toward joint ventures among the direct investments is indicated by the fact that from January, 1954 to April, 1958 all but 19, or more than 90 percent of the 227 applications for foreign investment approved by the Turkish authorities were joint ventures in one way or another. Though these data relate to applications approved rather than to investments actually made, it is safe to assume that there is no departure from the pattern as approved by the authorities once the investments are carried out. There are also some important investments being made in Turkey which are wholly foreign-owned, including a major oil refinery now being planned by three foreign oil companies.

Non-Equity Joint Ventures

The quantitative indications given relate to the extent of joint ventures involving the investment of equity capital by both foreign and domestic partners in the total of foreign investments in the less developed countries. There are other types of joint ventures which do not involve the investment of equity capital but which still are types of business arrangements characterized by a degree of continuity and close cooperation in enterprises that qualify them as joint ventures, such as technical services contracts, licensing and franchise arrangements, construction contracts, and management contracts. These are dealt with in some detail at a later stage in this report. At this point, the extent to which they have been found in our investigations in comparison with the equity type of joint venture is indicated.

With respect to the capital-exporting countries individually surveyed: About a third of the joint venture cases for West Germany involved no equity participation by the German partner. These included a technical services agreement with an Indian railroad car manufacturer for the construction of a new plant and an export credit and construction contract with the new government-owned steel plant in India. In Japan, technical assistance appears to have been rendered only in conjunction with its equity joint ventures; no instances were found of technical assistance arrangements without any financial interest by the Japanese partner. About 40 percent of the Japanese joint equity ventures also were accompanied by technical assistance contracts; this varied a great deal by region, depending upon the stage of development of the country or area of location of the enterprises; thus, in Latin America, 6 out of 44 cases included technical assistance contracts, while in South and Southeast Asia, 56 out of 58 cases included such contracts. Italian joint ventures generally involve some equity participation by the Italian partner, though frequently on a minority basis and in recognition of intangible assets contributed such as technical know-how and patent rights.

Among the Latin American countries, a minority of all the cases of joint ventures surveyed, ranging up to about one-third of the total, consisted of various types of non-equity joint ventures.

In Brazil, a few of the 65 cases reviewed were non-equity joint ventures. For example, a large domestically-owned glass manufacturing enterprise had patent rights agreements with American firms, with no financial investment or financial assistance by the latter, for the manufacture of specialized products.

In Mexico, some 10 out of the total of 65 cases were non-equity joint ventures. They consisted of agreements for the manufacture of consumer items including foodstuffs, wearing apparel, soft drinks, and washing machines, under license and involving the use of foreign brand names; technical process agreements for the manufacture of copper, brass, and bronze products, machinery items such as valves, and chemical products such as caustic soda and soda ash; franchise agreements for the manufacture of automotive vehicles; a design and construction contract, as well as loan financing, for a domestically-owned cement plant; and drilling contracts with the government petroleum monopoly.

The ratio was higher and the range broader of non-equity joint ventures in the total in the case of Colombia. About one-third of the total of 40 cases fell in this category. As in Mexico, they included a number of licensing and trademark utilization agreements covering paints, various paper specialties, typewriter ribbon, household appliances such as stoves, hot water heaters, washing machines and refrigerators, and soft drinks and ice cream. Plans for the local assembly of automotive vehicles were also designed for the most part on the pattern of franchise agreements with no foreign equity participation. There are also some important cases of management contracts in hotel operation and petroleum refinery administration.

About a fifth of the 25 cases surveyed in Cuba were also in this category. These cases included a foreign construction contract combined with loans for a harbor tunnel project, a technical assistance arrangement by a British airline with the leading domestically-owned Cuban airline, and management contract and rental arrangements in the tourist industry in the operation of hotels and gambling casinos.

In the Far East, there was also a minority representation of non-equity joint ventures found in the total of cases surveyed, but it was somewhat more difficult to establish any quantitative indications of their extent.

In the Philippines, eight representative cases were studied in detail, of which one was a non-equity joint venture, consisting of a Philippine enterprise that has entered into royalty agreements with a number of United States firms for the manufacture of crayons, pencils, paints, carbon paper, and typewriter ribbons. Royalty arrangements covering the exclusive manufacture of a product with a well-known brand name, as well as technical assistance on the local processing or manufacture, are quite common in the Philippines. The local manufacture of brand-name storage batteries is an important example. Somewhat less frequent arrangements include those involving royalty agreements for technical processes rather than for particular, differentiated products; management contracts in industries involving complex production processes; and construction contract arrangements, especially on government projects.

In India, the non-equity type of joint venture is particularly found in the foreign participation in fields reserved for state enterprise.

The two existing integrated steel plants in the country, which are privately owned, have also embarked on non-equity joint ventures through the use of foreign technical collaboration. The study of Pakistan, on the other hand, revealed no significant cases of the non-equity type of joint venture.

In Burma, the representative cases of joint ventures included no non-equity joint ventures, although they do exist to some extent. Most of the construction work for new industrial enterprises is carried out under construction contracts with foreign firms. There are also cases of management contracts with foreign firms, especially in government enterprises where the government wishes to retain complete ownership or where the enterprise manufactures commodities of prime necessity over which the government wishes to maintain distribution or price control, as in the case of pharmaceuticals.

In the Middle East, in Turkey, there is also apparently some minority representation of non-equity joint ventures. Although the representative cases studied do not include any of this type, the following statement of the British Chamber of Commerce of Turkey, in its December, 1957 publication on "Prospects for U.K. Investors," which generally recommends the joint venture as a desirable form of foreign investment in that country, is perhaps significant in this respect: "In certain cases, the investment of patent rights and manufacturing licenses is a suitable investment but, in general, investments in the form of machinery, plant, etc., are the preferred and recommended medium of investment" (p. 4).

Recapitulation

International capital movements, which in the early years of the postwar period consisted primarily of aid to the war-devastated industrialized countries for their economic rehabilitation, have in recent years shifted to the less developed countries. As this geographic shift has occurred, there has also been a greater participation by private capital in the movements, especially for direct investment. The trend has developed to the point where the magnitude of private direct investment in the less developed countries as a whole is about equal to the volume of public aid and loans to these areas. There is considerable variation in the relative importance of public and private foreign investment among the various less developed regions of the world. In this connection, there appears to be a fairly close and inverse correlation between the stage of economic development and the importance of the public capital component. Public investment is much more important than private investment in the least developed countries of South and Southeast Asia, while the reverse is the case in Latin America.

The United States has continued to be the major source of the capital invested, but other industrialized countries such as those of Western Europe and Japan are rapidly increasing their participation in the aid to and investment in the less developed countries. Considerable pressure to this end has been exerted since the onset of a substantial balance of payments deficit in the United States in 1958 and as other industrialized countries have strengthened their internal economic positions and added to their international reserves.

As private direct investment in the less developed countries has increased, the use of the joint venture form of investment has also increased, although it still constitutes only a minor portion of the total of such investment. Censuses of foreign direct investments of the United States indicate that some 17 percent of such investments in the less developed countries were in joint ventures in 1957, and that the ratio had increased from some 11 percent in 1950. Among other capital-exporting countries, West Germany's joint ventures abroad appear to constitute a small part of its total foreign direct investments, while most of Japan's and Italy's foreign direct investments are joint ventures with local partners. In the cases of West Germany and Japan, export credits and other forms of foreign investment have been much more important than direct investments.

Among the less developed countries themselves, available quantitative data also confirm the impression that joint ventures still constitute only a minority of the total of foreign direct investments, though with considerable variation among countries and with a general trend of increasing importance. In Latin America, joint ventures appear everywhere to be gaining importance. In Brazil, they are estimated to represent about one-fifth of total foreign direct investments. Among the countries in the Far East and Middle East, there appears to be an even greater emphasis on joint ventures than in Latin America. In the Philippines, about a third of the value of foreign capital in foreign investment enterprises formed in the period 1953–56 was in association with local capital. In Burma, and Turkey, the majority of all the foreign direct investments effected or reconstituted in the postwar period have been joint ventures. In India, there is a great emphasis on participation by nationals in foreign investments in the country, and assistance of foreign private capital has been sought and obtained by the government for the formation of State enterprises.

In addition to joint ventures that involve equity investments in the same enterprises by both nationals and foreigners, there are those that consist of other types of business cooperation such as design and construction contracts for new plants, licensing and patent or trademark agreements, management contracts, and technical assistance agreements without any joint capital investment. These types of non-equity joint ventures are estimated to represent up to about one-third of the total of joint ventures in the less developed countries.

With this background of indications, necessarily incomplete, concerning the quantitative importance that joint international business ventures in the less developed countries have assumed in recent years, the analysis in the succeeding chapters now proceeds to a consideration of various aspects of this form of foreign investment, based on the intensive studies that have been conducted of conditions in both capital-exporting and capital-importing countries and of representative cases of joint venture enterprises.

III. Distribution by Countries and Industries

FROM THE INDICATIONS of the over-all importance of joint ventures in the total of foreign investments in the less developed countries, we now pass to a consideration in detail of their significance in selected individual countries and in the policies of leading investing companies.

Joint Ventures in Local Economies

The largest number of joint ventures found in various areas of the world were in the Latin American group. This is a reflection of the greater volume of foreign private direct investment in Latin America than in other less developed areas. The bulk of foreign private direct investment in the postwar period has come from the United States, where there is greater familiarity with the Latin American area, compared with the more remote areas such as those in the Far East, and the political problems have generally posed fewer problems for the foreign investor than in areas closer to the frontiers of the cold war. Coupled with these factors have been the rapid rate of industrial development and the growing nationalism of Latin America. The combination of all these factors has stimulated the joint venture type of foreign investment.

Within Latin America, joint ventures have been widely used in Brazil and Mexico, the most highly industrialized countries of the area. Joint ventures are found to varying extents in all sectors of the Brazilian economy, especially in manufacturing, and they are of particular importance in certain basic sectors of industry such as primary iron and steel, the tire and rubber industry, machinery and vehicles, synthetic textile fibers, specialized footwear, and cigarettes and matches. The pattern is similar in Mexico, where joint ventures dominate in iron and steel, copper refining, aluminum smelting, tires and rubber products, refractories, newsprint, machinery and equipment, and synthetic textile fibers. The number of fields for joint ventures is fewer in less industrialized Colombia, but joint ventures are found in important lines of industry including tires, synthetic textile fibers, primary paper, asbestos-cement building materials, and durable household equipment. Until early 1959, there was less representation of joint ventures in manufacturing industries in Cuba, which had developed to a much more limited extent than in the other Latin American countries, but such ventures were found in other fields including mining and the tourist industry.

A common pattern is found in the Latin American countries in public utilities, such as electric power and telephone service, and in air transportation. These fields were originally generally developed by entirely foreign-owned enterprises. In recent years they have been converted into joint ventures in response to nationalistic trends, and to the difficulties in attracting additional capital from abroad for expansion under local policies of rate control and the declining exchange value of currencies.

In the Far East, especially in India, Burma, and Pakistan, there has been greater reluctance on the part of foreign private interests to invest because of graver problems arising from political unrest and instability, a less clearly favorable disposition toward private enterprise, and fewer investment opportunities with profitable prospects than in Latin America. Private investments have come from areas other than the United States, especially from the United Kingdom, because of its close historic ties with those countries. To the extent that foreign investments have proceeded, however, the joint venture form is perhaps even more prominently represented in the total than in Latin America, among other reasons because of stricter governmental control over the economy and over new investments. Also, at least in India, non-equity types of joint venture arrangements are of somewhat greater importance than in other countries, as illustrated by such arrangements as those for the new steel plants that are being developed as government-owned enterprises, pursuant to the general policy of governmental control over basic industries. In Burma, the mining sector of the economy is entirely dominated by joint ventures, which before the Second World War were exclusively British-owned enterprises. New activities of importance in these economies have been introduced by joint ventures, including deep-sea fishing in Burma, the production of high quality soaps in Burma and Pakistan, and the development of natural gas resources in Pakistan.

The Philippines presents a somewhat different pattern in the Far East, somewhat closer to that observed for Latin America, because of its historic ties with the United States. Former entirely foreign-owned public utilities have recently been converted into joint ventures, and joint ventures are of particular importance in manufacturing, in such fields as the production of tires, storage batteries, and aluminum products.

In Turkey numerous industries have recently been founded under joint venture arrangements, frequently arising from former exporter-importer relationships. Particularly important fields developed in recent years by joint ventures are the production of steel pipe, pharmaceuticals, electric light bulbs, and preserved food products, with important investments being represented especially by partners from West Germany and the United States.

BRAZIL

A number of important enterprises in primary iron and steel in Brazil are joint ventures. The first integrated steel plant of the country, the Companhia Siderúrgica Belgo-Mineira, founded in 1921, is a joint equity venture of Belgian, French, and Brazilian capital. The latest important addition to the country's primary steel-making capacity is the enterprise Usinas Siderúrgicas de Minas Gerais (Usiminas), organized in 1957 with Brazilian federal and state government capital and the equity participation of several Japanese industrial firms. Electric furnace steel and steel pipe are now manufactured by the Companhia Siderúrgica Mannesmann, organized as a German-Brazilian joint equity venture in 1952. Steel drums and related products, and consumer items such as household stoves and other cooking equipment, are made by Rheem Metalúrgica, founded in 1946 with United States and Brazilian equity.

The tire and rubber industry in Brazil is dominated by joint ventures, although some of the enterprises have only a small amount of Brazilian capital. The five foreign brands represented in this way are Goodyear, Firestone, General Tire, Dunlop, and Pirelli. The Pirelli enterprise (Pirelli S. A. Companhia Industrial Brasileira) also manufactures an entirely different line, that of electrical wire and cables which accounts for about three-fourths of total national consumption.

There is widespread representation of joint ventures in the rapidly expanding field of automotive vehicles and equipment. The largest automotive vehicle manufacturing enterprise in the country, Willys Overland do Brasil, is a joint venture with United States, French, and Brazilian equity, long-term loans from private lending agencies in the United States, and an investment by the International Finance Corporation. Other brands that are assembled or manufactured in the country are Ford, General Motors, Mercedes Benz, Volkswagen, and Simca. All of these brands are made by joint venture enterprises, with the exception of Ford and General Motors, whose enterprises are wholly foreign-owned. A plant opened in November, 1959 for the manufacture of automotive transmissions, gears, differentials, and other automotive components, said to be the first of its kind in Latin America, is that of Equipamentos Clark-Mac, with United States, French, and Brazilian equity. In the related field of agricultural vehicles and equipment, there is the joint German-Brazilian venture Vemag (Veiculos e Máquinas Agrícolas); and a large, diversified plant which manufactures railroad cars and parts and steel foundry products is the firm Cobrasma (Companhia Brasileira de Material Ferroviario), a United States–Brazilian venture which supplies about one-fourth of the country's railroad car requirements.

Other complex machinery and equipment industries in the country also have considerable representation of joint ventures. A recent case is the Japanese-Brazilian venture Industria Mecanica Howa do

Brasil, which manufactures textile machinery. In electrical machinery and equipment, including household appliances, there are the enterprises Eletromar, with Belgium and Luxembourg, United States (Westinghouse), and Brazilian capital, and Bendix Home Appliances do Brasil, with United States, Swiss, and Brazilian capital. The local manufacture of electric light bulbs and electronic equipment such as radios, record players, and television sets was introduced into the country by Philips do Brasil, which has some Brazilian capital.

Cigarette and match manufacturing are dominated by joint ventures, the former by a British–American–Brazilian group in the Companhia de Cigarros Souza Cruz, and the latter by several enterprises including the Companhia Fiat Lux de Fosforos de Segurança, a British-Brazilian firm dating back to 1914, which also holds an interest in a second match enterprise, the Companhia Brasileira de Fosforos. A more recent venture in this field, which for the first time is using the United States technique of advertising on match boxes, is the Companhia Universal de Fosforos, set up in 1953 by the Universal Match Corporation of the United States jointly with Brazilian capital.

In cement, the first modern plant in the country was set up in 1926 by the Companhia Brasileira de Cimento Portland Perus, a Canadian-Brazilian venture. United States capital is also represented in joint ventures in this industry, in the enterprises Cimento Aratú and Companhia Nacional de Cimento Portland, with investments by the Lone Star Cement Corporation. The most recently organized enterprise in this field, the Companhia Mineira de Cimento Portland, is a joint Israeli-French-Brazilian firm which received an International Finance Corporation investment commitment in December, 1958. There are also joint ventures in the manufacture of cement-based products such as concrete, with the Australian–United States–Brazilian enterprises Concreto Redimix do Rio de Janeiro and Usina Central de Concreto.

The pharmaceutical industry in Brazil has much foreign investment. Joint ventures are represented in the enterprises recently formed, while the older ones are wholly foreign investments. Among important enterprises formed in recent years are the United States–

Brazilian firms Indústrias Farmaceuticas Fontoura-Wyeth, which manufactures penicillin, and Laborterápica Bristol, which manufactures other antibiotics and pharmaceutical specialties.

The glass and glass products industry is generally nationally owned, but specialized products are manufactured by the domestic enterprises under patents agreements with foreign firms, for example pyrex by the Companhia Vidraria Santa Marina, and pharmaceutical glassware by the enterprise Vitrofarma.

The textile industry, one of the oldest in the country, has a tradition of joint ventures dating back to the late nineteenth century, when Portuguese cloth merchants bought into domestic textile enterprises to complement financing and marketing arrangements. There are also some more recent joint venture investments in this field (German, in S.A. de Teçidos e Bordados Lapa; and Japanese in Fiação e Tecelagem Kanebo do Brasil, and Toyobo do Brasil). The newer field of synthetic fibers has been developed by various joint ventures, such as the French-Brazilian Companhia Brasileira Rhodiaceta Fábrica de Raion and the Italian (Snia Viscosa)–Brazilian Fiação Brasileira de Raion-Fibra.

Specialized footwear is dominated by two joint ventures: the French-Swiss-Brazilian Companhia Industrial Brasileira de Calçados Vulcanizados, in rubber footwear; and São Paulo Alpargatas, in fiber shoes, representing a joint Latin American venture with capital from Argentina and Brazil.

In foodstuffs and beverages, there is some joint venture representation in specialized products. The Nestlé firm has such an enterprise that manufactures soluble coffee and processed milk products. One of the country's breweries (the Maltaria-Cervejaria Londrina of Paraná) has admitted a foreign partner to take advantage of foreign exchange regulations that favor the investment of machinery over its importation. Ice cream, soft drink concentrates, and dehydrated foods are also manufactured under joint venture arrangements.

There are also joint ventures in commerce, mining, electric power, air transportation, and communications.

In commerce, a small minority of Brazilian capital is found in Anderson, Clayton & Cia., one of the largest coffee and cotton exporters in the country. The distributors of imported equipment are to a large extent wholly-owned subsidiaries of the foreign manufacturing or exporting firms, but some distributing enterprises have been organized as joint ventures. Examples of these are the German electrical equipment distributors, AEG Companhia Sul-Americana de Eletricidade; and the distributors of Belgium-Luxembourg construction materials, S.A. Casa Domingos Joaquim da Silva-Materiais para Construção. In domestic retail trade, Mesbla, a pioneer in department stores originally formed by French interests, still has a small minority of French capital; and the local Sears, Roebuck is almost 100 percent foreign-owned.

Mining is not an extensively developed industry in Brazil, but it has assumed importance particularly in iron ore and other minerals for the steel industry, both local and foreign. In this area, joint ventures have been represented to an important degree in manganese, to which Bethlehem Steel (Icomi) and the United States Steel Corporation (Companhia Meridional de Mineração) are parties, as well as in scheelite, lead, and magnesite.

Electric power in Brazil, as in many other Latin American countries, was developed by foreign capital. The principal companies operating today are still either all or mostly Canadian- and American-owned. The group of companies controlled by the American interest, which is the American and Foreign Power Company, includes some which also have Brazilian equity; and it is of interest that the newest addition to the electric power companies, the recently formed Central Elétrica de Furnas, has been established as a Canadian-American-Brazilian joint venture, with a substantial amount of loan capital from the International Bank for Reconstruction and Development. This plant, which is being built in Minais Gerais, will be the largest in the country, with a capacity of 1.1 million kilowatts, compared to the present national total of about 3.5 million kilowatts.

One of the leading airlines of Brazil, Panair do Brasil, originally all United States-owned, is now a joint venture with equity participation by Pan American World Airways.

Telephone service, like electric power, was originally developed by foreign capital and has recently been moving toward conversion into joint ventures. The Companhia Telefonica Brasileira, formerly a branch of a Canadian corporation, was converted into a local corporation in 1956 as a first step toward the admission of local capital. This has become a pattern in public utilities in response to the difficulty of raising capital abroad for expansion because of the adverse effect on profitability of official rate control policies coupled with the depreciating foreign exchange rate.

MEXICO

The pattern of joint ventures in the economy of Mexico is similar to that noted for Brazil. Joint ventures, though still constituting only a minority of total foreign investments in the economy, are increasing in relative importance. They are prominent in heavy industries and in those involving complex production processes, and formerly wholly foreign-owned public utilities have been converted into joint ventures or have been completely nationalized.

In iron and steel, the largest primary mill in the country (Altos Hornos de México), organized during the Second World War, is a joint venture with United States equity participation, and it has also utilized American technical assistance and substantial loan funds from the Export-Import Bank. The oldest and now the second largest primary steel enterprise in the country (the Compañía Fundidora de Fierro y Acero de Monterrey) dates back to the turn of the century, when it was founded by Mexican and American interests. A third steel enterprise (La Consolidada) was mostly American-owned, with a small Mexican minority, until the latter part of 1959, when most of its shares were acquired by Nacional Financiera, the Mexican government development corporation. These three primary steel enterprises together accounted for almost two-thirds of total national production in 1958. Projects for new primary steel facilities in the country are also likely to develop as joint ventures.

The only enterprise in the country that produces seamless steel pipe for the petroleum industry (Tubos de Acero de México) was organized in 1952 as an Italian-French-Swiss-Mexican venture. Other steel products such as castings for railroad cars and concrete reinforcing bars are produced under joint venture arrangements, examples being Fundiciones de Hierro y Acero, and Aceros del Norte.

In non-ferrous metals, the only copper refiner in the country is the Mexican-American enterprise Cobre de México, established in 1943. Recently (November, 1959) the Aluminum Company of America announced it had joined Mexican and European investors for the construction of Mexico's first primary aluminum smelting plant at a total cost of nearly $20 million.

The tire and rubber industry in Mexico is dominated by joint ventures to varying degrees. This is the case of the five major enterprises, which produce the brands of Goodrich, Goodyear, General Tire, United States Rubber, and Firestone.

Four United States brands and two European brands have been represented in Mexico's automotive vehicle assembling industry. Two United States brands, Ford and General Motors, are turned out by wholly foreign-owned enterprises, while the other two, Chrysler and Willys, are produced under franchise arrangements by firms owned by Mexican capital. One European brand, the Italian Fiat, was made by the national enterprise, Diesel Nacional, under a franchise arrangement until the end of 1959, when the franchise expired and was replaced by one with the French Renault enterprise.

Joint ventures have been represented in Mexico's rapidly developing machinery and related industries. Examples are: Wormser-Suiza de México, the only enterprise in the country producing certain types of machinery and equipment for the construction industry; Toyoda de México, originally a Japanese joint venture, recently converted into an all-national enterprise, which is the only manufacturer of industrial textile machinery and accounts for about one-half of national capacity in household sewing machines; Industria Eléctrica de México, the Westinghouse joint venture which is the leader in local manufacture of electrical machinery and equipment and household appliances; and Bristol de México, a British joint venture which has the only modern facility in the country for the overhaul and repair of airplane engines. Other important enterprises in related fields are Worthington de México, a Mexican-American enterprise that manufactures deep well water pumps; and

Engranes y Productos Industriales, a Mexican-American venture (in which the International Finance Corporation made its first investment in Mexico) that produces parts for automotive vehicles.

In electrical products, aside from the leader, Industria Eléctrica de México, which is probably the largest enterprise of its kind in Latin America, there are other joint ventures manufacturing household appliances, and one of the principal firms in the manufacture of wire and cables is the American-Italian-Mexican enterprise, Conductores Eléctricos.

Cement is for the most part a nationally-owned industry in Mexico, but two large plants, which account for close to 20 percent of national capacity, are owned by the British-Mexican enterprises La Tolteca and Cemento de Mixcoac. These enterprises are old, dating back, respectively, to 1909 and 1931. A new cement enterprise, established in 1956, Cementos California, is owned by local capital, but has received American loans and technical assistance.

Glass is similarly a national industry, but there are some recent instances of joint venture arrangements for the manufacture of specialized products such as glass fiber insulation.

Refractories are entirely dominated by joint ventures. There are two important Mexican-American enterprises in this field: Ladrillos Industriales y Refractarios Harbison-Walker-Flir, and Compañía Mexicana de Refractarios A. P. Green.

Foreign interests are widely represented in the manufacture of chemicals and pharmaceuticals, generally without association with local interests, but there are some important instances of joint ventures in this area too. The recently formed French-Mexican enterprise for the manufacture of nitrogenous fertilizers, Fertilizantes de Monclova, will have a larger output than the only other existing producer, and will supply about 40 percent of the total national need. The only producer of soda ash and the leading producer of caustic soda is Sosa Texcoco, which has a technical assistance arrangement with Imperial Chemical Industries of Great Britain. Other firms in the field of alkalies that have recently been formed are also joint ventures. An important producer of naval stores is the Mexican-American enterprise Corbu Industrial, and the country's leading producer of aspirin and other salicylates is the Mexican-American venture Pyrina.

Mexico has only one firm that produces newsprint, the Fábrica de Papel Tuxtepec, recently organized as an American-Canadian-Mexican venture. Another important source of pulp for the paper industry and for rayon is the Italian-Mexican enterprise Celulosa de Chihuahua, which also produces rayon or viscose textile fibers in Viscosa de Chihuahua. The foreign partner in both enterprises is Snia Viscosa. The only other producer of synthetic fibers in Mexico is the American joint venture Celanese Mexicana, which specializes in the acetate fiber.

In ready-made apparel, there is a wide representation of foreign brands that are manufactured by nationally-owned enterprises under licensing arrangements. Some 30 foreign brands were represented at an exposition of the national clothing industry held in Mexico City in November, 1958.

Joint ventures are found to a limited extent in Mexico's food and beverage industries. They are usually franchise arrangements as in the case of the bottling of foreign brand soft drinks and the packing of brand-name breakfast cereals, but there are also some cases of joint equity ventures, as in processed milk (the Mexican-American Carnation de México) and crackers (Nabisco Famosa).

The nationalized petroleum industry in the country has permitted some foreign participation through arrangements between the government company and private foreign contractors.

Electric power was originally developed here too by foreign enterprise (Canadian and American), but in recent years the industry has become entirely nationalized. The American and Canadian interests were sold entirely to the Mexican government. The leading foreign enterprise, the Mexican Light and Power Company, started in 1955 to sell minority shares to Mexican investors. Its expansion had also been financed by Mexican government loans, which bore option rights for the conversion of some of the loan obligations into equity. Still another joint venture aspect of a different type involved the distribution through this private company of power from the new generating facilities that had been developed in the country over the last 10 to 15 years mainly by the government. The American-owned Impulsora de Empresas Eléctricas (American and Foreign Power) was the second largest privately operated system in the country.

Telephone service, also developed in Mexico for the most part by foreign enterprise, has moved through a joint venture phase to present ownership entirely by national capital.

The two leading aviation enterprises in Mexico, the Compañía Mexicana de Aviación and Aeronaves de México, which account for 80–85 percent of the aviation services in the country, are joint ventures, with participation by Pan American World Airways.

Joint ventures are represented to some extent in merchandising, and banking. Sears, Roebuck, which has numerous department stores throughout Mexico, has a small minority of local capital by virtue of an employees' profit-sharing scheme, and has invested jointly with some local firms which manufacture consumer goods sold in its stores. Another joint venture in this field is Sanborn Hermanos, well-known for its department store and restaurant services to American tourists. It was originally developed as an American venture but has since been sold to other American interests in partnership with local capital.

Banking is a national operation, except for the only foreign branch bank in the country, the First National City Bank of New York. There is one joint venture in the field, the recently organized Descuento Agrícola, with participation by the Bank of America, which specializes in medium-term credit for the acquisition of agricultural machinery.

COLOMBIA

Industrial development in Colombia has not proceeded quite so far as in Brazil and Mexico, and foreign investments have not been as important as a primary factor in the country's general economic development. Joint ventures have also been somewhat less widespread. However, in recent years the country's industrial development has been increasing rapidly, and, with its less nationalistic attitudes toward foreign investments, joint ventures are increasing and can be found in a wide variety of activities.

Heavy industry has had a limited development. The country has only one primary steel mill, Acerías Paz del Río, inaugurated in 1954 as a government-owned enterprise, but also having private Colombian capital by virtue of forced investments by income tax payers. There is no foreign equity in the enterprise, but a substantial loan from a French bank was obtained to finance the initial equipment, and foreign designers and construction contractors as well as individual technicians have been employed.

The country has no automotive vehicle industry or important machinery manufacture. In recent years there have been balance of payments difficulties which made it necessary to impose prohibitions on the importation of automotive vehicles, and projects have been developed for automotive assembly plants. None of these has as yet come into being because of government hesitation concerning the economic advisability of such projects, but they have all been planned as joint ventures with franchise arrangements with foreign manufacturers.

Small river boats are built in the country, primarily by a joint venture, the Unión Industrial y Astilleros Barranquilla, with equity participation by three American shipyard companies. This enterprise was developed by German capital, but was nationalized by the Colombian government during the Second World War.

The non-ferrous metals industry has also had a very limited development. There is one plant that rolls aluminum ingots, and is a joint venture with equity participation by the American Reynolds Metals Company (Aluminio de Colombia–Reynolds, Santo Domingo).

The tire industry in Colombia is dominated by foreign interests and particularly by joint ventures. The brands represented are Goodrich, Croydon, Seiberling, and Goodyear. The first three are manufactured by joint ventures; the Goodyear enterprise is wholly foreign-owned.

Another similarity with Brazil and Mexico is in the field of synthetic textile fibers, manufactured entirely by important joint venture enterprises (Celanese Colombiana, affiliated with the Celanese Corporation of America, and Indurayón Consolidada). Acetate yarns and fibers are produced by Celanese Colombiana, and viscose by Indurayón. Control of Indurayón was recently purchased by Celanese Colombiana. One of the leading producers of cloth of synthetic fibers in Colombia, Textiles Panamericanos, which accounts for somewhat more than one-fourth of the local market, is a joint United States–Colombian venture.

The cotton textile industry in Colombia is almost entirely national. However, one of the two principal enterprises that produces cotton yarns, the Compañía Textil Colombiana, is a French-Colombian venture, the other being an all-British enterprise; and the foreign partner (Burlington Mills) in the enterprise, Textiles Panamericanos, also has a technical assistance agreement with its Colombian partner in the Fabricato firm, which is a leading cotton cloth producer. W. R. Grace & Company, which held an important share in another leading cotton cloth enterprise, Tejicóndor, recently sold that investment to national interests to move on to other fields in Colombia.

There is also some joint venture representation in the less well-developed field of apparel, in ladies' hosiery (Berkshire Knitting Mills de Colombia), and in various arrangements with manufacturing firms by Sears, Roebuck.

The only primary paper and paperboard producer in Colombia is the joint United States–Colombian enterprise, Cartón de Colombia, with participation by the Container Corporation of America. There are two projects for the creation of additional primary pulp and paper facilities, both of which are being planned as joint ventures, one to which the Container Corporation of America is also a party, and the other a pulp-from-bagasse project of W. R. Grace & Company. Joint ventures are represented to a smaller extent in paper converting. Specialized cellophane and other fancy paper wrappings are manufactured by Shellmar de Colombia, a joint venture of the Continental Can Company of the United States. A large national distributor of paper products and office supplies, Carvajal y Compañía, has a process agreement with a United States firm for the manufacture of calendars, and is contemplating others for such items as carbon paper and typewriter ribbon.

Joint ventures are also found in various branches of building materials, especially in asbestos-cement products, lumber, and paints.

The basic building products, such as cement and bricks, are produced by national enterprises. Asbestos-cement roofing and other building materials are produced in the country by three enterprises (Eternit Colombiana, Eternit Atlántica, and Eternit del Pacífico) owned by the same joint foreign (Swiss–Belgian–United States) and Colombian interests. In lumber exploitation, until recently carried on in Colombia only on a primitive basis, a large new enterprise, Industria Forestal Colombiana, was formed in 1955 at foreign initiative (Mexican, United States, and Swedish) with Colombian participation. The first important paint enterprise in Colombia, Pintuco, was started as a United States–Colombian venture, but the foreign investor (W. R. Grace & Company) has since sold its interest to the domestic partner, and has started a new all-foreign paint firm in the country. In addition, Sherwin-Williams paints are manufactured under a licensing agreement by a firm owned by Colombian capital.

The local assembly of household equipment such as kitchen cabinets, refrigerators, stoves, hot water heaters, and washing machines, and the manufacture of office furniture have been stimulated in recent years by balance of payments pressures. Foreign participation has generally been sought by local entrepreneurs, and various types of joint venture arrangements have emerged. Prominent among such ventures are the Icasa, Induacero, Industria de Equipos de Acero, and Salazar & Manrique firms.

An important move toward the development of local chemical industries was made in 1958 when W. R. Grace & Company bought into two small ventures, originally started by resident foreign entrepreneurs, that produce solvents and resins.

Most of the food and beverage industries in Colombia are nationally-owned, but certain fields have foreign participation through joint venture arrangements. The largest brewery firm in the country, the Consorcio de Cervecerías Bavaria, now all nationally-owned, was originally a German-Dutch-Colombian venture. From one-fourth to one-third of the local soft drinks market is covered by four foreign brands—Coca Cola, Pepsi Cola, Canada Dry, and Citrus Products of Chicago—which are bottled by local enterprises under foreign franchise arrangements. There is a similar arrangement for a soft ice cream product (Crem Helado) that has been developed in recent years. Conservas California, originally a national investment in canned and bottled foods, has been converted into a joint venture by the entry of W. R. Grace & Company.

Foreign investments in petroleum are among the most important foreign investments in the country, and joint ventures have been represented in various of the activities of one of the important foreign companies, the International Petroleum Company Ltd., a Canadian subsidiary of the Standard Oil Company of New Jersey. This company held one of the oldest and most important oil concessions in the country, the De Mares concession, which, with all its installations, reverted to the government in 1951 after a period of some 32 years of operation, in accordance with its original terms. At first, the government conducted oil extraction on the concession with technical assistance from the former concession holder; this became unnecessary after a few years. The De Mares concession installations also included the country's only important oil refinery. The oil refinery is run on a rental basis by a subsidiary of International Petroleum, which also granted a large loan for expansion. International Petroleum has since built a second important refinery in the country as a wholly-owned operation. Another subsidiary of International Petroleum, Esso Colombiana, for years was the only distributor in the country of gasoline and other petroleum products. Part of its capital is now owned by the general public in Colombia, and it has encountered the competition of two other principal distribution networks—those of a foreign company (Shell) and of a domestic company (Codi), the latter having been promoted by a former high Colombian official of Esso. Another joint venture promoted by International Petroleum, the Compañía Colombiana de Gas, is the distributor of the only modern household fuel used in the country, liquefied petroleum gas. Finally, International Petroleum has developed a petroleum products pipeline, the Oleoducto del Pacífico, on a joint venture basis.

In service fields, joint ventures are prominent in hotel operation, sales financing, and aviation. The country's leading hotel, the Hotel Tequendama in Bogotá, was developed on a contractual basis by the Intercontinental Hotels Corporation utilizing equity capital of a local pension fund, that of army officers, and of various agencies of the Colombian government, and loan capital from the Export-Import Bank of Washington. The Intercontinental Hotels Corporation holds no equity in the Hotel Tequendama, but runs the hotel under a management contract. The Intercontinental Hotels Corporation has recently bought a majority equity interest in the Hotel del Prado in Barranquilla after having operated the hotel in the past on a management contract basis.

The institution of retail sales financing of durable consumer goods was started in Colombia in 1955, when Promotora Colombiana was organized by United States, French, and Colombian interests.

In aviation, Avianca, by far the country's leading enterprise in the field, is a joint venture with equity participation by Pan American World Airways. The firm, one of the oldest aviation enterprises in the world, was originally developed in 1919 by German initiative and Colombian capital.

CUBA

Policies and attitudes in Cuba toward foreign investments and private enterprise changed radically with the revolution of early 1959, and the future of joint ventures or any other foreign investments is quite uncertain at the date of this writing. This is to be borne in mind in reading the summary below of our findings on joint ventures in the Cuban economy prior to the revolution.

Cuba had not developed basic or even secondary manufacturing industries to the same extent as the other Latin American countries. Accordingly, joint ventures were less widespread. However, foreign investments in Cuba were extensive in the all-important sugar industry, and in other fields such as public utilities, and some trend toward the joint venture type of foreign investment became noticeable during the last decade.

The Cuban sugar industry had a large amount of foreign investment, but generally on a wholly foreign-owned basis. Nevertheless, some of the important enterprises, including Vertientes Camagüey, the Cuban Atlantic Sugar Company, and the Francisco Sugar Company, had national as well as foreign capital.

It is of interest that a new industry had developed in the use of bagasse, the sugarcane residue, for wallboard and other fiber products instead of being employed as a low-quality fuel. Substantial investments were made in this industry in Cuba beginning in 1955, especially to substitute for the country's large lumber imports, and many of the enterprises represented joint Cuban-American ventures by interests involved in the sugar industry. The most important were the Cuban Finance Company, formed in 1957, and Primadera Bagasse, organized in 1956.

An important minerals resource in Cuba was developed during the Second World War through the construction of a nickel processing plant by the United States government at a cost of some $85 million to utilize the country's extensive nickel deposits. The reserves of about 24 million tons of contained nickel are three times larger than those of Canada, the world's leading producer of nickel. The plant was shut down in 1947 as a surplus defense plant, but it was reactivated in 1951 during the Korean conflict. Upon its reactivation in 1951, the plant was operated under a management contract by the Nickel Processing Corporation, a joint Cuban-American venture. On September 15, 1959, the United States government announced that the plant was for sale.

Joint ventures also dominated in petroleum. Exploration for petroleum had been stimulated, until the advent of the revolutionary régime, by the construction of three new refineries in the country by foreign companies—Standard Oil of New Jersey, Shell, and the Texas Company. (These refineries were taken over by the Cuban government in mid-1960 in a dispute with the companies over the processing of crude oil from the Soviet Union; the Standard of New Jersey and Texaco refineries were subsequently expropriated). Production of crude petroleum in Cuba is small, amounting to less than ten percent of domestic requirements. The joint ventures in exploration generally consisted of "farm-out" arrangements with foreign companies by Cuban land or concession holders, and included large foreign companies such as Standard Oil of Indiana, the Gulf Oil Company, and Standard Oil of New Jersey, as well as smaller "independent" oil operators.

One of the leading sources of Cuba's foreign exchange was tourism, and joint venture arrangements were prominently featured in the industry, especially in hotel activities. The Hotel Nacional, the oldest modern tourist hotel (built in 1930) was American-owned and was operated by its leading shareholder, the Intercontinental Hotels Corporation, under a management contract to which Cuban interests were also a party. Other leading hotels more recently constructed are the Hotel Havana Hilton and the Hotel La Riviera, both of which were joint ventures. The Hotel Havana Hilton followed the pattern of the Hotel Tequendama in Colombia; the equity was Cuban (the retirement fund of the Restaurant Workers' Union, compared to the retirement fund of army officers in the Colombian case), but operation was on a management contract basis by Hilton Hotels International. The Hotel La Riviera was jointly owned by a Cuban government bank and an American hotel operator. Another joint venture aspect of the tourist business was the operation of gambling casinos by American interests on a concession basis. All of these activities have been taken over by the government since 1959.

Public utilities, developed in Cuba by foreign interests, followed the pattern of gradual assumption of joint venture characteristics. In electric power, the Cuban Electric Company, the country's leading enterprise in the field and a subsidiary of the American and Foreign Power Company, had expansion programs in recent years financed by loans from the Cuban government as well as from the Export-Import Bank of Washington. The only major hydroelectric plant in the country, owned and operated by the government, distributed its power through the Cuban Electric Company. Telephone service had for a long time been rendered in Cuba by the Cuban Telephone Company, a subsidiary of the International Telephone and Telegraph Company, which became a joint venture by virtue of being obligated to offer shares to the Cuban public under a modification of its concession in 1957. Both the Cuban Electric Company and the Cuban Telephone Company were expropriated in August, 1960.

Another important joint venture in the field of public utilities was the Havana Harbor Tunnel, recently completed to facilitate the flow of traffic to the business center of the city. The project was financed by specialized government development banks, and constructed by a French contracting firm which also purchased a substantial amount of bonds issued to help in the financing.

In transportation, the leading aviation enterprise (the Compañía Cubana de Aviación) was bought in 1954 from Pan American Airways by a local group, and it entered into a cooperation and technical assistance agreement with the British Overseas Airways Corporation. An agreement was signed in mid-1958 by the Cuban government with British interests for the construction of a shipyard and the creation of a national merchant marine.

In manufacturing, joint ventures were found in soaps and cosmetics, iron and steel, and copper wire and cables.

In soaps and cosmetics, a leading enterprise was a joint venture with participation by Colgate-Palmolive. Cuba's iron and steel industry is limited to plants that manufacture concrete reinforcing bars and steel pipe. In the former, the largest enterprise was the Antillana Steel Corporation, a joint Cuban-American venture that had been converted from a wholly domestic enterprise in connection with its expansion. Metalúrgica Básica Nacional was established in 1956 to manufacture steel water pipe by Cuban and Belgian interests. The only producer in the country of copper wire and cables was the enterprise Pheldrak, organized in 1956 as a Cuban-American-Dutch venture.

INDIA

Joint ventures are prominently represented in various branches of heavy industry in India, especially in the production of iron and steel, dyestuffs and pharmaceuticals, and automotive vehicles, and in certain branches of light industry, including the production of bicycles, fountain pens and ink, and tires.

The steelmaking capacity of India is growing. Projects include expansion of the two principal steel plants of the country, which are privately-owned, and the construction of three new plants by the Indian government. By the end of the second Five-Year Plan (1961), the capacity of ingot steel will be raised to 6 million tons. Each of the three government-owned plants is to have an initial capacity of one million tons, and together will represent one-half of the country's total production. One of the two privately-owned firms is the Tata organization, which has been making steel for over 50 years. This firm has had the technical collaboration of the

Kaiser Engineering Corporation of the United States. The three government steel projects are being built at Rourkela, Bhilai, and Durgapur, with West German, Russian, and British assistance respectively. The foreign assistance in no case involves equity investment, although, in the case of the Rourkela venture, a ten percent equity investment, gradually to be liquidated, was originally contemplated. The Indian government eventually decided to keep full ownership in its steel enterprises. The participation of the foreign interests therefore consists of technical services for designing and construction of the plants, plus deferred payments arrangements and loans for the imported equipment. Thus, joint venture arrangements have been prominently featured in the Indian iron and steel industry, but there are no instances of joint equity investments, and the arrangements with foreign interests have been of a limited and temporary nature.

One of the country's leading producers of dyestuffs and pharmaceuticals (Atul Products Ltd.) has joint venture arrangements with a number of firms from various countries. Atul was organized after the Second World War as a result of investigations of the possibilities of developing a local dyestuffs industry, and in this connection assistance was sought from abroad. Both technical and equity participation were obtained from the American Cyanamid Company in 1946, from Ciba Ltd. of Switzerland in 1948, and from Imperial Chemical Industries Ltd. of England in 1955. The arrangement with Imperial involved the formation of a new joint venture company, Atic Industries Ltd.

Also in pharmaceuticals is Merck Sharp & Dohme of India Private Ltd., set up as a joint venture with local private interests in 1958. The parent firm, Merck Sharp & Dohme International, also entered into a technical assistance and licensing arrangement with a government-owned plant for the production of streptomycin and derivatives. The initial production line of the private joint venture covers steroids, diuretics, some vitamins, and some sulpha drugs.

One of the leading manufacturers of automotive vehicles in India is the Automotive Division of Telco (the Tata Engineering and Locomotive Co. Ltd.). The Telco enterprise was first formed in 1945 for the manufacture of locomotive and heavy engineering products. It moved into the production of road vehicles in 1954 through an agreement with Daimler Benz of West Germany for the manufacture of Mercedes-Benz diesel truck and bus chassis.

An important light engineering industry is the production of bicycles. Demand for bicycles has quadrupled during the postwar period, and the country now manufactures nearly 700,000 bicycles per year, with demand still growing rapidly. Two new firms were added in 1951 to the one that was previously in existence. Both of these new firms were organized with technical and financial collaboration of well-known British bicycle manufacturers.

A leading producer of quality fountain pens and ink is the Pilot Pen Company (India) Private Ltd., which was organized in 1952 as a Japanese-Indian joint venture. This firm now turns out nearly 50,000 pens and 500 gallons of ink per month.

In tires, which are in short supply and for which present production capacity is insufficient, an important new joint venture project is underway. This is the Ceat Tyres of India Ltd. firm, established in 1957 with the participation of the leading Italian tire producer, Ceat Gomma S.p.A., which in turn has a technical agreement with the General Tire and Rubber Company of the United States.

BURMA AND PAKISTAN

Joint ventures in Burma dominate mining, and have also been of primary importance in deep-sea fishing, and the production of soap, pharmaceuticals, and tea.

Mining, particularly of tin, tungsten, lead and silver, and petroleum extraction were important industries in Burma before the Second World War, and were operated entirely by British enterprises. These minerals accounted for close to 40 percent of the country's total foreign exchange earnings. A great deal of physical destruction of the installations in this industry occurred during the war, and production came to a standstill. Political and military insecurity in the postwar period caused the British operators to hesitate on investing for the rehabilitation of facilities, and the eventual result was the conversion of the foreign operating companies into joint ventures in association with the Burmese government. Accordingly, mining and petroleum exploitation in Burma are now dominated by the following joint ventures: The Burma Corporation (1951) Ltd., whose principal product is lead; The Burma Oil Company (1954) Ltd.; the Anglo-Burma Tin Company (1956) Ltd.; and Mawchi Mines (1957) Ltd., which produces a mixed tin-wolfram-scheelite concentrate.

Deep-sea fishing was introduced into Burma in 1953 by a private Japanese-Burmese venture, the Martaban Company Ltd., with participation by the Taiyo Fishing Company of Tokyo.

The manufacture of high quality soaps is dominated by Burma Unilever Ltd., formed in 1958 after protracted negotiations as a joint venture by the Unilever enterprise of England and the Industrial Development Corporation of the Burmese government.

The Burmese government has sought foreign technical collaboration for the operation of certain industries which are run as government enterprises: The advice of the Lipton Tea Company has been obtained by the government's Tea Project Board; and a management contract, at least for a short period of time, was entered into by the Burmese government with Evans Medical Supplies Ltd. of England for the development of a pharmaceutical industry.

In Pakistan, quality soaps are produced almost entirely by a joint venture between the Unilever enterprise of England, the local government, and some local entrepreneurs. This is the enterprise, Lever Brothers (Pakistan) Ltd., which started operating on a joint venture basis in 1948 through some predecessor companies of different names. In addition to the high quality soaps, in which this firm is the leader in the field in Pakistan, it also produces 20 percent of the nation's edible vegetable oils, and has recently introduced the manufacture of "balanced cattle food."

An enterprise of basic importance to the economy of Pakistan is the Sui Gas Transmission Company Ltd., set up as a joint venture in 1954. Pursuant to new petroleum regulations enacted in 1949, Pakistan Petroleum Ltd. was set up as a joint venture, mainly with the local government, by the British-owned Burmah Oil Company Ltd. In the course of its explorations, this company came upon a large strike of natural gas in 1951. Its utilization led to the formation of the Sui Gas Transmission Company Ltd. Sui Gas was set up to purify and transmit the gas to two distributing companies, one owned entirely by the Pakistani government and the other by private local investors. The joint venture in Sui Gas was set up between the Burmah Oil Company and the Commonwealth Development Finance Company on the British side, and the Pakistan Industrial Development Corporation of the government and private local investors on the Pakistani side. The enterprise also obtained a large loan from the International Bank for Reconstruction and Development. The development of natural gas has permitted the curtailment of substantial imports of coal and petroleum, and new industrial installations (such as electric power stations and cement and fertilizer plants) are being planned on the basis of its availability.

THE PHILIPPINES

Foreign investments in the Philippines, concentrated in public utilities, mining, and manufacturing, have been converted into joint ventures. In public utilities, the outstanding firms are the Manila Electric Company and the Manila Gas Corporation, providing the respective utilities in the capital. The Manila Gas Corporation became a joint venture in association with the Philippine government early in the postwar period in connection with its rehabilitation requirements. The Manila Electric Company, still all foreign-owned, has announced plans, approved by the Philippine government, to raise additional capital in the local market because of difficulties in raising capital abroad under local controls on utility rates and on the remittance of profits. This is similar to the trend among foreign-owned electric power enterprises in Latin America.

Mining output in the Philippines has consisted of some copper and other base metals, but mostly of gold. A number of enterprises were started by resident Americans, but have generally become joint ventures through trading of securities in the local stock market. Philippine mining ventures, including Benguet Consolidated, Inc. and Lepanto Consolidated Mining Company, have become jointly-owned by American investors through the same mechanism. Some Philippine mining enterprise securities are listed on stock exchanges in the United States.

In manufacturing, joint ventures are found especially in the production of tires, storage batteries, aluminum products, and milk products. There has also been some joint venture entry into petroleum refining.

Foreign tire brands manufactured in the Philippines are those of Goodrich, Goodyear, and Firestone. Of these, the Goodrich and Firestone enterprises are joint ventures, while Goodyear is wholly foreign-owned, following a pattern observed for that firm in other countries. During the postwar period, new firms were formed in the Philippines by nationals to manufacture storage batteries, generally on the basis of royalty arrangements with foreign manufacturers. The rolling of aluminum ingots into products such as cigarette and candy foils, and corrugated sheets and circles was introduced into the country in 1954 by the joint venture known as the Reynolds Philippine Corp. In milk processing, a leading canned milk producer, the General Milk Company (Philippines), was established in 1956 as a wholly foreign-owned venture, but sold additional shares to a local investment group in 1958.

In petroleum refining, a wholly foreign-owned subsidiary of the Caltex firm was established in 1952, and the Standard Vacuum Oil Company soon followed suit. The Shell Oil Company attempted to do the same, but had trouble obtaining official approval since its project coincided with the Gulf Oil Company refinery project, which was planned on a joint equity basis with local investors. Shell was forced to abandon its original plans and to take on local equity.

The only domestic airline in the Philippines is Philippine Air Lines, and the government holds the majority share. It has been reported that Pan American World Airways has recently acquired a minority position. Pan American Airways, through its subsidiary, the Intercontinental Hotels Corporation, also has a project for the development of a tourist hotel to be known as the Rizal Intercontinental Hotel. This project will involve equity participation by IHC as well as a management contract arrangement with it. There has been much opposition to this project by local, domestic hotel interests, and its future is uncertain. In any case, Pan American Airways appears to have embarked on joint venture projects in the Philippines along the lines it has followed in a number of Latin American countries.

TURKEY

Joint ventures are found in Turkey in manufacturing industries. They have frequently arisen from former exporter-importer relationships between the foreign and Turkish partners, and subsequent decisions to undertake local manufacture. Thus, they are found especially in recently established fields, but some older enterprises, formerly foreign-owned, have also been converted into joint ventures.

In cement, the most important and one of the oldest enterprises in the country is the Anadolu Cement Corporation, founded in 1929. This enterprise was all foreign until 1956, when it was expanded and converted by its Belgian and Danish owners into a joint venture with the Industrial Development Bank of the Turkish government, pursuant to the desire of the foreign interests to minimize their commitment of new capital resources, and the emphasis on joint ventures in the official policy of the country. Anadolu is one of 14 cement plants in Turkey. A recently formed enterprise to manufacture concrete, the Turk-Betocel Company, is a joint venture with West German participation.

The only producer of steel pipe in Turkey is the joint venture of a West German firm and a local official bank (the Mannesmann-Sumerbank Steel Pipe Manufacturing Corporation), organized in 1954. Another older joint venture producing iron and steel products is the Belgian-Turkish enterprise, Turkiye Madoni Sanayi (established 1931), which manufactures wire, nails, and shovels.

Leading pharmaceutical firms have been set up in recent years as joint ventures. These are the recently established enterprise known as the United German Pharmaceutical Plants, with the capital participation of Bayer, Shering, Knall, and Merck; E. R. Squibb & Sons of Turkey (organized in 1951); and another West German joint venture, Turk-Hoechst, formed in 1954 with the capital participation of Farbwerke Hoechst.

The sole producer of electric light bulbs in Turkey is the General Electric Turkish Corporation, organized as a joint venture in 1948. The assembly of radios was introduced into the country by

Turk-Philips, organized in 1956 with a nominal amount of Turkish capital.

The only modern plant in the country engaged in canning and bottling of fruits, vegetables, and prepared foods is a joint venture. This is the Tamek Canning Company Ltd., originally formed in 1954 as a German-Turkish enterprise, and converted into a United States–Turkish enterprise in 1957. The leading firm in the manufacture of cotton thread, Santral Dikis Sanayii Turk, is also a joint venture, having been set up in 1952 with the participation of J. & P. Coats Ltd. of Scotland.

The major enterprises in the manufacture of toothpaste tubes are joint ventures, one an Israeli-Swiss-Turkish enterprise known as Metalum Sanayi Ltd., and the other a French-Turkish enterprise with the trademark "Perfect."

Other manufacturing fields in which there has been a development of new facilities in recent years on a joint venture basis include motorized agricultural equipment, jeeps, typewriters, and chemicals such as synthetic fertilizers, insecticides, and paints and resins.

Joint Ventures in the Foreign Operations of Investor Companies

Interviews were conducted with leading companies in the industrialized countries involved in foreign investments to determine their attitudes toward and experience with joint ventures.

UNITED STATES

Approximately 20 leading companies in the United States were surveyed. Most of them were companies engaged in a particular industrial line or field of activity and had extended their activities abroad in operations other than mere foreign trading. They represent petroleum companies, service industries, and such varied activities as the production of chemicals and pharmaceuticals, artificial textile fibers, business machines, electrical equipment and machinery, automotive vehicles, specialized steel products, soaps, and tires. In addition to the companies that are engaged in the production of goods or consumer services, the American Overseas Finance Company has been a provider of loan capital, the Panamerican Capital Corporation of venture capital.

The global statistical data presented in Chapter II on the quantitative extent of joint ventures among total United States foreign direct investments suggested that joint ventures constituted only a small minority of the total of investments in the less developed countries in 1950 (representing little more than 10 percent of the total), but that there was a trend toward this type of investment in the postwar period, the ratio having risen to some 17 percent in 1957. The increasing trend toward joint ventures was generally borne out in the interviews with the United States firms. About a third had either no joint ventures or practically none in their foreign investments in the less developed countries, a third had only a few joint ventures among all their foreign investments, and the remaining third was involved mostly in joint ventures in their foreign operations.

The soap, business machine, automotive vehicle, and petroleum companies were almost entirely without joint ventures. This does not imply that the particular firms in question are necessarily representative of the joint venture situation in their respective industries.

The soap producer, Procter & Gamble, conducts its foreign operations on a wholly-owned basis. In some cases, foreign interests were represented in preexisting enterprises that became Procter & Gamble operations, but these interests were entirely bought out, and no foreign equity remained in the firms. The company has made considerable use of foreign loan capital in the particular countries where it operates in order to protect itself from the depreciation of exchange rates.

The IBM World Trade Corporation is a party to no joint ventures in any of the less developed countries, primarily because of the highly specialized nature of its products. There has been less external pressure for local participation in its enterprises than in the case of other more familiar activities.

The Ford Motor Company similarly establishes plants abroad on a wholly-owned basis. It began in economically underdeveloped areas such as Latin America many years ago when there was not the pressure that exists today for participation by local capital. It has offered shares in its enterprises to the general public only in industrialized countries. In one instance, Ford formerly owned a majority stock interest in a Spanish company which in turn owned substantially all of the shares of a Portuguese company, but the joint equity was eliminated. By virtue of the Spanish company's control of the Portuguese company, profits from the latter were remitted to Spain, and were then subject to difficulties of transfer to the United States. This and other restrictions in Spain finally resulted in a transaction in 1954 under which Ford emerged with complete ownership of the Portuguese plant and with no equity interest at all in the Spanish venture. At the time the transaction was concluded, the equity interest of Ford in the Spanish enterprise was replaced by technical assistance and licensing agreements between Ford of the United States and its affiliate in the United Kingdom on the one hand, and the now wholly Spanish-owned enterprise, Motor Ibérica S.A., on the other.

General Motors also follows a deliberate policy of not entering into joint ventures in its foreign investments. The view is that participation in the fortunes and risks of the firm should take place through the acquisition of shares in the parent corporation. Separate participation in its individual foreign subsidiaries is regarded as no more justified than the acquisition of separate stock in any of the company's domestic divisions, and such participation is considered undesirable because of the potential interference with the determination of company policies on an overall, worldwide basis; the firm wishes to be free to set its policies in any given country in the light of its global policies. It has not encountered pressures for local participation in its ventures and, accordingly, has undertaken them on a wholly foreign-owned basis; this is true of a truck-manufacturing operation in Brazil, and of a similar plant being started in Argentina. Clamor for local participation in its ventures has been met only in Canada and Australia; in Australia, despite the clamor, a small local participation in the GM-Holden enterprise was recently eliminated when Australian-held preference shares (belonging to some local distributors of GM products) were bought back by GM, because the shareholders wanted participating profits rather than a fixed dividend of six percent.

American petroleum companies generally have not engaged in joint ventures with local capital in less developed countries, but have had to accept participation under special circumstances. For example, Standard Oil Company (Indiana) is party to a joint venture with the National Iranian Oil Company, the government company, in an offshore oil production venture in Iran. The Standard Vacuum Oil Company, in which Standard Oil Company (New Jersey) and Socony Mobil Oil Company, Inc. are 50 percent shareholders, has joint oil exploration ventures with the governments of India and Pakistan.

The Union Carbide Corporation has been increasingly looking upon its foreign operations in recent years as independent units rather than merely as extensions of its domestic operations, and, following upon this emphasis, has entered into a number of joint venture arrangements in India and Brazil. The firm generally prefers to take on foreign partners only after it has developed its new ventures to the point of becoming going concerns.

The Worthington Corporation, manufacturer of pumps and other machinery items, has approximately five enterprises in less developed countries, of which two (in Brazil and Colombia) are wholly-owned, while three (Argentina, Mexico, and Spain), are joint ventures. Although Worthington's general policy has been to set up ventures with outright ownership, it has accepted the joint venture arrangements under special circumstances.

In the field of chemicals, E. I. duPont de Nemours & Company had foreign manufacturing investments in Latin America (Brazil, Mexico, Cuba, Chile, Argentina, and Peru), aside from those in more highly industrialized countries such as the United Kingdom, Germany, and Canada. Although duPont prefers to operate through wholly-owned subsidiaries, it has by no means always adhered to this pattern. Of its Latin American investments, those in Brazil as well as Peru, and some in Mexico are wholly-owned, while those in Chile and Argentina are joint ventures with a duPont majority, and in Mexico duPont holds a 49 percent equity in one enterprise. In

Mexico all operations were conducted through wholly-owned subsidiaries until the formation of Pigmentos y Productos Químicos in 1959 to engage in the manufacture of certain pigments. The decision was initially made to construct the facilities on a wholly-owned basis, but, because of difficulties involving approvals and clearances from the Mexican government, a 51 percent Mexican equity participation was admitted. The firm's investment in Brazil was converted in 1954 from a partially-owned to a wholly-owned subsidiary.

Armco, a leader in the United States in the production of specialty steels, through its Armco International Corporation, similarly prefers wholly-owned subsidiaries, but has entered into some joint venture arrangements in Latin American countries. In some cases it has technical assistance agreements overseas but these have not precluded its simultaneous development of wholly-owned subsidiaries in the same countries.

The pharmaceutical house Merck & Co., Inc. has changed the emphasis in its foreign operations from exporting to the establishment of plants abroad. The objective of its international division, Merck Sharp & Dohme International, and of the company is to become a pharmaceutical house on a world-wide basis rather than merely an exporter out of its United States operations. Accompanying this shift of emphasis has also been a move away from manufacturing abroad through licensing agreements with foreign firms to manufacturing in plants in which the parent firm holds equity. The company has seven subsidiary plants in less developed countries: four in Latin America, in Argentina, Brazil, Mexico, and Colombia, and three in the Far East, in India, Thailand, and the Philippines. The four plants in Latin America are wholly-owned subsidiaries, the two plants in India and Thailand are joint equity ventures with local capital in which the parent firm directly or indirectly holds a 60 percent majority, and in the Philippines the firm has a wholly-owned subsidiary as well as a licensing arrangement with a national enterprise for the manufacture of a different line of products. While the company appreciates the advantages of the simplicity of control and lack of potential conflict of interest in a wholly-owned subsidiary, it recognizes the considerable advantages of joint ventures and anticipates more in the future. Although it favors only minority local participation, the company feels that the minority should be substantial enough to ensure the necessary degree of interest in the enterprise by the local investor. In this respect, one problem that it anticipates meeting in countries of only limited development is that of the availability of local partners who can make an effective contribution to the joint venture.

The Von Kohorn International Corporation, designer, supplier, installer, and operator of chemical yarn and fiber plants for other concerns, frequently takes joint stock participation in the establishment of such plants; the amount of the participation may range all the way from a moderate to a major share, or even to control of a given company. Such joint venture arrangements serve to assure local investors of Von Kohorn's continuing interest in the success of the plant after it has gone into operation. At times, the joint venture arrangements take the form of technical assistance agreements, guaranteeing the client continued professional operation for the term of the agreement.

Some of the leading electrical machinery and equipment and tire firms in the United States lean to wholly-owned foreign operations while others engage in joint venture investments, perhaps because of a weaker competitive position in foreign markets. The International General Electric Company has mostly wholly-owned subsidiaries abroad, while Westinghouse Electric International has mostly joint ventures, generally without participation in equity. Of the approximately 15 affiliated overseas companies of General Electric, only a few include participating local capital, such as those in Turkey, Chile, and Spain. Westinghouse has greatly extended its technical assistance and licensing agreements with foreign enterprises in the postwar period; it now has approximately 114 licensees in 25 different countries. In the few cases that have involved equity participation, it has come about through acceptance of shares in lieu of certain payments.

In the production of tires, a similar contrast is presented between the United States Rubber Company and the B. F. Goodrich Corporation. United States Rubber generally prefers wholly-owned foreign operations, but does go into joint ventures, usually regarding majority control as essential. B. F. Goodrich, on the other hand, which has about a dozen foreign affiliated manufacturing companies (to a large extent in Latin America), either holds only a minority of the equity in these enterprises or has no equity interest at all but simply technical assistance arrangements. Of the other three principal tire manufacturers in the United States, Goodyear generally operates abroad on a wholly-owned or mostly-wholly-owned basis, while Firestone and General Tire are more receptive to joint venture arrangements.

The Bettinger Corporation, a small but dynamic enterprise which has gained much public recognition in connection with its specialized coating processes applied to building materials and machinery parts, has developed its foreign operations by entering into a network of technical assistance and process agreements with various foreign companies.

A large involvement in joint ventures abroad is characteristic of Pan American World Airways, Inc. and its subsidiary, the Intercontinental Hotels Corporation. Pan American Airways, which pioneered in the development of air transport abroad, formerly was the sole owner of its foreign enterprises, especially in Latin America, but its holdings have been reduced to minority participation in most cases. In other areas of the world, such as the Middle East and Southeast Asia, it has had technical assistance contracts with local airlines. In a few instances the contracts have been combined with joint venture arrangements on an equity basis. The Intercontinental Hotels Corporation, now operating numerous hotels in Latin America and in other parts of the world, has generally followed a joint venture pattern involving varying amounts of its own capital, as well as its management of the hotels under lease or contract arrangements, local equity capital, loans from local institutions, and loans from United States institutions, generally from the Export-Import Bank of Washington.

W. R. Grace & Company is a highly diversified company engaged in a wide variety of activities in the United States and abroad. Its leading activity is the production of chemicals in the United States, and its other enterprises include its well-known steamship line, miscellaneous business activities in the United States, such as banking and insurance, a half interest with Pan American Airways in an international aviation company, and the production of paper, chemicals, textiles, food products, and trading and ship agency activities in Latin America. About a fifth of its capital is employed in the operations which are based abroad. A majority of the overseas operations is wholly-owned, but as much as $18 million, or slightly more than 25 percent of the total of its capital employed overseas at the end of 1957, represented its holdings in joint ventures. Its wholly-owned foreign operations are in trading and shipping, and in the production of sugar, paper, chemicals, and paints. Most of the joint venture enterprises are engaged in the production of textiles and food products. New Latin American ventures in chemicals and paper, either recently embarked upon or still in the planning stage, are in the joint venture category.

The American Overseas Finance Company, originally formed in 1955 as a specialized agency to grant medium-term credits abroad for the acquisition of capital goods, has not, of course, engaged in equity participation in joint ventures, but its lending activity has generally involved joint ventures due to the equity participation of other United States interests with local investors in the enterprises to which it has granted loans. By the end of 1958, it had disbursed or committed approximately $15 million for development financing (excluding its purely export financing), all in Latin America (Brazil, Chile, Cuba, Mexico, and Peru). The largest of these joint ventures has been an automotive vehicle manufacturer and a pulp plant in Brazil (Willys Overland do Brasil, and Celubagaço Industria e Comercio), a copper mine and smelter in Chile (Empresa Minera de Mantos Blancos), a Cuban acetate fiber plant (Acetafil), a cement plant in Mexico (Cementos California), and an iron ore mining enterprise in Peru (Pan American Commodities). The scope of activities of this enterprise was broadened to include direct equity ownership in foreign companies as a result of its consolidation in January, 1960 with the Transoceanic Development Corp., owned by prominent investment and banking interests in the United States, Canada, United Kingdom, Netherlands, France, Germany, Italy, and Switzerland. The new consolidated company is known as Transoceanic-AOFC Ltd.

The Panamerican Capital Corporation was organized in 1955 to provide equity capital for investments rather than loan capital in Latin America. This enterprise has to date operated on a much smaller scale than the American Overseas Finance Company, having invested only about $1.5 million. Its policy has been to enter where possible on a partnership basis with local capital. Most of its ventures have in fact been on such a partnership basis, including primarily a soluble coffee plant in Guatemala (Industria de Café), a sales finance company in Colombia (Promotora Colombiana), the same pulp plant in Brazil which received loan capital from the American Overseas Finance Company, and a shrimp fishing enterprise in Panama (Panama Fishing Industries).

OTHER CAPITAL-EXPORTING COUNTRIES

In the United Kingdom, interviews were conducted at company headquarters with Unilever Ltd., the large producer of soap and toilet products. The Unilever enterprise is a British-Dutch combine consisting of Unilever Ltd. of England and Unilever N.V. of Holland. In addition to its joint ventures in Burma and Pakistan, Unilever is also engaged in joint ventures in India, Chile, and Kenya. The enterprise in India is Hindustan Lever Ltd., which in 1956 as a wholly-owned subsidiary named Lever Brothers (India) Private Ltd., acquired the business of the other Unilever Indian subsidiaries, changed its name, and was converted into a public company. A minority of ten percent of the stock of the reorganized enterprise has been sold to the Indian public. The joint venture in Chile is with one of the country's leading industrial enterprises, Compañía Industrial. Unilever operated in Chile for many years through a small, wholly-owned company of its own before entering into a joint venture with Compañía Industrial. The enterprise in Kenya, East Africa Industries Ltd., was formerly a joint venture between the Colonial Development Corporation of the British government and the Industrial Development Corporation of the local government; Unilever joined the enterprise in 1953 and the two government agencies have continued as partners.

Unilever has also reported its widespread involvement elsewhere in Africa in joint ventures, especially in Nigeria and Ghana, through a holding company known as the United Africa Company Ltd., in which it is associated with other European investing interests. The varied fields covered by these enterprises include bulk oil plants, shipping, pig farming, and the manufacture of cement, concrete, plastic articles, mattresses, beer, and mineral waters. The local investors are usually government development corporations, but there are some instances of participation by individual private investors—most of whom are involved only in minority participation. There are a few cases of 50-50 participation or majority holdings by the local partners.

At one time it was Unilever's almost invariable policy to have its foreign enterprises wholly-owned by one or the other parent company. This attitude has been modified to meet present conditions and today Unilever welcomes the financial participation in its enterprises of the people of any country in which it is starting a new business or expanding an existing one. As the chairman of the parent companies put it at the Annual General Meetings in 1959, "if the people of the country, on their own account or through their Government, will join their resources with ours, then we are very glad to have their cooperation." In its partnerships with outside interests, Unilever still carries responsibility for running the business, a responsibility which it is anxious to discharge, as far as posible, through locally recruited managers.

Richard Costain Ltd. is one of the largest international construction firms, and over half of its business is from work overseas. It has conducted projects overseas jointly with construction firms from other developed countries and has, in a few instances, set up joint ventures with interests from the less developed countries. In its largest joint venture overseas, Costain, Ltd. of Nigeria, the firm's partners are a British trading company from Nigeria and an African merchant from the same area. This enterprise was formed as a joint venture to obtain the advantages of the sharing of risks, the facilitation of business contacts, and the good reaction in the local community deriving from the national participation. In Kuwait, Costain has yet another enterprise with a local partner in order to comply with a requirement for national participation to be able to bid on government contracts. In another instance, Costain joined forces with a Lebanese construction firm to pool specialized skills in connection with a hospital construction contract.

Imperial Chemical Industries Ltd. has an extensive network of some 28 overseas enterprises, including both manufacturing and selling organizations in less developed countries in the Far East, Near East, Africa, and Latin America. These are mostly wholly-owned subsidiaries of ICI or joint ventures with other companies from developed countries, but six of the enterprises are joint ventures with interests from the less developed countries themselves. Of the six, four are in India, one is in Africa, and one in Mexico. An outstanding case in India is the joint venture with the Atul enterprise. The other three are: the Alkali and Chemical Corporation of India Ltd., with a 30 percent participation by the Indian public; the Khewra Soda Company Ltd., with a similar pattern; and Indian Explosives Ltd., which is owned 20 percent by the Indian government. The enterprise African Explosives and Chemicals Ltd. is owned 50 percent by ICI and 50 percent by an African company. In Mexico, ICI has a technical assistance arrangement with Sosa Texcoco.

Another joint venture in Mexico with British participation is the enterprise Bristol de México, with participation by the Bristol Aeroplane Company Ltd. Bristol Aeroplane has been active in the exportation of the aircraft it manufactures ever since its beginnings in 1910. To promote and service these sales, it has set up subsidiary companies and shops in various strategically located points in the world. The enterprise in Mexico was set up with an eye toward all of Latin America. Some of its local plants, including those in France and Spain, were set up jointly with local interests, and the favorable experience in those cases, combined with the positive attitude in Mexico toward joint ventures, led it to set up its most recent affiliate in Mexico in cooperation with local interests.

In West Germany, interviews conducted with such leading firms as Mannesmann A.G. and Siemens & Halske A.G., indicated that they have begun to move in the direction of reëstablishing foreign equity investments, and that they are generally favorably disposed toward joint ventures. Mannesmann, one of the largest firms in West Germany, manufactures steel pipe, but is an integrated enterprise that also manufactures its raw materials and is engaged in the output of numerous finished products. It has important joint ventures in Brazil and Turkey, established respectively in 1952 and 1954. In Brazil, it actually has several joint venture affiliates, but the principal one is the Companhia Siderúrgica Mannesmann, which produces steel pipe, and in turn has various subsidiaries and affiliates in iron ore mining, construction, and sales. About 75 percent of this enterprise is held directly and indirectly by Mannesmann, and the balance is owned by local private interests. In Turkey, Mannesmann holds a 57 percent interest in the Mannesmann-Sumerbank Boru Endustrisi enterprise, formed jointly with the official Sumerbank of Turkey. Mannesmann also holds a two-thirds interest in an affiliate in Argentina.

Siemens, a manufacturer of electrical machinery and equipment, has gone farther in rebuilding its foreign subsidiaries since the end of the Second World War. It now has approximately 16 subsidiaries outside of Europe. A few of these are joint ventures, including two enterprises in Brazil with a Siemens majority, and one in Egypt in which the Siemens interest amounts to only 20 percent.

Hochtief, a construction firm, is also engaged in foreign jobs. Since these jobs are generally one-time affairs, the creation of permanent foreign subsidiaries or affiliates usually does not arise as in the case of manufacturing enterprises. Hochtief does have one such affiliate in a country that has had a great deal of construction activity in recent years—Venezuela—on a joint venture basis with local interests.

Farbwerke Hoechst A.G., a large manufacturer of chemicals, had invested a total of 76 million marks (about $18 million) by the end of 1958 for the development of its foreign operations. A substantial part of this amount was spent in Central and South America. Hoechst owns (partly or in full) 37 distributing agencies in 29 countries. Of the 76 million marks, 10 million have been invested, partly in joint ventures and partly in full ownerships in at least nine finishing plants in such countries as Turkey, Chile, India, and Brazil. More plants are under construction or in the planning stage.

In Japan, the relatively small amount of foreign direct investment in recent years has been on a joint venture basis. Illustrations are found in mining, fisheries, and the production of textile machinery, textiles, iron and steel, glass, and fountain pens. The joint ventures in mining have been prompted largely by Japan's need for imported industrial raw materials. Several of these projects are for the production and shipment to Japan of iron ore. Some are private, such as the project of Kokan Kogyo K.K. in Goa and of Nittetsu Mining K.K. in Hong Kong, while others have been official, for example, the Orissa project in India involving a credit by the government of Japan to the government of India for the development of iron ore production and shipment. There are also private joint venture projects in Thailand for the production of tin and tungsten.

Taiyo Fisheries K.K., the largest company in this field in Japan, is a party to a joint venture in Burma, and also has a similar affiliate in India, the New Indian Fisheries Company, established in 1954. Another Japanese company in the field, the Southern Fisheries Development Co., has entered into a joint venture with the government of Iran for fishing in the Persian Gulf. Still another fisheries company, Nanyo Boeki K.K., is a party to a joint venture on New Hebrides Island.

In textile machinery, there have been the joint ventures in Mexico and Brazil of the Toyoda and Howa Kogyo enterprises. In textiles themselves, Japanese enterprises have also ventured abroad in association with local interests; illustrative are a hemp fiber processing operation in Formosa set up in 1953 by Nippon Sen-i Kogyo K.K., and an enterprise to produce cotton thread and cloth set up in 1955 in El Salvador by Kureha Cotton Spinning K.K.

Several Japanese steel firms are participating in the new, large iron and steel project at Minas Gerais in Brazil.

The Asahi Glass Company of Tokyo is a party to a joint venture in India established in 1956, to manufacture sheet glass.

The Pilot Fountain Pen Company of Tokyo, party to the joint venture in India previously mentioned, has a similar venture in São Paulo, Brazil, set up in 1954.

Among the smaller capital-exporting countries, Italy is another country whose companies appear to have been very favorably disposed toward joint ventures. Examples are the Snia Viscosa and Fiat enterprises. Snia Viscosa is Italy's largest and one of the world's largest producers of artificial and synthetic textile fibers. During the last two decades, it has embarked on a number of ventures in the less developed countries of Europe, Latin America, and Africa on a joint venture basis with a Snia Viscosa minority. Snia Viscosa is involved in at least seven joint ventures: Its first such venture was set up in Spain in 1939 to produce fibers (the enterprise Sniace); a second joint venture was established in Spain in 1956 as a fabrics finishing enterprise (Fibracolor); in Argentina, the joint venture affiliate, which also produces fibers, is known as Sniafa; in Brazil, Fibra S.A. produces fiber as well as pulp; in Mexico, there are the two enterprises Celulosa de Chihuahua and Viscosa de Chihuahua, which produce pulp and fibers; and in South Africa, there is the South African Industrial Cellulose Corporation, first set up by Snia Viscosa, together with the British firm, Courtaulds Ltd. (which is a minority holder of Snia Viscosa), and the Industrial Development Corporation of the South African government; after its initial participation in helping to get this enterprise started, Snia Viscosa turned its share over to Courtaulds.

Fiat, the oldest and by far the largest enterprise in Italy in the production of automotive vehicles, is a vertically organized and highly diversified company, engaged in the production of numerous other products. It has participated in a number of industrial projects in the less developed countries since the Second World War, especially in Argentina, but also in other countries of Latin America, including Mexico, Brazil, and Chile. The Fiat operations have been set up generally with the financial participation of the local governments. In Argentina, Fiat Someca Construcciones Córdoba Concord was established in 1954 to produce tractors, with majority control by Fiat and its French affiliate Someca, and minority participation by the Argentine government. This plant was constructed at the site of Ferreyra in the Province of Córdoba, and gave rise to the creation of a new industrial zone at that site through the later development of other Fiat enterprises, engaged in the manufacture of engines for railways, railway rolling stock, and forgings and stampings. Fiat also has other enterprises in Argentina, engaged in the distribution and servicing of the Concord tractors, the servicing and repair of diesel engines, and the production of agricultural implements, and it has submitted a proposal to the Argentine government for the establishment of an automotive vehicle factory.

In Italy, the construction firm, the Societá Anonima Elettrificazione (SAE), is involved (as is Costain of the United Kingdom and Hochtief of Germany) in overseas work to a large extent. Its field is primarily the installation of electric power transmission systems. Because of foreign exchange and other restrictions, it has been led to establish some 13 overseas companies. These companies usually do not have any substantial local participation, but there is sometimes a nominal amount to conform to local restrictions. About ten of the enterprises are in economically underdeveloped areas in Africa, Latin America, and Asia.

In petroleum, a principal factor in Italy is the government agency, Ente Nazionale Idrocarburi (ENI), which, through various affiliates, has also extended its foreign operations in the less developed countries, often on a joint venture basis. Illustrations are the ventures with the Egyptian government in the Compagnie Orientale des Petroles d'Egypte set up in 1953 for exploration and production; with the Lebanese government in Gaz Orient, set up in 1956 for the distribution of natural gas; with the Iranian government in the Société Irano-Italienne des Petroles, set up in 1957 for exploration and production; with a Libyan group in the Societá Libica per il Petrolio, set up in 1957 for the distribution of petroleum products; and with the Moroccan government in the Societá Marocchina Italiana dei Petroli, set up in 1958 for exploration and production.

COMPARISONS AMONG INDUSTRIALIZED COUNTRIES

The greatest disposition toward entering into joint ventures in the less developed countries appears to exist in Italy and Japan. The more positive attitude toward joint ventures in these countries is probably a result of their limited finances, which makes foreign investment in association with local capital a more attractive proposition, and of their weaker competitive position in international markets vis-à-vis other investing countries. Because Italians have had considerable experience with partnership arrangements and foreign interests within their own country, they are probably less reluctant to enter into partnership arrangements with foreigners in other countries.

There appears to be a somewhat greater trend toward joint ventures in West Germany and the United Kingdom than in the United States, although not to the same degree as in the cases of Italy and Japan. However, there are certain firms in the United States which have been convinced of the advantages of joint investments over wholly-owned investments, and that engage in joint ventures as a matter of deliberate policy. This is especially true of firms that have had extensive experience in foreign operations.

Aside from capital shortages, the primary pull toward joint ventures appears to have come from the growing nationalism in the less developed countries. Enterprises in developed countries have tended to exhibit a considerable reluctance to engage in joint ventures. The reluctance has gradually broken down as it has been revealed either that this is the only form of foreign investment available or that it at least contains advantages for relations within the less developed countries over wholly-owned investments. The overcoming of the reluctance has been facilitated as experience has been gained with joint venture investments. The cases of outright failure of such ventures because of their inherent nature seem to be far fewer than those of success, even though the achievement of the success may involve somewhat greater initial difficulties than might be the case for wholly foreign-owned investments.

Distribution by Industries

It is difficult to establish a definite trend of the use of joint ventures by various industries. There are instances of firms involved in the joint venture form of foreign investment and other instances of similar firms involved in wholly-owned enterprises abroad; this is the case, for example, in the electrical equipment industry, where Westinghouse falls into the former category, and General Electric and the German firm Siemens & Halske fall in the latter. There are examples of the same firm utilizing the joint venture form in some cases and investing on a wholly-owned basis in other cases; thus, W. R. Grace & Co. is involved in both joint venture projects and in wholly-owned projects in the fields of production of paper and chemicals in Latin America. Generally, the reasons for the use of the joint venture are found more in the area of country policy or in the competitive position of individual companies rather than in the unique characteristics of specific industries.

Some common denominators based on industrial characteristics have nevertheless been found. Since the end of the Second World War joint ventures have been seen in the new manufacturing industries that the less developed countries have been bent on instituting or expanding. They have been used in primary iron and steel and steel products, other metalworking industries, artificial and synthetic textile fibers, tires, pulp and paper, pharmaceuticals, machinery and equipment, specialized building materials such as asbestos-cement products, electrical goods, and consumer durables. These are fields in which the establishment of the respective industries in the less developed countries requires large amounts of capital, technical knowledge from abroad, patents for specialized products, or the rights to trade names that have been extensively developed on an international basis. There is a growing desire by investors in the less developed countries to participate in new, dynamic investment opportunities: Where industries date back to before the Second World War in the less developed countries, they are frequently operated by entirely foreign-owned enterprises.

Another branch of activity in which joint ventures are popular is public utilities such as electric power, telephone service, and air transport. These are frequently cases of formerly foreign-owned enterprises having become joint ventures because of the need for capital for expansion. Under the conditions of nationalism, restrictions, and exchange depreciation characteristic of the less developed countries, it has been difficult to get additional capital from abroad. Local capital (when it is private capital) is forthcoming because it is not so much affected by these conditions, or (when it is government capital) because it is supplied by local government financing agencies concerned with expansion of the basic facilities to promote economic development.

Joint ventures are least found, in the older, simpler, and more traditional industries, such as textiles and foods, where the foreign contribution in the form either of capital or technical assistance is less needed. Even in these fields, joint ventures are prominently found in branches within the field that are concerned with newer or more differentiated products. Thus, while there is little foreign participation in the cotton textile industry, there is much foreign participation in synthetic textiles. Similarly, the production of basic foods is generally carried on by national enterprises, but the newer branch of food bottling and canning has much foreign participation. A similar phenomenon is noted in the glass industry where basic products are produced by national enterprise, but specialized products such as plate glass and glass insulation are being developed with foreign participation; and in soaps, where the lower-quality product for laundry purposes is a function of national enterprise and higher quality toilet soaps are produced by joint ventures. This is also true of some service activities, such as hotels, where side by side with national hotels they have been developed on a joint venture basis to cater especially to the international tourist.

Highly complex industries, such as the production of intricate business machines rarely utilize the joint venture form. If there is an absence of local familiarity with the products, there is less insistence on local participation, and the less developed countries are generally content to allow the foreign interests to proceed on their own. To a large extent this is also true of the extractive industries, which have been a traditional field for foreign investment, not only because of their complexity but also because of their heavy capital requirements. But in these cases, too, local participation has been increasing, and has taken the form of investment in the same enterprises with foreign interests.

Analysis of the distribution of joint ventures by industries seems to point to the conclusion that joint ventures are likely to increase in importance as the establishment of more complex industries in the less developed countries proceeds, and as former entirely foreign-owned social overhead capital facilities continue to expand. It may be that greater or complete reversion to national ownership in many fields will occur at a later stage, as more technical competence is attained in the less developed countries and as local capital markets develop. In the intermediate period of many years to come joint ventures appear likely to be the form in which private foreign capital will operate more and more in its participation in the expansion of new economic activities in the less developed countries.

IV. Types of Joint Ventures

JOINT INTERNATIONAL business ventures in the less developed countries are generally between private companies from the capital-exporting country and private firms or small groups of investors from the capital-receiving countries. There are numerous variations and qualifications of this general theme, for example the many important cases in which governments or public agencies, especially from the less developed countries, are parties to the ventures. About a third of the case studies of joint ventures cited as illustrative in Part II of this book are in this category.

Foreign Private Interests

The foreign parties to joint ventures in the less developed countries are generally manufacturing companies or public utilities. The reason for the establishment of the foreign investment is not always the extension abroad of manufacturing or service activities, and as a consequence the nature of the foreign party falls somewhat outside of the general pattern. This is true of some ventures of foreign manufacturing firms that invest abroad to develop a source of supply of raw materials, an important example being the Bethlehem Steel Company of the United States, which holds a 49 percent interest in the Brazilian manganese mining venture, Indústria e Comércio de Minérios. Investment for the acquisition of raw materials has also been largely characteristic of the joint ventures of firms in Japan. A Japanese investment in Goa is considered a prototype of this form of investment: It involves a joint venture in iron ore exploitation to which the foreign partner is Kokan Kogyo K.K. of Tokyo, a subsidiary of a company that manufactures steel pipe.

The bulk of foreign investments in joint ventures is by foreign operating companies involved in one field of activity, but there are also joint ventures by companies that operate in a diversified range of activities, by companies that are sources of venture capital for foreign investments generally, and even by individual investors or the public at large in capital-exporting countries.

W. R. Grace & Co., with its highly diversified activities in the United States and abroad, is perhaps the outstanding case of a diversified company that has been widely involved in joint ventures in less developed countries.

There have not been many cases of enterprises in the United States and in other capital-exporting countries entirely devoted to the use of venture capital for foreign investment, but some significant examples have been found. Outstanding in the United States is the Panamerican Capital Corporation, organized with the idea of paying special attention to the possibilities of associating with local capital in enterprises in Latin America. Similar to the Panamerican Capital Corporation, although engaging to a greater extent in the operation of enterprises itself, is the International Basic Economy Corporation (IBEC). In Industria de Café in Guatemala, which operates a soluble coffee plant, IBEC has invested jointly with the Panamerican Capital Corporation as well as with local capital. Another joint venture by the International Basic Economy Corporation is a concrete manufacturing enterprise in Brazil (Concreto Redimix do Rio de Janeiro).

In addition to foreign venture capital invested in this way on a risk or equity basis, capital is supplied to enterprises in the less developed countries on a loan basis by a growing number of specialized private financial institutions from the capital-exporting countries. These loans are frequently made to joint ventures. Outstanding among such institutions is the American Overseas Finance Company, which has been instrumental in developing sources of equity capital and technical know-how in the United States to associate with capital in the less developed countries. A merger early in 1960 with a venture capital firm has made it possible for AOFC to invest in foreign equities as well.

There are instances of non-institutional foreign venture capital which has been invested in enterprises jointly with local capital, either through small groups of individual foreign investors or by listing on stock exchanges of the developed countries. Illustrative are the Philippine mining enterprises, Benguet Consolidated Inc. and Lepanto Consolidated Mining Co., which are listed on United States stock exchanges, and Industria Eléctrica de México (the Westinghouse affiliate), a minority of whose stock was floated on the New York market by underwriters when the enterprise was first organized in 1945.

Local Private Interests

The parties to joint ventures in the less developed countries are frequently local manufacturers who have been operating in the field for some time, and the foreign investor who buys into the enterprise with the idea of expanding it. Thus, full advantage is taken of the existing facilities and status of the national enterprise, and it becomes unnecessary to develop a new venture from scratch. In Brazil, Bristol Laboratories of the United States associated in 1950 with a local pharmaceutical manufacturer that had been in existence since 1938 to form the joint venture known as Laborterápica Bristol. In that same country, the large government-owned steel mill at Volta Redonda is also a party to the new steel mill being developed jointly with Japanese steel firms in Minas Gerais. In Mexico, the Nabisco Products Corporation of the United States bought into an old established food products manufacturing firm in 1953 to form the Nabisco Famosa joint venture. The Hercules Powder Company in 1958 bought into a small Mexican enterprise that had been manufacturing naval stores since 1948. A number of the W. R. Grace & Company joint ventures follow this same pattern: In Colombia, Grace bought into a food bottling and canning enterprise (Conservas California), and into two existing chemical manufacturing enterprises in the country (Carboquímica and Probst y Cia.). Grace bought into a candy and biscuit company (Arturo

Field y Cia.) in Peru, largely motivated by its interest in distribution activities, and into a paper container enterprise (Envases San Martí) as an offshoot of its primary paper production there. In Chile, Grace holds a large minority in a national woolen cloth enterprise, the Fábrica de Paños Bellavista, the intention being to expand its participation in the enterprise in the future. Sears, Roebuck has bought into existing manufacturing firms to obtain supplies of various consumer goods for distribution throughout its stores in Mexico, Colombia, and other countries.

Outside of Latin America, there are also instances in which the local partner is an existing manufacturer in the same field as the foreign partner. This would, of course, be true of all royalty arrangements, as in the Philippines, where the firm H. G. Henares & Sons has entered into a number of royalty arrangements with foreign manufacturers covering a diversity of products including paints, writing implements, and other office supplies. In Turkey, the joint venture Metalum Sanayi (manufacturer of aluminum toothpaste tubes), was organized in 1954 after a considerable number of years of operation by the same national interests as tube manufacturers.

Another type of local interest associated in joint ventures is that which, although not having been engaged in the specific field of activity of the new venture, has been active in some related field. The new venture sometimes comes about because the foreign partner, exploring a possible investment in a given field, has sought out local associates who might logically be interested, or it may arise at the initiative of the local firm seeking an extension of its activities. In Brazil, a local gear manufacturing concern holds ten percent of the enterprise Clark-Mac, which opened a $4.5 million plant in November, 1959 to produce automotive transmissions. One of the parties to the venture building the new Brazilian steel mill in Minas Gerais is the important producer of iron ore, Cia. Vale do Rio Doce. One of the founding partners of the Cia. Brasileira de Material Ferroviario, organized in 1944 to manufacture railway equipment, was Cia. Siderúrgica Belgo-Mineira, the first integrated steel operation in Brazil, and itself a joint venture. In Mexico, in the organization of Descuento Agrícola, the bank established in 1955 to finance agricultural machinery acquisitions, the local interests in related fields that associated in the enterprise are private commercial banks (40 percent of the total), an association of distributors of agricultural machinery (30 percent), and the government development bank (10 percent). In Colombia, the local partner in Pantex, a leading joint venture that produces cloth of synthetic fiber, is a principal producer of cotton cloth. Cartón de Colombia, a joint venture that produces primary paper and paperboard, found its local capital subscription among paper dealers in the country. The initiative for the formation of Icasa, a joint venture in refrigerators, came from a large local distributor who had dealt in imported refrigerators and other consumer durables for many years. A local office supplies distributor in Colombia is the national partner in the Industria de Equipos de Acero, which manufactures filing cabinets.

Local participation of this type is also found in India and in the Philippines: In India the local partner, the Tata Engineering and Locomotive Company, had been manufacturing locomotives and heavy engineering products for some ten years before organizing an automobile division in 1954 in association with Daimler Benz of West Germany. In the Philippines, the local partner in the project now underway to construct a hotel with the Intercontinental Hotels Corporation is a Philippine real estate firm.

The relationship between the traditional field of activity of the local partner and that of the joint venture frequently involves some sort of integration of the two, such as a supplier-customer relationship in one direction or the other. The national partner often is a customer for the goods or service of the joint venture. This is the case with the Cia. Brasileira de Material Ferroviario which, in addition to having local primary steel producers as partners, also includes some railways that purchase its products, such as the privately owned Cia. Paulista de Estradas de Ferro. In Mexico, the local partner in a leading producer of refractories (the Fábrica de Ladrillos Industriales y Refractarios Harbison-Walker-Flir) is the Fundidora de Monterrey steel plant, which is an important customer for the firm's products. The local partners in Bristol de México, a modern aircraft engine overhaul and repair service, are the two leading local airlines, Cia. Mexicana de Aviación and Aeronaves de México, which, incidentally, are themselves joint ventures.

In many cases, joint ventures have been formed between foreign manufacturers and their former local distributors. In response to balance of payments restrictions and the trend toward local manufacturing in the less developed countries, these associations have been a natural outgrowth of the prior business relationship between the foreign and national parties. Examples of joint ventures with former local distributors as the national partners are found in enterprises in Brazil that produce electrical goods and automotive vehicles, in Mexico in the production of equipment for the construction industry, in Colombia in the manufacture of paints, in Pakistan in the production of electrical products, and in Turkey in the manufacture of pharmaceuticals, electric light bulbs, and cotton thread.

Still another type of local investor consists of interests that hold concession or other rights to valuable natural resources. In Mexico, the holders of forest concession rights joined with the Hercules Powder Company of the United States to form the Corbu Industrial joint venture for the manufacture of naval stores. In a forestry and lumbering operation in Colombia (Industria Forestal Colombiana), a local minority holding consists of Colombian interests with rights to extensive forest lands. A large iron ore exploitation project in Peru (Pan American Commodities) has interests with rights to exploitation of iron ore deposits through its local partners; these interests were able to obtain a large loan from the American Overseas Finance Company, which in turn arranged for other United States and British equity participation and technical direction. In Thailand, the New Cang Phra Tin Mining Company was formed in 1954 between Japanese mining interests and local holders of mining concession rights.

A great deal of local participation in joint ventures has been on the part of general investors in the less developed countries. The general investors usually consist of small groups that are prominent in the local financial community. Local investors are also currently being found through more institutional channels. The subject of participation in joint ventures by the general public on an open basis will be considered separately.

Association by Groups of Foreign Interests

In the majority of cases, the foreign interests in joint ventures consist of single foreign firms, as can be seen from the illustrative case studies cited in Part II of this book. Nevertheless, there is an appreciable minority of cases of association by groups of foreign interests and these include some ventures of considerable importance. The combination of firms generally arises from the allied operating interests of the combining parties, or as a means of obtaining additional capital for the investment.

The Willys Overland automobile manufacturing enterprise in Brazil involves a consortium of foreign interests. The principal foreign stockholders are the Willys Motors Company of the United States and the Renault firm of France but other United States companies, having supplied some of its equipment, also hold some equity. The substantial sum of $5.6 million was supplied to the enterprise on a loan basis by three important foreign agencies: the International Finance Corporation, Arcturus Investment Development Ltd., and the American Overseas Finance Company.

The foreign investment of some 40 percent of the capital of Usiminas, the new steel plant being built in Minas Gerais is being made by a combine of several Japanese firms, among which the following are the most prominent: the Yawata Iron and Steel Company, the Tokyo Shibaura Electric Company, Hitachi Ltd., and the Mitsubishi Company. Also, the new enterprise for the production of automotive transmissions, Equipamentos Clark-Mac, is owned 55 percent by a United States operating company, Clark Equipment International, and 35 percent by a French banking interest, the House of Rothschild. The nature of the association by groups of foreign interests may vary depending upon circumstances; in these cases in Brazil, they involve passive participation through the supply of equipment and the provision of finance, as well as a combination among operating firms in the same field.

In Mexico, Tubos de Acero de México and Bristol de México

involve an association by groups of foreign interests. In Tubos (engaged in the production of seamless steel pipe for the petroleum industry), 20 percent of the capital is held by four Italian enterprises connected with the steel industry, and 15 percent was placed with individual European investors from Sweden and France. In Bristol (engaged in overhauling and repairing aircraft engines), the investment was promoted by a Canadian subsidiary of the Bristol Aeroplane Company of England, which holds a majority of the capital, and there is also indirect participation by Pan American World Airways through its minority holdings in Mexico's two principal commercial aviation companies, which are minority partners in Bristol de México. In Fertilizantes de Monclova, an enterprise set up in 1956 to produce fertilizers, a one-third interest is held by French investors, consisting of the St. Gobain Company, which operates in this field, and other French financial groups; in addition, a substantial loan, in the amount of $8.75 million was obtained by the enterprise from a French bank, the Banque Nationale pour le Commerce et l'Industrie. Another case in Mexico involves bi-national foreign participation: Conductores Eléctricos (manufacturer of electrical wire and cables), has one-third of its capital owned by the Anaconda Wire and Cable Company of the United States, and one-third by the Pirelli enterprise of Italy. For Wormser-Suiza de México, formed in 1957 to produce equipment for the construction industry, resident European capital was tapped by the foreign promoting enterprise to hold a balance of power between itself and the Mexican group. The foreign operating company's holding, that of a Swiss firm, amounts to slightly more than one-fourth of the total, and the resident European capital to close to 50 percent. In the new aluminum smelting project recently announced, the Aluminum Company of America will have a 35 percent interest, and 10 percent will be held by a European group, the balance being held by a Mexican group.

Neither of the case studies for Colombia included in Part II involves association by groups of foreign interests, but there are other important joint ventures in this category. The complex of enterprises that produce asbestos-cement building materials in the country, the Eternit firms, all of the same ownership, started with a combined investment of Swiss and Belgian interests, and later the Johns Manville International Corporation of the United States joined the firms. In the important lumbering operation, Industria Forestal Colombiana, lumbering interests from various countries—Mexico, the United States (including Puerto Rico), and Sweden—combined for the investment. In the petroleum products pipeline company, the Oleoducto del Pacífico, the International Petroleum (Colombia) Company interested a local subsidiary of the South American Gold and Platinum Company in the investment, and half of the firm's equity is held by these two groups, 40 percent by the former and 10 percent by the latter. The Cia. Croydon del Pacífico, producer of tires and other rubber products, was originally formed by Swiss and Canadian interests associated with the Croydon Manufacturing Company of Canada, and later the United States Rubber Company joined the firm. In the shipyard enterprise Unión Industrial y Astilleros Barranquilla, three United States shipyard firms, the Todd Shipyards Corporation, the Baldwin Lima Hamilton Corporation, and the Charleston Shipbuilding Drydock Company, are joined to represent the foreign interest.

In one of the joint ventures in Latin America of W. R. Grace & Co., there is participation by another United States firm. The venture came about because of the complementary nature of the interests of the two firms: Electromat, S.A., of Chile, produces electric light bulbs; Grace had exclusive distribution rights in Chile for General Electric bulbs. When General Electric responded to pressures to produce locally, Grace joined in the investment. It is now held one-third by GE, one-third by Grace, and one-third by local investors.

Also in Latin America, there are some interesting examples of a joining together of United States venture and operating capital from a variety of sources with local investors. In order to promote a venture for the manufacture of soluble coffee in Guatemala, Compañía Financiera, S.A. was formed by a number of leading Guatemalan coffee growers and businessmen. The company sought capital and technical assistance from the United States and got them from Tenco (a company owned by ten leading United States coffee roasters) and from two sources of venture capital, the International

Basic Economy Corporation (IBEC) and the Panamerican Capital Corporation. The joint venture, Industria de Café, S.A. is owned 30 percent by the Cia. Financiera, 25 percent by Tenco, 25 percent by IBEC, and 20 percent by Panamerican Capital. Distribution of the firm's product in Guatemala and in the rest of Central America is handled by W. R. Grace & Company. The arrangement in Guatemala was inspired by a similar plant in neighboring El Salvador, previously formed by Tenco, IBEC, and local investors.

The cases in India are generally associations by single foreign firms. Multi-national interests have been parties to the arrangements of the new government steel plants and of Atul Products Ltd., but these have been really separate, individual arrangements and cannot be considered genuine consortia of foreign interests. In Atul Products, separate agreements were made by the Indian enterprise with American, Swiss, and British firms at different times and for the production of separate schedules of products; in the association with the British, a new, separate company was formed known as Atic Industries Ltd.; and the formation of separate joint ventures with the other foreign participants is being planned to replace the former arrangements under which the foreign companies were associated, though in fact separately, with the same single Indian firm.

In Burma too the joint ventures are generally with single foreign firms. However the Burma Oil Company (1954) Ltd. has for partners Burmah Oil Company Ltd., the Indo-Burma Petroleum Company Ltd., and the British Burmah Petroleum Company Ltd. The reason for this association is that all the British companies operating in the petroleum industry in Burma were beset by the same problems of instability that prompted them to combine for the formation of the joint venture with the government. Of the three, the Burmah Oil Company Ltd. was by far the most important factor in the preexisting situation, having accounted for 77 percent of Burma's output of crude oil and 75 percent of its output of refined products in 1941.

It was announced in Pakistan early in 1960 that a combination of foreign operating companies would construct a new petroleum refinery. Four companies, the California Texas Corporation, the Standard-Vacuum Oil Company, the Royal-Dutch Shell group, and the Burmah Oil Company, have combined to furnish 60 percent of the capital for the new refinery, which will cost about $35 million, and the rest of the capital is to be supplied by private sources in Pakistan. Also in Pakistan, a different type of association between foreign interests in a joint venture is found in one of the case studies in Part II. This is the Sui Gas Transmission Company, in which a foreign operating company has combined with a foreign source of finance. The Burmah Oil Company of London holds 24½ percent of the capital of this enterprise and another 24½ percent is held by the Commonwealth Development Finance Company of England.

In the Philippines, the General Milk Company (Philippines) involves an association between the Carnation Milk Company and the Pet Milk Company of the United States; these two firms had combined previously, not specifically for the venture in the Philippines, but for investments in milk plants in other countries in South America and Europe.

None of the four cases cited in Part II for Turkey includes groups of foreign interests. However, the Anadolu Cement Corporation is 75 percent jointly owned by Belgian and Danish interests. In the United German Pharmaceutical Plants, 70 percent of the equity is held by four German pharmaceutical companies, who were interested in the enterprise by a group of Turkish distributors of their products in the country. In Metalum Sanayi (toothpaste tubes), a foreign interest of 51 percent is held jointly by Swiss and Israeli partners, who are also associated elsewhere in the business of manufacturing similar products. The Turkiye Madoni Sanayi enterprise, which draws wire and manufactures various metal products, was established by various Belgian operating firms in this industry, two of which still jointly hold 30 percent of the investment.

Participation by the General Public

Association in joint ventures generally takes place by individual firms or small groups of interests on both the capital-exporting and the capital-importing sides, and the joint venture enterprises are therefore usually "closed" corporations. In the capital-exporting countries, there is little interest on the part of the general investing public in investments in the less developed countries. The situations are considered to be too unstable; there is too great a tendency toward depreciating currencies; there are too many restrictions on the free movement of foreign exchange; and, in any case, there has been little development of specialized institutional arrangements to facilitate direct investments by the general public in the less developed countries. In the less developed countries themselves, there is, of course, only a relatively narrow base from which funds can be obtained, and internal capital markets characteristically have not been created to any great extent.

Participation by the general public on an open basis, either from the capital-exporting or the capital-importing countries, therefore, is found only to a limited extent in joint ventures in the less developed countries. Nevertheless, some beginnings have been made. A few situations have been found in which it has been possible to float some securities of local enterprises on the general market in the United States. Institutional arrangements for broadening the capital markets in less developed countries are gaining ground through the expansion of stock markets and the development of companies for the underwriting of new securities issues. To some extent, the formation of underwriting companies has been promoted by foreign interests. For example, Deltec S.A., Brazil's leading investment firm, is a subsidiary of the Deltec Corporation of New York. A recent, interesting example of an all-national underwriting enterprise is the Corporación Financiera Colombiana de Desarrollo Industrial, established in December, 1958 by Colombia's leading banks, insurance companies, and some industrial concerns, to promote the formation and financing of new and expanded industrial enterprises. Another reflection of the broadening of capital markets that is taking place in some less developed countries is the recent formation of open-end or "mutual" investment companies, which depend for their success and have their reason for being in the existence of investment opportunities which are too diversified for broad participation in many of them by single, small investors. Such firms have been formed in recent years in Mexico, Venezuela, Colombia, and the Philippines.

At times, participation by the general public in joint ventures is promoted by the governments of less developed countries. This has occurred in connection with the expansion and conversion into joint ventures of formerly foreign-owned public utilities enterprises. It has also happened as a result of the operations of government-owned development corporations, which frequently sell their holdings in enterprises to the general public once the enterprises in which they invest have become successful, and then move on to new fields in order to "show the way" for new, productive investments in the economy.

In other cases, the intiative for participation by the general public on an open basis has come from the foreign investor. This has taken place especially in enterprises that produce consumer goods that have a mass market, as a means of promoting favorable public relations and wide acceptance of the enterprises' products. In some cases, the shares held by the general public are non-voting preference shares (for example, the Standard Vacuum oil refinery at Bombay, India).

Participation by the general public in joint ventures depends on the existence of a general investing public in the country in question, and so is found to a somewhat greater extent in the Latin American countries, whose level of development is generally higher than that of countries in the Far East.

When Industria Eléctrica de México, the Westinghouse affiliate, was formed in 1945, a minority of its stock was placed with United States investors through New York underwriting companies, led by Kuhn, Loeb and Company. Approximately 15 percent of its stock is now owned in this way. Mining enterprises in the Philippines have considerable general public participation in the United States.

Public utilities that became joint ventures through some participation by the general public in the local country were found in Mexico, Colombia, and the Philippines. The Mexican Light and Power Company, the largest private power enterprise in the country, took the decision in 1955 to sell part of its stock to the general public in Mexico; by the latter part of 1957, slightly less than ten percent of the total stock of the company was held in this way. Telephone service in Mexico, originally developed by United States and

Swedish companies, has run the gamut from all-foreign enterprise through joint venture enterprise to its present status of being almost entirely nationally-owned, as a result of a purchase by local financial interests in August, 1958. At the time of this recent purchase, 26 percent of the stock of Teléfonos de México was publicly held by subscribers to telephone service as a result of a forced investment decreed by the government in 1955. This decree provided for "priority" to new applicants for telephone service and to applicants for certain transfers of service who would provide financing to the company according to a prescribed schedule of investments, half in the purchase of stock and half in the purchase of long-term bonds—enacted as a means of facilitating the financing of expansion of telephone service. In Colombia, Avianca, the national aviation enterprise, is widely held—to the extent of 60 percent of its shares—by general investors, and its shares are among those most traded on Colombian stock exchanges. Pan American Airways, which originally held Avianca's majority, reduced its holdings to a minority by selling part of its stock to general investors because a law required that a majority interest in domestic air transport companies be held by Colombian nationals or by companies controlled by Colombian nationals. Concurrently there had developed a new company policy toward minority holdings by Pan American Airways in its affiliated enterprises abroad. In the Philippines, the Manila Electric Company, with the encouragement and approval of the Public Service Commission, recently increased and changed its capital structure to admit participation by the general public. A total of 40 percent of the expanded capital of the firm will be offered to the general public in the Philippines from time to time as required by the company's need for capital to meet its expansion and improvement program.

The role of a government development corporation in stimulating the participation of the general public is illustrated in the case of Icollantas, the Goodrich-affiliated tire manufacturing enterprise in Colombia. Icollantas was formed in 1942 with a 73 percent capital participation by the Instituto de Fomento Industrial, the development corporation of the Colombian government. By 1953 the Instituto had sold out its interest, primarily on the general market to private Colombian capital, and now holds no shares in the enterprise. The stock of Icollantas is also extensively traded on Colombian stock exchanges. In a recent project for the development of an enterprise to produce pulp from local timber, to which the Instituto is also a party jointly with the Container Corporation of America, 20 percent of the capital stock was reserved for subscription by the general public.

The development of wide public participation through the initiative of the private promoting partners in joint ventures is exemplified by the Willys Overland automotive vehicle manufacturing project in Brazil. More than 40,000 Brazilian stockholders have ownership in this enterprise by virtue of public flotation of its securities by the Deltec investment firm. In Colombia, Esso Colombiana, the major wholesale distributor of gasoline and other petroleum products, is owned in the minority (12.5 percent) by general investors as a result of the decision by the International Petroleum Company, its former sole owner, to start such a public offerings program in 1951. In the rubber products firm, Cia. Croydon del Pacífico, as a deliberate public relations policy, the stock of the company was registered on the stock exchange in 1953, and a small amount was sold to the general public which now holds 4 percent of its equity. A similar decision was taken by W. R. Grace & Company in connection with various of its consumer goods manufacturing enterprises in Latin America. In Peru, Grace owns 63 percent of the textile enterprise, Cías. Unidas, and 37 percent is held by local investors as a result of a public offering of shares. In Chile, Grace owns 70 percent of Tejidos Caupolicán, the textile enterprise, and 67 percent of the Cía. de Industrias y Azúcar (manufacturer of vegetable oils, lard, refined sugar, and paints), and the balance is held by general investors.

In India, the government insisted that ten percent of the stock of Hindustan-Lever Ltd. be sold to the Indian public. The corporation was formed in 1956 by a merger of four existing Indian corporations, all of them wholly-owned by Unilever Ltd. This public issue was for 5½ million rupees (more than $1 million), and was oversubscribed. Limitations were imposed on the amount that could be bought by any one buyer, in order to get the widest possible distribution, and there are now some 10,000 shareholders. The company reports that this distribution of stock had a pronounced salutary effect on the morale of its Indian staff. Two affiliates in India of Imperial Chemical Industries Ltd., the Alkali and Chemical Corp. of India, and the Khewra Soda Co., are similarly held to the extent of 30 percent of the total by the general public.

Foreign Majority versus Foreign Minority Participation

While it is difficult to generalize with respect to the frequency of occurrence of foreign majority participation or foreign minority participation in equity joint ventures, the cases surveyed for this study indicate that there is a greater incidence of foreign minority participation than is generally supposed. Just as there appears to be a continuing trend toward entering into joint ventures as opposed to wholly foreign-owned investments in the less developed countries, so there seems to be a greater occurrence of foreign minority participation. Firms in capital-exporting countries, which a few years ago would not consider anything but wholly-owned investments, have come to recognize that the advantages to be gained from joint ventures may offset the disadvantages, and even find themselves—usually as a result of pressures in the less developed countries—engaged in a minority position relative to their local partners.

More than half of the cases of equity joint ventures cited in Part II of this book involve foreign minority participation, and a few are 50-50 arrangements. This is not to imply that the same situation holds true for all joint ventures. However, the data do indicate that foreign minority participation is widely represented, and that 50-50 arrangements, which presuppose the fullest type of confidence and cooperation between the partners, also are found in a small number of important cases.

In Latin America the most marked tendency toward foreign minority participation appears to exist in Mexico. There is also a great pull toward this type of participation in Brazil. In Colombia, the greater number of joint ventures involves majority or at least 50 percent participation by the foreign interests.

In the Far East in India, Burma, and Pakistan the initial bias toward foreign minority participation that characterized the early years of independence has come to be attenuated to a considerable extent. The early insistence on local majority ownership of enterprises has been abandoned as the formation of enterprises of importance to the economies has run into problems of availability of local capital or managerial competence, especially in fields which are technically complex and require large investments of capital. In the Philippines, as in the countries of Southeast Asia, the important thing seems to be some participation by local capital, but not necessarily a majority local participation.

In most of the joint ventures in Turkey reviewed for this project, on the other hand, the foreign investor has a majority interest.

LATIN AMERICA

Of the seven cases reproduced in Part II for Brazil, all are equity joint ventures, and four involve minority participation by the foreign partners while three have foreign majority participation.

The four joint ventures with foreign minority participation are Cobrasma, Icomi, Panair do Brasil, and Willys Overland do Brasil. The Cobrasma enterprise was formed in 1944 during the Second World War at the initiative of Brazilian railways which were concerned with supply shortages from abroad. Foreign assistance was sought for this new, complex industry in the economy, and it was first obtained in the form of a licensing agreement. It was not until 1956 that the first foreign equity was invested in the enterprise—by American Steel Foundries International. The foreign participation amounted to only 15 percent of the total equity of the firm, and this level has been maintained to date. Icomi, the mining venture, similarly had its origin in Brazilian initiative. It was first set up in 1942 as an all-Brazilian enterprise to engage in iron ore mining in Minas Gerais. After it was awarded a concession by the government in 1947 for the working of a large manganese ore deposit, it sought both foreign capital and technical assistance to work the concession, and the Bethlehem Steel Company joined the firm in 1949 with a 49 percent equity participation. The aviation enterprise Panair do Brasil was originally a totally foreign enterprise. It was owned outright by Pan American World Airways from 1930 to

1943; in 1943 a 42 percent share was sold by the owners to Brazilian investors. In 1947, by voluntary decision of the parent company, the procedure was carried still farther, and Pan American remained with a minority participation of 48 percent. The Willys Overland enterprise was started in 1952 by the Willys Motors Company of the United States together with 11 local distributors of its vehicles, and Willys had only a 10 percent share of the original company. The foreign equity participation, both of Willys and others, has increased. It is still planned for Brazilian stockholders to have more than 50 percent of the voting stock by the time the expansion is completed.

The three cases of foreign majority participation are Laborterápica Bristol, Rheem Metalúrgica, and Cia. Siderúrgica Mannesmann. Although the Bristol joint venture came about as a result of a merger with a local firm that had been the distributor of its antibiotic products, a 51 percent majority was obtained by Bristol from the beginning in 1950. The Rheem Manufacturing Company first thought of establishing itself in the Brazilian market by purchasing an existing plant, which was formerly German-owned and had been expropriated during the Second World War by the Brazilian government. It finally rejected this plan, and decided to proceed by establishing a joint venture, although it kept a majority of 70 percent. The policy of Rheem appears to be to own foreign plants outright or to have a comfortable majority where it is in a joint venture. Mannesmann was established with a foreign majority of about 75 percent, and the local participants were mainly banking interests.

This almost equal distribution of foreign minority and foreign majority participation generally follows the pattern observed in other joint ventures in Brazil. Brazilian interests, in entering upon joint ventures, attempt to keep a majority of at least the voting stock. It is not always possible to achieve because of the problems of capital availability or because of the insistence on a majority by some foreign firms, and there are therefore also many cases in which a foreign majority prevails. But there is a tendency, even in the cases of a foreign majority, to accord participation in management to nationals which is greater than their participation in equity.

There is even a greater tendency toward foreign minority participation in joint ventures in Mexico. Of the seven cases in Part II, all of which are equity joint ventures, only one (Bristol de México) has a foreign majority. Two others which formerly had foreign majorities (Celanese Mexicana, and Toyoda de México), have had the foreign participation decline to a minority or be eliminated altogether.

The foreign majority holder of the Bristol enterprise (Bristol Aeroplane Company of England) has indicated that it is prepared to relinquish its majority financial control in the future. Bristol is operated under a management contract by the majority shareholder, and it would insist that this contract be continued if the majority control were relinquished.

The Celanese enterprise had a slight foreign majority when it was started in 1947, but the majority was relinquished in 1953 at the time of its merger with three other local firms. It is of interest to quote the attitude of the foreign partner, the Celanese Corporation of America, as expressed by its vice-president, Mr. Emery N. Cleaves, in a conference at Michigan State University held in February, 1957:

> There may be some question as to whether a foreign company should enter Mexico or any other Latin American country on a financially equal basis or in a majority or minority position. My company has done all three. Over the years I think the attitude has developed that the position of stock ownership should reflect the contribution made by the respective partners. There may also be the feeling that if you don't get along with your associates, it doesn't make much difference what proportion of the stock you own. As a matter of fact, Celanese Corporation of America, after originally owning a majority of the common shares of Celanese Mexicana, allowed its holdings to decline to a minority position when new issues of shares were made. To me that seems significant of the company's confidence in its Mexican associates.

The Toyoda enterprise until recently had a 59 percent majority holding by the Toyoda Automatic Loom Works of Japan. The enterprise had originally been established in 1954, with an even larger foreign majority. The majority was reduced as the enterprise expanded and as new shares issued were purchased by Nacional

Financiera, the Mexican government development bank, which sponsored the formation of the enterprise from the beginning. According to recent reports, Nacional Financiera bought out the foreign share entirely in November, 1959; the enterprise had been incurring heavy losses, and it was apparently decided to attempt to salvage it under government ownership.

The remaining cases in Mexico were formed with foreign minority participation from the beginning. Altos Hornos de México was the result of Mexican initiative during the Second World War when shortages prompted the promotion of a second integrated steel plant in the country. Foreign public and private assistance were sought. The public assistance was obtained in the form of loans from the Export-Import Bank of Washington; the main ingredient in the private assistance was participation of a technical nature. Accordingly, the foreign participation in equity amounted to only about 7.5 percent of the total, where it still stands today. Tubos de Acero de México was organized in 1952 with a foreign participation of 35 percent. The Mexican participation is both private and public; the government is especially interested in this enterprise, producer of seamless steel pipe for the petroleum industry, since the petroleum industry is a government monopoly. Industria Eléctrica de México, when it was organized in 1945, obtained foreign equity only through a stock flotation on the New York market in the amount of about 15 percent of total equity. The initial arrangement with Westinghouse was only for technical assistance. Later, in 1955, Westinghouse bought into the enterprise, to the extent of 26 percent of its equity. The total foreign participation now amounts to a minority of some 41 percent. Descuento Agrícola was organized at the initiative of the Mexican Association of Distributors of Agricultural Machinery, whose activities this specialized bank finances. The foreign participation is limited to 20 percent.

Aside from the cases described in Part II, about two-thirds of the joint venture enterprises surveyed in Mexico have foreign participation on a minority basis. Although there is considerable variation in the matter of foreign majority or minority participation, to the extent that it is possible to generalize, the favorite formula in Mexico seems to be for the foreign interest to invest capital in the joint venture on a minority equity basis, but to take an active part in management and technical direction.

In Colombia, one of the two cases cited has foreign minority participation; the other has no foreign equity participation at all. Icollantas, the foreign minority case, was organized at the initiative of the Instituto de Fomento Industrial, the government development corporation, which sought foreign technical assistance and to a lesser extent capital participation. The enterprise began with a one-fourth equity participation by foreign capital, which has since risen to the present level of about one-third. The greater number of joint ventures involves majority or at least 50 percent participation by the foreign interests, but there is also a considerable number of cases where the foreign participation is in the minority. It is safe to assume that local interests in Colombia would prefer only a minority foreign participation, but they have shown themselves willing to associate with a majority of foreign capital where there is insistence on this degree of participation.

FAR EAST

In India, for the private sector of the economy in which foreign equity participation is permitted, there was a rather rigid policy of the authorities in the early days of independence of insistence on an Indian majority ownership of enterprises, but this policy has become much more flexible in recent years, dictated by the necessities of the country's economic development. The joint ventures surveyed show about an equal distribution of foreign majority and foreign minority participation. Atul Products Ltd., which concluded its arrangements in 1947 with the American Cyanamid Company, involved only a ten percent participation in equity by the foreign partner; this participation has since declined. In its more recent arrangement (1955) with Imperial Chemical Industries of England for the establishment of a new firm, the equity distribution is on a 50-50 basis. The foreign participation amounts to 40 percent of the equity in the case of the Automobile Division of the Tata Engineering and Locomotive Company. The foreign participation in T. I. Cycles of India Ltd. was in the minority, amounting to 49 percent, but the foreign participation has been raised to a majority under a plan for expansion that has been in the process of development since 1955. In the joint venture in India established by Merck Sharp & Dohme International in 1958, the foreign participation is in the majority, amounting to 60 percent of the total. The majority control proposed by the foreign partner was accepted without question by the authorities and by the Indian partner; the Indian partner is acting as a general investor, is not actively engaged itself in the venture and has been content to leave control in the hands of Merck.

In Burma, the two cases in Part II involve a foreign majority in one and a foreign minority in the other. As a matter of general policy, foreign participation in enterprises in Burma is limited to 40 percent unless specific permission is otherwise obtained from the government. The Martaban fishing enterprise between Japanese and Burmese interests follows the general pattern, and the Japanese participation amounts to 40 percent of total equity. There seems to be little difficulty in obtaining the special permission to have a larger foreign participation if insisted upon by the foreign partner, when the enterprise is considered to be of sufficient interest to the Burmese economy.

The Burma Corporation (1951) Ltd., which has served as a prototype for similar joint ventures between British mining and petroleum interests and the Burmese government, was set up on a 50-50 basis. One other such enterprise, Mawchi Mines (1957) Ltd., was also organized on a 50-50 basis. In the two other cases, the government has a majority in one and a minority in the other. The Anglo-Burma Tin Company (1956) Ltd. was organized with a 51 percent share for the government and 49 percent for the foreign interest. On the other hand, the Burma Oil Company (1954) Ltd. has only a one-third government share and two-thirds for the foreign partners. Even in this case, the government has an option to buy any number of additional shares in the enterprise, and its bylaws provide for certain changes in administration whenever the government acquires at least 51 percent of the shares. The general policy seems to have been for the government to have a majority or at least a one-half interest if its resources permit; in the case of the oil enterprise, the capitalization, at 200 million kyats, or more than $40 million, was considerably higher than in the other cases.

The two cases in Pakistan are both equity joint ventures, one with a foreign majority and the other with a foreign minority. There appears to be no definite pattern in Pakistan, although investments are subject to official scrutiny, and there is at least an initial bias toward foreign minority participation, which nevertheless has shown itself to be subject to exceptions in important cases. Thus, in the case of Lever Bros. (Pakistan) Ltd., foreign majority participation was sanctioned by the government, after opportunity was given to local shareholders to raise their participation to a majority. Sui Gas Transmission Company Ltd. has a 49 percent foreign minority participation.

In the Philippines approval of investments by the Central Bank is sought in order to obtain assurances regarding remittance abroad of earnings, and the policy appears to be to require some participation by local capital—though not necessarily a majority. Of the four cases cited in Part II, three are equity joint ventures, two with foreign minority participation and one with a foreign majority. The Manila Gas Corporation was converted into a joint venture with government participation in 1948, because of the reluctance of the foreign owners of the enterprise to stand alone the cost of its rehabilitation after the destruction of the physical plant during the Second World War. The foreign owners offered to sell the enterprise entirely to the government, or to take the latter in as a minority partner. The government countered with the accepted offer of 60 percent participation by itself and 40 percent for the foreign partner. The Goodrich International Rubber Company also has a foreign minority, in the amount of 43 percent. The General Milk Company (Philippines), on the other hand, would probably have been set up as a wholly-owned foreign subsidiary had it not been for a requirement by the Central Bank to admit local capital. This was done by selling slightly more than 20 percent of the shares to a local insurance company as a passive investment.

TURKEY

In Turkey, a trend toward foreign majority participation in equity joint ventures was seen, although not as a result of official policy which is generally indifferent to the size of foreigners' holdings. Of the four cases described in Part II, three have a foreign majority and one a foreign minority. This order of proportion in favor of foreign majority participation is borne out in Turkey in other joint ventures. The General Electric Turkish Corporation was started with a foreign majority of 60 percent, and this has risen to two-thirds. The Mannesmann enterprise has a foreign majority of 57 percent, and the Squibb enterprise of 71 percent. Of the firms included in our survey, Tamek is the only enterprise that has a foreign minority (40 percent).

POLICIES OF INVESTOR COMPANIES

A considerable number of companies in the United States are quite definite in their insistence on majority financial control in their joint ventures, but an impressive number are either doubtful with respect to the need for having such control or show themselves quite willing to take only a minority participation as a matter of general policy. In the United Kingdom and West Germany, virtually all the firms interviewed prefer arrangements in which they have majority control; at the other end of the spectrum, most of the cases of joint ventures with Japanese firms as the foreign partners involve a minority Japanese position. Italy is found somewhere in between: One very important Italian participant in joint ventures abroad, Snia Viscosa, quite regularly takes only a minority position; others, such as Fiat, usually enter with majority control; the state petroleum enterprise, ENI, has to a large extent established a 50-50 pattern, and by this device has upset the traditional scheme of the international petroleum industry for sharing profits with host governments.

In the United States, Merck & Company has a 60 percent ownership in its two joint ventures in India and Thailand. DuPont has the majority in two of its joint ventures in economically less developed countries, but in its recent venture in Mexico it assumed a 49 percent minority in response to local pressures. The United States Rubber Company usually regards majority control as essential. The Worthington Corporation has always gone into joint ventures on a majority basis. The joint ventures of General Electric involve a foreign majority, either of the firm alone, as in the case of Turkey, or together with other foreign interests, as in the case of Chile where it shares a foreign majority with W. R. Grace & Co. Grace, in turn, prefers and has acquired majority financial control in its joint ventures except in some cases where it does not participate actively and has gone into an investment not because of its interest in the enterprise per se, but because of the relation of the enterprise to some other Grace activity in the country in question. Panamerican Capital Corporation, the venture capital enterprise, usually holds only a minority of the enterprises in which it invests, but it invests in enterprises in association with other foreign interests. Taken together, the investment of Panamerican Capital and of the other foreign interests often constitutes a majority, as in the case of the soluble coffee plant in Guatemala, Industria de Café, or the finance company in Colombia, Promotora Colombiana.

The B. F. Goodrich Company generally holds only a minority of equity in its joint ventures supplementing it by technical assistance and sometimes also by management contracts. Pan American World Airways is frequently in a minority position with its affiliated companies. While there is a somewhat greater variation in the investments of its subsidiary, the Intercontinental Hotels Corporation, the general pattern of IHC is to hold a minority of about one-third, although it usually insists on running the hotels under a management contract. The Armco International Corporation either has wholly-owned subsidiaries abroad, or, where it does go into joint ventures, does so on a minority basis. The equity positions assumed by Westinghouse are also generally in the minority, as in the case of its 26 percent holding in Industria Eléctrica de México. The American Overseas Finance Company, until its merger in January, 1960 with the Transoceanic Development Corporation, was engaged in lending abroad and not in any direct foreign investments, and showed itself well disposed to making loan funds available to joint venture enterprises which have a minority of foreign equity participation. This is the case of the large automotive firm in Brazil, Willys Overland do Brasil, of the large iron ore mining operation in Peru known as Pan American Commodities S.A., of a concrete reinforcing bar enterprise in Mexico known as Aceros del Norte, and of smaller enterprises set up in Chile (Soinbal) and Peru (Freno S.A.) to manufacture brake linings.

The Union Carbide Corporation has indicated that it is not particularly concerned with whether or not it has a majority position, but relies for control on the constantly changing technical information and assistance required by its joint venture enterprises. A similar attitude is held by the Celanese Corporation of America and by the Von Kohorn Corporation.

In the United Kingdom, Unilever has a clear majority in its affiliated enterprises in Burma (75 percent), Pakistan (61 percent), and India (90 percent), and in its Kenya enterprise, it holds 50 percent supplemented by a one-third share of the Colonial Development Corporation of England. Imperial Chemical Industries Ltd. has a 50 percent arrangement in its venture in India with Atul Products, but it has a clear majority in other enterprises—70 percent in the Alkali and Chemical Corporation of India and in the Khewra Soda Company, and 80 percent in Indian Explosives Ltd. The construction firm, Richard Costain Ltd., has a majority in the few cases where it has embarked on joint ventures in the less developed countries.

In West Germany Mannesmann has a majority in its principal joint ventures in Brazil (75 percent), Turkey (57 percent), and Argentina (66⅔ percent). The principal investment of Siemens in Brazil is slightly short of a wholly-owned subsidiary. The one permanent joint venture of the West German construction firm, Hochtief (Venezuela), is owned 60 percent by itself.

The Japanese trend toward minority participation ties in with its policy of supplying know-how and equipment in its foreign investments, rather than cash. Minority participation characterizes the investments of Taiyo Fisheries in Burma (40 percent), and in India (49 percent), and another Japanese fishing investment in Iran (33⅓ percent Japanese); the investments in tin and tungsten mining in Thailand (both 49 percent); the investment in the new steel mill in Minas Gerais in Brazil (40 percent Japanese); and the Pilot Pen ventures in Brazil (49 percent), and India (30 percent).

With respect to Italy, the pattern of Snia Viscosa's investments in joint ventures was set in 1939 by its first such venture—the Sniace enterprise in Spain—where its participation is 25 percent. In its second investment (1956) in Spain—the Fibracolor enterprise —70 percent is owned by Sniace (that is 17.5 percent indirectly by

Snia Viscosa) and 8 percent directly by Snia Viscosa. In its Argentine and Brazilian investments, Snia holds 21 percent and 23 percent respectively. In Mexico, it holds 50 percent of the Viscosa de Chihuahua enterprise, but only 18 percent of the related firm, Celulosa de Chihuahua. Fiat, on the other hand, more frequently holds a majority position except where it is rendering primarily technical assistance and where it might in some cases receive a minority of stock in payment for its initial services. In the important Concord tractor enterprise in Argentina, Fiat, together with its French affiliate Someca, originally held 75 percent and now has about 91 percent of the equity of the enterprise. The ENI petroleum enterprise of the Italian government has a 50 percent participation with a government company in Iran. This arrangement in effect means that 75 percent of the profits goes to the Iranian government—50 percent in accordance with the usual formula for sharing profits with the government in exchange for the concession rights and 25 percent by virtue of the government's one-half participation in the equity of the operating company. ENI's investments in Lebanon and Morocco are also on this basis, and in Libya a 50 percent holding in a joint venture is shared equally between ENI and Fiat.

Non-Equity Joint Ventures

The non-equity types of joint ventures discussed here include arrangements for the provision of technical services, franchise and brand use agreements (frequently combined with the provision of technical assistance), construction and other job performance contracts, and management contracts or rental arrangements. Although some of these arrangements are temporary, they partake of the essential characteristics of joint ventures by maintaining a close relationship of interests from both the developed and the less developed countries. They frequently constitute a prelude to a more permanent association involving a later investment of equity capital in the enterprise by the partner from the developed country. In numerous cases, equity joint ventures also involve a formal arrangement (in addition to the investment of capital) for the provision of one of the types of services mentioned; this type of combination appears to be much more frequent either than the pure equity type of joint venture or the pure non-equity type. The reason is that the partner in the less developed country is frequently as much in need of the technical services as of capital; and from the point of view of the partner from the developed country, an investment in equity in addition to the provision of services alone makes for a more permanent and successful arrangement and provides an opportunity for sharing in the profits of the successful enterprises. Furthermore, the non-equity agreements provide an opportunity for control of the enterprise that makes it less necessary for the partner from the developed country to have a financial majority.

TECHNICAL SERVICES ARRANGEMENTS

Technical services contract arrangements with foreign firms are usually found where the national firm is in need only of those services and not of foreign equity capital as well. Well-established private national firms may wish to modernize their operations or undertake a new line of production. Such arrangements are more frequently found among public enterprises wishing to limit foreign participation to temporary technical assistance, perhaps supplemented by loan funds.

In Mexico the only producer of soda ash and the principal producer of caustic soda is the domestically-owned Sosa Texcoco. This firm started production in 1947 and in 1952 entered into a technical assistance arrangement with Imperial Chemical Industries Ltd. of Great Britain. Following this, output by the firm increased substantially because of the installation of new techniques and equipment. In Colombia, there is a joint equity venture in Pantex, a firm that produces cloth of synthetic fiber, between Burlington Mills of the United States and Fabricato, Colombia's second largest cotton cloth producer. This arrangement worked out so satisfactorily that the Colombian partner later decided to enter into a technical assistance agreement with Burlington for its own cotton cloth operation, with the American firm holding no equity. A purely technical assistance contract in Colombia was also concluded between a subsidiary of the Standard Oil Company of New Jersey and the

Colombian government in 1951, when Standard's concession reverted to the government in accordance with the original terms. The technical assistance arrangement was to assist the government in the production of crude oil on the concession acreage. The contract had a duration of five years, but it was actually terminated by common agreement before three years, because of the technical ability of the government to take over the operation.

A technical services arrangement of limited scope has been found in Burma, where the development of a tea plant by the government is being assisted on a consulting basis by the Lipton Tea Company. Lipton does not actively participate in the management. In India, there are various instances of the rendering of technical assistance to state-owned enterprises by leading foreign firms. Some of these arrangements include the supervision of construction of new facilities, as in the case of the three new government steel plants. The German firm, MAN, which produces heavy machinery and engineering products, has a similar arrangement with Hindustan Aircraft Ltd. of the Indian government, which assembles railroad cars and manufactures and repairs airplanes. The MAN contract, signed in 1956, involves complete technical assistance for modernization of the railroad car manufacturing operation. The British enterprise Associated Electrical Industries Ltd. concluded a contract in 1955 with the Indian government to provide technical assistance for the establishment of a heavy electrical industry in the country. Merck Sharp & Dohme, the American pharmaceutical manufacturer, has entered into a contract to provide technical assistance to the Indian government for the construction of a streptomycin plant.

FRANCHISE AND BRAND USE AGREEMENTS

These are found in a number of countries in Latin America between foreign manufacturers of well-known brands of soft drinks such as Coca Cola, Pepsi Cola, and Canada Dry, and local factories that bottle the soft drinks under a franchise. In the Mexican apparel industry numerous local manufacturers produce a large number of foreign brands of apparel in their own installations. This makes it unnecessary for the foreign manufacturer to establish his own facility in the country, and provides additional use of capacity by local manufacturers. Franchise arrangements are also found in other fields, including automobile assembly, the manufacture of paints, paper products, and consumer durables. In Colombia, automobile assembly projects, which have not yet come to fruition, covering brands such as Austin, Nash, the Japanese or Toyota jeep, Volkswagen, and the American or Willys jeep, have all been planned on the basis of franchise arrangements with virtually no investment of capital by the prospective foreign partners. In other countries, automobile assembly or manufacturing arrangements frequently involve a combination of equity participation by the foreign partner and franchise arrangements. Paints in Colombia are manufactured by a local enterprise under a licensing agreement with the Sherwin-Williams Company of the United States. Paper products such as calendars and carbon paper are also made in Colombia on the basis of similar arrangements. In consumer durables, Westinghouse entered into a licensing arrangement in Colombia early in 1959 for the manufacture of electric stoves, hot water heaters, and washing machines with a firm that existed for several years as a service and repair shop and as distributor for Westinghouse appliances.

An outstanding illustration in the Far East of a firm with franchise agreements is H. G. Henares & Sons of the Philippines, a sole proprietorship which became a joint venture through royalty arrangements with American firms. This enterprise was organized in 1947 to manufacture an asbestos paint, but its initial operations were not very successful. It decided to negotiate for the manufacturing rights of well-known American brands of paints as well as other items, and obtained franchises for the following products during the period 1953 to 1956: Crayola crayons from Binney and Smith, Inc.; Wessco paints from the National Gypsum Company; Old Town carbon paper and typewriter ribbons from the Old Town Corporation; Mongol lead pencils from the Eberhard Faber Pencil Company; Universal paints from the Universal Paint and Varnish

Corporation; and Parker Quink from the Parker Pen Company. These arrangements resulted in a successful expansion of business for the local enterprise, and the foreign participants retained their position in the Philippine market.

CONSTRUCTION AND OTHER JOB PERFORMANCE CONTRACTS

Construction of factories and other large, complex facilities in the less developed countries is frequently carried out by foreign enterprises on a contract basis without any equity participation by the foreign interests. This is also true of other types of job performance activities carried out by foreign firms for national enterprises in the less developed countries. In Mexico, for example, Cementos California, established in 1956 on the Lower California peninsula, had its plant designed and the construction of it supervised by the Kennedy Van Saun Manufacturing and Engineering Company of the United States; it also received a medium-term loan of $1.2 million from the American Overseas Finance Company. In the petroleum industry—run as a government monopoly in Mexico—there has been joint venturing in the form of contracts with private foreign companies for well-drilling activity. For example, close to one-fourth of the total well-drilling activity from 1953 through 1957 was performed by such contractors. Under these arrangements, the contractor assumes all the risk; there is no return to him if no oil is found, and he receives, upon the discovery of oil, 50 percent of the value of total production until costs are recovered, and thereafter 15 percent of the value of total production for a period of 20 to 25 years. The collection of these royalties, however, depends upon decisions of the government with respect to wells it will work.

In the Far East three separate government steel projects are being constructed in India by private German and British interests and by the Russian government. The arrangements include contracts for the complex job of coordinating all the aspects of the construction, and also involve deferred payments arrangements for the equipment which is being imported, but there is no equity participation at all by any of the foreigners, and the plants are entirely owned by the Indian government.

MANAGEMENT CONTRACTS OR RENTAL ARRANGEMENTS

This type of arrangement is commonly found in the hotel industry in underdeveloped countries, and involves large international hotel operators such as the Hilton organization and the Intercontinental Hotels Corporation. Such arrangements are found in Latin America, in Mexico, and Colombia. An outstanding example is the Hotel Tequendama in Colombia, managed by the Intercontinental Hotels Corporation. The hotel is owned entirely by Colombian capital, and is managed entirely by the foreign interest on the basis of a management contract. The promotion of the hotel resulted from the initiative of the foreign party, which interested the local capital in the investment, and obtained substantial loans from the Export-Import Bank of Washington to help finance its construction. For its "pre-opening" services, including arrangements for the financing, design and construction of the hotel, IHC was paid a lump sum, received in installments during the first five years of operation of the hotel. For its continuing complete management responsibility, the corporation receives a fixed annual fee plus a participation in profits.

An important rental arrangement was also found in Colombia, in the petroleum industry. The foreign firm whose concession reverted to the government in 1951 turned over as part of the reversion a petroleum refinery, the only important one then existing in the country. The company then entered into a rental arrangement with the government for operation of the refinery. The arrangement involved payment to the government of a fixed annual sum plus a scale of payments based on the number of barrels of crude petroleum treated. The firm granted a loan of $10 million for expansion of the refinery, and was instrumental in obtaining an additional loan of $8 million from a New York bank for the same purpose.

In Burma, a new local industry (pharmaceutical) has been in the process of development by the government under a management contract arrangement with Evans Medical Supplies Ltd. of England on the basis of a fixed fee amounting to £25,000 per year or five percent of the value of products turned out by the enterprise, whichever is higher. The foreign company was required to make available all its technical and scientific knowledge. The contract, however, is reported to have run into difficulties, and it was expected that it would be terminated before the end of its initial period of seven years.

NON-EQUITY ARRANGEMENTS AS PART OF EQUITY JOINT VENTURES

In Brazil, Cobrasma, the manufacturer of railway equipment, has a participation of 15 percent in its equity by American Steel Foundries of Chicago, and a patents and technical assistance agreement with another subsidiary of the same firm, as well as similar agreements with other United States firms covering specialized products such as axles for railway cars, signal equipment, and brakes. Pan American Airways, in addition to its minority holdings in such enterprises as Panair do Brasil and the Cia. Mexicana de Aviación, has provided loan capital to them, has acted as their purchasing agent for the acquisition of equipment, and has mutual ground service arrangements with them. Formal patents and process agreements are also found in other important equity joint ventures in Brazil: in pharmaceuticals (Laborterápica Bristol), metal products (Rheem Metalúrgica), tires and tubes, and electrical wire and cables (Pirelli), automotive vehicles (Willys Overland do Brasil), and fountain pens (Brazil Pilot Fountain Pen Co.).

In Mexico, Conductores Eléctricos has equity, technical assistance, and patents participation by Anaconda of the United States and Pirelli of Italy. The Westinghouse affiliate, IEM, has equity participation by Westinghouse as well as a formal technical assistance and licensing agreement; Westinghouse began to supply equity in the enterprise when developments in the company required financial assistance. Tubos de Acero de México, producer of seamless steel pipe for the petroleum industry, has the financial participation of four Italian enterprises connected with the steel industry and there has been a technical assistance arrangement for the design and construction of the plant as well as for the production itself with another Italian engineering firm specialized in the field. The aircraft engine overhaul and repair firm, Bristol de México, in addition to being owned in the majority by a subsidiary of the Bristol Aeroplane Company of England, is operated under a management contract with that same subsidiary.

Technical assistance is combined with equity in Colombia in Icollantas. The B. F. Goodrich interest in equity amounts to about one-third and the technical assistance agreement with Goodrich provides for a fee of three percent of the annual net sales of all products manufactured by the enterprise during the life of the agreement. Similar formal technical assistance agreements are found in Colombia in the following equity joint ventures: Celanese Colombiana (artificial fibers), Unión Industrial y Astilleros Barranquilla (shipyards), Eternit enterprises (asbestos-cement building materials).

The combination of formal technical assistance agreements and other types of non-equity arrangements with foreign equity participation is found, perhaps even to a greater extent, in the joint ventures in the Far East. Formal agreements supplement the equity participation of the American Cyanamid Corporation, of Ciba of Switzerland, and of Imperial Chemical Industries of England in the dyestuffs and pharmaceuticals ventures of Atul Products Ltd. of India. There are also carefully drawn agreements for the technical assistance and franchise granted by Daimler Benz of West Germany to the Automobile Division of the Tata Engineering and Locomotive Company of India, for the manufacture of the diesel-engined commercial vehicles undertaken by this joint venture in 1954.

In Burma, in the joint ventures in extractive industries formed between British firms and the Burmese government, the Burma Corporation (1951) Ltd., the Burma Oil Company (1954) Ltd., the Anglo-Burma Tin Company (1956) Ltd., and Mawchi Mines (1957) Ltd., the foreign partners are the administrators of the enterprises by contract.

In Pakistan, Unilever Ltd. of England has a technical cooperation agreement, under which it receives royalty payments; and in the case of the Sui Gas Transmission Company Ltd., there is a managing agency agreement between the firm and a subsidiary of the Burmah Oil Company of London, under which the firm is to be managed by Burmah for a period of 20 years, and is to pay remuneration for these services on the basis of a sliding scale of percentages of net annual profits (7½ percent of the first 5 million rupees [slightly more than $1 million], 6¼ percent of the next 5 million rupees, and 5 percent of amounts in excess of 10 million rupees).

The Reynolds Metals Company of the United States owns 51 percent of the equity in the Reynolds Philippines Corporation and has an agreement with the Philippine enterprise covering management, technical assistance, and royalty arrangements. In the Goodrich International Rubber Company of the Philippines, the foreign partner holds a minority (43 percent), and there is a contract between the enterprise and B. F. Goodrich of the United States covering management and technical assistance, for which the fees paid are two and three percent (respectively) of net sales of manufactured products by the local firm.

In the joint ventures of the General Electric Company and of E. R. Squibb & Sons in Turkey, both of which are owned in the majority by the foreign partner, there are patent rights and technical information agreements, under which royalties are paid by the local companies (not to exceed 5 percent of net sales in the case of the General Electric enterprise; the amount has not been revealed in the case of the Squibb enterprise).

Public Agencies and Governments as Participants

The direct participation by official agencies as equity partners in joint ventures is quite widespread, especially in the less developed countries. Government agencies of the capital-exporting countries are generally not involved in joint ventures as equity partners, and their participation has usually been incidental to their role as providers of finance on a loan basis.

About a third of the cases of joint ventures cited in Part II involve equity participation by governments of the less developed countries. This does not necessarily represent the extent of all such public participation in joint ventures, but it does suggest their importance and fairly widespread occurrence.

In most cases, the participation is by general development institutes or corporations of the local governments, but there are also cases of equity investment by specialized agencies of the government or directly by the government itself. Frequently, the public participation in joint ventures is not so much a matter of ideology as of concern with stepping up the rate of development of the local economy. Organizations such as the Nacional Financiera of Mexico, the Corporación de Fomento de la Producción of Chile, the Pakistan Industrial Development Corporation, the Industrial Development Corporation of Burma, the National Development Company of the Philippines, and the Sumerbank of Turkey are not concerned with public ownership of enterprises per se, but rather with the encouragement of investment in basic sectors of the economy. The investment is made whenever possible in association with private enterprise, and because of the capital and technical contributions that foreign private enterprises have to offer the association is frequently made with them.

There are other countries where the participation by governments in joint ventures is more a matter of ideology, and in these cases the foreign participation is usually limited to technical assistance and perhaps loan capital. Illustrative are the activities of the Indian government, with some limited assistance from abroad, in certain sectors of the economy such as iron and steel, heavy electrical goods, and certain basic pharmaceuticals.

One of the most active development banks in the less developed countries is the Nacional Financiera of Mexico. This organization, which has been in operation since 1934, has been particularly active since the Second World War in the promotion and financing of new, basic industries. It has frequently sought capital and technical assistance abroad, and consequently many enterprises in which it has been interested have been set up as joint ventures, in most cases both with Nacional Financiera and with private Mexican equity. In addition to providing equity capital, Nacional Financiera has also been very active in supplying loan funds and in guaranteeing large credits obtained abroad from such sources as the Export-Import Bank of Washington or the International Bank for Reconstruction and Development. In some cases, its role has been limited to this form of assistance while in others it has granted loans and guarantees in addition to equity capital.

Nacional Financiera holds equity in five of the seven Mexican cases described in Part II. Its equity participation has been mostly on a minority basis, and it has generally not played an active role in the management of the enterprises. In two of the cases (the Altos Hornos steel mill and the Toyoda textile machinery plant), the Nacional Financiera position, at first in the minority to the extent of less than one-third, has moved up either to a very large majority or to total ownership. In the other three cases (the Tamsa steel pipe mill, the IEM electrical equipment manufacturing operation, and the Descuento Agrícola bank for agricultural machinery), the Nacional Financiera participation ranges from 10 to 20 percent. As suggested by the nature of these enterprises, Nacional Financiera participation is to be found in those joint ventures that have introduced new or basic lines of production into the country, and represent large capital investments, such as the fields of iron and steel, machinery and vehicles, fertilizers, copper refining, wood pulp, and newsprint.

Colombia also has a comprehensive public development institute, the Instituto de Fomento Industrial, but it has not played the important role in the Colombian economy that development institutes have assumed in other Latin American countries. Icollantas was originally formed at the initiative of the Instituto during the Second World War, and it held a majority of some 73 percent of the enterprise's capital. The majority share was always intended to be temporary, and the Instituto acted in the classic way in which development institutes are supposed to act in such situations; once the enterprise became successful and it was possible to do so, the Instituto started to sell its shares to general investors, and this process was completed by 1953.

One of the earliest (1938) development corporations and one which is frequently considered a prototype is the Chilean Corporación de Fomento de la Producción (Corfo). In addition to being very active in the development of basic sectors of the economy such as iron and steel, electric power, and petroleum, with its own funds and in some cases with loans from the Export-Import Bank and the International Bank, Corfo has also cooperated very widely with private capital, national and foreign, in a wide variety of fields including metalworking industries, electrical and electronic equipment, chemicals and pharmaceuticals, lumber products, pulp and paper, textiles, fisheries and fish products, cement, tires and rubber products, and air transport. Corfo has worked much the same as Nacional Financiera of Mexico, providing loan capital, equity capital, and obtaining and guaranteeing foreign loans.

In Pakistan, the main vehicle for carrying out the efforts of the government to promote industrialization is the Pakistan Industrial Development Corporation. The official participation in the Sui Gas Transmission Company Ltd. is by this organization. There are various official joint venture aspects to this enterprise. The discovery of large deposits of gas that gave rise to the formation of this company was made, too, by a joint venture with official participation. This was the Pakistan Petroleum Ltd. enterprise, which had been set up by the Burmah Oil Company Ltd. of London with a 30 percent participation by local capital, pursuant to petroleum regulations that were enacted by the government in 1949. Of the 30 percent local participation, only about one percent was taken up by private investors, and so the government of Pakistan subscribed to the remaining 29 percent. With this background, it is not surprising that the transmission company was also organized with official participation. The Pakistan Industrial Development Corporation holds 25½ percent of the investment (another 25½ percent is held by private Pakistani investors). In addition, the gas is sold to consumers through two distributing companies, both of which are Pakistani-owned, one being a wholly-owned subsidiary of the Development Corporation. The official participation in this joint venture is not only local, but also includes foreign and international participants: the Commonwealth Development Finance Corporation of the British government holds 24½ percent of the equity, and the International Bank for Reconstruction and Development granted the enterprise a loan amounting to $14 million. Thus, this enterprise is a complex of public-private participation, with the largest single shareholder being the Pakistan Industrial Development Corporation.

In addition to the official Development Corporation, there is another development corporation which is a privately-owned joint venture itself, although it has also received official assistance. This is the Pakistan Industrial Credit and Investment Corporation, owned

60 percent by private Pakistani investors and 40 percent by private American, British, and Japanese investors. The Investment Corporation has received loans from the Pakistan government, from the Development Loan Fund of the United States government, and from the International Bank for Reconstruction and Development.

In Burma, there is also an official organization known as the Industrial Development Corporation which concerns itself with investment for the development of certain sectors of the economy. Efforts to promote development in the pharmaceutical and tea industries, with foreign assistance, have been conducted by this organization. It is also the local equity partner in the Burma Unilever Ltd. enterprise. Aside from these cases, the Industrial Development Corporation has not been an equity partner in any of the important joint ventures that have developed in Burma. However, it is of interest to note that the Burmese equity investment in the Martaban fishing enterprise cited in Part II was loaned to the private Burmese investors by the Industrial Development Corporation, which has also supplied loan funds directly to the enterprise itself.

Government participation in enterprises in association with private investors in the Philippines is carried out through the National Development Company of the Philippine government. Participation by this organization in joint ventures has been limited. Its outstanding case is the Manila Gas Corporation, which was converted in 1948 from a wholly-American-owned enterprise of long standing to a joint venture, with a 60 percent participation by the National Development Company.

In Turkey, the Sumerbank has been responsible for the development of a number of basic industries including iron and steel, paper, glass, and rayon. Illustrative of its equity participation in joint ventures is the Mannesmann-Sumerbank Steel Pipe Manufacturing Corporation, formed at the initiative of the Sumerbank. This official bank holds 43 percent of the equity, and has also made important sums available to the enterprise on a loan basis.

The official participation in joint ventures in the less developed countries is not limited to that by general development corporations. There is also participation by government agencies concerned only with the operation of specific sectors of the economy, and directly by the governments themselves. It is frequently found in the petroleum sector, which has been earmarked in a number of countries for official operation or intervention. For a variety of reasons, the specialized government agencies charged with the operation of all or part of the petroleum activities in the country have frequently entered into arrangements with foreign participants. In Mexico, Petróleos Mexicanos, the official oil monopoly, has had arrangements with foreign drilling contractors. In Colombia, a government company, the Empresa Colombiana de Petróleos, was created to receive and administer the important petroleum concession that reverted to the government in 1951. In this connection, the government company entered into technical assistance and management arrangements with the foreign firm that had previously held the concession. In Iran, the petroleum industry was placed under the control of a newly formed government company, the National Iranian Oil Company (NIOC), in 1951. In the Anglo-Iranian Oil Agreement of 1954, the NIOC, jointly with the government of Iran, entered into a complex agreement with a consortium of major foreign oil companies. Unlike the later joint venture between the Iranian government and the Italian ENI, the parties did not form a new entity with jointly held shares. Instead they formulated an elaborate set of mutual rights and obligations on commercial, social, and technical matters. One aspect of the agreement is the incorporation by the oil companies of two operating companies in the Netherlands, whose boards of directors (totaling seven) include two Iranian representatives. Only to that extent does the agreement include a joint operation in the strict sense.

In India, too, specialized official statutory corporations have been organized to run enterprises in sectors of the economy marked out for government operation, as in the case of Hindustan Steel Ltd., which owns and will operate the three new steel plants being built with German, British, and Russian assistance.

In Burma and Pakistan, there are cases of direct participation in joint ventures by the governments themselves. The mining and petroleum joint ventures in Burma have direct government participation, pursuant to a Special Companies Act that was enacted in 1950 precisely to facilitate the formation and operation of such joint ventures with the government as a partner. This act exempted joint ventures of this type from the provisions of the Burma Companies Act, the general legislation which governs the formation and operations of companies in the country. In Pakistan, the local official participation in the joint venture of Unilever was first held by the state government of Bahawalpur, and was later taken over by the West Pakistan government, when that state became part of the Province of West Pakistan.

As indicated, foreign government equity holdings in joint ventures in the less developed countries are unusual, but they, too, are represented to some extent, as illustrated by the Sirip petroleum venture in Iran. The foreign participation in Sirip is by a subsidiary of the Ente Nazionali Idrocarburi (ENI) of the Italian government. ENI has entered into other joint ventures abroad in Egypt, Lebanon, Libya, and Morocco.

The role of foreign and international public agencies in providing finance to joint ventures is dealt with in Chapter VII. Reference is made now to some of the cases in Part II where there has been such participation. In the Icomi enterprise in Brazil, the Export-Import Bank of Washington has made a large amount of financing available, having disbursed as much as $55 million. This is because of the strategic interest of the United States government in manganese, as evidenced also by the marketing agreements between the enterprise and the United States Defense Materials Procurement Agency. The International Finance Corporation has made one of its largest loan commitments, in the amount of $2.45 million, to the complex joint venture Willys Overland do Brasil, which is in the process of becoming one of the largest manufacturers of automotive vehicles in that country. An IFC commitment, in the amount of $520 thousand, is also represented in the joint venture Bristol de México, which has inaugurated a modern aircraft engine repair facility in that country. A substantial Export-Import Bank loan, in the amount of $1.8 million, made to the Goodrich International Rubber Company in the Philippines, has permitted the foreign equity participation in that venture to be limited to a minority.

V. Attitudes and Motivations

THE REPORTED MOTIVES of participants in joint ventures cover only a part of the whole explanation. The complexity of the issues involved is very great, and motives in taking business decisions are not always comprehensively analyzed or even fully reported in a deliberate way. Although we are confined to a consideration of conscious and avowed motives, unconscious motives do play a significant role also. Decisions on joint venturing in less developed countries involve acceptance or rejection of a close quasi-fraternal partnership with foreigners who are of different cultural and often of different racial backgrounds. In such matters unconscious attitudes are understandably present, for example, attitudes toward familial patterns, racial and cultural differences, and hierarchical and impersonal relationships versus human relationships based on equality and face-to-face dealings. Indications of rationalization and other symptoms of unconscious motivation have not infrequently appeared in respondents' discussions, especially in their objections to joint venturing.

The explanations given by business respondents for joint venturing fall into two main categories: 1) non-specific motives, and 2) specific motives. Non-specific motives refer to general economic or business advantages of given joint ventures which are not necessarily connected with their being joint ventures. Specific motives refer to the advantages (or disadvantages) of a joint venture as such. There is also the matter of motives underlying the preference for a particular form of joint venture or degree of participation.

Non-Specific Motives

Local[1] legislation (for example, Burmese) may require joint ventures for foreign[2] investments—at least in certain industries—or government attitudes (for example, in the Philippines) may so strongly favor joint ventures that foreign investors are left with few attractive alternatives. The opportunity for a foreign investment may arise only through the initiative of a local firm or development bank or government agency which invites an investor company[3] to make the investment with local participation and financing. For the investor company, this specific opportunity makes its appearance in the form of a joint venture. In theory, the investor company could turn down the specific proposal and go in on a solo basis. In practice, this alternative receives no serious consideration—either because the financial or other contribution of the local group is viewed as indispensable, or because the political and public relations aspects would be too unfavorable. The advantages of joint venturing may appear so small or so nearly offset by disadvantages that the jointness seems an insignificant aspect compared with other advantages or disadvantages of the project which then get the main analytical attention. It was rare in our study for respondents to mention spontaneously the jointness of a given venture as the main or specific reason for entering it. Foreign operations are sometimes organized, for tax or other special reasons, as a foreign branch of the home company: The legal situation will then preclude sharing the ownership with local interests, and possible advantages of joint venturing may never be considered. When the company explains why it does not have a joint venture it may refer to considerations having no bearing on the advantages or disadvantages of jointness. For these or other reasons, investor companies will often explain their participation in joint ventures by reference to broad business considerations identical with those which would apply to solo ventures: markets, costs, control of supply of materials, tax advantages.

[1] "Local" here refers to the capital-importing country.

[2] "Foreign" here refers to investments by investor companies (from capital-exporting countries) in capital-importing countries.

[3] "Investor company" here refers to a company of a capital-exporting country.

Specific reference was made to profitability by respondents. Pan American World Airways stated that it had gone into an extensive program of hotel building and operation on a joint venture basis not only because it helps to break important bottlenecks in tourism, thereby rendering its main operations more profitable, but also because the hotel end of the business is especially profitable. It even goes so far as to build hotels in areas serviced not by itself but by rival airlines. Government authorities in Japan, France, and the United Kingdom indicated that a major consideration in approving their nationals' applications to invest in foreign joint ventures is the likely profitability of the ventures. In a few cases, the formation of joint ventures is explained by United States firms on the grounds that production abroad is cheaper. Large Japanese firms indicated that one reason why certain joint venture opportunities in Southeast Asia were not accepted was that local labor working with Japanese technicians have a third as high a productivity as would Japanese labor working with the same technicians.

Among the most common type of general business motive offered by business informants is integration—combining an existing operation with a preceding or following stage of production. W. R. Grace & Company's original ventures into manufacturing involved a logical extension of its shipping and other transportation business which, in Latin America, often constituted a strategic stage in the production process. An investment in manufacturing constituted a forward linking insofar as the transportation stage was required to bring materials to the factory, and a backward linking insofar as transportation was utilized in disposing of the finished product.

Grace has recently been following a policy of selling off its holdings in industries where it possesses no specialized know-how and therefore has no special advantage, and expanding into joint ventures in other industries where it possesses exceptional operating and research experience that can be put to profitable use. This illustrates a type of forward linkage. It has also been entering into joint ventures for the production or procurement of raw materials used in its other operations—illustrating backward linkage. It has entered into joint ventures in order to pick up distribution networks in areas not covered by its own distributive system—again illustrating forward linkage. In short, integration of operations appears to be a major motive for selection or retention of joint ventures by W. R. Grace & Company, which has had an especially wide and successful experience in the joint venture field.

In a good many cases, the motive emphasized involves neither general policy nor broad business advantage but the opportunity or challenge offered by a particular situation. Quite frequently, the challenge is a threat to continuation of an existing profitable situation. A profitable export business may, for example, be threatened by tariffs or other import barriers imposed by the local government, either for balance of payments reasons or for stimulating economic diversification and development. The exporting firm may have good reason to expect that unless it establishes or participates in a local production operation, it will be frozen out by other production set up either by local or foreign interests—sometimes with local government participation or financial assistance. The exporting firm is thereby faced with the long-range alternative of transforming its business into a local production operation or losing the business entirely.

Sometimes the challenge wears the guise of a positive opportunity. For example, a source of raw materials in rising world demand may be found or may have become commercially exploitable through the development of new means of transportation; or the rising costs of exploitation of reserves being worked elsewhere may provide the challenge. The degree of profitability of a project to exploit the new resource may be secondary to the strategic purpose of assuring a long-range dependable source of raw materials at reasonable cost. The development of collateral industries, a new transportation route, or the rising prosperity and purchasing power of an area may open new markets. The opportunity may arise from one of any number of special situations, which are not readily classifiable, such as the sale of a family firm through the death of the owner, or the availability of credit through the decision of a development bank to develop a new industry.

Two examples of foreign investment motives of this sort are: 1) A local family textile business in Colombia which made cloth out of imported artificial fibers had surplus funds to invest and proposed to the Celanese Corporation of America a joint venture for producing fibers locally. Celanese accepted the proposal because it offered a profitable opportunity, although until the situation arose it apparently had not contemplated establishing a production operation there, and would probably not have done so on a solo basis. 2) The Grace company had exclusive rights to distribute General Electric light bulbs in Chile. When the Chilean government exerted its influence to have the bulbs made locally, General Electric decided to set up a production operation in conjunction with local capital. Since Grace had the distribution system, it was natural to ask it to participate—which it was glad to do—on a minority basis.

Specific Motives

We turn now to an examination of the motives for (and against) establishing joint ventures rather than solo ventures and the reasons why some companies regard the opportunity to form partnership arrangements with local private interests (or, less commonly, with local governments) as a positive advantage, and why others consider it seriously objectionable—or at best as a disadvantage which can be compensated for only by favorable terms in other respects. Jointness is rarely viewed as the decisive advantage of an investment opportunity and is usually stated as an advantage only when the subject of jointness has been specifically brought up.

Jointness is acknowledged to have been particularly important in the formation of a venture when the investor company would not have been able to finance the project without the assistance of local capital, or when the contribution of a local partner was an indispensable part of the project in other ways. But if a project calls for a joint venture, this is at times a sufficient reason for its rejection by an investor who would not even take the trouble to analyze its profitability.

LESS DEVELOPED COUNTRIES

In the less developed countries, most governments seem to favor joint venturing on the broad grounds that it permits local capital to participate more fully in the benefits of economic development, and that it transmits technical and business know-how more rapidly and effectively than either purely local, or 100 percent foreign-owned ventures, and finally that it lessens the danger of foreign domination of industry.

Some of our informants observe that these motives may be somewhat inconsistent with the objective of attracting maximum foreign investment. They argue that joint ventures utilize local capital that could have found alternative employment and reduce the amount of foreign capital for projects. This does not apply when the outside investor cannot or will not finance the project by himself, even if he has that alternative—available local funds in such cases induce foreign investment. The inconsistency between the two sets of motives stands out sharply when local government pressure forces outside investors to divest themselves of part of their equity, either by open sales of stock to the local public or by inviting in specific local interests. Such pressure may result in true disinvestment, with the foreign investor repatriating part of the capital he would otherwise have left abroad.

In a venture in India where ten percent of the stock was, on the request of the Indian government, sold to the general public, it was noted by an official of the investor company that the Indian government had "played fair" by imposing no barriers on the repatriation of the proceeds of the sale. There were some genuine benefits derived from sharing part of the equity with local investors, but there was also a sacrifice made by India with respect to maximizing foreign investment in its economy.

The economic implications are quite different where a project would not be of sufficient interest to a foreign investor as a solo venture, either because the capital requirements are too large, or because the venture is too risky, or because the active participation of the government or the local business community is itself a major precondition of success. In such cases, the motive of the government in offering to contribute part of the equity capital—either directly or through a state development bank—may be to make possible a foreign investment that would otherwise not occur. By reducing the required investment for the foreign investor or by indicating its own willingness to carry part of the risk, and by giving its moral support to the project, it can powerfully stimulate foreign investor interest.

In the postwar period, when balance of payments problems have been intense in most developing countries, their governments have sometimes been concerned that any immediate benefit to the balance of payments arising from the inflow of foreign capital would be more than offset in the long run by the outflow of dividends.[4] This has sometimes been a motive for favoring joint ventures, since the burden of dividend transfers and repatriation of foreign capital is thereby reduced, while still achieving the gains in acquisition of techniques and management skills, as well as in industrial activity, that a solo venture would have provided.

Less developed countries have also insisted on joint ventures with government participation because of a lingering distrust of foreign investment and the fear that it may exert an improper political and social influence. A passive minority partnership for the government may be sufficient to allay anxiety, since their representatives sitting on the board are in a better position to scrutinize the activities of the business and to divine its intentions correctly than would be an external group of officials to whom the business might otherwise have to report. The allaying of such anxiety even if it is ill-founded, may become a valid motive for a prospective investor to offer a joint venture—assuming that the government's anxiety could not be dissipated in other ways. On the other hand, the use of really capable civil servants for the job of helping to run particular businesses (particularly those which are foreign majority-owned and for which there are adequate managerial resources provided by the foreign owners) may constitute a very expensive use of scarce resources from the point of view of the less developed country.

Insistence on joint ventures may reflect the desire to preserve the opportunity for local business interests to share in the profitable industries selected by foreign investors for exploitation. Where

[4] The limited studies so far made of the effects of direct foreign investment in the postwar period do not substantiate this fear, but appear to indicate that the net growth of the economy arising from such foreign investment has been sufficient to improve the net balance of payments through import substitution or new exports. However, the investments whose effects are being measured have generally been screened, and it could be argued that equally favorable results might not have occurred in the absence of such screening.

the market for a given product or group of products is too small to permit more than one plant large enough to reap the advantages of scale, there is a strong temptation to preempt by government edict a place for local business interests by insisting on a joint venture—whether or not this is the wisest course for rapid development.

CAPITAL-EXPORTING COUNTRIES

For the most part governments of capital-exporting countries have not discerned any need to adopt a general policy on the subject of joint ventures in less developed countries. The policy implications have hardly been appreciated as yet, and what consideration has been given to this subject has dealt chiefly with such incidental aspects as the effects on enforcement of currency controls.

An official of the Bank of England indicated that Her Majesty's Government is particularly concerned that foreign investments show profitability and permit sufficient dividend payments to warrant the initial export of capital from the point of view of the balance of payments. The government, while not opposed to joint ventures, has some preference for solo ventures for United Kingdom foreign direct investments. The rate of return and dividend repayment is thought likely to be higher on solo ventures, and screening the proposed investment and later administering the currency controls is likely to be easier. The consideration of bureaucratic convenience is not put forth as a socially justifiable motive of importance, but it is admitted to exercise some influence.

The motives of potential foreign investors from capital-exporting countries are of crucial interest in this study because they have the bulk of the capital to invest and transfers of technical and business know-how, constituting perhaps the most vital ingredient in economic development, usually go with the capital.

The range of motives expressed by investor companies is broad: At one extreme there is a strong opposition in principle to joint ventures; at the other, there is an acceptance of joint ventures as the most appropriate and rewarding way of doing business abroad. In between there are at least two intermediate positions: One prefers solo operations but accepts joint ventures as sometimes unavoidable; the other position is neutral, accepting without any preference either the joint venture or solo venture as opportunity, circumstance, and immediate advantage indicate.

The great diversity of viewpoints concerning joint ventures among experienced and thoughtful executives of major international companies is perhaps one of the most arresting observations in this study. Different viewpoints are sometimes expressed with great conviction and with indications of strong emotional adherence to the position stated.[5]

The trend is toward increased acceptability of joint ventures. A considerable number of informants indicated that company policy, formerly rigidly set in favor of solo ventures, had now yielded, or was yielding, or was expected soon to yield, to a more flexible policy of acceptance of joint ventures. In some companies interviewed, the policy was in a transitional stage and a subject for major differences within the firm, especially between the international division of the company, or the officers assigned to the international side of the operation, and the domestic side of the firm or top management or boards of directors, most of whom had grown up with almost exclusively domestic experience. The officers most experienced in international business were usually on the side favoring greater acceptance of joint ventures.

Important exceptions to the prevailing trend are found among the leading automobile manufacturers of the United States. The Ford Motor Company has entered into a few joint ventures, both in industrially developed countries and in less developed countries (Spain and Portugal). Currency restrictions and other difficulties impelled Ford to liquidate its Spanish venture in exchange for full ownership of its Portuguese company, formerly a subsidiary of the Spanish company.[6]

[5] In the case of those defending a purely solo venture policy, the emotional strength of the conviction seems often particularly intense, with manifest overtones of defensiveness in the way the case is put. This defensiveness may arise from a feeling of resisting what may now be becoming a majority trend, or from a fear of appearing insular, prejudiced, or uncooperative, overly nationalistic, or too exclusively concerned about maximizing the investor company's profits without regard to sociopolitical objectives or local aspirations.

[6] Ford's growing antipathy to joint ventures recently led it to buy out the British minority in its English subsidiary, at great expense and against the inclinations of both the British and American governments. The British were concerned that future operations of the firm might be jeopardized by subordi-

An outstanding and apparently uncompromising champion of fully controlled foreign subsidiaries is General Motors. The General Motors operations in Australia provide an example of outstanding psychological and practical importance. Some years ago GM transformed its former Australian distributing agency into a manufacturing enterprise. The product, a six-cylinder car named the Holden, proved an overwhelming success, and the enterprise expanded beyond all expectations. GM chose to finance the expansion entirely through reinvestment of profits. Far from offering even a minority of shares to the Australian public, GM made an attractive offer for the redemption of the 20 percent of non-voting preferred stock held since 1931 (long before manufacturing was started) by some Australian distributors. The insistence of GM on full capital control has become a major national issue in Australia—a scientifically and technically developed country with a high sense of national pride—and has provoked fears of a currency crisis if and when General Motors should choose to transfer a major part of its earnings.

The motives of investor companies for participating in joint ventures in less developed countries may be analyzed in various ways —usually with considerable overlap. The advantages usually mentioned are: 1) the achievement of capital savings and the reduction of business risks; 2) the obtaining of management skills and the maintenance of employee morale; 3) the facilitating of sales; 4) the improvement of governmental relations; and 5) the achievement of good public relations. There are additional miscellaneous advantages.

The saving of capital involved in a joint venture is obvious, but it is more often stressed as a motive by investor companies concerned with investment in developed, rather than in less developed, countries. It is frequently mentioned, for example, that a United States firm seeking to establish capacity in Europe today will be in for extremely heavy initial capital charges, and that the capital requirements may be very greatly reduced if a joint venture is arranged: An existing facility might simply be modernized or expanded. It is not merely the plant that is expensive to construct *de novo;* the assembling of a trained work force and an experienced management team

---

nating its welfare to that of Detroit. Washington was concerned at the sizable adverse effect of the transaction on the United States balance of payments.

may pose difficulties and involve a substantial investment in salaries before the productive unit begins operating as an efficient team.

There are several reasons why this factor is less emphasized in the less developed countries: 1) Local plants and operating companies rarely exist in a form requiring only adaptation and expansion to operate successfully. The proposed joint venture is commonly a brand new production operation. Even if a local management team is available, it will ordinarily not be experienced in the new industry, nor can it operate on the scale necessary for the proposed venture. 2) Most of the equipment will have to be imported and, for foreign exchange reasons alone, the foreign investor will probably have to pay for it. 3) The local group often is unable to make a sizable contribution to the total capital required. It can often finance only a small minority position in the new company. 4) The ventures in less developed countries are likely to be attempted only by quite large investor companies, and the capital requirements for a single venture may be small in relation to the total capital of the investor company. In relation to the resources of the investor, the amount of capital required for the investment may look less impressive than a similar proposition in a developed country. 5) In a less developed country, there are so many other major hazards and difficulties that the amount of capital required for the investment does not have the same relative importance as other factors in making a decision.

Despite the qualifications, it remains true that important capital savings may result from joint venturing. It is particularly true where capital from additional sources is required in order to interest foreign or international financing agencies in supplementing the equity.

Closely connected with capital saving is the reduction in business risk. By sinking less capital into a venture and diversifying investments between industries, areas, and countries, the investor company obviously gains an element of protection. In addition, the entrepreneurial skills and experience of local partners permit easier adaptation to the particular dangers of a new business environment with which the investor company may be relatively unfamiliar. Geographic diversification is heavily relied upon for protection by some of the big investor companies who have sometimes indicated that they regard it as offering superior protection to that offered, for example, by the United States Foreign Investment Guarantee program. Grounds for this conclusion are that the guarantee program protects only against certain rather narrowly delimited types of risk, whereas the protection offered by diversification is broader.

With a given amount of capital available for foreign investment, an investor firm may achieve a greater degree of diversification of holdings if it spreads its investments over a larger number of joint ventures, instead of a smaller number of solo ventures. If only minority holdings are taken risks may be further reduced by the greater mobility and flexibility afforded, since minority holdings can more easily be disposed of in case of adverse business developments or threatening government policies.

Reduction of risk as a motive involves the notion that a company with a local partner is less subject to the danger of adverse action by the local government. If the government or a national development bank is the local partner, there is an added element of protection, not only against the gross risks of outright expropriation, but also against the often more dangerous risks of bureaucratic harassment and gradual strangulation in red tape which sometimes afflict foreign investors who are out of favor with the governments of the countries in which they are operating. This motive was noted by an important international construction firm in relation to contract terminations, failure to honor contracts, or to make payments. In such cases, having local partners could reduce considerably the risk of unfavorable developments.

A second major type of investor company motive is the desire to aid in the attainment of various management objectives. Where the investor company accepts a small minority position and takes a passive role in the new company it may lack management resources for the new project or feel that it cannot spare management personnel and the time and attention of the head office for running the new venture. Having confidence in the caliber of the local management, it is glad to leave the direction of the new company in its hands. Even the largest international companies frequently feel that capable managerial talent is their rarest and most valuable resource. They may welcome an opportunity to economize on management, without foregoing an attractive business opportunity, by allowing an existing local management team to retain or assume direction. Occasionally, a company will do this even when it has a majority control.[7]

The excellence of existing local management was a consideration in forming joint ventures by W. R. Grace & Company. Despite Grace's majority control, management responsibilities were at least for a time left in local hands. Examples are the Compañía Colombiana de Conservas California, and Carboquímica in Colombia, Arturo Field y Compañía in Peru, and the International Mining Company in Bolivia.[8]

In most cases, however, where management objectives play a part in motivating a joint venture, the aim is not to avoid management responsibilities entirely so much as to supplement the investor company's managerial resources with resources locally available. The supplementation may have a quantitative or a qualitative dimension. Quantitatively, it may simply be that a local management team is a welcome addition possibly because the investor company lacks the managerial resources to take on the additional responsibilities immediately. More significant than this is the qualitative supplementation which a local management team may give. Local management can contribute a knowledge of local conditions and an ability to deal with labor, government, and suppliers, which no foreign management could match.

This was one of the motives mentioned by Mr. Emery N. Cleaves, Vice-President of the Celanese Corporation of America, in discussing the formation of the Mexican joint venture Celanese Mexicana, S.A. In explaining his company's favorable attitude toward joint ventures, he said: "Local partners will help one avoid mistakes and handle local problems better."

It is fair to ask why similar advantages could not be obtained by assembling local people as managerial personnel and advisors under the direction of a group from the investor company. Sometimes,

[7] This situation is to be distinguished from the very frequent case where the investor company, while retaining control and direction of a foreign subsidiary, employs local personnel as officers of administration. Such officers are still subject to close control by the home office, where policies, budgets, and investment programs are normally determined.

[8] The original promoter and director of the International Mining Company was made a Grace official and ran the joint venture in that capacity.

this is the only or best alternative. However, first class managerial talent is usually hard to find in less developed countries outside the owner groups—the separation of ownership and management has not proceeded nearly as far as it has in the United States or in Europe. The desired caliber of local management is usually obtainable, if at all, only by associating with a group of existing owner-managers, who insist ordinarily on obtaining or retaining an ownership position in the new firm. Although potential managerial talents may be available in profusion, time is usually lacking to train them. Moreover, local employees without an ownership position often lack the status and personality either to press views on behalf of the local company where these views conflict with those of the management of the investor companies, or to obtain favorable local treatment or public relations for the company. They may be less useful than local partners in helping the firm to make the necessary—and sometimes difficult—local adjustments.

There is an important managerial advantage of joint ventures of a relatively intangible kind: the favorable effect on the morale of the local employees of inviting local capital participation. In a venture in India, it is reported that the sale of ten percent of the stock of the company to the Indian public had a markedly beneficial effect on the morale of the Indian staff.

National pride is not ordinarily considered an economic motive—yet it may have substantial economic effects. Where local interests, especially the employees themselves, are permitted participation substantial favorable effects may be noted. This is because acceptance of local investors as partners is a major step in the process sometimes referred to as: "ization" (as "Indianization," etc.), by which a foreign investment assumes a local character and status. When this happens, the local employee may be able to integrate his loyalties more easily, with a consequent reduction in tension and improved work performance.

There is also a widespread impression that a foreign venture may find it easier to sell its products in the local market if it assumes a joint venture form, particularly if the product is a consumer good. This was adduced as a major motive for certain joint ventures of the British firm Associated Electrical Industries by its chairman.

Speaking in particular of AEI firms producing consumer durables in the British Commonwealth, he stated that it was company policy to allow local investors to participate when possible, and emphasized as an important reason that it improved sales by creating an incentive to buy, and strengthening brand loyalty. This was the chief reason given for the sale of 30 percent of the ownership of AEI Ltd. of Australia to the Australian public.

This type of influence is probably strongest where the local stock participation is widely diffused and where the market is small and relatively undynamic. The creation of additional incentives to buy, even in a few hundred families, could have a significant influence on sales in a small market, especially when the imitation effects are considered. The influence would be particularly important where new products were being introduced and in a business community where price competition between brands was not intense.

Whether the admission of local capital has a significant effect in improving product acceptability generally, even among those who do not become stockholders, is nevertheless open to question. In less developed countries, preference is frequently given to products with a foreign name on the grounds of assumed higher quality. Business buyers are concerned mainly about price and quality, and the general consumer is often badly informed about the national ownership of local industries. And, as the case of General Motors' Holden car in Australia testifies, strong national identification of consumers with a product is possible despite 100 percent foreign control of the company producing it.

Another important motive for joint ventures has been the hope of obtaining more favorable treatment from the local government. In the extreme case, the laws of the country are such that it is legally impossible for an investor company to invest locally at all, or impossible to invest in particular industries, except on a joint venture basis. Laws forbidding wholly foreign-owned ventures exist in several less developed countries. (These are examined in detail in other parts of this study.) Such laws provide a clear-cut motive for the investor company to choose a joint venture since no investment is otherwise possible. In effect, they result in a limitation of choice rather than an incentive. In other cases, the choice of solo ventures is legally open, but the local government policy so strongly and openly favors the joint venture form that the investor feels the chances of doing business are slight unless that form is chosen.

Thus, in the Philippines, no law is on the books requiring joint ventures, and United States investments have a legally preferential position. Yet the approval of a substantial investment project by the Central Bank and National Economic Council (with the necessary assurances regarding transfer of dividends and repatriation of capital) has been getting harder and harder to obtain even for United States investors if the proposed project is *not* a joint venture. The General Milk Company (Philippines), which began as a wholly-owned United States subsidiary, found it necessary upon reorganization in 1958 to admit Philippine capital—in the form of a passive minority holding by a group of Philippine insurance companies.

International construction companies sometimes have to form a local joint venture in order to qualify for government contracts, since these can by law be given only to national citizens or companies.

Aside from such extreme cases, investor companies quite frequently indicate that they have been motivated to establish joint ventures by the hope of obtaining better treatment from the host government. Companies are rarely explicit about what benefits they expect to obtain and how they expect their actions to exercise a favorable influence on the government. And, for obvious reasons, they are rarely willing to be quoted on the subject. The following analysis must therefore be mainly in general terms and involve a degree of interpretation of meanings.

One of the main advantages sought is protection against various kinds of actions by the government, allowable under local law, which would be seriously detrimental to a new venture. The most obvious example is nationalization, without adequate compensation—and in practice compensation is almost never adequate, because it does not compensate for the loss of future profits, appropriately rewarding the bearing of the risks of initial establishment. There are other types of harassing action which the local government can take to make the conduct of the business difficult or unprofitable. Examples are refusals of foreign exchange allocations or import permits for essential materials, machinery, and spare parts, or refusals of necessary work or residence permits for managerial or technical personnel, and arbitrary and burdensome labor legislation.

Aside from negative actions by the local government, the success of the venture will often be crucially affected by the positive actions which the local government takes or fails to take. Important examples are: protective tariffs to protect the new industry; tax burdens imposed on the industry; authorized transfer of dividends and repatriation of capital, and the exchange rate at which such transactions are permitted. Tax payments are sometimes negotiated with government officials and do not necessarily coincide with tax liabilities implicit in the tax legislation on the books. Here, government attitudes could be of great importance.

In order to obtain favorable governmental action in these and other respects, it has often seemed highly desirable to give a foreign investment a joint form. But how, exactly, is it supposed that the formation of a joint venture will exert a favorable influence on the local government? There are three distinct ways in which it may be hoped such influence will be exerted.

The first and most obvious way is by evoking greater friendliness on the part of the government. By the foreign investor's doing what the government favors, by acceding to strong and widespread nationalistic sentiments, it is hoped that the government will regard the venture more favorably and will refrain from measures harmful to it, and even, perhaps, take measures favorable to it. Friendliness and cooperativeness on the part of the investor company will, it is hoped, elicit friendliness and cooperativeness in response. Where the government is highly centralized, as it usually is in the less developed countries, and where the government may for practical purposes be equated with a handful of leaders and officials, this kind of thinking may make much practical sense. Friendship with such a group may be achievable and rewarding. If achieved, it may provide more solid protection against discriminatory or damaging treatment than any amount of protective legislation.

A second and quite different motive for bringing in a local investor (or even the local government itself) as part owner of the new venture, is to create an incentive in the government to avoid actions damaging to the venture, since not only foreigners but also local interests will be hurt. The local interest here serves the purpose of a sort of lightning rod: It deflects or dissipates harmful emotional charges which the foreign venture may attract because it is big, successful, and foreign. By becoming more "national," it hopes to avoid discriminatory treatment and obtain the more favorable governmental treatment accorded to members of the "in-group."

A third mechanism of action on the government through joint ventures is different again from the other two. The local interest associated in the joint venture is viewed not merely as a passive protector or "lightning rod" but as an active agent to favorably influence government policies and treatment. The influence may be exerted through the normal channels of political action—by appeals made to the legislature, and by working through organized business groups and political parties. The foreign investor company is in a much less strong and much more delicate position when it comes to exerting political influence on the local government. Such activities can backfire and become extremely dangerous, especially in areas with a strong anti-colonial tradition. A local interest within a joint venture is subject to no such inhibitions, and may appropriately take action in political defense of its business interests.

Local partners may influence government action by private negotiations with government officials and politicians. This function is better performed by local partners than by the investor company because they are experienced—"know the ropes," have well-established connections, and have the "feel" of the situation—and also because such activities on their part are more readily accepted by government and public opinion, than if carried on by foreigners. Matters like these can be—and often are—entrusted to local intermediaries, lawyers, or company officials of local origin, even without formation of a joint venture. But the impression is that influence may be exerted and negotiations conducted more effectively if the local representatives have a financial stake in the outcome and are acting on their own account.

Interestingly enough, a positive influence on government can be exerted even when the government itself is the partner in the joint venture. One enterprise reported that the civil servants on the board of directors representing the government played a very helpful role in obtaining favorable action from the government on the vital matters of import permits and price increase permissions. Their reports on the objective needs of the firm for imported materials and for more lenient margins were based on first-hand observation and were believed by other officials in the government, whereas reports by the investor company's own representatives gained less credence. In a more general way, the government of a less developed country can sometimes gain a sounder conception of the objective problems of an enterprise and a more generous appreciation of the contributions made by the investor company when it actively associates itself with the conduct of the business and learns to look at its problems from the inside, from the viewpoint of one seeking to run an organization at a profit.

Favorable public relations are occasionally cited as a motive for joint ventures, without too specific indication of just how this is expected to benefit the company. The Grace Company reports that in industries of prime necessity, the local investing public has sometimes been invited to participate for public relations reasons. (Compañías Unidas in Peru and Compañía de Industrias y Azúcar in Chile are mentioned as specific examples.) In such industries it is thought to be particularly desirable for an enterprise to be "closely identified with the country." Our own interpretation is that a company such as Grace, with widely diversified holdings in Latin America, is concerned with creating a favorable public image of its activities, and finds that partnership with local interests is helpful. This would be particularly important in items with a wide consumer sale, and some of the benefits of a favorable public image, once established, might be expected to extend to concerns of Grace which were not joint ventures. The benefits might include enhanced acceptability of the products, more favorable reception and treatment by governments, and improved employee morale.

Exchange controls have stimulated the formation of joint ventures, an example being the Goodrich International Rubber Company of the Philippines: The head of a Philippine company became interested in the manufacture of automobile tires when the imposition of exchange controls and import restrictions threatened the flow of imports. The company interested B. F. Goodrich in associating with them in a joint venture. Goodrich's motive was partly the desire to utilize various blocked funds. The fact that a joint venture was chosen probably reflected certain other factors including the general Goodrich policy in this respect and the positive attitude of the Philippine government toward joint ventures.

According to charges by the Philippine Central Bank, a joint venture was established for the purpose of exchange control evasion; or at least it was charged that it was rapidly adapted to this purpose soon after its formation. The Roxas-Kalaw Textile Mills in the Philippines received over $4 million of foreign exchange allocations at preferential rates, of which nearly $3 million were intended for raw materials to be used in manufacturing operations. Much of the foreign exchange obtained was diverted to other uses, particularly the illegal importation of finished textiles for sale at inflated prices in the highly protected Philippine market which was then suffering from an extreme shortage of goods. As charged by the country's Central Bank, the enterprise's evasion of regulations was facilitated by its dealing mostly through foreign supplying firms, either managed or owned by some of its shareholders: the joint venture form was advantageous.

When a local government or development bank has the necessary capital or land to undertake a new project but does not have the technical know-how or administrative resources to set up the business on a purely local basis, it may invite a foreign interest to supply the missing ingredient. The project could be arranged without joint participations by procuring the necessary foreign technical or managerial know-how via a licensing or management contract arrangement. Alternatively, a foreign company could be invited in on a solo basis, and the necessary capital made available as a long-term loan; or government-owned land could be sold to the foreign company. If a joint participation is adopted, it is usually not because it offers the only possible way to exploit the special situation, but because it offers subsidiary advantages or is the most practical way to handle the situation.

The joint equity venture usually arises when two parties own or control different elements required for a successful operation; they prefer to enter into a partnership rather than have one party sell or rent the element it controls to the other because there may be a nationalistic or other block against the sale or rental of a particular element. For example, land may not willingly be sold to foreign interests, or there may be an emotional block against selling out a traditional family business. There are also genuine reasons of an economic or business kind: The true value of a given factor in the business may be too difficult to measure; its value in the particular venture may be far higher than its "market value" in alternative uses, and its value within the venture can be ascertained only in experience. Establishing a partnership permits the rewards to the separate elements to be determined in large part by the success of the enterprise. It is still necessary to make an initial evaluation of the capital contribution of each of the partners, but agreement on this is more easily obtained.

Arrangements are possible for one party to rent the element it controls to the other party on a sliding scale of rentals, or to provide other devices for profit sharing. A more straightforward partnership relation will often be preferred—to reduce the likelihood of one party's taking advantage of the other and to give both parties an opportunity to contribute (and be remunerated for) managerial services which they have available.

Another special type of motivation falls, in part, outside the profit-making objective. The creation of joint ventures is sometimes motivated by the desire to aid in the process of transferring technical and managerial knowledge and skills to less developed countries as a contribution to their economic development. This has been a legitimate and important motive of various development banks. They assume, and often with good reason, that the creation of a strong entrepreneurial group in the country will be aided by the encouragement of joint ventures. This view is part of the philosophy of the International Finance Corporation, and explains the extent to which it has financed joint ventures.

The private International Basic Economy Corporation began with developmental rather than profit-seeking goals and has encouraged participation of local capital in its projects. The American

Overseas Finance Company (now known as Transoceanic-AOFC Ltd. and partly owned by the International Basic Economy Corporation) has also been involved in development financing, and most of its projects have been joint ventures. Aside from its desire to stimulate economic development, AOFC is motivated by the desire to make sound investments. Investments in a less developed country, all other things being equal, may well be more successful if carried out in participation with local capital.

The idea that joint ventures are intrinsically more profitable could become an important motive for choosing joint ventures, but no such general expectation was reflected in the views of our informants. Some see clear advantages in joint ventures, which might well make them more profitable, but they did not go so far as to state that experience indicated that they *were* more profitable. Sufficient experience is certainly lacking to draw satisfactory overall conclusions regarding profit comparisons between solo and joint ventures.

Investor companies frequently were more spontaneous in citing motives against rather than for joint ventures. Even those companies which have joint ventures seem more aware of their difficulties than of their advantages, and indicated that they entered joint ventures reluctantly, hesitantly, under pressure, or against their better judgments. In spite of this, they were hard pressed to enumerate particular difficulties that they had encountered in their own joint ventures. In any case, one can hardly interview a substantial sample of companies on this subject without obtaining an impression that joint venturing is still something of a novelty, and, as such, distrusted to a considerable extent by conservative management. Often the objections to joint ventures are given with great assurance by companies which have never tried joint ventures, and have therefore never themselves experienced the difficulties which they cite.

It is very hard to distinguish between rationalization and true motives. For one reason or another, many companies distrust or dislike the *idea* of joint ventures, and the reasons they cite for avoiding them are often convenient excuses invented to conceal the real motive or to lend additional justification to the real motive. If a concern has had an unfavorable experience with a joint venture, it is understandable for it to wish to avoid further joint ventures. However, the unfavorable experiences cited are often no worse than those that have been philosophically accepted by other companies which continue to believe in and accept joint ventures. Sometimes the damage suffered seems insufficient to justify the extremely negative position adopted, and one may suspect that the unfavorable experience brought a welcome confirmation to a basic attitude of distrust of joint ventures; the attitude itself probably accounted for a part of the bad experience with them.

It is interesting to observe that companies which cite unfavorable episodes with joint ventures from their own experience, generally continue to utilize them. Their unfavorable experiences do sometimes lead them to be more cautious in the kind of joint ventures they are willing to enter, and to avoid certain conditions which they are able to recognize as inauspicious. Unfortunate experiences do not invariably turn companies against joint ventures. The blankly negative appraisal of joint ventures in less developed countries came, in all but a very few instances, from informant companies that were totally inexperienced with them.

Motives for avoiding joint ventures are often the obverse side of the coin of the same reality which provides a positive motive for joint venturing. For example, joint venturing reduces capital requirements, but correspondingly reduces the profit potential. It provides additional local managerial resources, but poses difficult problems of cooperating with them. It may induce good employee morale, but it may lead to problems of nepotism; and it may be in a position to utilize connections with the local government to good advantage, but changes in government personnel may result in official hostility.

Some strong and very wealthy companies see little benefit in the capital-saving aspect of joint venturing since they are always able to raise additional capital for projects they consider profitable enough to bother with. They are less impressed with capital saving and more concerned with reduced profit potential for the investor company. They claim that local capital is often hard to find and is apt to ask for more in the way of reward than is really justified. There is also concern over the "free rider" type of situation where the local interest benefits from certain affiliations, know-how, technical abilities, and patents, of the investor company, which were not and could not be adequately capitalized in the initiation of the joint venture. In the course of time the joint venture may expand into new fields where the contribution of the investor company is disproportionately large and from which the local investor group gains a return incommensurate with its contribution.

One large company feels that it is not entitled to utilize its limited managerial resources and its own capital except in ways which maximize the return. It does not feel justified in utilizing them in enterprises where part of the benefits go to others. "If a venture is worth doing, it is worth doing alone." A particular difficulty with a joint venture is that whereas you can initially make some evaluation of the contribution of each partner, you gradually lose sight of their relative contributions, and after a while one party is contributing more than its share, and the other party is receiving disproportionate benefits. The firm in this instance feels itself likely to be on the short end with local partners because it deals with many fields of industry; the firm may be able to contribute more if the venture diversifies. At the same time, the contribution of local partners in their political, cultural, and social influence, can be a waning asset, becoming less and less indispensable with the course of time.

The choice of partners may be very limited in less developed countries. One firm noted that it has been difficult to obtain additional local directors for its joint venture even in Canada and that it would be glad to have a large Canadian capital participation if it could find it. Lack of available local private capital is cited quite often as a leading reason for not having more joint ventures in less developed countries. Investor companies are sometimes loath to enter joint ventures with local governments because of the disproportionate benefit thesis, and the feared political instability of less developed countries.

While the opportunity to obtain local management is sometimes regarded as a major advantage of joint venturing, the need to work with local management is sometimes regarded as a major disadvantage. If viewed as a disadvantage, the emphasis may be either on the general difficulties of a nonunified management, the inevitable conflicts of interests between partners, or the specific difference in management philosophies between investor companies and local interests.

One company without joint venture experience reports a fear of dilution of responsibility as a motive for resisting the joint venture. It notes that outside equity capital is not utilized by the company even within the United States, where presumably a closer congruence of management philosophies could be expected to be found. Companies which have tried joint ventures admit that the tasks of administration may be made far more difficult by the need to explain and justify company policies to a local minority. Even companies which consider this a desirable challenge to which they have successfully responded, recognize that the additional wear and tear on the management represents a real cost. (Some joint venturers report incipient differences between the diverse interests are easily and amicably settled entirely without strain, and that the ventures have not involved any unusual administrative burdens.)

There may be a real and inevitable conflict of interest between the partners, or there may be differences in management philosophy. One type of conflict of interest occurs when the partners own rival distribution outlets for the products manufactured by the joint venture. This was the source of the difficulty in Pinturas Colombianas, which led the Grace Company to sell out its share to its Colombian partners.

Different tax laws and foreign exchange considerations affecting the two partners can be sources of conflict. For example, the investor company may desire the joint venture to retain surplus and not to remit dividends in order to be free of United States profits taxation at a given time; the local partner may need cash. Conversely, the investor company may prefer to avoid accumulating profits for working capital, out of fear of losses from currency depreciation, whereas the local investor might dislike the idea of incurring heavy interest payments by borrowing for working capital requirements. Having to be concerned with local partners curtails the flexibility of the investor company, which can no longer respond swiftly and easily to exploit profit opportunities from tax and currency situations as they arise. (Some of the largest international companies, on the other hand, consider that frequent shifts in a firm's policy, designed to exploit such opportunities, are not truly worth-while, and distract attention from the essentials.)

The potential conflict of interest over the relative rates of reinvestment of earnings and of dividend distribution is very widely referred to by our informants, although, as indicated in a subsequent chapter, experience has demonstrated this fear to be considerably exaggerated. There may, of course, be such conflict between an investor company, especially a United States investor company, which desires a substantial period of heavy reinvestment of earnings in order to achieve rapid growth, while local partners press for immediate and large dividends. The attitude of the United States company in such cases may be partly influenced by United States tax laws. These laws are more favorable to capital gains than to high incomes, and, of course, entirely exempt reinvested income of foreign subsidiaries from tax until distributed to the United States parent. The company's attitude is also, however, frequently based on a management philosophy which puts heavy emphasis on growth, and maintenance (or improvement) of market shares.

Staffing and employment policies and, in particular, the problems of nepotism are further causes for controversy. Substantial conflict occasionally arises when the investor company wants to impose professional criteria of selection for its staff and the local owners want to give influential posts to their relatives. Disagreements also arise when local partners hasten the replacement of foreign staff by nationals more rapidly than the foreign partners feel is warranted by the technical training and capacity of the local employees.

Some firms averse to joint ventures discount heavily the promise of a favorable influence on the local government. They feel that the special connections of locals with the government and their ability to pull political strings, constitute an asset of temporary and declining importance. With changes of governmental regimes such special connections may be lost and may even create difficulties for the firm that has used them. A firm which has been "in" with one government will almost certainly be "out" with its successor, if the change is of a revolutionary character.

Where joint ventures involve acceptance of the local government as a partner, many United States firms, even those well-disposed toward joint ventures with private local interests, often draw the line. It is felt that there is something inherently unsuitable about mixed governmental-private enterprises, since the government "wears two hats"—as regulator and partner. Others refuse to enter partnerships with governments because they feel they would be subjecting themselves to the dangers of frequent changes in government policy.

Occasionally, but rarely, antitrust dangers were cited as one of the reasons why joint-venturing was avoided. This subject is dealt with in detail in Chapter VII.

The extremely technical nature of the product was mentioned by the International Business Machines Company as a reason for not utilizing joint ventures. Governments and local businesses in economically underdeveloped countries have not pressed IBM to accept them as local partners because they felt they would not be able to understand the problems involved. In other cases, it was asserted that a highly technical industry facilitates joint ventures. Advanced technical know-how and continuing research give investor companies effective control of joint ventures without majority ownership or legal control of the board. This makes the companies less concerned about the disadvantages of associating with local interests and facilitates the administration of their enterprises.

The Type of Joint Venture

The limited amount of capital investment involved in looser forms of joint ventures (licensing agreements, management contracts, etc.) makes them attractive to small companies with no spare capital but with an advanced technical specialty. Other companies financially able to make foreign investments prefer a form of association which minimizes capital investment abroad because of the fear that such investment is peculiarly risky—particularly in less developed countries which have only recently achieved self-government. The fear may be unfounded; the postwar history of direct investment in such countries is reassuring. Furthermore, the greater political risks are offset by lower commercial risks; there is usually little competition owing to tariff protection, import quotas, and government restrictions on the establishment of additional enterprises in the same industry. The growth of industry and sales is likely to be rapid, and the profits, tax, and depreciation rates may be favorable enough to permit total repatriation of the investment in a relatively short period. For companies inexperienced with foreign investment and operation, the hazards may appear too great, and a form of association with minimal capital investment may be preferred.

Some firms are precluded from joint participations not only through lack of capital, but also through lack of managerial resources. While this burden might be minimized by the use of minority participation, the investor company may hesitate to commit any of its capital to a foreign venture unless it exercises a considerable degree of surveillance and supervision.

Some companies, of which Westinghouse is a prime example, have specialized in licensing as the preferred form of joint venturing. The reason is the disinclination to commit large amounts of capital abroad—especially in view of the capital-intensive nature of the industry and the high cost of new plants—and because of the research program being conducted. The research and development effort is so extensive and successful that Westinghouse can count on retaining a long lead in product development over its licensees, thereby minimizing the risk that the technology transferred will build up a dangerous rival, or that the licensees will wish to terminate the relationship at the end of the licensing period.

Other licensors with less imposing research programs have expressed concern that their technological advantages may be dissipated without commensurate long-term benefits, since the licensee, if a good one, will assimilate the know-how and technology during the licensing period, and may even make improvements on them. He may then either choose to operate independently or demand a heavy cut in royalty rates as a condition for renewal. Other motives for avoiding licensing are that the licensee's government will intervene to limit or reduce the royalties, and that there may be antitrust hazards arising from the strong desire of most licensees for an exclusive assignment of particular markets.

There is considerable agreement that, for firms which can afford the investment of capital and managerial resources required, a joint participation is generally preferable to a looser form of participation in the long run because of maximized profits. Technical know-how, patents, trademarks, good will, capital, and managerial services make a valuable package. To sell separately one or two pieces may reduce the risk, but it also greatly reduces the bargaining power which possession of the whole package gives. Possession of a wanted technology may provide the leverage for the sale of the whole package, the returns to which may be quite incommensurate with the returns to the technological component sold separately. An integrated production operation permits profiting from every phase of the foreign operation, including lower labor costs and lower levels of managerial remuneration.

There is a consensus (though far from a unanimous one) among investor companies that majority participations are best. The essential motive here is the desire for control. If the investor company is confident of retaining control either through a management contract, through simple technical leadership, or because the stock is shared by other interests from developed countries, concern about the majority position is less.

The desire of the investor company to exercise control is understandable. The investor company assumes that its contribution in the field of management is likely to be a superior one, and that the chief purpose of direct foreign investment in less developed countries is to permit such countries to benefit from the managerial resources and talent and know-how of the advanced countries. This contribution may be more important in the long run than the capital invested and is most easily and effectively made if the investor company retains control. To spare local susceptibilities, the existence of investor company control is often disguised in the form of technical assistance agreements which do not overtly convey managerial powers.

A considerable number of large investor companies have expressed themselves as willing to accept minority participations under certain circumstances. It is possible to sell out to local interests if the outlook is unfavorable—without wrecking the operation—

and it is possible to shift resources to take best advantage of currency, tax, or other opportunities as they arise. One firm has expressed itself as favoring a minority position if a 100 percent control is not available—if a joint participation is involved, it prefers a minority position. The rationale of this preference was not clearly stated. It may be the desire to avoid the probable frictions and wear and tear of joint venturing by surrendering the burden of management to a foreign interest in which they have confidence, or it may be the desire for the enterprise to be identified as a national one.

One might well suppose that a 50-50 arrangement, in which either party may veto the initiative of the other party, would be a perfect recipe for frustration and a guarantee of inefficient administration, and would be avoided at all costs. But it is more common than is generally supposed. Its adoption is usually at the insistence of the local interest, motivated primarily by nationalistic concern not to relinquish control. Often the local government is directly or indirectly involved, insisting that the foreign interest shall not acquire full control over the project. This may create difficulties: The local partner might be unable to finance additional capital investment required for the company's growth, and the investor company is often not permitted to increase its investment to a majority holding.

Despite the obvious difficulties of such a setup, investor companies are at times willing to accept them. The motive is the greater confidence which 50 percent ownership gives to the local interest and the greater sense of responsibility for decisions which it helps to create. A disgruntled minority can be a dangerous thing, particularly if this minority is of the same nationality as the government which controls the company's destinies. The "engineering of consent" is a major part of the job of managing a joint venture and is easier if the local interest can be dealt with on terms of full equality, with the knowledge that it stands to gain or lose as much as the investor company by the decisions taken.

VI. Internal Operations of Joint Ventures

ATTENTION IS first paid to the operating experiences of private joint ventures in which the foreign partner holds a minority of the equity of the enterprise, a form which is constantly growing in importance and one in which greater problems might be expected than where the foreigner controls the enterprise by a majority. Actually, there has been considerable success in avoiding problems under this form of participation. The 50-50 type of participation is found only to a limited extent in private joint ventures; it exists to a greater extent in special arrangements with governments as participants.

Minority Participation by the Foreign Partner

In numerous cases, the foreign partners who participate in joint ventures on a minority basis find that their interests are adequately represented despite the fact that they do not exercise a majority of the voting power in the enterprise: The enterprises are dependent on the foreign partners—for proper technical operation, for financial assistance other than through investment in equity, or in other ways. As a result, the enterprises are usually managed to the satisfaction of the foreign partners without their exercising actual formal control. But there are some instances where special provisions protect the minority partner's interests.

The *de facto* control exercised by the foreign partners may be as a result of a formal technical assistance or other type of agreement, or it may exist without formal agreement by virtue of the ability of the foreign partner to be of some special assistance to the enterprise as, for example, in obtaining loans from foreign or international lending agencies. In other instances, there may be business transactions between the joint venture enterprise and the enterprise of the foreign partner which yield such decided advantages to the joint venture that the influence of the foreign partner in it is greater than would be expected from its minority financial participation alone.

In Brazil, Cobrasma has a technical assistance agreement with its minority foreign partner, American Steel Foundries International, which holds a 15 percent interest in the enterprise. The proper functioning of the firm depends upon this agreement and technical assistance agreements which it has with other American firms specialized in certain aspects of railway car manufacture. American Steel Foundries International, which originally participated only with technical assistance, later invested its relatively small amount of equity because of the successful development of the enterprise. The investment was not primarily to give financial assistance to the joint venture. The prospect of participating in the venture's success not only in the form of royalties but also through dividends motivated the investment. The relatively small financial participation of the foreign partner was thus effected without any prospect at all of voting control in the enterprise.

Willys Overland do Brasil also has only a minority foreign participation in its voting stock. Despite this fact, it is obviously dependent upon the Willys Motors Company of the United States and the Renault enterprise of France, with which it has technical assistance and franchise agreements. The Brazilian participation is very widely distributed among the public, so that the possibility of bloc voting by the national partners is somewhat less than in closely held corporations.

The Celanese Corporation of America holds a minority of the stock and has a technical assistance and process agreement in Mexico with Celanese Mexicana. This permits adequate control of the enterprise by the foreign partner despite its minority financial position, and has made it possible for the local interests to take advantage of very diversified technical experience and to broaden the range of products produced in Mexico. When the enterprise began in 1947, its production was limited to acetate yarns and fibers, and it has since expanded into the production of viscose yarns and fibers, nylon, various chemical products, plastics, and cellophane.

The pattern is similar in Industria Eléctrica de México. The share of the principal foreign partner, Westinghouse, is even smaller than in the Celanese case, but effective control is exercised through a technical assistance agreement as well as through an administrative device: There is a total of 16 members of the board of directors, of which seven represent Westinghouse and other foreign shareholders; the total foreign holdings amount to slightly more than 40 percent; however, this board of directors is only a *pro forma* group, and the real policymaking body of the firm is an operating committee of five, on which Westinghouse holds a majority of three. The Mexican majority interests have accepted this arrangement in view of the dependence of the enterprise upon the technical and management contributions of Westinghouse.

In Bristol de México the foreign partner holds a majority and runs the enterprise on the basis of a management contract, but is prepared to relinquish its majority while continuing the management contract.

In Colombia the technical assistance and information agreement between B. F. Goodrich and Icollantas supplements Goodrich's minority investment and there are provisions for special voting rights to further protect the interests of the minority shareholder. As in other cases, the technical information aspect of the agreement has permitted the local enterprise to branch out into diverse fields of production in addition to the original one of rubber tires: It is now producing such items as rubber hose, rubber soles for shoes, automotive battery cases and batteries, rubber tile, plastic cloth and bags, and rigid plastic pipes. The shares of the enterprise are divided into two classes, one of which (class B) relates to the Goodrich stock, which amounts to about one-third of the total. Despite the minority represented by this one class of stock, a 60 percent vote of each of the two classes is required for certain matters, including changing the rules of election and composition of the board, changing the preferential rights of the existing shareholders to subscribe to new shares, and dissolving the company. Thus, although Goodrich holds a minority of only one-third, its influence is considerably greater, and it is protected against being forced out through a dissolution of the company.

Turning to the Far East, foreign minority participation usually has technical assistance arrangements to supplement the equity investment. Most often, participation in management by the foreigners is minimal, and main reliance is placed by them on the technical assistance arrangements to protect their investments. In Atul Products Ltd. in India, the two foreign minority shareholders, American Cyanamid and Ciba of Switzerland, have technical assistance agreements with the firm for their respective products, but they do not participate on the board of directors. Atul is actually managed under a managing agency agreement with the separate enterprise of the Indian partner. In the Telco enterprise, there is a joint venture arrangement with respect to its manufacture of Mercedes-Benz vehicles. Their manufacture is carried on by the automobile division of the firm, which is managed simply as a division of the larger company. The 40 percent interest of Daimler Benz of Germany is limited to the automobile division, but it has two directors on the larger Telco board. In Tube Investments of India, until an expansion and reorganization that was effected in 1959, the British interest amounted to 49 percent but the British had equal representation on the board of directors. There were also strict provisions for quality control of the product pursuant to franchise and technical assistance agreements.

In Burma, in the Martaban Company there is a minority Japanese participation of 40 percent, pursuant to general legal limitations of foreign participation. The Japanese favored a 50-50 arrangement, but went along with the legal restriction. This is also a case where there is heavy reliance on the foreigner for technical aspects of the enterprise. Deep-sea fishing is an activity that has not been pursued in Burma, and the Japanese partner is one of the leading enterprises in this field in Japan. At first, all the personnel on the firm's fishing trawlers were Japanese. Local personnel have now been trained, and fewer Japanese are required in the operation of the enterprise.

In the Philippines, the Goodrich International Rubber Company follows a similar pattern to that of the Goodrich joint venture in Colombia. Goodrich holds only a minority in the enterprise, but its investment is protected by a technical assistance and information agreement and by provisions for special voting rights. Although Goodrich holds a 43 percent interest in the enterprise, its consent is in effect required to change the articles of incorporation or to dissolve the company since these actions require a two-thirds majority vote. In addition, this enterprise is managed by Goodrich under a management contract.

There are similar arrangements in the Snia Viscosa joint venture in Spain. Although Snia Viscosa holds only 25 percent of the capital, the enterprise is dependent upon it technically via a technical cooperation agreement, and the company cannot be dissolved nor can its bylaws be amended without the consent of the foreign minority partner.

In certain cases, the protection of the minority interest of the foreign partner is achieved through the special legal form of the company, or through other private law devices. Protection through the use of a particular company form is illustrated in the case of the Tamck Canning Company Ltd. of Turkey. The United States partner holds a 40 percent interest. Nominally there are three Turkish partners, but in effect they are all members of the same family and can be considered as one. As a limited company with fewer than five shareholders, all decisions of the firm's board must be unanimous, pursuant to the Turkish Code of Commerce. The fact of the minority holding by the foreign partner therefore is of little practical effect in the management of the enterprise. The day-to-day affairs are managed by the Turkish partners, but there is constant and continuing cooperation with the foreign partner in the administration.

The dependence upon foreign minority partners for financial assistance in particular is well illustrated in Icomi of Brazil. There is a very high ratio of loan capital to equity in the enterprise, and the substantial loans required have been obtained abroad. For example, as of the end of 1958, the paid-in equity capital amounted to only about one-eighth of outstanding long-term loans. Foreign assistance was sought from the beginning by the enterprise to work its large manganese deposits, not only because of the requirements for know-how but also because of the very large financing that was involved. The Bethlehem Steel Corporation of the United States entered with a 49 percent equity participation. Rather than increase this participation, it extended a loan to the enterprise of close to $2 million at an interest rate of only 3 percent per year. The bulk of the financing came from the Export-Import Bank of Washington, in the form of a loan of approximately $55 million. Undoubtedly the presence of Bethlehem in the enterprise was instrumental in the decision to extend a loan of such magnitude. With its ability to provide and tap this type of financial assistance, aside from its ability to contribute technically, the influence of Bethlehem Steel is much greater than might be supposed from its minority participation.

In the Hotel Tequendama in Colombia, the foreign partner has no equity interest at all, only a management contract arrangement, but there has been considerable financial dependence on the Intercontinental Hotels Corporation. IHC was instrumental in obtaining financing for the project from the Export-Import Bank of Washington in the amount of $4 million, which was almost equal to the total equity invested in the enterprise. Most of this financing has a term of about 20 years, and the duration of the management contract coincides with this term. The probability is that the financing could not have been obtained without such a condition, and it is obvious that the foreign partner had a special leverage in the situation because of its ability to obtain the financing.

Business relations between a joint venture enterprise and the enterprise abroad of the foreign partner are of considerable importance in the case of Panair do Brasil and Pan American World Airways. Pan American's interest in Panair is 48 percent. The two firms have a mutual services agreement for the utilization of each other's facilities in connection with their respective international flight operations. The arrangement has yielded Panair large net payments which are important in its over-all financial position. Pan American has been of great assistance to the Brazilian enterprise, both technically and financially, in the acquisition for it of aircraft and parts. In addition to acting as its agent abroad in this complex matter, Pan

American has made loans to finance the acquisitions and has been instrumental in obtaining loans from United States banking sources. With these kinds of supplementary relations, the influence of Pan American Airways on Panair do Brasil is again greater than that arising merely from its minority equity holding.

Majority Participation by the Foreign Partner

Where the foreign partner has a majority of the equity in a joint venture, there is of course no problem of control from his point of view nor any need to seek supplementary devices to achieve the control as in the case of minority participation. For practical purposes, the situation is much like that of a wholly foreign-owned enterprise. As with a wholly foreign-owned enterprise, there is the problem of achieving an identification of the firm with the local economy so as to reap the benefits of good public or governmental relations. With this in mind, foreign majority partners frequently leave the management of the enterprise largely to nationals. This is a practice also followed to a large and increasing extent by wholly foreign-owned enterprises, not only for reasons of local identification but also because of the frictions that can arise from the presence of foreign personnel, and because of the different and lower-cost labor market from which the local personnel is recruited.

There is the question among companies from the capital-exporting countries of whether the local identification that is sought can really be attained in anything except a joint venture in which the foreign interest is in the minority. Some feel that this objective has not been achieved when minority local participation has been admitted by formerly all-foreign enterprises—the enterprises tend to continue being looked upon as foreign. Pursuant to this view, the choice should be one between a solo operation and a joint venture with only minority foreign participation; the intermediate step of a joint venture in which the foreign partner retains a majority incurs the disadvantages of joint ventures without achieving their benefits. This does not necessarily indicate that joint ventures with majority foreign participation are a rapidly passing phenomenon, just as the wholly foreign-owned venture is not, but the problems of operating wholly-foreign ventures frequently are also present to a large extent in foreign majority-owned joint ventures.

The use of practically all-national management in joint ventures having a majority of foreign equity is illustrated in Brazil in the Laborterápica Bristol and Rheem Metalúrgica enterprises. The foreign partner in Bristol holds 51 percent of the equity but only one position on the board, and that in the person of a Brazilian lawyer who had previously represented its interests in the country. The arrangement was facilitated by the previous history of the local partner as a successful national pharmaceutical manufacturer. When a new line of antibiotics was introduced for manufacture by the joint venture, all-national operation was quickly achieved for this line too by an intensive training program involving the presence in Brazil of foreign technicians as well as the training of Brazilians in the United States facilities of the foreign partner. In Rheem, where the foreign partner holds 70 percent of equity, the foreign firm again has only minority participation on the board and then through its Brazilian lawyer. The enterprise was managed by Americans only during its first years of operation. A similar policy is followed by Rheem even where it has wholly-owned subsidiaries.

The use of local management despite foreign majority ownership is further illustrated in a number of the joint ventures in South America of W. R. Grace & Co. Grace desires to control management, but this does not necessarily mean management by Grace itself. The essential element from Grace's point of view is the power to decide who shall manage the enterprise. In various cases where Grace bought into existing enterprises, it was content to let the local management continue to run the enterprise. This is true in the following companies: Arturo Field y Cia., Peru (Grace, 50.08 percent); Cia. Colombiana de Conservas California, Colombia (Grace, 51 percent); Carboquímica, Colombia (Grace, 51 percent); Probst y Cia., Colombia (Grace, 86 percent).

In Merck Sharp & Dohme of India, the foreign partner has a 60 percent majority, and the local partner, in view of his lack of experience in the manufacture of pharmaceuticals, has been content to leave management entirely to Merck. Nevertheless, the foreign partner has been running the enterprise with only a few key foreign personnel (about 3 out of a total of some 185).

There are other cases where local minority participation is in the form of a passive investment, and there is no problem in the foreigner's being able to run the enterprise with the same type of free hand as if it were a wholly foreign-owned venture. This is the case, for example, in the General Milk Company (Philippines), where the local minority investor is an insurance group, which does not interfere at all in the management of the enterprise.

50-50 Participation

In Atic Industries Ltd. there is a 50-50 participation by Imperial Chemical Industries of the United Kingdom and Atul Products of India. Pursuant to this equal sharing of the equity, there is equal representation of the two interests on the board of the enterprise. By agreement, the chairman of the board for the first five years is named by the Indian partner, and thereafter there is to be an alternation in the appointment of the chairman by each of the two partners every three years. As would be the case even if the foreign partner held a minority, the foreign participation in the management of the enterprise is enhanced by the fact that there is a technical assistance agreement for the control of production, which involves the technically complicated field of dyestuffs.

Changes in Type of Participation

Joint ventures frequently come about through the conversion of formerly all-foreign enterprises. Also, in the course of their operation, it is at times found desirable to change certain of their basic characteristics.

FROM LICENSING AGREEMENTS TO INVESTMENT IN EQUITY

Licensing agreements are sometimes entered into because they permit the licensor to retain a position in the local market without the problems of investing capital or managerial resources. By the same token they mean that the licensor's yield is exclusively in the form of royalties. When the enterprises of licensees become profitable and licensors have capital to invest, it is not infrequent for the original licensing agreement to be supplemented by an investment in the equity of the licensee. At times the reason for the investment may be to provide financial assistance, but this usually involves only a minority financial participation by the foreign interest. The coupling of licensing and minority equity investment permits the licensor firm to share to a greater extent in a growing market, and to diversify its position in relation to the treatment it receives under exchange controls or taxation, one or both of which may treat royalties and dividends differently.

The change from a purely licensing participation to a minority investment in equity in addition to the licensing arrangement is illustrated by Cobrasma. In 1948, American Steel Foundries International had only a licensing agreement with the Brazilian firm. In 1956, it made an investment amounting to 15 percent of equity by supplying equipment. As the total capital of the enterprise has increased, it has maintained its 15 percent interest by supplying both additional machinery and cash; it supplied new funds from abroad as well as royalties accumulated under the Cobrasma licensing agreement.

When Industria Eléctrica was organized in 1945, Westinghouse participation was limited to the provision of technical assistance, patent rights, and distribution rights for certain products which would not be manufactured locally. Some ten years later, Westinghouse made its investment in equity. In this instance, the reason was not the immediate profitability of the enterprise, but rather the need to put it on a sound financial footing. The technical assistance, patent, and distribution agreements were continued, and a special device was worked out for administrative control despite the minority Westinghouse investment. Since this step was taken, Industria Eléctrica has done very well, and it is felt that the success is due to the greater interest and participation by Westinghouse.

Akin to the trend of change from licensing agreements to investment in equity is the phenomenon sometimes observed of change from a management contract to an investment in equity by the foreign partner. The Intercontinental Hotels Corporation has only a management contract with the Hotel Tequendama in Colombia, but IHC may also make some equity investment for the expansion of the enterprise. IHC appears to favor some equity investment in combination with its management contracts, not only because the investments themselves are good propositions, but also to facilitate its management task through having some representation on the board. In the Hotel Del Prado, IHC had only a management contract for some years, but in 1957 invested in the equity of the hotel, buying a majority of slightly more than 60 percent. The decision was influenced to some extent by the devaluation of the peso, and by the consequent incentive to reinvest in the country proceeds which the firm was earning from its management contract with the Hotel Tequendama, rather than to remit them at the new and less favorable exchange rate.

FROM WHOLLY FOREIGN-OWNED OPERATIONS TO JOINT VENTURES

Wholly foreign-owned operations have often been converted into joint ventures. The process has sometimes stopped with the admission of a local minority participation, but in others it has continued to move until the local participation has become a majority.

This phenomenon has characterized many of the overseas investments of Pan American World Airways. Pan American developed numerous aviation enterprises abroad in the early 1930s on a wholly-owned basis. As a culmination of the growing nationalism of the thirties which became even more intensified during and after the Second World War, Pan American admitted some minority local participation, and later reduced its own holdings to minority positions. From 1929 to 1943, Panair do Brasil was a wholly United States-owned operation. In 1943, when the capital of the enterprise was increased, 42 percent was transferred to Brazilian ownership. Between 1943 and 1947, the local share was increased to a majority of 52 percent and Pan American extended considerable financial assistance in the form of loans and grants to put the enterprise on a more solvent basis and to make it more attractive to local shareholders.

FROM FOREIGN MAJORITY TO FOREIGN MINORITY

There is some feeling on the part of firms in the capital-exporting countries that joint ventures with a foreign majority fail to achieve the benefits of local identification. Pursuant to this view, there are cases where joint ventures set up with a foreign majority have passed the majority interest to local investors. Celanese Mexicana was organized in 1947 with a slight majority by the Celanese Corporation of America. In 1953, the enterprise merged with three other local firms, and Celanese allowed its position to decline to a minority. In Bristol de México, the majority foreign partner (a Canadian subsidiary of the Bristol Aeroplane Company of England) has indicated that it is prepared to relinquish its majority at an appropriate time in the future.

As a corollary development, it has also been found that deliberate efforts are sometimes exerted by the foreign partner to limit his participation to a minority in the face of circumstances that might otherwise lead to his acquiring a majority. Normally in a business enterprise in need of substantial additional amounts of capital, it is not uncommon for a partner with large resources to supply the funds required and consequently to increase his participation in the equity of the enterprise. In the less developed countries where the foreigner holds a minority to begin with, this situation runs into the pressure frequently exerted for the foreign interest to continue as a minority. Rather than permit the foreign minority position to change, the solution to the financial problem is sometimes found in other ways. Goodrich supplied long-term loan capital to the Goodrich International Company of the Philippines and used its good offices to obtain a substantial loan from the Export-Import Bank of Washington, at the same time maintaining a minority position in the enterprise.

FROM FOREIGN MINORITY TO FOREIGN MAJORITY

There is much less representation of shifts in joint ventures from a foreign minority to a foreign majority position. They do occur to some extent, and are frequently a result of the need for substantial additional amounts of capital, which the foreigner is in a better position to supply. Such a shift occurred in T. I. Cycles of India, renamed Tube Investments of India Ltd., in connection with a substantial expansion effected in 1959. The British partners emerged with a 60 percent holding compared to their previous holding of 49 percent; it was planned that the 60 percent holding would decline to 52.5 percent in the future, but it was to continue as a majority. The fact that the need for capital was the prime consideration in this case is also reflected in a commitment by the British associates to extend to the enterprise a ten-year loan of £1 million.

FROM CLOSED TO OPEN CORPORATIONS

Most joint ventures are closed corporations, especially because of the limited nature of capital markets in the less developed countries. But capital markets are developing, and joint ventures that were previously closed corporations are admitting more and more participation by the local investing public. This is especially true of enterprises that manufacture consumer goods—among other reasons to achieve wide consumer acceptance of the products.

Willys Overland do Brasil was organized in 1952 between the Willys Motor Company of the United States and its local distributors to engage in the assembly of automotive vehicles. When the Brazilian government developed the National Automobile Industry Plan and when the enterprise decided to expand and become a genuine automobile manufacturing operation, it opened the corporation through public offerings to wide local participation. There are now in this corporation over 40,000 Brazilian shareholders who hold a majority of the voting shares.

Managerial Functions and Nationality of Personnel

There is a noticeable tendency in joint ventures to allocate managerial functions to the local partners, even if the foreign partner has a majority financial control. Where the foreigner is the minority, there is a tendency for his intervention in management to be less than proportional to his degree of financial participation. It is also a growing characteristic for wholly foreign-owned enterprises in the less developed countries to use national personnel as much as possible even in key management positions. The participation of nationals in the direction and management of enterprises tends to be greater where they have an equity interest, either because of the stronger position of nationals when they are partners in the enterprise, because of the higher quality of nationals that it is possible to associate in a joint venture as compared to a wholly foreign-owned enterprise, or because of a greater sensitivity by foreign investors to the requirements of the local scene when they are parties to joint ventures.

In Brazil, the minimal participation of the foreign partners in Laborterápica Bristol and Rheem Metalúrgica, despite their majority financial control, has already been cited. In the Companhia Siderúrgica Mannesmann, the foreign partner holds an interest of approximately 80 percent and three of the five members of the board are Brazilians, although not necessarily representing the Brazilian equity. An interesting balance has been achieved here between foreign and Brazilian directors in that two of the directors are Germans, two are native Brazilians, and the president of the board is a naturalized Brazilian citizen of German origin.

The use of national personnel is illustrated in a particularly interesting way in Bristol de México. The foreign partner has majority financial control and operates the enterprise under a management contract. Even though the nature of the business is highly complex and exacting, there are only 5 foreigners in a total personnel of 135. These include the general manager, the assistant general manager, the production manager, and the senior overhaul engineer. Other key posts are held by Mexicans, including those of superintendent, chief inspector, and chief of finance. These results have been achieved through intensive training, including the use of a school maintained at the Mexico City airport by the International Civil Aviation Organization and the sending of selected workers abroad. The success of the training program is indicated by the fact that among the first 100 aircraft engines overhauled by the firm, there was only one liability arising from carelessness in the plant.

In Industria Eléctrica de México, although the minority foreign partner (Westinghouse) exercises administrative control through the operating committee, there are very few foreigners working in the enterprise: only about 7 persons out of a total of 1,800 personnel are foreigners. The principal executive officer of the firm, the director general, is Mexican, as are 4 of the 5 chiefs of operating divisions. The only top American personnel are the vice-director general, and the engineering director.

Icollantas utilizes national personnel even though the foreign partner controls production through a technical assistance agreement. As of the end of 1957, there were only two American technicians out of the total of 850 personnel. There was one American in the executive hierarchy: the vice-president, who was formerly a Goodrich man, but in his current capacity has no formal connection with Goodrich at all.

The same tendency is noted in the Goodrich enterprise in the Philippines, where there are now only about 10 Americans out of the total personnel of somewhat more than 500, despite the technical assistance agreement with the United States firm and despite the fact that B. F. Goodrich actually runs the enterprise pursuant to a formal management contract.

The allocation of managerial functions to nationals and the use of local personnel are seen also in India, where the investment or technical assistance agreements usually provide for the use of foreign personnel on a temporary basis—long enough to train national technicians to take over. This was the case in the joint venture arrangements of the Atul Products enterprise. In the Telco Automobile Division, the general manager is Indian, and the German managers and technicians were subordinate to him and were required to train Indian counterparts to replace them within a period of three years. In the Tube Investments enterprise, with a total personnel force of about 1,500, there are only a few top-level foreign technicians.

The tendency to utilize local personnel is found in Turkey in the General Electric and Squibb majority joint ventures where the only resident American in each firm is the managing director in one case and the executive director in the other.

Conflicts of Interest

Conflicts of interest between the foreign and national partners arising from their different intrinsic positions are more potentially inherent in joint ventures, than in wholly foreign-owned companies. The conflicts can arise because of differences in general attitudes toward business, or because of the different influences to which the partners are subject. The foreign partner may be a company that operates in numerous countries, whereas the national partner most likely is limited to his own country. The foreign partner is affected by the taxation policy of his own country as well as that of the country of the investment, whereas the national partner is concerned with the taxation of only one country. The foreign partner is concerned with conditions in the local money market of the host country as well as with trends relating to the external value of the country's currency because of remittance considerations; the local partner is less concerned with foreign exchange trends. The foreign and the national partners may have other conflicting business interests. The foreign partner may have interests abroad that integrate with the joint venture operation, whereas the local partner may not be concerned with the integration. For these and other reasons, conflicts of interest can arise because of the very nature of joint ventures.

The evidence that it has been possible to develop concerning actual conflicts of interest is limited. Most of it points to the conclusion that the conflicts tend to be minimized and to be worked out to the satisfaction of both parties. In evaluating this conclusion, it is important to bear in mind that it is difficult to develop objective data because there is a natural tendency for informants to speak about successes and not of failures.

Although conflicts arising from different business attitudes cannot be ignored, the fact is that business attitudes in the less developed countries are generally approaching those that exist in the economically advanced countries as the pace of development increases; experiences in joint ventures indeed provide an opportunity for the approach of attitudes to a common ground. The more important conflicts of interest arise from the different specific influences to which foreign and national partners are subject, such as taxation, exchange remittances, and the interests of stockholders in different countries.

Efforts are sometimes made beforehand to include provisions

in joint venture agreements in order to avoid conflicts. For example, in the Telco Automobile Division in India, the agreement provides that the parties are bound to one another in their operations in India, Pakistan, Burma, and Ceylon. Telco has exclusive manufacturing rights and is the sole selling agent in this territory for Daimler-Benz products. Neither party is to manufacture, buy for resale, or sell automotive products or parts in the area without mutual agreement. Furthermore, Telco is not to export outside the area without the consent of Daimler-Benz.

In various cases, one would expect that the interest of the foreign partner *prima facie* would have been better served in a wholly-owned operation. For example, Bethlehem Steel is an important buyer of Icomi's product. It would therefore probably have been to its advantage to minimize rather than to maximize the profitability of the enterprise in Brazil, in contrast with the national partners. Other considerations apparently outweighed this interest; the venture, which arose from Brazilian initiative, was set up on a joint basis, and there is no conflict of interest reported with respect to price policy.

At times conflicts of interest arise from separate holdings in other enterprises in the same country by each of the partners in the joint venture. In a joint venture of W. R. Grace & Co. in Colombia, the conflict eventually led to Grace's withdrawal from the enterprise. The disagreement occurred in the paint manufacturing firm known as Pintuco, and arose from the desire of Grace to use its own distribution facilities in the country while the local partner also had such channels that it wished to use. Grace finally sold its interest to the local partner, and later established another paint enterprise in the country, as a wholly-foreign venture in association with another United States firm.

Conflicts of interest that can arise in connection with franchise agreements are illustrated with H. G. Henares & Sons of the Philippines, which has such agreements with half a dozen United States manufacturers. One set of problems related to the exclusive distributors in the country of the United States manufacturers. The arrangements were continued for the distribution of the products to be manufactured under license by Henares, and conflicts arose between the distributors and the Philippine manufacturer over pricing policy. In an effort by the licensors to exert some on-the-spot control of the activities of the licensee, the distributors were given certain audit powers over the Henares firm, which inevitably led to conflict and were eventually abandoned. An additional source of problems was the desire by the United States manufacturers to supply raw materials to the licensee, while the licensee wanted a free hand in purchasing raw materials to take advantage of the most favorable sources of supply. This problem was eventually resolved by permitting the licensee to purchase raw materials where it was most advantageous to do so.

The matter of general differences in business attitudes is most frequently cited in relation to the question of reinvestment of earnings versus the payment of dividends. Enterprises from the more developed countries are said to favor a policy of liberal reinvestments, at least in the early stages of enterprises, to promote their growth, while investors from the less developed countries are allegedly used to and demand early and high dividends. On this point, there is considerable evidence that serious conflicts have not arisen and that joint ventures have followed a policy of liberal reinvestment for growth. It is questionable whether this concept of the investor is not a myth which is rapidly disappearing. Enterprises in the more advanced countries do not ignore altogether the interest of their stockholders in dividend distributions and the effect of dividend payments on the value of their securities on the public exchanges.

Cases are not totally absent where the relative attitudes of the foreign and local partners toward reinvestment policy are the reverse of what is expected. In a situation of sharp exchange depreciation, the foreign partner may wish to remit dividends rather than reinvest profits, while the local partner may prefer to reinvest profits for working capital rather than to borrow locally.

The cases in Brazil indicate a liberal reinvestment policy by the joint ventures. The dividends distributed by Rheem Metalúrgica have rarely exceeded eight percent of the paid-in capital, which, by Brazilian standards, means a heavy rate of reinvestment. Cobrasma, with an 85 percent Brazilian majority, has consistently ploughed back 25 to 30 percent of its profits. In Panair do Brasil, profits have been entirely reinvested in certain years, and when dividends have been distributed, they have usually amounted to no more than six percent of the capital. The Bristol pharmaceutical enterprise reinvested 58 percent of its profits in 1957 and 79 percent in 1958. Willys Overland do Brasil has been paying a relatively high dividend of 12 percent, but this has been a deliberate policy to pave the way for public acceptance of its shares in connection with the substantial expansion program that it has had underway.

The cases in Mexico similarly indicate a liberal reinvestment policy, even where the majority financial interest is held by local partners. The original capital of Celanese Mexicana of 21 million pesos had grown to 333 million pesos in twelve years; at the end of 1959, the firm also had surplus and reserves in the amount of 150 million pesos. Part of its profits had been reinvested almost every year, and the substantial growth of capital had come about partly from these reinvestments. In Industria Eléctrica de México, reinvestments in recent years have consistently amounted to close to one-half of total profits; more than half of the total cost of close to $1.5 million of a new factory to be built in 1961 will come out of past earnings. On the other hand, experiences in enterprises that operate in fields similar to that of Industria Eléctrica de México indicate that the avoidance of conflicts of interest on dividend distribution policy is dependent to a large extent on the particular partners involved. Thus, Square D de México, which produces industrial control equipment and switchgear, was at first a 50-50 joint venture, but is now a wholly foreign-owned enterprise—the local share having been bought out because of differences over reinvestment policy. The local partner later started to manufacture transformers under a licensing arrangement with Allis Chalmers of the United States, and was again bought out by the foreign participant.

A liberal reinvestment policy is also found in Colombia in cases where the local partner holds a majority. In Icollantas, owned two-thirds by Colombian stockholders, earned surplus at the end of 1956, excluding the profits of that year and depreciation reserves, amounted to close to half of the paid-in capital. In the Hotel Tequendama, where the equity is all national, the Intercontinental

Hotels Corporation has been successful in having adequate sums devoted to maintenance, which is quite frequently difficult to achieve in the operation of hotels in Latin America.

Liberal reinvestment policies also characterize the joint venture enterprises in India. In T. I. Cycles, even before the assumption of a majority by the British, dividend distribution was limited and ample provision was made for reinvestment reserves. During the two fiscal years 1957–58 and 1958–59, of total profits of 5.3 million rupees, only 2.3 million rupees or less than half were distributed as dividends. In the Merck Sharp & Dohme enterprise, organized in the fall of 1958, the plan of the parent firm was to apply a policy of substantial reinvestment of earnings for long-range growth, and full agreement on this policy by the Indian partner was obtained from the very beginning.

Governments as Partners

Governments are the local partners in joint ventures in a considerable number of less developed countries in Latin America, the Far East, and the Middle East. Government participation has sometimes arisen from a policy of promoting new economic activities through official development institutions, and sometimes the government's presence in the venture is more the result of ideological or doctrinaire considerations.

Private investors in the capital-exporting countries are generally reluctant to enter into joint ventures with governments of the less developed countries as partners, but in many cases have done so either because it was the only way in which a particular investment could be effected, or because there was some specific advantage to be gained. There has been less reluctance to enter into such ventures when the government is represented by an autonomous institution such as a development bank or corporation, for the reason that the danger of having business decisions based on political considerations is minimized. Frequently it has been the local government or official development institution that has taken the initiative in interesting the foreign partner in the venture.

Joint ventures with local governments have generally proven to be no less successful than entirely private joint ventures. With some exceptions, it has been possible to run the enterprises entirely on a businesslike basis. In most cases the ventures have not received privileged treatment from official regulatory agencies dealing with taxation or foreign exchange control, and in some instances they have had the same problems as those encountered by entirely private enterprises. Nevertheless, there are advantages that are almost inherent in the fact of the government participation; one in particular is the availability of favorable loan financing from the same development institution that is the partner in the enterprise.

Aside from the vagaries of politics, foreign investors are concerned about having governments as partners because of the lack of general business experience or specific technical competence by government personnel. Generally the government agencies recognize this weakness and are content to leave management to the experienced foreign partner, at times through formal management contract arrangements.

There are instances where the government participation, through a development corporation, turns out to be temporary, remaining long enough for the enterprise to be developed to the point of profitable operations at which time the government's shares are sold to private investors. This is the classical type of function for a development corporation to perform in a less developed economy organized along private enterprise lines: to assist in the promotion, financing, and organization of new industries; to broaden the opportunities for private investors; and to move on to new investments with the rotation of its funds from earlier investments. However, the development corporation is a relatively new institution in the less developed countries and private capital markets are slow to develop. Consequently, there are not many cases where government participation in joint ventures has been eliminated in this way.

MEXICO

The government participation in the Altos Hornos de México steel mill is in the form of an equity interest in the amount of approximately 81 percent by Nacional Financiera, the official development corporation. When the enterprise started, the government interest was in the minority, amounting to a little more than a fourth of the equity. The need for additional capital because of losses during the initial years of operation of the enterprise and because of its need for expansion led to the increase in the government participation. Other reasons for the increasing official participation have been ideological considerations in Mexico with respect to government ownership of certain basic industries. Altos Hornos is the largest steel mill in the country. Early in 1960 the government expanded its operations in steel by buying La Consolidada, the country's third largest steel enterprise, which had been a private joint venture owned mostly by foreign interests. Altos Hornos became almost entirely an official enterprise, and the Mexican government has taken a dominant position in the national steel industry, a trend which is unlikely to be reversed.

As an enterprise owned to the extent of about four-fifths by the government, Altos Hornos is managed by the government corporation that holds the shares for the state. As far as can be determined, it is managed in an autonomous fashion, and political considerations in management are either at a minimum or are nonexistent. Despite the four-fifths ownership by Nacional Financiera, during the last few years only half of the company's directors have been Nacional Financiera representatives, and the technical cooperation with the minority foreign shareholder has worked out satisfactorily.

The government participation in Altos Hornos through the investment by Nacional Financiera has been useful financially in another way: Large amounts of loan capital have been obtained from Nacional Financiera and it has provided guarantees for important loans obtained abroad. There is evidence that the enterprise has not been granted undue advantages because of the government interest in it: It is paying full taxes to the government after having enjoyed an initial ten-year period of tax concessions arising from its nature as a "new or necessary" industry, concessions which have also been obtained by numerous qualifying private firms in the country.

In Tubos de Acero de México, the Nacional Financiera participation amounts to only 20 percent, and this limited participation has been retained despite substantial increases in the firm's capital. Tubos de Acero has the special characteristic of producing an item, seamless steel pipe for the petroleum industry, for which the only customer in the country is the government. The government petroleum company, Pemex, has one director on the board of 15 of Tubos de Acero, though Pemex holds no equity in the firm. Nacional Financiera has two directors. The usefulness of having government participation in such an enterprise is obvious in view of the special situation of the petroleum industry in Mexico. In addition, Nacional Financiera has taken up large debenture issues of the firm. While the initial 20 percent government participation has not increased, it appears most likely that it will continue because of the special nature of the situation.

Nacional Financiera first held 30 percent of the equity of Toyoda de México in order to help finance the enterprise, but has since bought out all of the 59 percent interest of the foreign partner, the Toyoda Automatic Loom Works of Japan. The move was apparently necessary because there were difficulties in getting the enterprise to a stage of profitable operations. As in other cases, in addition to its equity investment, Nacional Financiera granted substantial loans and guaranteed the loans of the enterprise obtained from abroad. On the other hand, despite the government participation, the enterprise was unable to get benefits that have been obtained by numerous other new firms in the country, including tax concessions and protection against the competition of imported goods. Despite its minority financial participation, Nacional Financiera had veto rights with respect to certain policies of the firm. Whatever the reasons may have been, the operation of the enterprise as a joint venture with government participation turned out to be a failure, and, as in the case of the Altos Hornos enterprise, it has become almost entirely a government-owned operation.

In contrast is the situation of Descuento Agrícola, where the Nacional Financiera participation amounts to only ten percent. Its participation in management is also minor: Nacional Financiera has one director on an eleven-man board, though it has the right to name the chairman of the board on a rotating basis for one out of every four terms; and it has one representative on a six-man credit committee. This enterprise is operating in a field (agricultural credit) in which there has been activity only by official banks. The minor participation by the government via Nacional Financiera was undoubtedly looked upon by the promoters as a desirable feature in view of this background, and because the Nacional Financiera could be an important source of additional finance for the enterprise.

COLOMBIA

Icollantas represents the type of participation by a government development corporation which is strictly in accordance with the way such institutions ideally are supposed to behave in private enterprise economies. The enterprise was promoted at the initiative of the government Instituto de Fomento Industrial, which held 73 percent of its capital. Icollantas was run autonomously even at the beginning without political interference and the government stayed out of management. The Institute's interests were protected by special voting powers which it would have as long as it held at least a 25 percent interest in the firm. As the enterprise became successful, the Institute started to sell its shares to the general public, and eventually disposed of them all. It completed its mission of having promoted and having helped to finance a desirable new industry in the country, and then sold it to private investors once it had become sufficiently attractive. It recouped its own investment for activities in other fields.

Somewhat more than two-thirds of the equity of the Hotel Tequendama is owned by the Retirement Fund of the Armed Forces, and by this token it takes on a somewhat semi-official character. The balance is owned by various agencies of the government, such as the Municipality of Bogotá and the Stabilization Fund of the Central Bank. The combination of the semi-official and official interest in the enterprise has undoubtedly been helpful in various ways, including its ability to import its initial furnishings and equipment duty-free, and its use as an important community center for social and official activities. On the other hand, it has, like any privately owned hotel, run into problems arising from the policies followed by the government in fixing hotel rates. It was only after a considerable lag that it was able to obtain rate increases following the substantial devaluation of the peso in mid-1957, a circumstance which increased considerably its local currency obligations in servicing the large Export-Import Bank loans that had been secured to finance it.

INDIA

In India, partnership arrangements between the Indian government and foreign interests are illustrated in the Bhilai, Rourkela, and Durgapur steel ventures. These are limited partnership arrangements in that the foreign participation consists of contracts for the supply of equipment and construction of the mills, the provision of credits, and technical assistance for the training of personnel and the placing in operation of the plants. The equity of the enterprises is owned entirely by the Indian government. With the policy pursued in India of reserving the expansion of certain basic economic activities such as steel for ownership and operation by the public sector, the government has nevertheless called upon foreign interests to assist it, although only in these limited ways.

They are important ventures, involving as they do steelmaking capacity in the amount of 3 million tons annually and a total cost of close to $1 billion. Being projects of such magnitude, they posed great administrative problems for the Indian government and for the foreign participants in their relations with the government. They are now all realities, in varying stages of completion. The essential success of the operating experience in these ventures is evidenced by the plans that have been formulated under the government's third Five-Year Plan for expansion of the capacity of all three plants, and by the willingness of the German, British, and Russian interests to cooperate with the expansion plans.

Given the nature of these situations, which are considerably different from cases in other countries where governments are partners in joint ventures on a much more limited basis, the Indian government is very active in management. A government corporation, Hindustan Steel Ltd., was set up to operate the three plants. An elaborate program of training was evolved for workers to run the plants. Training establishments were set up in cooperation with existing, privately owned steel mills. Training was provided also by the German, British, and Soviet interests under their arrangements with the government for construction of the plants. Additional training assistance was received under the Colombo Plan, from the Ford Foundation, and from the United Nations.

The lack of experience of government personnel in the administration of this type of enterprise gave rise initially to difficulties and to frictions with foreign personnel who were administratively subordinate to the national managers. The frictions were minimized where the foreigners limited themselves, as was reported to be the case with the Soviet venture, to a discreet advisory capacity and gave more initiative and responsibility to the national personnel. In the case of some of the arrangements, such as the German one, there were numerous independent firms included in various aspects of the operation, and difficulties of coordination were great. In other cases, for example, in the Russian one at Bhilai, there was tighter coordination on the foreign side and cooperation with the Indian authorities was consequently easier.

There is no issue in these situations, in view of the nature of the arrangements, of the possibility of an indefinitely continuing association between the foreign interests and the local government in the enterprises. The fact that the steel mills have been constructed and have been brought to the point of operation is an impressive demonstration of the possibility of working with a government as the partner in large and complex projects. The demonstration is further reinforced by the likelihood of a renewal of the arrangements between the foreign interests involved and the Indian government for expansion of the plants.

PAKISTAN

Both joint ventures in Pakistan described in Part II have local government participation. The government holdings are in the minority (about 30 percent in the Lever Brothers enterprise, and 25.5 percent in the Sui Gas Transmission Company), but the government is the largest single shareholder in Sui Gas where there are several different groups of partners. Management of the enterprises is left largely to the private foreign partners, even in the case where the government is the largest single shareholder. In Lever Brothers, the government is contemplating selling its shares to private interests.

The participation of the government in these enterprises has arisen mainly from the limited availability of local private capital rather than for doctrinaire reasons, and it has not interfered with the successful development of the enterprises as autonomous and essentially privately run operations.

In Lever Brothers (Pakistan) Ltd., the official participation is not by the central government but by the local government of West Pakistan. Most of the participation is in the form of the preference shares of the enterprise, all of which are held by the government. This fact reduces the government's voting power to less than its share of some 30 percent in equity since the preference shares have only one-half the voting power of the common shares. The entry of the provincial government into the enterprise had been to promote the organization of this type of industry in its territory, and it is now reportedly contemplating selling its share to private interests.

The Lever Brothers enterprise received some concessions from the government as a new industry, but it might have obtained the concessions even if the local participation had been private. The enterprise has not been able to work to capacity because, like most other enterprises in Pakistan dependent on imported raw materials, it has not been able to import all of its requirements in view of national exchange shortages. It received some state tax concessions from the provincial government, but the participation of the government of West Pakistan does not appear to have resulted in any special treatment by the central government in taxation, import licenses for raw materials, or the remittance of profits. The central government did sanction an exception from general legislation applicable to the production of vegetable oils for Unilever's participation to exceed a 49 percent limitation, but this exception might have been obtained regardless of the local partner.

The Pakistan government's participation in the Sui Gas Transmission Company is through its Industrial Development Corporation, which holds 25.5 percent of the company's stock. A like amount is held by private Pakistani capital, and the balance of 49 percent is held in equal shares by a private British firm (the Burmah Oil Company) and by the British government's Commonwealth Development Finance Corporation. The influence of the Pakistan government on the board of the enterprise is somewhat greater than would be warranted by its share in the equity alone; the Industrial Development Corporation elects three of the nine directors, and one of its nominees is always the chairman. On the other hand, the enterprise is administered under a managing agency agreement by a subsidiary of the Burmah Oil Company [BOC (Pakistan Trading) Ltd.]. Because of the technical nature of the firm's activities, the government has left administration entirely to the experienced private partner.

Sui Gas does not appear to have obtained any unusual concessions from the government's participation in it. It has received generous depreciation allowances for income tax purposes, but these are generally granted to newly created industrial undertakings. Since it is a public utility, its prices are controlled by the government, although due regard has been paid to the need for a reasonable return on the investment, and a satisfactory level of profits began in the 1956–57 fiscal year. Considering the basic and very valuable natural resource that the firm is exploiting, it is questionable whether it would have been possible or desirable to proceed without the participation of the government, which has in any case been limited and has probably been quite advantageous in working out the numerous arrangements necessary for bringing the resource to the stage of profitable exploitation.

BURMA

A unique type of government participation in joint ventures is found in Burma. The case is one of several in the extractive industries in which British firms that had operated in the country on a solo basis before the Second World War found it advantageous to enter into joint ventures with the Burma government when they resumed their activities after the war. The risks arising from the unsettled political conditions in the country during the postwar period were diminished. Special legislation governing this type of joint venture and exempting it from general company law was adopted in the form of the Special Companies Act of 1950.

In the Burma Oil Co. (1954) Ltd., the Burmese government holds a 33 percent interest and names two of the five directors. Management is left to the Burmah Oil Co. Ltd., the private British 55 percent shareholder, under a managing agency agreement. Pursuant to the Special Companies Act of 1950, any modification of the company's charter requires the approval of the President of the Union of Burma. The privileged position in the enterprise of the government is also indicated by the fact that it has an option to buy any number of additional shares at a fixed price. This is of great potential advantage since it could mean that the government might be in a position to buy out the entire company at favorable terms if a large oil strike were made.

During the prewar period, there were severe labor problems in the operations in Burma of the private British oil companies. The largest of them, the Burmah Oil Co. Ltd., now also the principal British interest in the joint venture, was looked upon by labor as a symbol of British "imperialism." These suspicions and conflicts have been largely eliminated by the government's participation in the joint venture. The leaders of the Trade Union Congress of Burma have shown a much more understanding attitude toward the problems of the company and tend to think of them in relation to the broad national interest rather than purely in partisan terms.

In Burmese joint ventures in extractive industries with government participation—the most important foreign direct investments now in the country—the government is in a privileged position disproportionate to the extent of its equity participation, but the private foreign companies involved apparently felt the advantages to be gained made these arrangements worthwhile in view of the unsettled conditions in the country. Management has been left to the experienced private firms under managing agency agreements.

PHILIPPINES

In only one of the four Philippine cases cited in Part II for the Philippines (the Manila Gas Corporation) is the government a party to the joint venture. Before the Second World War, the company was entirely foreign-owned. After the destruction of company facilities during the war, the American owner was reluctant to undertake the extensive work of rehabilitation without government participation. Negotiations led to the government's entry into the venture with a 60 percent interest held by the official National Development Company.

The government's participation has proven to be useful in a number of ways. It has facilitated the securing of supplementary financing from the official Rehabilitation Finance Corporation, and it has made the handling of transactions with regulatory government agencies comparatively easy to accomplish.

TURKEY

A government agency is the local partner in the Mannesmann-Sümerbank Steel Pipe Manufacturing Corporation. Mannesmann of Germany holds a 57 percent interest; the balance is held by the Sümerbank. The enterprise has been successful, and the experience of the foreign partner with the official development bank has been a happy one. Less than five years since its formation, the enterprise is now raising its capital from 5.6 million to 35 million Turkish lire, with the proportionate shares of the partners remaining the same. The capacity of the firm is being raised from 15,000 tons of pipe per year to 60,000 tons, and the variety of sizes produced is being increased from a range of ½″ to 2½″ to 6″.

The enterprise originated at the initiative of the Sümerbank, which approached and interested the Mannesmann firm. The factory site was owned by the Sümerbank and was sold to the new venture at favorable terms. The Sümerbank also proved to be a useful source of loan funds for working capital. There is little interference in management by the Sümerbank. It names two of the venture's five directors. Regulatory agencies of the Turkish government have been helpful to the enterprise, because of the importance to the economy of its output as well as because of the nature of the Turkish participant. For example, the foreign partner has had no difficulty in remitting profits, though the enterprise has encountered occasional difficulties in importing raw materials because of the country's scarcity of foreign exchange.

IRAN

In the Société Irano-Italienne des Petroles (Sirip), both partners are government agencies. On the foreign side, the partner is Agip

Mineraria, an Italian government-controlled corporation engaged in petroleum exploration and production. The local partner is the National Iranian Oil Company (Nioc), organized in 1951 at the time that the petroleum industry was nationalized in Iran. The nationalization has not meant operation of the industry by the government, but rather greater intervention by the government in the activities of private foreign petroleum companies, and it has resulted in some joint ventures between the government and foreign companies. After the nationalization, the activities of the international oil companies in Iran were regulated by an agreement executed in 1954 between the Iranian government and Nioc and a consortium of the companies. Pursuant to this agreement, certain operating companies were set up with representation of the Iranian government in the form of two directors on their boards of seven, and a 50-50 profit division between the government and the petroleum companies was established.

In the Sirip venture, 50 percent of the capital was put up by Nioc, thus entitling it to 50 percent of the firm's profits. Since the profits retained by Sirip can amount to only 50 percent of its total profits, after turning one-half of profits over to the Iranian government in lieu of taxes, the effect of the arrangement is a 25-75 percent division of profits between the foreign partner and the Iranian government.

The risk assumed by Nioc in putting up half of the capital of Sirip is very limited. The total capital of Sirip is only $200 thousand. The heavy risk capital is to be put up by Agip Mineraria, which is required to spend no less than $22 million on exploration over a period of twelve years in carrying out plans which it must draw up in consultation with Nioc. Sirip is to refund these costs only if commercially recoverable reserves are found, and one-half of any such refund is to be paid to Nioc; Sirip bears operating expenditures currently only after reserves are discovered.

Nioc is represented on the six-man board of Sirip by three directors, and it names the chairman of the board; the deputy chairman is named by Agip Mineraria. The firm also has a three-man board of auditors, of which one is named by Nioc, one by Agip, and the third is named by a Swiss trust company or auditing agency, and he must be neither Persian nor Italian nor connected with either party to the venture, nor may he have any interest in the petroleum industry.

There is also provision for neutral conciliation and arbitration procedures in the event of disputes between the partners.

Actual administration is left to the director of Agip Mineraria. The managing director of Sirip is appointed by Agip in the person of one of the three directors it names to the board, and the technical managers are appointed by the managing director from personnel designated by Agip.

The Sirip arrangement, concluded in September, 1957, represented a considerable departure from the traditional practices governing relations between foreign petroleum companies and host governments, because of the more onerous profit-sharing formula and the greater degree of intervention of the government in industry operations. Agip Mineraria accepted it—presumably because it was unable to enter the promising Iranian petroleum industry on more favorable terms. The venture is still too young to permit any appraisal of its operating experience, but it is significant to note that it has been followed by similar arrangements with some other foreign petroleum companies.

VII. Governmental Policies and Legal Factors

WE HAVE SHOWN that the attitudes and policies of governments affect joint ventures. In this chapter we shall discuss these attitudes as well as the legal and administrative measures of governments. We shall also consider how the official financing institutions react to joint ventures.

Capital-Exporting Countries

With few exceptions industrial countries have not developed an affirmative policy toward joint ventures. This is not because the opportunity has not existed. The flow of equity capital from major industrial powers often takes place through government guarantees of foreign investment, or is assisted by governmental or semi-governmental credit institutions. For example, most foreign investments made by Japanese principals are dependent on lines of credit from the Export-Import Bank of Japan. German foreign investors frequently get finance for their overseas ventures through the Hermes credit insurance organization, which is closely associated with the German government. In Britain, this is frequently done by the Export Credit Guarantees Department of the Board of Trade, and counterpart institutions in France and Italy are similarly involved. In the United States, institutions such as the Export-Import Bank and the Development Loan Fund are active in providing resources for American overseas investments; the guarantee program of the International Cooperation Administration has insured many American foreign investments against war risk, inconvertibility, and expropriation. The various governmental institutions which directly or indirectly manage these sources of credit, and/or guarantees, are in a position to encourage foreign investment in the direction of joint ventures, but there is little evidence that they have been doing a great deal along this line. They have followed the lead of borrowers, but they have rarely developed their own policies on this subject.

While there is no evidence of unfriendliness toward joint ventures, the governments have generally put themselves into the position of leaving the form of business organization to the investor's own decision. They realize that there is no consensus among private investors themselves as to the appropriateness of this form of business. Although joint ventures have a particular appeal to the governments of the less developed countries, the policies and laws of the industrial countries generally do not favor one particular form of investment for the economically less developed areas and another for the developed areas.[1]

In three countries—Italy, Britain, and France—all proposals for foreign investment must clear government agencies before they can be carried out, whether or not government sources of credit are used, and the policies of some of these and of other industrial countries toward foreign investment tend unconsciously to favor joint ventures or to find them almost an inevitable form of investment.

The government of Italy requires full details of the business to be set up abroad before any foreign exchange is made available to the investor. The government strongly prefers the export of equipment and services rather than the flow of liquid capital to establish the foreign investment. In practice this frequently means that the Italian foreign investor establishes his equity by furnishing plant and equipment, for he is rarely able to acquire from Italian sources the working capital needed by the new company. For this reason the

[1] Germany must be counted as an exception. The Bundestag has recently passed legislation affording insurance against various types of risks in connection with German foreign investment. This insurance is available *only* for investments in economically less developed countries. But this in and of itself does not constitute a preference for the joint venture.

Italian company is likely to set up a joint venture and to secure its working capital from the participation of local interests.

No government examination or clearance is needed for a British foreign investment within the Sterling Area. All proposals for foreign investment outside of the Sterling Area must be cleared by the Exchange Control Department of the Treasury. The Treasury generally takes the position that a British foreign investment should be able to acquire its working capital in the country of the investment. The Treasury does not insist that the British company should give up equity in return for working capital, but this often occurs.

The government of France also requires approval of all foreign investments by its nationals. The function is delegated to the Foreign Assets Division of the Ministry of Finance. Prior to 1959, its major concern was to prevent the use of foreign investment as a means of smuggling foreign exchange out of France; it had to be sure that each case represented a bona fide transfer of assets. Since the economic reforms instituted early in 1959, the policy of the Ministry of Finance has been to interest itself in the foreign exchange earnings of the investment and to prefer the remission of profits in the form of "serviceable" currencies. The government also likes investments with a good growth prospect and those which are likely to continuously use products of France, either in the form of semi-finished materials or components. Foreign investments which will service French capital equipment and machinery in foreign countries also enjoy favor.

West Germany does not require government clearance for foreign investment. Official statements repeatedly direct German investors, wherever possible, to have at least 51 percent of the shares in an overseas enterprise. It appears to be the view of the Economics Ministry that the effective control of a corporation is a prerequisite to the transfer of know-how and techniques to an overseas venture. This does not imply an official declaration in favor of joint ventures, but it does indicate the German government's acceptance of the form of business if the German investor is in a protected position—a controlling one where possible.

There are several reasons why most Japanese postwar foreign investments have taken the form of joint ventures. The shortage of capital and foreign exchange available to Japanese foreign investors makes it necessary to accumulate as much capital as possible in the country of the investment. Since Japan was inactive in this field for a long time, her would-be foreign investors strengthen their position by bringing in nationals who are well acquainted with the local scene, markets, and government regulations. The government of Japan, through the Ministry of Finance (and when required, through such additional agencies as the Ministry of International Trade and Investment and the Ministry of Agriculture), must approve all foreign investments, whether in cash or in kind (machinery, equipment, services). A number of factors are first considered: whether the investment is likely to be amortized within a reasonable period out of profits; whether profits will be remitted in a "serviceable" currency; whether the investment provides a source of raw materials for Japan; whether the investment will be accompanied by the utilization of Japanese personnel and labor; whether the investment will increase trade with the country in which it is made; whether the investment will hinder or be a substitute for normal trade. Both the Japanese business community and the government have been very alert in replacing declining exports by foreign investments and the manufacture of Japanese products abroad. This has been true, for example, in the cotton textile field and in the manufacture abroad of textile machinery.

Japan is the only industrial country that has openly favored joint ventures. In the course of concluding reparations agreements with Indonesia, the Philippines, and Burma, the government of Japan agreed to use its best efforts to induce the Japanese business community to enter into joint ventures with nationals of these countries. The area, commonly referred to as "Economic Cooperation" in the reparations agreements, is a substantial one. Japan agreed to try to stimulate the flow of capital (in money or in kind) to Burma by $50 million, to the Philippines by $250 million, and to Indonesia by $400 million. In spite of these provisions, there have been no significant results as yet.

The United States government does not examine the foreign investments of its nationals unless the investor buys insurance against the risks of inconvertibility, expropriation, or war and revolution. Under these circumstances, the International Cooperation Administration, through its Investment Guarantee Division, examines all particulars of the proposed investment.

A similar situation would arise if the American investor sought to raise some of his capital from the Export-Import Bank, the Development Loan Fund, or from other ICA programs. The investor then becomes a petitioner on much the same grounds as he would before a private lending institution—he must show the potential profitability of his investment. With the DLF and ICA, there are additional areas of questioning which include the suitability and acceptability of the investment for the country in question. All such proposals for loans (and guarantees as well) ultimately must be reviewed by the National Advisory Council, composed of the United States Treasury, Export-Import Bank, State Department, Commerce Department, and Federal Reserve Board. Political, economic, and foreign policy considerations are all involved in assessing the investment.

United States government lending agencies have shown a coolness toward assisting state-owned manufacturing industry, including joint ventures where the government exercises substantial control. Occasionally, overriding considerations have set such attitudes aside, especially in ICA aid. But there is a growing tendency to insist on private control of manufacturing industry as a precondition of assistance or loans.[2]

Except for these qualifications, the United States government has no general official position concerning joint ventures. The officials who administer loans and the guarantee program are well aware that joint ventures are often the only way in which a business can be carried out in some less developed countries. They do not quarrel with this, and indeed perform a useful service to American investors by pointing out the areas in which a joint venture may be a *sine qua non* of going into business.

[2] The same policy is followed by the World Bank. The International Finance Corporation, an affiliate of the World Bank, does not rule out joint private-government ventures, providing it is demonstrated that the government has no major voice in management and does not have a member on the board of directors.

Generally speaking, the governments of the industrial countries have made no attempt to reverse or to challenge the joint venture movement. Their encouragement has grown out of the changed attitudes, ideologies, laws, and institutions which have emerged in the less developed areas in the postwar world. This new social, political, and economic climate has set the rules for investment, and the industrial nations have had to work within these rules. The only initiative taken by the governments of the industrial countries has been to create countermeasures which make foreign investment more secure and attractive.

GOVERNMENT PROTECTION AGAINST LOSS OF FOREIGN INVESTMENT

Although industrial countries have not been able to secure treaty assurances from governments of the less developed countries that the property of their nationals will not be expropriated, they have unilaterally set up insurance schemes designed to compensate their nationals for expropriations.[3] Fair compensation in the event of nationalization or expropriation is usually guaranteed in a general way by the basic laws of less developed countries, but such compensation is often open to the vicissitudes of administration. It is for this reason that industrial countries create their own insurance schemes. No government offers protection against war and revolution except for the United States and West Germany, which do offer insurance to their nationals against these risks on a purely unilateral basis.[4]

[3] Certain less developed countries give special guarantees against expropriation for a limited period of time; others, such as India, are giving special undertakings with respect to compensation for expropriation which in effect gives the owner of nationalized property a measure of compensation decided upon by his *own* government, which India then accepts or negotiates with his government. Such arrangements are in effect with the United States and have been offered to other governments.

[4] In connection with insurance administered by the ICA under its Guarantee Program against expropriation, inconvertibility, and war risks, the United States government negotiates an agreement with the country covered by the insurance. The government in question recognizes the United States government's interest in its nationals' property and, among other things, agrees 1) to the transfer of local currency (in the absence of convertible currencies) to the United States government; 2) to give national and most-favored-nation treatment to United States property in the event of war; and 3) to enter into diplomatic negotiations and/or international arbitration in the event that compensation for expropriated property is not equal to the valuation put on it in the ICA insurance contract.

The industrial countries continue to try to secure protection for their nationals' investments and property through national and most-favored-nation treatment under treaties of commerce, friendship, and navigation. And it is precisely here that great difficulties arise. The less developed countries do not always propose to give foreign nationals treatment on a parity with their own nationals and with their state-owned industries. Special provisions applying to the foreigner exist, such as the refusal to let foreigners own land, the requirement that foreigners must train local personnel and management, the requirement that management must include nationals of the country where the investment is located, special treatment regarding remission of profits, and, in some countries, a commitment required of the foreign investor not to invoke the diplomatic protection of his own government in the protection of his property. Most-favored-nation treatment has been more generally accepted by the less developed countries, though there are exceptions here, too. For example, the government of the Philippines vigorously discriminates against all foreigners except Americans, who enjoy a special status under treaty obligations.

Occasionally an economically less developed country needs an industry or facility so badly that it is obliged to give far-reaching concessions that extend beyond rights normally granted even to its own citizens. This has been true in oil refining, public utilities, and mining. The government of India, for example, has given rights to foreign oil companies when capital and equipment could not be supplied by its own citizens. There are a number of other old foreign investment situations with a similar background, for example, in the electric power field and in mining in Latin America, where the foreigner originally secured complete control over his investment. But a process of attrition is generally taking place. Governments may directly or indirectly force the foreign investor to share his equity with local investors, and may at times go into business as outright competitors, for example in electric power. This has been true in Mexico and Argentina. But the process is not consistent—the same government may actually be furnishing loan capital to the foreign company or cooperating with it in other ways. In any case, the prospect of coming into the less developed countries with an investment on one's own terms is rapidly disappearing. The present-day situation makes the investor usually a bargainer and petitioner, and rarely, if ever, a master.

Capital-Importing Countries

In a number of less developed countries the governments have by law, or announced policy, required that foreign investment in general take the form of joint ventures.

Foreign participation is not indiscriminately welcome in India. It is sought as a scarce resource to be allocated to strategic areas, and the terms of any collaboration are carefully scrutinized to insure that the price India pays is commensurate with the value received. Decisions regarding foreign investment are not left exclusively to private negotiation; the government has ultimate sanction. A new foreign investment must give definite assurances on the terms of capital participation, on the terms of payment for imported materials, on a program of eventual manufacture within India of components for the product involved, and on the training of Indians for responsible managerial positions. Though statistical data are not available on the extent of joint equity ventures in India, it is clear that the policy since independence has been geared to the promotion of foreign investment in this form. Prime Minister Nehru, in a now famous policy statement of April 6, 1949, stated among other things that "the major interest in ownership and effective control of an industrial undertaking should, as a rule, be in Indian hands." Despite this, actual majority Indian participation has in fact not always been insisted upon; there has been considerable flexibility depending upon the nature of the enterprise, but government policy in India, almost without exception, favors at least some Indian capital participation in foreign direct investments.

Pakistan has a similar firmly announced policy. In a basic declaration of industrial policy issued by the government of Pakistan in April, 1948, it was stated that "Pakistan would welcome foreign capital seeking investment from a purely industrial and economic objective and not claiming any special privilege . . ." with the condition that "opportunities for participation of indigenous capital are provided and monopolies avoided." The condition means that nationals of Pakistan should ordinarily be given the option to subscribe at least 51 percent of all classes of share capital in some 13 specific industries,[5] and 30 percent in other industries. But "if the Government is satisfied that the requisite amount of indigenous capital is not forthcoming the balance might, with their prior approval, be subscribed by foreign investors." The insistence on local equity participation was made somewhat less rigid in a policy statement of November, 1958, by the new military regime; however, even in that statement it was pointed out that "normally the Government will expect that the required local expenditure [in a new enterprise] will be met from local equity capital" and that "in the case of oil refining the Government will expect substantial participation of Pakistani capital in equity."

All major foreign investments since independence in Burma have taken the form of joint ventures. Most of them have resulted from reorganization of British-owned enterprises into which Burma government capital has been injected. A few entirely new enterprises have also been formed as joint ventures.

Two motives seem to have been uppermost in Burmese government decisions: 1) Existing British mining and petroleum operations required extensive investment because of wartime destruction, and the areas in which they operated needed security against guerrilla operations. The British companies were themselves unwilling to provide the necessary capital, so Burma responded by participating in the enterprises. 2) The Burma government also became convinced that one of its primary problems was a lack of trained technicians and a managerial class, and it decided to encourage foreign capital in the form of joint ventures in order to help overcome the lack; this is still a strong motivation behind the government's policy.

In the reparations agreement between Japan and Burma, the government of Japan agreed to use all possible means to encourage its business community to invest in Burma, in the form of joint ventures, the sum of $50 million at an annual rate of $5 million for ten years. Thus far, not a single joint venture between Japanese citizens

[5] The specified industries are: cement, coal, cotton spinning and weaving mills, fish canning and fish oils, electric power generation (other than hydroelectric), glass and ceramics, heavy chemicals and dyestuffs, minerals, preserved and prepared foods, power alcohol, shipbuilding, sugar, tanning and leather.

and the Burmese government or citizens has materialized. The main difficulty encountered appears to be that Burma has not formulated any policy regarding the selection of industries and projects for development under the Japanese Economic Cooperation Agreement. It is likewise alleged that the Japanese are not keen on making large investments where major financial risks are entailed. They feel that projects in Burma will not bring substantial profit because of government-controlled prices, high costs of production, and generally unfavorable economic prospects.

Burma recently announced that it would not itself directly engage in joint ventures with Japanese nationals. It has formulated a new policy which encourages joint ventures between Burmese private interests and Japanese nationals in small-scale industrial operations. It is too early to evaluate this decision, but it is probably going to be handicapped by the very limited availability of private capital resources and business know-how in Burma, compared to the substantial resources available to the country under the Economic Cooperation Agreement with Japan.

The Philippine government appears more interested in foreign loans than in foreign equity investments. In direct investments there is a distinct preference for the joint venture. These attitudes have been in effect since 1957; earlier attitudes toward foreign investment were more liberal.

The Philippine policies with respect to aliens are primarily directed to removing Chinese nationals from business activities. The effect has been to discriminate against all foreign investment other than American—a result of the preferred status given to American nationals under the Bell Trade Act. All non-American foreigners suffer not only from discriminatory action on the administrative level but also from antagonistic legislation. As a result, it is believed that since 1949 there has been a net outflow of Chinese and perhaps also of other non-American capital. Most Chinese capital affected is likely to have been of domestic origin. Non-Chinese foreign nationals (except for Americans) are generally incidental casualties of the anti-Chinese policy. The fact is that there is almost no antagonism against Europeans as a group that even remotely compares with the one existing toward the Chinese.

Though there is no legal requirement for foreign investment to take the form of joint ventures, and though Turkish officialdom denies influencing investment into this channel, a substantial amount of foreign investment in the postwar period has taken the form of joint ventures. (This is demonstrated in Chapter II in this book.)

REQUIREMENTS FOR JOINT VENTURES IN CERTAIN INDUSTRIES

In a number of less developed countries, a foreigner is precluded by law or policy from investing in certain industries except on a joint venture basis. This requirement may stand alone, or it may be in addition to a general policy favoring joint ventures.

India has reserved a relatively large number of fields for exploitation by the state. The reserved industries are the manufacturing of iron and steel, shipbuilding, power generation, railroads, arms and ammunition, atomic energy, heavy capital goods, heavy electrical machinery, coal and lignite, mining of iron ore, aircraft, air transport, telephone, telegraph, and wireless. Because the Indian government does not have the technological and capital resources to go into all of these fields, it has had to form joint ventures with foreign governments and companies. The establishment of the three new Indian steel mills has been with British, German, and Soviet assistance; in the field of the manufacture of heavy electrical equipment, a British consortium (Associated Electrical Industries) is furnishing technical assistance and training of Indian personnel and management. In addition, the Indian government has had other offers of technical assistance and loans for the exploitation of various aspects of heavy capital goods industry by Soviet, Czechoslovakian, and British groups. There are similar tie-ups with Western companies for most of the other fields reserved by the Indian government for its own ownership.

A second area of industry which is open both to the Indian government and to private industry, but where the Indians were to take the initiative was announced in the second Five-Year Plan.[6]

[6] For a complete list of the fields reserved for the government, and for the fields to be jointly exploited by the government and private industry, see Government of India Planning Commission, *Second Five-Year Plan* (1956), p. 50. It should be noted that the Indian government's regulation about reserved industry applies to *new* investments and not to the existing ownership

The industries involved are the following: aluminum, machine tools, ferro-alloys, synthetic fertilizers, synthetic rubber, carbonization of coal, and road and sea transportation. A number of these fields have gone entirely to the private sector and have resulted in joint ventures between private Indian and private Western companies. Some of these include aluminum (Kaiser-Birla) and synthetic fertilizers (Montecatini and private Indian). In the field of machine tools, the Indian government is the sole owner but important technical assistance and management arrangements have been made with Swiss, German, French, and British machine tool manufacturers. In the field of synthetic rubber, the Indian government is not in the picture at all, and Firestone of the United States has begun production.

Most of the recent large-scale heavy industrial undertakings in India have been carried out with European partners. The International Bank for Reconstruction and Development, and some United States government lending institutions have followed a policy of not financing government-owned manufacturing industries. The same hesitations are not present among Europeans, and for this reason the government-owned industrial sector in India has been built largely with West European or Soviet participation.

The Industrial Policy Statement of the Pakistani government (April, 1948), reserved some 13 specific fields of industry for control by Pakistan nationals and also required other industries to have Pakistan national participation. The policy was substantially amended and no longer rigidly applies. However, there have been indications that the Pakistani government is applying a policy of having trading activities and banking controlled by Pakistan nationals. Also, the November, 1958 statement of the government reserved the fields of arms and ammunition, and the production of atomic energy for exploitation by official agencies only. Railway and air transport, and telecommunications are to continue as government-owned enterprises. The Pakistani government has left all other areas of industry for private exploitation, but it reserves the right, when private industry does not come forward, to own and operate basic industries, at least temporarily.

---

patterns. For example, Tata, a private company, continues to operate the largest steel mill in India.

Burma generally requires that there be 60 percent Burmese control in any corporation involved in the following fields: exploitation of timber, minerals, forests, fisheries, coal, petroleum and other mineral oils, sources of energy, and other natural resources. The President has the power to amend this percentage.

The Philippines has a constitutional provision which states that no foreigner can hold more than 40 percent of the shares in a corporation engaged in agriculture, banking, timber exploitation, mining, or exploitation of other natural resources. Philippine law gives preferential treatment to Philippine-controlled corporations in bidding for Philippine government contracts. Thus, no public works contract may be awarded except to companies which are 70 percent controlled by Filipinos. (United States nationals are treated on a national basis in these respects.)

The Turkish government will not permit 100 percent control by foreigners in any "defense industry." Defense industry is defined as any form of metal-working, assembly of tractors, vehicles, metal processing, and power generation. To the extent that foreign interests are involved in these industries, they are in joint ventures.

Mexico has a constitutional provision that a foreigner may not hold more than 49 percent of the shares in an agricultural operation. This formula also applies to radio broadcasting and television, motion pictures, publishing, advertising, fishing, transportation, the production and distribution of soft drinks, and the manufacture of tires. Banking, mining, and forestry must be carried on by a Mexican corporation, although the corporation may be wholly-controlled by foreign interests.

The Brazilian government requires domestic control varying from one-third to one-half for newspapers, radio, television, and aviation companies. Telegraphic and radio communication must be managed by Brazilians. The corporation may include foreign stockholders.

NATIONAL MANAGEMENT REQUIREMENTS

Many of the less developed countries require that their nationals take part in the management of enterprises in which foreigners have an interest—not only to provide maximum employment opportunities for nationals but also to upgrade their skills. The word "management" is defined differently in different countries and sometimes refers to the board of directors and senior business managers; at other times it refers to technical management.

Nationals are used in the management of enterprises to give them a local character, to shroud as far as possible their foreign origins, and to build up a cadre of local trained personnel. These considerations often force the foreign investor to allow the local management to participate in the ownership of the company. If a foreign investor is obliged to have local nationals as part of the management, he may reason that the only way to get really loyal managers is to give them an equity in the business.

Some such circumstances have been at work in the widespread minority holdings of Turkish nationals in foreign corporations in Turkey. Turkish law merely requires that the board of directors of any company must include a Turkish national.

In the Philippines, no foreigner (except American) can be a member of the board of directors of a company exploiting natural resources; furthermore, Philippine law has been interpreted to require any foreign director of a Philippine corporation doing business in fields other than the exploitation of natural resources to be a permanent resident in the Philippines. The extent to which such provisions can frustrate large-scale foreign investment can be seen in the case of the reparations agreement between the Philippines and Japan. Under the 1956 agreement, Japan agreed to encourage its business community to establish joint ventures in the Philippines and to make available through the Export-Import Bank of Japan credits to finance such joint ventures up to a total of $250 million. Philippine law prohibits Japanese nationals from establishing permanent residence in the country. Under these conditions it is not surprising that there have been no Philippine-Japanese ventures. Thus, the local residence requirement is holding at bay $250 million in development capital, along with the skills and know-how of highly industrialized Japan.

Colombia, in its labor code, requires, for foreign firms that employ more than ten persons, that at least 80 percent of the specialized or executive personnel be Colombian. If the personnel is not available for these high posts, corporations may appeal to the Ministry of Labor, which can lower the percentage on a temporary basis for the period required to train Colombian personnel.

Brazil requires that top management be resident in Brazil. It is reported to be customary for Brazilian industrialists to want to control the positions on the board of directors in companies in which they are involved, and for them to be averse to submitting their policies for review to anonymous stockholders. Though this is not directed against foreigners, it nevertheless stiffens the resolve of Brazilians to hold a majority in joint ventures.

One of the major objectives of Indian industrial policy is that Indian personnel should be, in the words of Prime Minister Nehru (1949) "trained for highest posts in the quickest possible manner." The government program of "Indianization of staff" requires foreign enterprises to gradually reduce the number of their own nationals in positions of responsibility, and to replace them with trained Indians. The necessity for the foreigners to periodically secure re-entry permits gives the government an opportunity to check upon the progress of the firm's program. In general, government policy has not been one of sacrificing efficiency for ideology so long as it is convinced that the firm is making a reasonable effort to comply. On the other hand, it is also true that India is no longer the place where the young Englishman goes to improve his fortune, retiring at an early age to the "auld sod." Acceptance of the Indian program is a necessary part of the plan of operations for any foreign investment in the country.

In Burma the foreign investor is under obligation to rapidly pass on technical and management skills to Burmese nationals. In part this is the rationale for the official joint ventures policy of the Burmese government, but it also reflects the hostility of Burmese trade unions toward foreign investors and the desire to dispose quickly of reliance upon foreigners.

Though it is difficult to prove that joint ventures grow out of the obligation to include local nationals in mangement, this is frequently the result since the best national in management is the one who is risking his own money in the venture. If the requirement for local management is a serious condition which cannot be met by dummies or other devices, there is the opportunity to make a virtue out of necessity. Local management becomes a partner, with special skills and know-how, and tries to reduce the risks of a business which it shares with the foreigner. Foreign investors do not have a single mind on this issue. Nationalization of staff is sometimes complied with, without giving local participants an equity in the business, and the use of dummies and other nominal tokens of compliance suffice in some countries to meet the requirements of nationalization of staff.

FOREIGN EXCHANGE DIFFICULTIES

Regulations pertaining to foreign currency transactions are generally found in less developed countries. They affect many phases of business owned by foreigners, including the remission of profits, the salary of non-local personnel, the repatriation of capital, and the ability to import raw materials, parts, and components. These regulations may induce the joint ventures form in order to have local know-how and influence in obtaining foreign exchange. Sometimes governments will be more liberal in allocating foreign exchange to companies with a substantial local character.

The precarious balance-of-payments situation in less developed countries, for example, in such countries as Pakistan, Turkey, Colombia, the Philippines, Brazil, and India, has been an important cause of foreign investments and joint ventures. When companies in Germany, Japan, the United Kingdom, and the United States find their markets shrinking because of local foreign exchange difficulties, they frequently decide to produce in foreign markets: They are able to hold their markets and make a minimum claim on the foreign exchange holdings of the less developed country. Furthermore, foreign investment caused by balance-of-payments difficulties frequently takes the form of joint ventures. The investor in an uncertain monetary situation tries to keep his investment to a minimum and to round out his capital position with local capital. At the same time, there is less of a claim on the country's future foreign resources when part of a given investment is local. Thus, there is pressure for joint ventures from both sides.

India has in effect a number of measures to husband foreign exchange. Importers, whether Indians or foreigners, in order to qualify for foreign exchange, are required to buy equipment from abroad on deferred payment plans, with a maximum down payment of 20 percent and the remaining 80 percent to be paid on a seven-year line of credit. The Indian government also tries to influence foreign-owned corporations to produce their materials, parts, and components within India—again a result of scarce foreign exchange. In a very few cases, foreign investors have rejected the pressure of the Indian government and have decided to leave the country, rather than comply with what they consider unrealistic attempts to produce parts and components locally. General Motors took this decision several years ago.

Turkey has been of keen interest to European and American exporters and investors, and under the pressure of the foreign exchange situation, joint ventures have been prominent among postwar investments. The partners are frequently the former Turkish importer and the European or American exporter-producer. Because of the exchange difficulties, there has been a tendency for foreigners to keep their equity position no larger than is needed by the foreign exchange requirements of the new business. Local capital is not hard to get, and whatever can be secured locally reduces the hazards of Turkey's volatile economy.

Pakistan is another country suffering from recurring foreign exchange problems and investors frequently attempt to associate themselves with one or another Pakistani government agency or corporation on the assumption that foreign exchange will then be found to maintain essential production. Foreign companies supplying machinery, equipment, and services have frequently accumulated local currency which they could not remit, and they have used these funds to go into production.

Colombia, which at times has also suffered from foreign exchange difficulties (for example, having accumulated several hundred million dollars in debts to foreign creditors in 1956 and 1957), is another country where investments have been made in order to preserve traditional market positions.

The Philippines has encouraged the investment of blocked peso accounts. Other limitations have promoted a "Buy Philippine" policy, and so have also encouraged investments.

Brazil is another country in which the shortage of foreign exchange available for ordinary trade has led to joint ventures. Several large Japanese investments made in Brazil in recent years were based on this consideration, as was the establishment by German interests of a local steel pipe mill; both the Japanese and German investments took the form of joint ventures. Numerous other joint ventures here have been motivated by this consideration.

LAND OWNERSHIP AND LEASES, AND MONOPOLIES

One of the typical measures taken by newly independent countries is to limit the right of foreigners to own and lease lands. This device, designed presumably to effect security objectives or to prevent the unauthorized exploitation of agriculture, mineral deposits, and oil, also, of course, has its effects on any type of productive enterprise where relatively large investments are made at a permanent site. These and other restrictions have induced companies to have local nationals as partners. In Mexico a foreign company or any corporation which has foreign shareholders is forbidden by constitutional provision from owning land within a certain distance from the country's borders; leases of more than ten years are subject to the same provisions. In the Philippines, no foreigner may own land of any kind. In Burma, constitutional provisions provide that a foreigner may not acquire land, and that he may not lease land for a period of more than one year, although exemptions can be granted by administrative act of the government.

Sometimes the governments of less developed countries offer foreigners an inducement that becomes in and of itself a basis for joint ventures. If a foreign investor can secure a monopoly position for his product, or if he can get a protective tariff, which may amount to the same thing, he has an interesting business situation. But by the same token he is open to the potential charge of monopoly coming from local consumers. Under such circumstances, there is a strong tendency to associate local nationals with the operation in order to give the company as much domestic character as possible. This has occurred in Pakistan and Turkey. However, monopolies or near monopolies achieved through high tariffs are not easy to come by. The government must be convinced that this is a *sine qua non* for getting investment in some field which it regards as vital. Furthermore, United States investors may shy away from such situations because of their concern with anti-trust legislation.

The motives for a joint venture do not proceed from a single cause to an effect. Many factors simultaneously enter into such decisions. The foreign investor examining a less developed country finds a ring of controls which single him out for special treatment. He finds also that the whole economy, including his business, is in some cases subject to central planning and day-to-day government intervention. The controls over his business and the power of government to give or refuse the essential ingredients which he needs to conduct his business of necessity turn his thoughts from purely business considerations to considerations of his relations with the government.

In most less developed countries a business must be able to petition for foreign exchange allocation for raw materials and for import permits for essential materials, machinery, and parts in order to survive. The relation of labor to management is complicated not only by the protective legislation of governments, but also by the social, cultural, and religious background of the work force. In addition, a business may be successful or unsuccessful to the extent that it is able to get protective tariffs, a favorable tax situation growing out of skillful negotiation with the government, or the transfer of dividends and the repatriation of capital at a favorable exchange rate. These considerations have prompted numerous foreign investors to take on local partners, while others still feel that they can be more successful by "going it alone."

Public Financing Agencies

The principal international agency for the financing of economic development in the postwar period has been the International Bank for Reconstruction and Development. The range of the bank's activites was broadened in mid-1956 by the creation of a new, affiliated agency, the International Finance Corporation. The chief foreign lending agency of the United States government has been the Export-Import Bank of Washington, and a second institution, the Development Loan Fund was established in 1957. These agencies have worked with joint international business ventures in various ways.

INTERNATIONAL BANK FOR RECONSTRUCTION AND DEVELOPMENT

The World Bank makes loans for the most part to governments or government agencies. Loans made directly to private enterprise have been limited by the requirement of the bank charter that any loan made by it to a borrower other than a government must be guaranteed by a government, central bank, or by other comparable agencies. Private borrowers are not inclined to come to the World Bank for fear that a government guarantee would lead to government interference in their business. And governments are unwilling to guarantee loans to private borrowers at the expense of loans for projects considered to be of higher priority. They have also hesitated to place their guarantee on loans for private projects, however useful, for fear of being charged with favoring one private firm over another. This situation led to the formation in July, 1956, of an affiliated institution of the World Bank, the International Finance Corporation, which undertakes the financing of private projects without government guarantee.

Despite the limitations on World Bank lending for private enterprise, it is estimated that loans made for the ultimate account of the private sector amounted by February 29, 1960, to $1.1 billion, net of cancellations and refundings.[7] These loans have been made for the most part for the production of steel and electric power. Some of the largest private recipients have been: the Indian Iron and Steel Corporation, $50 million; Tata, India (power plants and steel mill expansion), $131.3 million; Brazilian Traction (power), $109 million; Kawasaki Steel (Japan), $28 million; and Kansai Electric Power (Japan), $57.6 million.

Although the bank has not developed any policy specifically favoring joint ventures, some of its loans have gone to them. An example is the case of the Sui Gas Transmission Co., Ltd., Pakistan, a venture consisting of the Burmah Oil Company of Great Britain, the Pakistan Industrial Development Corporation (a Pakistani government corporation), private Pakistani capital, and the Common-

[7] This figure does not include postwar reconstruction loans amounting to $497 million or certain loans for general development purposes amounting to $205 million.

wealth Development Finance Company of Great Britain. A majority of 51 percent of the capital is held by PIDC and private Pakistanis, and 49 percent of the capital by Burmah Oil and CDFC. The World Bank made a loan equivalent to $14 million to this group.

In addition to its direct loans to private enterprise, the World Bank makes loans to various government institutions and public and private banking institutions, including development banks, which in turn relend the receipts to private companies within their country. Examples are loans to the following institutions (as of February 29, 1960): the Industrial Development Bank of Turkey, $17.7 million; Banco Central of Costa Rica, $6.5 million; Cassa per il Mezzogiorno of Italy, $196.6 million; Banco de Fomento of Peru, $10 million; Iceland Bank of Development, $1.35 million; the Industrial Credit and Investment Corporation of India, $20 million; the Pakistan Industrial Credit and Investment Corporation, $14.2 million; and the Development Bank of Ethiopia, $2 million. Institutions such as these have been widely represented in financing joint ventures. Some of these development banks themselves are joint ventures, examples being the aforementioned Indian and Pakistani institutions.

INTERNATIONAL FINANCE CORPORATION

The International Finance Corporation has been in operation since mid-1956. As of June 30, 1960, it had made 33 commitments for projects in 17 countries in the total amount of $42 million (including portions of investments sold to others in the amount of $6 million).

As was previously indicated, the operations of the International Finance Corporation differ from those of the World Bank in that it deals exclusively with private business and neither lends to, nor accepts guarantees from, governments. The IFC's purpose is to further economic development by encouraging investment in productive private enterprises in its member countries, particularly in the less developed areas such as Africa, Asia, and Latin America. It invests only where sufficient private capital is not available on reasonable terms and does so in association with local or foreign capital. It particularly seeks private capital in its investments and endeavors to revolve its funds by selling investments out of its portfolio to private investors whenever it can obtain a reasonable price for them. Only enterprises which are predominantly industrial have been considered eligible for financing; the IFC does not engage in operations which are essentially for the purposes of relending or refinancing or for the direct financing of exports or imports.

The IFC's investments may take any form, except that, under its articles of agreement, it may not invest in capital stock.[8] Its investments, therefore, take the form of loans; and these are usually repayable in United States dollars and are unsecured. But, since the IFC invests risk capital, it seeks equity features and so, in addition to fixed interest, IFC's investments usually provide for a participation in profits, either by means of a right to additional income (normally payable in local currency) based on earnings for example, or an option to subscribe to equity capital, or both. Conversion and option rights may not be exercised by the IFC, but they may be sold. There is no set pattern, and terms are matters for negotiation to suit particular circumstances.

About a third of all the enterprises which have received financing from the IFC have been joint ventures. This incidence of joint ventures is not the result of a deliberate policy, although the IFC is favorably disposed toward them because it believes that foreign capital is, in any particular country, in a stronger position commercially and politically if it acts in partnership with local capital. The IFC recently expressed itself on this subject as follows:

> There is an unquestioned trend toward joint ventures under international and local sponsorship, based on growing evidence that the advantages outweigh the difficulties. With full realization that each case must be judged in the light of its particular circumstances and of local conditions, including appropriate timing, IFC considers that wherever practicable joint enterprises are desirable.[9]

The location and types of joint ventures partly financed by the IFC are as follows: Argentina (pulp and paper); Brazil (cement, motor vehicles); Chile (cement); Mexico (foundry products, aircraft engine overhaul); Pakistan (steel products); Peru (synthetic

[8] The articles of agreement are now in the process of being amended to permit IFC investment in equities, as a result of a decision taken by the corporation's board of governors at its September, 1960 meeting.

[9] International Finance Corporation, *Fourth Annual Report 1959–1960* (Washington, D.C., September 29, 1960), p. 5.

ammonia and fertilizers, building materials); and Tanganyika (sugar).

EXPORT-IMPORT BANK

In the five years 1955–59, the Export-Import Bank made a total of 532 dollar loans valued at some $876 million to private groups and companies. Only nine of these loans amounting to $36 million can be identified as going to joint ventures in which some change in the equity position or structure of the borrower occurred at the time the loan was granted. (Thus, these data do not separately indicate loans made to existing joint ventures where no change in the equity position occurred.) The bank's total lending to private and public borrowers during the five-year period exceeded $3.6 billion. Thus it appears that Export-Import Bank lending to the joint venture type of enterprise has been relatively unimportant. This does not, however, stem from any deliberately unfavorable attitude toward joint ventures by the Export-Import Bank; the bank has sometimes tried to encourage its borrowers to join with local capital.

The conclusion is borne out by the "local currency" lending of the Export-Import Bank. Such lending has arisen from Public Law 480, which provides for the sale abroad for local currencies of United States surplus agricultural commodities, and for the lending of most of the local currency proceeds for economic development projects in the countries in question. One-fourth of these proceeds is administered directly by the Export-Import Bank in loans to enterprises, pursuant to the Cooley Amendment (1958) to P.L. 480. Only a few joint ventures were financed under this program by the end of 1959.

There have been four such joint ventures in Israel in petroleum distribution, steel processing, cotton spinning, and the manufacture of animal feeds and medicines. These companies received loans totaling 3.5 million Israeli pounds. This represented about 13 percent of all loans made with Israeli Cooley funds (total of 21.5 million Israeli pounds). In Pakistan, on the other hand, one Cooley loan of one million rupees to a joint United States–Pakistani pharmaceutical plant represented well over one-half of all Cooley loans (1.4 million rupees). In Turkey, a loan to a Turkish-American joint venture to produce sewing machines (1.6 million Turkish lire) represented only a small part of the Cooley loans actually made (22 million Turkish lire). In Peru, one Cooley loan was made to a joint venture for the construction of housing (4 million soles), representing about 10 percent of all Cooley loans made (44 million soles). In France, a loan of 6 million new French francs made to a joint venture manufacturing agricultural and industrial machinery represented about 20 percent of the total Cooley French loans (28 million new French francs).

DEVELOPMENT LOAN FUND

This bank is a relatively new lending agency of the United States government. It began operations early in 1958 and finances specific projects as well as broader programs for economic development in the less developed countries. As of May 30, 1960, the DLF had made loans in excess of $1.2 billion, of which $879 million went to the public sector and $339 million to the private sector. Private sector loans were of three types: 1) direct loans to the private sector, $97.8 million; 2) loans to development banks relending to the private sector, $107 million; and 3) loans to public borrowers relending to the private sector, $134 million.

Included among the banks that have received loans for relending in turn to the private sector are the following: the Banco de Guatemala, $5 million; the Industrial Finance Corporation of India, $16 million; the Industrial and Mining Development Bank of Iran, $5.2 million; the Industrial Development Bank of Israel, $5 million; the Reconstruction Bank of Korea, $5 million; the Banque de Credit Agricole, Industriel et Foncier of Lebanon, $5 million; the Pakistan Industrial Credit and Investment Corporation, $4.2 million; the Bank of Monrovia (Liberia), $250,000; the Central Bank of the Philippines, $5 million; Credito Somalo (Somalia), $2 million; the China Development Corporation (Taiwan), $10 million; the Peru Savings and Loan Association, $1 million; and the Industrial Development Bank of Turkey, $10 million. As in the case of similar lending by the World Bank, some of these institutions are themselves joint ventures and their lending activity has been directed to joint venture enterprises among their other clients.

The DLF has made 28 loans directly to joint ventures (including six loans to banks and development corporations which are themselves joint ventures. This represents almost one-half of all loans made to the private sector (62 loans). The overwhelming majority of loans to joint ventures have been to the equity-type of joint venture (21 cases); only 7 loans have been made to joint ventures involving technical assistance and lines of credit.

American private investors have been participants in 11 of the 28 joint ventures. In the following list of these joint ventures, it will be seen that a considerable variety of other nationals has also been involved in joint ventures supported by the DLF.

Country	*Activity*	*Foreign Nationality*
Costa Rica	resettlement	Italian
Ethiopia	cotton weaving	Italian
Greece	hydropower	German, Italian
Guatemala	kenaf bags	American
Haiti	sugar mill	American
India	cement and jute processing	British
India	railroad modernization	German
Jordan	phosphate mining	Yugoslav
Liberia	sawmill	American
Pakistan	water supply & sewage	Australian
Pakistan	gas pipeline	British
Pakistan	high tension grid	Canadian
Pakistan	railroad rehabilitation	German
Paraguay	meat packing, ranching, quebracho	American
Philippines	pulp and paper	American
Spain	hydroelectric power plant	French
Spain	switchgear plant	French, Swiss
Sudan	cotton textiles	Greek, American
Taiwan	shipbuilding	American
Taiwan	cement	British
Taiwan	by-product coke	Japanese
Thailand	meat packing	Danish
Tunisia	pulp	American
Turkey	carbide, plastics plant	American, Italian
Turkey	plastics materials	Italian, American
UAR/Syria	worsted textile plant	Netherlands
Yugoslavia	plastics & chemical plant	British

As this activity indicates, the DLF looks with favor on joint ventures. In the brochure on its activities dated February, 1960, the DLF made the following statement:

Joint ventures between private American investors and local private investors or investors from third countries will be looked upon with favor.

American participation in such ventures brings production and management know-how to the enterprise and local participation brings a knowledge of local economic and political conditions including local markets and distribution systems.

The "Buy American" policy which was adopted by the DLF early in 1960 requires borrowers to use DLF funds, save under exceptional circumstances, for services and equipment originating in the United States. The policy does not affect the willingness of the DLF to make loans to joint ventures composed of Europeans and local nationals. For example, the preceding list includes cases where the DLF has co-financed projects in Greece with German and Italian participation; in Pakistan with German participation; and in Spain with French participation. The DLF is attempting to induce Europeans to act as co-financers of other projects as well.

Once the decision has been made to establish a joint venture, the attention of the participants will be directed to the problems associated with the selection of organizational arrangements and control mechanisms for the enterprise. It is here that the local law dealing with forms of business organizations and related commercial matters becomes of key importance. Each participant, whether holding a majority or a minority interest, will seek to maximize the degree of control and the degree of protection which will be available to it. The resulting structure and control mechanisms will reflect the relative strength and negotiating skill of each participant, and if the venture is to be effective, they will also reflect judicious compromises made by each participant in the interest of making the enterprise viable.

Form of Business Organization [10]

In the great majority of cases, a joint venture in a less developed country involving local interests and foreign investors will be organized under one of the forms of business organization available under

[10] For a fuller discussion of this subject, see "Comparative Analysis," in Friedmann and Pugh, *Legal Aspects of Foreign Investment* (Little, Brown & Co., 1959), pp. 754–79.

the law of the country concerned. It is also possible that the participants will wish to organize the enterprise under the law of a second country, in order that the enterprise may be able to function in the less developed country as a branch of a foreign business organization. Reasons for this form of organization often include a desire to minimize taxes or to withdraw profits to a second country where they may be accumulated free of the danger of currency depreciation, political instability, or a tightening of exchange controls. Such arrangements are not uncommon if joint ventures are established in industrially developed countries but they are rare in less developed countries, partially because governmental bodies charged with screening foreign investment applications generally will either not approve investments or will deny investment incentives if the proposal involves the organization of an enterprise in a foreign country to which profits can be withdrawn.

In the unusual case where this type of organization is a genuine alternative in a less developed country, there may be local private law considerations which will bear on its adoption or rejection. The requirements for the qualification of a foreign company may be highly burdensome, and indeed considerably more burdensome than would be the setting up of a local company. For example, the company charter and by-laws, and even the laws dealing with business organizations in the state where the company is incorporated may have to be translated and filed, and in some cases extensive reports on the world-wide operations of the enterprise may be required. On the other hand, operation as a branch may avoid certain restrictive provisions of local commercial law which would otherwise create substantial problems. Often tax considerations also will provide either an incentive or a deterrent to operation in a less developed country in the form of a company organized in a second country.

In the typical case—a joint venture organized as a company under local law in the country where business operations are to be conducted—the local and foreign participants will generally find a wide range of alternatives available. The French-German civil law system and the British legal system, which have been adopted with modifications throughout most of the world, offer a wider range of distinct organizational forms than are recognized in the United States.

The typical civil law business forms include the corporation (*société anonyme*, *sociedad anónima*, or *Aktiengesellschaft*); the limited liability company (*société à responsabilité limitée*, *sociedad de responsabilidad limitada*, or *Gesellschaft mit beschränkter Haftung*); the limited partnership (*société en commandite simple*, *sociedad en comandita simple*, or *Kommanditgesellschaft*); the limited partnership with shares (*société en commandite par actions*, *sociedad en comandita por acciones*, or *Kommanditgesellschaft auf Aktien*); and the general partnership (*société en nom collectif*, *sociedad colectiva*, or *offene Handelsgesellschaft*). In addition, contractual joint ventures [11] are generally possible and other business forms are sometimes available.

In those countries whose legal systems have English roots, such as Australia, Burma, India, the Union of South Africa, and Israel, the available business forms include, in addition to the public company or corporation, and the various types of partnership and contractual joint ventures utilized in the United States, the so-called private company, which resembles the limited liability company of the civil law system, but has no close counterpart in the United States.

Generally speaking, any of the available business forms in a given less developed country may be suitable as a vehicle for a joint venture. Rarely will any legal provision alone make the choice of a particular form mandatory; rather the choice will depend upon a consideration of a variety of non-legal as well as legal factors, some of which will now be considered.

CORPORATION OR PUBLIC COMPANY

The civil law corporation (*société anonyme*, *sociedad anónima*, or *Aktiengesellschaft*) or English law public company is the business form most often selected for productive enterprises organized as

[11] The term "contractual joint venture" is here used to refer to the particular form of business organization known in the United States as the "joint venture" in order to avoid confusion with the generic "joint ventures" which are the subject of this study.

joint ventures. The flexibility of the corporation or public company and its adaptability to effective centralized management, notwithstanding dispersed ownership, generally make it the most advantageous form of organization for large-scale joint ventures. A non-technical factor which encourages the use of the corporation is the fact that it often enjoys greater prestige in the public eye than other business forms. Where the equity participation of the local interests is to be widely held by the public, the corporation or public company will be the only practicable alternative because it is usually the only company form in which the shares are readily transferable.

Another factor which may influence the use of the local law equivalent of the corporation is that the laws relating to such matters as minority stockholder rights, preemptive rights, capitalization, and rights and duties of directors are commonly spelled out in much greater detail in code or statute, and have been more fully worked out in practice and in judicial decision for the corporation than for other business forms. For the minority participants the fact that their rights as minority stockholders and their preemptive rights are clearly defined is significant. On the other hand, because the law relating to the corporation has been more fully developed, it may be difficult to use corporate control devices such as cumulative voting which may be unknown in local practice. Innovation may be easier in the case of the limited liability company since the details often have not been worked out in law or practice and are left to agreement between the participants. The requirement that all the authorized capital of the civil law corporation be subscribed and paid for at least in part, at the time the corporation is organized, results in a certain inflexibility in the capital structure of the corporation. If it is necessary to issue additional shares, an amendment of the corporate charter (with its attendant formalities and expense) is required. Accordingly, it will often be impracticable to use corporate shares for executive compensation or for the purchase of assets. In the case of at least one country (Mexico), a civil law corporation with flexible capital has been developed. Here the corporation with variable capital may increase its capital pursuant to a decision by a special shareholders' meeting.

LIMITED LIABILITY COMPANY AND PRIVATE COMPANY

The limited liability company (*société à responsabilité limitée, sociedad de responsabilidad limitada*, or *Gesellschaft mit beschränkter Haftung*) is a business form peculiar to civil law systems and often the preferred vehicle for joint ventures of modest size where the equity participations are to be closely held. This type of company combines certain features of the corporation with features more characteristic of the partnership. Like the corporation, the limited liability company affords limited liability [12] and continuity of existence. Unlike the corporation, whose capital is divided into readily transferable shares, the limited liability company's capital is divided into members' quotas which usually can be transferred to a non-member only with the consent of a fixed percentage of the other members or after the other members have declined to exercise a prior option to purchase. No transferable certificates representing these quotas are issued. The limited liability company generally does not have a board of directors.

The limited liability company is usually subject to less regulation and fewer requirements for publicity than the corporation and may also bear a lower tax burden.

One serious disadvantage of a limited liability company is the lack of flexibility in the capital structure. Capital devices such as separate classes of stock with different voting rights normally may not be used to finance the company. Since the utilization of shares with preferred voting rights is a standard device of granting management control to a party supplying a minority of the equity capital, its non-availability may dictate against the use of the limited liability company as the preferred form of business organization. In addition, financing through the sale of bonds or debentures is not possible in some civil law systems. In some less developed countries, for example, those in which the Belgian legal system has been adopted, the limited liability company is of restricted utility because a mem-

[12] In most civil law systems, the member of the limited liability company enjoys liability limited to the amount of his equity participation only when the company capital has been paid up in full. Until that time, all members are jointly and severally liable to the extent of all unpaid subscriptions.

ber cannot be a juridical entity such as a corporation, but must be a physical person.

The private company found in the English legal systems bears certain similarities to the civil law limited liability company. For example, the transferability of its equity participations is restricted, and, in its organization and operation, it is subject to fewer formalities and requirements for publicity than the public company. Unlike the limited liability company, however, its basic structure is the same as that of the public company or corporation. A private company issues shares represented by transferable certificates, is managed by a board of directors, and confers the same limited liability on its shareholders as the public company. The private company differs from the public company only in that the number of its shareholders is limited to 50, the transferability of its shares is subject to certain restrictions, and no public offering of shares or debentures is permitted. The private company was devised to meet many of the needs which have been answered, at least in part, in the United States by the *de facto* development of the so-called closed corporation.

PARTNERSHIPS AND CONTRACTUAL JOINT VENTURES

While the various forms of partnership and contractual joint ventures are almost never utilized as vehicles for joint ventures in manufacturing enterprises, certain of these business forms are often employed in extractive enterprises—primarily for tax considerations.

The contractual joint venture is particularly common in joint ventures whose purpose is mineral exploitation. The device, although seldom dealt with as a distinct form of business organization in the civil law or common law countries of the world, is nonetheless nearly always available under general principles of contract law. The contractual joint venture, which depends almost entirely upon the mutual agreement of the parties, is highly flexible. Its major disadvantages from the point of view of the investor are basically the same as those of the simple partnership (*société en nom collectif*, *sociedad colectiva*, or *offene Handelsgesellschaft*), namely, unlimited liability, the lack of continuity of existence, and non-transferability of partners' shares.[13] The limited partnership (*société en commandite simple, sociedad en comandita simple*, or *Kommanditgesellschaft*), does afford the advantage of limited liability to the partners who do not participate in management. In the case of the limited partnership with shares (*société en commandite par actions, sociedad en comandita por acciones*, or *Kommanditgesellschaft auf Aktien*), moreover, another business form which is peculiar to the civil law, the capital of the partnership is divided into transferable shares.

THE BURMA SPECIAL COMPANIES ACT

In the case of one less developed country, legislation has been enacted to provide for a special business form under which certain joint ventures may be conducted. This legislation is the Burma Special Companies Act of 1950. The primary purpose of the act was to create a form of "special company" to serve as the vehicle for joint ventures between the Burmese government and private interests—foreign as well as local.[14] The key feature of the special company is that its memorandum (charter) and articles of association (by-laws), which must be approved by the government, prevail over inconsistent provisions of the Burma Companies Act. There are no limits on the flexibility of the arrangements which may be adopted, and the law governing the company will depend upon negotiation between the government and the private participants. The joint ventures which have been set up under the Special Companies Act between the government and foreign companies have usually involved the issuance of two classes of shares: fully-paid shares issued to the foreign companies concerned and non-fully-paid shares allotted to the government. Normally, dividends are payable in proportion to the amounts paid up on each share. The memorandum and articles of association usually specify which party shall nominate a majority of the directors. The right is given to the Burmese government to acquire the shares held by the private participants

[13] In some joint ventures, of course, non-transferability of participants' shares may be desired.

[14] The first joint venture incorporated under the act was the Burma Corporation (1951) Limited, a joint venture between the Union government and the Burma Corporation; cf. section on Burma in Chapter III and the case study of the Burma Oil Company (1954) Limited in Part II of this book.

subject to certain conditions, including the requirements that the government pay for its shares in full before exercising this option and that it pay prescribed amounts in sterling for the shares to be acquired.

Problems of Control and Minority Protection

In addition to the choice of business form, the foreign or local participant in a joint venture will be concerned with the problem of how best to insure continued effective control over the enterprise without denying basic protections to the minority participant. The objectives of all participants will be to maximize the degree of control and protection they each enjoy. One of the safeguards which will often be sought by minority and majority participants alike is protection against the transfer of a participation to an independent party without the approval of all or a specified number of the other participants. If a portion of the equity of the joint venture is widely held by the public of the less developed country concerned, restrictions on the transfer of shares representing the publicly held portion would, of course, be inappropriate.

EFFECTIVE VOTING CONTROL

If a participant in a joint venture has effective voting control, he will usually own a majority of the equity of the enterprise as well. But it is often possible for one participant or group of participants to own a majority of the equity while the voting control remains in the hands of a minority participant, for example, when one class of shares has no vote or is vested with multiple votes. In some cases, such an arrangement will be impossible because of local law prohibitions. The same result can be achieved through a voting trust or a shareholders' agreement. However, in civil law countries, except in rare cases such as Venezuela where legislation introducing trust concepts has been adopted, the voting trust will be unavailable. Also in most, if not all, civil law countries the shareholders' agreement will usually not be a satisfactory control device. In some cases, a shareholders' agreement involving any restriction on a shareholder's right to vote is void, and in others, even if the agreement is valid, it will be inadequate because the remedy of specific enforcement is not available; consequently the only means of enforcement would be an action for damages, the existence and quantum of which often would be extremely difficult to establish.

One of the primary concerns of the participant or group of participants holding voting control will be to insure that effective management of the enterprise cannot be blocked. This can best be accomplished by insuring that, to the extent possible under local law, the majorities required by the corporate charter or by-laws (which in civil law systems are combined in a single instrument) for director and stockholder action are such that they can be readily produced by the controlling participants.

CONTROL BY MINORITY PARTICIPANTS

When participants accept a minority position in the voting equity of a joint venture, they will frequently endeavor to exercise as many controls as possible over the management of the enterprise. In some cases these controls may result in effective management by the minority participants; in others they will consist merely of the right to veto acts inimical to their interests; and in still others they may mean only an extra measure of influence over management decisions. The forms and combinations of these controls are numerous, and their effectiveness will vary according to the circumstances.

Where the equity participation of one group of participants is widely held by the public, it will often be possible for a minority participant to exercise effective control without the aid of devices extrinsic to its voting powers.[15]

If the majority participation is closely held, probably the most direct method by which a minority investor can retain effective control is by a management contract under which he will direct and will have control over the day-to-day operation of the enterprise.

There are many ways to subject the management of a joint venture to the direction of minority participants without formally

[15] For example, in the case of the Willys-Overland venture in Brazil, the United States parent company owns less than half of the voting shares, the majority being held by more than 40,000 Brazilian shareholders.

depriving it of its freedom to act. The devices are often in the nature of ultimate sanctions. For example, the joint venture may be the licensee under a patent license from the minority participant. When the enterprise cannot operate effectively without the license and the license is terminable by the licensor, the significance of the license to the control of the enterprise is obvious. The same result can often be achieved through a lease of equipment or agreement for the supplying of technical assistance necessary to the joint venture's operation that could be terminated by the lessor or party furnishing the services. A substantial degree of control could also be effected by a minority participant if he serves as the exclusive sales agent for the products manufactured by the joint venture.

Interdependent devices may be adopted to accord a measure of control to a minority participant. For example, a participant who holds a minority of the equity but who is in a position to supply additional capital and patents and know-how essential to the enterprise may lend capital to the joint venture subject to his holding a security interest in a controlling portion of the stock which would enable him to vote this portion on some or all questions of business policy during the period the loan is outstanding. In addition, a patent and know-how license from the minority participant to the joint venture may be set up for a period coinciding with the term of the loan and thereafter terminable at any time with a short period of prior notice by the licensor. In this way, the measure of control represented by the right to vote a controlling portion of the stock while the loan was outstanding could be replaced after repayment of the loan by the less direct, but still effective, measure of control represented by the right to terminate the license.

PROTECTION OF MINORITY PARTICIPANTS LACKING CONTROL

Where the joint venture participant enjoys neither technical nor effective control, he will be primarily concerned with protection of his minority rights. The rights available to minority shareholders differ greatly from country to country. In some cases, highly effective protective mechanisms exist;[16] in others, virtually no legal or administrative protections are available.

[16] See Friedmann and Pugh, *Legal Aspects of Foreign Investment*, pp. 772–79.

However well or badly the minority shareholder's rights may be protected under local law, the minority participant will want to buttress his legal position. It is sometimes possible to insure a representation of the minority on the board through a shareholders' agreement, although the shareholders' agreement is likely to be unenforceable or enforceable only through an action for damages. Accordingly, the foreign or local minority investor will try to provide for minority representation in the charter and by-laws of the enterprise. In some cases this may be accomplished by cumulative voting. Where this is not possible, it may be feasible to provide in the charter for a special class of stock to be issued to the minority participant and to state that a prescribed number of directors is to be elected from a slate proposed by the holders of this class of shares.

It may also be important to provide in the charter and by-laws that specified corporate acts such as amendment of the charter, sale of assets, contracts with affiliates or stockholders, and new investments, can be taken by a directors' or shareholders' meeting only by prescribed majorities which are large enough to vest in effect a veto power in the minority. In addition, if this point is not covered in the local corporate law, preemptive rights may be expressly included in the charter as a protection against being frozen out, and it may be provided that the charter and by-laws can be amended only by stated majorities.

SPECIAL PROBLEMS OF THE 50-50 JOINT VENTURE

The most serious problem of the 50-50 venture is a deadlock between the parties. The possibility of deadlock on day-to-day corporate problems can be substantially reduced by providing that one of the parties may elect one more than half the directors, by providing that day-to-day management is to be supervised by an executive committee of the board on which one party has a majority, perhaps on an alternating basis, or by having the board delegate substantial management powers to a president or general manager acceptable to both parties.

It is not easy to predict the cause of a deadlock. Provisions are sometimes made for arbitration. Dissolution is, of course, a possibility normally available under local corporate law. The participants usually endeavor to work out some arrangement whereby one may buy out the other so that the drastic step of dissolution can be avoided. One technique which is sometimes utilized is to provide that in the event of deadlock either party may initiate the buy-out procedure by offering to purchase the other party's equity at any price set by the former. The latter party then has two alternatives. He may agree to sell his equity for the stipulated price or he may purchase the initiating party's equity at the same price. Thus, the initiating party, by making his offer, loses the right to determine whether he will buy the other party's participation or sell his own; he determines merely the price at which he will sell or buy. This mechanism can also be set up so that the selling participant will sell not all its equity but merely enough to enable the other party to gain control.

RESTRICTIONS ON THE TRANSFERABILITY OF PARTICIPANTS' SHARES

Participants in joint ventures usually insist on retaining a veto power over the transfer of the equity participation of any other participant except where the latter is a member of the public exercising no active role in the enterprise. Provision must be made for the acquisition of the equity of a participant whose legal existence ceases through death or dissolution. Where the participants are corporations or other business entities enjoying continuity of existence, the latter problem is seldom presented on a significant scale—although it is often encountered in smaller enterprises because of the existence of qualifying shares held by individuals.

The problem of giving each participant a veto over a transfer of the equity of another participant is often handled by giving the remaining participants a right of first refusal. This arrangement may be embodied in a shareholders' agreement, but because of the problems of enforcement it is often preferable to incorporate the right of first refusal in the charter and by-laws. In many countries it will be impossible for a corporation or public company or a limited liability company or private company to purchase its own shares. Accordingly, the right of first refusal must often be vested in the participants rather than in the entity conducting the joint enterprise.

Occasionally, the necessity of imposing restrictions on the transferability of shares may have a bearing on the form of business organization selected for the joint venture. For example, the law relating to the limited liability company may provide that if the members representing a stated portion of the equity agree to a transfer of a member's participation to an outsider, such transfer will be valid notwithstanding any provisions in the company's constitutive documents to the contrary. Where this is the case, a minority participant will, of course, seek to have the joint venture organized in a form other than the limited liability company.

The problem of acquiring the equity of a participant upon death or dissolution is most often handled through an option agreement under which the remaining participants or the joint venture itself (where this is possible under local law) have the right to purchase the equity of the withdrawing participant at a price to be determined in accordance with a prescribed formula or fixed by appraisers.

The investor contemplating a foreign investment jointly with local interests must be concerned with a wide range of tax considerations. These considerations will normally be centered in the capital-importing country, the capital-exporting country and, in many cases, in a third country which may be used as a base for some or all of the investor's international business operations. The interrelation of tax factors in these various countries through such mechanisms as the United States foreign tax credit and international treaties for the avoidance of double taxation are also of importance.

In some cases, tax considerations within the capital-importing countries will affect the choice of the country in which the investment will be made, and will determine whether the enterprise is to include local interests. But the tax question is generally not a prime factor in these basic decisions. Once the situs has been selected and the decision to have local participation has been reached, the problems of choosing the form of organization and other operational arrangements to be adopted must be faced. It is in this area that tax factors assume key importance. In the discussion which follows, it will be assumed that the foreign participant in the joint venture will be a corporation organized under the laws of one of the states of the United States. A considerable portion of the discussion will also be germane to the situation of investors from other capital-exporting countries.

Tax Factors in the Capital-Importing Country

A natural starting point for the prospective investor abroad is an examination of the tax burden imposed upon business income in the capital-importing country concerned. If the foreign investor has some freedom of choice as to where the investment will be made, and when economic and non-tax legal factors create no strong preference for a particular country, a relatively low tax burden on business income may significantly influence the location of the proposed investment. In order to ascertain what this over-all tax burden will be, the prospective investor must—in addition to determining the applicable income tax rates—study carefully such other matters as the depreciation rates, the existence of taxes on accumulated earnings, the availability of loss carry-overs, and the existence of non-income taxes such as capital taxes, property taxes, or turnover taxes.

The existence and nature of special tax incentives to investment must also be investigated. In most, if not all, countries of the world there are such incentives. In the case of industrially developed countries, these incentives are generally available to domestic as well as foreign investors. Often special incentives are offered to encourage investment in areas within the countries which are industrially underdeveloped or economically depressed. Special incentives are available in Italy, to encourage investment in Southern Italy and Sicily, and in France, to encourage investment in Algeria.

In the less developed countries and in some highly developed countries which particularly want to attract foreign capital, special incentives may be devised. Often they are embodied in special legislation and in many cases they form part of broader programs which include such features as interest-free or low-interest loans by the government of the capital-importing country, exemptions from import restrictions, governmental guarantees of the remittance of profits and the repatriation of capital, and governmental guarantees against expropriation.

The tax incentives cover a wide range. Some of the most common devices are outright reductions in the applicable tax rates, exemption from certain taxes, accelerated depreciation, authorization to revalue assets for depreciation purposes to reflect currency depreciation or devaluation, and allowance of depreciation deductions in excess of the cost of the depreciated property. Tax reductions and tax exemptions are generally granted for limited periods of time after which the normal tax rates become applicable. This approach enables the investment to obtain tax relief during the formative stage, at the same time preserving the right of the capital-importing country to obtain revenue later on if the investment is profitable.

Typical of the incentives are those which are embodied in the Israeli Law for the Encouragement of Capital Investment of 1959. Under this legislation, enterprises approved by the Israeli Investment Center will be subject to the annual company profits tax at a maximum rate of 28 percent (with no additional taxes levied upon distribution of profits as dividends to non-resident shareholders) and will be exempt from all other taxes (including real estate taxes on buildings built or acquired by the enterprise) for a period of five years. In addition, the rate of depreciation is 200 percent of the normal rate in the first five years of operation, and where unusual wear and tear is involved, the depreciation rate may be increased up to 250 percent of the normal rate.[17]

The foreign investor is, of course, interested not only in the present existence of tax incentives but also in their continuity. In a majority of cases, it is probable that the most the foreign investor can hope for is an informal assurance by the tax authorities of the capital-importing country that the obligation not to alter the tax incentives to the detriment of the foreign investor will be respected. The obligation is sometimes embodied in legislation. For example, the Greek Investment Law provides for the freezing of income tax rates in effect at the time the investment is approved, for a period of ten years with downward readjustments if taxes are lowered.[18] A similar result is achieved under the provision of the Chilean Statute on Investments that the order signed by the President of the Republic authorizing the investment shall constitute a con-

[17] See United States Department of Commerce, *Foreign Commerce Weekly* (December 14, 1959), p. 7.

[18] See Lambadarios, "Greece," in Friedmann and Pugh, *Legal Aspects of Foreign Investment*, p. 245.

tract between the State of Chile and the foreign investor, which incorporates all current tax legislation.[19]

Another aspect of tax incentives in the capital-importing country of significance to the foreign investor (and particularly to the personnel who will be involved in the management of the enterprise) is the privileged tax treatment, which includes such features as tax reductions or special deductions, that may be granted to foreign technical and managerial personnel who are considered necessary for the effective operation of the enterprise.

The over-all tax burden in a particular country and the existence of special incentives may have considerable influence on the location of a joint venture. But whether the prospective participant in such a venture is concerned with where to set it up or with what organizational structure to adopt, he cannot isolate his study of the tax situation in the capital-importing country from the tax considerations in the capital-exporting country (here assumed to be the United States), and in any third country which is involved in the alternative organizational arrangements which may be available.

Tax Factors in the United States

Usually, a United States corporation is subject to its country's taxation at the regular corporate rates on its income from all sources, foreign as well as domestic.[20] Accordingly, a United States corporation which operates through foreign branches is subject to the United States corporate income tax in the year that income is realized. In the case of a foreign corporation which is partially or wholly-owned by a United States corporation, however, the foreign profits are subject to United States corporate tax only when they are remitted as dividends, royalties, interest, or as a distribution in liquidation by the foreign to the United States corporation. This deferral of United States tax on the profits of a foreign corporation is of paramount importance to the United States corporation participating in a foreign investment, for, assuming the foreign taxes are less than those in the United States, such a corporation is able to

[19] See Aramayo, "Chile," in *ibid.*, p. 139.

[20] It will be assumed, in the interest of simplicity, that the over-all United States corporate income tax rate is 52 percent.

increase its investment each year by the amount of tax which, but for deferral, would be payable to the United States Treasury.

When profits are distributed as dividends the device which mitigates double taxation is the foreign tax credit.[21]

FOREIGN TAX CREDIT

Under the operation of the foreign tax credit, the United States corporate taxpayer receives a credit against the United States tax which is due on its foreign-source income in an amount which represents the foreign income, war profits, and excess profits taxes that have actually been paid or deemed to have been paid with respect to such income.

There are two distinct elements of the foreign tax credit, the "direct" credit and the "indirect" or "deemed paid" credit. The direct credit is that applicable to foreign income, war profits, or excess profits taxes which are considered to have been paid directly by the United States corporate taxpayer receiving the foreign-source income. For example, the direct credit applies with respect to qualifying foreign taxes which are levied on the profits of a foreign branch of a United States corporation or which are withheld from dividends paid by a foreign corporation to its United States stockholder. If we assume a gross dividend from a foreign corporation of 100 to a United States corporate stockholder, which is subject to a withholding tax of 20 percent in the source country, the dividend would be subject to a tax of 52 percent in the United States reduced by the direct credit of 20, with the result that the tax to be paid in the United States would be 32 and the over-all tax burden would be 52 percent. The effect of the direct credit is to insure that the total burden of the taxes paid to both the foreign and the United States government will be no greater than 52 percent in any case in which the foreign tax rate is 52 percent or less. If the foreign tax rate is equal to or higher than the United States 52 percent rate, no additional tax is payable in the United States.

The indirect credit enables the United States corporate taxpayer to obtain a credit not for the taxes *it* has paid to the foreign coun-

[21] United States Internal Revenue Code (hereafter referred to as I.R.C.), Sections 901–5.

try, but rather for taxes actually paid by the foreign corporation but which, for purposes of the tax credit, are "deemed to have been paid" by the United States corporation. Specifically, Section 902(a) of the Internal Revenue Code provides that:

> a domestic corporation which owns at least 10% of the voting stock of a foreign corporation from which it receives dividends in any taxable year shall be deemed to have paid the same proportion of any income, war profits, or excess profits taxes paid or deemed to be paid by such foreign corporation to any foreign country . . . on . . . the accumulated profits of such foreign corporation from which such dividends were paid, which the amount of such dividends bear to the amount of such accumulated profits.

The operation of the deemed paid credit can best be clarified by a simple example. If we assume that the before-tax accumulated profits of a foreign corporation are 100, that it has paid foreign income taxes with respect to such profits in the amount of 20, and that a dividend of 80 is paid to a United States corporate stockholder owning all of the voting stock in the foreign corporation, the computation of the foreign tax credit may be reduced to the following formula: [22]

$$\frac{\text{Amount of dividend}}{\text{Accumulated profits before foreign income tax}} \times \text{Foreign income taxes levied on accumulated profits} = \frac{80}{100} \times 20 = 16$$

Computing the United States corporate tax with respect to this dividend, we find that the United States tax before the foreign tax credit would be 41.60 (52 percent of 80). Deducting from this figure the indirect credit (16), the net United States tax payable is 25.60, the total taxes paid to the United States and the foreign government with respect to the 100 profit are 45.60, and the over-all effective tax rate is 45.60 percent. This illustration points up a highly important fact for the United States taxpayer—that the method of computation of the indirect foreign tax credit often results in an over-all tax burden of less than 52 percent on foreign earnings received as dividends. The corporate taxpayer first receives in effect a deduction of 20 because his United States tax is computed not on

[22] This formula is a simplification of the formulas contained in paragraph 1.902–1 (e) of the United States Income Tax Regulations.

the full accumulated profits out of which the dividend is paid, namely 100, but rather is computed on the basis of the after-tax accumulated profits of the foreign corporation, namely 80. The indirect credit received by the corporate taxpayer is nonetheless based on the full amount of foreign tax with respect to the entire accumulated profits of 100.

This tax saving is maximized when the foreign tax on corporate income is exactly half the United States rate, namely, 26 percent. If the foreign tax rate is at this optimum figure, the ultimate tax burden on dividends received by the United States corporate taxpayer is only 45.24 percent. The advantage remains very substantial as long as the foreign tax rate is within approximately 10 percentage points either way of 26 percent and it gradually disappears as the foreign tax rate approaches 0 percent, on the one hand, or 52 percent on the other.

The indirect tax credit is available to a United States corporate stockholder owning 10 percent of the voting stock of a foreign corporation not only with respect to taxes paid directly by that foreign corporation, but also with respect to taxes paid by a 50 percent-owned subsidiary of the foreign corporation since such taxes are deemed to have been paid by the foreign corporation on dividends received by it from the subsidiary.[23] By virtue of this double application of the indirect credit computation just described, the over-all tax burden imposed on accumulated earnings of such a subsidiary which are paid out as dividends to the foreign corporation and then in turn to the United States corporate stockholder can be reduced to approximately 41 percent.[24]

The significance of the tax savings which can be achieved through the operation of the indirect foreign tax credit is apparent, and it is particularly important where the United States participant wants to maximize the after-tax income that is ultimately realized by the United States corporation upon repatriation of the foreign earnings. In order to receive the benefits which result from the computation of the United States indirect foreign tax credit, the United States

[23] I.R.C., Section 902 (b).

[24] See Statement of Professor Stanley S. Surrey, *Hearings Before the House Ways and Means Committee on H.R. 5*, 86th Congress, 1st Session (1959), p. 537.

participant must obtain at least 10 percent of the voting equity if its investment is directly in the operating enterprise, and if a base company is utilized, that base company must own at least 50 percent of the voting equity of the operating enterprise.

The tax reductions which result from the computation of the indirect foreign tax credit are, along with the 14-point tax reduction granted to the Western Hemisphere Trade Corporation,[25] open to criticism on the ground that they constitute unwarranted tax subsidies to United States corporations investing abroad. Those supporting the enactment of tax incentives by Congress to encourage foreign investment are understandably reluctant to see the preferential tax rate eliminated, even though they are often willing to admit that the preference resulted from legislative carelessness rather than design and that it lacks any rational basis. If other tax devices could be adopted to encourage foreign investment without distorting our tax system with preferential tax rates for foreign-source dividends, there would seem to remain little in the way of justification for retaining the present anomalous mode of computing the indirect credit.[26]

There is another aspect of the foreign tax credit which is of particular significance in regard to joint ventures in less developed countries, many of which, as pointed out above, have enacted tax incentives to encourage foreign investment. If and when profits are remitted as dividends from a foreign corporation to a United States shareholder, the effect of the United States foreign tax credit is to nullify most tax incentives in the form of reductions in, or exemptions from, the normally applicable income taxes. The United States foreign tax credit tends to penalize capital-importing countries which enact tax incentives to foreign investment: When foreign profits are remitted to the United States investor, it results in the

[25] I.R.C., Sections 921 and 922.

[26] One of the original provisions of H.R. 5, often referred to as the "Boggs Bill," an act "to amend the Internal Revenue Code of 1954 to encourage private investment abroad," would have revised the method by which the indirect credit is computed so as to eliminate the possibility of realizing an over-all tax rate of less than 52 percent on dividends received by a United States corporate stockholder from a foreign corporation. This provision was eliminated by the House Ways and Means Committee before reporting the bill to the House. See Commerce Clearing House, *Federal Tax Reporter*, Vol. VI, paragraph 6332.

payment of the increment by which foreign taxes are reduced to the United States government rather than to the government of the capital-importing country—with no tax saving to the United States investor. Thus, if a capital-importing country enacts an investment incentive statute under which the normal corporate income tax rate of 40 percent is reduced to 20 percent, the effect of the foreign tax credit is that the 20 cents on the dollar which represent the foreign tax reduction must be paid to the United States Treasury. In order to view this problem in proper perspective, it is important to emphasize two points: 1) this effect of the tax credit is encountered only if and when profits of the foreign corporation are remitted to a United States shareholder. As long as profits are retained abroad and devoted to the expansion of the enterprise, the full benefit of tax concessions is obtained. 2) In the great majority of cases the earnings of a foreign enterprise are retained and reinvested during the early years of operation, the very years in which such tax concessions are usually applicable.

TAX SPARING

In an effort to eliminate the problem of the nullifying of tax incentives adopted in capital-importing countries by the United States foreign tax credit, considerable support has developed in recent years for the concept of "tax sparing." Under the tax-sparing concept, the tax credit available against United States taxes for foreign taxes paid or deemed to have been paid to a foreign government would be computed as if the foreign taxes had been imposed at the normally applicable rates, notwithstanding that in actuality such taxes were either reduced or eliminated under an investment incentive program.

The first attempt to adopt the principle of tax sparing was contained in the double taxation treaty between Pakistan and the United States, signed July 1, 1957. The report of the Department of State which accompanied the submission of this treaty to the President stated in part:

> Pakistan tax law, in order to attract capital and encourage investment for the development of Pakistan's economy and natural resources, offers an incentive for establishment of approved new enterprises. . . . More spe-

cifically, . . . a business qualifying as a new enterprise may obtain tax exemption for a 5-year period on profits up to 5 percent of invested capital, and dividends paid from such profits may be tax exempt. At present an American corporation qualifying for such treatment under Pakistan law may find that United States taxes will be increased and thus offset the effects of the Pakistan tax law. The concession by Pakistan, therefore, is no special attraction to the United States investor. Under article XV(1) of the proposed convention this situation would be remedied within limits and on certain conditions by treating, as though paid for foreign-tax-credit purposes, the amount of income tax and supertax by which the American taxpayer's Pakistan tax is reduced.[27]

Although the Senate's advice and consent to the ratification of the Pakistan Treaty included a reservation to the second sentence of Article XV(1) which contains the tax-sparing feature, this reservation was based on the fact that the Pakistan tax incentive law had expired subsequent to the signing of the convention but prior to action by the Senate and did not reflect any decision by the Senate on the tax-sparing principle.

More recently, the tax-sparing principle has been adopted with respect to the tax incentives of India, in Article XII of the Double Taxation Treaty between India and the United States. The treaty is awaiting action by the United States Senate. It has been reported that double taxation treaties with tax-sparing provisions are in an advanced state of negotiation with six countries in Latin America, the Middle East, and Asia and that preliminary negotiations on similar treaties have been held with four other countries in Latin America and Asia.[28] A tax-sparing provision relating to certain Indian tax incentives to investment is contained in Article XI(3) of the

[27] Commerce Clearing House, *Tax Treaties*, p. 6215.

[28] See Statement of David A. Lindsay, Assistant to the Secretary of the Treasury, *Hearings Before the House Ways and Means Committee on H.R. 5*, 86th Cong., 1st Sess. (1959), p. 41; and *Business International* (December 4, 1959), p. 3. It is noteworthy that Section 6 of H.R. 5 in its original form contained a tax-sparing feature. During public hearings on H.R. 5 by the House Committee on Ways and Means, officials of the Department of State and the Department of the Treasury indicated support for the tax-sparing principle, but they urged that the committee amend the bill to limit the allowance of a credit to specified waivers of tax by a foreign country which are covered by an Executive Agreement on a selective basis. They also indicated that such agreements should be limited to "less developed" countries, including those in Latin America, Asia, the Middle East, and Africa. The Ways and Means Committee eliminated Section 6 before reporting the bill to the House. See C.C.H., *Federal Tax Reporter*, Vol. VI (1960), paragraph 6332.

Double Taxation Treaty between India and Japan, signed January 5, 1960.

Tax sparing has, however, been severely criticized. Professor Surrey, for example, has stated:

> The proposal for tax sparing treaties, granting a foreign tax credit for taxes not paid to foreign countries, is . . . unsound. It involves a discrimination between the investor at home and the investor abroad, since the tax not paid to the foreign country becomes, when a credit is given for its amount, equally a tax not paid to the United States and hence a reduction in the U.S. tax. In addition, it involves bizarre discriminations among U.S. investors abroad, for it favors investors in one foreign country as against another foreign country depending not on the need for investment in one or the other country nor on the level of tax rates in the foreign countries but whether or not a country has adopted a tax concession law containing a particular form of concession. . . . Moreover, tax sparing by stressing foreign tax concessions and lower rates places a serious obstacle in the way of the reform of foreign fiscal systems. Such reform is needed in underdeveloped countries so that they can both raise revenues commensurate with their needs and also provide the stable tax system required to promote capital formation and investment. Since tax sparing works in just the opposite direction, by favoring the unstable system and revenue reduction, it is contrary both to the needs of underdeveloped countries and to our objectives in assisting those countries.[29]

While there is much in what Professor Surrey says about the inconsistency between special tax concessions and rational tax administration, the fact remains that a large number of countries have adopted special concessions involving elimination or reduction of income taxes for a limited period with respect to certain foreign investments. They are apparently satisfied that such concessions constitute an effective investment incentive and will have a salutary effect on the tax base in the long run. This being so, a persuasive argument can be made that the adoption of steps by the United States government to encourage United States private investment abroad should include some means of preventing the cancellation of foreign tax concessions by the United States foreign tax credit. But even if this is accepted as a legitimate objective, it does not follow that tax sparing is the most desirable means to its realization.

A deferral of tax for a United States, rather than a foreign, base

[29] Surrey, *Hearings*, p. 543.

company may be preferable to tax sparing. The utilization of a United States base company would parallel the pragmatic approach now being adopted by a great many companies which use foreign base companies, but would avoid the discrimination among United States investors. This discrimination is inherent in the tax-sparing proposal and results from the fact that the foreign tax credit applies only to foreign taxes on income and, accordingly, affords no relief with respect to other tax concessions which relate to taxes not based on income.

BASE COMPANY OPERATION

The United States corporation contemplating a joint venture abroad will generally consider having its equity participation owned not directly but by a wholly-owned base company incorporated in a "tax haven" or "profit sanctuary" country such as Switzerland, Luxembourg, Panama, the Bahamas, or Liberia. In these countries corporate income and accumulated profits are subject to little or no taxation; free currency convertibility and political and economic stability prevails.[30] The income received by such a company is not subject to United States tax unless and until it is remitted to the United States parent company.

Thus, the profits of a joint venture may be drawn down as dividends to a base company and accumulated there free of the danger of political instability, currency depreciation or devaluation, and future exchange controls in the country in which the joint venture is carrying on its operations, and free of United States income taxes and penalty taxes on accumulated earnings.[31] Base company operation also permits the transfer of earnings from one foreign subsidiary to another, free of United States income tax. In the absence of an intermediate base company, such a transfer would be open to treatment as a taxable dividend to the United States parent corporation, followed by a capital contribution by the United States corporation to the second foreign subsidiary.

The use of a base company would be a particular advantage in

[30] For a thorough analysis of the tax and non-tax factors bearing on base company operations, see W. J. Gibbons, *Tax Factors in Basing International Business Abroad*, Harvard Law School, 1957.

[31] I.R.C., Sections 531–37.

the case of a joint venture in country x involving, on the one hand, a United States corporation whose primary objective is maximizing the accumulation of funds outside country x for additional investment in other countries, and, on the other hand, parties in country x whose primary objective is the realization of immediate income. Through the use of a base company, dividends could be paid to the local participants (thus enabling them to obtain immediate income), while the United States participant would not have his income reduced by United States corporate taxes since it would be paid as dividends to the base company and accumulated there.

If the United States corporation is to receive income from a joint venture in the form of dividends, the interposition of a base company will result in the realization of a larger after-tax profit by the base company than would be realized by the United States corporation in all cases in which the taxes imposed in the capital-importing country on the income of the joint venture distributed as dividends are significantly lower than the United States corporate tax rates. If the United States participant wishes to accumulate profits outside the capital-importing country, the existence of income-tax concessions in the capital-importing country creates a special pressure toward having the United States corporate participant own its share of the enterprise equity through a wholly-owned foreign base company. If the United States investor owns stock in the joint venture directly, the computation of the United States foreign tax credit will cancel the effect of the tax incentives when the foreign earnings are remitted to the United States.

Furthermore, it is often possible to mix base company income which is subject to relatively high taxes in the source country, with other income which is subject to lower or no taxes at the source. The result is that the over-all foreign tax burden on the income mixture received by the base company produces the maximum advantage in the computation of the United States foreign tax credit, when profits are remitted from the base company to its United States parent.

Until recently, the so-called per-country limitation on the United States foreign tax credit created an additional incentive toward the utilization of a foreign base company. Its effect was to prevent the taking of any greater credit for foreign taxes than that portion of the United States tax before credit attributable to the taxpayer's income from a particular foreign country.[32] Thus, if a United States corporation directly owned stock in one joint venture in country X where the over-all tax rate was 60 percent, and in another joint venture in country Y where the tax rate was 40 percent, it could not, because of the per-country limitation on the foreign tax credit, take any credit for the country X tax in excess of 52 percent. As a result of a ruling by the Internal Revenue Service that all income taxes paid by a foreign base company's subsidiaries are deemed to have been paid by the base company itself,[33] the utilization of a base company in which the dividends can be mixed and the taxes averaged enables the United States corporation to avoid the restrictive effect of the per-country limitation. The averaging of foreign taxes can also be effected when dividends from a high tax country are mixed in a base company with royalties under license agreements, or fees under technical assistance agreements from the same country, which are subject to low taxes or are free of tax in the source country. The importance of the restrictive factor represented by the per-country limitation in the planning of foreign operations has, however, been greatly reduced by the recent passage of H.R. 10087 which amends Section 904 of the Internal Revenue Code to permit taxpayers to elect an "over-all" rather than a "per-country" limitation on the foreign tax credit.[34]

[32] The per-country limitation, as set forth in I.R.C., section 904a)1), is expressed in the following formula:

$$\frac{\text{Taxable Income from Foreign Country Concerned}}{\text{Total Taxable Income}} \times \begin{matrix}\text{Total United States Tax}\\ \text{before Credit}\end{matrix} = \begin{matrix}\text{Maximum Foreign}\\ \text{Tax Credit}\end{matrix}$$

[33] "Income Tax 4089," in *Cumulative Bulletin,* II (1952), 142, 144. This ruling is now embodied in paragraph 1.902-1(c) of the United States Income Tax Regulations.

[34] The "over-all" differs from the "per-country" limitation in that it applies to the amount of taxes paid to all foreign countries taken together, and allows as a credit against the United States income tax the same proportion of the United States tax (before the credit) which taxable income from sources outside the United States is of the total taxable income of the taxpayer. The taxpayer may make the initial shift from the per-country to the over-all limitation at any time, but thereafter can change from the over-all to the per-country limitation, or vice versa, only with the consent of the Treasury Department.

There are often strong tax motivations toward using a base company for the licensor or supplier of technical or managerial services to a joint venture. These motivations derive from the fact that royalties and fees are commonly subject to taxation in the capital-importing country at rates very much lower than the rates applicable to profits distributed as dividends. Consequently, if a given amount can be drawn down from a joint venture in the form of royalty or fee paid to a base company in a country where no tax will be imposed, a much higher after-tax profit will be realized by the base company than if the same amount were drawn down as dividend. The after-tax profit of the base company will also in this case be much larger than would be realized by the United States corporation if the same amount were paid to it as dividend or royalty. The accumulation of royalties or fees in a base company is obviously attractive to a United States corporation desiring to maximize its immediate after-tax profit for reinvestment abroad. When this objective is present, the United States corporation will often attempt, in joint venture negotiations, to bargain not only for an equity participation but also for a licensing or technical assistance arrangement under which its base company will be paid royalties or fees.

Considerable support has developed in the United States for the enactment of tax legislation which would enable an investor to obtain many, if not all, of the advantages afforded by a foreign base company through a United States, rather than a foreign, corporation. The legislative proposal on which recent attention was particularly focused was H.R. 5 or, as it was more commonly designated, the "Boggs Bill." The key feature of this proposed legislation, as originally introduced in the House of Representatives, was its provision for the qualification as a "foreign business corporation" of United States corporations which receive certain types of foreign-source income including dividends, interest, and royalties, and which fulfill certain other requirements. Under the proposed legislation, a corporation qualifying and electing to be taxed as a foreign business corporation, would enjoy the highly important advantage, now afforded by the foreign base company, of having United States tax on its foreign-source income deferred until such income was distributed to its stockholders. Hence, foreign profits could be accumulated by the foreign business corporation for reinvestment abroad, free of United States income and accumulated earnings taxes and such corporations would gain the benefit of the United States double taxation treaties which are far more numerous than those to which any foreign tax-haven country is presently a party.

The foreign-business-corporation concept provided for in the original version of the Boggs Bill held considerable promise of being a highly effective incentive to foreign investment. Once the deferral principle is accepted—and it has been a feature of United States tax law since its inception—it becomes difficult to defend the present situation under which investors must base their international business in a foreign tax-haven country in order to obtain the full advantages of deferring United States taxes until foreign profits are remitted to the United States stockholders. In addition to the other advantages inherent in foreign base company operations, the adoption of the foreign-business-corporation device would allow the profits of foreign investment to accumulate for reinvestment abroad in a United States corporation free of the dangers of political instability and future exchange controls which are less likely to arise in the United States than in tax-haven countries. At the same time, since the foreign business corporation would involve only the deferral of United States taxes on foreign income, it would not entail further distortion of our tax system with special rate preferences.

The adoption of the foreign business corporation would also meet in part the problem at which the tax-sparing proposal is aimed, for as long as profits from a foreign investment were accumulated in a foreign business corporation, the United States foreign tax credit would not cancel the benefits of foreign tax reductions. Deferral of United States tax through a foreign business corporation not only affords an effective and adequate solution to the problem caused by the interaction of foreign tax concessions and the United States foreign tax credit, but it also affords a solution which is preferable to the adoption of tax sparing and all the discrimination and anomalies there involved.

The Boggs Bill, passed by the House of Representatives on May

18, 1960, in a form which differed fundamentally from the original version of the bill, was not acted on by the Senate. Under the form of the bill passed by the House, a foreign business corporation was defined restrictively to include only corporations which derive 90 percent or more of their gross income from sources within "less developed countries"; in addition, deferral of United States taxes applied only to income of foreign business corporations invested in "less developed countries." "Less developed countries" were defined as any foreign countries (outside the Sino-Soviet Bloc) designated as such by the President, but excluding Austria, Belgium, Canada, Denmark, France, Federal Republic of Germany, Italy, Japan, Luxembourg, Monaco, the Netherlands, Norway, Portugal, Sweden, Switzerland, and the United Kingdom. The aforementioned restrictions on the foreign business corporation were supported by the Treasury [35] primarily because of a fear of substantial immediate revenue losses if the foreign-business-corporation concept were adopted without geographical limitation.[36]

Few would quarrel with the encouragement of United States private investment in the less developed countries of the free world to help these countries develop economically. But, it is by no means clear that the Boggs Bill as passed by the house would be an effective means to this end. It is a basic fact that most investment occurs, at least at the outset, in industrially developed countries where the skills, the materials, and the market are available for manufactured products. Once substantial profits have been realized from such investments, the utilization of profits in relatively underdeveloped countries becomes more probable. It is also generally true that the United States corporate investor prefers to centralize his foreign operations to the greatest possible extent. Since the foreign business corporation, as limited in the House version of the Boggs Bill, would be useless for much investment abroad and since centralization is de-

[35] Report of the Secretary of the Treasury on H.R. 5, *Hearings Before the House Ways and Means Committee on H.R. 5*, 86th Cong., 1st Sess. (1959), p. 50.

[36] "Although recognizing the merits of section 2 of H.R. 5, the Treasury Department nevertheless is compelled to oppose unlimited deferral at this time because of the substantial revenue losses involved in extending the deferral provisions to include investments in and exports to all regions of the world by American firms" (*ibid*).

sirable, the foreign base company would probably continue to be used for investments in "less" as well as "more" developed countries of the world.

A basic policy decision which must be reached before the problem of tax incentives can be dealt with effectively is whether it is desired to encourage foreign investment *generally* or only in the less developed countries of the free world. If general encouragement is the objective, and if tax law provisions are deemed a suitable incentive device, it would appear desirable to adopt the foreign-business-corporation concept with no geographical limitations. Conversely, if it is determined that only investment in less developed countries is a proper subject for legislative incentives, then adopting the foreign business corporation in broad form would not be effective since it lacks any means of funneling investment. More useful would be a provision under which the foreign business corporation could earn its income in industrially developed countries of the free world, but could obtain the applicable tax advantages only if that income were reinvested in the less developed countries. Such a device would be ineffective, however, as long as it remained possible for an investor to use the base company in a foreign tax haven. Since the foreign base company would afford deferral of United States taxes with no geographical limitations, it would obviously be preferred by investors in most cases. Thus, in order to make the foreign business corporation an effective instrument to channel investment into less developed countries of the world, complementary legislation will have to be adopted to end the tax advantages now afforded by the base company organized in a foreign tax haven.

DOUBLE TAXATION TREATIES

There have been numerous bilateral international treaties to eliminate or mitigate double taxation, but most of them are between industrially developed countries—so that if a joint venture in an underdeveloped area is contemplated, double taxation treaties may not be significant.

The United States corporate participant in a joint venture abroad may be concerned with three double taxation treaties: 1) the treaty between the United States and the capital-importing country concerned; 2) the treaty between the capital-importing country and the country in which a base company is incorporated; and 3) the treaty between the base-company country and the United States.

These treaties can be important to the tax planning of a joint venture because they eliminate or reduce the income taxes otherwise withheld at the source on dividends, interest, and royalties, fees for technical assistance, and similar commercial payments. In addition, they generally define the degree of commercial activity that is required to subject a foreign entity to taxation. If the tax-sparing principle becomes a regular feature of United States double taxation treaties, the treaties will acquire a special importance for the investor.

FORM OF BUSINESS ORGANIZATION

Once the United States corporate investor has decided in what country to establish the joint venture and whether to utilize a base company and, if so, where to establish it, the problem of organizational structure remains. We are assuming the enterprise will be owned partly by the United States corporation and partly by local interests.

The most common broad alternatives would be: 1) the organization of a jointly-owned base company in a tax haven outside the country in which the actual business operations will be conducted, with such operations being carried on by a branch of the base company, and 2) the organization of a joint enterprise in the country where operations are to be conducted in one of the forms of business organization available with the equity of the United States investor owned directly or by a wholly-owned foreign base company. Of these broad alternatives the latter, which offers many variations, is far more often encountered in practice. In addition, features such as licensing arrangements, technical assistance agreements, and management contracts will often form a part of the over-all organization.

The organization of a joint venture in country X (a tax haven), to operate through a branch in country Y, may result in the advantages to the United States partner usually associated with base company operation. The country Y interests participating in the enterprise may have similar reasons for seeking to accumulate their profits in a base company.

There are other tax factors which bear directly on the desirability of branch operation.[37] For example, in Brazil, the net income of a branch is taxed at the normal corporate rates and the full amount credited to the head office is taxed again as income of a non-resident (whether or not it is actually remitted), subject only to a narrow exclusion for earnings devoted to certain reinvestment in plant.[38] In Belgium a branch with large profits may incur a smaller tax burden than a Belgian subsidiary corporation with the same profit since profits distributed by the branch are subject to a flat tax rate of 40 percent, whereas profits distributed by a Belgian company are subject to graduated tax rates up to 45.3 percent.[39]

In some cases a local company will have to be organized for non-tax reasons. This will be true where certain business activities (mining is a common example) can be carried on only by a locally organized enterprise. Non-tax considerations may also determine the form of business organization to be used.[40]

The tax burdens imposed in the capital-importing country may, of course, be an important factor in the ultimate choice. But for the United States corporate investor, his own country's tax considerations are likely to be even more important. In some cases uncertainty is created because the form of organization may not fit clearly into one or another of the classifications which will determine tax consequences in the United States.

For example, the tax savings which can be realized through the computation of the indirect foreign tax credit will influence the United States investor. Such savings, however, apply only to dividends paid by a foreign "corporation" to a United States corporate stockholder. The question arises as to which of the civil law forms of business organization will be treated as a "corporation." Cases have indicated that both the civil law corporation and limited liability company will qualify.[41] It is highly doubtful whether a

[37] See Friedmann and Pugh, "Comparative Analysis," in *Legal Aspects*, p. 754.
[38] Nattier, "Brazil," in *ibid.*, p. 78. [39] Blondeel, "Belgium," in *ibid.*, p. 59.
[40] See p. 212 ff. in this book, and footnote 38 in this chapter.
[41] See Abbott Laboratories International Co., 160 F. Supp. 321 (E.C. Ill. 1958).

limited partnership or even a limited partnership with shares would be treated as a "corporation." No doubt this is one of the factors responsible for the United States corporate investor's favoring the corporation and the limited liability company over other forms of business organization. Another factor is that deferral of taxes until foreign profits are remitted to the United States applies only to the profits of a foreign "corporation."

If the joint venture is in the extractive sector, quite contrary tax considerations are present. The Internal Revenue Code offers very substantial advantages to United States taxpayers engaged in the exploration, development, and exploitation of mineral resources anywhere in the world. These advantages include the right to deduct currently exploration and development expenditures which would otherwise be subject to capitalization,[42] and the right to deduct currently intangible drilling and development costs (in the case of oil and gas wells),[43] and the right to percentage depletion.[44] These benefits are available only to United States taxpayers, and they are lost if the investor participates with foreign interests in an enterprise organized in a form which is recognized as a separate entity for United States tax purposes. Thus, if the extractive joint venture is organized as a local corporation or limited liability company (or if a base company is utilized), these benefits will be lost.[45] On the other hand, if the enterprise is organized in a form, such as a local partnership or a contractual joint venture, which is not recognized as a separate taxable entity, the United States corporate investor will be able to enjoy these tax benefits.

The desire for these benefits may have an important effect not only on which form but also on the time that a particular form of local business organization is adopted. In certain mineral operations, a local contractual joint venture may be used during the exploration and development stage (so that expenses incidental thereto may be deducted currently), after which the enterprise will be incorporated.

[42] I.R.C., Sections 615 and 616.

[43] I.R.C., Section 263(c).

[44] I.R.C., Section 613.

[45] In the case of *William F. Buckley*, 22 T.C. 1312 (1954), *aff'd* 231 F.2d 204 (2d Cir. 1956), it was held that the holders of certificates of ownership in an enterprise formed under the laws of Venezuela as a *compañía anónima* were not entitled to depletion allowances in respect to foreign mineral properties owned by the *compañía anónima*.

Similarly, the expectation of losses in the early years may dictate operation through a local partnership or contractual joint venture so that losses may be offset against the current income of the United States investor. This factor will, of course, tend to lose importance in capital-importing countries which offer liberal loss carry-overs.

Antitrust Law

As our previous analysis has shown, there is a definite shift of foreign capital investment from the formerly prevailing pattern of branches or wholly-owned subsidiaries of foreign corporations to various forms of equity participation. Increasingly, as a result of local legislation or administrative pressures or, in some instances, of long-term policy considerations, American and other foreign investors will choose or will be compelled to hold a strong minority interest rather than a majority share. It is therefore a matter of considerable concern that the Sherman Act, as currently interpreted, may, in an already extremely difficult international situation, impede the very form of American enterprise abroad that is most acceptable to a majority of the less developed countries and is most likely to destroy the real or imagined fear of "imperialist" foreign capital domination in the developing economies. This form is the joint venture.

Of the industrially developed countries, only Canada and the United States have had antitrust legislation other than of very recent origin. It is significant that these laws were enacted at times when, in the United States and Canada, foreign trade and investment abroad were subordinate in significance and preoccupation to the expansion of domestic markets and the threatening monopolization of vital domestic utilities and industries. In contrast, the restrictive trade practices laws that have been passed in recent years, as in the United Kingdom and West Germany, display an awareness of the necessity of separating foreign trade and foreign investment from domestic trade. The British Act of 1956 specifically exempts from the range of potentially illegal restrictive agreements "the production of goods, or the application of any process of manufacture to goods, outside the United Kingdom." The German Act of 1957 exempts contracts and resolutions "designed to secure and promote exports, insofar as they are limited to the regulation of competition in markets outside the area of application of this law." Permission may be granted by the cartel authority to contracts that legitimately fall within this exception even when they affect conditions of competition within Germany "insofar as such regulation is necessary in order to ensure the desired regulation of competition in the markets outside of the area of application of this law." Also, the antitrust provisions of the European Economic Community [46] apply only to agreements and actions restrictive of free trade within the area of the community. These provisions will not become operative until the relevant regulations have been issued by the community.

Quite apart from the text of these laws, it can be stated with confidence that the whole tradition and outlook of European legislators, courts, and administrative authorities would militate strongly against an imputation of illegality to either the transformation of an existing foreign enterprise into a joint venture, or to the starting of a new one designed to promote the foreign production of German, French, or British machinery or goods, unless such a venture were coupled with extraneous and specifically restrictive agreements affecting internal trade.[47]

It may well be that the situation is not very different for those subject to United States law, but they have to consider the potential applicability of sections 1 and 2 of the Sherman Act to joint ventures abroad.

The American decisions dealing with joint international business ventures are very few and their import is doubtful. Mainly they are concerned with joint ventures entered into either by several American firms or by major American and European firms who dominate between them a certain field of industry rather than with the type of joint ventures here examined.

In the *I.C.I.* case,[48] an American and a British manufacturer, both

[46] Treaty Establishing the European Economic Community (1957), Arts. 85, 86.

[47] Even this would seem to be unconditionally permissible under the section of the British Restrictive Trade Practices Act.

[48] United States v. Imperial Chem. Indus., Ltd., 100 F. Supp. 504 (S.D.N.Y. 1951).

giants in the chemical field, had formed a jointly-owned company in Canada to which they contributed capital and patents and processes. This combination in itself was accepted as legal "with a dubious nod." [49] What made the venture illegal, however, was the agreement between du Pont and I.C.I. designed to eliminate existing, or to preclude potential competition in Canada. A similar situation led to a similar result in the *National Lead* case.[50] Price fixing or a division of territories between competing American manufacturers in the country of the joint enterprise, would certainly be illegal unless there were extenuating circumstances. Statutory control of maximum or minimum prices, or both, as occurs frequently in countries faced with economic shortages, would be such a circumstance, for it would certainly be absurd to hold responses to statutory requirements illegal. Indeed there could hardly be any question of "conspiracy" when there is no voluntary agreement.

Again, in the *Timken* case,[51] American Timken owned a controlling interest in its former British competitor, British Timken, and together they acquired all of the stock in a French company manufacturing the same product. The reason for invalidating the arrangements was "the explicit agreement governing the partners, not their partnership, which formed the basis of liability." [52] In *Minnesota Mining*,[53] four-fifths of the American manufacturers in the abrasives industry had formed, through a holding company, joint manufacturing subsidiaries in Canada, Britain, and West Germany, and had abstained from exporting in competition with these foreign manufacturing companies. Once more the elimination of competition between the American companies, through the implied agreement to abstain from any business other than that done through the jointly owned foreign factories, impugned the arrangement.[54]

[49] *Ibid.*, p. 557.

[50] United States v. National Lead Co., 63 F. Supp. 513 (S.D.N.Y. 1945), *aff'd*, 332 U.S. 319 (1947).

[51] United States v. Timken Roller Bearing Co., 83 F. Supp. 284 (N.D. Ohio 1949), *modified*, 341 U.S. 593 (1951).

[52] Kingman Brewster, *Antitrust and American Business Abroad*, McGraw-Hill (1958), p. 211.

[53] United States v. Minnesota Mining & Mfg. Co., 92 F. Supp. 947 (D. Mass. 1950).

[54] Wilbur L. Fugate, *Foreign Commerce and the Antitrust Laws*, Little, Brown & Co. (1958), p. 263.

Moreover, in this case, the agreement joined together virtually an entire American industry, a situation that will not often occur in foreign investment.

These few cases in which foreign joint ventures of American manufacturers were held partly or wholly illegal are certainly remote from the actual or potential cases of joint international business ventures here considered. And even these few decisions have not gone unchallenged. The strong dissenting judgments of Justices Frankfurter and Jackson in *Timken* are very much concerned with the situation that will very frequently occur in the less developed countries. In Justice Frankfurter's words:

> When as a matter of cold fact the legal, financial, and government policies deny opportunities for exportation from this country and importation into it, arrangements that afford such opportunities to American enterprise may not fall under the ban of a fair construction of the Sherman Law because comparable arrangements regarding domestic commerce come within its condemnation.[55]

Similarly, Justice Jackson observed:

> In a world of tariffs, trade barriers, empire or domestic preferences, and various forms of parochialism from which we are by no means free, I think a rule that it is restraint of trade to enter a foreign market through a separate subsidiary of limited scope is virtually to foreclose foreign commerce of many kinds. It is one thing for competitors or a parent and its subsidiaries to divide the United States domestic market which is an economic and legal unit; it is another for an industry to recognize that foreign markets consist of many legal and economic units and to go after each through separate means. I think this decision will restrain more trade than it will make free.[56]

There is no reported decision dealing with a partnership arrangement entered into between an American firm, either singly, or in combination with another American or foreign firm, and public or private local capital in an economically less developed country. This is not an accident and it is not due to the predominantly recent origin of such joint venture arrangements. The major reason lies in their economic and commercial background. Whether joint international

[55] United States v. Timken Roller Bearing Co., 341 U.S. (1951), pp. 593, 605–6.

[56] *Ibid.*, pp. 607–8.

business ventures in less developed countries are transformations of a formerly wholly-owned branch or subsidiary of a Western enterprise [57] or are new ventures with local participation, they are often a response either to statutory requirements for majority or minority national participation, or to national economic and administrative policies which make the granting of import licenses, the allocation of foreign exchange, or other necessary conditions for the operations of a local enterprise dependent upon national capital participation. Increasingly, American investors now anticipate legal or moral compulsion and enter into joint ventures voluntarily. This trend is openly encouraged by government agencies, such as the Export-Import Bank and the Development Loan Fund. It hardly requires legal authority or precedent to demonstrate that, when the formation of a joint venture is the only alternative to the elimination of the American enterprise from business, manufacture, or trade in the country concerned, it should not, even by the most strained construction, be interpreted as a restrictive practice.

Generally, joint ventures are at least a partially successful response to the new nationalism, which seeks an increasing national control of manufacture and services. In support of their legality, it may be sufficient to refer to two American decisions that are strongly imbued with antitrust sentiments. In the *I.C.I.* opinion it was stated that:

> It is settled that joint manufacturing ventures, even in domestic markets, are not made unlawful *per se* by the Sherman Act, but become unlawful only if their purpose or their effect is to restrain trade or to monopolize. . . . It is also clear that absent this wrongful purpose or harmful effect there is nothing *per se* unlawful in the association or combination of a single American enterprise with a single local concern of a foreign country in a jointly owned manufacturing or commercial company to develop a foreign local market.[58]

And even in the most radically antitrust minded judicial opinion of recent years, Judge Wyzanski admitted that:

[57] The various Latin American operations of Pan American World Airways and public utilities enterprises in the Philippines provide examples of such transformations.

[58] United States v. Imperial Chem. Indus., Ltd., 100 F. Supp. 504, 557 (S.D.N.Y. 1951).

It is axiomatic that if over a sufficiently long period American enterprises, as a result of political or economic barriers, cannot export directly or indirectly from the United States to a particular foreign country at a profit, then any private action taken to secure or interfere solely with business in that area, whatever else it may do, does not restrain foreign commerce in that area in violation of the Sherman Act. For, the very hypothesis is that there is not and could not be any American foreign commerce in that area which could be restrained or monopolized.[59]

It would therefore seem that only in very exceptional situations might a joint venture in a less developed country acquire the taint of illegality under the United States antitrust laws, and it is hardly conceivable that it would ever do so, when, as in most cases, the venture is between a single American firm that holds the majority interest, and one or a group of public or private local participants.

A curious irony is inherent in the conspiracy concept of the Sherman Act, according to which only a combination of two or more independent legal entities can create an illegally restrictive agreement. The subsidiary of a single firm—even if economically it is an enterprise many times more powerful than a combination of a number of smaller manufacturers—does not by itself fall under the prohibition of section 1.[60] However, because in the situation in which the American firm has only a minority participation the joint venture is legally independent of the American participant, this arrangement is theoretically most vulnerable. Even in such cases, it would certainly have to be shown that the minority participation of the American firm had an injurious effect upon American business by excluding competition and thereby negatively affecting exports or imports. In the situations considered in this study this will hardly ever occur.

When several American firms combine with each other, or when

[59] United States v. Minnesota Mining & Mfg. Co., 92 F. Supp. 947, 958 (D. Mass. 1950).

[60] Despite certain dicta that might cast doubt on this assertion, see United States v. Timken Roller Bearing Co., 341 U.S. (1951), pp. 593, 598; Kiefer-Stewart Co. v. Joseph E. Seagram & Sons, Inc., 340 U.S. (1951), pp. 211, 215; "the government has not yet based a prosecution or fashioned a decree in foreign commerce solely on the basis of internal conspiracy between parent and majority-owned subsidiary," Brewster, *Antitrust*, p. 86. The situation in which the parent company and the foreign subsidiary both participate in international cartels might be different. Cf. *ibid.*, pp. 186–87.

one or several American firms combine with a British, German, French, or some other enterprise from a capital-exporting country to form a joint venture in a less developed country, United States antitrust laws could affect the American partner. The most vulnerable situation—far from hypothetical—arises when a legal or factual monopoly for production is enjoyed by the joint venture in an economically weak country. There are certainly many countries in Latin America, Asia, or Africa in which there is, at present, a profitable market for only one manufacturer of steel tubes, diesel trucks, or nylon stockings. Governments in these countries quite frequently not only tolerate but actually desire manufacture to be concentrated in one efficient unit, for they are unwilling to multiply such incidents of manufacture as licenses for import and allocation of foreign exchange. We could go further and imagine a situation in which a government wishes to replace the local manufacture of a multiplicity of more or less luxurious automobiles by a single mass produced product—a kind of "Volkswagen." Let us further assume that this government exerts strong pressure upon, for example, General Motors and Ford, to combine their local facilities and resources in a joint enterprise concentrated entirely on such an inexpensive mass produced car. If Ford and General Motors respond to this pressure as the price to be paid for continuing their business in this country, is United States antitrust law violated thereby? If we regard the dictum of Judge Wyzanski in *Minnesota Mining* [61] as more than a dictum, the answer would probably be "yes." The pooling of resources by Ford and General Motors would certainly constitute "a combination of dominant American manufacturers to establish joint factories for the sole purpose of serving the internal commerce of that [foreign] country." From this Judge Wyzanski deduced that

> it may therefore be subject to condemnation regardless of the reasonableness of the manufacturers' conduct in the foreign countries. . . . Joint

[61] United States v. Minnesota Mining & Mfg. Co., 92 F. Supp. 947 (D. Mass. 1950). Judge Wyzanski stated that "it may very well be that even though there is an economic or political barrier which entirely precludes American exports to a foreign country a combination of dominant American manufacturers to establish joint factories for the sole purpose of serving the internal commerce of that country is a *per se* violation of . . . the Sherman Act." *Ibid.*, p. 963.

foreign factories like joint domestic price fixing would be invalid *per se* because they eliminate or restrain competition in the American domestic market. That suppression of domestic competition is in each case the fundamental evil, and the good or evil nature of the immediate manifestations of the producers' joint action is a superficial consideration.[62]

It is more than doubtful that this reasoning would allow the defense that the combination of the manufacturers in the foreign country occurred in response to strong pressure from the local government as a clear alternative to the impossibility of doing any business at all. Judge Wyzanski's reasoning implies that the foreign advantages or necessities of joint ventures are totally and absolutely subordinate to the potential restriction of competition in the domestic market. Even if it were shown that the parties to the joint venture were continuing to compete everywhere else in the United States and abroad, this might not make any impression, for the mere fact of collaboration *somewhere* is said to have a debilitating effect on the zeal and methods of competition in the domestic market. There would be general agreement that if joint venturers accompany their joint arrangement with specific restrictive arrangements, there is some justification for the application of the Sherman Act. However, when the conclusion is deliberately stripped of such accessories, as the Wyzanski dictum is, it is surely untenable and objectionable as a matter of legal policy. As has been pointed out by Professor Brewster,[63] this dictum strayed from the issues then at bar. Yet, it has to be admitted that uncertainty about the reach of the legal prohibition in itself acts as a barrier to American participation in joint ventures abroad.

Quite often, the desire of a foreign government to concentrate manufacturing possibilities in one enterprise or a special consortium will not be formulated in laws or regulations but will be a matter of administrative policy, manipulated through the handling of import licenses, currency transfer regulations, tax arrangements, and the like. For the American investor, as for example an oil company or a group of oil companies, the resulting factual situation may be as dangerous as an open agreement, looked upon with suspicion by the Department of Justice.[64]

[62] *Ibid.* [63] Brewster, *Antitrust*, pp. 209–10.

[64] It is difficult to assess with any degree of statistical precision how many potential American investors abstain or withdraw from a joint venture abroad

It is urgently necessary to reassess and clarify the application of antitrust legislation to foreign investment, and in particular to joint ventures, in the light of contemporary international realities.

In an age in which intense nationalism and rising resentment against foreign economic domination is coupled with a desire for national economic development, the conditions that compel to an increasing degree the adaptation of foreign investors to the local situation and the demands of governments are totally different from those contemplated by the Sherman Act. As with the interpretation of the United States Constitution, the legal evaluation of the situation existing in 1960 in the light of formulas evolved more than half a century earlier would be bad law as well as bad policy. It is submitted that a clarification, rather than any significant change in the present law, is required. The state of the authorities does not command a condemnation of joint ventures in less developed countries, which, if undertaken in the United States, might be illegal. None of the authorities, as distinct from isolated dicta, condemns a joint venture abroad as such, unless it is coupled with specific restrictive features such as the elimination of factually possible competition, price fixing, or the division of territories. Several of the cases have specifically declared foreign joint ventures to be legal as such and, as in *Minnesota Mining*, admitted the relevancy of political or economic barriers to the problem of restraint of commerce.

The view that joint ventures, in the absence of specific restrictive agreements or practices, even if they carry the implication of a restriction of free competition in theory, are permissible is supported by the two most serious studies of the problem. Mr. Fugate, a member of the Department of Justice, suggests that "in considering the

---

because of possible antitrust implications, at times with the result that a European, Japanese, or Soviet enterprise steps in. Counsel for a number of important United States corporations, notably in the oil, chemical, air transport, and automobile industries, have repeatedly stressed the importance of these considerations. There is at least one recent case in which a major American manufacturer of basic chemicals sold out its minority interest in a prospering and developing joint enterprise with Indian industrial interests because the stock interest might at some time be found to be objectionable under the United States antitrust laws. This happened at a time when the Indian group was busily extending its joint ventures with a number of British and other European chemical companies.

legality of the operations of a joint company, the question should be asked whether the parents, through the company, are doing something which they may not legally do in its absence—for example, fixing prices or dividing markets." [65] Professor Brewster suggests that "the essential measure of United States commerce restraint would seem to be whether, but for the jointness, the exports would have been substantially different or greater." [66] Again, "the desire to present a common front to foreign governments, or, the converse, foreign governmental pressures for multifirm participation, may also dictate a joint vehicle." [67] Another test is whether, "but for the restraint, there would have been no commerce forthcoming from this facility." [68]

This approach accords with that of the report of the Attorney General's committee on the antitrust laws, which has suggested that the Sherman Act should apply "only to those arrangements between Americans alone, or in concert with foreign firms, which have such substantial anti-competitive effects on this country's 'trade or commerce . . . with foreign nations' as to constitute unreasonable restraints." [69]

A great deal might depend on the kind of commerce that is potentially affected by the joint venture arrangement. To expect an American investor to compete actively with its own subsidiary by exporting to the country of investment the very product that the joint venture is manufacturing would be an absurdity, even though this contingency seems to be included in the Wyzanski dictum. This would cut the ground from under the feet of the foreign venture. An agreement or understanding that would limit or exclude sales to the United States from the country of investment would be more objectionable and, therefore, application of the Sherman Act would be more acceptable.

It is important that American enterprises be as unobstructed as other Western enterprises in solving the difficult problem presented by the transformation of existing enterprises or the launching of new ones in economically less developed countries by an uncertainty

[65] Fugate, *Foreign Commerce*, p. 264. [66] Brewster, *Antitrust*, p. 216.
[67] *Ibid.*, p. 220. [68] *Ibid.*, p. 218.
[69] Att'y. Gen. Nat'l. Comm. Antitrust Rep. 76 (1955).

about possible antitrust effects that is neither warranted by existing precedent nor desirable as a matter of legal and economic policy. As joint international financing and risk-sharing enterprises between the Western powers develop, it will also become increasingly desirable that the antitrust policies and laws of the countries concerned should be broadly in accord. This is possible only on a "rule of reason" basis. In every case, the test should be whether the venture, on balance, promotes rather than hinders the legitimate economic interests of the country of jurisdiction, which here would be the United States.

A standard of this kind is, of course, subject to the criticism of uncertainty. What the American investor wants above all is reasonable assurance about the legality of a contemplated foreign venture. However, the present situation, with the paucity of relevant decisions and the sweep of a few dicta of doubtful validity, does not promote certainty either. It is, on the other hand, apt to deter American enterprises, especially some large ones sensitive to antitrust accusations, from engaging in foreign ventures that are desirable as a matter of both national and international policy.

As the problems are so much on the borderline between business and politics, and the number of cases that raise possible antitrust objections is rather small, it would seem advisable to obtain clarification through the use of diplomatic procedures at the negotiation stage rather than to take a chance, or to abstain as a matter of superabundant caution. In the Iranian Oil Agreement of 1954, a case in which the position of the Justice Department was made known prior to conclusion of the negotiations, the United States government indicated its approval of the agreements, which, in the words of a former legal adviser to the State Department, "might otherwise have been called into question under the antitrust law,"[70] by making known the opinion given to the President by the Attorney General that the proposed arrangements, other than marketing, distribution, further manufacture, and transportation, would not contravene the antitrust laws.[71] Mr. Becker has suggested that this

[70] L. E. Becker, *The Antitrust Law and Relations with Foreign Nations*, 40 Dep't State Bull. 272, 278 (1959).

[71] See *Hearings Before the Antitrust Subcommittee of the House Committee on the Judiciary*, 84th Cong., 1st Sess., pt. 2 (1955), p. 1559.

procedure should be used more often, and that the Department of State, which tends to take a more international view than the domestically-oriented Department of Justice, should act as an intermediary between foreign governments and the American authorities involved.[72] This could solve difficulties in the politically and diplomatically most important cases, but, generally, the Department of Justice prefers not to give opinions, and private firms might be reluctant to involve the government in transactions having slight, but possible, antitrust implication.

In view of the likelihood that joint ventures between Western capital-exporting countries in less developed areas will increase in the years to come, the approximation of equivalent antitrust standards between such countries as the United States, Canada, and the nations of Western Europe will become more and more important. The desirability of some measure of coordination, at least between the antitrust policies of the capital-exporting countries, is further emphasized by the incidents that have, in recent years, arisen from certain judicial attempts to make decrees in United States antitrust suits with international implications effective abroad.[73]

It may be that the North Atlantic Treaty Organization [74] or another essentially Western international organization could be the framework for a formulation of common antitrust standards. Eventually, a general international antitrust machinery, as was envisaged in the abortive International Trade Organization that was designed to form part of the Havana Charter, might materialize, possibly

[72] Becker, *The Antitrust Law*, pp. 276–77.

[73] The best known of these is the *I.C.I.* case, United States v. Imperial Chem. Indus., Ltd., 105 F. Supp. 215 (S.D.N.Y. 1952), in which the final decree ordered Imperial Chemical Industries in Britain to reassign to du Pont the British nylon patents under which another British firm had been granted an exclusive licence by I.C.I. This led to a polite but firm rebuke by the English Court of Appeal, see British Nylon Spinners, Ltd. v. Imperial Chem. Indus., Ltd., [1953] 1 Chapter 19 (1952), as an improper invasion of foreign sovereignty. Other reactions have included Ontario and Swiss legislation prohibiting nationals from disclosing records in response to foreign court orders, and a protest from the Netherlands government about the decree proposed by the Attorney General in United States v. General Elec. Co., 115 F. Supp. 835 (D.N.J. 1953). See Becker, *The Antitrust Law*, p. 274.

[74] Article 2 of the treaty states that the parties "will seek to eliminate conflict in their international economic policies and will encourage collaboration between any or all of them." But this has hitherto remained a dead letter.

under United Nations auspices. Here, however, as in other fields of international organization, it would be futile to aim at general international conventions before there is a reasonable measure of agreement on standards and practices. In a few years' time, for example, the trends in the application of recent antitrust legislation in Britain, France, Germany, Italy, the Netherlands, Norway, and Sweden may be much clearer than they are at present. It would seem that joint coordinating committees, on official as well as private levels, between governments, bar associations, chambers of commerce, and universities could do a great deal to help in the development of common standards.

VIII. Some General Conclusions

IT WOULD BE tempting to conclude this rather detailed survey and analysis of joint international business ventures in many countries and types of industry by saying that no general conclusions can be drawn at all, that the variety of countries, situations, and conditions is too great to permit any generalizations.

Such a conclusion would be as unwarranted as oversimplified generalizations. The general assumption underlying this study was that the joint international business venture *might* constitute an important expression of changing relationships between the industrially developed and less developed countries. That hypothesis has been abundantly confirmed by our country surveys and case studies.

There is reason to believe that the very fact of placing this problem into the center of a comprehensive and comparative study has helped to articulate many problems as yet half conscious in the minds of the decision-makers in government and in industry. No amount of pragmatism or scepticism should obscure the plain fact that, in politics as in philosophy, in economics as in physics, significant ideas and aspirations dominate and symbolize certain times while others fade away. Politico-economic relations are dependent upon changing relations of nations and people as well as on changing conditions of production.

Joint ventures are not an invention of the postwar period. They existed before, although predominantly between industrially developed countries. But as a significant phenomenon of international business relations, the joint venture is overwhelmingly a postwar phenomenon, one of many attempts to bridge the gap between the vast material and technological superiority of the industrially developed nations and the urgent needs and aspirations of the less developed nations.

Most of the case studies in this volume deal with joint ventures launched in the last decade or even the last few years. Data have been presented to show, as far as is possible on the basis of still inadequate statistical material, the increase in joint venturing that appears to have taken place, and the apparently still increasing momentum of this transformation in international business enterprise.

The real difficulty is not that of deciding whether the joint international business venture is a significant phenomenon, but to articulate as precisely as possible the conditions under which it does and can contribute to a successful and harmonious relationship.

The Problem of Definition

In the introductory chapter, we defined the joint venture as comprising "any form of association which implies collaboration for more than a very transitory period." Such a deliberately wide definition emphasized the human and psychological rather than the legal aspects. It was in accordance with the principal objective of the work—to explore the problems and prospects of partnership, in the broadest sense, in business associations between the developed and the less developed countries. It is equally possible to define joint ventures more narrowly and emphasize the risk-sharing of joint venture capital.[1]

In our case studies and analysis, the emphasis has been overwhelmingly on joint ventures in the stricter sense, that is, on enterprises in

[1] Even in such a case questions might arise as to the minimum percentage that would qualify a participant as a "joint venturer." Cf. the rather arbitrary definition by the United States Department of Commerce of direct investments as "foreign enterprises in which American investors or parent companies have a controlling interest, consisting of an ownership of 25 per cent or more of the voting stock of foreign subsidiary companies, or unincorporated foreign branches" (United States Department of Commerce, *Factors Limiting U.S. Investment Abroad*, Part I [1954] p. 1). Our study has not chosen such a mechanical test, which often does not correspond to the actual degree of jointness in relations between partners.

which rights, liabilities and responsibilities are shared, without ignoring entirely the looser types of association. Legally, the former, closer type of association is expressed in the forms of company law as distinguished from contract law. The various partners form a lasting association—usually one with limited liability—in which minimum rights and responsibilities are defined by law (with considerable latitude for contractual variations) and by which they must to some degree share gains and losses. In the majority of cases, the link created by company law certainly represents a closer partnership than one established by contractual arrangements. Yet legal form should not overshadow psychological and political reality.

A good example of a contractual partnership is seen in the three Indian steel mill ventures. In the narrow sense these projects would not be joint ventures, but psychologically they are. The impact of these ventures on the Indian public, and on its attitude toward foreign aid and economic development probably surpasses the impact of many joint equity ventures. This is so not only because of the basic importance of steel in a country's economy; it is mainly due to the opportunity afforded the Indian people for experience with the technical methods, managerial principles, and human relations involved in the collaboration with three groups of foreign nationals. The selection of the supervising staff, the methods of training, the approach to human and social relations between disparate customs and traditions—these factors imply in some cases, for better or worse, a degree of jointness far greater than that of some ventures in which the financial participation is not paralleled by shared human endeavors.

At the other extreme, there is the wholly foreign-owned subsidiary, a form of foreign equity investment once overwhelmingly predominant and still quantitatively more widespread than the joint venture. Critics of the joint venture as a generally desirable form of partnership between developed and underdeveloped countries have rightly pointed out that a wholly foreign-owned subsidiary which makes the maximum use of local personnel on all levels, which avoids discrepancies in the remuneration and standard of living between foreign and local personnel, and which is guided by experience and understanding of the country and its people, can be a far more successful experiment in partnership than a joint venture which is merely a financial device. For example, an airline is not likely to gain in efficiency or in harmony of relationships by having the local government or public or both share the control with the foreign operator. Technically, the operation of a wholly foreign-owned subsidiary will often be simpler than the division of financial and managerial responsibilities. Sometimes local (public or private) financial participation increases rather than diminishes the problems of the country. The concentration of our study on joint ventures in the strict sense should not be interpreted as an adverse judgment on the many successful Western enterprises in less developed countries that continue to be wholly foreign-owned.

The Growing Significance of the Joint Venture

The joint capital venture still remains the principal symbol of partnership. The reasons, as they have emerged from the detailed discussion in the various chapters, may be summed up in the following general propositions.

1. In a significant proportion of cases, there is an immediate business advantage in the association of local capital with the enterprise. The foreign investor may be short of capital, or he may be unwilling to bear the entire risk alone.

2. Closely allied are cases in which availability of the best local entrepreneurial or managerial talent is linked with local participation.

3. The acceptance of a joint venture is sometimes the only alternative to desisting from or abandoning an existing enterprise by a foreign investor. A joint venture may be "forced" upon a foreign investor, either through legislative requirements for local participation, or by administrative measures which make the granting of the necessary licenses and currency allocations contingent upon jointness. Such forced ventures are generally disliked by the foreign investor because they hamper his freedom of decision and movement. It is all the more important for the foreign investor to appreciate the noneconomic factors which, in the great majority of

the less developed countries, create the psychological pressure for jointness. Such understanding will eliminate the less desirable alternative of a forced joint venture.

4. To many of the governments and peoples of the less developed countries, partnership in the full sense, that is, jointness in ownership, control, and responsibility, is a symbol of equality.

5. Such symbols are important, regardless of the immediate business aspects because they help to reduce deeply ingrained suspicions of foreign economic domination. Whether such suspicions are justified in a particular case or not, they are a real and an important aspect of that national sensitiveness which characterizes many emancipated peoples who were formerly held in a state of political or economic dependency.

6. Overwhelmingly, the new nations want economic development. In the world of today, they will get support from either the Western or the Communist world. The joint venture is a vehicle, though not the only one, for helping these aspirations and for influencing the course they will take.

Is the joint venture likely to be a permanent or a transient phenomenon in the economic evolution of the less developed countries, and in the transformation of their relationships with the industrially developed countries of the Western world?

From the point of view of the less developed countries, the joint venture serves three essential purposes: 1) It stimulates the engagement of responsible local capital in productive enterprises; 2) it helps to develop a nucleus of experienced managerial personnel in the public and in the private sectors, in proportion to the participation of public authorities and private capital in joint ventures; 3) it helps to advance the training of native labor and technicians.

As the less developed countries advance in these respects, their need for joint ventures is likely to decline. Some of our most experienced collaborators from the less developed countries have pointed out that it is advisable for foreign investors to begin their enterprises in the form of joint ventures from the outset rather than later on as a belated concession or as a result of pressure. They believe that local enterprises will eventually exploit a growing proportion of industrial production without the participation of foreigners, unless the foreigners are associated with the enterprises from the start.

It is not possible to estimate with any degree of precision how many joint ventures now existing or developing are likely to endure. Probably many of them will, in the course of years, give way to entirely locally-owned and managed enterprises as a result of organic developments or of legislative or administrative pressure. It is also likely that the most successful joint ventures will endure because the sharing of risk capital often will be an advantage to both parties; successful partnership association will be advantageous to both sides in the intricate network of business decisions, public relations, and social adaptation that constitute so characteristic a feature of the joint venture; and the human associations formed through joint endeavors in critical periods of development may endure beyond the period of immediate necessity.

Some Arguments For and Against Joint Ventures

To say that the proportion of joint ventures appears to be on the increase is not to imply that the joint venture either does or should form the normal pattern of foreign investment in the less developed countries. A number of investors from the developed countries tend to favor one or the other of two extremes: On the one hand—like General Motors—they insist on wholly-owned subsidiaries, even though they may be quite ready to substitute local for foreign personnel up to the managerial level. On the other hand, they may find it preferable to abstain or withdraw from equity investment and to confine their participation to licensing and technical assistance arrangements. The decision to insist on full ownership may stem from the desire to maximize the dividends coming to the original shareholders, or sometimes from old-fashioned ideas of management. Solid business reasons may also militate against joint ventures. The major oil companies of the Western world resist joint venturing mainly for two reasons: 1) because oil exploration is a risky business attended by many failures which a large organization with world-wide affiliations and capital reserves can sustain better than local interests concentrated on one venture only; and 2) because the requirements of established world-wide operations and markets cannot be taken into account in joint ventures in individual, less developed countries.

Another important factor is the nature of the product or service involved. Generally, the establishment of a separate and continuing enterprise with shared equities and responsibilities is appropriate to a standardized product with a continuous market, rather than to a nonrecurring project. There are many joint ventures in the manufacture of such products as chemicals, drugs, plastics, bicycle tubes, diesel trucks, and radio equipment. The construction of a dam or a steel mill, while involving a prolonged period of close collaboration in matters of finance, technical services, and equipment, does not lend itself to the establishment of a legally and financially separate enterprise.

Quite often the question of joint venturing will be decided by the nature of a previous relationship between the parties concerned and the degree of intimacy to be achieved in continuing collaboration. As Chapter VI has shown, joint ventures may develop from a variety of earlier relationships, such as the exporter-importer relationship, or that of licensor with licensee.

Political and psychological conditions sometimes militate against joint ventures. Where difficult and unstable conditions prevail in a country, the association of a foreign investor with local interests may increase the precariousness of the situation. Pressure on the foreign firm may be increased through the local interests involved. The chosen partner may fall out of favor with a new government and prove to be a liability rather than an asset. Conditions of this kind generally would jeopardize the foreign enterprise altogether, regardless of the form of its operation. It is doubtful, for example, whether jointness—even with minority participation—would have proved effective protection for United States industry in the revolutionary conditions prevailing in Cuba. Some of the enterprises expropriated in Cuba, such as the Cuban Telephone Company, were partly owned by Cubans.

Perhaps the most unanimous and widespread argument against joint ventures is a disparity of outlook between the foreign investor and the local partners. In joint ventures between industrially developed countries, such as the United States, Britain, West Germany, the Netherlands, Italy, or Sweden, there is a certain community not only of tradition and of scientific, technical, and legal standards, but there has also been more experience with responsible investment practices and legal supervision, although such standards have often evolved only after disastrous experiences with unscrupulous speculators. In many of the less developed countries, this stage has not yet been reached in the business environment. Power and wealth are often concentrated in relatively few hands, and they are not matched by a corresponding sense of responsibility. The partner from the industrialized country, usually a large corporation with world-wide interests and long experience, generally takes a long-term view of profits, placing the development of the enterprise before quick dividends. Tax considerations may provide an additional incentive to reinvest in a developing foreign enterprise.

Inflationary conditions may produce the reverse situation: The local partner will want to leave his investment in the enterprise where it is relatively inflation-proof, while the foreign investor will be anxious to take out his earnings before devaluation decimates them. The relevant investigations of our study [2] tend to show that the conflict of interest between foreign and local investors is not nearly so frequent as often assumed.

The most ubiquitous and essential criteria are flexibility of mind and attitude, and the ability to appraise the elements inherent in a particular country, a particular situation, and for a particular product or service.

The joint venture is an important symbol of the changing relationship between the developed and the less developed countries, but it cannot be regarded as a panacea. It is a device to be adopted, rejected, or modified after a sober consideration of the many legal, psychological, and technical factors prevailing in a given situation. Confidence between the partners will overcome the most difficult obstacles; lack of confidence will destroy the most perfect devices.

[2] See Chapter VI.

Forms and Modalities

It is only after the basic considerations have been given their due weight, and have led to a decision in principle to attempt a foreign joint venture in a less developed country, that the question of forms and modalities becomes important.

The question of the proper legal form has been discussed in a brief account in this book.[3] The modalities of corporate organization in the less developed countries—all based on patterns of the common law or the civil law systems developed in the principal countries—allow for enough flexibility to accommodate the different variations of joint ventures. The Special Company Act of 1950 of Burma appears to be the only case of a general law enacted specifically to facilitate joint ventures between a government and approved foreign investors, but such specific legislation seems to be neither desirable nor necessary.

Those favoring the expansion of the joint venture in international business have sometimes advocated an express linking of the credit operation of public United States or international agencies with the constitution of joint ventures. The conclusions of our study would support the prevailing opinion that it is undesirable to substitute legal or administrative directives of this kind for the individual decision, based on the facts of the case—which sometimes do and sometimes do not favor a joint venture. Where legislation restricts foreign participation to a certain percentage, the joint venture is a necessary condition of investment. Whether and to what extent such legislative restrictions (from which no country is entirely free) [4] are desirable, is a matter of policy, not of legal technique.

Majority and Minority Participation

A rather more complicated issue, from a psychological as well as a practical point of view, is the proportion in which the respective

[3] See Chapter VII, pp. 212–19.

[4] For the restrictions by federal and state legislation in the United States, see Cary and Cohen, in Friedmann and Pugh (editors), *Legal Aspects of Foreign Investment*, Little, Brown & Co. (1959), pp. 621 ff.

shares should be held by the foreign and local investors once a decision has been made in favor of a joint venture. Even a few years ago, the overwhelming view of those Western—and in particular, American—firms which had reluctantly decided to accept a joint venture would not consider anything but a majority interest. The reasons which have produced a gradual change and led to an increasing proportion of foreign minority participation are complex but can perhaps be summed up under the following major categories.

1. Local legislation may stipulate a stated minimum majority to be held by nationals in certain industries or services.[5] The alternative for the foreign investor is either to accept a minority interest or to stay out.

2. National prestige factors may account for strong pressure to reduce a foreign interest to a minority holding, at times resulting in specific legislation to that effect. This is notably so in air transport, where national prestige is strongly involved. Foreign firms such as Pan American Airways, which once dominated Latin American air transportation, have gradually come to accept a minority interest (usually one-third) in many cases.

3. Some firms, in industries particularly suitable to joint venturing such as chemical products, draw a distinction between specialty products (a patented drug) and a general production line (plastics). For specialties they will insist on majority control, but for general products they are prepared to accept a minority interest.

4. Experience has shown that the apparent disadvantage of a minority interest is, in many services and industries, countered by the continuing advantage of know-how and technological superiority.

5. The apparent minority interest, say of 49 percent or even 33⅓ percent, can mean effective majority control if the local holdings are scattered among many participants. It is only where the foreign investor accepts a minority participation with one local investor, that he faces possible majorization.

In the course of our inquiry it was pointed out by some experienced Western investors that to hold a substantial minority interest in a foreign enterprise has compensating advantages. In many of the

[5] For examples see Chapter VII, pp. 195–202.

less developed countries, the foreign investor is apt to be looked upon with greater suspicion than the domestic investor in the conduct of his operations. As a minority shareholder, the foreign investor escapes the responsibilities for the often complex and cumbrous procedure of minority protection.[6] As long as the foreign investor is needed because of his capital investment, his managerial experience, and his technological know-how, he is not likely to suffer from the position of a minority stockholder, and he is not subject to the accusation of dominating the enterprise at the expense of the minority holders. A foreign minority participation will usually classify the joint enterprise as "national" and thus save it from general legislative or administrative measures directed at foreign enterprises. It is largely for this reason that some of the largest enterprises of the United States have accepted minority positions in joint ventures, for example, the Celanese Corporation of America and duPont in enterprises in Mexico, and Gulf Oil in the Filoil refinery in the Philippines.

Political Problems

Our analysis has revealed the multitude of complex considerations that influence the making and development of any international business enterprise: government controls and assistance mechanisms on one side or the other, the "pros" and "cons" of majority or minority participation, the type of product or service, and the availability of partners. In addition, certain basic problems relating to the proper mixture of business and politics in contemporary enterprises abroad, and especially in those that are based on permanent collaboration with public and private elements in the country of investment must be considered.

Many entrepreneurs, especially in the United States, would answer that the question is improper, that a business enterprise investing abroad must be guided by business considerations and must leave wider policy questions to governments. But such an answer evades the question. We do not suggest that the board of an American, British, French, or Dutch company should consider its foreign enter-

[6] For details on these, see Friedmann and Pugh, *Legal Aspects of Foreign Investment,* pp. 772 ff.

prises primarily as humanitarian ventures, or as direct contributions to the foreign policy of its country. It could not justify such a decision either to itself or to its stockholders. But closer reflection shows that the mixture of politics and business in foreign investment —especially in the less developed countries—is inevitably different from that prevailing in domestic enterprises.

The investment decision presupposes basic political evaluation. The overwhelming majority of decisions concerning foreign investment are long-term decisions, and the long view is all the more necessary, the less developed the country of investment is. A decision, by an American, British, or German manufacturer or—as is increasingly the case, by a consortium of Western enterprises—to start the production of diesel trucks in Brazil, or pharmaceuticals in India, or of bauxite in Guinea, presupposes a careful appraisal of a number of factors which would count for little or nothing in any purely domestic decision. The relevant considerations will include an estimate of the political stability and the likely direction of political development of the country in question, an appraisal of the quality of the public service, the possibilities of long-term economic growth, the attitude of government and people toward foreigners in general and toward the nation of the prospective entrepreneur in particular. The host's attitudes must be considered in the light of the history of the country, its past experience with foreign political power and economic interests, and of the social, and, in some cases, the religious traditions that influence attitudes toward business and toward Western methods of enterprise. Not only the answers to these questions, but also the relative gravity and importance of the different considerations will vary from country to country.

Many of these factors have too often been neglected, or even contemptuously ignored by Western businessmen. In contemporary foreign investment, good long-term business planning involves good political judgment. It is not sufficient to have a correct estimate of, and confidence in, the chosen foreign business partner. It is at least as important to assess the attitudes and policies of his government, the degree of internal social stability, and the measure of external or internal threats to the continuity of the enterprise. There are also the subtler psychological phenomena of national pride and sensitivity, sometimes ignored by the most experienced of Western enterprises. The technical and financial arguments which make General Motors maintain an inflexible 100 percent control over its foreign subsidiaries may well be solid and cogent; the wisdom of its decision to exclude even the Australian or Canadian public—nations far closer to American and Western standards of culture and development than the vast majority—from any chance of participation in its enterprises in these countries may well be doubted, even though it has recently been reinforced by Ford's decision to acquire full control of its prosperous British enterprise, hitherto a joint venture. The great majority of Western enterprises have come to take a less dogmatic attitude. They have, often reluctantly, come to assign due weight to the political and psychological imponderables. The very decision taken by the foreign firm—the form of investment, the type of association, its approach to government and to public and private capital, its employment policies—will contribute to legislative, administrative, and policy developments in the host country. Sometimes it will significantly influence political relations between the countries concerned. Responsibilities are inevitably placed on the investor's shoulders.

Considerations of national policy may sometimes clash with immediate business interests, and a joint venture may be advisable from one point of view and not the other. But such conflicts should not arise too often. Precisely because of the close interweaving of policy and business considerations in international business, wise business planning will usually accord with long-term national interests. Nor should there be frequent clashes between the political interests of the capital-importing and capital-exporting countries. The economic development of the less developed nations in free and equal association is a declared objective of Western policy.

Governmental Policies and Private Investment

Any foreign enterprise presents an intricate interweaving of governmental and private business decisions.[7] On the governmental side in the capital-exporting countries, there is usually a combination of

[7] See, in particular, Chapter VII.

open public policy decisions, expressed in foreign aid and grants, and commercial or semi-commercial decisions, expressed in the amount and duration of credits, the rates of interest, or the conditions attached to loans.

Of the numerous national and international public bodies that today play a more or less conspicuous part in foreign economic development, some are essentially or overwhelmingly guided by international public policy. Outright aid is offered by the Technical Assistance Administration and the Special Fund of the United Nations, by the Colombo Plan, and by the military and economic assistance programs of the United States. But the majority of national and international financial agencies are ostensibly directed by commercial considerations in their loan and investment policies—considerations that by their very nature involve the most careful political, economic, and sociological studies. A survey, for example, of the various decisions made by the World Bank to grant or not to grant a loan for government-owned steel mills in India, the Aswan Dam in Egypt, public or private power development in Japan, or irrigation in Pakistan reveals an intricate mixture of commercial and policy decisions similar to those that affect contemporary private business.

National governments become more directly involved with foreign investment insofar as they set up export credit guarantees or, like the United States and more recently West Germany, devise public guarantee schemes designed to insure the national investor in foreign countries against certain major vicissitudes.

The interlocking of government policy and business decisions is more ubiquitous in the capital-importing countries. That government is a crucial and generally at least, a directive factor in the economic development of the less developed countries is one of the facts of life in the present phase of international economic relations. This is quite independent of the extent to which the government may directly engage in the operation, ownership, and management of business and industry.

That the government of the capital-importing country can make or break a wholly or partly foreign-owned enterprise—as indeed it can any domestic enterprise—through its manifold levers of control (import licenses, currency regulations, employment permits) is today grudgingly but definitely accepted by any foreign investor. No Western businessman could do otherwise without by implication denying his own government powers that it constantly exercises. His main concern is that the controls should be exercised in such a manner that will not hamper the development of a promising enterprise and will operate with a minimum of bureaucratic red tape. Many of these matters (concession agreements, instruments of approval, contracts of guarantee) are now handled by specific agreements between the government of the capital-importing country and the particular foreign enterprise.

The question of direct participation by the government or a government-owned corporation in a capital-importing country is still viewed differently in many Western business circles—definitely unfavorably in the United States. Our case studies include successful joint ventures between foreign private enterprises and local governmental enterprises, such as a government bank or a national development corporation. In countries where private entrepreneur capital is scarce or lacking, such partnership—at least during a long transitional period—should be welcomed as guaranteeing a higher level of responsibility and long-term vision than an association between an experienced foreign enterprise and an inexperienced, often speculative-minded local partner. On the whole, European entrepreneurs accept such association pragmatically, judging it on the merits of the situation. United States entrepreneurs are still inclined to reject any such association as inherently evil, as a token of socialism, and unacceptable to a free enterprise economy. It may be—and indeed, it must be hoped—that, with a growing insight into the great variety of conditions prevailing in the less developed countries, such *a priori* prejudices, characteristic of a domestic-oriented rather than of an international outlook, will gradually give way to a more experimental and pragmatic approach. Objections are slightly less pronounced where the foreign government partner is not a government department as such but a semi-autonomous governmental corporation with separate legal personality, budget, and business experience. Some of these, like the Nacional Financiera of Mexico, the Corporación de Fomento of Chile, the Instituto de Fomento

Industrial of Colombia and the Sümerbank of Turkey have established a fine record of stimulating industry, often by initial capital association with a foreign enterprise. In some cases, these development corporations have subsequently disposed of all or part of their holdings to the public.

Be that as it may, it cannot be denied that in some of the least developed countries, the only alternative to initial participation by the government is no local participation at all. Quite often (in Ghana, for example) the government is content with a relatively small minority participation, if it is in association with an experienced and a responsible foreign enterprise, such as the Unilever concern. Outside of the Soviet Bloc, few people today see the panacea in a wholly government-controlled and government–operated economy. But there is hardly any country, even in the industrially developed world, and most emphatically in the less developed world, where a mixed economy is not, at least for a long transitional period, a necessary concomitant of planned economic development. That countries like India, Pakistan, Mexico, or Nigeria—to name but a few representative examples—must base the general tempo and direction of their economic development on long-term plans and governmental participation in enterprises and seek to find a reasonable balance between ambitions and resources is today no longer seriously denied in Washington any more than in London, Paris, New Delhi, or Accra. The proper degree of public participation in industrial development is a delicate matter, to be judged in the light of a mixture of political and economic conditions.

It is regrettable that the public United States lending agencies and the international agencies in which United States influence is dominant should have adopted a dogmatic rather than a pragmatic attitude that could be interpreted as an attempt to force United States economic philosophy on other countries.

The World Bank has consistently refused to lend to publicly-owned "industries" (including basic ones such as steel mills) as distinct from "utilities" (dams, power development, etc.). The United States-owned International Cooperation Administration and Development Loan Fund have made loans for certain industries on the condition that they be privately owned (for example, a recent steel venture in Turkey). The test should be individual creditworthiness, not a dogmatic preference that is unlikely to alter the basic pattern of development of the countries concerned and might well make them turn to other sources for help: India's largely state-owned steel industry will be developed and influenced overwhelmingly by the Soviet Union and West European groups.

There is evidence that, with experience, maturity, and greater national self-assurance, many of the less developed countries are coming to take a less dogmatic attitude on the proper proportion of public and private enterprise in their own economic development. Many of the original, more radically socialist policy statements or laws were not due so much to doubt in the efficiency of private, especially foreign private, enterprises as to political resentment or suspicion. Such emotional reactions are today repeated in a country like Cuba. In countries like Burma, India, Pakistan, Brazil, and Mexico, the practical experience of partnership enterprises has contributed to the modification of earlier attitudes and to a greater readiness to accept foreign investment with less cramping restrictions. Much remains to be done by both sides, but the rigidity of the earlier postwar period seems to have given way to a more experimental and practical approach.

Joint Ventures and Mutual Understanding

More important even than the technicalities of legal, financial, and technical arrangements is the question of how much the joint venture can contribute to the vital battle for the progress of the less developed countries, a battle that is fought simultaneously on the political, economic, and personal levels.

At its lowest, the joint venture is a device of financial arrangements or company law, a minor variation of equity investment. At its highest, it can be an important experiment in the sharing not only of legal and financial but also of human responsibilities. It expresses well the idea of partnership, and it is only on the basis of partnership that the economic progress of the less developed countries can be achieved, and that it will be possible to impart the experience and resources of the more developed countries to nations that want to bridge the gap, without sacrificing national pride and human dignity.

Ultimately in that battle—in which the Western world faces the growing competition of a more purposeful, more ruthlessly directed, and increasingly efficient Communist world—the legal financial arrangements are likely to be less crucial than the achievement of human partnership. The multitude of national and international financing agencies that have sprung into existence in recent years is far from satisfying the long-term needs of the less developed world, but it is expressive of a vastly sharpened understanding of these needs and of a greater readiness to meet them. National public financing agencies such as the Export-Import Bank, the Development Loan Fund, or the International Cooperation Administration in the United States—now partly paralleled by similar developments in West Germany, Japan, and other countries—join hands with the international financing agencies led by the World Bank and flanked by its affiliates (the International Finance Corporation and the International Development Association), and such regional financing institutions as the Inter-American Development Bank, the European Investment Bank, the Overseas Territories Fund of the European Economic Community, and the Colombo Plan. To these must be added the slowly growing number of private international financing companies and consortia formed for the promotion of economic development.

It is with regard to the mutual understanding of traditions, outlooks, and approaches on the part of government servants as well as business managers, engineers, and labor that most of the work remains to be done.

We do not yet know how far the spirit and methods underlying the development of Western industrial enterprises—capitalist or socialist—can be translated to the world of Hinduism or Buddhism or Islam. Nations comprising many hundreds of millions of people are attempting not only to industrialize their traditional rural economies, but also to change age-old habits and philosophies. Whether Burma, for example, can achieve the evolution of a Western industrialized society without abandoning the deeply ingrained religious, ethical, and social habits of an intensely Buddhist culture is as yet an open question. How far India should retain or revive the village community as a center of life and production, or concentrate on Westernized production methods, is a question much debated among Indian leaders. The acquisitive industrial society of the Western world developed on the basis of the philosophical, moral, and religious individualism characterized by the Renaissance, the philosophy of Descartes, Hume, and Kant, and the religious attitudes of Calvinism which found it possible to see in material wealth a proof of the grace of God. The world of Buddha or Siva is certainly a very different one. The clash of traditions is bound to produce agonizing conflicts. Perhaps they are insoluble. At the very least, the Western businessman or government servant working amidst alien traditions and cultures should attempt to understand the problem. The attempt has already been made by some; it should be made by all. They should seek to understand, for example, that the Burmese concept of Pyidawtha is an endeavor to harmonize religious values and traditional ideas of community with economic progress and development. The attempt to solve these problems in the practical and continuous association of joint enterprises is likely to promote far more mutual understanding than general exhortations by visiting executives or politicians.

Only a few years ago, a lamentably large number of Western business executives and politicians thought it sufficient to preach sermons on the superiority of their system and methods without the slightest attempt to understand either the needs or the traditions of the people to whom they were speaking. Happily today, as a result of many partnership experiences in joint enterprises and far more articulate efforts of mutual understanding, such demonstrations have become less frequent. Practical experience and continued cooperation have made the more mature in most less developed countries—their government servants, their businessmen, their scientists, and their engineers—aware that some of the suspect qualities of capitalist Western societies are required for an industrialized society, that profitability is in the long run a test of efficiency, even in a socialized country.

It is only if the partnership idea in the form of the joint venture is implemented not only by appropriate financial, legal, and technical arrangements, but also by a spirit of human partnership, that a significant contribution can be made by it in the transformation of the relations between the developed and the less developed countries of the world.

PART II. *Case Studies*

I. Latin America

Altos Hornos de México, S.A.

ORIGIN OF THE ENTERPRISE

Mexico was the first country in Latin America to engage in the integrated production of iron and steel. It was undertaken shortly after the turn of the century, in 1903, by the Compañía Fundidora de Fierro y Acero de Monterrey. Until the Second World War, this company was the only integrated producer of steel in the country. The shortage of steel abroad early in the war prompted a group of Mexican industrialists and users of steel to investigate the possibilities of establishing another steel mill. This second integrated steel mill, Altos Hornos de México, S.A., has since come to be the leading steel mill in the country, with Fundidora in second position.

The original idea of the Mexican promoters was to establish a plant for the manufacture only of cold rolled sheet and tin plate, based on semi-finished steel to be imported. Foreign technical assistance was sought, and was obtained from a leading United States steel producer, the Armco International Corporation, a subsidiary of the Armco Steel Corporation. The promoters thought that the enterprise should be limited in its operations because they wanted to avoid the high costs and complications inherent in an underdeveloped economy of a truly integrated steel operation. Despite these objections, preliminary studies led to the conclusion that limited manufacture based on the importation of semi-finished steel would be subject to much the same risks in the situation of war scarcities as the importation of the finished products themselves. Accordingly, a plan was developed, with the blessing of the government through its development bank, Nacional Financiera, for an integrated plant with an annual capacity of 18,000 tons of tinplate, 15,000 tons of cold rolled sheet, 15,000 tons of steel plates, and 7,000 tons of centrifugal pipe. This total of 55,000 tons of finished products for the enterprise has since grown to an actual output of about 300,000 tons of these products.

A site was selected close to sources of coal and iron ore at the city of Monclova in the northern state of Coahuila, with reasonably good transportation facilities to Mexico City and environs, the main area of consumption in the country.

At the end of 1941, agreement was reached among the Mexican industrialists who were promoting the idea, Mexican bankers, the Nacional Financiera, and the Armco International Corporation for formation of the enterprise. The enterprise was legally constituted on July 6, 1942. The first units of the plant were completed and production began in mid-1944.

ORIGINAL CAPITAL STRUCTURE AND TECHNICAL ARRANGEMENTS

The initial capital of the company was 22,310,000 pesos, of which common stock amounted to 16,490,000 pesos (32,980 shares at 500 pesos each), and seven percent preferential shares amounted to 5,820,000 pesos (11,640 shares at 500 pesos each). At the same time, the enterprise issued 30 million pesos worth of six percent, 15-year bonds, and obtained an equipment loan from the Export-Import Bank of Washington of $8 million in 1942.

Of the original equity, Armco took 10 percent of the common stock (or about 7.4 percent of the total equity), 90 percent of the common stock was subscribed by private domestic investors (66.5 percent of the total equity), and Nacional Financiera took all of the preferential shares (26.1 percent of the total equity), and assumed the task of placement of the company's bonds.

Armco, in addition to its minority participation in the equity, entered into a technical assistance contract with the enterprise, with a duration of some five years, to supervise construction and operation of the plant. It has not been possible to obtain the terms of this contract. Armco delegated one of its engineers (Harold R. Pape) to supervise the operation and supplied the technicians required to occupy key posts and to train Mexican personnel. Mr. Pape has continued to this day as general manager of the company, a post which involves technical direction of the plant; general administrative direction is the function of a "director-general." It is reported that Mr. Pape is the only foreigner now in the enterprise.

The task of arranging for the equipment for the enterprise was especially difficult since this was being attempted during the war when such equipment was extremely scarce. Through Armco and other connections, steel mill equipment was obtained in such diverse places as St. Louis, Missouri; Indiana Harbor, Indiana; Cincinnati, Ohio; southern Illinois; Kentucky; and Coatesville, Pennsylvania. Special emphasis was given by the company in reporting on its history to the ingenuity involved in making these diverse arrangements for the supply of equipment; a similar project for Brazil was cited (Volta Redonda), the idea for which started earlier than Altos Hornos, and which could be completed only several years after Altos Hornos was in full production. The first chairman of the board of directors, Abelardo Rodríguez, a former President of Mexico, is reported to have expressed the hope in 1942 that there might be someone who could make some order out of the "mountain of scrap" that had been collected as equipment for the new steel mill.

The first lines of production were plates, certain types of sheets, and pipe. Another two years were necessary before production could be begun of cold rolled sheet and tinplate. Altos Hornos supplied thousands of tons of plates during the war to the United States Maritime Commission for shipbuilding.

DEVELOPMENT OF CAPITAL STRUCTURE

During the first three years of operations (1944–46), losses were incurred in the total amount of 8.5 million pesos. These losses and the continuous need for expansion of the productive facilities of the enterprise resulted in a successive series of increases in the capital of the company.

On February 15, 1944, the capital was raised from the original 22,310,000 pesos to 40,000,000 pesos. This was achieved by raising the issue of preferential shares from the original 5,820,000 pesos to

23,510,000 pesos. Thus, the enterprise emerged from this capital increase with the original amount of 16,490,000 pesos of common stock, and 23,510,000 pesos of preferential shares. The additional issue of preferential shares was taken up by Nacional Financiera, which thus raised its participation from the original 26.1 percent to a majority, of about 59 percent. At the same time, the issue of the company's bonds was raised from 30 to 40 million pesos through the facilities of Nacional Financiera.

Another increase of capital was effected on October 27, 1947, from 40 million pesos to 70 million pesos, and the preferential shares outstanding were reduced to 10 million pesos through an exchange for an equivalent amount of common stock. With this change, common stock outstanding amounted to 60 million pesos, and preferential shares to 10 million pesos. Also, the majority share of Nacional Financiera was increased to 80 percent; the share of Armco continued at 7.5 percent and the balance of 12.5 percent was held by private Mexican industrialists and bankers.

On June 24, 1952, the 10 million pesos of preferential shares were retired, and the common stock was increased to 70 million pesos. Later, the capital was doubled to 140 million pesos through the issue of a 100 percent stock dividend, involving the capitalization of 70 million pesos of reserves.

On March 26, 1956, the capital of the enterprise was once again raised, this time to 175,000,000 pesos, divided into 350,000 common shares with a nominal value of 500 pesos each. In 1958, the par value of shares was reduced to 100 pesos each, and old shares were exchanged for new ones at a one to five ratio; on January 9, 1960, the capital was raised to 300 million pesos, through a reinvestment of 65 million pesos of reserves and a revaluation of assets in the amount of 60 million pesos. The division of these shares among stockholders at present is the following: Nacional Financiera, 80.7 percent of the total; Armco International Corporation, 7.5 percent of the total; and the balance of 11.8 percent of the total is held by private Mexican investors, including some employees of the enterprise.

The balance of Nacional Financiera credits to the firm outstanding at the end of 1957 was 166 million pesos. Most of these credits involved discount of paper of government customers of Altos Hornos. Altos Hornos has a regular line of credit with Nacional Financiera in the amount of 20 million pesos for the discount of customer paper.

The Export-Import Bank of Washington has extended substantial credits to Altos Hornos. These have amounted to a total of $29 million, consisting of the original credit of $8 million of 1942, a credit of $5 million granted in 1951, and a recent credit of $16 million, granted on February 7, 1957. The initial loan has been entirely repaid. The 1951 loan bears an interest rate of 4 percent and is repayable in 20 semi-annual installments that began in November, 1953. The 1957 loan bears interest at 5½ percent, and is repayable in 30 semi-annual installments which began in January, 1960.

MANAGEMENT AND PERSONNEL

The technical assistance rendered by Armco was invaluable in the organization of the enterprise, particularly with respect to the handling of the original production equipment under the difficult conditions that then prevailed. Armco also supplied the necessary technical men at the outset, and this involved many problems because of the manpower shortage resulting from the war, and because of the unattractive living conditions in the small town of Monclova where the plant was located. The enterprise reports that the only foreign technical man now on the payroll is the general manager.

The board of directors consists of twelve members, elected by majority vote in the general assembly of shareholders. Each minority group of shareholders representing at least 25 percent of the shares nevertheless has the right to elect one director. During the last few years, the board has been made up of only six representatives of Nacional Financiera, although it is an 80 percent stockholder. Among the other six, one is a representative of Armco, and he is the only non-Mexican on the Board.

The chief executive officers of the company are a director-general and a general manager; the former is the principal general executive officer, while the latter is more specifically responsible for technical direction of the enterprise. As previously mentioned, this post is still held today by Mr. Pape, the man first named by Armco to supervise the operation.

The total work force of Altos Hornos numbered 6,312 persons at the end of 1959. More than 50 percent of these had a seniority of more than five years. Labor-management relations have generally worked out smoothly; there has been only one serious labor conflict which occurred in 1949. The company has built 500 houses for its workers, which are sold at payment terms of ten years with an interest rate of six percent per year, a very low rate for Mexico. The company has a program for adding 100 houses every year to this stock. In addition, it provides school and hospital services, scholarships, sports facilities, and has financed a consumers' co-operative for the workers. Labor conditions are set by collective contracts with the workers' union, which are revised every two years.

FINANCIAL RESULTS

Altos Hornos earned profits of 40.8 million pesos, after taxes, in 1957. This was the first full year after the increase in capital to 175 million pesos in March 1956; these profits thus represented the substantial return of 23 percent on equity. The ratio of long-term capital to equity has been high in the case of Altos Hornos, undoubtedly facilitated by its close connection with the Mexican government. The balance sheet at the end of 1957 showed long-term capital of 245 million pesos, compared to the equity of 175 million pesos. It is, on the other hand, also significant that Altos Hornos is now paying full taxes to the Mexican government; 1955 was the last year of the tax concessions it enjoyed for a period of some ten years as a "new or necessary" industry.

The company has followed a policy of reinvestment of substantial portions of its earnings. Reference has already been made to the capitalization of 70 million pesos of reserves in raising the capital from 70 million pesos to 140 million pesos, and to the reinvestment of 65 million pesos of reserves in the latest capital increase to 300 million pesos. The reinvestment record of the years 1955–57 was as follows: in 1955, all of the net profits of 32.2 million pesos were reinvested; in 1956, 26 percent of the net profits of 32.9 million pesos were reinvested; and in 1957, 41 percent of the net profits of 40.8 million pesos were reinvested.

The distribution of approximately 59 percent of the net profits earned in 1957 represented a dividend of 60 pesos per share net of all taxes or 12 percent of the par value of the stock. A 12 percent distribution was also effected in 1959. The company intends to maintain this rate as its dividend policy. In the past years, the rate had been from 5 percent to 8 percent in cash dividends, in addition to the stock dividends previously indicated.

ALTOS HORNOS AND THE MEXICAN STEEL INDUSTRY

The production of steel ingots by Altos Hornos in 1958 amounted to some 350,000 tons, which is almost double the output of the second most important steel enterprise, Fundidora de Monterrey, and represents close to one-third of total production in the country. In 1959, the production of Altos Hornos increased to 415,368 tons. The volume of output of Altos Hornos has almost doubled since 1954, a rapid rate of increase which has been characteristic of the steel industry as a whole in Mexico. The production of Altos Hornos, of five other principal steel producers, and of the industry as a whole in the years 1954–58 is given in the following tabulation.

PRODUCTION OF STEEL INGOTS IN MEXICO, BY PRINCIPAL ENTERPRISES, 1954–58 (*metric tons*)

Enterprises	*1954*	*1955*	*1956*	*1957*	*1958* [a]
Altos Hornos	219,174	256,075	314,172	355,636	353,533
Fundidora	145,766	160,844	179,447	210,794	220,000
Consolidada	81,403	94,145	105,131	119,493	160,000
Hojalata y Lámina	66,876	96,526	118,895	156,288	180,000
Aceros Nacionales	30,429	37,754	53,788	60,186	62,000
Aceros Ecatepec	19,927	25,664	35,860	38,252	40,000
	563,575	671,008	807,293	940,649	1,015,533
Total National Production	609,450	725,350	888,412	1,049,446	1,195,000

[a] Estimated, except for Altos Hornos.

Early in 1960, Altos Hornos purchased a controlling interest in the important Consolidada steel enterprise.

Despite the substantial increase in local production of steel ingots, imports have also had to increase substantially to keep pace with increases in consumption, which have occurred in total and on a per capita basis as well, as shown in the following figures. Imports in 1957 still represented as much as 39 percent of total consumption.

PRODUCTION, IMPORTS, EXPORTS, AND APPARENT CONSUMPTION (TOTAL AND PER CAPITA) OF STEEL INGOTS IN MEXICO
1953–57 (*metric tons*)

	(1) *Production*	(2) *Imports*	(3) *Exports*	(4) *Apparent Total Consumption* (1) + (2) − (3)	(5) *Consumption Per Capita* (*kilograms*)
1953	525,030	348,400	1,676	871,754	31
1954	609,450	358,477	3,451	964,476	33
1955	725,350	377,088	8,586	1,093,852	36
1956	888,412	648,060	18,661	1,517,811	49
1957	1,049,446	663,873	23,641	1,689,678	53

A recent expansion program of Altos Hornos, financed in part by the 1957 Export-Import Bank loan of $16 million, and designed to increase its ingot capacity to 600,000 tons per year, was virtually completed by the end of 1959. Studies have been completed for a further expansion in ingot capacity to one million tons, to be executed by 1964, at a cost of some 400 million pesos.

AFFILIATED COMPANIES

In connection with the development of its raw materials supplies, Altos Hornos has organized a series of affiliated companies, generally on a joint basis with Nacional Financiera. The principal ones, for mining of iron ore and coal and the production of coke, are La Perla, Minas de Fierro, S.A.; Compañía Minera de Guadalupe, S.A.; Compañía Minera Las Alazanas, S.A.; Carbonífera Unida de Palau, S.A.; Carbonífera de Barroterán, S.A.; and Mexicana de Coque y Derivados, S.A. In one of these enterprises, the Carbonífera Unida de Palau, there is also capital of the Fundidora de Monterrey.

Aside from these enterprises, Altos Hornos has a joint investment with the government's Federal Electricity Commission in Eléctrica de Monclova, S.A., which supplies electric power to the plant as well as to the towns of Monclova and Frontera on a public service basis. Another Altos Hornos subsidiary, Ahmsa Comercial S.A., takes care of the distribution of its products.

EVALUATION

Altos Hornos, the leading integrated steel mill in Mexico, specializing in flat products and centrifugal pipe, was originally promoted during the Second World War by private Mexican interests which, because of the magnitude of the investment involved and the highly technical nature of the enterprise, enlisted the participation of the government through Nacional Financiera and of the Armco International Corporation of the United States. Initially, a majority of the capital was from private Mexican sources, but continuing large financial requirements for expansion have reduced this participation to a minority, and 80 percent of the enterprise is now owned by the government, through Nacional Financiera. The position of Armco has always been a minority one, having been maintained at about 7.5 percent of the total equity throughout the period of substantial expansion of the enterprise. Armco supervised the installation and operation of the plant at the beginning under a special contract, and the original Armco supervisor is still technical manager of the plant today. The enterprise has obtained substantial loans from the Export-Import Bank of Washington. The administration of the enterprise, as might be expected, is dominated by Nacional Financiera, the 80 percent shareholder, but full advantage has been taken of the technical advice of Armco, despite its small minority position, as evidenced by the continuation of Mr. Pape as Technical Manager of the plant.

Altos Hornos is an interesting case of a joint venture involving cooperation between a foreign private enterprise and a national government agency in a basic industry. The government agency has assumed a very active role in the venture, and has provided most of the large amounts of financing continually required for expansion. This official national financing has been supplemented to a very important extent by foreign official financing, from the Export-Import Bank of Washington. The role of the foreign private company has been of some significance financially, but its more important contribution to the enterprise has been technical.

Bristol de México, S.A.

ORIGIN OF THE ENTERPRISE

Bristol de México, S.A. was organized in March, 1956 at the initiative of the Bristol Aeroplane Company, Ltd., of England, to engage in aircraft engine overhaul and repair operations. Bristol of England has been active in foreign operations ever since its beginnings in 1910. The decision to engage in such an operation in Mexico was made by Bristol after it had conducted a survey of potential markets in the Latin American area. Aside from the engine overhaul business to be obtained in Mexico, from other Latin American countries, and from international operators passing through Mexico, it was felt that a plant in Mexico would provide useful support for the sale of the Britannia aircraft and other Bristol products in Mexico and elsewhere in Latin America.

The detailed activity for the formation of the enterprise in Mexico was carried out for Bristol by its Canadian subsidiary, the Bristol Aeroplane Company of Canada. Bristol also has local plants, in Spain and France, where the investments are joint with domestic investors. The past experience with joint ventures plus the favorable attitude toward such ventures in Mexico led to the decision to form Bristol de México. The plant is located at the central airport in Mexico City and started functioning on July 1, 1957.

CAPITAL STRUCTURE

Bristol de México was set up with an equity of 13 million pesos, the majority of which was contributed by Bristol of Canada. Aeronaves de México, a leading Mexican airline and itself a joint venture (about 20 percent Pan American World Airways capital), participated with an investment of 1.5 million pesos, or 11.5 percent of the total. Individual Mexican investors also hold a small part of the total. During the last months of 1958, agreement was reached for entry into the company of the Compañía Mexicana de Aviación (CMA), the principal Mexican airline and, like Aeronaves de México, also a joint venture (about 40 percent Pan American World Airways capital). CMA was to contribute 2.5 million pesos, which would raise the company's capital to 14.5 million pesos (1 million pesos was to be acquired from Bristol), and make the combined CMA and Aeronaves share about 27.5 percent of the total. CMA and Aeronaves, incidentally, together account for about 85 percent of total domestic air traffic in Mexico. CMA and Aeronaves also have a stock purchase option agreement with Bristol de México, under which their combined share of the enterprise can rise to more than that of Bristol of Canada, although it is to be less than 50 percent of the total.

In addition to the equity, the investment of Bristol de México includes a loan equivalent to 6.5 million pesos ($520 thousand, half in pesos and half in United States dollars) from the International Finance Corporation. The IFC loan bears interest at the rate of seven percent per annum, and is to be amortized in 13 semi-annual installments beginning October 1, 1960; in addition, IFC is to receive certain interest payments above seven percent per annum contingent upon the amount of earnings of the company. It also has a nine-year option on the purchase of shares for one-half of its total investment.

MANAGEMENT AND PERSONNEL

Bristol de México is administered by Bristol of Canada under a management contract, which has a fixed fee basis. To insure proper technical control of the operation, Bristol would probably want this management contract to continue indefinitely, although it is prepared to relinquish its majority financial control in the future. The general manager and assistant general manager are foreigners furnished by Bristol of Canada. Other key posts in the organization are those of the superintendent, production manager, chief inspector, senior overhaul engineer, and chief of finance. The majority of these posts is manned at present by Mexicans; Canadians hold the positions only of production manager and senior overhaul engineer.

The board of directors of Bristol de México consists of six members, four of whom are named by Bristol of Canada, one by Aeronaves de México, and the remaining post is reserved for CMA, in accordance with the arrangements made toward the end of 1958 for entry of the latter firm as a stockholder. This distribution of directors is the result of an unwritten agreement; there are no special rules for election of the board. All the stock of the enterprise is common stock, with no special voting rights appertaining to any particular blocks of shares.

The nucleus of the work force of Bristol de México consisted of 23 men who were taken from an aircraft repair shop that had been operated at Torreón, State of Coahuila, by Aeronaves de México. When Bristol was formed, Aeronaves closed its plant, and its personnel, with their seniority rights and labor contract, were taken over by Bristol.

The present total work force of Bristol amounts to some 135 people, of whom 75 are "productive" and the balance concerned with administrative and service operations. Some 50 "productive" people were obtained from the training facilities of the International Civil Aviation Organization School conducted at the Mexico City airport. In addition, Bristol has started a program of sending selected workers abroad for further training.

The management of Bristol de México is very satisfied with the quality of the work it has been able to obtain from Mexican personnel trained in this way. Of the total work force of 135, only five are foreigners, including the four in top management previously mentioned. This is particularly impressive considering the new nature of the activity in Mexico and its relative complexity and need for highly exact work. There have been some problems arising from the intrinsic nature of the situation: The main problem of the enterprise has been an understandable lack of versatility on the part of technical personnel, which can be corrected only through training over a period of time; also, there has been a need for closer supervision than in more highly industrialized countries.

ROLE IN THE ECONOMY

Prior to the establishment of Bristol de México, the only similar facility existing in Mexico was that of Aeronaves. This shop worked only on certain types of engines, and most of them, particularly the heavier types, had to be sent to the United States for overhaul. This is no longer necessary. Bristol is equipped to handle all the engine work in the country, and handles all the work of CMA and Aeronaves, by far the two leading airlines in Mexico, as well as that of some smaller lines, such as Aerolíneas de México. Furthermore, Bristol de México hopes to obtain the business of international aircraft calling in Mexico.

The total number of engines overhauled by the end of 1958 was slightly over 100. In only one of these cases was there a liability because of carelessness in the plant. Under present arrangements, Bristol has a guaranteed market of from 20 to 30 engines per month. Its financial break-even point is at about 20 engines per month. With present machinery, which occupies only one-half of its plant, its capacity is 40 engines per month. The cost of overhauling engines in Mexico is much cheaper than in more industrialized countries, principally because of the lower wage rates in Mexico; productivity is quite comparable with that in the more developed countries.

FUTURE PLANS

The site on which the Bristol plant is located was leased to the enterprise by the airport authorities at the Central Airport of Mexico City. The area of the site consists of 36,000 square yards, and the main building covers 32,000 square feet. There is, thus, room for the construction of another building on the site which can be nearly twice as large as the present one. Expansion can take place even within the present building, in only one-half of which machinery has been installed.

As has been indicated, Bristol de México is now assured of virtually all the piston engine work arising in Mexico. With the development taking place in the use of other types of aircraft engines, such as the turbo-prop and turbo-jet, Bristol is beginning to think in terms of accommodating these non-piston types of engines, at least for aircraft of international routes.

Aside from the principal work on aircraft engines, there are also possibilities for engaging in other activities and servicing other industries. For example, Bristol may at some future time assemble diesel engines. Also, because of its excellent machine and plating shops, it has already begun to do precision machining for the airlines, and it is hoped to absorb work from customers outside the aviation industry.

EVALUATION

Bristol de México has developed a line of activity which had previously been practiced in the country only to a limited extent. It has successfully developed cooperation with the leading airlines of Mexico, which are also joint ventures and are important to it both as participants in the enterprise and as customers for its services. It also was successful in obtaining the assistance of the International Finance Corporation.

Bristol of Canada, a subsidiary of the Bristol Aeroplane Company of England, is the majority stockholder and runs the enterprise under a management contract. It has been able to carry out its management functions with a very limited number of foreign personnel, and the training of Mexican operatives has been very satisfactory. The major problems to date have been related only to the need for developing more technical versatility among the local personnel.

From the joint ventures point of view, the enterprise has worked out very well in the cooperation between the Mexican and foreign interests involved. Although Bristol now has majority financial control, it is prepared to relinquish this in the future, although it will be interested in some sort of technical and management control to insure operation up to its standards of the precision type of activity in which the enterprise is engaged.

Celanese Mexicana, S.A.

ORIGIN OF THE ENTERPRISE

The Celanese Corporation of America initiated production in Mexico in 1947 through Celanese Mexicana, S.A., an enterprise which it formed together with Mexican capital and in which it first had a slight majority interest. The enterprise was first set up at the invitation of the Mexican government, which was interested in the development of local production of synthetic fibers as part of its industrialization program especially after the difficulties experienced during the Second World War in obtaining these materials abroad. The Mexican government assisted in the formation of the enterprise by granting it loan capital and tax concessions pursuant to its Law for the Development of Manufacturing Industries. The Mexican capital was placed with private Mexican investors through an underwriting operation by Mexican banking groups.

Prior to the Second World War, the manufacture of cloth based on synthetic fibers was little developed in Mexico, and such imports of the fibers as were effected came primarily from Japan and Italy. These were mostly viscose rather than acetate fibers. During the war, it was necessary to turn to the United States for these supplies, and this development permitted the Celanese Corporation of America to enter the Mexican market through exports and to develop greater utilization of its synthetic fibers.

Prior to the formation of Celanese Mexicana there were some efforts at local production of synthetic fibers. The first of these enterprises, Productora de Artisela, S.A., was set up in 1941. Later, in 1944, another enterprise, Artisela Mexicana, S.A., took over the same plant; it was more successful than the first enterprise, and reached the point of filling some 13 percent of domestic demand. These efforts were later abandoned because of inability to meet the competition of Celanese Mexicana once its production got underway, and Artisela Mexicana was merged with Celanese.

The initial investment of Celanese Mexicana amounted to 21 million pesos, and at first the company had only one plant, located at Ocotlán, State of Jalisco, and produced only one product, acetate yarns and fibers; its capacity was equivalent to about one-third of domestic consumption of all synthetic fibers.

CAPITAL STRUCTURE

The original capital of 21 million pesos has grown to 333 million pesos, and the original single plant and product to 7 plants and 29 diversified products.

By 1953, three other enterprises, viz., Viscosa Mexicana, Celulosa Nacional, and Claracel, had merged with Celanese Mexicana. They had been engaged in the production of viscose fibers and yarns as well as cellulose from cotton linters, and plastics products, and these lines were added to the acetate production of Celanese Mexicana. At the time of the merger, the Celanese Corporation of America decided to relinquish its majority control. At present,

Mexican stockholders hold the majority of Celanese Mexicana, and the balance is held by Celanese of America. By the end of 1957, the original loans of the Mexican government had been fully repaid.

The present capital of 333 million pesos is represented in 3,300,000 shares with a par value of 100 pesos each. There is only one class of common shares.

MANAGEMENT AND PERSONNEL

The Celanese Corporation of America has a technical assistance and process agreement with Celanese Mexicana.

The board of directors of the company, elected by the general assembly of stockholders, numbers 16 directors, of whom the majority are Mexicans. There is also an executive committee which is empowered to set policies and to make decisions, subject to the approval of the board. Until 1959, the position of director-general of the company was occupied by an American, but he was then succeeded by a Mexican national.

The total work force of Celanese Mexicana amounts to over 4,000 persons today, compared to 427 at the time it started production in 1947. As Mexicans have become more familiar over the years with the company's operations at the technical and managerial levels, the number of foreign employees has declined. There are now only about 40 foreigners in all in the company. To some extent, the foreigners are residents of Mexico who simply happen to have been employed by the company.

Celanese has maintained harmonious relations with labor. Working conditions are set by collective agreements with the union of its workers. It has followed a policy of providing financial assistance for special projects of the union, and a pension plan was instituted in 1958. It has followed a policy of cooperating financially and materially in community housing, welfare, and other projects of civic interest in the localities where its plants are situated.

FINANCIAL RESULTS

The rapid growth of Celanese Mexicana during the past decade or so has been fostered by its favorable financial experience. With its paid-in capital of 333 million pesos, it is one of the largest joint international business ventures in Mexico and one of the largest enterprises in the country outside of public utilities. In addition to its capital, Celanese Mexicana had surplus and reserves at the end of 1959 in the amount of 150 million pesos. Some of this expansion has been financed by a reinvestment of profits, which in the company's early years was facilitated by the "new industry" tax concessions it enjoyed. It did not, however, receive tax concessions for its nylon and plastics plants, and others have now run out. The company has sustained a policy of reinvesting a substantial part of its after-tax profits in virtually every year of its productive existence.

Actual data on earnings are not available: The company's published annual reports do not include a profit and loss statement, and there is no profit or loss item separately indicated on the liabilities side of its balance sheet. The profitability of its operations is adequately indicated by the impressive growth it has undergone, part of which, as stated heretofore, was financed by the reinvestment of profits. Some criticism of the high profits of the enterprise has been expressed in nationalistic quarters in Mexico, but, in the absence of published data on profits, it is not possible to evaluate this criticism.

ROLE IN THE ECONOMY

Celanese Mexicana now has seven plants distributed throughout the country at the following locations: one in Mexico City, three in the State of Mexico (Naucalpan, Toluca, Tulpetlac), one in the State of Michoacán (Zacapu), one in the State of Jalisco (Ocotlán), and one in the State of Tamaulipas (Río Bravo). In addition to the acetate yarns and fibers which were its original line of production, Celanese Mexicana produces viscose or rayon yarns and fibers as well. Its production is about equally divided between these two types of synthetic yarns and fibers. In 1957, it also started the production of nylon, which will soon permit imports to be eliminated. The acetate, rayon, and nylon fibers are used by the Mexican textile and apparel industries. Acetate is also utilized by the cigarette industry for the manufacture of filters, the use of which is increasing in Mexico. Rayon is used, too, by the tire industry in the form of tire cord. Celanese also produces various chemical products, such as anhydrous sodium sulphate, a product used by the paper and detergent industries; polyvinyl acetate emulsions used for paints, textiles, and adhesives; polyester resins and formaldehyde used in the plastics industry; cellulose from cotton linters, which provides some of its own raw material requirements; various plastics products for the construction and other industries; and cellophane.

The process agreement that the enterprise has with the Celanese Corporation of America has permitted it to diversify into these various fields, and will permit continued growth and diversification in the future.

Celanese Mexicana is the only producer in the country of acetate fibers and supplies all of local consumption requirements. In rayon fibers, it has the competition of two other enterprises: Viscosa de Chihuahua, a joint venture set up recently with Italian (Snia Viscosa) technical assistance and capital participation, and Celulosa y Derivados.

When Celanese Mexicana first started production, consumption in Mexico of chemical fibers of cellulose origin was almost entirely dependent on imports. Since that time consumption has tripled, and all of the demand can be more than supplied by the local industry. The import substitution process has been completed, and future growth of the industry will depend only upon growth of national consumption, unless export markets can be developed.

There has been considerable development concurrently of local raw materials for the industry, and a large percentage of the total can be supplied from domestic sources. However, the size of the market is not large enough to warrant investment in certain installations to make the country self-sufficient in raw materials for the manufacture of all synthetic fibers.

Since the beginning of the enterprise, protection against the competition of imports has been provided by a system of import licensing controls. This system has frequently worked imperfectly, but generally has provided the type of protection that an infant industry requires.

Local prices of rayon and acetate staples and fibers are in line with world prices. In nylon, despite the very recent inception of production, price comparisons are also favorable. For denier 15, a type which constitutes about one-half of local consumption, prices are slightly lower than in the United States.

EVALUATION

Celanese Mexicana, after a period of slightly more than thirteen years of operation, has grown to be one of the largest joint ventures in Mexico. The enterprise was originally formed at the invitation of and with the assistance of the Mexican government. The investment of the American interest originally constituted a majority of the total investment in the enterprise, but has since been consciously allowed to decline to a minority.

The enterprise, assisted by tax concessions, has expanded continuously, through new capital and the reinvestment of earnings, and has greatly diversified its output. It will undoubtedly continue to expand into new fields, particularly as a result of the availability to it of the research and technical facilities of the Celanese Corporation of America, as Mexican industries become more diversified and integrated.

Celanese of America is thoroughly convinced of the desirability of the formula it has followed in this investment in Mexico. In a Conference at Michigan State University held in February, 1957, Mr. Emery N. Cleaves, then Vice-President of the Celanese Corporation of America, expressed the following attitude toward joint ventures:

> I have a strong opinion that every company establishing a manufacturing facility in Mexico, or anywhere else for that matter, should organize it as a venture jointly owned with local capital. In the first place, the capital is available. In the second place, it becomes possible to stimulate national pride when selling the product. Local partners will help one avoid mistakes and handle local problems better than he. An affiliated company is not likely to become a political target whereas a foreign subsidiary may become fair game for anyone. . . .
>
> There may be some question as to whether a foreign company should enter Mexico or any other Latin American country on a financially equal basis or in a majority or minority position. My company has done all three. Over the years I think the attitude has developed that the position of stock ownership should reflect the contribution made by the respective partners. There may also be the feeling that if you don't get along with

your associates, it doesn't make much difference what proportion of the stock you own. As a matter of fact, Celanese Corporation of America, after originally owning a majority of the common shares of Celanese Mexicana, allowed its holdings to decline to a minority position when new issues of shares were made. To me that seems significant of the company's confidence in its Mexican associates.

Companhia Brasileira de Material Ferroviário (Cobrasma)

ORIGIN AND DEVELOPMENT OF THE ENTERPRISE

Cobrasma is a corporation organized under the laws of Brazil, domiciled in São Paulo, and it has its plant at Osasco, a suburb of São Paulo.

Cobrasma was founded to improve the precarious situation of the Brazilian railways during the Second World War, when they were obliged to transport ever increasing loads, and could not import needed materials from their traditional foreign suppliers.

The directors of various railways sought a solution in a plan for the domestic supply of these materials, at prices and qualities comparable with imports. A project to carry out the plan was approved in October, 1943 by the coordinator of Economic Mobilization, the director of the Export-Import Department of the Bank of Brazil, and the directors of the Paulista Railway Company, the Mogiana Railway Company, Northwest of Brazil Railway, São Paulo Railway Company, Central of Brazil Railway, São Paulo Goiaz Railway, and various leaders of Brazilian industry.

According to the project, a company was to be founded for the manufacture of railway equipment, and it was agreed that the Brazilian railways would hold the majority of its shares.

The company was founded on September 1, 1944. All the necessary facilities to assemble freight cars were prepared by 1946, and in the middle of that year the first freight car assembled by Cobrasma was delivered.

Cobrasma then signed an agreement with American Steel Foundries, under whose license railway trucks, couplers, and draft gears were to be manufactured in Brazil. A steel foundry was set up. On March 23, 1948, the first pouring was made.

Since 1951, after the railways sold their majority of shares in Cobrasma to an industrial group that now controls it, there has been a program of diversification of production to supply parts for the growing automobile industry of the country. With this program in view, a forge shop was built; it started production on June 1, 1954. A building was later constructed and equipment was purchased for the machining of automotive parts. The present automobile parts machine shop, which started production on July 16, 1956, marked the beginning of this development. This arrangement culminated in November, 1957, in the formation of a new enterprise between Cobrasma and the Rockwell firm, known as Cobrasma Rockwell Eixos S.A. (Cresa). Cresa was capitalized at 720 million cruzeiros, held to the extent of 68 percent by Cobrasma and 32 percent by Rockwell; Rockwell contributed its share entirely in the form of equipment. The enterprise also obtained a loan, in the amount of $5.32 million from the Export-Import Bank of Washington. Cresa began production in mid-1959, and was expected to be in full production in 1961. At the same time, Cobrasma expanded its forge shop, for which it obtained a loan of $1.62 million from the Export-Import Bank. Both Export-Import Bank loans were guaranteed by the Brazilian government's National Economic Development Bank.

The government's policy for the progressive development of a national automobile industry, starting with trucks, was decisive in the company's taking a stronger interest in that industry.

In November, 1955, an agreement was signed with the Timken-Detroit Axle Division of the Rockwell Spring and Axle Co. for the production in Brazil of front and rear axles for trucks and, simultaneously, the first steps were taken for the organization of this new industry.

CAPITAL STRUCTURE

Cobrasma was founded with a capital of 40 million cruzeiros, divided into 40,000 common shares with a par value of cr$1,000 each.

Subsequent capital increases were all effected through issuing the same type of shares. In all the increases, the old shareholders had a preferential option to new shares in proportion to the lots they already held.

The capital increases, from the company's foundation to April 1, 1959, were as follows:

On August 6, 1946, to cr$80 million.

On September 10, 1951, to cr$120 million.

On September 19, 1956, to cr$240 million.

On October 9, 1956, to 480 million cruzeiros. This capital increase was affected through two operations, namely a revaluation of the company's lands and industrial installations and equipment, whose book value was thereby increased by cr$98,904,530.20, and a reinvestment of the reserves accumulated in previous years in the amount of cr$141,095,469.80. The sum of these two operations is cr$240 million, permitting a 100 percent increase in the capital, to cr$480 million.

On September 9, 1957, to cr$600 million.

On February 16, 1959, the latest increase of Cobrasma's capital, to cr$900 million, became effective.

The main shareholders of the original capital, of cr$40 million, and those of the present capital, of cr$900 million are cited:

The original shareholders were Companhia Paulista de Estrada de Ferro and Companhia Mogiana de Estradas de Ferro, cr$10 million each; Cia. Siderúrgica Belgo-Mineira, cr$5 million; Monteiro Aranha & Cia. Ltda., cr$3 million; Hime Comércio & Indústria S.A., cr$1.3 million; Klabin Irmãos & Cia., cr$1.1 million; Cia. Central de Administração e Participações and Raul Veiga de Barros, cr$1 million each. Another 51 shareholders, all of Brazilian nationality, held the balance of cr$7.6 million (19 percent), their holdings ranging from lots of cr$900,000 down to cr$10,000.

With the latest capital increase to cr$900 million, voted on February 16, 1959, the distribution is the following: Cia. Melhoramentos Norte do Paraná, cr$512,130,000 (57 percent); American Steel Foundries, of Chicago, Ill., cr$135,000,000 (15 percent); Monteiro Aranha & Cia. Ltda., cr$71,460,000 (7.9 percent); S.A. Indústrias Votorantim, cr$22,650,000 (2.5 percent); Klabin Irmãos & Cia., cr$21,519,000 (2.4 percent); Maritima Companhia de Seguros Gerias, cr$10,950,000 (1.2 percent); Siderúrgica Barra Mansa, cr$10,238,000 (1.1 percent); the balance of cr$116,053,000 (12.9 percent) of the capital is held by 188 minor shareholders holding shares in lots ranging from just under cr$10 million down to cr$10,000.

According to the balance sheet of December 31, 1958, the company's assets stood as follows:

Real Estate	cr$ 19,508,620.40
Constructions and Installations	208,237,923.30
Equipment, etc.	172,072,819.90
Participations, Bonds, etc.	266,407,353.30
Total, Fixed Assets and Investments	666,226,716.90
Current Assets	766,950,264.30
Total Assets	cr$1,433,176,981.20

Besides American Steel Foundries, there are no other foreign shareholders in Cobrasma.

By April 1, 1959, American Steel Foundries had made three capital investments in Cobrasma, and had been credited with one stock dividend, as follows:

1st—in 1956, American Steel Foundries made its first capital investment in Cobrasma, buying 36,000 shares for $880 thousand thus becoming a shareholder with 15 percent of the total capital, which at that time was cr$240 million. The investment was made in the form of equipment.

2d—in October, 1956, through a revaluation of assets and reinvestment of profits, the total capital was raised from cr$240 to cr$480 million, with a total stock dividend of 240,000 shares of cr$1,000 each. American Steel Foundries was granted a dividend of 36,000 shares, that is, the amount corresponding to its 15 percent share.

3d—in 1958, American Steel Foundries, again through the supply of equipment for Cobrasma's foundry, raised its capital investment in Cobrasma by $246,320, to maintain its previous 15 percent participation, since by 1957 the total capital had been raised to cr$600 million. As of December, 1958, American Steel Foundries' participation in Cobrasma was cr$90 million.

4th—again in February, 1959, through a capital issue, Cobrasma raised its capital to cr$900 million. To maintain its 15 percent participation, American Steel Foundries decided to subscribe to 45,000 shares, which, at the value of cr$1,000 each, increased its investment to cr$135 million.

Of the total profits earned by American Steel Foundries in the enterprise, 25 to 30 percent is ploughed back, as is the case also with the Brazilian shareholders.

ROLE IN THE ECONOMY

The area on which Cobrasma's industrial shops stand is about 300,000 sq. mts. (74 acres), and it is served by railway lines of 1.00 meter and 1.60 meter track gauges. The plant tracks have three rails, thus serving both gauges, and have a length of about 11 kms. (6.5 miles). They serve various plant sections and are connected with the Osasco Station tracks of the Sorocabana Railway. Through this railway's system, Cobrasma's plant is also connected with all other railway lines of the southern, western and central states of Brazil, and will in the near future also be connected with those of the north of the country.

Electric power is supplied by the São Paulo Light and Power Company. The incoming power is transformed in a primary sub-station, and then distributed to the plant through eight secondary sub-stations. The water supply comes from two deep wells, and a water tower of 66,000 gallons capacity distributes it.

The total area covered by buildings is roughly 40,000 sq. mts. (10 acres). The principal hall of the car shop covers about 86,000 square feet. The sectional plan, resulting from a careful study of local conditions, was worked out in accordance with advice and technical assistance supplied by the Pressed Steel Car Company Inc., of Pittsburgh, Pennsylvania, and Messrs. Giffels and Vallet Inc.

The main body of the building is occupied by the assembly line, which is served by a complex system of overhead traveling cranes and overhead rails. On one side of the main body is the wheel, axle and truck section, and on the other, the shop equipped with shears, bending cylinders, and drills.

The car shop began to work in the middle of 1946. Hundreds of freight cars of the most diverse types have emerged from it since, such as refrigerated cars, ore cars with bottom and lateral discharge, tank cars, flat cars, gondolas and box cars, and cane cars.

The steel foundry was designed by Messrs. Giffels & Vallet under the supervision of American Steel Foundries and Cobrasma's own specialized engineers. American Steel Foundries are the biggest producers of cast steel parts for railway material in the United

States, and Messrs. Giffels & Vallet's engineering offices have been in charge of large projects of similar kinds in various parts of the world.

Quality control and the testing of basic materials are carried out at a chemical laboratory, at a mechanical testing center, an installation for metallographical tests, and a sand control laboratory. These laboratories carry out all routine tests and are also engaged in research work, principally concerning the substitution of imported basic materials by local ones.

After a meticulous study made of the equipment that would be required for a forge shop producing automobile parts, Cobrasma's engineers selected in the United States the most modern available for this purpose, and constructed the forge shop and the die shop, which were inaugurated in June, 1954.

The items produced include railway draft gears, trucks, and other railway materials; cast steel parts in general; cast iron parts in general; manganese steel parts for the cement and other industries; steel ingots; railway passenger cars; all types of railway freight cars; wagonettes; railway side track equipment; forged parts for trucks, automobiles, tractors, and general purposes; railway signal equipment; heat exchangers; high pressure piping forged flanges; and items of industrial equipment.

The monthly planned capacity output for the steel foundry was 1,000 tons of finished parts, a figure often surpassed. The forge shop was originally equipped to turn out 500 tons of forged parts, weighing from a few grams to two or three tons.

The railway car shop can manufacture any type of railway car (gondolas, flat cars, box cars, tank cars, ballast cars, sugarcane cars). The shop can produce up to 100 railway cars per month, in addition to the wagonettes and repair and reconditioning services.

Cobrasma's actual production of railway equipment in the period 1954–57 is shown in the following table:

	Units Produced			
Product	*1954*	*1955*	*1956*	*1957*
Cars	364	564	447	352
Trucks	4,907	2,215	5,128	6,632
Draft gears	8,157	9,566	9,378	18,849
Others	3,524	5,252	13,691	15,648

Besides the railway equipment, other industrial facilities such as the foundry, forge, and rolling mill are quite active in total production.

As to the national market for railway cars, it is estimated that Cobrasma supplies about 25 percent. In parts such as forged axles, draft gears and others, its participation is much larger since Cobrasma supplies other existing railway car factories in the country.

Raw materials used are: Volta Redonda (government-owned steel mill) steel plates and bars; small bars from other domestic mills; iron and steel scrap; pig iron; ferro-alloys; steels for forgings and coil springs. All these materials are domestically produced.

The graphite electrodes for the electric furnaces are the sole raw materials imported and used in large quantities.

TECHNICAL ASSISTANCE

The corporation has a patent use agreement and a technical assistance agreement with American Steel Foundries International, S.A., with headquarters in Venezuela and offices in Chicago, Illinois; with the M. W. Kellogg Company; with the Peerless Equipment Company; the General Railway Signal Company; and the Union Asbestos & Rubber Company.

The American Steel Foundries contract has been in operation for more than ten years, and has enabled the company to manufacture approximately 40,000 railway trucks and 65,000 couplers for the Brazilian railroads, in addition to railway equipment for export to Argentina.

The contract with M. W. Kellogg has been in force for about three years. Inasmuch as the technical assistance for the manufacture of heat exchangers provided for in this contract is one of a permanent nature, and considering the availability in Brazil of basic products such as steel, pipes, etc., Kellogg had to resort to a detailed study of their specifications to permit the use of these raw materials.

Royalties on both contracts are paid in cruzeiros, converted on the free dollar market and remitted to the headquarters of the companies involved.

For years American Steel Foundries International S.A. kept the proceeds of such royalties in Brazil. Using these accumulated royalties together with a substantial dollar investment from the United States, American Steel Foundries International S.A. made its 15 percent investment in Cobrasma.

None of the foreign organizations has a director or representative in the corporation.

The contracts with Peerless Equipment and General Railway Signal cover licenses to produce railway equipment parts such as traction gears, railway signal equipment, and brakes.

EVALUATION

The technical and commercial relationships between the engineers and directors of Cobrasma and those of the foreign organizations cooperating with the enterprise have been continuously harmonious.

Especially in the case of American Steel Foundries, the experience has been excellent. Technical problems are studied either in American Steel Foundries or Cobrasma laboratories for the mutual benefit of both organizations. Royalties have always been paid on the basis of Cobrasma financial records sent to American Steel Foundries, even before their association as equity partners. This background of understanding and honest collaboration by both parties led to a capital association based on complete trust. For this reason, although American Steel Foundries tries to maintain its proportion of the capital stock at 15 percent, mainly for profit reasons, it never thought it necessary to have one of its officers on the joint venture's board of directors.

With respect to the matter of foreign versus domestic personnel, as a matter of policy, Cobrasma prefers to work with local people. Of 44 engineers working in its plants, only 3 are foreigners (Polish), but they are by now Brazilian-naturalized. At the beginning of the foundry operations, Cobrasma imported 5 Italian skilled workers, but as of today only one remains.

It is felt in Cobrasma that "know-how" can be transmitted to local personnel with relative facility. Therefore, for cost reasons as well as for reasons of human relations, it is considered more desirable to have domestic labor and management, especially since there is no question of impairing productivity levels, which are comparable with those of the United States, with the same industrial processes and equipment as in that country.

Companhia Siderúrgica Mannesmann

ORIGIN AND DEVELOPMENT OF CAPITAL STRUCTURE

The paid-up capital of this firm amounts to cr$1,680,000,000, with the following distribution: The foreign participation is by Overzee Holding Maatschappij N.V., of Curaçao, Netherlands West Indies, a subsidiary of Mannesmann A.G. of Germany, with 79.4 percent of the total in registered common shares. The remaining 20.6 percent is in the hands of Brazilian citizens or Brazilian enterprises. The main shareholders of this part are the Banco de Crédito Real de Minas Gerais, the Banco Hipotecário e Agrícola do Estado de Minas Gerais, and the Banco Mineiro da Produção.

At a general assembly held on February 15, 1952, the corporation was organized, with headquarters in the city of Rio de Janeiro, and a capital of cr$400,000,000 (400,000 shares of cr$1,000 each), for the main purpose of setting up in the country a steel mill for the production of Mannesmann seamless pipes.

This venture was the result of the combined efforts of Brazilian and German industrialists and businessmen, the latter on behalf of Mannesmann A.G., of Germany.

The founders were: the Banco de Crédito Real de Minas Gerais, with 35,000 shares; the Banco Mineiro da Produção, and the Banco Hipotecário e Agrícola de Minas Gerais, also with 35,000 shares each; the Banco Holandes Unido, with 25,000 shares; the Banco do Distrito Federal, with 10,000 shares; and the Comércio e Indústria Mannex do Brasil (a Brazilian subsidiary of Mannesmann), and Sampaio & Kahn, with 210,000 and 50,000 shares respectively.

The first board of directors consisted of a director-president (Sigmund Weiss); a director-secretary (Jorge de Serpa Filho); and a director-treasurer (Joaquim Mendes de Souza).

Once the studies for the mill project were terminated, the cornerstone for the venture was laid during a ceremony on May 31, 1952. Construction proceeded at a rapid pace, making possible the inauguration in August, 1954 of the pipe extrusion press and related installations.

The post of industrial director was created at an assembly meeting on April 30, 1953, and was filled by Rudolf Mooshake, a German engineer. Upon his retirement in 1959, he was replaced by Hermann Kleinheisterkamp, also of German nationality.

In view of the rapid rate of construction, and in response to a request of the government and private entities of Minas Gerais, the board of directors proposed a change in the corporation's headquarters to Belo Horizonte, and the proposal was accepted at a general assembly on August 28, 1953.

At this general assembly, Odilon Behrens was elected director-treasurer, replacing Joaquim Mendes de Souza, who had resigned from the post of his own accord. Both are Brazilians. Pursuant to the financial scheme initially drawn up, the capital was increased to cr$700,000,000, the general assembly authorizing on September 30, 1954, the issue of 300,000 shares, 150,000 of which were common shares and the other 150,000 preferred shares. The by-laws were altered for the creation of preferred type of shares. This issue was well received in the Brazilian capital market, and there was ready subscription to the capital increase.

During 1955, the main industrial installations were set up, including the automatic mill, the round bar rolling mill, the steel works, and reduction furnaces, with a total of 27,390 tons of machinery and installations.

At a board of directors meeting on June 13, 1955, José Machado Freire was appointed acting director-treasurer. He replaced Odilon Behrens, who had resigned from his post. Mr. Freire, a Brazilian, was elected for another term on April 23, 1956.

Once the installation of the industrial equipment was terminated, the corporation started its commercial operations, creating for this purpose the post of commercial director, to which Walter Schnabel, of German nationality, was elected on April 23, 1956.

In view of the increase in business and with the purpose of providing greater financial support for the plans of the administration, the board of directors presented for the consideration of the shareholders a new proposal for a capital increase up to cr$1.26 billion.

The general assembly approved this proposal on May 12, 1958, and appointed as commercial director Edwin May, of German nationality, to replace the former director who had resigned.

On August 18, 1959, the general assembly authorized another increase in the capital to cr$1.68 billion by a revaluation of the fixed assets. Aside from an initial loan of cr$265 million negotiated with the Bank of Brazil, no other financing has been requested of Brazilian credit institutions.

The shares of the corporation, with a par value of cr$1,000 each, include both common and preferred, and can be issued either to the bearer or registered. Preferred shares have no voting rights and cannot be redeemed, but enjoy the following advantages:

a) Priority in the collection of non-cumulative dividends of ten percent a year, on their face value;

b) Right to participate on an equal footing with common shares in the distribution of the remaining profit from each year of operations, after certain deductions as set forth in Article 32 of the corporation's by-laws;

c) Right to participate on an equal footing with common shares in the distribution by the corporation of stock dividends or any other securities or advantages, including the capitalization of reserves and the revaluation of assets;

d) Preference in capital reimbursement up to their nominal value at the time of liquidation of the corporation; common shares are reimbursed up to their nominal value after the preferred. The balance is distributed on an equal footing between common and preferred shares, but observing the special rights of founders' shares, in accordance with the corporation law;

e) Right to attend the general assembly, and to discuss the subjects brought up for analysis, in accordance with Article 90 of Law 2627 of 1940.

In addition to common and preferred shares, the corporation also issued founders' shares. These 40,000 founders' shares issued to the bearer by the corporation entitle their holders to the rights mentioned in Article 31 and those following of Law 2627 of 1940. These founders' shares have, in general, the right to a participation of five percent of the annual net profit of the corporation. Net profit, for the purpose of the percentage to be distributed to founders' shares, means the profit shown in the balance sheet after the deduction of amounts destined to reserve funds and redemption of founders' shares themselves and of the dividends to be paid to the shareholders. The redemption fund for founders' shares is constituted by the allocation for this purpose of five percent of the net profits. The corporation may, at any time, totally or partially redeem the founders' shares, taking as a basis for the redemption price, the average of the amounts distributed to them in the last three years. The capital that would be necessary to produce the net profit attributed to them, on the basis of a return of 12 percent per annum, determines the redemption price. Should the amount reached by the redemption fund be higher then the amount figured according to the provisions of this Article, redemption is effected on the basis of the amount in the fund. In the event of a partial redemption of founders' shares, the portion of net profit that would correspond to the redeemed founders' shares is applied to the strengthening of the founders' shares redemption fund. Founders' shares cannot be converted into common or preferred shares. In the event of liquidation of the corporation, founders' shares have the rights prescribed in the corporation law.

Mannesmann has not issued any debentures or bonds, either in the country or abroad, but only common and preferred shares, and founders' shares.

The business year coincides with the calendar year. Net profits are distributed as follows:

Five percent for the legal reserve fund until it reaches 20 percent of the corporation's capital.

Five percent for depreciation allowances and installations maintenance.

The amount required for the payment of the ten percent guaranteed to preferred shares.

The amount required for the payment of dividends up to ten percent to common shares, calculated on their face value.

Five percent for the redemption fund of founders' shares.

Five percent for the earnings of founders' shares.

Seven percent for the varying remuneration of the directors.

Three percent for the varying remuneration of the advisors' council.

The destination of the balance is determined by the general assembly, on the basis of proposals of the board of directors and opinions of the fiscal council.

There are no payments of royalties or special costs for technical assistance.

FINANCIAL RESULTS AND ROLE IN THE ECONOMY

As previously indicated, on February 15, 1952, the Companhia Siderúrgica Mannesmann existed only in the minutes recording its organization. In 1953, ground was cleared and the mill foundations were begun. In 1954, industrial activities were started and subsequently developed until 1958, when capacity production was attained.

The Brazilian market is growing by leaps and bounds. Brazilian steel production is today ten times as large as at the time the industry was begun. It is predicted that in 1963 it will surpass the 3,000,000 ton mark. The tightening of exchange facilities and high importation costs coincided with the tremendous development in the country of the steel consuming industries. Owing to the good quality of Brazilian steel and to its low cost, it was expected, and this actually happened, that these industries would prefer to use the domestic product. However, the continuous demand being larger than supply, imports are still necessary, though on a decreasing scale. Between 1900 and 1940, Brazil regularly imported from 150,000 to 250,000 tons of steel per annum. Imports were higher after the Second World War, having reached 500,000 tons in 1956. Hence a production deficit still exists, making it necessary to effect an increase in production to balance supply and demand. This situation is in general favorable to the corporation. It remains for it to increase its production capacity, and studies are being conducted and arrangements are being made to increase its steelmaking capacity to 300,000 tons per year.

The first commercial year for Mannesmann was 1957, and in 1958 there was a thorough consolidation of its production capacity. In 1957, the monthly average of orders was 3,206 tons; in 1958, orders stepped up to 9,279 tons monthly: 4,840 for steel and 4,439 for pipes. Raw steel production rose by 39.5 percent between the two years, reaching 91,000 tons in 1958. Pipe production remained practically stable at 34,266 tons, while constantly growing demand for round and square steel bars made 1958 output of those items increase by 350 percent, reaching 30,375 tons. A total of 71,716 tons of products was shipped in 1958.

It was only after April, 1958 that the mill worked at full capacity. Hence the favorable results mentioned correspond to a period of about eight months of full activity, and the results in 1959 were still better. In 1959, the output of round and square steel bars increased by 36 percent, reaching 41,173 tons, and of pipe by 22 percent, reaching 41,779 tons. A total of 86,271 tons of products was dispatched—20 percent more than in 1958.

While output in 1958 and 1959 reached or even surpassed forecasts, no less encouraging were the financial results, as shown in the balance sheet data. The small accumulated loss at the end of 1957 was converted into a profit of cr$315 million by the end of 1959.

BALANCE SHEET DATA, 1957–59 (*millions of cruzeiros*)

	End of 1957	*End of 1958*	*End of 1959*
Assets			
Fixed Assets	1,115.6	1,358.5	2,111.9
Disposable Assets	14.8	15.7	31.9
Current Assets	778.6	1,265.1	1,734.4
Inventories	416.5	586.6	957.1
Receivables and Others	362.1	678.5	777.3
Liabilities			
Capital	700.0	1,260.0	1,680.0
Reserves	119.8	75.8	95.7
Depreciation	51.9	118.4	254.1
Current Liabilities and Long-term Loans	1,047.1	1,023.9	1,533.1
Loans (including long term)	361.9	420.8	386.5
Other Current Liabilities	685.2	603.1	1,146.6
Profits and Losses	—9.6	161.2	315.3
Cash Distributed	—	—	—

EVALUATION

Mannesmann emphatically makes a point of the ever-growing "nationalization" of its manufacturing processes. The enterprise was planned for maximum use of domestic raw materials and power sources. Minas Gerais, with its rivers and waterfalls, offers outstanding power possibilities, and has made it possible to ignore the traditional blast furnaces and to give preference to electric furnaces, which consume less coal for ore reduction. Minas Gerais, and particularly Belo Horizonte, provided ideal characteristics for the mill location due to their rich iron ore mines, sources of electric power, and abundant manpower. Thus, looking at the list of raw materials that went into the manufacture of pig iron, steel, and pipes during 1958, out of the 15 elements needed, only 5 were imported while the other 10 were all supplied domestically. The corporation manufactures the tools needed for the maintenance of its output, which also means a substantial saving in exchange.

Relations between the three Brazilian directors and the two foreign directors, as well as between Brazilian and German technicians, have developed in the most cordial atmosphere. Subordinate personnel has willingly accepted foreign technical supervision, which has been necessary because of the nature of the enterprise. The director-president, Dr. Sigmund Weiss, is a Brazilian naturalized citizen of German origin who has resided in Brazil for about 20 years.

The reaction of the Brazilian capital market to the issues launched by Mannesmann has been most favorable, and there has been rapid public subscription to the corporation's shares.

With respect to Mannesmann's experience in Brazil, it is significant to quote from a statement made by Hermann Winkhauss, president of Mannesmann A.G. of Germany, at the time of his visit to Mannesmann do Brasil in the middle of 1959:

> Cooperation with Brazilians is a real source of pleasure. This nation's government has always shown the utmost understanding. In the people of this country we have always found collaborators of high human and individual value. Among the 2,000 or more workers of the steel and pipe mill of Barreiro (Belo Horizonte) there are today approximately 50 German nationals. In the next years, this contingent will become only 1.5% to 2% of the entire staff. This proves how highly we value the cooperation of the Brazilian group.

Descuento Agrícola, S.A.

ORIGIN OF THE ENTERPRISE

Descuento Agrícola, S.A. was set up in September, 1955 as an institution to extend credit for agricultural purposes, especially the acquisition of agricultural machinery. The idea for this institution originated in the Mexican Association of Distributors of Agricultural Machinery, an association made up of importers and agents for agricultural machinery, most of which is of United States origin. The Mexican Association had obtained credit facilities from time to time from the Bank of America for the importation and sale on credit terms of its machinery. Recognizing the need for continuous use of credit facilities, not only for the importation of agricultural machinery but also for its sale internally, the Mexican Association took the initiative and approached the Bank of America, the Nacional Financiera, and local private banks with the idea of forming a credit company that would extend medium-term facilities for its machinery. Descuento Agrícola was, in fact, later formed as a joint venture of these four groups: the Nacional Financiera, the Bank of America, private Mexican banks, and the Mexican Association of Distributors of Agricultural Machinery.

As a credit institution licensed by the Mexican Ministry of Finance, and subject to the supervision of the National Banking Commission, Descuento Agrícola is known as a "financing, savings, and trust institution" (*institución financiera, de ahorro y fideicomiso*). It is thus empowered to receive savings from the public, and to engage in trust operations. To date, however, it has only been engaged in lending operations.

CAPITAL STRUCTURE

The authorized capital of Descuento Agrícola amounts to 20 million pesos, the distribution of which is as follows: 10 percent Nacional Financiera, 20 percent Bank of America, 40 percent private Mexican banks, and 30 percent the Mexican Association of Distributors of Agricultural Machinery. The Mexican banking group consists of five of the most important private commercial banks of the country: Banco de Comercio, Banco de Londres y México, Banco Comercial Mexicano, Banco Mexicano, and Banco Comercial de la Propiedad.

Of the 20 million pesos of authorized capital, only 10 million pesos have been paid in to date. In addition to this source of funds, Descuento Agrícola has obtained resources for its lending operations from various of the banks associated with it. These lines of credit have amounted to date to 20 million pesos, or twice the amount of the paid-in capital of the institution.

MANAGEMENT

The board of directors consists of 11 members, one named by Nacional Financiera, two by the Bank of America, three by the Mexican Association of Distributors of Agricultural Machinery, and five by the private Mexican banks (one by each bank). This distribution is pursuant to the rule that each million pesos of paid-up shares gives the right to name one director (and an alternate), with the exception that the five private Mexican banks have specifically been given the right to name one director each (they would otherwise have a total of only four). Aside from this, there are no particular voting privileges for any specific groups of shares, which are all of one, common type. The president of the board is named, in rotation, by each one of the four shareholding groups. At present, he is the representative of the private Mexican banks.

For operating purposes, there is a credit committee with the following representation: one permanent member named by Nacional Financiera, one permanent representative of the Bank of America, and four representatives who change every two months, two named by the private banks and two by the importers of machinery. Every two months, two of the private banks name one such representative each, and there is similar rotation for this purpose among the various companies that make up the Mexican Association. The credit committee meets once a week; its decisions with respect to credit applications are subject to review and change by the board of directors.

The director-general, or chief executive officer of the company, is named on the basis of general voting procedures. At present, this post happens to be occupied by one of the directors named by the Bank of America, who is a Mexican; as director-general, however, he does not represent the Bank of America.

FINANCIAL RESULTS

During the period of about 2½ years from its inauguration in September, 1955 to April, 1958, Descuento Agrícola extended loans in the amount of 57.5 million pesos, of which 31.9 million pesos were repaid, leaving an outstanding balance of 25.6 million pesos. These loans were extended to more than 1,100 farmers, whose properties amount to about 50,000 hectares (125,000 acres). The credits have financed the purchase of a wide range of agricultural machinery and tools including tractors, plows, harrows, sowers, cultivators, threshers, combines, harvesters, and levelers.

The purchase of the machinery financed by these credits is effected through members of the Mexican Association of Distributors of Agricultural Machinery. These loans have been made mostly to farmers with individual holdings, but two loans have also been made to groups of communal farmers, and the experience has been entirely favorable. As of April, 1958, only 1½ percent of the portfolio of Descuento Agrícola was in arrears, and the prospects were for 100 percent collections.

The loans are generally made at terms of two years, with repayments during the period as follows: repayment of 30 percent after 6 months, 35 percent after a year, and the remaining 35 percent after 2 years. Interest and all other charges in no case exceed 12 percent per annum. This is considered a favorable rate in Mexico; credit institutions that supply medium-term credits to industry are not authorized to charge more, but the maximum rate established by law is frequently circumvented through special, hidden charges of various types.

Descuento Agrícola has been able to pay moderate and increasing dividends to its stockholders: operations in 1956 permitted a dividend rate of 3½ percent; in 1957, 6½ percent; and in 1958, 8 percent.

ROLE IN THE ECONOMY

Mexico has a large part of its population devoted to agricultural pursuits, and the use of machinery and the availability of credit to agriculture are limited. It is estimated that 52 percent of the economically active population of Mexico is devoted to agriculture. Most of its total cultivated land in 1950 was worked with animal power. Agricultural machinery was used on only some 4 percent of the one-third that had any power at all. The remainder of this one-third overwhelmingly utilized only animal power, to the extent of 80 percent of the total, and 16 percent used mixed animal and mechanical power. In absolute figures, only some 430,000 hectares (1,075,000 acres) used agricultural machinery, while 7.1 million hectares (17.8 million acres) remained to be mechanized. The scope for increasing sales of agricultural machinery is obvious.

Existing credit facilities for agriculture are very limited, and are practically all of a short-term character. The main sources of agricultural credit are two government-owned banks, the Banco Nacional de Crédito Agrícola y Ganadero, and the Banco Nacional de Crédito Ejidal. The former institution extends credit to individual landowners while the latter works with communal farmers. The limited extent of agricultural credit, and the predominant role of these two institutions in the total of agricultural credit, are indicated in the following figures: At the end of 1957, total credits outstanding of the country's banking system amounted to 22.5 billion pesos, of which only 3.6 billion pesos were nominally listed as agricultural (much of the "agricultural" credit was probably actually used for other purposes). The total of agricultural credit outstanding of government-owned credit institutions was 2.2 billion pesos on the same date. Although the figures previously indicated for the credits of Descuento Agrícola are still small in relation to these totals, it is obvious that they are of some significance, and will be even more so in the future.

Furthermore, these global comparisons tend to minimize the significance of Descuento Agrícola since it is in the business of extending medium-term credits, which are practically totally unavailable elsewhere. Even the two government agricultural credit institutions generally limit their operations to crop loans with a maturity not exceeding one year, and the private bank loans to agriculture generally do not exceed six months. There is, of course, also usury financing available to small farmers from individual lenders, and some of the larger farm units dealing in commercial crops such as cotton, tobacco, and truck crops obtain credit facilities from their customers.

In short, Descuento Agrícola, with its medium-term credit facilities for the acquisition of agricultural machinery, is virtually filling a vacuum in the Mexican credit structure. It is hoped that it may enter other phases of agricultural financing in the future for which present facilities are either very limited or non-existent, such as the construction of rural housing and other edifices, the establishment of agricultural processing industries, and the opening up of new areas to planting. The foreign investment and participation are on a relatively small minority basis, but constitute an interesting supplement in local currency financing in a field where the foreign bank involved was previously engaged only in foreign exchange financing. Another interesting aspect of the venture is its predominantly private character, although there is some minority investment and participation by the Mexican government through Nacional Financiera, in a field such as agricultural credit where previously government institutions have been virtually the only suppliers because of a lack of interest in private banking quarters.

Fábrica Nacional de Maquinaria Textil Toyoda de México, S.A.

ORIGIN OF THE ENTERPRISE

One of the oldest and most important manufacturing industries in Mexico is the cotton textile industry. It employs some 50,000 workers, and produces about 100,000 tons of cloth per year. The industry has approximately 1,300,000 spindles and 50,000 looms. The majority of this equipment is, however, obsolete, being more than 25 years old. Shortly after the Second World War, much consideration was given by the government in Mexico to the need for replacement and modernization. Except for a few parts, textile machinery had to be imported into the country, and it was considered desirable by the government, in view of the large machinery requirements of the local cotton textile industry and to conserve foreign exchange, to investigate the feasibility of undertaking the manufacture of the machinery in Mexico.

Nacional Financiera, the official development bank, investigated the possibility of interesting textile machinery producers in various countries, and finally came to an understanding with the Toyoda Automatic Loom Works Limited of Japan. Intensive studies at the Toyoda Works in Japan were carried out by engineers and technicians both of Nacional Financiera and of the Central Bank of Mexico.

Toyoda of Japan, with more than 50 years of experience, is one of the largest textile machinery manufacturers in the world. It employs 4,300 workers and produces annually 8,000 automatic looms and 600,000 spindles. The Japanese textile industry is equipped with Toyoda products to the extent of 60 percent of its total machinery. Toyoda, furthermore, is engaged in important overseas operations, with respect both to the export of its machinery and to royalty arrangements for the use of its patents.

The Fábrica Nacional de Maquinaria Textil Toyoda de México, S.A., was formed on June 4, 1954. The site selected for the plant was Cuidad Sahagún (formerly Irolo), in the State of Hidalgo, at a distance of 120 kilometers from Mexico City. This is a new industrial site in the country, where other important enterprises have been established in recent years, including a railway car plant, the Constructora Nacional de Carros de Ferrocarril, S.A., and a plant that produces diesel engines and trucks, Diesel Nacional, S.A. Construction of the plant was begun in October, 1954, and completed in June, 1956. With the recent nationalization of Toyoda de México, the plan is to coordinate its activities closely with those of the two plants at Ciudad Sahagún.

CAPITAL STRUCTURE

Toyoda de México was first set up with a capital of 35 million pesos. Originally, all of this capital was supplied in the form of machinery by Toyoda of Japan, although Nacional Financiera had committed itself to financing even before the company was formally organized.

The Nacional Financiera participation became effective in April, 1955, when the capital of the enterprise was raised from 35 million pesos to 50 million pesos through subscription by Nacional Financiera of 15 million pesos of eight percent preferential shares. Later, at the beginning of 1958, the capital was once again raised, this time to its present level of 60 million pesos. Nacional Financiera took another 3 million pesos of preferential shares, to make its total investment in the enterprise 18 million pesos. Until November, 1959 Toyoda of Japan held 59 percent, Nacional Financiera 30 percent (the 18 million pesos of preferential shares), and the balance of 11 percent was held by private Mexican investors. In November, 1959, Nacional Financiera bought the Toyoda 59 percent share, and thus became an 89 percent shareholder in the enterprise.

In addition to its equity, Toyoda de México has obtained medium-term loans amounting to 47 million pesos, of which 25 million pesos have been obtained from Nacional Financiera and 22 million pesos from private foreign banks, the latter guaranteed by Nacional Financiera.

MANAGEMENT AND PERSONNEL

Toyoda de México manufactures machinery for the textile industry, domestic sewing machines, and also runs its own iron and steel foundry. For each of these divisions, it has had formal technical assistance contracts with foreign firms. Toyoda of Japan had a technical assistance contract for the textile machinery, on the basis of a royalty of five percent on the sales of such machinery, which lapsed in April, 1960. Another Japanese enterprise, Aichi Kogyo Limited, had a similar technical assistance contract for the sewing machines, and the American Steel Foundries International of the United States supplies technical assistance for the foundry operations.

Until November, 1959, the company's board of directors consisted of ten members, of which six were Japanese and four Mexican; the chairman of the board was Japanese. The preferential shares, held by Nacional Financiera, had the right to name two of the directors as well as a financial inspector (*comisario*). They also had the right to veto certain important decisions of the board, including those relating to distribution of profits, reinvestments, and the contracting of loans. The important executive officers of the enterprise were an executive director, and two general managers, one of which was the plant manager and the other a sales manager; only the sales manager was Mexican. These arrangements have changed with the nationalization of the enterprise.

The personnel of the enterprise numbered 625 by the latter part of 1959, of which 53 were Japanese, consisting mostly of the top executive officers and technical personnel. Originally, almost all the technical personnel were Japanese, but later, considerable progress was made in moving Mexican personnel into technical positions.

The workers of the enterprise are organized in a union, with which there is a collective labor contract, providing for important fringe benefits such as housing, restaurant and health facilities, sports activities, work clothing, educational facilities for the children of workers, and certain loan availabilities.

ROLE IN THE ECONOMY

Toyoda de México has a capacity for annual output of 3,600 looms, 120,000 spindles, 36,000 domestic sewing machines, and foundry products for rolling stock and other purposes to the extent of close to one-fourth of its total productive capacity. The break-even point for the enterprise is estimated to be at an annual value of total production of 40 million pesos. This point has not yet been reached. During the last half of 1956, the value of output at 19 million pesos approximated this annual rate; in 1957, however, the total value of production amounted to only about 13 million pesos; and during 1958, it amounted to under 30 million pesos. By the end of 1958, accumulated losses amounted to some 36 million pesos. Aside from the difficulties involved in the initiation of a new line of production in Mexico, there were some difficulties in acceptance of the machinery of the enterprise in the local market in competition with imports. Because of the wide range of textile machinery items, there has been little effective customs or import licensing protection in this field against imported products. Furthermore, although the enterprise seemed clearly to qualify for tax concessions as a new industry and applied for them, these concessions were not granted.

The Toyoda capacity in textile machinery, including 3,600 looms and 120,000 spindles, would permit a replacement rate of somewhat less than ten percent per year of the obsolete equipment in use in the Mexican cotton textile industry.

With respect to domestic sewing machines, in addition to the annual capacity of 36,000 units of Toyoda, and probably in response to the competition of the Toyoda enterprise, the Singer Sewing Machine Company set up a wholly-owned subsidiary in Mexico in 1958 with a present capacity of 40,000 units per year and a projected future capacity of 80,000 units. In this field, there are effective import controls, in contrast with the industrial textile machinery, since sewing machines are a much more uniform and clearly definable item.

Toyoda produces a variety of foundry products for internal combustion engines, railway rolling stock, and for its own raw materials requirements in textile machinery. Customers for its products include the two other important manufacturing enterprises located at the same site in Sahagún as well as Industria Eléctrica de México (the joint venture with participation by Westinghouse) and the General Electric subsidiary in Mexico. Because it has its own foundry, Toyoda is able to obtain about 80 percent of its raw materials domestically.

At the time of its agreement with the government to set up an enterprise in Mexico, Toyoda committed itself not to set up a textile machinery factory in any other country of Latin America and to use products from its Mexican plant in an assembly operation planned for Brazil. Future plans included export operations to other countries of the Latin American area.

Toyoda textile machinery manufactured in Mexico is able to sell at prices competitive with or only about 10–15 percent higher than the prices of European machinery, and at prices well below those of United States products.

EVALUATION

Toyoda de México is the only manufacturer of textile machinery in Mexico. It also produces domestic sewing machines, and in this field has since been followed by the Singer Sewing Machine Company, which recently set up a wholly-owned manufacturing subsidiary in the country. Supplying most of its own raw materials requirements from local sources, it will result in substantial savings of foreign exchange for the country, at prices for its products which are competitive with the prices of imports. Its foundry department supplies some of these raw materials for other Mexican industries as well.

The enterprise was formed, at the invitation of the Mexican government, with a majority of Japanese capital, although the Mexican minority participation, both official and private, was substantial. Toyoda of Japan, on this account as well as through a formal technical assistance agreement, ran the enterprise. However, Nacional Financiera, the important official Mexican minority stockholder, holding the preferential shares of the enterprise, had certain veto rights with respect to important decisions of the company's board of directors. Aside from its equity, Nacional Financiera had also supplied substantial credits as well as guarantees for credits obtained abroad.

Under these arrangements Toyoda de México had difficulties in developing its production to capacity, primarily because of the problem of acceptance of its products in the market. Eventually, a little more than three years after it started production, the enterprise was nationalized by the government development bank purchase of the majority foreign interest. Thus, though the joint venture has not persisted, it has resulted in the formation of an important new industrial facility in Mexico. The reorganization of the enterprise scheduled for 1960 was also to include its assumption of a new company name.

Hotel Tequendama

This joint venture involves no capital participation by the foreign partner. The hotel is owned entirely by Colombian capital, and is managed entirely by the foreign interest on the basis of a management contract. The promotion of the hotel resulted from the initiative of the foreign interest, which obtained the local capital for the investment as well as a substantial foreign loan to help finance the construction of the hotel. The result has been a hotel in the capital of Colombia which is in a class well above that of the other hotels that previously existed. Despite a level of rates which has been moderate by international standards, the hotel has yielded a good return to the investors and has been maintained very well through the investment of adequate sums out of earnings for this purpose. The need for such a hotel in Bogotá is reflected in the very high occupancy rate that the Hotel Tequendama has enjoyed, and by the importance that the hotel has assumed in the community as a center of social activities.

ORIGIN OF THE ENTERPRISE

The Hotel Tequendama has been in operation since May, 1953. The hotel is the result of the initiative of the Intercontinental Hotels Corporation, a subsidiary of Pan American World Airways, which operates hotels in a number of Latin American countries. In connection with its own interest in hotel operations and also because of the interest of its parent company in stimulating travel to Colombia, the IHC undertook to promote the organization of a first-class hotel in Bogotá. To this end, it set about looking for an appropriate local group of investors. It was finally successful in interesting in this investment the Caja de Sueldos de Retiro de las Fuerzas Armadas, the pension fund for officers of the armed forces in Colombia.

A corporation known as Hotel San Diego S.A. was set up for the venture in November, 1948. The stock was subscribed almost entirely by the Caja de Sueldos de Retiro. IHC did not participate as an investor. A loan was obtained from the Export-Import Bank of Washington to help finance construction.

CAPITAL STRUCTURE

The corporation Hotel San Diego S.A. was formed with a capital of 6 million pesos, of which the subscription by the Caja de Sueldos de Retiro amounted to 5.8 million pesos. Small amounts (20,000 pesos each) were subscribed by two other official or semi-official agencies of the Colombian government, the Fondo de Estabilización of the Central Bank and the Instituto de Fomento Industrial; and a small token amount of 6,800 pesos was subscribed by eight private Colombian investors.

Steady increases in the capital of the corporation were made during the course of construction of the hotel. At the time of its completion, the paid-in capital amounted to 11.3 million pesos; in addition to new capital contributed by the Caja de Sueldos de Retiro and by the Fondo de Estabilización, the Municipality of Bogotá had also become a small shareholder. At the end of 1959, the paid-in capital amounted to 11.9 million pesos, of which the Caja de Sueldos de Retiro held slightly more than 98 percent.

MANAGEMENT

The IHC was completely in charge of the work involved in planning and constructing the hotel; it undertook to contract the services of a United States firm of architects, and took the responsibility for seeing the project through to completion. It was also instrumental in obtaining financing for the hotel from the Export-Import Bank of Washington. In 1949 the Export-Import Bank granted a loan of $3,057,600, repayment of which was to begin in 1954 and to be completed in 1971. An additional medium-term loan of $942,400, to make a total of $4 million, was obtained from the Export-Import Bank during the course of construction in 1952; the last installment in repayment of this loan was made in June, 1958. The total Export-Import Bank financing was almost equal in amount to the peso financing of the hotel contributed by the local investors.

IHC has had a management contract for operation of the hotel. For this service, which involves complete management responsibility, it receives a fixed annual fee plus a participation in profits. The management contract, which at first had a term of 5 years, was extended as of January 1, 1959, for a period of 15 years.

FINANCIAL RESULTS AND ROLE IN THE ECONOMY

The Hotel Tequendama has a total of 387 rooms, of which 378 are in service for guests. At the time of its construction, there was considerable public doubt as to whether Bogotá could support a first-class hotel of this size. The operating experience of the hotel has clearly shown that the more optimistic expectations of the promoters were correct.

The Hotel Tequendama is "the" hotel in Bogotá, and is a leading center for social activities in the capital. During the year 1959, its average occupancy rate was 82.8 percent. The break-even point for hotels in general is an occupancy rate of between 40 percent and 50 percent, and for a hotel of the characteristics of the Tequendama, it is considered to be closer to 40 percent. The average occupancy rate for hotels in the United States of over 500 rooms, with which the Tequendama is comparable, is about 71 percent.

Total profits from operation of the hotel, after deduction of depreciation reserves, amounted to 3.5 million pesos in 1959. This represented a rate of return of about 13 percent on invested capital (paid-in capital plus the Export-Import Bank loan). Available for distribution to the shareholders was the amount of approximately 2.7 million pesos, representing a return of about 21 percent of paid-in capital.

IHC has been successful in having adequate sums devoted to maintenance of the physical plant of the hotel. In this connection, it follows the standards of the "Uniform System of Accounts for Hotels" as prescribed by the American Hotel Association. The excellent physical condition of the hotel reflects this policy.

IHC purchased a majority interest of the Hotel del Prado in Barranquilla, another principal city of Colombia on the North Coast, in August, 1957. To finance this investment, it took a local loan in pesos, and is repaying the loan out of the management fees it earns for operation of the Hotel Tequendama. Thus, it is reinvesting the proceeds of one of its operations in Colombia to expand into other hotel operations in the country.

PROBLEMS AND FUTURE PLANS

As indicated, the Hotel Tequendama is entirely owned by Colombian capital. IHC, with no capital investment in the enterprise, and only a management contract, is therefore not represented on the board of directors. Its recent purchase of the majority of the Hotel del Prado, with which it also had only a management contract in earlier years, suggests that it prefers, in connection with its operation of hotels, to participate in the ownership as well.

One of the problems that hotels encounter in Colombia (and elsewhere in Latin America) is that rates are controlled by the government. As with public utilities in general, this frequently results in a lag in rate increases behind economic conditions that justify them. In connection with the devaluation in June, 1957 of the exchange rate of the peso, the Hotel Tequendama was finally granted a rate increase as of September 1, 1957, largely because of the directly proportionate increase in the peso cost of repaying the loan from the Export-Import Bank. A further increase was granted effective October 1, 1959, to compensate partially for the steady increase in prices and wages. Even the new rates are moderate by international comparisons for luxury hotels; they range from 60 to 84 pesos daily single and from 88 to 109 pesos double (without meals); these rates, translated into dollars, amount to about 9 to $12, and 12.50 to $15.50 respectively.

The fixed annual fee received by IHC could be transferred into dollars at the official 2.50 pesos per dollar rate of exchange as long as that rate was in existence, but its participation in profits had to be serviced through a less favorable free exchange market. Since the reform in Colombia's exchange system in June, 1957, all of its earnings are subject to the free market rate. This was one of the considerations in connection with its decision to reinvest earnings from the Hotel Tequendama in its investment in the Hotel del Prado.

With respect to supplies for the hotel, the initial furniture and equipment were exempt from import duty and were imported with no problems. Subsequently, every attempt has been made to utilize local supplies for the hotel, but problems have been encountered in connection with the quality of some local articles. This has been partly true of linens, and from time to time problems have arisen in connection with the importing of such articles because of import restrictions. In foods, the experience has been much more favorable; arrangements have been made with selected local purveyors of food items, and these arrangements have had a noticeable effect on improvements in local quality of some of these items.

Initially, there were considerable difficulties in obtaining personnel that could adequately be trained for hotel employment, since such skills are scarce in Colombia, but much progress was made in on-the-job training during the early period of operation of the hotel. At present, most of the personnel is Colombian, but the key positions, such as those of heads of departments, are held by foreigners experienced in the hotel business, some of whom were resident in Colombia and could be hired locally.

There have been plans under discussion for some time for the construction of an addition to the Hotel Tequendama. It was announced in April, 1960 that plans for such a 215-room addition, at an estimated cost of 12 million pesos, are close to completion and that construction might start in January, 1961.

Industria Colombiana de Llantas, S.A. (*Icollantas*)

Icollantas was first organized 18 years ago and has been in production for the last 15 years. During this period, Colombia has achieved virtual self-sufficiency in tires and tubes, which are the principal items of production of Icollantas, and Icollantas is the major producer in the country. The enterprise was formed at Colombian initiative. It was promoted by a government development corporation, which at first held almost all of the Colombian interest and constituted the majority. When the enterprise subsequently became firmly established, the interest of the government was gradually sold out entirely, primarily to private Colombian investors. Foreign investment in the enterprise has always been in the minority, has been combined with a formal technical assistance arrangement, and there have been certain provisions in the corporate by-laws to protect the minority interest. Management has worked harmoniously, largely under Colombian direction. Technical control of production, which has been exercised pursuant to the technical assistance agreement, has been retained by the principal foreign investor, even though technical aspects of the operations have been gradually taken over more and more by Colombian personnel trained over the years. The technical assistance arrangement has enabled the enterprise to undertake the manufacture of new products developed by the United States producer.

ORIGIN OF THE ENTERPRISE

The enterprise had its origin during the early years of the Second World War when there were difficulties in obtaining tires and tubes from abroad. All tires and tubes consumed in Colombia at that time were imported. It was felt that the small amount of local production of natural rubber might be increased substantially as a result of the war effort, and, with the shortages of imported products, there was great interest in the formation of a local tire and tube industry. The Instituto de Fomento Industrial, a government corporation that had started functioning shortly before to promote the formation of new industrial enterprises, was the agency that took the initiative for the industry's creation.

The Instituto delegated to one of the leading tire distributors the task of exploring with United States tire producers the possibilities of obtaining technical cooperation for the development of a tire factory. The distributor, who happened to deal in products of the B. F. Goodrich Company, explored the matter with some major United States companies and finally recommended acceptance of the Goodrich proposal.

ORIGINAL CAPITAL STRUCTURE AND TECHNICAL ARRANGEMENTS

In November, 1942, the Instituto de Fomento Industrial and the B. F. Goodrich Company entered into a technical assistance contract. Simultaneously, the local corporation named Industria Colombiana de Llantas, S.A. (Icollantas) was formed, with majority financial participation by the Instituto, and minority participation by the Goodrich Company, a New York State corporation, and the Compañía Hulera Euzkadi of Mexico, a tire factory in that country with minority participation by Goodrich. There was also a token investment by several private Colombian investors to complete the five shareholders required by Colombian law to form a corporation, including the tire distributor who had investigated the matter for the Instituto. The technical assistance contract between the Instituto and Goodrich was automatically transferred to the new company in accordance with a clause of the contract which provided for this transfer.

The company was formed with a capital of 1.5 million pesos, of which 75 percent was subscribed by the Instituto and Colombian private capital, and 25 percent by Goodrich and its Mexican affiliate. The exact percentages were as follows:

Instituto de Fomento Industrial	72.7
Colombian private investors	2.3
	75.0
B. F. Goodrich Company	16.7
Compañía Hulera Euzkadi	8.3
	25.0

Two classes of shares were provided for, A and B. The shares of the Instituto and the other Colombian investors were class A, and those of Goodrich and its Mexican affiliate, class B.

These two classes of shares both consisted of common stock, with no difference in financial participation in the enterprise. The differences related to rights to elect members of the board, and to certain other voting rights.

The corporate by-laws provided for a board of six members, four to be elected by class A shares and two to be elected by class B shares.

In order to provide for protection of the minority class B shares, a 60 percent majority vote of each of the two classes was required for decisions to change the rules for election and composition of the board, and to change the preferential rights of existing shareholders to subscribe to new shares of the company. Quorums for meetings to decide on such changes similarly had to consist of a majority of the shares of each class. The same voting requirements held true for dissolution of the company. The minority class B shareholders were protecting themselves against the possibility that the majority might dissolve the company once techniques had been learned and go off on its own in the production of tires.

The intent was clearly to preserve these rights for the Goodrich group. Class B shares would automatically become class A shares if transferred by the initial subscribers, except for transfers to companies associated or affiliated with the initial subscribers. If more than 50 percent of the class B shares were transferred, all the class B shares would automatically become class A shares.

Similarly, to preserve rights of the Instituto, it was provided that it would elect two of the four class A board members, present a slate for election of the corporation's financial inspector, and for acts requiring a 60 percent vote of each of the two classes of shares, the Instituto's affirmative vote was required, all so long as it continued to hold 25 percent of the company's shares.

The technical assistance contract with Goodrich provided for two types of services: technical assistance in getting the factory under way and with respect to certain aspects of its continued functioning; and technical information with respect to Goodrich products and processes. In connection with the first, Goodrich was to assist in the selection of a site for the factory and furnish designs, drawings, blueprints, and specifications for the factory. Also, it was to supply engineers and technical men to be employed by the Instituto or the new company for construction and equipment of the factory; it was to advise on the kind, type, and sources of supply of raw materials, other supplies, machinery, and equipment; it was to select, inspect, and purchase such items for the enterprise; and it was to provide the same sort of services for the enlargement of the factory or expansion into the manufacture of new products. These services were to be provided by Goodrich on a cost-plus-expenses basis, including the prorating of overhead expenses of its departments that might render such services.

With respect to the technical information phase, Goodrich was to supply all knowledge and data known to it and used by it in its manufacturing methods for automotive tires, tubes, and rubber products. It would also make available for employment such technicians as might be necessary for directing the operation of the factory, and provide a testing and analysis service for products manufactured by the factory. Goodrich would keep the Instituto or the tire company fully informed of all its new developments in the manufacturing of rubber products. The Instituto or new company would be entitled to continue using after the expiration of the agreement all such technical data gathered during the life of the agreement. For this type of assistance, Goodrich was to receive a fee of three percent of the annual net realized sales of all products manufactured.

The cost-plus-expenses reimbursement for the first type of service was to be paid in United States dollars and thus protected against exchange losses. The 3 percent fee for the second type of service was to be paid in Colombian pesos, but this fee was to be increased by any amounts that might have to go for payment of taxes in Colombia by Goodrich.

The Goodrich trademark could be used by the Instituto or new company provided it was accompanied by the words "Made by the Instituto" or their equivalent, in letters at least one-third as high and of the same type, color, and style as the Goodrich mark. Such use could be made only during the life of the agreement (plus an additional six months as a "close-out" period).

The agreement was made for a period of 15 years from the end of the year when manufacturing started (1945); thereafter it was to continue automatically subject to cancellation by either party on notice of no less than one year.

DEVELOPMENT OF CAPITAL STRUCTURE

Before the enterprise began production in 1945, it was found necessary to raise its capital from the original 1.5 million pesos to 3 million pesos; this was done in June, 1944. Thereafter the steady expansion of the company was reflected in a series of increases in its capital. By June, 1956 the authorized capital reached 30 million pesos.

Against this amount of authorized capital, Icollantas had a paid-in capital at the end of 1956 of 17.8 million pesos, and total assets of 77.7 million pesos. Of these total assets, quick assets amounted to 16.9 million pesos, inventories to 24.7 million pesos, fixed assets to 18.3 million pesos, and good will to 15.2 million pesos. On the liabilities side, in addition to the paid-in capital of 17.8 million pesos, it had an earned surplus of 15.2 million pesos, including net profits of 6.9 million pesos earned in 1956.

In the course of the development of the enterprise, Goodrich expanded its share of the investment, and the Instituto de Fomento Industrial sold out its interest, primarily on the general market to private Colombian capital but also to private foreign investors in the United States and in Mexico. The sale to general investors in Mexico was effected through purchase and resale of blocks of the stock by the Compañía Hulera Euzkadi. The sale to general investors in Colombia was effected through local stock exchange brokers. This was done gradually so as not to depress the price of the shares.

The B. F. Goodrich Company, at the end of 1956, owned 5.9 million pesos (nominal value) out of the paid-in capital of 17.8 million pesos, or one-third of the total. The Instituto now holds no shares in the enterprise; its shares were gradually sold out over the years and the process was completed by 1953.

Both classes of stock and special voting rights have gone through certain changes, especially in connection with the intention of the Instituto to sell out its shares on the general market. The situation today is that two classes of stock, A and B, still remain. Class A stock is that of the general investor, both in Colombia and abroad, and class B stock is primarily that of Goodrich. The original shares of the Compañía Hulera Euzkadi of Mexico were converted into class A, and aside from Goodrich, only a small portion of class B stock (4.2 percent of all company shares) is held by a private bank in Mexico, the Banco de Londres y México.

The six members of the board continue to be elected as in the original by-laws: four by class A stockholders and two by class B stockholders. The 60 percent rule for quorums and voting on dissolution of the company and on changing rules regarding election and composition of the board still holds true. A certain fraction of class B stock (12.5 percent) can be transferred into class A stock if requested by the seller, in selling to persons or companies other than the initial subscribers or companies associated or affiliated with them.

MANAGEMENT

The board of the company has one-third of its members elected by class B shareholders (primarily Goodrich), which more or less matches their present capital participation. One of these two members of the board is an American who has for many years been vice-president of the company. The president of the company, who has also had this post for many years, is the Colombian former tire distributor who originally was entrusted with the negotiations for formation of the company by the Instituto de Fomento Industrial.

The company has always followed a prudent policy of reinvestment of some of its earnings for expansion of the enterprise. This is of special significance in Colombia where the interest of investors is usually in having a high and immediate return on their investment. It seems that both objectives have been borne in mind by the company. For example, the 6.9 million pesos of net profit in 1956 was what remained after deduction of 4.5 million pesos for depreciation and other reserves. Out of this net profit, some 5 million pesos were distributed as dividends, and therefore an additional 1.9 million pesos were transferred to reserves. Thus, transfer to reserves amounted to more than half of total profits (including depreciation), compared to the legal requirement of ten percent. Accumulated reserves at the end of 1956, excluding depreciation reserves and 1956 profits, amounted to 8.3 million pesos, or 47 percent of subscribed capital. At the same time, the 6.9 million pesos of net profits (after depreciation and certain other reserves) in 1956 represented a return of 18.4 percent on invested capital. This left an ample margin for a profitable return to investors (especially since part of the invested capital, 4.6 million pesos, was long-term debt) with the distribution as dividends of 5 million pesos out of the 6.9 million pesos.

The technical assistance arrangement with Goodrich has worked out well as provided for in the original agreement. The association of the Mexican affiliate of Goodrich from the beginning has made it possible to render this assistance, furthermore, from a proven Latin American background. In rendering the technical assistance, Goodrich has always placed emphasis on the training of Colombian personnel to take over. At present only two technical men on the payroll are Americans, recommended and loaned to the enterprise by Goodrich. The number of foreign technicians was substantially greater in the early years of the enterprise.

Although the agreement provides for the use of the Goodrich trademark, the technical assistance fee of 3 percent of sales is looked upon as a fee for technical services rather than as a royalty for the use of the Goodrich name.

ROLE IN THE ECONOMY

Icollantas began production in October, 1945. At about the same time, another enterprise—wholly United States-owned, Goodyear de Colombia S.A.—also began production of tires in Colombia. At present, Icollantas is the major tire producer in the country, accounting for probably a little more than one-half of the total national output, almost double that of Goodyear, its major competitor. There are now two other domestic tire producers, which are also joint enterprises with United States technical assistance and capital participation. These are the Compañía Croydon del Pacífico, an old enterprise that previously specialized in other rubber products with capital and technical assistance of the United States Rubber Company, and which began the production of tires in 1955; and Productos de Caucho Villegas, which started the production of tires in 1956 with the technical and financial cooperation of the Seiberling Rubber Company. With these four enterprises, Colombia is now virtually self-sufficient in the production of tires and tubes, although the local development of natural rubber hoped for during the war did not materialize and the industry is heavily dependent on imported raw materials.

With the exception of a small amount of raw rubber, all of the important raw materials of the tire industry in Colombia are imported. Development of plantation rubber in Colombia has never progressed. Such rubber as is produced is gathered in jungle areas in the southern part of the country by a few promoters who employ local labor in the area. Some five to ten percent of the rubber used in the tire industry is obtained in this way. This small industry is protected by the government through requirements on the tire companies that they utilize certain quantities of this domestic rubber in combination with imported rubber. Natural rubber is imported from the Far East through New York brokers in dollar transactions, and some synthetic rubber is imported directly from the United States. During the last few years, when synthetic rubber became available for export from the United States, about one-fourth of total rubber imports by the local tire industry has consisted of synthetic.

Other important raw materials, such as carbon black and tire cord, are imported, primarily from the United States. To date, the volume of demand by the local tire industry has never been sufficient to justify the establishment of local industries in these fields. In addition to the limited volume of total demand, there is the problem of individual specifications required by the various tire manufacturers, which has made it even less attractive to set up local production. The situation, however, may change in the future as the volume of consumption grows. This is particularly true of carbon black, a relatively uniform product in which local petroleum operators might become interested.

The Colombian tire industry developed during its early years with very limited protection against imports. From 1946 to 1950, duties on all tires amounted to a specific rate of five centavos per kilogram, which was equivalent to about two percent of the unit value per kilogram of imported tires. During this period, there were also moderate exchange taxes, but these taxes, added to the import duty, gave a total protection of only 6 percent in 1946–48 and a maximum of 28 percent in 1949–50.

In 1951 a new import tariff was enacted in Colombia. The rate of duty since then has been compound, at one peso per kilogram plus ten percent ad valorem on most tires of the type produced by the local industry, and 30 centavos per kilogram plus ten percent ad valorem on other tires, including some produced by the local industry. During these latter years, however, exchange taxes and import prohibitions have been far more important as instruments of protection than import duties. This has been especially true during years of exchange difficulties, in the period 1951–52, and since 1955. Import duties plus exchange taxes have amounted to a total of about 20 percent since 1951 on the category in which there is some local production, and have ranged up to 130 percent for the category entirely competitive with local production. In addition, from time to time, there have been outright prohibitions on the importation of tires of the type produced in the country, and this is the case at present. These exchange restrictions and import prohibitions were imposed primarily for balance of payments reasons, but naturally have had a protective effect on the local tire industry.

Assuming that the present prohibition on imports were not to exist, the price of locally produced tires would be reasonably competitive with the cost of imported tires, ex duty. For example, as of a few years ago, the laid down cost at a Colombian port, ex duty, of the popular size 6.70 x 15, 6 ply tire would have been approximately 117 pesos (assuming an exchange rate of 5 pesos per dollar). To this dealers' markups would be added. The retail price all over the country of a locally produced tire of these specifications was 130 pesos. Similarly, with a popular truck tire, 7.50 x 20, 10 ply, the laid down cost for an imported tire would have been about 295 pesos, and the retail price for a local tire was 324.30 pesos. The quality of local tires compared to imported tires is excellent; only 6 ply tires are manufactured because of the rough condition of roads. This ability of the tire industry to compete is attributed to the modern nature of equipment in the factories, to the lower labor rates in the country, and to the degree of labor efficiency that it has been possible to achieve.

Bearing in mind these cost comparisons, the contribution of Icollantas to the Colombian economy can be measured primarily in terms of the amount of more than $54 million in foreign exchange it claims to have saved the country during the first decade of its production. Furthermore, there is the possibility of future development of local raw materials.

Icollantas employs about 850 personnel. Its job classifications were set up on the basis of United States techniques. Salary levels are based on the going rates in the country, as determined by periodic salary surveys the firm has conducted, and have also been influenced by collective bargaining with the union of its employees.

A total of some 120 commercial firms, with about 100 branches around the country, distribute Icollantas tires. The agreement with Goodrich prohibits marketing outside of Colombia.

In recent years Icollantas has gone into the manufacture of a number of related products, such as rubber hose, rubber soles for shoes, automotive battery cases and batteries, rubber tile, plastic cloth and bags, and rigid plastic pipes, in connection with which the technical information arrangement with Goodrich has been very valuable.

PROBLEMS

The original association between a private foreign company and a government development corporation worked out well because there was an understanding that the enterprise would be managed autonomously without political interference. The Instituto stayed out of everyday management problems and placed its confidence in the Colombian president, who had been a Goodrich distributor and had been entrusted by it with promotion of the enterprise. A good working relationship was established between the Colombian president and the American vice-president, who had been a Goodrich employee.

Because of its heavy dependence on imported raw materials, the enterprise has had problems periodically in obtaining import permits and exchange for imports, especially in periods of national exchange stringency. Also, it has had to contend to some extent with a nationalistic policy that has forced it to purchase small amounts of national wild rubber, even though it is more costly than imported rubber. The main effect of these difficulties has been the need to maintain larger stocks and more working capital than might be the case in a tire factory in the United States, with some consequent increase in the costs of operation.

Also, like all other foreign enterprises and joint ventures in the country, it has suffered delays from time to time in the remittance of dividends. The country's record in this respect, however, is generally good, and the delays have not worked undue hardship. Under current conditions, Goodrich, as a previously registered foreign investment, can remit profits freely at the certificate rate of exchange (the more favorable of two exchange rates) now in existence in the country.

Note: The foregoing data were obtained several years ago, primarily from the Illocantas enterprise. Recent information obtained in Colombia has revealed that basic disagreements have developed between the foreign and national partners, that the enterprise is now owned in the majority by the foreign partner, and that the Colombian president of the company has been replaced by an executive from the United States.

Indústria e Comércio de Minérios, S.A. (Icomi)

ORIGIN AND DEVELOPMENT OF THE ENTERPRISE

The paid-up capital of the firm amounts to 200 million cruzeiros, of which 98 million cruzeiros (49 percent) has been contributed by the Bethlehem Steel Company of the United States and its subsidiaries, and 102 million cruzeiros (51 percent) represents the Brazilian share, invested by the Companhia Auxiliar de Emprêsas de Mineração. However, the total investment of Icomi is much larger, and this has been made possible by a large loan from the Export-Import Bank of Washington, and by a loan from the Bethlehem Steel Company in the amount of $1.9 million, to be amortized starting in 1962 at an interest rate of three percent per year.

Icomi was organized in 1942, in Belo Horizonte (State of Minas Gerais), by a Brazilian group devoted since 1937 to mining activities in that state.

Since its inception, Icomi has concentrated on the development of raw materials for the steel industry (both for the domestic industry and for export), such as iron ore, manganese ore, and limestone deposits. As the Companhia Siderúrgica Nacional (Brazil's national steel company) started functioning, Icomi became not only one of that firm's largest suppliers, but also grew in importance and structure in other ways to become one of the outstanding mining companies in the country.

In 1947, when manganese ore was discovered in the Amapá Territory, on the border of French Guiana, the Icomi group had already had ten years of experience in mining and had also acquired some experience in international trade through exports from Minas Gerais.

As the Amapá deposits became a national reserve, pursuant to Decree-Law 9858 of September 13, 1946, their development came under the control of the Conselho Nacional de Minas e Metalurgia (National Mines and Metallurgy Council). In 1947, bids were called for and proposals were submitted by Icomi and several foreign concerns. Icomi was awarded the bid. Upon its approval by the President of the Republic, it was written into a contract, on December 6, 1947, between Icomi and the Federal Union, the latter represented by the Amapá Territory Government. This contract, amended in certain respects, was approved in 1950 by the President of the Republic, registered in the Court of Official Accounts, and unanimously ratified by the National Congress.

It should also be pointed out that the Conselho de Segurança

Nacional (National Security Council) deemed the Icomi project in Amapá to be of great interest for Brazil's economic security and development.

In 1948, Icomi started geological surveys and the first studies on the possibilities of transportation for the manganese ore. This preliminary work was extremely arduous. The deposits are located in the heart of the jungle, 200 kilometers (124 miles) away from any civilized point, and their transport had to be effected partly (100 kms.—62 miles) through savannas, and partly across the Amapari and Araguarí rivers, the rapids of which allowed the use of small craft only.

The initial operations of the first work crews involving the clearing of the jungle, the construction of buildings, the transportation of personnel, supplies and equipment, and the maintenance of a small community under primitive conditions, were accomplished in the face of unusually great difficulties.

After more than a year of work and studies, when an idea was gained of the potential of the deposits, it became clear that there was need for capital, know-how, and experience which the country lacked.

The Icomi group was determined to give the venture the highest standards of efficiency. Of equal or even greater importance than foreign capital was the need for foreign technique and know-how from similar ventures.

After studies and inquiries in Europe and North America, Icomi found it possible to associate with the Bethlehem Steel Company under equitable and suitable conditions.

Eleven years of experience have proven the wisdom of this association to the extent that both groups continue to consider it absolutely satisfactory. They believe further that the same formula of cooperation ought to be adopted should they decide to embark jointly on any other new venture.

After the preliminary agreement with Bethlehem, in August, 1949 the two groups intensified geological research and studies for a project involving the installation of the mine, a railroad (200 kms.—124 miles), and an Amazon river port.

In the first approach to the project, the work was estimated at about $35 million, and a loan was negotiated for this amount with the International Bank for Reconstruction and Development. A guarantee from the Brazilian government, secured through Congressional Law (No. 1235 of November 14, 1950), was one of the conditions of the loan.

While the loan negotiations proceeded and the guarantee law was going through Congress, more complete studies were undertaken, including revisions of the previous projects and preliminary budget, and more resources were found to be needed.

The revised estimate reached $48 million, and new negotiations were undertaken with the International Bank for Reconstruction and Development. At this stage of the negotiations, the interested parties became concerned over the ever-increasing inflation in the country and its consequences on the project costs during its execution (four years). The amount of $12 million (25 percent) was added to the basic budget because of inflation anticipated during construction. The budget was then raised to $60 million.

Considering the interest to accrue during construction, $7.5 million were further added, making a total of $67.5 million for the credit to be secured to assure the completion of the project.

Icomi eventually obtained a credit in this amount from the Eximbank, which dispensed with the Brazilian government guarantee. The credit previously negotiated with the International Bank was, therefore, given up.

The Eximbank loan to Icomi was at an interest rate of 4.5 percent a year, and the term was seven years, payments to start upon initiation of the operations.

Because of the meticulous planning of the work and of the exceptional efficiency of the construction company (Foley Brothers Inc.), the project was completed in three years only, and its cost, including interest during construction, did not exceed $55,250,000, thus requiring the use of only a part of the credit extended by the Eximbank, and permitting the company to commence selling at the relatively high market price then in effect.

Out of this loan, $15,615,000 were brought to Brazil to pay for expenses in cruzeiros, and $39,635,000 went into the payment of expenses in dollars.

Another important point in the arrangement was the market guarantee secured from the United States Government Defense Materials Procurement Agency (DMPA), which committed itself to buy up to 5,500,000 tons of ore, a sufficient quantity to assure the repayment of the loan should the market or prices fall to such an extent that Icomi would be unable to service the loan. The guarantee set forth basic prices, to fluctuate along with the inflation ratios, which were sufficient to cover all production expenses, transportation costs, and the loan interest and amortization. It was actually an insurance against commercial risks that cemented the structure of the venture. It should also be pointed out that the DMPA guarantee may be used at Icomi's option, thus allowing the ore to be placed on the market at the most favorable price.

With the credit and market guarantee problems solved, construction started in January, 1954. Three years later, in January, 1957, the industrial installations were completed, and full capacity operations were begun. The export of ore reached 658,000 tons in 1957, carried in 69 bottoms.

Today, more than three years after the beginning of operations, the corporation is devoting its efforts to the strengthening of its organization, to personnel training in the various fields of activity, and to the improvement of cost control. Rapid progress has been made in the construction of residential facilities, including schools, medical centers, and commercial and recreation centers, representing a total investment of more than one billion cruzeiros. Most of these facilities were scheduled for completion by the end of 1960.

The following can be mentioned as some results of the venture:

The dollar value of export during the first three years of operations, FOB-Santana, were: 1957—$35,000,000; 1958—$30,000,000; and 1959—$27,000,000.

The liquidation of the loan made by the Eximbank commenced on schedule and has continued without interruption. Payments of $7,000,000 in 1957, $7,000,000 in 1958, and $9,000,000 in 1959 represent a reduction of approximately 42 percent of the original liability.

As a consequence of contractual obligations, Icomi has paid royalties to the Federal Territory of Amapá in excess of cr$400,000,000 on account of the manganese ore produced up to December 31, 1959. These funds are being used by the territory for an extensive electrification program. It is estimated that by the end of 1961 total royalties will have amounted to more than cr$1 billion.

Due to Icomi's activities, the Amapá Territory, which was one of the lowest income areas in the country, became the highest, with an income of about 40,000 cruzeiros per capita in 1957. Approximately 6,000 persons (12 percent of the territory's population), including the corporation's employees and their dependents, attained a standard of living thus far unknown in the Amazon region and hard to compare to the rest of the country, not only in the betterment of individual incomes and material comforts, but also in health, educational, and social standards.

One of the most encouraging results of this venture is the rapid training of Brazilian personnel in new working methods. Men who only recently used the most primitive methods and were unable to handle even rudimentary tools such as the pick and shovel, today run, with an amazing sense of responsibility, machines that cost scores of millions of cruzeiros. This preparation embraces not only the workers, who gradually become specialists, but also all types of professionals, such as engineers, physicians, lawyers, accountants, who are daily improving their professional standards. One of the most valuable contributions of the venture is this educational aspect, which perhaps even surpasses its direct economic consequences.

Foreign know-how is responsible for most of the success of the venture. This contribution has been made by individual experts, by the concerns that planned and executed the work, and by the manufacturers of the diversified equipment, and is reflected in the low cost of production and in the high rate of ore recovery, which amounts to 97.3 percent of all the metallic manganese contained in the materials extracted from the mine.

MANAGEMENT

Being a corporation, Icomi's profit distribution is based on the number of shares of each stockholder. Icomi does not pay royalties for the use of foreign patents, but only those due to the Amapá Territory Government as stipulated in the concession contract.

In the cases where Icomi had to resort to the technical assistance of third parties, as in the instances of the port, the railway, and the mine installations, it paid for such services through contracts.

From the beginning, Bethlehem Steel has been rendering assistance to Icomi in the most varied ways, such as laboratory research, providing mining specialists and experts in administration, accounting, civil construction, and port installations. Such assistance has been rendered gratis by Bethlehem, although Icomi has remunerated the individual experts.

BALANCE SHEET DATA, 1956–59 (*millions of cruzeiros*)

	End of 1956	*End of 1957*	*End of 1958*	*End of 1959*
Assets				
Fixed Assets	1,956.2	2,279.2	2,525.6	2,909.2
Disposable Assets	63.5	616.1	488.8	350.0
Current Assets	66.1	507.6	410.2	770.6
Inventories	19.2	27.8	41.8	71.2
Receivables and Others	46.9	479.8	368.4	699.4
Liabilities				
Capital	39.2	200.0	200.0	200.0
Reserves	—	167.3	244.6	439.1
Depreciation	—	315.5	680.7	1,079.3
Current Liabilities and Long-term Loans	3,077.1	3,407.0	3,591.0	7,316.9
Loans (including long-term)	2,873.1	2,793.9	3,062.1	6,669.8
Other Current Liabilities	204.0	613.1	528.9	647.1
Profits and Losses	—212.2	379.8	405.3	447.5
Distributed	—	50.0	50.0	na [a]

[a] na = not available.

The board of directors is composed of four directors, at present three Brazilians and one American. The relationship among the directors has developed in an atmosphere of cordiality and understanding.

One hundred and twenty foreign technicians were working for Icomi during the construction phase of the project. As of the beginning of 1960, the number had been reduced to 18, with the expectation that it would be further curtailed.

Icomi's experience points to the fact that language differences present some difficulties in the cooperation between Brazilian and foreign technicians, but such difficulties can be overcome to a great extent through an understanding attitude on the part of the directors.

The relationship between subordinate personnel and supervisors has also been a problem of persuasion and enlightenment. The problem has been not so much one of nationality but rather one of the actual ability of the supervisors involved, regardless of their nationality.

Industria Eléctrica de México, S.A. (IEM)

ORIGIN OF THE ENTERPRISE

IEM was constituted on August 25, 1945. The plant was completed and production started in April, 1948. The enterprise had been developed by a group of Mexican bankers to produce electrical equipment both for industrial and for domestic use. The initiative of the Mexican group was stimulated during the Second World War when such equipment was in short supply and was developed in the atmosphere that then reigned in Mexico of expansion into new fields of manufacturing.

CAPITAL STRUCTURE

IEM was set up with a capital of 65 million pesos. Most of this was raised locally by the promoters of the project, but some of the capital was also obtained in the United States. Some 15 percent to 20 percent of the capital stock was placed with United States investors through New York underwriting companies, led by Kuhn, Loeb and Company.

The enterprise was formed with the technical assistance of the Westinghouse Electric Corporation. Westinghouse supplied complete design information, and arrangements were made for Mexican personnel to be trained by Westinghouse in the United States. For this technical supervision and the use of its patents, Westinghouse received a percentage of sales receipts. The technical assistance and royalty arrangement was a continuing one; in addition IEM was named the exclusive distributor in Mexico of special Westinghouse products. The original arrangement with Westinghouse was limited to technical assistance, patents, and distribution aspects, and Westinghouse had no participation whatsoever in the capital of IEM.

The growth of IEM is reflected in the doubling of the original amount of capital. By the end of 1957, IEM's authorized and outstanding capital stock amounted to 130 million pesos, consisting of 1,300,000 common shares with a par value of 100 pesos each.

In 1955, in connection with a financial reorganization of the company, Westinghouse bought into the enterprise by bringing in fresh capital. The capital of the company was raised at that time from 75.5 million pesos to the present level of 130 million pesos. Westinghouse now owns 26 percent of the stock of the company. The original investment by general investors in the United States has continued, and about 15 percent of the capital stock is now owned in this way. Thus, the foreign ownership of IEM amounts to slightly more than 40 percent of the total.

The majority of the capital is owned in Mexico: Nacional Financiera holds 16.5 million pesos of the stock, or close to 12 percent of the total; and approximately 48 percent of the stock is held by private Mexican investors.

Upon the entry of Westinghouse into the company as an investor in 1955, the formal technical assistance contract was somewhat modified, but continued essentially as it had been from the beginning, with Westinghouse technical direction on the basis of a royalty arrangement. IEM continued to be the exclusive distributor in Mexico of special Westinghouse products.

The increase in the company's capital in 1955, made possible largely by the Westinghouse investment, permitted the company to improve its financial position by eliminating an accumulated deficit, part of which consisted of accumulated dividends on preferred stock. With the financial reorganization, the preferred stock was retired, and the company emerged with only one class of common stock.

MANAGEMENT AND PERSONNEL

The company is governed by a board of directors, consisting of 16 principal directors and 11 alternates. By formal agreement, 7 of the principal directors and 3 of the alternates are elected by the American stockholders. Although this board is theoretically the supreme management body, the real policymaking group of the company in effect is an operating committee of 5 members, 3 of whom, by agreement, are elected by Westinghouse. Nacional Financiera takes no active part in the management, although its president is one of the directors of the company, and its vice-president is an alternate director.

The chairman of the board of directors is a Mexican, very prominent in the local financial community, who was the prime mover in the formation of IEM. He is also the chairman of the board of the largest private banking institution in the country. The principal executive officers of the company are a director-general, who is a Mexican, and a vice-director general, who is an American. There are no special agreements or voting rules for the election of these officers, who, like other officers of the company, are simply named on the basis of the general voting procedures of the board of directors.

There are five other principal officers of the company, each in charge of an operating division: the treasurer, engineering director, manufacturing manager, public and employee relations manager, and sales manager. These posts are all occupied by Mexicans, with the exception of that of the engineering director, which is held by an American.

IEM has three plants, all located at Tlalnepantla, State of Mexico, which is an important industrial suburb of Mexico City, located about fifteen miles from the capital. Its personnel force consists of 1,800 persons, most of whom are Mexicans. From the very beginning, there has been a deliberate and active program of training of local personnel. The result is that there are only some seven foreigners employed. The training program is still being conducted actively at present, both in Mexico and in sending key personnel for training in the United States. The experience in sending personnel abroad has been quite successful; there has been little turnover among returning technicians whom the company has wished to retain.

Labor relations have been cordial. The present contract with the union representing IEM workers, providing for increases in wages as well as in certain fringe benefits, was signed on December 9, 1959, with a duration of two years.

FINANCIAL RESULTS

The company's financial experience since the reorganization of 1955 has been quite satisfactory. Net profits after taxes amounted to 12.3 million pesos in 1956, 13.1 million pesos in 1957, and 17.5 million pesos in 1958. The earnings in 1958 represent a return of some 13 percent on equity. The company has utilized little long-term capital in relation to its own equity and accumulated reserves. Long-term capital liabilities at the end of 1957 amounted to only 6 million pesos.

There has been no difference of opinion among the various stockholders with respect to the reinvestment of substantial portions of the profits of the company to finance its continuous expansion programs. During the last few years, reinvestments have been consistent at close to one-half of total profits. Under present expansion plans, it is hoped to finance a factory in 1961 partially through the reinvestment of profits of previous years.

ROLE IN THE ECONOMY

IEM produces two broad lines of electrical equipment and apparatus: industrial, including such items as motors, transformers, switchgear, circuit breakers, and control apparatus; and household items, including refrigerators, stoves (both gas and electric), heaters, irons, and washing machines. It is the largest company in this field in Mexico, and is probably the largest of its type in Latin America. The value of its sales has steadily increased from 32 million pesos in 1948 to 223 million pesos in 1958. During the last few years, the sales of imported Westinghouse products, principally generators and turbines, which IEM does not produce, have averaged 60 million pesos annually. About 60 percent by value of IEM's total production consists of the industrial equipment and 40 percent of the domestic appliances. The company has six regional branch offices in the country, and its products are sold by 280 independent dealers.

During the period of IEM's existence, there has been considerable expansion in Mexico in manufacturing industries in general and in the utilization of electric power. Electric power generating capacity in the country doubled from some 1,100,000 kilowatts in 1948 to 2,200,000 kilowatts at the end of 1958. The increase in electric power facilities has been matched by a considerable growth in the manufacture of electrical equipment. It has been possible for local output to meet virtually all demands in domestic appliances, but local production has not been able to keep pace with the sharply rising demand for electrical equipment for industry. For example, in 1957, imports of domestic appliances amounted to only 19.2 million pesos (about $1.5 million), but imports of electrical equipment for industry in that year amounted to as much as 269.7 million pesos ($21.6 million).

There are various manufacturing enterprises in Mexico whose output overlaps in certain respects with that of IEM. One of the principal ones is Manufacturera General Electric, a wholly-owned subsidiary of the International General Electric Corporation of the United States that manufactures domestic appliances as well as some motors and transformers. Another is Square D de México, also a wholly United States-owned subsidiary, of the Square D Company. This enterprise is limited to industrial items such as control equipment and switchgear. The Square D Company had also started out as a joint venture, with 50 percent of the enterprise held by one Mexican investor. Differences over reinvestment policies later led to the purchase of the complete interest of the Mexican investor by the United States party. The Mexican investor then undertook to manufacture transformers under license by Allis Chalmers, and this enterprise similarly was later bought out by Allis Chalmers. Other enterprises in the field, especially in domestic appliances, are Frigidaire–GM (100 percent United States-owned) and Kelvinator, which is a joint venture (20 percent Kelvinator, 20 percent Sears Roebuck, and 60 percent Mexican capital).

The growing integration of Mexican manufacturing industries has permitted IEM to come to the point where only about 20 percent of the total of its raw materials is now imported. This represents almost a precise reversal of the original situation, when only about 20 percent of the raw materials could be obtained locally, and the trend of decline in the utilization of imported materials is continuing.

As a new industry in the Mexican economy, IEM obtained tax concessions from the Mexican government, but the ten year period of concessions ran out in April, 1958, and the enterprise is now subject to normal tax rates.

The company's domestic line generally sells at about 25 percent more than retail prices in the United States, and the industrial line is generally competitive with United States prices. This favorable price position, coupled with the substantial exchange savings to the Mexican economy resulting from establishment of the enterprise and the stimulation it afforded to the development of other, complementary industries in the economy, indicates the advantages that have accrued to Mexico through the development of IEM.

FUTURE PLANS

IEM has consistently followed a policy of expansion to keep pace with the dynamic development of the Mexican economy. It has been concerned with increases in productivity as well as in total output.

Changes made in factory layout in 1957 are estimated to have resulted in an increase in production per employee of 16 percent over 1956 and 47 percent over 1955. Also, the company is constantly expanding into new lines of production. For example, in 1957, two new types of air conditioners were introduced, as well as a complete line of radio receivers, television sets, and high fidelity equipment. Some of these items are produced in cooperation with the Philco manufacturing facility in Mexico. New types of transformers, motors, washing machines, and gas ranges were introduced in 1958. The company completed a factory in 1959, and has plans for another to be completed in 1961 which will increase its capacity by some 40 percent over present levels. As previously indicated, part of this expansion is being financed by a reinvestment of profits (about 10 million pesos, or $800 thousand), and the balance is being financed by a loan from the Export-Import Bank of Washington in the amount of $640 thousand which was granted in November, 1958.

EVALUATION

IEM pioneered some ten years ago in the establishment of a new line of production in Mexico. It was organized at the initiative of Mexican entrepreneurs, although a minority of its capital was raised from the beginning among general investors in the United States. Technical direction of the enterprise was obtained by a formal arrangement with the well-known Westinghouse Electric Corporation of the United States, although there was no capital investment by Westinghouse.

It is felt that some of the initial difficulties of the enterprise resulted from insufficiently active participation by Westinghouse because of the limited nature of its arrangement with the company. In those early years, the enterprise attempted to develop simultaneously too many lines for the Mexican market. It also failed to obtain adequate protection against imports, a condition which later was remedied.

The entry of Westinghouse as an investor in 1955 is felt to have resulted in an improvement in the management of the enterprise, because of greater managerial participation by Westinghouse. Even though Westinghouse financial participation is limited to only about one-fourth of the total equity of the company, it has, by agreement, worked out an arrangement for close participation, principally through naming a majority of the members of the key operating committee. It is generally accepted in the enterprise that Westinghouse, although it does not have financial control, should participate in a decisive way with respect to technical and management control. This *modus vivendi* has worked out very well.

The success in general of this joint venture can be measured in terms of the key position it has assumed in the Mexican economy after only some ten years of life. It will undoubtedly continue to grow in important ways in the future as the Mexican economy expands and as the extent of industrialization and household purchasing power increase.

Laborterápica-Bristol S.A., Indústria Química e Farmacêutica

ORIGIN AND DEVELOPMENT OF THE ENTERPRISE

The paid-up capital of this firm amounts to cr$400 million, owned to the extent of 51 percent of the total by Bristol Laboratories, Inc., of Syracuse, New York, and 49 percent by a Brazilian group represented by firms owned by members of the Pires de Oliveira family, and a small number of other shareholders.

The corporation is engaged in the manufacture of pharmaceutical specialties and antibiotics. Before the entry of Bristol, Laborterápica was set up as a limited liability partnership in 1938 and transformed into a corporation in July, 1943, the founders having been Messrs. José e Domingos Pires de Oliveira Dias, who for a long time had been engaged in the pharmaceutical industry. Theirs was the first and only laboratory to produce insulin in Brazil, crystallizing it from domestic cattle pancreas. They isolated the lypocaic hormone, on the basis of which a new product was launched on the market; they made extracts of vitamins K and E from natural sources, as well as of vitamin A; they manufactured natural folic acid, and produced para-amino salicylic acid, one of today's most widely used chemotherapics for the treatment of tuberculosis. Besides the usual opotherapic extracts, the firm's extraction section produces natural hormones and vitamins, hydrochloric acid, cholesterin, and many other kinds of raw materials for the preparation of its pharmaceutical specialties.

With the advent of the antibiotic era in 1948, Laborterápica S.A. was appointed the exclusive representative in Brazil of Bristol Laboratories, Inc., for the distribution of their antibiotic products. In view of the well-equipped condition of Laborterápica for such representation, Bristol Laboratories had rewarding results, and paved the way for the formation of a mixed capital venture in Brazil for the manufacture, distribution, and sale of their products.

In 1950, Bristol-Labor S.A. was formed with a capital of cr$2 million, 51 percent of which belonged to the American company, and 49 percent to the Brazilian group headed by Laborterápica S.A., which rendered technical and administrative assistance, publicized the products through its organization and distributed them throughout Brazil. The merging of Laborterápica S.A., Indústria Química e Farmacêutica and Bristol-Labor S.A., Indústria Química e Farmacêutica, was accomplished in March, 1957, and the new firm was registered under the name of Laborterápica-Bristol S.A., Indústria Química e Farmacêutica. The shares were initially issued as registered, a part was later changed to bearer shares (those belonging to the Brazilian group), and the other part remained as registered (those of the American group, as required by law). The capital was increased during 1959 from cr$340 million to cr$400 million.

The Brazilian corporation pays a five percent royalty on sales to Bristol Laboratories, holders of the patents for the manufacture of the firm's antibiotic-based products. The royalty contract has a duration of 15 years.

ROLE IN THE ECONOMY

When the venture was simply Laborterápica S.A., its sales amounted to cr$43 million in the first two years of operation, and they reached cr$380 million in the last two years before its merger (1955 and 1956). At its inception, Bristol-Labor S.A. registered, in 1951 and 1952, a sales volume of 170 million cruzeiros, which reached the sum of cr$593 million in 1955 and 1956. The total sales of the new firm, Laborterápica Bristol S.A., reached cr$691 million in 1957. Laborterápica-Bristol S.A. occupies one of the first places in Brazil in production and sales capacity for pharmaceutical products. Its share in national production and consumption amounted in 1957 to 4.6 percent of the total of cr$15 million. There are 525 laboratories in Brazil contributing to this total figure. Of the total market, 60 percent is accounted for by 31 laboratories, 25 percent by another 82 laboratories, and the remaining 15 percent by 412 laboratories.

In view of the ever increasing use in Brazil of broad spectrum antibiotics, Laborterápica-Bristol S.A. set up the first South American tetracycline plant in São Paulo. The most modern techniques were applied in this factory, and it is one of the finest such plants in the world. The plant was designed by engineers of Bristol Laboratories of the United States, and was constructed and installed by Brazilian companies using 95 percent domestic materials. The plant started operations in February, 1958. It utilizes 99 percent national raw materials.

MANAGEMENT AND PERSONNEL

The administration and direction of the corporation are exclusively the responsibility of the Brazilian group. All technicians in the new plant are Brazilians, highly specialized in their lines and trained in the United States.

The long background of good commercial relations between Laborterápica and Bristol Laboratories, even before their association, is probably the main reason why the foreign partner, despite its majority position in the voting stock, has no representation on the firm's board of directors. The only representative of Bristol Laboratories in Laborterápica-Bristol is the Brazilian who was formerly the lawyer for the Bristol branch; he holds a non-executive position on the Board.

As for technical personnel, Bristol Laboratories' intervention did not go beyond the antibiotics plant—for which the Brazilian group had no experience at all. For all other lines of production, Laborterápica needed no help from Bristol Laboratories. Foreign technicians were in Brazil for only a few months during the period of installation of the antibiotic equipment. At the same time, Laborterápica's technicians were sent to Bristol Laboratories in the United States for training to be able to handle the new equipment. The quality of these trainees and their instructors was such that after about six months they were prepared to take over the Brazilian plant.

A basic contribution of Laborterápica Bristol to the country has been the technical knowledge acquired concerning the production of antibiotics.

BALANCE SHEET DATA, 1957–58 (*millions of cruzeiros*)

	End of 1957	*End of 1958*
Assets		
Fixed Assets	221.3	259.7
Disposable Assets	38.2	46.2
Current Assets	466.5	519.5
Inventories	130.6	163.4
Receivables and Others	335.9	356.1
Liabilities		
Capital	340.0	340.0
Reserves	170.2	268.1
Depreciation	22.8	35.1
Current Liabilities	193.0	181.8
Profits	80.9	127.6
Cash Distributed	34.2	28.4

Panair do Brasil, S.A.

ORIGIN AND DEVELOPMENT OF THE ENTERPRISE

The paid-up capital of this firm is cr$88 million, of which the foreign participation amounts to cr$42,240,000 (48 percent), represented by 211,200 shares (200 cruzeiros each) owned by Pan American World Airways, Inc., of the United States. The Brazilian participation amounts to cr$45,760,000 (52 percent), represented by 228,800 shares (cr$200 each), including the Banco de Minas Gerais with 44,000 shares.

Toward the end of the 1920 decade, the United States government announced its intention of subsidizing an airline to operate between the United States and Argentina along the east coast of the Americas. Two organizations endeavored to qualify for the concession of the proposed line: the New York, Rio and Buenos Aires Line (Nyrba) and Pan American, both American-owned. In view of the long distance to be covered by the airline along the Brazilian coast—approximately 5,000 kilometers (3,107 miles)—and considering that travel between Brazilian territorial points was reserved by law to Brazilian organizations, Nyrba decided to organize a Brazilian subsidiary to use as a means of operating the route between Belem in Brazil and Buenos Aires in Argentina. Founded October 22, 1929, this Brazilian subsidiary was called Nyrba do Brasil S.A.

In January, 1930, the Nyrba Line and Nyrba do Brasil started their operations. Upon the call for public bids on the international route Miami-Buenos Aires, Pan American was awarded the contract.

Once the concession was decided upon, in August, 1930 Pan American acquired the Nyrba Line assets as well as those of its Brazilian subsidiary, Nyrba do Brasil, absorbing the former and changing the name to Panair do Brasil S.A. Panair's capital (cr$500,000) was then owned entirely by Pan American.

Since the air service rendered by Panair was an integral part of the international line Miami-Rio-Buenos Aires, Panair was, from a technical standpoint, considered a division of Pan American.

In 1932–33, Dr. José Américo de Almeida, Brazil's Minister of Transport and Public Works, foresaw the important role commercial airlines could play in opening up the immense Brazilian hinterland and also in facilitating communications between the cities in the more developed region of the coast. Through frequent contacts with the directors of the two outstanding airlines then in existence in the country, Panair do Brasil and Sindicato Condor Ltda., Dr. Almeida tried to find the means of inducing the two organizations to establish airlines which might have as their exclusive purpose travel within Brazilian territory. The solution agreed upon included the granting by the government of customs duties and tax exemptions on fuels and aviation equipment imports, besides a subsidy for each kilometer flown by the contracting parties.

Since Dr. Almeida wanted Panair do Brasil S.A. to establish its own line along the coast, separate from the one under operation as a trunk of Pan American international lines, it was further agreed that Panair would establish such a line and, as a compensation, the government would grant PAA special permission to travel, in the course of its international routes, between Brazilian territorial points.

As a result of this arrangement, Panair consolidated its objective (air routes between Brazilian territorial points), cutting loose, as of 1934, from the international line, and from its status as a mere division of Pan American.

Until the Second World War, when the Brazilian government requested Panair to widen its operations to eliminate air services performed by German-controlled aviation enterprises, which were then considered dangerous to domestic security, Panair had extended its lines considerably in Brazil. Thus, it became the sole regular connection between the south, and northeast and northern regions of the country.

In 1943, Pan American decided to increase Panair's capital to cr$80 million, and to relinquish its rights to underwrite the increase and to keep control of all of the shares, thus allowing the transfer of 42 percent of the capital to Brazilian ownership.

In 1946, already enjoying considerable prestige among domestic airlines, Panair undertook the organization of a route between Brazil and Europe.

In 1947, through a new capital increase, the majority of Panair's shares shifted to Brazilian ownership. From then on Pan American became just a strong Panair shareholder.

By the end of 1959, Panair was operating a large air fleet, with twenty four-engine airplanes. Of these, twelve were used in domestic routes and eight in international flights; besides Panair owned a special amphibious fleet used in a wide air network in the Amazon Basin.

As an illustration of this corporation's contribution to the Brazilian economy, it is of interest to note that, before the inauguration of the Panair airline—now the sole means of transportation between Rio de Janeiro and Manaus—a ship required 20 days to cover this distance. Upon the inauguration of the airline, this time was cut down to 3 days; today, with the four-engine planes extensively used by the enterprise in Brazil, the same distance between Rio and Manaus is covered in a little over 7 hours.

As for international routes, Panair operates at present a daily service between South America and Europe. To maintain its leadership in this tremendously important route, the corporation was to receive by the end of 1960 two DC-8, Douglas jet planes, which can fly directly from Rio de Janeiro to Lisbon in 9 hours, and have a capacity of more than 100 passengers.

CAPITAL STRUCTURE AND FINANCIAL RESULTS

As previously stated, in 1943, Panair's capital was increased to cr$80 million, to permit a 42 percent Brazilian participation. When this increase was effected, Pan American had an investment in Panair amounting to 72,903,266 cruzeiros, as a result of invested capital, accumulated profits, and loans made to Panair. Pan American never withdrew any profits from Panair and never charged any interest on loans to the latter during the period 1930–43. Consequently, Pan American made financial contributions to Panair in the total amount of 72,903,266 cruzeiros with the following breakdown:

Capital and Reinvested Profits	cr$42,600,000
Loans and Current Account Credits	30,303,266
	cr$72,903,266

To complete its participation in the new capital structure, Pan American purchased additional shares to make its total participation 58 percent. The balance of 42 percent was subscribed by Brazilians.

Pan American held its majority position for four years (to 1947), when the majority passed to Brazilian shareholders. During this four-year period, Pan American assumed the obligation of paying to Panair, as a grant subsidy, at the end of each year, the difference between the total net profits earned by Panair before income tax and interest deductions, and the amount corresponding to ten percent per year on capital invested in the material used in the operation of the services as well as in airports and other installations.

The encouragement and incentive derived from this guaranteed income were demonstrated by the speedy purchase by the public of Panair shares on the open market.

On the strength of this guaranteed income, Panair was able, during the period 1944–47, to declare and pay dividends to its shareholders. Pan American and the Brazilian shareholders received their participation in the declared dividends as follows:

Year	*Dividend Rate (Percent)*	*Received by Pan American*	*Received by Brazilian Shareholders*	*Total Distributed*
		(values in thousands of cruzeiros)		
1944	7	3,248 (58%)	2,352 (42%)	5,600
1945	5	2,320 (58%)	1,680 (42%)	4,000
1946	8	3,712 (58%)	2,688 (42%)	6,400
1947	10 (in shares)	3,840 (48%)	4,160 (52%)	8,000
Total		13,120	10,880	24,000

Under the guaranteed income arrangement, Pan American paid to Panair, during the same period, the following amounts:

1944	cr$21,148,183
1945	26,802,132
1946	17,251,809
1947	23,027,689
Total	cr$88,229,813

Panair would not have been able to declare and pay dividends during this period, had it not been for the Pan American-guaranteed income agreement. The figures indicate that Pan American paid to Panair cr$75,109,813, after the deduction of dividends it received (cr$88,229,813 less dividends cr$13,120,000). Out of this amount, Panair paid cr$10,880,000 to the Brazilian shareholders, and the balance went into strengthening its financial position. In other words, Pan American rendered financial assistance to Panair in the amount of cr$75,109,813 in 1944–47, besides loans for the purchase of equipment during the same period.

Also noteworthy is the fact that Panair started obtaining Federal subsidies for its domestic routes in 1939; from this year until 1947, the total received by Panair from the Federal government in subsidies amounted to some cr$25,998,000, compared to the income guaranteed and paid by Pan American of cr$75,109,813. Thus, both the Federal government and Pan American contributed to the development of Brazilian commercial aviation during the period 1939–47.

In 1947, the majority of Panair's capital was transferred to Brazilians, as a consequence of a voluntary policy decision by Pan American. The proportion of 48 percent Pan American and 52 percent Brazilian capital still holds good as of today.

From 1948 to 1954, Panair declared the following dividends:

Year	*Received by Pan American*	*Received by Brazilian Shareholders*	*Total*
		(*cruzeiros*)	
1948 [a]	—	—	—
1949 [b]	—	—	—
1950 [b]	—	—	—
1951 [a]	—	—	—
1952 [b]	—	—	—
1953	2,534,400	2,745,600	5,280,000
1954	2,534,400	2,745,600	5,280,000
Total	5,068,800	5,491,200	10,560,000

[a] Profits were entirely reinvested.

[b] There were losses in these years as well as from 1955 through 1959.

The distributions in 1953 and 1954 amounted to only six percent per annum on the invested capital of cr$88 million.

Besides the capital invested in Panair and the grants made to it, Pan American has assisted Panair in the purchase of aviation equipment, not only from a technical but also from a financial standpoint.

The first five Constellations acquired by Panair during 1946–47 were originally financed by Pan American. In 1947, Panair secured a credit from the Bankers Trust Company, thus enabling it to refinance this operation.

In February, 1953, January, 1954 and April, 1954, an additional three Constellations were purchased in the amount of $2,550,000, financed entirely by Pan American; the first one was paid for by Panair in 12 monthly installments and the other two in 36 installments.

In January, 1955, Panair purchased three more Constellations at a total cost of $2,550,000. This purchase was financed by the Chase Manhattan Bank of New York, through 48 monthly installments and with a Pan American guarantee, as required by the Bank.

Thus, Pan American directly or indirectly participated in the financing of the following acquisitions:

5 Constellations—Bankers Trust	$3,200,000
3 Constellations—Pan American	2,550,000
3 Constellations—Chase Manhattan Bank	2,550,000
Total	$8,300,000

The average interest rate charged for these financing operations was five percent a year.

For many years, Pan American and Panair have maintained a mutual services agreement in connection with ground facilities as well as interline arrangements for passenger, mail, and cargo traffic.

Under the mutual services and other arrangements, the following payments were made:

During the ten-year period, 1944–54, Pan American paid to Panair:

1. Airport expenses for ton-landings of Pan American flights in Brazil, including supervision tax; depreciation of the Brazilian airports used by both companies; interest on capital; payments under the guarantee arrangement; radio service	cr$400,025,561
2. Commissions on Pan American sales; services rendered to Pan American passengers; publicity services rendered to Pan American; Panair ticket agency expenses; interest on Pan American/Panair current account	cr$142,674,763

Total received by Panair for services rendered to Pan American	cr$542,700,324

During the ten-year period, 1944–54 Panair paid to Pan American:

1. Airport expenses for Panair plane landings outside of Brazil; airport depreciation participation outside of Brazil	cr$88,985,916
2. Commissions on Panair sales; interest on the Pan American/Panair current account balance	cr$48,596,199
Total received by Pan American for services rendered to Panair	cr$137,582,115

Comparing the payments made by one to the other, the following net balance results:

Payments made by Pan American to Panair	cr$542,700,324
Payments made by Panair to Pan American	cr$137,582,115
Difference in favor of Panair	cr$405,118,209

The average annual income received by Panair from Pan American during the ten year period 1944–54 thus amounted to about cr$40,000,000 or a sum equal to two-thirds of the annual subsidy obtained by Panair during that period from the Federal government.

Ever since the acquisition of the Constellation fleet, Pan American has granted all facilities to Panair for the purchase and financing of equipment, spare parts and engine repairs, always providing such services despite the scarcities of foreign exchange in Brazil. During the period January, 1950—March, 1955, the total cost of such materials, parts and engine repair services amounted to $9,340,000. On several occasions during this period, Panair's debt to Pan American went as high as $3,350,000. Panair has endeavored to maintain this credit on a perfectly solvent basis, but such efforts depend on exchange availability. Had it not been for the facilities offered by Pan American, Panair would have met with serious difficulties in maintaining its fleet in proper condition.

SELECTED OPERATING STATISTICS

	1939 [a]	*1940* [a]	*1957*	*1959*
Kms. flown (thousands)	1,701	2,014	22,223	na [b]
Hours flown	8,245	9,325	77,504	na
Passenger-kms. (thousands)	10,205	13,291	487,815	476,253
Cargo (thousands of ton-kms.)	1,009	1,326	53,672	na [b]
Income (millions of cr$)	19.7	20.8	1,703.7	2,910.5

[a] Income for 1939 and 1940 converted from dollars into cruzeiros at the rates of 19.90 and 20.70 cruzeiros respectively.
[b] na = not available.

MANAGEMENT

The relationship between the Brazilian director and the director representing the foreign shareholder is highly satisfactory, being based on mutual trust and personal friendship.

As for foreign technicians, the policy of the corporation is to contract them only for short and fixed periods, usually to provide for the solution of some specific technical problem. In such contracts, it is always specified that there must be due regard for the solutions offered by Brazilian technicians occupying the positions involved on a permanent basis.

BALANCE SHEET DATA, 1955–59 *(millions of cruzeiros)*

	End of 1955	*End of 1957*	*End of 1959*
Assets			
Fixed Assets	497.6	1,174.8	1,836.1
Disposable Assets	157.5	168.5	184.1
Current Assets	350.9	762.6	1,849.5
Inventories	35.1	69.4	179.1
Receivables and Others	315.8	693.2	1,670.4
Liabilities			
Capital	88.0	88.0	88.0
Reserves	82.3	97.8	172.5
Depreciation	302.4	358.3	616.8
Current Liabilities and Long-Term Loans	587.6	1,561.7	3,456.4
Profit and Losses	51.4	−5.0	−255.9

Rheem Metalúrgica, S.A.

ORIGIN AND DEVELOPMENT OF THE ENTERPRISE

The paid-up capital of the firm amounts to cr$120 million, 70 percent of which is owned by the American group, the Rheem Manufacturing Company, and 30 percent by Brazilian stockholders.

When Rheem Metalúrgica was organized, the initial capital was owned in the same proportions by Rheem and by Dr. Heitor S. Bergallo, Dr. Euvaldo Lodi and, to a small extent, by other shareholders. This capital, cr$8 million in all, was successively increased, but the original proportions were maintained and the undistributed reserves were capitalized. The increases were as follows:

On November 30, 1947, to cr$16 million.
On July 19, 1949, to cr$20 million.
On August 8, 1952, to cr$30 million.
On November 30, 1956, to cr$60 million.
On December 30, 1958, to cr$120 million.

The constant, large reinvestments show the expansion policy followed by the shareholders, and have made the corporation grow in a relatively short period to an enterprise with impressive resources and potential.

Rheem Metalúrgica was founded on June 8, 1946. The early postwar period witnessed the mushrooming of new enterprises in all the industrial centers of Brazil. Rio de Janeiro, at the time of Rheem Metalúrgica's foundation, offered favorable conditions for the development of a steel containers industry. At first the founders of Rheem Metalúrgica attempted to buy an already existing and similar enterprise, the Fábrica Nacional de Tambores (national drum factory), an enterprise with German capital expropriated during the war by the Brazilian government. Its obsolete equipment could be modernized, but this plan was eventually abandoned for economic reasons. In the process of study of the possibilities of adaptation of this plant, the promoters were afforded an opportunity to evaluate the vast potential of the Brazilian market for the establishment of their industry.

It was decided to form a new company with mixed capital. The Rheem Manufacturing group associated with two well-known Brazilians and formed Rheem Metalúrgica, on June 8, 1946, with the initial capital of cr$8 million.

The decision to install a plant in Rio de Janeiro was preceded by intensive market studies. To permit efficient operations, the raw materials supply problem, especially for steel sheets, the electric power supply, which had to be especially good, the location in relation to consumption markets, and other factors, were all carefully analyzed. The location of the plant was selected on the basis of low transportation costs for the finished products, ample electric power through high tension lines, the availability of water, and proximity to areas with available manpower and to the source of main raw materials (the Volta Redonda steel plant).

Rheem did not receive any government subsidy for its installation in the country. Since it started operations prior to 1953, the type of exchange subsidy to speed up Brazilian industrialization inaugurated with the 1953 exchange system had not as yet been instituted. Rheem considers that this type of subsidy granted to other industries which, directly or indirectly, compete with it, has contributed to disturbances in the market, creating either shortages of raw materials essential to its activities or misunderstandings with its traditional customers, who once in a while succeed in securing supplies at more favorable prices in view of the exchange subsidies granted to its competitors.

Rheem's association with the two Brazilian groups, the total participation of which represents 30 percent of the corporation's capital, is primarily a result of headquarters policy in the United States in favor of such associations in the countries in which it operates. This allows the American enterprise not only to benefit from local experience in aspects such as marketing, tax problems and others involving government contacts, but also to take advantage of the good will that accrues to such associations, in relations with personnel, customers, banks, and others connected with its activities.

It is interesting to note that, although 70 percent of the capital belongs to the American group, there is not a single foreigner in Rheem Metalúrgica, S.A. Both its technical and administrative personnel, and even its board of directors, are made up entirely of Brazilians. The reason for the large American participation in the enterprise's total investment is reported to be the considerable amount of capital needed at the time it was first raised. As previously stated, the initial capital was cr$8 million, which, in 1946, at the prevailing rate of exchange, was equivalent to about $500 thousand.

At present, its capital is cf$120 million. At the free market rate of exchange, this is about $1 million. All the increases were effected entirely through the reinvestment of profits.

The partners in Rheem Metalúrgica are also associated in two other enterprises: Parmet-Participações Metalúrgicas, a holding company capitalized at cr$60 million, with about the same division of stock as in Rheem Metalúrgica; and Rheem Senotubo, at São Paulo, which produces spiral welded pipes, held 95 percent by Parmet. Thus the original investment of cr$8 million in the one enterprise Rheem Metalúrgica has grown, through reinvestment, to more than cr$150 million in these three enterprises.

Since the corporation has its capital, both Brazilian and American, in the hands of closed groups, the distribution of dividends follows a rather conservative course. With rare exceptions, the dividends distributed to the shareholders have been on the basis of eight percent of the paid-up capital. For the Brazilian market, this percentage means there has been a high rate of reinvestment of profits.

Besides its participation in the venture's profits, Rheem of the United States has a licensee production contract with the enterprise involving the use of the parent company's original processes on the basis of royalty payments; this contract is of indefinite duration. There is also a technical assistance contract on a two-year renewable basis, which also involves the payment of a percentage on sales.

Starting with a sole product (the steel drum), Rheem later went into the production of small painted pails, lithographed pails, stoves, automotive parts, architectural porcelain-covered steel panels, and, more recently, with the acquisition of Rheem Senotubo at São Paulo, into the manufacture of tanks and pipes made of steel sheets (rolled and welded spiralwise, a process patented in Brazil).

MANAGEMENT

During the first years of operation, Americans managed the factory. The results were excellent, and in a short time, due to the adaptability of the Brazilians, the Americans turned over their functions to Brazilians, including the operation and maintenance of the plant as well as management and other operations. Today, despite the majority of Rheem Manufacturing, all the policies of Rheem

Metalúrgica are set and executed by local personnel, who are enthusiastically and loyally devoted to the corporation they helped to develop. This policy has been followed by Rheem Manufacturing all over the world with excellent results.

Rheem Metalúrgica is today operated by a director-president (Dr. Heitor S. Bergallo) and a director-manager (Dr. Fernando Pernambuco), each with his own specified functions.

At the beginning of its operation, the firm's board of directors consisted of three directors: director-president (Dr. Euvaldo Lodi), founding partner, Federal Deputy for the State of Minas Gerais, well-known mining and industrial engineer, now deceased; director-vice-president (Dr. Heitor S. Bergallo), also a founding partner, electrical and mechanical engineer, a graduate of the Electro-Technical School of Porto Alegre University and a man with vast industrial experience; director-manager (Mr. Mario Capelli), American citizen, Italian by birth, responsible for the start of the venture, having directed the research studies that resulted in the establishment of the corporation. Today, he is vice-president in charge of the International Division of Rheem Manufacturing in New York.

ROLE IN THE ECONOMY

The manufacturing lines at present and their respective capacities are:

Drum Line. 200 and 100 liter drums, manufactured in accordance with ICC specifications; daily average production of 2,000 units of each type. Lithographed pails, of 2, 2½, 5, and 7½ gallons. Manufactured in accordance with ICC specifications; daily average production of 9,000 units of each type.

Home Products Line. Stoves for liquefied petroleum gases or manufactured gas, with four burners, Rheem Master trademark; daily average production is 100 units. Broilers. Rheem Grill trademark; daily average production is 240 units.

Industrial Products Line. Rings for the rear wheels of trucks, purchaser's design; daily average production is 150 units. Architectural porcelain-covered panels. Seaporcel and Seaporclad trademarks, of varied sizes, types, and colors; daily average production is 50 sq. meters.

The petroleum products distribution industry, the paint and varnish industries, chemical industries, and others, such as refractory cements, constitute the market for receptacles. The home products are sold to the market in general and especially to the liquefied petroleum gas distributors. Some of the largest organizations in this field are among Rheem's customers.

EVALUATION

Rheem Manufacturing considers its experience in Brazil extremely favorable, especially its decision to entrust to Brazilians the management of the venture. This is a deliberate policy which it has followed with success in all countries where it operates. Even in Peru, where Rheem's capital is 100 percent American, the subsidiary's management is entrusted to nationals. In this manner, it has been possible to maintain very satisfactory relations, not only inside the company but also in the domestic market where it operates.

This deliberate orientation toward the "nationalization" of the direction and operation of its plants is based on the experience it has acquired during many years of activity outside the United States. In Brazil, there were at the beginning some misunderstandings between the two nationality groups entrusted with the task of going ahead with the venture. The repetition of this type of experience in other countries as well led Rheem to its present policy.

The problem of administration became one of the selection of local personnel who would take over the corporation's management, and training and adapting this personnel as fast as possible to replace foreign personnel. The cost of local personnel is much lower than that of foreign personnel, who require special incentives to leave their country.

Problems of relations between subordinate personnel, especially laborers, and their foreign supervisors, were of rather short duration. The American technicians who came to Brazil to start the venture, as well as the personnel recruited in the country, were of such high caliber that in a short time the presence of the foreign technicians became unnecessary, and local personnel, both in management and technical functions, have since taken over the entire responsibility of the joint venture.

BALANCE SHEET DATA, 1956–58 (*millions of cruzeiros*)

	End of 1956	*End of 1957*	*End of 1958*
Assets			
Fixed Assets	86.2	92.1	107.1
Disposable Assets	2.2	1.8	11.5
Current Assets	102.4	100.8	119.6
Inventories	59.4	68.8	48.2
Receivables and Others	43.0	32.0	71.4
Liabilities			
Capital	60.0	60.0	60.0
Reserves	43.9	64.7	74.6
Depreciation	18.6	25.7	29.4
Current Liabilities	68.3	44.3	74.2
Loans	21.5	10.3	10.0
Other Current Liabilities	46.8	34.0	64.2
Profits	53.4	56.1	19.8
Cash Distributed	3.6	—	—

Tubos de Acero de México, S.A. (*Tamsa*)

ORIGIN OF THE ENTERPRISE

This enterprise was promoted for the production of seamless steel pipe for the petroleum industry by a group of industrialists and investors in Mexico headed by Bruno Pagliai, a leading local investor of Italian origin. There had been considerable interest in the Mexican government, especially in Petróleos Mexicanos, the official petroleum enterprise, in the establishment of such manufacture in the country because of its total dependence upon imports to meet requirements of oil line pipe. Italian investors were obtained by the promoters, presumably through the connections of Mr. Pagliai, and Nacional Financiera joined the enterprise because of the special interest of the government in this new field of manufacture. The enterprise was organized on January 30, 1952, and began producing during the last half of 1954.

CAPITAL STRUCTURE

The company was formed with a capital of 50 million pesos, of which 45 percent was subscribed by private Mexican investors, including the promoting group and Mexican banking interests; 20 percent was subscribed by Nacional Financiera (this was actually effected about a year and a half after the enterprise was formed);

20 percent by four Italian enterprises connected with the steel industry (Finsider of Rome, Dalmine of Milan, and Ilva and Ansaldo of Genoa); and the remaining 15 percent was placed with individual European investors from Sweden and France. Thus, the majority of the investment was by Mexican interests, both private and official, and a minority by European interests, principally Italian.

In the development of the enterprise, it has been necessary to increase the equity capital from the original 50 million pesos to the present level of 230 million pesos, and to obtain substantial amounts of loan capital.

The first increase of capital was effected on August 30, 1954, when it was raised from 50 million pesos to 120 million pesos. The original 50 million pesos had been represented in 500 thousand common shares with a par value of 100 pesos each. The additional 70 million pesos was made up of 40 million pesos of common shares, and 30 million pesos of five percent preferential shares.

On August 17, 1955, the capital was raised by another 20 million pesos, to a new total of 140 million pesos, through a revaluation of the peso value of imported assets as a result of the exchange rate depreciation decreed in April, 1954, and through the issuance of 200 thousand common shares for this amount. This brought the total of common shares to 110 million pesos, while the value of preferential shares continued at 30 million pesos.

Because of continued expansion of the enterprise, another increase in capital was effected on April 12, 1957. This increase, in the amount of 30 million pesos, brought the total to 170 million pesos. Of the total increase of 30 million pesos, 20 million pesos consisted of new capital and 10 million pesos corresponded to the reinvestment of accumulated reserves. At the same time, the preferential shares were retired, and the 170 million pesos of capital was therefore represented exclusively in 1,700,000 common bearer shares.

Another capital increase, to 200 million pesos, was effected on March 31, 1959, through the reinvestment of 5 million pesos plus a new investment of 25 million pesos. Finally, on March 31, 1960, a 15 percent stock dividend raised the capital to 230 million pesos; the dividend represented almost the total of 1959 profits.

Throughout these various changes in the capital structure, the original distribution of the capital among the various shareholders has remained the same.

With respect to loan capital, a total of 30 million pesos of long-term bonds was placed through Nacional Financiera in 1957. Most of these bonds continued to be held by Nacional Financiera, but considerable amounts were placed with private Mexican individual and institutional investors. The outstanding balance amounted to 24 million pesos at the end of 1959. Also, an issue of dollar bonds was effected during the first half of 1957. The amount of the issue was $3 million, and by the end of 1959 it was totally placed. These are ten-year bonds with a minimum annual interest rate, also payable in dollars, of 5 percent, plus additional interest up to another four percent annually depending upon the extent of profits of the enterprise. According to the information supplied, these bonds were sold locally. The reason given for their denomination in dollars is the fear of exchange rate devaluation in Mexico and the lack of interest in investments in peso obligations.

The enterprise was the first of its kind in Mexico, and it was, therefore, necessary to obtain technical assistance for the design and construction of the plant as well as for the process of production itself. Although the various Italian investors in the firm are involved in the steel industry, the technical assistance arrangements concluded were not with any one of them but rather with an Italian engineering firm specialized in the field, the Compagnia Tecnica Internazionale (Techint). Techint was awarded a contract for supervising the installation of the plant, for which it was remunerated by being granted stock in the enterprise, and has had continued technical supervisory functions through a contract that has been renewed on a yearly basis.

MANAGEMENT AND PERSONNEL

The board of directors consists of 15 members, named by majority vote of the general assembly of shareholders. The assembly also names the chairman of the board, who at the same time is the president of the company. Since the beginning, the board has had the following composition: four members from the Italian group; two from the group of other European investors; 2 representatives of

Nacional Financiera; three representatives of the Mexican private banking interests in the enterprise; one representative of Petróleos Mexicanos, the largest customer of the company; two representatives of other Mexican investors; and Bruno Pagliai, the leader of the group that promoted the enterprise, who is also chairman of the board and president of the company. The company has one general manager in charge of production and one in charge of administration, commercial matters, and finance. The technical manager is an Italian, while the other manager is Mexican.

The total personnel of the enterprise at the end of 1959 was 2,057. Of this total, only 45 are foreigners, in technical and administrative posts. The foreign personnel makes up about 20 percent of the total in technical supervision and administration.

Labor-management relations have been satisfactory, and there has been no strike or other serious labor conflict during the life of the enterprise.

The enterprise has paid special attention to the technical training of workers, for which it has a school, the Escuela de Capacitación Tamsa, which supplements the practical on-the-job training in the company.

FINANCIAL RESULTS

Since 1955, the first full year of production by Tubos de Acero de México, net profits after taxes have risen continuously as the volume of operations has expanded, from 7.0 million pesos in 1955 to 9.1 million pesos in 1956, 22.2 million pesos in 1957, and more than 30 million pesos in 1959. These profits represent a return on equity of 5.8 percent, 6.5 percent, 13.1 percent, and more than 15 percent respectively, in each of these years. The enterprise, as a new industry in the Mexican economy, obtained from the outset tax concessions from the Mexican government ranging in duration from five to ten years.

Despite the profits indicated, no distribution of earnings was effected until 1957, when 15.9 million pesos out of an accumulated net total of about 37 million pesos (taking into account losses incurred during experimental production in 1954) were distributed. This represented a payment of close to 10 percent on the par value of the company's stock. As previously indicated, almost all 1959 profits were reinvested.

ROLE IN THE ECONOMY

Tamsa is located at the east coast seaport of Veracruz. Its site consists of 1,790,000 square meters, with a constructed area of some 102,500 square meters, leaving room for considerable expansion in the future.

The company's output of seamless steel pipe has steadily increased from 36,000 tons in 1955 to 50,000 tons in 1956, 73,000 tons in 1957, 99,000 tons in 1958, and 109,000 tons in 1959.

The products of Tamsa were approved by the American Petroleum Institute in March, 1955, and the enterprise, therefore, has the right to utilize the initials "A.P.I." on its pipe to indicate conformity with the standards set up by the Petroleum Institute.

For raw materials, Tamsa has recently installed two electric furnaces which will make it almost completely self-sufficient. The first furnace was completed in March, 1958 and the second in November of the same year. These furnaces will not only meet the problem of raw materials supply for the enterprise, but will also mean utilization of the scrap produced in the pipe making process itself. With this development, it is estimated that Tamsa may save the country close to $30 million per year in foreign exchange. Steel ingot production rose from 42,460 tons in 1958 to 100,001 tons in 1959. Future plans include the installation by 1962 of a plant to produce steel from iron ore, both domestic and imported.

Tamsa has two subsidiary enterprises, one known as Inmobiliaria Tamsa, and the other Siderúrgica Tamsa. Inmobiliaria Tamsa was set up in 1953 with a capital of 35 million pesos to take care of the construction activities related to the organization and operation of the parent company itself. This enterprise also owns the land on which the installations are located. Its shareholders are all Mexicans, consisting of Mexican stockholders in the parent company in order to comply with the legal requirements that lands within certain distances of the coast of the country may be held only by nationals. Siderúrgica Tamsa was set up in 1956 with a capital of 5 million pesos to conduct exploratory activities, especially for iron ore in connection with the raw materials requirements of the parent company. The proportions of stock ownership in this enterprise are the same as in the parent company.

Another enterprise set up by the same Mexican and Italian interests as those involved in Tamsa is Metalmecánica, S.A., which purchases pipe from Tamsa for further processing.

EVALUATION

Tubos de Acero de México was set up at the initiative of private Mexican investors and promoters in cooperation with Italian and other European capital and with capital from the Mexican government through Nacional Financiera, to engage in a new and basic line of production for the important petroleum industry of the country. The European investors have a minority holding in the enterprise. Technical assistance has been obtained abroad from a firm in Italy which is independent of the Italian investors in the enterprise. Although continuing technical assistance is furnished on this basis, the management responsibilities of the enterprise are widely distributed among the various Mexican and foreign groups. Tamsa has been able to expand the rate of its production satisfactorily, and, consequently, to attain a remunerative rate of return on its investment, which has permitted a substantial reinvestment as well as the payment of attractive dividends to its stockholders. Government representation in the enterprise has had the double significance of providing a source of both equity and loan capital, and of creating an assured market for the output of the firm since the petroleum industry is a government monopoly in the country.

Willys-Overland do Brasil S.A., Indústria e Comércio

CAPITAL STRUCTURE AND DEVELOPMENT OF THE ENTERPRISE

The paid-up capital of this firm amounts at present to cr$5,610,000,000 composed of cr$1,260,144,000 of non-voting preferential shares and cr$4,349,856,000 of common shares. The Brazilian public (over 40,000 shareholders) owns 50.92 percent of the common and 6.55 percent of the preferential shares. The remaining shares are held by foreign investors, principally Willys Motors, Inc. of Toledo, Ohio, and Régie Nationale des Usines Renault of France. The following table shows the composition of the present capital and its distribution between the Brazilian and foreign shareholders:

	Preferential Shares cr$1,000	*Common Shares cr$1,000*	*Total cr$1,000*
Brazilian Public	82,500 (6.55%)	2,214,856 (50.92%)	2,297,356
Willys Motors, Inc.	584,544 (46.39%)	1,570,000 (36.09%)	2,154,544
Régie Nationale des U. Renault	305,800 (24.26%)	565,000 (12.99%)	870,800
Other Foreign	287,300 (22.80%)		287,300
	1,260,144	4,349,856	5,610,000

The foreign shareholdings in Willys-Overland do Brasil represent the investment of machinery and equipment with a value of more than $27 million; those of the Brazilian public represent cash subscriptions. In addition to the direct investment in machinery and equipment, the sum of $5.6 million was acquired abroad from the International Finance Corporation, the American Overseas Finance Company, and Arcturus Investment Development Ltd.

In number of vehicles produced, and facilities for in-plant manufacture, Willys-Overland is the largest automotive company in the country. The present program of the company embraces the production of four-wheel drive vehicles: the jeep, which has been in production since 1956, and the station wagon, the manufacture of which was initiated in July, 1958; a two-wheel drive model of the station wagon is also being produced. The company produces two passenger cars, the Renault-Dauphine, the manufacture of which was initiated in November, 1959, and the Aero-Willys, which started in March, 1960.

Willys-Overland has been the leader in the Brazilian automotive industry in attaining "nationalization" of the vehicles it produces. The jeep and the station wagon have national material components of over 95 percent of total weight; the Renault-Dauphine, which started in November, 1959 with 25 percent, and the Aero-Willys, which started in March, 1960 with 85 percent were both scheduled to be over 95 percent national before the end of 1960.

In 1952, Willys Motors, Inc. and its distributors in Brazil organized Willys-Overland do Brasil S.A., with an initial capital of cr$50,000,-000 for the purpose of assembling and gradually manufacturing in Brazil the jeep line of vehicles. During the postwar period automobile and truck imports into Brazil were substantially reduced, the availability of transportation was diminished, and the country's economic growth was impaired. The government developed a national automobile industry plan which created broad opportunities for solving the problem of supplying means of transportation to the country. The program envisaged the production of a progressively increasing quantity of vehicles in the country up to an annual rate of 170,000 units by the end of 1960.

The company's preferential shareholders are entitled to an 8 percent annual dividend. Both preferential and common shares participate equally in the distribution of additional dividends after the payment to both of an annual 8 percent dividend. The policy of the company, however, is to pay dividends at the rate of 12 percent, and this procedure has been followed. The relative facility with which the company's shares have been sold on the market may be attributed, to some extent, to this dividend policy.

The ratio of net profits to sales in the year ending June 30, 1960, was 5.6 percent, reflecting the company's policy of limiting the margin of profits and increasing volume.

The company has an agreement with Willys Motors which provides for the payment of royalties for the use of patents, registered trademarks, and other property rights. The royalty calculation is based on a percentage of sales and components, and the agreement has a duration of 20 years. For the manufacture of the Renault-Dauphine, the company has a license and royalty agreement with the Régie Nationale des Usines Renault, which is based also on a percentage of sales and components.

ROLE IN THE ECONOMY

Since 1954, the sales of units produced by the company have been as follows:

Year ending	*Jeeps*	*Station Wagons*	*Dauphine*	*Aero-Willys*
December 31, 1954	1,405			
December 31, 1955	1,258			
June 30, 1956 [a]	409			
June 30, 1957	4,605			
June 30, 1958	10,631	228		
June 30, 1959	14,510	7,282		
June 30, 1960	16,548	6,757	2,606	1,053

[a] First half of calendar year 1956 only.

The company's present production program calls for the manufacture of 4,350 vehicles per month, as follows:

900 Aero-Willys passenger cars
1200 Renault-Dauphine passenger cars
1500 jeeps
750 station wagons

Willys-Overland now has more than 600 domestic suppliers of production materials, from whom it purchases over cr$800,000,000 worth monthly. The total disbursements in June, 1960 for both directly productive items and others, reached over cr$950,000,000 paid to some 1,300 domestic suppliers.

The company's industrial development program is designed for facilities with a capacity for the yearly manufacture of 110,000 units, comprising 25,000 jeeps, 15,000 station wagons, 20,000 Aero-Willys passenger cars, and 50,000 Renault-Dauphine passenger cars. This program, which is virtually completed, embraces a total of 139,000 square meters of buildings and 1,045,000 square meters of land, which include the following facilities:

Willys Engine Plant, with an area of 9,454 square meters, and a capacity of 22 engines per hour.
Axle and Transmission Plant, with an area of 20,187 square meters.
Press Plant, with an area of 11,350 square meters.
Foundry, with an area of 13,473 square meters, with the capacity to produce all of the major castings.
Dauphine Engine Plant, with an area of 8,064 square meters and a capacity of 10 engines per hour.
Assembly Plants for the several vehicles now being produced, which have a total combined area of 39,300 square meters.
Tool and Die Shops, Quality Control Laboratories and Testing Facilities, Experimental Engineering Department, and other miscellaneous installations.

Relations between the national and foreign directors, as well as between the Brazilian workers and foreign technicians, are excellent. The adaptation of the Brazilian workers for the handling of the industry's complicated machinery and equipment has been accomplished within a short training period and is noteworthy. The number of employees on June 30, 1960 was 6,977.

Willys-Overland shares have an excellent acceptance on the Brazilian market. Since October, 1956, shares amounting to over cr$2,-200,000,000 have been placed with over 40,000 Brazilian shareholders. To place Brazilian company shares abroad, however, is almost an impossibility due to the instability of the cruzeiro and its depreciation in relation to other currencies. A stable currency would surely enable Willys-Overland shares to be placed on foreign markets. This is suggested by the success in obtaining substantial dollar loans abroad to finance the purchase of machinery, equipment, and spare parts for the enterprise.

BALANCE SHEET DATA, 1957–59, Fiscal Year Ending June 30
(*thousands of cruzeiros*)

	1957	*1958*	*1959*
Current Assets			
Cash on hand and in Banks	61,779	178,755	544,626
Accounts Receivable	481,139	402,672	246,107
Inventories	343,062	645,105	2,365,520
Other Short Term Accounts	176,116	222,049	403,342
Total Current Assets	1,062,096	1,448,581	3,559,595
Current Liabilities			
Promissory Notes and Unpaid Imports	559,130	591,062	1,436,440
Supplies and Other Unpaid Accounts	75,202	262,030	902,567
Reserves	29,367	84,332	324,830
Total Current Liabilities	663,699	937,424	2,663,837
Net Worth	398,397	511,157	895,758
Plus			
Long Term Capital Repaid	4,326	80,922	89,167
Miscellaneous Investments	384	32,488	161,742
Fixed Assets	445,287	1,017,404	5,782,198
	449,997	1,130,814	6,033,107
	848,394	1,641,971	6,928,865
Less			
Long-Term Liabilities	61,553	293,604	1,549,160
Miscellaneous Reserves	53,316	70,101	142,601
	114,869	363,705	1,691,761
Shareholders' Ownership	733,525	1,278,266	5,237,104
Shareholders' Ownership			
Capital	580,000	1,001,000	4,844,613
Capital Balance outstanding on Shares	—	—	765,387
Pending Profits and Reserves	153,525	277,266	580,431
	733,525	1,278,266	6,190,431

PROFIT AND LOSS STATEMENT, 1957–59, Fiscal Year Ending June 30
(*thousands of cruzeiros*)

	1957	*1958*	*1959*
Sales	1,313,110	2,784,778	7,853,072
Less Sales Costs (Exchange premiums and importation expenses, national parts, and production expenses)	770,170	1,971,343	5,717,870
Sales Tax and Consumption Tax	205,917	118,193	755,387
	976,087	2,089,536	6,473,257
Gross Profit from Sales	337,023	695,242	1,379,815
Disbursements			
Miscellaneous Taxes	56,939	89,736	—
Sales and Administration Expenses, and Other Disbursements	134,253	370,684	721,639
Doubtful Debtors Provision	38,491	1,509	40,000
Interest	—	—	72,418
	229,683	461,929	834,057
Profit from Operations	107,340	233,313	545,758
Other Income			
Discounts	3,305	9,813	36,416
Miscellaneous Income	—	12,277	15,000
	3,305	22,090	51,416
Profit During the Year	110,645	255,403	597,174
Less Legal Reserve	5,532	12,770	15,855
Net Profit	105,113	242,633	581,319

II. Far East

Atul Products Ltd.

ORIGIN OF THE ENTERPRISE

It is now little more than a decade since Atul Products Ltd. was established on September 5, 1947. Today Atul is one of the leading producers of dyestuffs and pharmaceuticals in India.

The importance of developing the dye industry as an integral part of the industrial economy of India was realized during the war years when supplies from abroad were virtually non-existent. The Planning and Development Department created by the government of India in 1943 had given consideration to this question and investigated the possibility of setting up India's own dye industry. A number of private concerns also explored the possibility, especially regarding available foreign know-how. Kasturbhai Lalbhai was one of the most prominent among those interested in the project. A leading industrialist and financier in India, Mr. Lalbhai took the initiative of contacting foreign concerns with a view to enlisting their collaboration in establishing a new dye industry in the country. He was successful in this endeavor and the foreign company that agreed to collaborate with him was an American one, the American Cyanamid Company. Later, additional arrangements were made with Swiss and British firms as well. Thus, Atul has become a successful multi-national venture.

The factory and establishment of Atul Products are located at Parnera, Bombay State, on a spacious 700-acre plot of land.

AGREEMENTS WITH FOREIGN PARTNERS

1. With the American Cyanamid Company.

A general and preliminary agreement was entered into in October, 1946, between the American Cyanamid Company and Mr. Lalbhai. The main provisions of this agreement were:

(i) Mr. Lalbhai will organize a new Company under the laws of India for the purpose of manufacturing, purchasing, and selling chemicals, dyestuffs, etc.

(ii) After the organization of the new Company, Cyanamid will purchase a portion (less than one-half) of the total number of shares of the new Company.

(iii) Cyanamid and the new Company will enter into a contract dealing with the details of the nature and extent of the collaboration.

The detailed agreement was entered into immediately after the formation of the new company, Atul Products Limited, and contains the following provisions:

(i) Cyanamid will furnish Atul with technical data and information for the plant layout, equipment specifications, and organization to construct the plant and to purchase and install such equipment. Cyanamid will also act as Atul's agent for purchases in the U.S.A. if necessary. It will provide these services at cost borne by Atul.

(ii) Cyanamid will, in addition, furnish descriptions of the processes for the production of the products and technical operating data for the operation of the plant. For this purpose, a competent chemist with a staff will be made available at the cost of Atul.

(iii) Throughout the continuance of this agreement, Cyanamid and Atul shall each, from time to time, disclose to the other any improvements made in the processes or methods of manufacture employed.

(iv) Cyanamid will train technicians on behalf of Atul. Expenses involved are to be borne by Atul.

(v) Atul will use "due diligence" to insure that both during and after this agreement, no information dealing with the processing, etc., is divulged by its technical personnel.

(vi) For the services of each engineer or chemist furnished by Cyanamid, Atul shall pay to Cyanamid in U.S. currency and at New York such funds as are agreed upon as compensation before the departure of such engineer or chemist. Atul will also bear the costs of first-class transportation, living accommodations and subsistence for such persons. Atul will also bear all incidental and other expenses including all taxes paid by or on behalf of such persons.

(vii) As compensation for the processes, technical data, information and advice furnished by Cyanamid and Atul's right and licenses to use the same, Atul shall pay to Cyanamid sums equal to two and one-half per cent of the "net sales value" of each of the initial products manufactured and sold by Atul for a period of ten years whether or not this agreement has expired or been terminated during this period. Such sums are to be paid at New York in dollars at the prevailing rate of exchange of the rupee within 90 days after the 1st of December every year, minus any Indian taxes which Atul may be required by the laws of India to withhold from such payment.

(viii) During the continuance of this agreement, Cyanamid shall sell to Atul upon mutually agreed terms intermediates and other chemicals required for the operation of Atul's plants in India to the extent that Atul may desire to purchase from Cyanamid.

(ix) Atul can make use of Cyanamid's name and goodwill in advertising its products. But Cyanamid will have the right to inspect the Atul products to ensure that Cyanamid's goodwill and high reputation are not impaired by products of inferior quality.

(x) The agreement is to continue for ten years from the date of the completion of the initial plant of Atul unless terminated earlier by either party upon written notice to the other given at least six months prior to the effective date of such termination.

2. With Ciba Ltd. of Basle, Switzerland.

On July 9, 1948, one year after the agreement between Atul and Cyanamid, Atul entered into another agreement with a new foreign collaborator, a Swiss concern, Ciba Ltd.

The main provisions of the general agreement were as follows:

(i) Atul recognizes CIBA's special knowledge and experience in the field of chemical production and desires collaboration. CIBA, recognizing the importance of India in the sphere of chemical production, desires to collaborate with Atul.

(ii) CIBA will subscribe to the capital stock of Atul to a specified portion and will be entitled to have a Director on the Board of Atul.

(iii) It is agreed that, should CIBA decide no longer to import any one or more chemical products into India, nor to manufacture either itself or through a subsidiary in India, then Atul will be the first to be offered the right to produce such products.

(iv) Atul undertakes not to enter directly or indirectly into the distribution field with respect to such products.

(v) Atul will make every effort to keep secret during and after the termination of this agreement, any processes or information received from CIBA.

(vi) The agreement is to last for twenty years.

(vii) If during the period Atul's management, ownership or control changes and as a result CIBA's interests are seriously impaired, the latter may terminate the agreement with three months notice in writing.

(viii) After termination of this agreement, Atul will not be entitled to use any process or information received under this agreement.

(ix) This agreement shall be construed and enforced according to the laws of Switzerland.

(x) All differences touching this agreement shall be settled in Switzerland by three arbitrators, one to be appointed by each party and an umpire to be appointed by the parties' arbitrators. The parties agree to be bound by the award of the arbitration.

Pursuant to the general agreement, a detailed agreement was entered into on the same date covering a specific product. Subsequently, more such specific agreements covering particular products followed on the same terms and conditions. The provisions of the specific agreement of July, 1948 are as follows:

(i) The first specific product, the production of which is to be undertaken by Atul, is Sulfatheazole (Cibazol).

(ii) Within a period of two years Atul will construct and put into operation the facilities necessary for the production of Cibazol and CIBA undertakes to make available to Atul all the scientific and technical knowledge necessary.

(iii) Atul will not sell Cibazol to third parties or through distribution facilities of its own without the prior consent of CIBA. If such consent is given Atul is prepared to pay CIBA a royalty on such sales at a rate to be determined when the case arises. (Atul does not in fact sell Cibazol).

(iv) The price to be charged to CIBA or CIBA's nominee in the purchase of this production from Atul is to be the full cost of production plus an amount equal to 15% of the prime cost, provided always that this price is not unreasonably in excess of the delivered world price, in which latter event CIBA reserves the right to buy elsewhere. On the other hand, if Atul can produce and deliver at a cost plus the percentage described more than 10% below the delivered world price from other sources, then CIBA agrees that the price differential shall be divided between Atul and CIBA in a proportion to be decided when and if the situation arises.

(v) Atul undertakes, in order that CIBA's position in the market for Cibazol may be maintained, to do everything in its power to facilitate the obtaining by CIBA of the necessary approvals and permits, so that CIBA can continue to import Cibazol in the interval before Atul reaches production in sufficient volume and of satisfactory quality.

The agreement also includes a schedule which defines the full cost of production and the method of calculating it. By the end of 1951, production of Cibazol had commenced at Atul.

3. With Imperial Chemical Industries Ltd.

The initial agreement was signed by Kasturbhai Lalbhai, Atul Products Ltd., Imperial Chemical Industries (ICI) India Ltd., and Imperial Chemical Industries Ltd., London.

The signing occurred on August 4, 1955. The main provisions were as follows:

(i) A new Joint Company to be called Atic Industries Ltd. will be formed between the I.C.I. and Atul. It will be registered in India.

(ii) The equity capital will be held 50 percent by I.C.I. (India) Ltd. and 50 percent by Atul.

(iii) The authorized capital will be Rs.50 million. The issued capital will be in the first instance Rs.20 million in the form of ordinary shares.

(iv) Atic will raise loans as required.

(v) The Board of Atic will consist initially of six Directors, three each from Atul and I.C.I.

(vi) Atul will make available on terms to be negotiated an area of about 20 acres of their site at Bulsar after approval of the area by I.C.I. technical staff.

(vii) Atic will negotiate with Atul for the supply by Atul on terms to be agreed of certain services such as steam, power, water, and facilities for waste disposal.

(viii) *Manufacture:* (a) Atic will manufacture Jade Greens from imported advanced intermediates first; then intermediates for Jade Greens; then a series of other Vat Dye stuffs and their intermediates.

(b) These products will not be manufactured by the parties anywhere else than in India unless otherwise agreed by the parties.

(c) The parties will be free to discuss with each other the possibility of further expansion in the field of dyestuffs.

(ix) The I.C.I. will enter into a Technical Agreement with Atic on the following (actually signed in October 1955):

(a) Designing of the plant and equipment.

(b) Providing technical staff to supervise the construction of the plant.

(c) Providing all information connected with the operation of the plant.

(d) Making appropriate arrangements for the training of personnel for the management of the plant.

(e) Making available all technical information required for the manufacture of the agreed products.

(f) To cover the expenses involved in these services, Atic will pay I.C.I.

their out-of-pocket expenses in design work, ordering, inspection, shipping, and erection of the plant.

(g) No royalties will be sought for information given in connection with the manufacture of the agreed products but it is understood that this clause will not prejudice the rights of both parties to negotiate separate technical agreements for the manufacture by Atic of dyestuffs and intermediates outside the field of this agreement.

(h) For the time being Atic will rely on I.C.I.'s continuing to give information within the scope of the agreement, and Atic will therefore make contributions to I.C.I.'s research in this field of 2 percent of the net sales value of the products manufactured and sold by Atic other than Jade Greens. These contributions will be made mutually for a period of ten years from the date on which the first of such products (other than Jade Greens) is first sold in commercial quantities by Atic.

(x) Atic will enter into an agreement with I.C.I. (India) Ltd. (Actually signed in October 1955) under which:

(a) I.C.I. (India) Ltd. will process and pack the whole of Atic's production initially and for as long as Atic so desires.

(b) I.C.I. (India) will be offered on terms to be agreed, 70% of the production for purchase and resale; the remaining 30% will be available to other dyestuffs distributors on terms to be agreed.

(c) In the event of the distributors' being collectively unable to dispose of the 30%, the excess will be similarly offered to I.C.I. (India) for sale.

(xi) I.C.I. (India) will provide specifications of all intermediates and other chemicals required for the manufacture of the agreed products. Atic will be free to make its purchases of the appropriate intermediates and chemicals from any sources available.

ROLE IN THE ECONOMY AND FINANCIAL RESULTS

After the registration of the company in 1947, its main problem was the acquisition of its site. As the plot was fairly extensive and there were already a few villages within it, the proceedings unavoidably involved delay. The government of Bombay finally gave possession of the lands to the company in September, 1949.

By November, 1949, building operations began and considerable progress was made during the next year. Two extensive reservoirs, the store building, and the mechanic shop building were completed in 1951. The foundations of the power house, the azo, alizarine, sulphur black and the sulfa finishing buildings had been laid in 1949. These were completed in 1951.

During 1950, the company acquired a free controlling interest in the Ameer Trading Corporation Ltd., Bombay, which was the sole distributor in India for the dyestuffs, pigments, and intermediates of the Calco Chemical Division of the American Cyanamid Company. This step was taken to make use of the Ameer Trading Corporation as a competent medium of distribution for Atul Products.

During the same year, the company entered into two agreements, one with Ciba and the other with Lederle Laboratories (India) Ltd., a wholly-owned subsidiary of American Cyanamid, under which pharmaceuticals including aureomycin, sulfadiezine, and folic acid, were to be manufactured by Atul.

The company went into production early in 1952. The Prime Minister of India, Jawaharlal Nehru, performed the formal opening ceremony of the plant on March 17, 1952.

By the end of 1952, the first year of production, the company had made a small profit, about rs5,000. By that time, the company had put on the market 12 different dyes and the market was receptive due to their standards, quality, and strength.

By the end of 1953, the company had made good progress in two directions: 1) establishing the qualities of the dyes manufactured, and 2) insuring a good and steady demand for its products. Despite the fact that Atul products were competing with imported dyestuffs from advanced countries which enjoyed many advantages, the company made a substantial profit during the year (about rs125 thousand). There was also an increase in the number of its products, which stood at 29 at the end of the year.

The first year in which the company functioned smoothly in matters of production and prices was 1954. As a result, there was a profit of some rs1.24 million. There was also a vigorous policy of expansion and additions to the plant, machinery and production in 1954. To promote these objects, the company negotiated a preliminary agreement with ICI (India) Ltd., and submitted to the government a further program of expansion mainly concerned with the manufacture of intermediates.

In 1955, the company produced a profit of rs2.06 million. The directors set apart a substantial part of this for depreciation reserves, and the rest was distributed as a 5.25 percent dividend on the ordinary shares of the company for the year ending December 31, 1955. It was during this year also that Atic Industries Ltd. was established by Atul and ICI (India) Ltd., with an authorized capital of rs50 million, for the purpose of manufacturing vat jade greens and other vat dyestuffs. A further agreement was later entered into between Atic and ICI (England) for the manufacture of several other vat dyes and their intermediates. The manufacture of jade greens began in August, 1956, and has progressed satisfactorily to date. The plant to manufacture the further range of vat dyes was opened in April, 1959, and is being gradually brought into full production.

Net profits for 1957 amounted to rs3.45 million, and a dividend at the rate of 8 percent per share of rs100 was declared for the year, after providing a substantial amount for depreciation. The dividend paid for 1959 was 12 percent.

The company now has a definite program of expansion in new products that is estimated to require capital expenditures of some $20 million over the next four to five years. There are at present being constructed a sulfuric acid plant and an electrolytic plant for the manufacture of chlorine and caustic soda. Both of these plants are primarily to supply raw materials to Atul Products. With the production of these basic chemicals, not only will the cost reductions be substantial, but also the company will possess the base for the production of a much wider range of chemical products than ever before.

CAPITAL STRUCTURE

The original authorized share capital of the company was rs50 million in 500,000 shares of rs100 each. Of the total, 100,000 were initially issued and subscribed. The American Cyanamid Company had a ten percent share in the original capital of the company, but has not subscribed to subsequent issues, and by the end of 1959 held only a five percent share.

Early in 1960 American Cyanamid sold on the open market stock purchase rights it obtained by virtue of the company's decision to increase the number of its shares by 50 percent; and in mid-1960 it was reported to be selling its remaining stock in Atul, although at the same time it was selling to Atul up to a 24 percent interest in its wholly-owned Lederle Laboratories (India). Of the total rs10 million initially subscribed, only rs5 million was called for in the year 1948. It was with this amount that the company began its operations.

At the beginning of 1950, the capital invested was rs10 million. By 1954 it had increased to rs14.13 million; by 1957, to nearly rs42 million; and early in 1960 the number of shares was increased by 50 percent. In mid-1960, Atul's shares were being quoted on the stock exchange at rs500 per share for stock with a par value of rs100.

In 1954, Atul adopted a resolution to request a loan of rs30 million from the government of India, which has always been very interested in having an operative dye industry in India. The government agreed in principle with the request for the loan, and advanced a sum of rs7.5 million in 1955. Toward the end of 1956, Atul applied to the government of India for a further loan of rs5.7 million from the sanctioned amount of rs30 million; this was received in 1957, and applied toward the development program. Pursuant to the loan agreement, the company agreed to place a nominee of the government of India on the board of directors.

With respect to Atic Industries (Private) Ltd., in 1956 the government of India issued a license to that firm for the manufacture of several other vat dyes in addition to the originally agreed varieties, and the capital of the company was increased to rs20 million.

MANAGEMENT

The general direction and control of Atul's management is vested in a board of directors, which has at present nine members. Originally the number of directors was eight, the additional member being the government director. Of the original eight, two represent the managing agents, Lalbhai Sons & Company, who are in charge of the day-to-day management of the concern, and the remaining six directors represent the shareholders.

No special qualification is fixed for the government director or the two directors of the managing agents. Other directors must be shareholders of at least 100 ordinary shares.

The Cyanamid Company did not insist upon a nominee of its

own on the board of directors although it had a substantial capital investment (10 percent). Nevertheless, one of its senior officials was a director of the company until 1954. Ciba has had no director of its own on the board. Of the board of directors of Atic Industries, 50 percent of the directors are nominees of ICI, and 50 percent are nominees of Atul. The chairmanship of the board is to be held by Mr. Lalbhai for the first five years and then will alternate between a nominee of ICI and Atul every three years.

Although the policies of Atul are determined by the board of directors, it is the managing agents who run the concern on a day-to-day basis. The terms of the agreement with the managing agents are as follows:

(1) Lalbhai Sons & Co. are appointed Managing Agents of the company for a period of twenty years from the date of Registration of the Company.

(2) The firm cannot be removed from the position during these twenty years except if found guilty of fraud or willful misconduct in the management of the business of the Company and in the discharge of their duties as Managing Agents.

(3) The remuneration of the firm shall be:

(a) a sum of Rs.3000 per month as allowance for holding office as Managing Agents;

and

(b) a commission of 10% of the net annual profits of the Company.

(4) The Company shall pay to the firm all preliminary expenses incidental to the formation of the Company.

(5) The Company shall further pay all expenses incurred in the management of the business of the Company.

(6) The firm shall keep proper and complete books of account for all transactions of the Company.

(7) The firm shall prepare the profit and loss account and balance sheet to be set before the Company in a General Meeting.

(8) The firm shall have charge of all property belonging to the Company.

(9) Subject to the supervision and direction of the Directors, the firm shall control the general conduct and management of the business of the Company.

(10) During the period of the agreement two representatives of the firm shall be on the Board of Directors.

(11) If the services of the firm are terminated earlier than twenty years, it is entitled to compensation.

(12) In case of any dispute between the Company and the firm in respect to this agreement, such dispute shall be arbitrated by two arbitrators, one to be named by each party to the dispute.

GOVERNMENT RELATIONS

The relationship of the company with both the government of India and the government of Bombay State and their agencies, on the whole, has been smooth and cordial. In fact, it has been the policy of the state to give all possible assistance to important industries of this nature. Mr. Kasturbhai was encouraged to enter the field because of this favorable attitude of the government of India.

At the inception of the enterprise, the company needed the government's help in acquiring the extensive site where the factories and offices are located. The legal procedure involved in the acquisition of land in India is, to say the least, dilatory and complicated. Considering this, the fact that the company got possession of the land by September, 1949 is indeed a significant achievement. The government of Bombay was extremely helpful to the company in this respect.

The factory construction, machinery installation, and commencement of production proceeded without delay due to the promptness with which the Indian government issued the licenses for importation of the requisite machinery and raw materials. The government showed its goodwill and particular concern toward the company when the Prime Minister performed the inauguration ceremony in March, 1952.

The market for the company's dyes was unfavorable during 1952, the first year of its production. The principal reasons for this condition were the increased activity on the part of foreign suppliers who were re-entering the market after the war, and the import policy of the government of India, which became liberal in granting import licenses for all types of dyes. The company brought this as well as other factors affecting the industry to the notice of the Tariff Commission, and asked for a protective tariff. The Tariff Commission considered the request in the beginning of 1954, and submitted its report to the government in that year. The commission's report was favorable and the government reduced import duties from 38.2 percent to 10 percent ad valorem on some of the specific intermediates used by the company and raised existing duties of 12 percent to 20 percent on imports of direct and acid dyes and sulphur black. Also, in 1954, the government imposed some restrictions on imports of dyes of the varieties which the company was manufacturing. At times, however, the Customs Authorities' interpretation of the tariff has greatly reduced its efficacy as a protective device.

PERSONNEL

There are about 800 laborers employed by the factory, most locally recruited. A sizeable proportion are provided with living quarters by the company and the rest live in nearby villages.

There have been no strikes or lock-outs in the factory to date. The relationship between labor and management has been, on the whole, very satisfactory. The workers overwhelmingly belong to the Indian National Trade Union Congress, an associate of the Indian Congress Party which at present holds the political power both in the Indian Union and in Bombay State. The union has exerted its influence in minimizing areas of conflict between management and labor.

Considering the international composition of the personnel working in the company, particularly during its early stages, personnel relationships have been more than satisfactory. At present, the number of foreign personnel is very small, but most of them hold key technical positions.

Atul is a telling example of how Indians can cooperate in industry with foreigners of diverse backgrounds. There are members of at least four nationalities working in the company. Foreign personnel and Indians attest to their excellent understanding. In the beginning, there were the usual problems deriving from absence of full confidence and trust. Many of these were the result of ignorance, prejudice, or misunderstandings. To a great extent, the varying sociological and political backgrounds accounted for the differences in approach, attitude, and behavior, but intimate contacts, exchange of ideas, and mutual problems soon built up a new bond, a new trust, and a new outlook.

The British, due to their long association with India and its people, know more about them and, therefore, are potentially more adaptable. On the other hand, some of the British personnel have certain prejudices which are not helpful to the tackling of many situations. The Americans, on the contrary, being generally unorthodox in their approach and relative newcomers to the Indian scene, can perhaps more easily adapt themselves to the local conditions. However, their background knowledge of India is rather superficial, and they are likely to have initial difficulties, as was the case in the early stages at Atul. Once these are resolved, the relationship becomes intimate and abiding. On the whole, the British tend to stay for longer periods than the Americans, who have frequent changes of personnel. For example, ICI maintains a permanent British staff at Atul.

EVALUATION

One of the most important results of Atul's work so far has been the training imparted to Indian personnel for them to become qualified to take over the responsibilities of operating the concern. Today, the foreign technical personnel working with the company are few.

Atul products are now fully established in the market. The steady progress the company has made during a period of about a decade is an index of its strength as a business concern. Since the time the company went into regular production, it has made quite reasonable profits, despite the fact that it had to face stiff competition from more advanced concerns abroad. With the present tariff protection and import control, Atul's financial future is bright.

The management of the company, almost exclusively under Indian direction, has worked smoothly, and the interests of the foreign collaborators have been adequately protected. On the whole, Atul Products has established itself as a model joint international business venture.

Burma Oil Company (1954) Ltd.

ORIGIN OF THE ENTERPRISE

Immediately before the Second World War, the petroleum industry, though accounting for only ½ of 1 percent of world production, was the third largest industry in Burma. Its importance to the economy is shown by its employment of about 25,000 workers in 1942, and the government in 1940 collected approximately rs10¼ million or the equivalent of $3.1 million in taxes (excluding taxation on profits, which amounted to approximately rs8.5 million or the equivalent of $2.6 million) from the Burmah Oil Company (B.O.C.), the Indo-Burma Petroleum Company (I.B.P.C.), and the British Burmah Petroleum Company (B.B.P.C.). These taxes constituted about one-tenth of the total revenue of Burma. The total production of crude oil by the B.O.C., I.B.P.C., and B.B.P.C. was about 275 million gallons in 1941. In contrast, "native" production was 4 million gallons, and "others" produced 0.75 million gallons. The B.O.C. refinery at Syriam had a refining capacity of 800,000 gallons daily.

In 1941, 77 percent of Burma's crude oil output (and 75 percent of refined products) was produced by the Burmah Oil Company Limited, 12½ percent by the Indo-Burma Petroleum Company, 8½ percent by the British Burmah Petroleum Company, and about 2 percent by the Nath Singh Oil Company.

The Burmese oil industry dates back to the thirteenth century, but production of crude oil began only after the Burmah Oil Co. Ltd. was formed and became a lessee of land in upper Burma.

The Burmah Oil Co. Ltd. was founded in 1886, and was registered in Edinburgh in 1902. It had subsidiaries such as B.O.C. (Burma Concessions) Ltd., B.O.C. (Refineries) Ltd., B.O.C. (Pipe Lines) Ltd., B.O.C. (Burma Trading) Ltd. Its oil wells were in Central Burma, and the company laid a 325-mile pipe line between the oil fields and Syriam, where its refinery was located. B.O.C. Ltd. was one of the four leading British companies in Burma. The company's assets in Burma, including oil wells, boring plants, tanks, buildings, pipes, refineries, etc., were destroyed when a "scorched earth" policy was adopted in 1942. The Indo-Burma Petroleum Company Limited started its operations long after the formation of B.O.C. Ltd. It had two refineries, the main refinery being situated near Syriam in Seikkyi. The British Burmah Petroleum Company Limited had its own refinery at Thilawa, a few miles from the Syriam refinery.

The British oil companies had severe labor problems. Although they paid higher wages and provided better working conditions than any other industry in Burma, they had more labor disputes than any other industry in the country. Most of the prewar labor disputes were related to the political movements of the day. The labor problem dates back to 1920. There were a number of disputes from 1921 to 1924 and in 1926, involving work stoppages, strikes, and civil disorder. The clash of labor and management in the oil fields area culminated in the great strike and civil unrest of 1928. The oil field strikers received strong moral support from the people of the country, who regarded the strikers as freedom fighters. Eventually, the workers returned to work without having won material improvements. But the nationalist feeling increased, and the people came to regard the Burmah Oil Company as a symbol of British capitalism which exploited Burma and Burmese labor.

When the British reoccupied Burma in 1945, the distribution of products was being managed by the civil branch of the military administration. The oil companies took over the fields, and the B.O.C. and I.B.P.C. took over the management of distribution from the military administration. The Burmah Oil Company discovered that the conduct of the "denial policy," in 1942, had been so thorough that the company's facilities had either been totally destroyed or extensively damaged, and major replacements and rehabilitation were required before substantial production could be restored.

Progress on the reconstruction of distribution facilities was made by the end of 1947, and the reconstruction of fields, pipe lines, and refineries was expected to be completed in 1951. The oil companies also foresaw that exploration for new reserves of oil to replace the wastage of existing sources would soon become necessary.

One of the difficult problems in the relationship of the B.O.C. and the government at that time was the "denial" claims. The company's reconstruction policy was based on the assumption that it would receive equitable war compensation from the government. However, before the company could make any substantial headway with the British government, Burma became independent (1948), and the government of the Union of Burma became responsible for the affairs of the country and the people of Burma. The company, together with other oil companies, filed legal suits in the Burmese courts for claims against the Union government. The oil companies claimed £40 million. However, the oil companies had received payment of £4.5 million from the British government, and said that the claims from the Burmese government would be reduced by that amount. Reconstruction was started and the companies' officials stated that the companies had spent £7.8 million up to the end of 1948, and trusted that the compensation would be forthcoming, that conditions would be stable, and that the government treatment would be favorable.

Meanwhile, insurrection in Burma broke out and the oil field area was occupied by insurgents for some months. In 1949, the companies were about to discontinue rehabilitation in the oil fields because of insecurity and lack of communications. They informed the Burmese prime minister accordingly. The prime minister invited them to put forward proposals for a scheme whereby the government of Burma would furnish the remaining capital required to complete the reconstruction and thus acquire an interest in the industry for the state.

The oil companies suggested a plan which the government accepted after some deliberation. The government then had the problem of getting funds for financing the projects. Burma at that time was trying to negotiate a loan from the British government. Britain, intending to help both parties work out an amicable solution, agreed to underwrite any expenditure incurred by the companies after March 7, 1949 while the negotiations were still going on. The companies stopped operations at Yenangyaung in 1949, and discharged 2,000 employees because security conditions were not satisfactory. Later, the government could not raise funds for this project, and the project finally failed in January, 1950. As a result of this failure, 6,000 employees at both fields and refineries were discharged in 1949. These discharges were referred to the Industrial Court. The court decided in favor of the workers, but the decision was set aside by the Supreme Court.

The work stoppage and discharge of employees created a bad impression on the Burmese public. The Burmese newspapers accused the companies of deliberately stopping reconstruction work and diverting their resources to other areas. At the same time, the war claims against the government dragged on in the courts without much progress. During this period, relations between the companies and the Burmese government were strained and there was public resentment over the companies' decision not to continue the rehabilitation of the fields and refineries.

The companies dropped the plan for the reconstruction of Syriam's refineries, and proposed to limit themselves to a small scale production of just enough to supply the upper Burma market.

In 1950, the government of Burma again expressed the desire for a joint venture between the government and the oil companies, and the oil companies responded with a new proposal for a joint venture. They valued their properties and assets at £15 million, and the government accepted the companies' valuation after considering the reports of a commission appointed to study the proposal.

The British government then offered the government of Burma a loan of £2½ million to help finance its share in the proposed joint venture. The Burmese government needed only £2½ million more to finance the proposed share of one-third in the company. The oil companies in turn suggested a scheme by which the Burmese government could pay the remaining portion of the share over a number of years. The government under this scheme would pay the oil companies a sum in pounds sterling equivalent to two-thirds of the total taxation on profits paid by the company. The government accepted, and the only remaining question was whether this minority participation of the government (one-third of the shares) was contrary to the constitution of Burma, which requires that, in companies exploiting the natural resources of the country, the Burmese government or citizens hold sixty percent of the shares. To solve this problem, the Union Minerals Resources Enabling Act was passed in 1949, empowering the Union government to grant licenses to foreigners and companies and associations where more than forty percent of the capital is owned by foreigners. The Supreme Court of the Union of Burma has held that this act is valid and not in violation of the constitution.

AGREEMENT WITH FOREIGN PARTNERS

The immediate objective of the enterprise is to make Burma self-sufficient in petroleum and by-products. To achieve this objective, the joint venture company was to restore refining capacity of 4,500 barrels per day and make all other necessary arrangements. The long-term objective of the company is to produce and refine 10,000 barrels of petroleum per day, either through the rehabilitation of the Syriam refinery destroyed during the war, or through construction of new plants and other facilities, and to revive Burma's export trade in petroleum products. Since the oil reserves of Burma in known fields were estimated to be about 90 million barrels, which would be exhausted in 20 years at a production rate of 10,000 barrels per day, further exploration would be required to reach and maintain the proposed rate of production.

The joint venture between the government of Burma and the oil companies includes the Burmah Oil Company Limited, the Indo-Burma Petroleum Company Limited, the British Burmah Petroleum Company Limited, and their subsidiaries. A joint venture company was formed in January, 1954, with the name of the Burma Oil Co. (1954) Ltd.

All the fixed, tangible, and other assets in the Union of Burma of the Burmah Oil Co. (Burma Concessions) Ltd., the Burmah Oil Co. (Pipe Lines) Ltd., the Indo-Burma Petroleum Co. Ltd., the British Burmah Petroleum Co. Ltd., and the Pyinma Development Co. Ltd., which were to be transferred to the new company, were valued at £15 million, or the kyat equivalent of 200 million. In addition, the oil companies agreed to make a cash payment of k10 million to the new company. The oil companies entered into a sales agreement with the joint venture company by which all the assets of the oil companies were transferred to the joint venture company in return for 2 million fully-paid shares at the par value of k100 each.

The company has a nominal capital of k300 million (k4.76 = United States $1.00), and an issued capital of k200 million. From the 2 million issued shares (k100 each) held by the oil companies after the transfer of property, one-third—666,667 shares—were transferred to the government of the Union of Burma at a price of £5 million payable in sterling.

The government of Burma paid a sum in sterling of £2½ million and undertook to pay the balance, also amounting to £2½ million, by installments. The payment of the balance was to be made by yearly installments in pounds sterling equivalent to two-thirds of the total taxation on profits paid each year by the joint venture company. However, the government in any calendar year is not obliged to pay to the oil companies more than the sum of £200,000, and it has the option to pay in part or in full the amount outstanding of the balance.

At present, the respective share holdings of the company are approximately as follows:

The Burmah Oil Company Limited	55 percent
The Government of Burma	33
Indo-Burma Petroleum Company Ltd.	10
British Burmah Petroleum Company Ltd.	2

At any time after the shares already transferred to the government have been paid, the government can, upon giving one month's notice, acquire any number of additional shares in the joint venture company. To do this, the government shall pay the Burmah Oil Company acting for and on behalf of the oil companies, in sterling in London, a sum corresponding to a price of £750 sterling for every 100 shares.

Except for the obligation of the oil companies to complete arrangements for the full refining of 4,500 barrels of petroleum a day, neither the oil companies nor the government is under obligation to contribute further capital for the joint venture. However, the government and the oil companies will consider any proposal for further capital expenditure put forward by the board of directors or by either party. If both are willing to contribute, new shares will be issued to the extent of the additional capital required and be taken up and paid for by the oil companies and the government in a ratio corresponding to their existing holdings in the joint venture company.

On the other hand, if one party, either the government or the oil companies, decides not to participate, the other party may provide all additional capital required by taking up and paying for all of the new shares issued. In such a case, the party who is not willing to subscribe to new shares must cooperate in every way in achieving the objective for which the additional capital is raised.

The new shares shall rank *pari passu* with the original shares for all purposes.

The board of directors of the joint venture company consists of five directors, including the chairman. Until the government of Burma acquires 51 percent of the shares, B.O.C. acting for and on behalf of the oil companies has the right to appoint three directors, and the government is entitled to appoint two directors. When the government acquires 51 percent of the shares, it will have the right to appoint three directors, and the company two directors. The chairman will be nominated by the directors representing the government or the oil companies—whichever is the majority shareholder.

Directors are not subject to retirement by rotation, and no qualifications for the directors have been prescribed. The chairman has one vote as director, but not a casting vote. The parties concerned also are empowered to appoint alternate directors who are entitled to receive notices of all meetings of the directors, and to attend and vote as directors at any meetings at which the directors for whom they are alternates are not personally present.

The administration of the joint venture company was entrusted to a subsidiary company of B.O.C. Ltd., which would act as agent for the joint venture at a fee to be agreed upon between the parties. The contract with the agent will be terminated six months after the government's paid-up holdings in the company amount to 51 percent of the total shares. However, the joint venture may invite the agent to continue its administration of the company.

The parties agreed that the affairs of the joint venture company shall at all times be conducted in accordance with the recognized rules of sound commercial practice.

Under the terms of a formal agreement, the B.O.C. (Burma Trading) Ltd. was appointed agent of the joint venture company. In addition to being reimbursed for the cost of administering the affairs of the company, the agent receives a token fee of k100 per month.

Most cases involving technical and policy matters are referred for advice by the agent to its London office, whose recommendations are submitted to the board of directors for approval. The board usually approves the recommendations of the London office in view of its experience and technical ability.

The routine administration of the company is left entirely to the agent, subject to the control and direction of the board of directors.

At the present time, the chairman of the board is also the general manager of B.O.C. (Burma Trading) Ltd.

The agent's responsibility extends to the engagement and dismissal of all staff, but senior appointments and promotions must be approved by the board of directors.

The creation of the joint venture company has not changed the internal organization of the oil companies. The significant changes are in ownership and policy. The board of directors has taken the place of the London office, but its responsibility is reduced since most of the problems which fall within its jurisdiction (such as capital expenditure, investment policy, and Burmanization) must be referred to the government and the oil companies. Even in matters which are within the powers of the board of directors, the technical advice of the London office and the experience of the oil companies' representatives carry a geat deal of weight.

The frequent changes of Burmese directors affect the continuity of interest and experience of these directors. An alternate directorship could hardly remedy this condition since the directors in this sort of undertaking must themselves maintain a continuous interest.

B.O.C. (Burma Trading) Ltd. and the I.B.P.C. Ltd. were appointed exclusive marketing agents in the Union of Burma for the distribution and sale of the refined products of the company, on a commission basis of 2½ percent of gross proceeds. These agents account to the company for the proceeds of sales after deducting the costs of packaging, handling, storage, distribution, marketing, and a rental to be agreed upon by the parties for the use of all facilities (the plant for manufacturing and filling packages, etc.), in addition to the 2½ percent commission. The board of directors may review the arrangements, terms and other conditions for distribution and marketing, but cannot accept terms and conditions less favorable to the agent than those indicated.

The government of Burma also has the right to purchase an interest in the marketing installations and other facilities in the Union of Burma of the B.O.C. (Burma Trading) Ltd. and the I.B.P.C. up to the percentage of interest which the government currently possesses in the joint venture company. Such a purchase is possible only after Burma has become independent of imports of oil products, or after the government has acquired a majority share in the present joint venture company. Any joint enterprise resulting from such acquisition shall continue as agent for distribution and sales on terms no less favorable to the present joint venture company than before. The price for such purchase is to be set after negotiation and mutual agreement, or by an independent appraiser in case of failure to agree.

The joint venture company is a company limited by shares. As it is a private rather than a public company, the membership is limited to 50. The public cannot subscribe to shares or debentures, and the right of a member to transfer his shares is also restricted.

Since the joint venture company is incorporated under the Special Companies Act of 1950, its articles of association could and did exclude certain provisions which would have been required under the general Burma Companies Act. Moreover, under the Burma Companies Act, articles of association can be altered by a special resolution of the company, but the articles of the joint venture company cannot be altered merely in this way. The approval of the President of the Union is also required. On the other hand, the Burma Companies Act creates intricate and difficult procedures for altering the memorandum of association of a company; but the memorandum of association of the joint venture company can be altered by a special resolution with the approval of the President of the Union.

One of the striking features of the joint venture is the overwhelming advantage of one party over the others in the question of future ownership. The government has the right to buy out other shares in the venture at fixed rates at almost any time. This means that one party—the government—can buy out the whole company in case new oil reserves are found, while the risk of loss in unsuccessful explorations, or from ordinary operations, is shared by all parties.

This feature has also resulted in the absence of provisions for reinvestment of earnings. It is stipulated that, after deducting income tax, all profits shall be distributed to the shareholders. This is because the government can buy all shares at fixed rates. There is no incentive for the other parties to set aside any earnings as reserves when it is not possible for them to recover these reserves if the government purchases control of the company. This inability to create reserves can put a financial strain on the company in times of emergencies and unforeseen needs.

LABOR RELATIONS

Since the start of the joint venture, labor relations have been relatively harmonious. Fewer cases have been referred to the Industrial Court than in previous years: Only one case was referred to the Industrial Court in 1954; two cases were referred in 1955. The labor situation has not necessarily improved, since disputes and unrest are not always referred to the court. However, from interviews with labor leaders, personnel officers of the company, and labor officers of the government, it appears that there has been a change of attitude among the top leaders of the T.U.C.B. (Trade Union Congress of Burma) and a decrease of labor agitation in the oil fields since the joint venture was started.

The company's officials pointed out that the leaders of the T.U.C.B. now consider problems more from the point of view of national economic importance rather than from the point of view of immediate partisan benefits. They are said no longer to view the company interest as being different from the interest of the nation. They now emphasize the mutuality of interest rather than the conflict of interest. They are consequently more appreciative of the problems of the company. The company officials believe that this change in attitude of the leaders has affected the unions in their dealings with the company. The union and management are more inclined to settle their difficulties between themselves rather than to refer cases to the Industrial Court. At the same time, union officials recognize that they have a problem of education, and they still have difficulty making the workers realize their social responsibilities.

ROLE IN THE ECONOMY

The refinery at Chauk, which was under construction during the negotiations and was formally opened in January, 1954, has a minimum refining capacity of 3,000 barrels a day. In 1955 the reconstruction of the new refinery at Syriam with a minimum capacity of 3,500 barrels of crude oil a day was started. The refinery was completed in March, 1957 at a cost of k11.7 million (£900 thousand or $2,520 thousand).

Now that this refinery is in full operation, Burma is self-sufficient in gasoline, kerosene, and fuel oils, and there is spare refining capacity to take care of the expected annual increase in local consumption for the next few years.

Beginning in April, 1956, the company carried out a seismic survey of part of the Irrawaddy delta at a cost of k3 million. The company also made plans during 1956, subject to a grant of satisfactory concessionary rights by the government, to drill a test well at Ondwe in central Burma. Negotiations were successful and the company started drilling the test well at the end of 1957.

TAXATION

The company from the beginning of its plan to carry out exploration work asked the government to allow it to treat exploration expenditures as current expenditures. The government recently decided to allow exploration expenditures to be deducted from current income in calculating taxable income, thus giving tax deduction on mineral exploration expenditures to all mining companies.

In Burma, the tax rates on individual incomes are graduated, but for companies both income tax and super-tax are flat rates. The joint venture company, like any other company in Burma, pays 32 percent and 18 percent of income as income and super-tax respectively.

The company also pays the business profits tax. Prior to 1956, the rate was 16⅔ percent of income after allowing an abatement of 6 percent of the company's share capital plus reserves. This abatement came to about k12.4 million for the company, and the 16⅔ percent was levied on income from which an abatement of 12.4 million had already been deducted. However, in 1957, the government made an amendment in the business profits tax retroactive to 1955, by which the joint venture company was given only k300 thousand as abatement, and it had to pay for 1956 about k2 million more than would have been owed under the old system. The reason for this increased taxation is unknown, but it is thought that the government's financial stringency and the ability of the companies to pay prompted the increase. There were only three companies affected by this taxation—the Burma Oil Company (1954) Ltd., the Burmah Oil Company (Burma Trading) Ltd., and the Burma Corporation. The B.O.C. (1954) Ltd. pays k1 million, which is 70 percent of total tax receipts from this source.

FINANCIAL RESULTS

The company had a sales volume of 52.4, 62.4, and 66.9 million kyats in the years 1954, 1955, and 1956, respectively. The profits available for distribution were k5.9 million in 1954, k7.8 million in 1955, and k4.4 million in 1956. The reasons that the profit available for dividends in 1956 decreased from the previous years are the considerable rise in business profits tax as a consequence of the Burma Profit Tax Amendment Act 1957, and the inability in 1956 to charge the survey and exploration expenditures to the profit and loss account.

The dividends earned by the government and the oil companies and the return on their investment are as follows:

	1954	*1955*	*1956*	*1956*[a]
	(millions of kyats)			
Government's dividends	2.0	2.6	1.5	1.9
Oil companies' dividends	3.9	5.2	2.9	3.9
Average dividend rate on the total investment (200 millions)	2.9%	3.9%	2.2%	2.9%
Dividend rate on the government investment	5.9%	7.7%	4.0%	4.7%

[a] Dividends available after exploration expenditures have been taken as a deduction.

B.O.C. (Burma Trading) Ltd. and I.B.P.C. are responsible for the distribution and marketing of oil products, for which they receive profits in addition to the dividends from the joint venture company. The oil companies received k1.3 million in 1954, k1.5 million in 1955, and k1.6 million in 1956, as commissions, which were subject to Burma taxation at a rate in excess of 50 percent.

PERSONNEL

B.O.C. has had from the beginning a relatively progressive policy with respect to Burmanization, compared with other Western enterprises in the country. As early as 1926, the B.O.C. endowed an engineering college in the University of Rangoon. Starting from the year 1935, the company has employed men with local degrees and diplomas.

There are four different kinds of staff in the company: 1) executive, 2) local covenanted, 3) clerical, and 4) laborers and tradesmen. The executive staff includes the people at the top management level while the local covenanted staff refers to middle management.

While most of the staff in the local covenanted grades are Burmese citizens, the majority of the executives are still non-Burmese.

The joint venture company is to adopt a policy of Burmanization throughout all its branches, including its administrative and technical branches. The ultimate objective is to have the oil industry manned by citizens of the Union of Burma. It was agreed to evolve and implement a program for training Union citizens both at home and abroad. Such a training program is to be periodically reviewed by the government. Subject to such factors as availability of suitable candidates, the amount to be allocated by the joint venture company for training is to be no less than k400 thousand per annum, at least half of which is to be used for training abroad.

GOVERNMENT RELATIONS

There are two important problems which any foreign company in Burma must face—obtaining import licenses for equipment, stores, etc., and remitting profits. As to the import licenses, the company has enjoyed better treatment since the joint venture agreement. With the help of the Ministry of Mines, which is directly concerned with the company, it has been able to obtain liberal import licenses for bringing in stores, equipment etc.

As to remittance of profits, the joint venture agreement states that "the President agrees to provide the oil companies with facilities to remit to the United Kingdom and to India and Pakistan any dividends received by them from the Joint Venture Company." The oil companies had some problems at the beginning, but now the situation has much improved. Compared with other companies, the joint venture company enjoys better treatment in this as well as other respects.

EVALUATION

This analysis has been concerned with the many technical aspects and problems of a joint enterprise between the government of a country which gained political independence only just over a decade ago, and old established British companies, which not only had to decide whether to rebuild their destroyed plants but also had to adapt themselves to greatly changed and fluctuating conditions. That the joint venture has overcome most of its major problems, and that it is today progressing to the satisfaction of both the national interests of Burma and the interests of the British companies, cannot be fully explained by any of the technical arrangements which have been described in this study. The success of the enterprise has been made possible only by an atmosphere of harmony and understanding between the Burmese government and its British associates, which has gradually displaced the conflicts and suspicions of the past.

General Milk Company (Philippines)

ORIGIN OF THE ENTERPRISE

The General Milk Company (Philippines) was established by an American milk producer as a step designed to maintain a favored competitive position in the Philippine market. Before the Second World War, the Carnation Milk Company of the United States enjoyed the major share of the Philippine market for imported canned milk through the distribution of its own brand. After the imposition of controls in 1949, however, the future of imported canned milk in the Philippines became more uncertain.

The Carnation Milk Company is the majority shareholder (65 percent), along with the Pet Milk Company (35 percent), in the General Milk Corporation (USA), an American firm which owns and operates several milk factories located in South America and Europe. On October 31, 1956, the General Milk Corporation (USA) was granted a license to do business in the Philippines by the Securities and Exchange Commission, after which the Philippine branch of the company commenced construction of a factory as well as the installation of the necessary machinery and equipment for milk-processing and can-making operations. These units were completed in August, 1957, and by the succeeding month the Philippine branch had begun manufacturing operations. The four-million-peso plant was located at Mandaluyong, Rizal, a suburb of Manila, and featured a modern milk-processing plant with an output of 2,400 cases of milk for each 8-hour shift, and a high speed can factory with an output rate of 22,000 cans per hour. The plant also featured the only milk evaporator in the country.

In accordance with the terms under which the General Milk Corporation (USA) had been permitted by the Central Bank of the Philippines to establish the plant, the General Milk Company (Philippines) was organized and incorporated on November 22, 1957 for the express purpose of taking over the Philippine operations of the General Milk Corporation (USA). At the time of its incorporation, the new company had an authorized capital stock of only 20,000 pesos, divided into 200 shares of 100 pesos par value, with a subscribed capital of 4,000 pesos, and a paid-up capital of 1,000 pesos. All incorporators were American; the seven directors were also American citizens. Thus, the General Milk Company (Philippines) began as a wholly owned subsidiary of a parent American corporation.

ROLE IN THE ECONOMY

Like most other recently established manufacturing enterprises, the company was granted tax exemption privileges as a new and necessary industry with respect to its manufacturing operations, the exemption extending until December 31, 1958. Taxes would be gradually increased after that date until exemption privileges would disappear completely by December 31, 1962, except for the income tax which would be applicable in full by September 17, 1961.

On December 9, 1957, the articles of incorporation were amended to include a stipulation that no stockholder could dispose of his share without first offering the stock in writing to the other stockholders at book value; at the same time, transfers to affiliated or subsidiary corporations were excepted from this ruling. The effect of the amendment was to increase the "closeness" of the corporation.

An interesting aspect arose with the decision by the company to market its processed milk under a new trade name, "Liberty Milk," in spite of the fact that the product of the majority shareholder of the company, Carnation Milk, already enjoyed wide favor in the Philippine market, especially as an infant food. One reason which was advanced is the use of coconut oil for the fat content of Liberty Milk, which could result in less uniformity of quality than would have been possible with the Carnation Milk formula. Another factor was the joint aspect of the parent General Milk Corporation (USA), which included equity owned by another milk company, the Pet Milk Company; Carnation Milk Company may have been understandably loath to share the proceeds from the use of its valuable trade name with the Pet Milk Company. A third reason could be advanced in terms of future possible eventualities. At present, Carnation Milk enjoys the privilege of unlimited importation into the Philippines, and Liberty Milk could well represent a supplementary product (in terms of product and price differentiation) which would augment total income rather than replace part of it. Should imported Carnation Milk be banned in the future, there is little to prevent either partial or complete diversion of the facilities of the General Milk Company (Philippines) to the processing of Carnation Milk locally. In any case the General Milk Company (Philippines) faces the unique situation of actually competing against a product of its major stockholder; however, some differentiation does exist since Carnation Milk is still being marketed in the Philippines at a premium over Liberty Milk. The price of Liberty Milk has been influenced downwards by the competition of other locally processed brands.

Both imported Carnation Milk and Liberty Milk are distributed by Connell Brothers, the same firm which held the prewar distributorship of Carnation Milk. So far, no restrictions have been imposed on the importation of canned milk, the item still being in the "decontrolled" category of the Central Bank classification system. Although the present policy of the Central Bank is to utilize price competition as a means of displacing imported canned milk with locally processed canned milk, certain local milk canners have approached the Central Bank on the possibility of additional restrictions on canned milk imports, to improve further their competitive position.

CAPITAL STRUCTURE

On June 5, 1958, the authorized capital stock was increased to 4 million pesos divided into 40,000 shares with a par value of 100 pesos per share. At the same time, the paid-up capital stock was increased to slightly less than 2 million pesos. A domestic insurance group composed of the Insular Life, Filipinas, Guaranty, and Universal insurance companies acquired 4,594 shares of stock for 544,400 pesos, thus purchasing the stock at a premium. With this equity acquisition by a domestic group, the General Milk Company (Philippines) was transformed into a joint venture.

EVALUATION

The significance of this transaction lies in the fact that the participation of local capital in the venture was one of the conditions laid down by the Central Bank of the Philippines in approving the project in the first place. The joint venture form of organization did not seem to have occurred to the original planners of the project; the distributing firm, Connell Brothers, a most logical choice for participation, was not even approached on the possibility. For its part, the insurance group seems to be content with its investment in the form of equity participation without the intention of indulging in or influencing managerial operations.

The future for domestic canned milk in the Philippines is relatively bright. With a number of competitors producing domestic canned milk already in the market, further restriction or the outright banning of canned milk imports does not seem too far off. Bottled fresh milk plays an insignificant role in the Philippine market, and early acceptance of a brand name will prove to be a great advantage. On the basis of these conditions, the General Milk Company (Philippines) has favorable prospects for the future.

Goodrich International Rubber Company (Philippines)

The Goodrich International Rubber Company (GIRC) represents one of the first cases in the Philippines in which a wholly-owned subsidiary of an American company has been converted into a joint venture with a local majority participation to engage in the local manufacture of formerly imported products.

ORIGIN OF THE ENTERPRISE

The B. F. Goodrich Company of Akron, Ohio established in 1927 a wholly-owned branch in the Philippines in order to expand the distribution of B. F. Goodrich products. This branch was changed to a Philippine corporation in 1935, which then became known as the Goodrich International Rubber Company. This company, with a capital of 500,000 pesos, was wholly-owned by B. F. Goodrich.

After the imposition of exchange controls and import restrictions in December, 1949, the head of J. M. Tuason and Company, a Philippine corporation, became interested in the local manufacture of tires and related products. Mr. Tuason approached several United States firms in the industry and eventually came to an agreement with B. F. Goodrich for the establishment of a joint enterprise in the Philippines. The willingness of B. F. Goodrich to undertake such a venture was partly motivated by its interest in using undistributed profits which could not be remitted on account of exchange controls. The formalization of the agreement was delayed until mid-1955, first, due to the unsettling effects of the Korean War, later, because of prolonged negotiations with the Central Bank and the National Economic Council. The final approval of the Central Bank was eventually obtained in April, 1955. It was made subject to the condition that the company is to use, after a reasonable period (about seven years), only locally produced raw rubber. The maximum annual foreign exchange allocation allowed for by the Central Bank showed the following distribution:

Raw materials	82.9 percent	Royalty fee	7.4 percent
Technicians' salaries	0.8	Interest on loans	3.2
Management fee	5.7		

In May, 1955, B. F. Goodrich, GIRC, and J. M. Tuason and Company, together with certain local associates, concluded an investment agreement and a technical assistance and management agreement.

CAPITAL STRUCTURE

Under the investment agreement, the authorized capital stock of GIRC was increased from 500,000 pesos to 12 million pesos, represented by 1,200,000 common shares with a par value of 10 pesos. All shares were to represent an equal interest in GIRC and were to have equal voting rights.

The Filipino party, J. M. Tuason and Company, was to subscribe to 6 million pesos in not more than four installments prior to the commencement of manufacturing operations.

In lieu of the 500,000 pesos original capital of GIRC owned by B. F. Goodrich, the latter was to be given 3½ million pesos in stock, which represented the net worth of the company.

Subject to the subscription of the Philippine party and the payment of at least 25 percent thereof, B. F. Goodrich committed itself to subscribe and pay in cash (United States currency) 1,200,000 pesos additional shares of the capital stock of GIRC. Consequently, the Philippine party acquired a majority of 56 percent and B. F. Goodrich a minority of 44 percent.

The board of seven directors was to be composed of five Filipinos and two Americans.

The principal problem encountered in the reorganization was not the finding of local investors but rather one of limiting to a minority interest the participation of B. F. Goodrich. The establishment of manufacturing facilities required substantial dollar resources which, if invested by B. F. Goodrich, would have given it a large majority, which would have been contrary to its intentions and established policy in regard to foreign ventures. On the other hand, the Central Bank was not willing to make available foreign exchange for the import of equipment.

The problem was solved by B. F. Goodrich's committing itself, subject to subscription by the Philippine party, to grant a loan of $600,000 at four percent to GIRC, repayable in five installments after six to ten years. Also, B. F. Goodrich agreed to use its best efforts to assist GIRC in obtaining a loan of $1,800,000 from the United States Export-Import Bank. B. F. Goodrich's participation in the venture was made conditional upon the obtaining of the loan, which was granted in November, 1955, at 5½ percent interest, repayable in 16 quarterly installments beginning November 15, 1957. Both loans provided sufficient dollar resources to enable the company to import equipment into the Philippines on a no-dollar basis. B. F. Goodrich's participation was also made subject to the granting of appropriate approvals of the Philippine government with respect to the venture.

MANAGEMENT

GIRC also entered into a technical contract with B. F. Goodrich, which was patterned after various contracts which the latter has with foreign associates in other countries. The contract covers a period of 15 years, and is renewable for successive periods of 5 years thereafter. In the case of the Philippine company, the arrangement also included a management contract since the local shareholders were not interested in running a tire factory and administering and selling the product. Accordingly, a fee of three percent of net sales of all manufactured products was charged for furnishing technical assistance, and a two percent fee of all net sales, including imported products, for managing, administering, and furnishing personnel. The contract included the furnishing of all designs, drawings, and specifications for the new factory, as well as engineering layout of the plant, and technical information pertaining to the manufacture of rubber products, administration and sales procedures, sources of supply of materials and equipment, excluding, however, information with respect to the manufacture of raw materials, ingredients, or intermediaries. In addition, the contract provided for the selection, inspection, and purchase of machinery, equipment, and supplies for the account of GIRC, and the testing and analyzing of rubber products and materials, on the basis of cost-plus-expenses reimbursement.

B. F. Goodrich agreed to furnish any technical personnel needed to put the plant in running condition and to operate it afterwards. Under the contract, one engineer and one accountant-paymaster were sent from Akron in order to complete the project. They stayed until the plant was operating completely, at which time the engineering was turned over to a Filipino plant engineer. The plant is now operated with four American technicians, and the company is administered with six American personnel. B. F. Goodrich also agreed to furnish GIRC with non-exclusive, non-assignable, unrestricted licenses for all patents of B. F. Goodrich filed in the Philippines for payment of mutually acceptable royalties. In addition to all fees due B. F. Goodrich, GIRC is required to pay a sum equal to any amount by which any Philippine tax exceeds the tax credit which B. F. Goodrich obtains from the United States government with respect to those fees. GIRC is to make all payments, including compensation of persons furnished by B. F. Goodrich, in United States dollars, except whatever portion of their compensation they may wish to take in pesos. The agreement also provides that the articles of incorporation are not to be changed nor the company dissolved without a two-thirds majority vote.

ROLE IN THE ECONOMY

Present production at capacity is about 550 tires daily or 150,000 annually. This output is estimated to supply about 50 percent of local requirements. (Goodyear Philippines, which commenced operations at about the same time, in the fall of 1956, has an equal capacity.) In addition to tires, GIRC produces an equal quantity of inner tubes and 650,000 pounds of camelback.

The company has somewhat more than 500 employees in all capacities. This includes not only the factory but also tire recapping and repair facilities in Manila and Iriga, Camarines Sur, branch sales offices, and warehouse workers in the Port Area, Manila. These employees are all Philippine citizens, except for the ten Americans previiously mentioned. The cooperation between Filipinos and Americans appears to have been smooth on all levels of the corporation.

The company anticipates no capital structure changes, but will be expanding shortly into the manufacturing of other products. This is being brought about principally by the entry of one other manufacturer (Firestone) with a capacity of about 120,000 tires into the Philippine market, which will prevent GIRC from operating at full capacity. The possibilities of other products are now being studied.

The company agreed, in obtaining the initial approval of the Philippine Central Bank, to engage in the establishment of a rubber plantation. It is now developing one on Basilan Island which, eventually, will constitute 1,024 hectares or approximately 2,500 acres. A nursery of approximately 100 acres is presently being established, which will take care of planting requirements for the plantation. In this nursery, high-yielding varieties which have been found to prosper in the Philippine climate are being developed. Other varieties were obtained from Coco Grove, Florida through the United States Department of Agriculture.

Eventually, the company plans to sell seedlings to local farmers in the plantation area in order to encourage greater local production of raw rubber. It is estimated that this plantation will provide about one-half of the requirements of the company. The other half is scheduled to be supplied by the local American Rubber Company.

EVALUATION

The company started operations in the second half of 1956. During the period 1952–55, the Philippines imported annually, on the average, 31 million pesos worth of rubber manufactures, and about 112,000 pesos of crude and synthetic rubber. In 1956 and the first half of 1957, imports of rubber manufactures dropped somewhat while imports of crude and synthetic rubber increased sharply; in 1956 they amounted to 2,100,000 pesos or almost 20 times the average during the immediately preceding years. It may be expected that this trend will continue until the local output of raw rubber has been sufficiently expanded. Total annual requirements are presently estimated at 21 million pounds, of which tire manufacture consumes about 16,800,000 (Goodrich and Goodyear, 6,000,000 each; Firestone, 4,800,000) pounds.

Annual local output of crude rubber is estimated at about 4 million pounds. Thus, there remains a deficiency of 17 million pounds. Once domestic production of raw rubber has been increased, the resulting dollar savings, which for GIRC is presently estimated at 50 percent of the cost of alternative tire imports, is likely to become substantially greater.

The greatest significance of GIRC, however, may be that it is one of the first cases in this country where a foreign minority has successfully established and is operating a manufacturing enterprise under the trademark of a well-known foreign company.

H. G. Henares and Sons

ORIGIN OF THE JOINT VENTURES

H. G. Henares and Sons is a sole proprietorship which has entered into joint ventures through royalty arrangements with American firms. It was organized in 1947 to manufacture an asbestos paint which had been invented by the wife of the owner in 1939. The company itself is family-oriented: The founder is the president, one son is the vice-president, the other the general manager.

Under the brand name "MC Asbestos Paints," the product was sold to the public through various distributors, but the primary purchaser was the government. Initial operations were not very successful, and to improve its position the company decided to negotiate for the manufacturing rights to well-known American brands. The motivation behind this decision was twofold. First, the company wanted to acquire technical know-how, and it felt that with the assistance of well-established companies it would be able to do so. Secondly, the manufacture of brand name products would alleviate the selling problems of the company.

In negotiating for royalty agreements, the company did not limit itself to paints but branched out into school supplies and office supplies. Throughout the period from 1953 to 1956, the company negotiated and was able to secure the following franchises for manufacturing rights, under which it paid royalties:

February, 1953	Crayola crayons from Binney and Smith, Incorporated
February, 1954	Wessco paints from the National Gypsum Company
March, 1955	Mongol lead pencils from the Eberhard Faber Pencil Company
June, 1955	Old Town carbon paper and typewriter ribbons from the Old Town Corporation
November, 1955	Universal paints from the Universal Paint and Varnish Corporation
August, 1956	Parker Quink ink from the Parker Pen Company

There were primarily two reasons that the American companies granted franchises to H. G. Henares and Sons to manufacture these products. First, in view of import restrictions which favored local manufacturers and limited imports of finished products, the American companies were anxious to maintain their share of the Philippine market. Second, in view of various nationalization measures, a Filipino manufacturer was in a better position to secure the necessary foreign exchange to import the raw materials needed for the manufacture of the products concerned.

PROBLEMS

The manufacturing agreements were initially beset with problems. Since Henares was limited to manufacturing rights and most of the products they were manufacturing had exclusive distributors that were dealing directly with the United States companies, conflicts arose in pricing. Likewise, audit privileges given to the exclusive distributors caused friction between H. G. Henares and Sons and the distributors. Furthermore, since most of the United States companies insisted on supplying Henares with the raw materials (perhaps for the purpose of maintaining quality control), Henares did not have the flexibility it needed to canvass the market and secure the lowest prices for comparable qualities of raw materials.

As experience was gained under the various franchise agreements, each of these problems was eventually solved to the satisfaction of the United States companies and H. G. Henares. Pricing to the distributor by Henares is now on a fixed-price basis, subject to revision every six months. Audit privileges of the distributors have been dispensed with. Henares has also been given the flexibility it needed in purchasing raw materials from any source.

One problem that has remained and will probably remain for some time is the utilization of local raw materials. Henares, in justifying its applications for foreign exchange to import the raw materials, has committed itself to the Central Bank to secure the assistance of the United States companies in conducting research on the possible replacement of imported raw materials by local raw materials. This it has been able to accomplish in some of the paints it manufactures, and also in the cheap grade of pencils that it manufactures for the Eberhard Faber Pencil Company. Some of the American companies, however, have been slow, if not actually reluctant, to provide the facilities for conducting research on the substitution of local for imported raw materials.

EVALUATION

Overall, it would seem that the expectations of both parties at the time the franchise agreements were entered into have been substantially borne out, and the agreements have worked to their mutual advantage. Henares has been able to secure the technical know-how, and has been able to sell the brand name products it manufactures with relative ease; sales rose from 40,000 pesos in 1947 to about 4 million pesos in 1957 at the same time that the labor force increased to over 600 employees. The American companies, at the same time, have been able to maintain their markets in the Philippines and their products have not been affected by the various nationalization measures that have been and will probably continue to be imposed on the economy.

Indo-Foreign Steel Ventures

Nothing symbolizes industrial power and prestige to Indians more than the production of steel. Steel production in India has an almost mystical quality, although in recent years it has been rapidly assuming a very tangible quality. Three new steel mills have been under construction for the government of India. The Russians have been building one at Bhilai. A German combine (Krupp-Demag) has been constructing a steel complex at Rourkela. And, at Durgapur, a British group has been putting up a third steel plant. All three of these projects are being managed by a government-owned statutory corporation, Hindustan Steel Ltd.

There were already in existence in India two steel plants in the private sector. The Tatas have been making steel for over fifty years. The Indian Iron and Steel Corporation is a more recent addition to the field. Both of these enterprises are currently engaged in substantial expansion programs. Both are receiving financial assistance from the International Bank for Reconstruction and Development. Tata has had the collaboration of the Kaiser Engineering Corporation of the United States. It is expected that, with the expansion programs undertaken by these two concerns and the addition of three steel plants in the public sector, Indian steel production will reach 6 million tons of ingot steel by the end of the second plan period—in March, 1961—resulting in a saving of about $315 million in foreign exchange annually thereafter.

The administrative problems involved in setting up the three government-owned steel plants, all at about the same time, severely tested the ability and experience of the Indians. Detailed planning and protracted negotiations were undertaken with foreign governments, plant suppliers, and contractors, to secure the best deals. Solutions had to be found to the problems of securing large numbers of contractors, engineers, workers, and technicians for engineering works unfamiliar in type and magnitude. Imports arriving at port, railway transport operations at ore mines, arranging for coal and other essential materials to arrive at the proper places on time, taxed the ingenuity of the government people. Although mistakes were made, the projects have gone ahead and have taken concrete shape.

Apart from completing the projects, the government was faced with the task of finding the people to run the plants once they were completed and the foreign collaborators had finished their job. India needed approximately 700 engineer officers for each plant, that is, a total of about 2,100 engineers—metallurgical, mechanical, chemical, and electrical. Some, at least, of this number had to have extensive steel works experience. At a lower echelon, it was necessary to have 6,300 skilled workers per plant, that is, about 19,000 in all, of whom about 3,000 had to be operatives with previous steel experience. In order to train these people, the government set up training establishments in Jamshedpur (where the Tata steel works are located), Burnput, and Bhadravati. These three plants have been training approximately 1,000 operatives a year for the government. Further, the railway workshops, 78 engineering works around Calcutta and Bombay, and other industrial centers in the country have been giving practical training to the skilled workers expected to be employed in the three steel plants. The engineering works are all members of the Indian Engineering Association and the Engineering Association of India and, hence, are the most qualified such operations in India. The trainees are mostly young men who have done 18 months basic training in the Labor Ministry's training centers. It was expected under this intensive program to turn out per year 4,000 reasonably well qualified workers for the steel plants.

At a more advanced level, with the assistance of the Ford Foundation, 900 Indian engineers have been trained in the United States. The Soviet Union has been training nearly 700 men for Bhilai; under the Colombo Plan, the United Kingdom has been training 350 engineers for Durgapur. West Germany has taken about 150 men for Rourkela and a further few have gone to Canada. More than 1,200 men have already gone abroad, of whom more than 600 have returned to the project sites. Much of the cost of training these Indian engineers has been borne by the host countries themselves. The Ford Foundation and the United Nations Technical Assistance Board have also contributed. The cost of training has, therefore, absorbed barely one percent of the total investment.

Within India, the government has drawn upon the Tata works for about 100 experienced steel men, many of whom have been assigned to posts as departmental heads.

In addition to the steel plants proper, the government has been building three steel towns for a community of 100,000 people each. Town planners have been employed. In the initial stage, 7,500 homes were designed in several blocs, each of which is a self-contained neighborhood unit, with its own health centers, schools, shopping centers, and other services.

The three projects are in varying stages of completion. At Rourkela, certain important installations were inaugurated in January, 1960, and the plant was to be completed by the end of 1961. At Bhilai, 60 percent of the total plant construction was completed by the end of 1959, and the balance was to be completed in 1960. At Durgapur, the first stage of the construction schedule was completed at the end of 1959, with other installations to be completed in 1960, and the entire plant by mid-1961. There has been keen competition, especially between the Germans and Russians, at Rourkela and Bhilai respectively, as to whose installations would be completed earlier.

A technical committee has recently been set up by the government of India to coordinate the further expansion of the three plants under the third Five-Year Plan to get underway in mid-1961.

ROURKELA (WEST GERMAN COOPERATION)

The Rourkela steel project was the first of the three projects to be negotiated. It is the result of an agreement between the government of India and the West German combine of Krupp and Demag. At one point, in the early stages of negotiation, there was the possibility that the IBRD would participate in the financing of the project. The IBRD, however, has adopted a policy of refraining from lending to entirely public-owned industrial enterprises in India. As a result, the bank took the position that if Krupp would raise one-third of the capital requirements, and the government of India one-third, the IBRD would make a loan for the remaining one-third. It was the bank's expectation that eventually the loan would be converted into stock and sold on the Indian market to private investors when the steel mill became a proven enterprise. At the same time, Krupp would have a sufficiently large stockholding in the enterprise to permit it to be in control of the technical and managerial aspects.

The government of India, however, would not accept virtual IBRD-Krupp control of a steel mill in India. Krupp, in turn, was willing to reduce its equity to ten percent of the paid-up capital. This, however, was unacceptable to the IBRD as it was contrary to its policy of not financing government-controlled industrial enterprises.

A government company, Hindustan Steel Ltd. was formed in December, 1953 for this project, with an authorized capital of rs1 billion and an issued paid-up capital of rs500 thousand, the government contributing rs400 thousand and the German participants rs100 thousand. But it was later decided to make the plant a wholly government-owned one. The agreement with Krupp-Demag was accordingly revised and their shares purchased. The management of the other two projects, Bhilai and Durgapur, previously managed departmentally, was transferred to Hindustan Steel in March, 1957, and the capital of the company raised to rs3 billion.

The German combine has been acting as technical consultant for the designing and erection of the integrated steel works at Rourkela. It is also in general charge of the construction.

As the first experiment, Rourkela produced a number of problems. Initially, the Krupp-Demag combine did not have final technical responsibility for the plant. The Indian manager of construction was taken from the Indian state railways. He had had no experience in steel mills. There was also a lack of responsibility in decision making; there was no one central supervisor who had the final power of decision. Compounding the problem was the fact that the Indians wanted Rourkela built with extreme haste. Krupp-Demag therefore engaged a great many more subcontractors than they otherwise would have. There were, thus, fifteen German firms supplying equipment and machinery. Each one of these subcontractors was on the site supervising his own particular segment of the project and hiring his own Indian civil contractor. Until very recently, the lack of coordination and central direction created a situation of relative inefficiency.

Part of the problem has been related to factors having nothing to do with management on the spot. Bottlenecks in the Indian harbors, where turn-around time varies from 10 to 30 days, posed a major problem. The congestion on Indian railways was an added obstacle. The second Five-Year Plan has emphasized the necessity of developing secondary ports to relieve the pressure on Bombay and Calcutta; the World Bank has sanctioned loans for this purpose. It has also approved loans for projects aimed at improving the situation with respect to the railways. These loans will, however, not bear fruit until well after Rourkela is completed.

The plant is to have a capacity of one million tons (against ½ million tons originally planned), and the consultants will receive a fixed fee of rs28 million (24.11 million deutsche mark), plus reimbursement for the actual expenses of their Indian office, subject to a ceiling of rs7 million.

The revised final project report for the one million ton plant, which recommended the adoption of a new process of steelmaking, called the "L.D. Process," to the extent of 75 percent of the plant's capacity, was accepted by the government with some modifications. This process is stated to have the advantage of lower capital and operating costs, a higher rate of production, and savings in space and equipment. While 750,000 tons of ingots will be produced by the new process, 250,000 tons will be produced by the conventional "open hearth" process. These will be rolled into plates of 3/16 inch and above (200,000 tons), sheets and strips, hot rolled (300,000 tons), sheets and strips, cold rolled (170,000 tons), and tinplate (50,000 tons). The plant will be capable of expansion to 1,250,000 tons, and layout is such that ultimately the capacity could be raised to 2,500,000 tons of ingot steel.

To utilize the surplus gases available under the "L.D. Process," it is proposed to set up a factory which will produce 600,000 tons of various fertilizers. To use the waste gases and to meet the demands of the fertilizer and steel plants, 75,000 kw. of power will be generated at a thermal station within the perimeter of the steel works. In addition, about 50,000 kw. will be obtained from the Hirakud electric project.

The first blast furnace started producing iron in February, 1959. In January, 1960 the "L.D." steelmaking plant and a blooming mill were inaugurated. The plant will be completed in all other respects by the end of 1961.

The estimated cost of the project has increased from an initial $256 million to close to $400 million. West German banks have granted medium-term credits in the amount of some $160 million at an interest rate of 6.5 percent per annum. The Krupp interests have indicated that further credits on a liberal basis will be offered to the government of India for expansion of the Rourkela plant.

BHILAI (RUSSIAN COOPERATION)

The integrated iron and steel plant at Bhilai (Madhya Pradesh) is being set up with Russian assistance. An agreement was signed by the governments of India and the Soviet Union in February, 1955. The $262 million plant (originally estimated at $226 million) will have an initial capacity of one million tons of ingots, to be rolled into some 750,000 tons of rolled products, with provision for expansion to a capacity of one million tons of rolled products.

The plant and equipment costing $104 million and structural steel work for $16 million are being supplied from Russia, and the value of these is to be paid back in 12 annual installments, with 2½ percent interest for the amount outstanding each year.

The Indo-Russian agreement provides for association of Indian experience and talent in all stages of planning, designing, and execution of the project. A team of Indian experts visited the Soviet Union to examine plants of similar nature in operation there. A sufficient number of Indian technicians are being trained in India and the Soviet Union, so that the Indian personnel can operate the plant to the maximum extent possible.

The Soviet organization is receiving $4 million for its technical services, including the project report, apart from the salaries and the allowances for the Soviet technical staff that is in India for the project.

The project report that was received in December, 1956 was accepted with some modifications. Provision is being made in the layout for the ultimate expansion of the capacity to 2,500,000 tons. In the first phase, the plant will produce rails (standard gauge 100,-000 tons, narrow gauge 10,000 tons); railway sleeper bars (90,000 tons); standard and broad-flanged beams, channels, angles and other light and heavy structural section-beams with section height up to 24 inches (284,000 tons); rounds of 7/8 inch to 3 inches and squares with sides from 7/8 inch to 3 inches (121,000 tons); flats from 2 inches to 5 inches wide (15,000 tons); billets for re-rolling at outside rolling mills from 2″ x 2″ to 3″ cross section (150,000 tons); and pig iron (300,000 tons).

By the end of 1959, the units of the plant completed included two blast furnaces, two coke oven batteries, two open hearth furnaces, a blooming and billet mill, two chemical plants for manufacturing sulphuric acid and ammonium sulphate fertilizers, and a foundry. During 1960, a blast furnace, a coke oven battery, and four open hearth furnaces were scheduled to be opened.

The Madhya Pradesh Electricity Board has been putting up a 90,000 kw. capacity thermal station in Korba mainly to supply power for this plant. A stand-by power plant of 24,000 kw. is also being located within the perimeter of the steel works. During construction, a diesel station put up in Bhilai is supplying the power.

The Russians, at Bhilai, have operated on a much different basis from the Germans at Rourkela. The Russian plant is a much simpler steel mill than the German, and is a duplication of what might be called the standard Soviet mill. Hence, every item in the mill is a duplication of an existing plant. The Soviets have thus been able to supply practically every bolt and nut with appropriate insert number. They have also had unquestioned supervision over the entire job even though they have associated Indians with them at the various levels. In contrast to Rourkela, the number of Indian subcontractors for civil construction has been 3 (Rourkela has had 15). Great care has also been taken to brief Soviet technicians in working with Indians.

The governments of India and the Soviet Union have already agreed in principle to raise the capacity of the Bhilai steel works to 2,500,000 tons per annum, to be financed partly by Soviet credits.

DURGAPUR (BRITISH COOPERATION)

The integrated steel plant at Durgapur (West Bengal) is being set up with British assistance. Following the recommendations of a technical team from Britain under the Colombo Plan, it was decided to locate the one-million ton plant at Durgapur. The plant is so designed that its capacity can be raised to 1,300,000 tons of ingots. There is also room in the layout for an ultimate expansion to 2,500,000 tons of ingots.

To insure speedy execution of the project, it was thought advisable to arrange with a single agency for the supply of plant and equipment. A contract for the setting up of the plant was entered into with a consortium of British firms, the Indian Steel Works Construction Company, in October, 1956. This firm is responsible for the entire erection of the plant, while the government is responsible for the works outside the perimeter of the plant.

The foreign exchange component of the rs1,330 million ($280 million) project comes to around rs850 million. Besides a loan of rs200 million (£15 million) offered by the British government for the project, a syndicate of British banks has extended a loan of rs153.3 million (£11.5 million).

Production in the first phase will consist of heavy forging blooms (10,000 tons), merchant sections (240,000 tons), forging billets (60,000 tons), light sections (200,000 tons), forging blooms (30,000 tons), wheels and tires (28,000 tons), axles (12,000 tons), billets for sale (150,000 tons), and pig iron (350,000 tons).

The Damodar Valley Corporation is putting up a thermal station of 150,000 kw. in Durgapur to supply power for the project. This station will use the surplus gases and middling of coal arising from the steel works. The DVC is also arranging a common system of water supply from the Damodar River.

A battery of coke ovens was inaugurated in August, 1959, and a blast furnace in December, 1959, to complete the first stage of the construction schedule for the plant. The remaining facilities are to be completed in three stages by mid-1961, including two coke oven batteries, two blast furnaces, seven open hearth furnaces, various rolling mills, a special casting shop, and a wheel and axle plant.

The Durgapur steel works is also expected to undergo expansion during the third Five-Year Plan period, and it is understood that the British are prepared to cooperate in connection with this expansion as well.

Lever Brothers (Pakistan) Ltd.

ORIGIN OF THE ENTERPRISE

Prior to August, 1947, when British India was partitioned into two independent countries, Pakistan and Bharat or India, Unilever of England was manufacturing and distributing vegetable oils and soaps through two subsidiaries, namely the Hindustan Vanaspati Manufacturing Company, Ltd., for vanaspati and vegetable oil, and Lever Brothers (India) Ltd. for soaps. The products of these two companies had captured a substantial part of the Indian market because of their superior quality and highly competitive price.

Some of the areas which came to form West Pakistan after partition were rather distantly situated from the HVM and Lever Brothers plants, and hence their products could not effectively compete with those of their rivals. The installation by Unilever of a new plant in the region, therefore, appeared to be a profitable proposition.

Before 1947, the princely states were encouraging the setting up of industry within their territories on concessionary terms in order to come into line with the rest of the country with respect to general economic development and employment opportunities for their subjects. Thus, there were numerous instances of a variety of industries, particularly the cigarette, cotton textiles, and sugar industries, finding their way into princely states scattered throughout the country. Bahawalpur, situated in the region where Unilever was interested in extending its manufacturing operations, had obtained permission from the government of India for the installation of a vegetable oil plant in its territory.

At the time of partition, Bahawalpur State acceded to Pakistan, and its government, which now owed allegiance to the government of Pakistan instead of to the British Crown, wanted to go ahead with the setting up of a vegetable oil plant. It approached Unilever for collaboration in the project. Two private families, namely those of Syed Amjad Ali and Sir William Roberts, both inhabitants of West Pakistan, offered to join the government of Bahawalpur and Unilever. They entered into a legal agreement on February 10, 1948, as a result of which Sadiq Vegetable Oils and Allied Industries Ltd. was registered in Bahawalpur under the Companies Act of 1913. At the initiative of Unilever, the parties also agreed to create the Sadiq Soap Company Ltd. Both were public limited companies, and their registered offices were located at Rahim Yar Khan, a small rural town in Bahawalpur State.

The government of Bahawalpur was clearly motivated in its negotiations with Unilever for the creation of a vegetable oil plant by the prospects of utilizing the extensive experience of Unilever in the matter of technical know-how, management and sales, and was impressed by Unilever's general reputation as a business partner and by the goodwill its products generally commanded; Unilever was interested in getting into the market of West Pakistan areas and in making the venture more economic and profitable by the addition of a soap company.

CAPITAL STRUCTURE AND TECHNICAL ARRANGEMENTS

According to the 1948 agreement Sadiq Vegetable Oils and Allied Industries Ltd. was to be purely a manufacturing concern. The distribution of its products was to be handled by a separately created private limited company, the HVM Company Ltd., registered in Pakistan. Similarly, the marketing of soap in Pakistan was given to Lever Brothers Ltd. (Pakistan). These two private limited concerns were financed exclusively by Unilever of England. The government of Bahawalpur State was to provide Sadiq Vegetable Oils and Allied Industries Ltd. with the following:

1. Assistance in obtaining licenses, import permits, and permission to issue capital from the appropriate authorities; also assistance in obtaining the highest priority possible for the import of machinery and plant and for the release of fuel and materials for the construction of necessary buildings for the company.

2. Water for the purposes of the company from its irrigation canals, at the usual volumetric charges.

3. The site selected by the promoters for the purpose of setting up the factories, on payment at stipulated rates.

The government of Bahawalpur was further under obligation to grant exemption to the company for a period of ten years after the start of manufacturing processes from the state income tax and the state corporation tax to the following extent (central government taxes were not applicable in Bahawalpur State at that time):

1. Exemption for the first five years to the extent of 50 percent of the state income and corporation taxes ordinarily leviable.

2. Exemption for the next five years to the extent of 25 percent of the state income and corporation taxes ordinarily leviable.

3. The amount of tax actually levied during the periods mentioned in (1) and (2) above was not to be less than 50 percent and 75 percent respectively of the income and corporation taxes which would be leviable under the law of Pakistan at Pakistan rates if that law were applicable.

4. The amount of tax actually levied during periods mentioned in (1) and (2) was not at any time to exceed the income and corporation taxes which would be leviable under the law of Pakistan at Pakistan rates if that law were applicable.

The capital of the two companies was to consist of cumulative preference shares and ordinary shares. The total authorized capital for the two companies was rs20 million, out of which 1.4 million was in the form of preference shares and 18.6 million in ordinary shares. The preference shares were to be held entirely by the state government. The distribution of the total share capital after it was fully paid up in 1952 was as follows:

	Sadiq Vegetable Oils		*Sadiq Soap*		*Total*	
	rs	*%*	*rs*	*%*	*rs*	*%*
5% Preference						
State Government	1,000,000		400,000		1,400,000	
Ordinary State						
Government	2,766,800	27.67	1,900,000	22.09	4,666,800	25.09
Sir William Roberts	210,000	2.10	300,000	3.49	510,000	2.74
Amjad Ali	1,050,000	10.50	200,000	2.33	1,250,000	6.72
Unilever	5,973,200	59.73	6,200,000	72.09	12,173,200	65.45
Ordinary Shares	10,000,000	100.00	8,600,000	100.00	18,600,000	100.00
Total Capital	11,000,000		9,000,000		20,000,000	

Although under the law of the country effective in 1948 foreign capital participation in the vegetable oil industry could not generally exceed 49 percent, in the soap industry it could be as high as 70 percent.

Unilever's equity participation in Sadiq Vegetable Oils was more than 49 percent because at the time its capital was increased (to the authorized limit), other shareholders did not buy the new shares offered to them in proportion to the existing shares held by them, and consequently the new shares were allocated to Unilever. The government sanctioned the increase in Unilever's participation.

Unilever thus had the controlling interest in the two companies as its equity investment in them amounted to about 61 percent of the total. The structure of the capital in the two companies taken together remained unchanged until the Sadiq Soap Company Ltd. was liquidated in 1955 and Sadiq Vegetable Oils and Allied Industries Ltd. took over the manufacturing of soap as well as vanaspati.

In addition to taking over the activities of the Sadiq Soap Company Ltd. in 1955, Sadiq Vegetable Oils and Allied Industries Ltd. also assumed the functions of Lever Brothers Ltd. (Pakistan) and the HVM Company Ltd. In the same year, consequent upon the merger of Bahawalpur into the province of West Pakistan, the West Pakistan government became the legal owner of the shares hitherto held by the Bahawalpur state government in Sadiq Vegetable Oils and Allied Industries Ltd. and the Sadiq Soap Company Ltd.

On October 12, 1955, Unilever Ltd. of England entered into a new agreement with Sadiq Vegetable Oils and Allied Industries Ltd. (hereafter called Sadiq), which company was now not only manufacturing vegetable oils and soap but was also marketing the two categories of products. This new agreement is called the royalty agreement, under which Unilever agreed, among other things, to:

(1) make available to Sadiq such secrets and processes, inventions and improvements as are necessary to enable Sadiq to manufacture all or any of the agreement products with efficiency, and to the standards of quality required by Unilever.

(2) furnish Sadiq with the information, know-how, and assistance that Unilever considers necessary for the satisfactory production, distribution, marketing, and advertising of products manufactured by Sadiq.

(3) make available to Sadiq technical, marketing, advisory, buying, insurance, accounts, and other appropriate advice.

In return, Sadiq agreed to pay a royalty (in sterling after December, 1956 and in rupees until then) with respect to soap and edible oils and fats at stipulated rates. Sadiq also agreed to disclose to Unilever from time to time any inventions, improvements, or secret processes relating to the products manufactured by it. The agreement was to cease to have effect if, among other things, Unilever or its subsidiary companies for any reason ceased to hold effective share voting control of Sadiq.

Until 1958 the joint venture continued to operate under the name of Sadiq Vegetable Oils and Allied Industries Ltd. It was, however, being gradually realized that the international prestige of Lever Brothers products did not generally attach to the Sadiq products, and, consequently, the name of the joint venture was changed in 1958 by the consent of all parties to Lever Brothers (Pakistan) Ltd.

Lever Brothers (Pakistan) Ltd. is a public company limited by shares, incorporated under the Companies Act of 1913. Ordinarily, at least in part, a public limited company's share capital, as against that of a private limited company, is subscribed by the public at large, and there is no restriction as to the number of its shareholders. However, the minimum number of original shareholders in a public limited company must be seven. This condition was met by Lever Brothers, as the original subscribers to its capital numbered twelve. They were the government of His Highness the Amir of Bahawalpur; E. Penderel Moon, revenue minister, Bahawalpur State; Unilever (Commonwealth Holdings) Ltd., London; C. S. Pettit, Gold Croft, Warden Road, Bombay; W. Roberts, Khanewal, Punjab; T. J. Roberts, Khanewal, Punjab; Sir Syed Maratib Ali, Lahore; S. Amjad Ali, Lahore; Syed Afzal Ali, Lahore; Syed Wajid Ali, Lahore; Syed Akhtar Ahsan, Lahore; and Syed Babar Ali, Lahore.

Thus, the general public was not given an opportunity to buy the joint venture's shares. According to paragraph 7 of the memorandum and articles of association of the venture, "the unissued shares shall be under the control of the Directors, who may allot or otherwise dispose of the same to such persons, on such terms and conditions and at such times, as the Directors think fit." So far, the directors have not disposed of the unissued or any other shares to the general public. The original subscribers to Lever Brothers' capital have clung to their shareholdings. Currently, however, the government of West Pakistan, which inherited the shares of the state government in 1955, is contemplating the possibility of ceasing to be a business partner in industry. If it does so, its shareholdings may, in case the directors so decide, come to the general public through open sale.

The capital structure of Lever Brothers has undergone some change since 1952. The total value of five percent preference shares has risen from rs1,400,000 to rs4,783,500. The ordinary shares of category A stand at a total of rs3,043,300, and of category B at rs12,173,200. The total share capital, however, remains unchanged at rs20 million. Both preference and ordinary shares carry voting rights on the principle of one vote per share. However, the preference shares are valued at rs100 each and ordinary shares at rs50 each, and this valuation thus confers twice the voting power on the holders of ordinary shares compared to preference shareholders of equal value.

The classification of ordinary shares into A and B has a definite purpose. Unilever owns the ordinary B shares exclusively, and, under Articles 112 and 120, the holders of ordinary B shares enjoy the right to appoint managing directors and the chairman of the board of directors.

MANAGEMENT AND PERSONNEL

There can be 11 directors on the board of directors of Lever Brothers (Pakistan) Ltd., 6 of them representing Unilever, and the remaining 5 representing local interests. The existing qualification of a director is that he must hold shares of Lever Brothers in the amount of rs25,000, except for directors representing the government. In 1948 this requirement was fixed at rs5,000.

At the moment Unilever has its full quota of six directors on the board. Of these six directors representing Unilever, two are Pakistanis and four Englishmen. They are all, except one Englishman, working as directors. In principle, there is no restriction on the number of Pakistani directors that may be appointed by Unilever.

The other five directors representing local interests are all Pakistanis. Their appointment is effected by written notice signed by the holders or the representatives or proxies of the holders of not less than three-quarters of the preference and ordinary A shares taken together.

In the senior managers' category there are three foreigners and two Pakistanis at present.

The company has nine managers in all, out of which six are Pakistanis and three are foreigners. All assistant managers are Pakistanis.

The technical side is handled by Unilever completely at the top level, although it is obliged by its contract with the company to use its best endeavors to insure that the company has an efficient administrative, technical and marketing management recruited from Pakistan nationals to the extent that suitable nationals are available. "Pakistanization" of the senior personnel is proceeding rapidly. On the marketing and advertising side, the entire personnel is Pakistani.

In the initial years of the venture, the progress of Pakistanization of personnel was a bit slow due to inadequate housing facilities at Rahim Yar Khan. A large number of houses were built in 1955, and this facilitated recruitment.

The senior Pakistani executives of Lever Brothers were trained both locally and in the United Kingdom. Their training in the United Kingdom was only for a short period—usually from six months to one year. Among the assistant managers, six out of fourteen have been to the United Kingdom. While these trainees are abroad, they are paid their salaries in Pakistan by Lever Brothers (Pakistan) Ltd., and their expenses abroad are met by Unilever.

The total number of operatives of Lever Brothers at Rahim Yar Khan is at present about 550. The ratio of skilled to unskilled laborers in the plants is 30:70. The labor force has organized an independent union which is not affiliated with any of the existing labor federations. However, the Lever Brothers Employees' Union, though independent, is not a company union. In fact, Lever Brothers (Pakistan) brings to bear on its personnel policies the experience and wisdom gained over the centuries in the West. Collective bargaining has been encouraged by the management of the joint venture and some tangible gains have been secured by the employees through it. Among them are a rise in the wage rate and the setting up of two family wards in the local civil hospital for the use of laborers' families. Unlike many Pakistani firms, Lever Brothers (Pakistan) Ltd. has on its staff a highly paid personnel officer.

Wages of unskilled laborers in Lever Brothers are relatively high. Pakistani firms do not generally pay as high wages. The fact that Rahim Yar Khan is a low-living cost area turns the comparison still more in favor of Lever Brothers. The minimum total monthly wage of an unskilled laborer of Lever Brothers is rs105, and in addition he is entitled to the use of the canteen where he brings his tiffin and is supplied free tea.

Laborers of Lever Brothers are entitled to three weeks' leave on full pay in the year in addition to 11 festival holidays. This compares favorably with the leave conditions obtaining in the country and provided by the law. If a laborer avails himself of two weeks' leave out of the allowable three weeks at a time when he wants it and leaves the remaining one week to be given to him at the convenience of the management, then another week's leave is added to his leave account.

The joint venture has a liberal sickness benefit scheme, which gives the employees substantial benefits. A cooperative credit society was organized by the management for the laborers. A liberal provident fund scheme has also been introduced for the employees with ten percent of basic salaries contributed by the employees and an equal amount by the management. Preventive medicines are distributed in sufficient quantities to prevent malaria, smallpox, and other such epidemics in the labor colony.

About 20 percent of the labor force lives in quarters built by the management with satisfactory ventilation, water supply, etc. The rest of the employees live in nearby villages. The occupants of the quarters pay rent to the management at a reasonably low rate and those who do not live on the company estate receive rent assistance. An area of about nine acres of land has been set apart in the estate area for use by the laborers as sports fields.

In 1954, there was a strike among some of the Lever Brothers employees on the grievance of retrenchment effected by the management after the construction on the mills was completed. The strike was a failure and since then relationships between the management and the labor force have been quite smooth.

GOVERNMENT RELATIONS

There are two aspects to Lever Brothers' relations with the government, that with the government of West Pakistan as a party to the joint venture, and that with the central government on general matters. So far as the first relationship is concerned, it is perfectly smooth and gives rise to no problems. The relationship with the central government is of a different nature. It involves tax laws, protection to the industry, problems of remittance of profit, price control, and issue of import licenses.

The venture does not face any special problems regarding tax laws. Taxes on industry have been generally high and all industries are equally affected by them. Substantial tax relief has now been afforded to industry under the revolutionary regime, and lower taxes became effective from July 1, 1959. The business profit tax has been abolished, but a part thereof has been included in the basic tax structure. The tax on profits from subsidiaries has been lowered from a maximum of 31.5 percent to a maximum of 20 percent.

With respect to protection, Lever Brothers is in an exceptionally favorable position since the import of soap and vanaspati is prohibited.

Lever Brothers did not face any problem of remittance of profits up to 1958 since no dividends were declared by it. The company was concentrating on the building up of reserves. It applied for the government's permission for the remittance of 1958 profits, which was subsequently granted on May 19, 1959.

The general position with regard to import licenses in Pakistan has been rather tight since after the Korean boom. Import licenses are needed by Lever Brothers for tinplate, coconut oil, essential oils, chemicals, and spare parts. Licenses for these purposes are not issued to them in full. The government has assessed the capacity of Lever Brothers' plant and issued licenses for about one-third of the soap raw materials of the total assessed capacity. Lever Brothers has been receiving these licenses reasonably regularly. The actual capacity of Lever Brothers is, in fact, higher than the capacity assessed by the government. However, in view of the general shortage of foreign exchange, this lower assessment on the part of the government has not been resented by Lever Brothers.

Martial law has actually opened up new sources for the acquisition of import licenses by Lever Brothers. The government has introduced an export bonus scheme, according to which exporters of various categories of goods from Pakistan have been promised import licenses, the value of which would form a specified percentage of the total value of exports, depending on the category of goods exported. Lever Brothers (Pakistan) Ltd. feels particularly encouraged by this measure because it is confident that its contacts abroad and experience in the area of foreign trade will enable it to gain from this scheme more than its competitors.

With the imposition of martial law, price controls were clamped on most articles constituting necessaries of life, and vanaspati (an edible oil product) was one of them. "Dalda" is the chief vanaspati brand which Lever Brothers makes, and a substantial part of the national market for vanaspati is supplied by Lever Brothers. Since the control on vanaspati was not related to the manufacturing costs, "Dalda" is not covering its total costs at the moment. However, Lever Brothers expects that when oilseeds are available at controlled rates and its capacity to import increases due to the export bonus scheme, it will be able to make a good business of "Dalda."

The 20 percent maximum gross profit allowed on soap by the government under price controls is not being currently realized by Lever Brothers because it has never allowed itself this rate of profit. Furthermore, the venture is cooperating with the government in keeping down prices as it regards itself as an integral part of Pakistan's economy and is therefore as anxious as anybody else in the country to see that it emerges from its difficulties.

FINANCIAL RESULTS

Following are selected indicators of the financial experience of the enterprise:

	1956	*1957*	*1958*	*1959*
		(thousands of rupees)		
Sales	21,400	23,900	28,700	34,400
Depreciation on fixed assets charged to profits	824	905	1,005	1,010
Net profit before tax	3,312	1,884	2,416	3,465
Provision for tax	—	250	1,340	2,163
Profit retained in the business at the year's end	—	4,850	5,060	6,202
Dividend preference	239	164	164	167
Dividend on ordinary shares	—	—	760 (5%)	1,065 (7%)
Stores and stocks on hand and in transit	7,734	6,490	7,080	13,244

The company has provided depreciation of rs3.7 million on its fixed assets in the last four years. In addition it has created general reserves of rs6.2 million. The present general reserve (retained profits) will be available for expanding the business without raising further capital.

The preceding table shows that the company has made progress and that its sales are increasing. In 1956 sales were rs21 million and they went up to rs34 million rupees in 1959—61 percent higher than in 1956.

The net profits of the company declined in 1957 and 1958 compared to 1956, mainly because of rising prices of indigenous raw materials, which have since been controlled at reasonable levels. Profits recovered appreciably in 1959. During the first years, reserves were being built up. Subsequently a dividend of five percent was declared for 1958 and one of seven percent for 1959.

ROLE IN THE ECONOMY

The main lines of production of Lever Brothers are vanaspati and soaps. Obviously, these categories of goods are of vital importance to the consumer in general. The major portion of the raw materials used in the manufacture of these products is indigenous. In fact, Bahawalpur ordinarily provides a sufficient quantity of oilseeds for edible oils. The total production of Lever Brothers with respect to these two goods forms a substantial proportion of their total domestic supply. However, in the inferior quality bar-soap used widely for washing purposes by most of the population, Lever Brothers' share is small.

The principal competitors of the joint venture in oil products and vanaspati are the Sind Oil Mills Ltd., the Ganesh Flour Mills, the Punjab Vegetable Ghee, and the Crescent Vegetable Oil Mills, all located in West Pakistan. In the field of soap, Crescent Pak Soap and Oil Mills is the principal rival in southern West Pakistan and Behtreen Soap Company in northern West Pakistan. Incidentally, none of these rivals is a joint venture, and the installed plant capacity of Lever Brothers is much larger than that of any one of them.

With respect to both vanaspati and soaps, excepting the inferior variety of bar-soap, the contribution made by Lever Brothers to the economy of Pakistan is particularly noteworthy. The joint venture has acted as price and quality leader in the two fields. Even though its supply of vanaspati is currently only about 20 percent of the total production in Pakistan, Lever Brothers has set standards of quality and price which its competitors have to respect and follow. If the total plant capacity of Lever Brothers were utilized, the supply of vanaspati and better quality soap in the country would increase significantly. Lever Brothers is looking forward to the day when greater regularity in availability of raw materials at home and of licenses for the import of raw materials from abroad will enable it to expand its production in accordance with its installed capacity.

In Pakistan at the moment the production and consumption of fats in all forms does not exceed seven pounds per head per annum, while this is higher than forty-five in the United Kingdom. Pure "ghee," a milk product used as a cooking medium, is becoming increasingly scarce and the consumers are more and more turning to vanaspati and vegetable oils in one form or another in the two wings of Pakistan. This fact sheds further light on the significant role of Lever Brothers in the economy of Pakistan.

With respect to soaps, the superior quality soaps are almost a monopoly of Lever Brothers, and their prices are not at all high in relation to the general price level and to the cost of production. It has already been mentioned that Lever Brothers has not been making the allowable 20 percent profit on soap.

The contribution which Lever Brothers has made to the balance of payments situation derives from the fact that its products, as is apparent from the foregoing, are essentially foreign exchange savers, although they have not reached the point of being foreign exchange earners.

EVALUATION

Lever Brothers (Pakistan) Ltd. is hopeful about its future operations in Pakistan. Its minimum target with respect to edible oils and soaps is to work its plants to full capacity.

In recent years the joint venture embarked on the production of balanced cattle food, a product for which it does not need additional plant or any imported raw materials. The total production of balanced cattle food during 1957–58 and 1958–59 was rather small. However, productive capacity for this product is quite large. The introduction of the product will indirectly lead to an increase in the supply of fats in the country and so will increase Lever Brothers' contribution to the total national economy.

The legal arrangement under which Lever Brothers (Pakistan) Ltd. is operating appears to be a permanent one under normal circumstances. In the absence of any now unforeseen eventuality of nationalization of economic activity in general or of foreign industrial assets in particular, Lever Brothers' role in the economy will perhaps be ever expanding.

The major problems of Lever Brothers seem to be irregular supplies of domestically produced raw materials and inability to get import licenses. However, these problems are by no means insoluble. With the increase in agricultural productivity which is at present the main preoccupation of the National Planning Commission of Pakistan, the supply of indigenous agricultural raw materials is bound to improve. The import license problem cannot be expected to be completely resolved in the near future in view of the fact that the balance of payments position will continue to be a major problem of the country as a result of the industrial development program in hand. Nevertheless, the export bonus scheme introduced by the present regime should definitely go a long way to afford relief to Lever Brothers in this respect.

Apart from these two problems, the joint venture does not seem to face any other very significant problem. Pakistanis in general have faith in the products of Lever Brothers and therefore their demand is likely to expand.

Lever Brothers is carrying out its contractual obligation to achieve Pakistanization with respect to responsible posts as and when the requisite staff are available. With all its experience by now of international collaboration in over 40 countries, Unilever has developed the ability to identify itself with local conditions and interests. For example, in its plant at Rahim Yar Khan, Lever Brothers closes on Fridays, and its entire European staff works on Sundays along with the local labor force. The joint venture favors this practice out of respect for the sentiments of its Muslim employees.

Manila Gas Corporation

ORIGIN OF THE ENTERPRISE

Under Act no. 2039 of the Philippine Legislature, a franchise to construct, maintain, and operate a gas system for the city of Manila was granted for a period of 50 years from January 2, 1912 to Schweizerische Gasgesellschaft, A.G., a corporation of Zurich, Switzerland. It soon became apparent, however, that the American governor-general of the Philippine Islands, then the chief executive of the land, favored some participation by Filipinos in the operation of the franchise. A corporation was therefore organized in Manila, the Manila Gas Corporation, on September 27, 1912 with some shares reserved for purchase by Filipinos. This corporation then acquired the franchise of Schweizerische Gasgesellschaft, the transfer being approved on October 19, 1912 by the American governor-general. Shares of stock which were not reserved for purchase by the Filipinos were purchased by Schweizerische Gasgesellschaft. Only a negligible number of shares reserved for Filipinos were eventually purchased, however, so that the Schweizerische Gasgesellschaft was virtually the sole owner of the corporation.

The management staff from 1912 to 1927 was made up entirely of Swiss engineers and technicians. In 1927, the Islands Gas and Electric Company of Maryland purchased the shares of Schweizerische Gasgesellschaft to become the sole owner of the Manila Gas Corporation except for the few outstanding shares that had been bought by Filipinos in 1912. About the middle of 1930, a few Americans joined the staff in representation of the new owners.

No material interruption in the serving of gas from its start on November 12, 1912 was experienced until the destruction of the plant and distribution facilities early in 1945 during the war for the liberation of the city of Manila between the United States Armed Forces and the Japanese Imperial Army. After the liberation of the city of Manila had been completed, the Islands Gas and Electric Company was reluctant to invest any additional funds to rehabilitate the corporation. Late in 1946, a representative of Islands Gas and Electric came to Manila, and presented to the government two propositions: 1) an offer to sell to the government or to any of its instrumentalities or agencies all that was left of the Manila Gas Corporation, or 2) an invitation to the government to come into the company as a minority stockholder.

The late President Manuel A. Roxas appointed a special committee to make a study of the proposals, as well as to examine the condition of the remaining properties of the Manila Gas Corporation. For the latter purpose, the committee availed itself of the services of engineers from the government-owned National Development Company (NDC).

CAPITAL STRUCTURE AND REHABILITATION

The NDC engineers reported that the underground pipes of Manila Gas were still in a serviceable condition and that the rehabilitation of the plant and that portion of the company's distribution facilities which had been damaged would cost approximately 3,200,000 pesos. After holding a number of meetings, the committee created by the late President Roxas recommended that the government, through the NDC, acquire majority control of the corporation subject to the following conditions:

(1) That the existing authorized capital stock of the Company, which was 1,500,000 pesos, be written down to 1,000,000 pesos, so that the Islands Gas and Electric Company would take an immediate loss of 500,000 pesos on its pre-war capital investment.

(2) That the authorized capital stock of the Company should then be increased to 2,500,000 pesos divided into 25,000 shares, and that the

Government, through the NDC, subscribe to 1,500,000 pesos, thus acquiring 60 percent control of the Company.

(3) That the 1,500,000 pesos subscription of the NDC be paid as follows:

660,000—in cash, and

840,000—by surrendering to the Treasurer of the Manila Gas Corporation the Company's bonds held by the Government which had a par value of 840,000.

(4) That the NDC be given by the Islands Gas and Electric Company a 5-year option within which to purchase the remaining shares of the latter in the enterprise.

The committee further recommended that a loan be obtained from the Rehabilitation Finance Corporation in the amount of 3.2 million pesos to help finance the rehabilitation program of the company. In computing the money that had to be obtained to complete the company's rehabilitation program, however, the President's committee did not take into consideration the 1,349,962.23 pesos that Manila Gas eventually received from the War Damage Commission.

The Islands Gas and Electric Company accepted the government's proposal and, on March 2, 1948, an agreement was drawn up with the NDC embodying the foregoing terms. Immediately thereafter, the corporation's capital stock was increased to 2,500,000 pesos. At the same time, the Islands Gas and Electric Company surrendered to the treasurer of Manila Gas for cancellation 5,000 shares worth 500,000 pesos. Thus, the company's capital structure became as follows:

Authorized capital	2,500,000 pesos
Amount held by Islands Gas and Electric Company	1,000,000 pesos
Amount of capital stock available for subscription by the National Development Company	1,500,000 pesos

Immediately after the foregoing steps were taken, Manila Gas advised the NDC that it was ready to receive the government's subscription and that, as soon as this was obtained, the company's rehabilitation program could get underway.

It was not until January, 1951 that the government paid its subscription. As soon as the NDC became the controlling stockholder, the company's board of directors was reorganized to provide for representation of the government. One of the conditions included in the agreement between the NDC and the Islands Gas and Electric Company was that for the first five years after rehabilitation of the plant, the company would engage the services of an experienced engineering firm in the United States to supervise the company's rehabilitation program and operations. The company designated for that purpose was the Stone and Webster Service Corporation of New York. This is the same firm which had supervised the company's activities for many years prior to the Second World War.

Soon after the reorganization of the Manila Gas Corporation in March, 1951, the management proceeded with the task of placing the underground gas system and production facilities once again in operating condition.

In December, 1951, negotiations were commenced with the Rehabilitation Finance Corporation for a loan of 2 million pesos for the purpose of providing funds with which to redeem all outstanding bonds, to pay off prewar bank overdrafts, and to complete the rehabilitation program. As a result of these negotiations, a 2 million pesos five-year loan was made available to the company in May, 1952. This loan was secured by a first mortgage on all physical properties of the company, and had an interest rate of six percent.

All of the company's outstanding bonds amounting to 264,000 pesos were redeemed, and all prewar bank overdrafts were settled for the amount of 274,278.55 pesos, both paid out of the proceeds of the loan.

The Stone and Webster Service Corporation, in its report of May 15, 1951 on the rehabilitation of the company's property, estimated the cost of rehabilitation at 2,510,690 pesos. This amount was exclusive of the cost required to redeem outstanding bonds and settle prewar bank overdrafts and other outstanding indebtedness.

The company's reconstruction schedule proceeded so that by early 1953 resumption of gas service was made possible in a large portion of the areas formerly served by the company prior to the Second World War.

EVALUATION

As a government-controlled corporation, the company suffers disadvantages arising out of certain restrictions imposed on its operations. The most significant restriction is that of not competing with private businesses unless a clear and present danger to its stability can be demonstrated. A restriction of lesser significance, nonetheless a disadvantage, vis-à-vis private businesses, is the standardization of personnel administration to the government pattern as supervised by the Office of Economic Coordination, Government Service & Insurance System, and the Administrative Code. A very minor restriction is that imposed by the General Auditing Office. On the other hand, because it is a government corporation, financing from government-owned financial institutions and the handling of transactions with government agencies have been comparatively easy to accomplish.

As an American-Filipino corporation, certain disadvantages have been encountered in the acquisition of machinery and equipment and the provision of technical services. With the present composition of ownership, 60 percent Filipino and 40 percent American, it is to be expected that some influence will be brought to bear on the procurement policies of the corporation to favor American equipment. The development of American equipment for the manufacture of gas out of bunker oil has understandably lagged behind development by European manufacturers on account of the almost total replacement of manufactured gas by natural gas in the United States.

The present structure of the company has also created certain financial problems which hinder expansion plans. It is rather difficult for the company to raise capital through public sale of stock due to the disadvantages imposed on government corporations. It is likewise doubtful that the American company would be willing to invest more money. On the other hand, government ownership has significantly minimized a drain on funds that might otherwise have occurred for the payment of dividends if the company were entirely privately owned.

Martaban Company

The Martaban Company was organized as a private limited company in 1953 under the Burma Companies Act. The two groups in the venture are private Burma shareholders and the Taiyo Fishing Company Limited, a well-established Japanese firm from Tokyo. The Martaban Company is the first and only company in Burma to be engaged in the deep-sea fishing industry. The life of the venture was not specified at the time the company was registered.

ORIGIN OF THE ENTERPRISE

The deep-sea fishing industry is entirely new to Burma, where the people have been consuming only river fish, although imported sardines often serve as an important constituent of the Burmese diet. Investigations carried out by the Fisheries Department of the government indicated that the Burmese coasts were promising fishing grounds, particularly south of the delta area, due to the presence of fish food and weed brought down by the waters of the Irrawaddy. Here, the swift current of the river meets a warm clear current coming up from the Admans, establishing a long tide line which spreads out east and west and which is 20 to 30 miles off the coast. The Fisheries Department discovered the feasibility of exploiting these fishing grounds and anticipated the substitution, to a considerable extent, of sea fish for river fish in the diet of the Burmese people.

The promotion of a fishing industry in Burma was first initiated by Bo Let Ya, the chairman and major shareholder of Let Ya and Company Limited. Let Ya and Company Limited was registered in 1952 as a private limited company under the Burma Companies Act with an authorized share capital of k2,000,000 divided into 2,000 shares of k1,000 each. The issued share capital of k1 million is held by 33 shareholders, all of whom are Burmese. The company came into existence to engage in diverse fields of business activities, and it trades in numerous types of merchandise, namely, timber, rice, mineral ores, fuel, iron and steel, electrical wires, cables and accessories, electrical equipment and appliances, communications equipment and apparatus, machinery, fertilizer, foodstuffs, chemicals, and textiles. Its scope of activities also extends into shipping and banking. Its charter specifically covers such activities as joint enterprises with foreign firms.

Bo Let Ya himself is an energetic and enterprising businessman who became interested in the research carried out by the Fisheries Department and realized the potentialities of the Burmese fishing grounds. Early in 1953, he inquired of the secretary of the Ministry of Industries regarding the feasibility of establishing such an industry, since it not only would curtail the import of fish and fish products from overseas and thereby save foreign exchange, but also would encourage the development of subsidiary industries such as fish meal, canning, and fertilizers. The yearly import figures of fish and fish products in Burma were as follows:

Year	*Value* (*thousands of kyats*)	*Volume* (cwt.)
1940–41	4,719	165
1947–48	9,961	94
1951–52	14,097	110
1953–54	29,053	247

The Ministry of Industries indicated its willingness to give assistance to Bo Let Ya and instructed the Industrial Development Corporation of the government to implement the project. Negotiations were begun between Bo Let Ya and the Industrial Development Corporation, and the form and terms of aid to be extended by the corporation were discussed.

The Industrial Development Corporation agreed to extend a loan of k300,000 in the name of Bo Let Ya to provide for initial investment in the venture, at an interest rate of 5 percent per annum and repayable, in equal installments, over a period of 10 years. The corporation agreed to issue fishing licenses as well as licenses for the import of such fishing equipment as would be needed for the fishing operations.

Bo Let Ya invited a Japanese expert from the Taiyo Fishing Company, who came to Rangoon in 1953, to study the prospects of the fishing industry in Burma. He confirmed the richness of the fishing grounds and the existence of a potential market for the fish. Late in 1953, Bo Let Ya and U Ba Tin went to Japan to negotiate the venture. Bo Let Ya invited the Taiyo Fishing Company of Japan to enter into a joint venture with his own firm. The Japanese firm favored a 50-50 ownership interest with the Burmese investors, which was, however, impossible under the provision of the constitution which requires that, for the exploration of natural resources, at least 60 percent of the ownership interest be held by Burmese citizens, and to this the Japanese partners finally agreed. Although the Japanese partners agreed to provide fishing equipment and personnel, specific arrangements were later made through individual contracts for chartering and manning the trawlers.

Established in 1916, the Taiyo Fishing Company is one of the two leaders in the Japanese fishing industry, and has a paid-up share capital of 4½ billion yen (k60 million). The company is engaged in deep-sea fishing, canning and refrigerating, and supplies, in large quantities, all sorts of fish and fish products to the Japanese and world markets. It has agencies established in various parts of the world, including Hong Kong, Manila, and Singapore. It recently entered into joint venture agreements with foreign firms in Bombay and Brazil, and is interested in similar undertakings elsewhere.

CAPITAL STRUCTURE

The authorized share capital of the Martaban Company is k10,000,000, divided into 10,000 ordinary shares of k1,000 each, of which k500,000 has been paid in. Sixty percent of the paid-in capital is held by the Burmese interest and the remaining 40 percent by the Japanese. There are altogether 26 shareholders in the Martaban Company, including the Taiyo Fishing Company, which constitutes a singe shareholder.

The initial investment of k300,000 came from Bo Let Ya, who obtained the sum in the form of the loan from the Industrial Development Corporation in his own name. This investment was made in the names of his 24 associates as well as himself. Bo Let Ya's associates did not contribute any sum to the joint venture, but Bo Let Ya included them in the list of shareholders, because he wanted to encourage his associates to take an interest in the undertaking and to make some financial contributions at a later date. Further financial assistance to the company was obtained from the corporation in 1957.

The Japanese partners remitted the equivalent of k200,000, and it was agreed that at the time of liquidation, such proceeds from the sale of assets as they were entitled to would be remitted to them. The government had agreed to provide foreign exchange facilities for these transactions. The dividends accruing to the Japanese would be remitted to them if and when declared, while the dividends accruing to Bo Let Ya would be used to repay the loan that he had obtained for his initial investment. Though the ownership ratio between the two parties is to be maintained, there are no specific provisions concerning contributions by the parties in case of expansion or if additional investment becomes necessary. In case of purchase by the Burmese, the Burmese shareholders would buy the Japanese shares at par.

MANAGEMENT AND PERSONNEL

The Martaban Company is managed by a board of directors composed of four Burmese and three Japanese. According to the provisions of the articles of association, the posts of chairman of the board and managing director are filled by Burmese directors. The vice presidents' posts are filled by Japanese. Two of the three Japanese directors live in Rangoon, and they receive free housing and transportation in addition to their salaries (k1,100 per month). They are allowed to remit two-thirds of their salaries to their families in Japan. In addition to policy matters, one of the two directors is in charge of accounts, while the other is held responsible for actual fishing operations. The office of the company is in Rangoon, and the headquarters staff are mostly Burmese.

The salary payments for administrative personnel of the Martaban Company amount to about k6,400 a month, of which k2,300 goes to Japanese personnel. Of the total monthly operating and selling expenses of k29,000, about k19,000 are incurred for the Japanese technicians who are engaged in the fishing operations.

The company started by chartering three trawlers from the Taiyo Fishing Co. Ltd., one of 250 tons called the "Taiyo Maru No. 11," one of 117 tons called the "Akashi Maru No. 1," and a larger one named the "Ginga Bawga." The three work in rotation, two being in operation at any given time and the third one in dock. Operations have been carried out at two excellent fishing grounds, one south of Bassein and Pyapon, and the other off the coasts of Tavoy and Mergui. Test trawling was also carried out in areas west of the Arakan coast and in the Gulf of Martaban. Trawling results showed average catches of 240 boxes or about 10,800 pounds per day, with maximum catches of 446 boxes or 20,070 pounds, and a minimum of 113 boxes or 5,085 pounds. The total quantity of catches from the beginning of fishing operations in November, 1953 to the end of September, 1956 was about 5,500 tons of 56 varieties of fish.

When fishing operations started in 1953, the trawling crews were all Japanese. It has always been the intention of the company, however, eventually to man the trawlers with Burmese crews. The more important posts on board a trawler, the captain, chief mate, boatswain, and second officer, are all filled by Japanese at present, while the less important posts such as those of oiler, sailor, engineer, wireless operator, etc., are filled by Burmese. On board the "Ginga Bawga," two-thirds of the total crew members are Japanese. They fill all the important posts. The turnover in the Burmese portion of the crew has been high, in spite of the favorable wage scale, probably due to the monotonous and wearing nature of the work. The fishing operations require technical skill which takes at least five years for an average employee to acquire. The company has arranged training programs for Burmese crew members. However, there are difficulties partly due to a lack of interest on the part of the Burmese, who do not usually stay long in their jobs, and partly due to a general reluctance on the part of their Japanese counterparts to spend a lot of time training others since they are more interested in increasing production. In the training itself, language was found to be another barrier which made the program less effective. The two groups at times developed antagonisms toward each other, although, on the whole, the relations were cordial and satisfactory.

To meet its Burmanization objective, the company recently sent two trainees to Cochin, India, for one year's training. The company plans to send four more for training, but has not been able to recruit the required men. Lacking experience and skill in fishing, the Burmese in general feel it a real hardship to work at sea and are not adaptable to sea life.

PROBLEMS, AND FINANCIAL RESULTS

When sea fish was introduced into the Burmese market, the reception from the consuming public was most unfavorable; since most Burmese are unaccustomed to eating sea fish, there was practically no demand. Intensive advertising campaigns were formulated and employed as a remedial measure. Though effective to a certain extent, this could not save the venture from heavy losses in its first two years of operation.

A contributing factor to this initial failure was the fact that taking life is very strictly prohibited by the Buddhist doctrines. Burmese Buddhists react unfavorably to Bo Let Ya and his associates, even though criticism is not expressed openly or strongly.

There has been a steady sale in the Rangoon-Prome-Pegu market. The demand for sea fish is showing an upward trend, and the market has been extended to Mandalay and Upper Burma. The average price of the sea fish (k0.99) is far less than that of river fish (k2.50). The company distributes its products through the Fish Marketing Cooperative Society Limited, for which it pays a commission of 4 percent on net sales.

There is a thriving by-product industry producing dried salted fish in the summer months and *ngapi* (fish paste) during the rains, about 46,800 pounds per month finding a market in Upper Burma. The production of fish sauce is also being planned.

In 1954 the company incurred a loss of k132,000, and in 1955 an additional loss of k118,640.

PROFIT AND LOSS STATEMENT, 1954–56

	1954–55	*1955–56*
Total Revenue	k652,300	k582,300
Operating and Distribution Expenses	559,480	358,300
Gross Profiit	92,820	224,000
Other Income	1,540	50,500
	94,360	274,500
Non-Operating and General Expenses	213,000	156,900
Profits and Losses	−k118,640	+k117,600

Operating expenses include charterage, crews' salaries and allowances, pilotage, and wharfage. Non-operating expenses include directors' salaries, office expenses, electricity, stationery, and audit fees.

The Profit and Loss Statement for 1956 shows a credit balance of k117,600. The company was unable to declare any dividend out of this because of the debit balance of more than k250,000 carried over from the previous years.

In addition to the loan of k300,000 to Bo Let Ya, the Industrial Development Corporation granted to the company a loan of k1,800,000. The loan carries an interest charge of 5 percent, and is to be repaid over 20 years in 40 equal half-yearly installments. The loan has been used to purchase the fishing trawler "Ginga Bawga" for k1,200,000, and cold storage equipment for k280,000.

The Martaban Company does not enjoy any concessions whatsoever and has had to pay the following fees, duties, commissions and charges:

1. Import license fees for trawlers, ship's stores, fishing equipment and gear, under charter from abroad.

2. Customs duties on the foregoing with the exception of the trawlers.

3. Port charges such as wharfage, pilot fees, river duties, landing and unloading charges, harbor duties, buoy charges and light duties payable regularly whenever a trawler returns from fishing grounds.

4. Commission of four percent on sales payable to the Fish Marketing Cooperative Society Limited.

FUTURE PLANS

The long-term plans of the company include the following:

1. Acquisition of additional trawlers, and other craft for surface fishing, as well as in-shore or coral fishing. Arrangements are under way for experimental operations with an Okinawan fishing company.

2. Establishment of a chain of cold storage facilities at selected centers and acquisition of cold storage railroad cars for effective and widespread distribution throughout Burma.

3. Establishment of subsidiary industries for by-products such as fish meal, fertilizers, fish oil, and canning.

4. Development of an export program.

EVALUATION

The various attitudes of the Burmese shareholders, the Burmese government, and the Japanese partners have developed in somewhat different patterns. The Burmese shareholders feel that state aid in the form of a long-term loan is not sufficient; they feel short-term facilities for working capital are also needed. They believe that the industry needs assistance and protection in many other ways, such as reduction of concession rates, duties, fees, charges, etc., procurement of trawlers by the government for charter to the company, and special tax rates and policies.

The company would highly favor a system of repayment of loans in increasing installments, with either a small amount of amortization or none at all at the beginning and an accelerated amortization rate at a later stage, since the growth of the company was retarded in the earlier stages by the present system. At present, there is little opportunity for ploughing back earnings, and amortization stands as a fixed charge. The burden of repayment should be less heavy in the earlier part of the company's existence when assets are not fully productive or utilized, and accelerated later when the company can stand on its own feet. And, in the first stages, the industry should, it is felt, be exempted from taxes for a certain number of years, or subject to especially favorable tax rates.

The annual charter fees amount to over k100,000, and wharfage and port charges to over k15,000. The company has argued that if the trawlers were bought outright by the Burmese government, the payments for charter fees to the Japanese could be saved. The company would then be able to charter the trawlers at more economical rates. This would also save the company the license fees on trawlers, gear, and fishing equipment which are incurred repeatedly when the trawlers undergo docking. The fishing trawlers are treated equally with merchant ships so far as port duties and wharfages are concerned. It is the feeling of the company that all these charges could be done away with or reduced as a token of encouragement and effective assistance to a struggling industry.

The problems of recruiting, training, and remunerating Burmese personnel for the fishing industry have always been serious. The company considers that the government should recruit and send people abroad for such training since the company itself cannot provide sufficient training facilities on its own boats. On return to Burma, these personnel could train other Burmese. The company finds it too expensive to train people abroad, and assistance in this respect from the Burmese government would be very effective.

The government, on the other hand, feels that it has given enough encouragement and assistance with the loans of ten and twenty years and that the industry should now be able to stand on its own feet. The government has promised to speed up the granting of sanctions in order to avoid further hindrance of the company's activities. It cannot immediately provide trawlers, amend income tax rules, change depreciation policies, or reduce port and customs duties. It is nevertheless interested in helping to build separate port facilities and wharves for the fishing trawlers.

The Japanese party is satisfied with the present venture because it receives annual charter fees of about k100,000, and the Japanese crews are afforded employment.

Merck Sharp & Dohme of India Private Ltd.

ORIGIN OF THE ENTERPRISE

Merck Sharp & Dohme of India was formally constituted in the fall of 1958 to undertake the manufacture of certain pharmaceuticals and related products. Prior to its organization, the operations in India of the parent firm had been limited to the export of finished goods, which it had been carrying on for many years through two local distributing firms. One of the local distributing firms was owned by resident British capital, and the other, at first a branch of a Swiss firm, later itself became a joint venture with participation by the original Swiss owner, by the Tata interests of India, and by the general Indian investing public. The existence of the two local distributors is traceable to the activities of Merck and of Sharp and Dohme as separate firms prior to their merger in 1953; both distributors were retained after the merger.

The initiative for the formation of the manufacturing joint venture came from Merck Sharp & Dohme in response to the interest of the Indian government, expressed in connection with its second Five-Year Plan, in the local manufacture of drugs, to provide employment, to build up native skills, and to save foreign exchange. In view of the environment in India, Merck Sharp & Dohme planned from the beginning to undertake its investment in that country on a joint basis with local capital, and its proposal in this respect was ratified by the Indian government in granting approval for the investment.

The conversations between representatives of the United States firm and the Indian government coincided with conversations that were also taking place with representatives of the Soviet Union, who offered to lend substantial sums at very long term and very low interest rates ($20 to $25 million, at a term of 40 years, and at an interest rate of two percent per annum) to help the Indian government develop the manufacture of drugs through State enterprise. The original Indian proposal was for the American firm to go into partnership with a government-owned corporation to produce a long list of needed drugs. The proposal was met by an alternative presented by the American firm for the formation of a private joint venture (Merck Sharp & Dohme of India), plus a technical assistance and licensing arrangement with a government-owned plant for the production of streptomycin and derivatives. The government corporation, Hindustan Antibiotics Ltd., was already in existence at the time of the Merck Sharp & Dohme conversations; it had been producing penicillin for the preceding five or six years. The streptomycin plant is now being built by the government, pursuant to this licensing arrangement.

The local partner for the private joint venture was found in the Tata group, which has highly diversified interests in the country. Merck Sharp & Dohme had already worked with Tata through one of its distributing companies. The distributing company (Voltas Ltd.) is also the distributor of the products of the manufacturing joint venture.

CAPITAL STRUCTURE

The joint venture company has a total authorized capital of rs42 million (close to $9 million), divided into 4,200,000 shares with a nominal value of rs10 each. The initial project, however, which is scheduled for completion during the next three or four years, involves the investment of only one-half of the authorized amount. Approximately $1.5 million have been invested to date. The shares consist of only one class of common stock, with no differentiation whatsoever with respect to voting or any other rights.

The investment in the equity of the enterprise is distributed 60 percent to Merck Sharp & Dohme and 40 percent to the Tata group. This distribution is the one originally proposed by the parent company, and was ratified without question by the Indian authorities. The policy of the parent firm is to have a clear majority, but not to such an overwhelming extent as to result in only perfunctory interest in the enterprise by the local minority investor.

The investment to date by Merck Sharp & Dohme of approximately $900 thousand (60 percent of $1.5 million) has been all in the form of cash, and has covered the requirements of the enterprise for imported capital goods and initial inventories, and has also met some of the local currency requirements of the investment.

In connection with this investment, Merck Sharp & Dohme obtained a convertibility guarantee from the International Cooperation Administration of the United States government in the amount of $5 million. Also, early in 1960, the Indian enterprise received a loan of rs5 million out of the local currency funds administered by the Export-Import Bank of Washington under the program of sales of surplus United States agricultural products.

There is a formal agreement between the parent firm and the subsidiary for the provision of technical assistance, and patents and trademark rights, but no royalties are paid for these services and rights, at least for products covered by the "initial project." Out-of-pocket expenses incurred in the provision of these services, however, are reimbursed, but there is a ceiling to the amount that may be paid by the subsidiary for this purpose, which in fact has already been exceeded, with the parent company having absorbed the excess.

MANAGEMENT AND PERSONNEL

The composition of the board of directors reflects the 60-40 distribution of the stock. Management of the enterprise is left entirely to the American partner by the Indian investors, who, except for the knowledge of their affiliated company, Voltas Ltd., in connection with the distribution of pharmaceuticals, did not have any specialized experience in pharmaceuticals. With the exception of a few key members of the staff, the personnel is entirely Indian. The total staff consists of about 185. The managing director is a

British national, the sales manager is Canadian, the chief of production is American, and the remainder of the employees are all Indian, with just a few exceptions. The firm had no difficulty in accumulating a staff of technically qualified people. From the beginning, the detailing staff of its distributors was drawn upon, and in addition it received many solicitations of employment from qualified people, so that it was easily able to gather together the necessary staff for its operations. It feels that scarcities of qualified personnel exist in India only with respect to upper management functions and high-level financial specialists. Its personnel program has included the bringing of Indian staff members to the United States for training in its own facilities in this country.

ROLE IN THE ECONOMY

The production line of the "initial project" covers steroids, diuretics, some vitamins, and some sulpha drugs. The steroids are to be manufactured from imported intermediate products, while all the others are to be manufactured from the raw material stage, and it is expected that most of the raw materials will be available in India by the time of completion of this phase of the project. Compared to other pharmaceutical manufacturing facilities now in existence in India, of which there are a number involving other American and European firms, this joint venture, representing an investment of about $4.5 million by the time of completion of its first phase, will be one of the largest in the field. It is anticipated that its expansion will be rapid to keep pace with the growth of the Indian economy and the tremendous potential for the use of pharmaceuticals as living standards improve.

EVALUATION

The parent firm intends to follow a policy of long-range growth and accordingly plans to apply profits liberally to reinvestment to achieve that objective. This philosophy was expressed from the beginning of negotiations to the Indian partner, and there was full agreement at the outset on this point. The financially powerful Tata group is similarly not primarily concerned with immediate profits. Accordingly, no problems have arisen on this score by virtue of the joint venture nature of the investment. It has also been possible to work out all other policy questions without the development of any serious problems although, naturally, looking at the situation from a very short-run point of view, more time has probably been involved discussing matters and getting exchanges of points of view than might be the case in a wholly-owned operation where intra-company directives might be sufficient to determine policies with the expenditure of somewhat less time.

The management of the firm has presented no problems different from what the case might be with a wholly-owned investment since for practical purposes the enterprise has been managed the same as if it were a wholly foreign-owned investment.

Except for pharmaceutical rules and regulations which are applicable to all pharmaceutical houses in India, problems with respect to government regulations have been no greater than those of other enterprises that operate in the country, with its myriad official controls deriving from the government's efforts to promote a rapid rate of development and from the recent attainment of independence, which has been accompanied by a pattern of considerable state intervention in the economy. One special problem, which it is believed is in the process of solution, is related to the classification by customs authorities of imported intermediates, which at times have been treated less favorably even than finished products.

This recently formed joint venture enterprise, of considerable magnitude and potential scope, is already obviously a valuable adjunct to the Indian economy, and is likely to make an even greater contribution as it expands in the future. An interesting aspect of it is that relating to the fact that it has been successful in getting allocated to private enterprise an activity that might easily have been taken over entirely by public enterprise, considering the philosophy and pressures in India at the time of its formation, and the interest of the Soviet Union in cooperating with India in this industry. It seems unlikely that this could have been achieved just as easily by a wholly foreign-owned investment, even if the Indian authorities had not insisted that the enterprise be constituted from the beginning with participation by local capital.

Sui Gas Transmission Company Ltd.

ORIGIN OF THE ENTERPRISE

At the very outset in Pakistan's march toward industrialization, there was a severe bottleneck as a result of the shortage of industrial fuels. Coal was mined in Baluchistan, West Pakistan, only in small quantities and was, moreover, of an inferior quality. A British oil company, the Attock Oil Company Ltd., incorporated in England in 1913, was operating in northern West Pakistan, and its total production of oil was 330,082 barrels in 1947. The development of hydro-electric power and the further discovery of oil were the two main hopes of the nation, and policies were therefore framed for their realization. Projects were developed for the generation of hydro-electric power, and for the discovery of oil the government framed petroleum rules which came into effect on September 1, 1949. According to these rules, any exploration or prospecting licenses or mining leases applied for were to be issued only to companies registered in Pakistan, and on the condition that 30 percent of the initial issue of shares be offered to nationals of Pakistan. The Burmah Oil Company Ltd. of London (BOC) set up a subsidiary under these rules by the name of Pakistan Petroleum Ltd., which became the successor to BOC's previous prospecting subsidiary, that is, BOC (Pakistan Concessions) Ltd. Seventy percent of Pakistan Petroleum Ltd.'s share capital was owned by the Burmah Oil Company Ltd., and since only about one percent of the Pakistani share was taken up by the public, the government of Pakistan took up the remaining 29 percent.

In the course of drilling for oil at Sui in the Bugti tribal territory of Baluchistan in West Pakistan, Pakistan Petroleum Ltd. struck large reserves of natural gas in 1951. This event was of far-reaching importance to the economy. Drilling for natural gas was started in October, 1951, and at a depth of approximately 5,000 ft. a thick porous limestone containing reserves of natural gas was discovered. Further development wells were then drilled, and it became an established fact that the reserves were very large.

Both the government of Pakistan and BOC thereupon set out to exploit this find for use in industry generally; not only was this natural gas a cheap and efficient fuel, but, being local, it also afforded a means of saving considerable amounts of foreign exchange which were being paid out for imports of coal and oil. After careful study, it was decided that a separate company, that is, the Sui Gas Transmission Co. Ltd., should be formed to purify this natural gas and transmit it via two independent distributing companies, namely the Indus Gas Co. Ltd. (owned by the Pakistan government) and the Karachi Gas Company Ltd. (owned by private Pakistani investors), to industrial centers of West Pakistan. The Sui Gas Transmission Co. Ltd. was incorporated on February 13, 1954. The Burmah Oil Company (Pakistan Trading) Ltd.—written as BOC (PT) hereafter—incorporated in London and another subsidiary of the Burmah Oil Co. Ltd., was appointed managing agent to the new company, not only because of Burmah Oil's financial interest in the company that discovered the gas, but also because, through its world-wide connections with the oil industry, it was in the best position to provide the technical know-how and equipment needed for effective operation.

CAPITAL STRUCTURE AND TECHNICAL ARRANGEMENTS

The Pakistan Industrial Development Corporation (PIDC) and BOC (PT) were the promoters of the Sui Gas Transmission Company Ltd. and negotiated all matters relating to the formation of the company. The following three contracts were entered into:

1. Managing Agency Agreement dated March 6, 1954 between the company and BOC (PT).

2. Under an agreement contained in correspondence dated January 9, 1954 and February 13, 1954 between Pakistan Petroleum Ltd. and the promoters, arrangements were made for the supply of natural gas by the former to the latter. This agreement sets forth the price of the gas and other conditions of supply. Later, a formal agreement was entered into between the parties.

3. An agreement contained in correspondence dated February 12, 1954 and March 9, 1954 between the Commonwealth Development Finance Company Ltd. of England and the company whereby the former agreed to subscribe to 92,610 shares on the conditions therein stated.

The total authorized capital of Sui Gas was rs150 million, divided into 1.5 million ordinary shares of rs100 each. The value of the issued capital was rs37.8 million, in 378,000 ordinary shares. The entire issued capital was paid up. BOC and the Commonwealth Development Finance Company each subscribed to 24½ percent of the issued capital. The remaining 51 percent was subscribed to by PIDC and Pakistani nationals equally.

The managing agency agreement signed between Sui Gas and BOC (PT) on March 6, 1954 included the following provisions.

(1) The Managing Agents shall serve the Company as sole and exclusive Managing Agents for a period of 20 years, but shall not, as such, have any representation on the Board of Directors of the Company. Any officer of the Managing Agents, however, may be appointed to the Board of Directors as representative of BOC and/or the Commonwealth Development Finance Company Ltd.

(2) Subject to the general control of the Directors of the Company or resolution of the Company in General Meeting, the Managing Agents shall undertake and manage all the business and affairs of the Company.

(3) The Managing Agents shall be responsible for the general administration of the Company's property, books, papers, effects, etc., and shall have full power to purchase and obtain all necessary plant, machinery, equipment, stores, goods and materials of any kind whatsoever.

(4) The Managing Agents shall be responsible for engaging and dismissing all officers and other personnel for the conduct of the Company's business and determining their remunerations and terms of appointment.

(5) The Managing Agents shall have power to institute and defend any legal proceeding by or against the Company, and to act on behalf of the Company in all matters relating to liquidation and insolvency.

(6) The Managing Agents shall be entitled to charge and shall be paid by the Company:

(a) all sums actually disbursed and incurred by the Managing Agents on behalf of the Company;

(b) by way of remuneration for their services a sum equal to: 7½% on the first Rs.5 million of net annual profits; 6¼% on the next Rs.5 million of net annual profits; 5% on any amount by which the profits exceed Rs. 10 million net; and—

(c) an office allowance of Rs.2,500 per month.

(7) If any differences shall arise between the parties hereto touching these presents or the constructions thereof or any clause or thing herein contained or any matter in any way connected with these presents or the operation thereof, then and in every such case the matter in difference shall be referred for decision to two arbitrators, one to be appointed by each of the parties in difference, or in case of the said arbitrators not

agreeing, to an umpire appointed by such arbitrators before proceeding on the reference, and the decision of the arbitrators or of the umpire, as the case may be, shall be final and binding on the parties. The arbitration shall be held in Pakistan and shall be conducted in all respects according to the law in force in Pakistan.

The Sui Gas Transmission Company is a public company limited by shares, registered and incorporated at Karachi under the Companies Act, 1913.

As noted earlier, the total paid-up capital of the company is rs37.8 million of which BOC and the Commonwealth Development Finance Company Ltd. hold 24½ percent each, and PIDC and the Pakistani public 25½ percent each. The BOC and the Commonwealth Development Finance Company Ltd. paid for their shares in pounds sterling.

In accordance with the voting rights stated in the prospectus of Sui Gas on a show of hands every member present has one vote. On a poll, every member has one vote in respect of each share held by him. No member is entitled to vote at any general meeting unless all calls and other sums presently payable by him in respect of shares in the company have been paid.

In addition to the equity capital, the company obtained a loan from the International Bank for Reconstruction and Development in various foreign currencies equivalent to £5 million ($14 million), repayable by installments over approximately 20 years. The rupee equivalent of the loan was rs46.2 million at the official exchange rate obtaining up to July 31, 1955, when the Pakistani rupee was devalued and consequently, the rupee debt of the company to the IBRD went up to a total of rs66,812,112. The IBRD loan was made in the following currencies:

Currency	*Value*	*Sterling Equivalent at Rate Charged by IBRD*
Pounds Sterling	4,274,669	4,274,669
American Dollars	1,998,066	713,595
Dutch Guilders	124,755	11,736
		5,000,000

The amortization schedule provides for the repayment of the loan and interest thereon by half-yearly payments, commencing from August 1, 1956 and ending August 1, 1974, repayment being in the original currencies of withdrawals. The loan is guaranteed by the government of Pakistan and is secured by a trust deed constituting a first charge on all assets of the company.

In addition, it was announced on February 19, 1960 that an agreement had been signed whereby the Development Loan Fund of the United States government will lend $2 million to Sui Gas to cover the foreign exchange costs of expanding the company's natural gas purification plant.

MANAGEMENT AND PERSONNEL

It has already been stated that BOC (PT) is the managing agent of Sui Gas. The day-to-day management of the company thus rests with the BOC (PT) under the overall control of the board of directors. The composition of the board of directors is as follows:

Elected from among the nominees of the PIDC, including the chairman:	3
Elected from among the nominees of BOC:	2
Elected from among the nominees of the Commonwealth Development Finance Company Ltd.:	2
Elected from among the nominees of the remaining shareholders from Pakistan:	2
Total:	9

Thus, out of the nine directors, including the chairman, five represent PIDC and Pakistani shareholders. The chairman of PIDC has so far been chairman of the board of directors. The representatives of the BOC and Commonwealth Development Finance Company Ltd. are British.

A qualification for a director is that he must hold Sui Gas shares in the nominal amount of rs25 thousand but this qualification does not apply where the director is a nominee of a holder of shares to the value of not less than rs2.5 million.

Two main concerns of the board of directors so far have been to increase sales of gas, and the Pakistanization of the company personnel up to the highest levels. Extension of distribution lines to areas farther north is being made and new uses of gas are being developed. This objective has been pursued in collaboration with the government.

In the top administration of the managing agent, there are three Englishmen, occupying the positions of general manager, chief accountant, and technical manager. The administrative manager, however, is a Pakistani. In the next highest category, there are five non-Pakistani and four Pakistani officers. The lowest category of officers, called the covenanted officers, consists of five Pakistanis alone. All these executives serve Sui Gas on a part-time basis, under an integrated service plan with Pakistan Petroleum Ltd. effected by BOC on August 18, 1958. The motive behind this integration was to render managerial control by BOC over both Sui Gas and Pakistan Petroleum more economic and effective.

A second category is of full-time executives and officers working for Sui Gas, though some of them are on loan from BOC. In all, there are 17 executives and 40 covenanted officers working full time, nine of the former class are non-Pakistanis and the remaining 48 are Pakistanis.

Technical direction, in the main, is still in the hands of non-Pakistanis. However, there are seven Pakistani engineers holding responsible jobs, one of them having been to the United States for training as a gas technician. The company is actively carrying out a policy of training Pakistanis with the ultimate object of their replacing their British counterparts.

The hiring of Pakistanis in covenanted positions and also as executives has steadily increased. Pakistani staff are trained on the job usually for a period of six months before they are confirmed.

Besides the officers' category, there are at present 400 employees of the company, including 75 clerks and peons and 325 laborers. Of the 325 laborers, 234 are skilled. These employees are scattered over a distance of about 345 miles from Sui to Karachi, along the path of the Sui-Karachi pipeline.

The wages of employees are made up of a basic wage and a cost-of-living allowance. An unskilled laborer gets a total of about rs112 per month.

The company has a provident fund scheme for its employees, both sides contributing equally. The contribution from each for those earning up to rs200 as basic wage is 1/12th of the basic wage and for those above rs200, 1/20th of the basic wage. In addition, the company has a pension scheme whereby at the age of 55 or after 20 years service with the company, employees earn a life pension which is 40 percent of the average of their last five years' basic salary. A reduction is made in the pension amount where 20 years has not been served provided that the total number of years of service is not less than 15. No pension is earned for service under 15 years.

The company maintains a very liberal medical scheme according to which its employees and their families are entitled to medical attention and full reimbursement of treatment expenses. At Sui, the laborers get free houses and food at subsidized rates at the food shop. Water is carried to Sui from a distance of about 40 miles through a pipeline which cost rs6 million.

The labor force of the company appears to be well satisfied with conditions, and there have been no strikes or other serious conflicts.

GOVERNMENT RELATIONS

The joint venture has a twofold relationship with the government of Pakistan: 1) that from being partly owned by it, and 2) that of being subject to its tax laws and other regulations. The first relationship presents no problem. The government, represented by PIDC, has three directors on the company's board, one of them being its chairman. In fact, the government, being the largest single shareholder of the joint venture, has given its utmost attention to its smooth operation. This has partly accounted for the extraordinary speed with which the joint venture's plans have been executed, particularly with respect to the laying of the pipelines.

As to the second relationship, the situation has also been favorable. The company has not had to pay any taxes to the government so far because of the generous depreciation allowances granted to newly created industrial undertakings by the Income Tax Act. The joint venture does not need any protection as the price of Sui Gas, in terms of heating value, works out to be less than that of coal or oil.

In concert with the government, the price of gas to the public is fixed by the board of directors of Sui Gas, and the two distribution companies, namely, Karachi Gas and Indus Gas. Because these companies are public utilities, the government keeps a close watch on the prices charged. Prices are fixed at the lowest possible limit which will allow them to meet their costs and afford them a reasonable profit. Here it may be noted that Sui Gas started to pay dividends out of profits in its third year of operation.

FINANCIAL RESULTS

Fiscal Years Ending March 31 (*thousands of rupees*)

Item	*1955*	*1956*	*1957*	*1958*	*1959*
Sales	—	5,094	17,236	20,582	23,860
Depreciation on fixed assets	127	1,041	4,347	4,481	4,414
Net profit or	—	—	2,806	3,914	4,192
Net loss	567	1,931	—	—	—
Dividend	—	—	—	2,835	3,780

The table shows that the company is making good progress with respect to sales, which have increased almost fivefold over the period 1956–59. The trend of sales is upward, and it is expected that this trend will be maintained in future years. The company suffered a loss in the years 1955 and 1956. In the fiscal year ending March 31, 1955, there were no sales; sales of gas did not commence until October 1, 1955. Therefore, the loss shown was anticipated by the company in view of operational and administrative expenses and interest payable on the IBRD loan. Again in 1955–56, sales had occurred only for six months—October 1, 1955 to March 31, 1956—and, moreover, due to the devaluation of the rupee, the company's liability with respect to interest on and repayment of the IBRD loan had increased. Thus, the loss in fiscal year 1956 is also easily accountable. The first complete year of operation was 1956–57, which showed a net profit of rs2.8 million. In 1958, profits were 39 percent higher than in the previous year, and in 1959 they increased by 7 percent as compared to 1958. There is an obvious correlation between sales and profits. With the increase in sales, economies have accrued in the purification and transmission costs per cubic foot of gas.

ROLE IN THE ECONOMY

Sui Gas was incorporated on February 13, 1954, and received its certificate to commence business on July 20, 1954. However, before the product of the company could come to the market, pipelines had to be laid from the gas field to the distribution centers. Consequently, a 347-mile gas pipeline from Pakistan Petroleum's gas field in Sui to the industrial centers of Karachi, was laid, and gas began to be supplied to industrial consumers in Karachi on October 1, 1955. As previously indicated, the distribution of gas was given to two new companies—the Indus Gas Company and the Karachi Gas Company. The former is a subsidiary of PIDC and distributes gas to consumers outside the Federal Capital Area of Karachi, and the latter is a public limited company whose entire share capital is owned by Pakistani nationals, and which distributes gas to consumers in Karachi. Sui Gas could not itself handle the distribution of gas (except in the case of certain large consumers and even this only as a temporary measure) in accordance with the agreement entered into with the IBRD.

Another 218-mile pipeline was laid by Sui Gas from Sui to Multan—an upcountry city in the north of West Pakistan—and was turned over to the PIDC in August 1958.

Sui Gas sold to the two distribution companies the distribution lines installed by it along with the auxiliary equipment necessary for their operation, for rs12.1 million. The sum was realized in installments.

Over the years, the total supply of gas by Sui Gas to the Karachi Gas Co. and the Indus Gas Company has shown a marked increase. From 1957 to 1958 the annual sales to the former company increased from 5,053,527 to 6,875,896 thousand cubic feet, an increase of 36.1 percent, and in 1959 the sales increased to 8,831,871, or by 28.45 percent over 1958. To Indus Gas, the sales increased from 2,765,541 to 3,947,757 thousand cubic feet in 1958, representing an increase of 42.8 percent, and in 1959 the sales increased to 4,286,158, or by 8.57 percent over 1958.

Sui gas is natural gas, the most convenient form of fuel nature has provided. It has a high calorific value, burns cleanly and evenly with a higher heat efficiency than either coal or oil, requires the simplest type of equipment for burning (this enables quick and economical conversions of installations which are presently operating on coal or oil), and can be transported cheaply in large volumes over long distances through pipelines. It is an ideal fuel for steam power plant installations, and is a convenient fuel for internal combustion engines and gas turbines of all sizes. In addition, it is an excellent raw material for the chemical industry, in which its most urgent use is for manufacturing synthetic fertilizers in order to increase the production of foodstuffs.

It replaces coal and furnace oil, which were being imported into the country. Prior to the supply of gas, the estimated total production of coal (all in West Pakistan) was some 600,000 tons per year, whereas the total consumption in West Pakistan was some 1,200,000 tons per year. The balance of approximately 600,000 tons had to be met by the import of foreign coal. Similarly, the production of furnace oil in West Pakistan, which was about 100,000 tons, fell far short of the total requirements of West Pakistan, which were over 600,000 tons per year. It is estimated that Sui Gas now affords a saving of about rs27.5 million per year in foreign exchange because of the curtailment of imports of coal and oil.

More importantly, it has made possible a whole new range of industrial planning which otherwise would have been entirely out of the question. New power stations using gas have been planned for three important cities in southern West Pakistan, namely, Karachi, Hyderabad, and Sukkur. Two more cement kilns will be installed at the Zeal-Pak Cement Factory in Hyderabad. In the north, gas will be supplied to a new power station at Multan, and also to a fertilizer factory to be established there. Practically all industries north of Sui now run on Sui gas. The use of natural gas as a household fuel is also expected to grow in the large cities, particularly in the Federal Capital.

Since the business of Sui Gas is confined to the purification and transportation of gas purchased from the Pakistan Petroleum Company at Sui and to its sale to the distribution companies, its plans for expansion are essentially determined by the total demand for gas in West Pakistan. The designed joint capacity of both the Sui/Multan and the Sui/Karachi lines is about 150,000,000 cubic feet of gas daily, but this figure can be increased by compressor stations to about 230,000,000 cubic feet daily. The total demand for gas falls well short of this capacity. However, it can be taken for granted that, as new uses are developed for natural gas, and also as the total intake in the already established uses increases, the demand for gas will also rise and it is expected that by 1962–63 the consumption figure will be on the order of 130,000,000 cubic feet per day.

The present capacity of the company's purification plant is 70,000,000 cubic feet daily, but in order to meet the increasing demand expected, the company has embarked on a process of plant expansion. In this connection, as previously indicated, the company has recently obtained a $2 million loan from the United States Development Loan Fund.

EVALUATION

The relationship between the principal collaborators, namely, the government of Pakistan acting through PIDC and BOC (PT), appears to be quite smooth and stable. A unique feature of this joint venture in Pakistan is that the Commonwealth Development Finance Company of England was persuaded to buy its shares in substantial amount. The loans from the IBRD and the DLF further assure the stability of the venture.

The present estimate regarding the available deposits of gas at Sui indicate that, even if the consumption of gas is built up to about 130,000,000 cubic feet per day, these deposits will last 75 years or so. This gas has already had a material impact on the economy of Pakistan and, like coal in England, it will provide the basis for the continued growth of industry in the country.

Tata Engineering and Locomotive Company Ltd. (Telco)—Automobile Division

ORIGIN OF THE ENTERPRISE

The Automobile Division of Telco at Jamshedpur (Bihar) was organized in 1954 to manufacture diesel road vehicles.

Telco had been formed in 1945, with registered offices at Bombay, primarily to develop the manufacture of locomotive and heavy engineering products. By 1954, the manufacture and supply of railway underframes had become unprofitable, and the demand for steam road rollers was no longer sufficient for their economic production. Upon termination of government contracts, the production of these items ceased, and the facilities and space were available for an alternative field of production. The future of cheap, economical road transportation as a supplement to the overworked railroads and a means of connecting vast stretches of rural areas with urban markets and industrial centers seemed assured particularly in the light of the country's first Five-Year Plan for the integrated development of national resources.

Since there was no native supply of capital equipment and technical knowledge, foreign collaboration was essential. The government of India's Industrial Policy Resolution of 1948 and the Prime Minister's subsequent statement in Parliament assuaged fears of expropriation by nationalization, and assured remittance facilities for profits on foreign capital. Negotiations with Daimler-Benz A.G. of West Germany for the manufacture of diesel-engined commercial vehicles (truck and bus chassis with capacities from 3.5 to 5.2 tons) were initiated, and an agreement was reached on March 2, 1954. The agreement covered a period from April 1, 1954 to March 31, 1969, and was formally signed on October 3, 1955, by the representatives of Daimler-Benz A.G., Telco, and Tata Industries Ltd. (the managing agent of Telco).

CAPITAL STRUCTURE, AND TECHNICAL ARRANGEMENTS

The agreement provides, *inter alia*, that:

(i) Telco shall be appointed the sole selling-agents for Daimler Benz products in India, Pakistan, Burma and Ceylon, and the price to be paid for such products will not be higher than that charged to any other market, except under certain special circumstances;

(ii) Daimler Benz will give technical advice, information and assistance as regards the layout of additional factory buildings and extensions for the automobile division to be set up at Tatanagar (Jamshedpur) and with regard to the selection and arrangement of the plant, equipment, services and facilities for manufacturing Daimler Benz trucks and other products. Mercedes Benz trucks of three tons and above will be the first items produced, although later programs may extend to passenger cars;

(iii) The production program will provide for successive stages of manufacturing parts and components with a view ultimately to attaining manufacture of complete units by Telco; the components and parts must conform to Daimler Benz standards of quality;

(iv) Daimler Benz will grant Telco, on an exclusive basis, the necessary manufacturing rights including patents and patent rights and will supply secret and other information relating to the manufacturing program; they will also supply all necessary drawings and designs and will assist Telco in obtaining the manufacturing and other licenses for turning out any parts or components procured by Daimler Benz from outside sources; the parts to be purchased and to be manufactured in India will be selected by mutual consent and Daimler Benz will promptly communicate to Telco all technical information relating to improvements and developments within the field of actual or prospective manufacture;

(v) Daimler Benz will supply at cost price all jigs, tools and fixtures or drawings and designs thereof needed by Telco for the manufacture of components and parts; they will also make available to Telco the parts and components to be incorporated into Telco's product in accordance with the approved manufacturing program;

(vi) The parties are exclusively bound to each other in regard to manufacture and sale of automotive products within the territories of India, Pakistan, Burma, and Ceylon; neither party will in its area of manufacture, buy for resale or sell automotive products or parts thereof without mutual agreement nor shall it negotiate with third parties in regard to manufacturing and selling rights in the automotive field covered by the agreement; Telco will not export, directly or indirectly, complete units or parts obtained from Daimler Benz outside its area of operation without the written consent of its associates;

(vii) Telco may develop its own designs of automotive parts (without payment of royalty to the associates) after consultation with Daimler Benz and if their production does not encroach upon the space needed for manufacture of Daimler Benz parts;

(viii) Telco shall be entitled to the use of the trade name, Tata-Mercedes-Benz in addition to the Mercedes Benz Star when the Telco proportion of manufacture becomes 30% or more; parts manufactured in India may bear the word Tata besides the Mercedes Benz Star;

(ix) On the expiration or termination of the agreement, Telco may continue production with the benefit of all technical information and experience acquired but without the use of the Daimler Benz name or trade mark in any manner;

(x) During the time that suitably qualified and trained Indian personnel are not available, Daimler Benz shall, within their ability to do so, place at the disposal of Telco the required technical personnel (who will in their turn train Indian personnel) and will also provide training facilities in their Mannheim plants and establishments for Indian personnel who will be paid on the same basis as German trainees;

(xi) Telco will be responsible for obtaining from the Government of India the licenses and permits required for setting up the Automobile Division within three months of the date of agreement, which is entered into subject to the approval of the Government of India and the Government of the Federal Republic of West Germany.

The agreement also provides for further issue of capital shares and management participation by the foreign associates, payment to them of a royalty for the first five years of commercial production (the royalty is fixed at one percent when Telco manufacture of parts accounts for 50 percent or less of the total value of the vehicle unit, and 1½ percent when the proportion exceeds 50 percent); payment to them of a fixed percentage of the net profits in addition to the royalty (7.5 percent of the net profits of the Automobile Division. No period limit is laid down in this case. In addition, as holders of shares worth rs8 million, the associates are entitled to dividends); a formula determining the price to be paid for the parts and components received from them; and separation of the Automobile Division's accounts from Telco's other accounts. In the territory covered by the agreement, Telco products are to be given priority for sale; to meet any extra demands, Telco is to endeavor to obtain necessary import licenses for products of Daimler-Benz for sale in the territory. The agreement is terminable at six months' written notice in case of a serious breach of terms or conditions, *force majeure* supervening for a period of six months, or the government of India's or any statutory corporation's confiscating the enterprise or a substantial part of it.

ROLE IN THE ECONOMY

Preparatory work for setting up the assembly line had been done early in 1954, and on May 1, the government of India's approval of the progressive scheme of manufacturing Tata-Mercedes-Benz diesel vehicles (the name given to the collaborative product) with an annual output of 3,000 units was received. On October 1, assembling began and the first complete vehicle was turned out on October 15.

Various shops have since been erected and machines installed for the dual purpose of assembly and manufacture; the assembly line was completed in October, 1954; a painting shop was erected in December following; a frame shop, press shop, sheet metal shop, and machine shop were erected in March, 1955; the storage arrangements for the vehicles and a spare parts warehouse were ready in 1954; and the experimental and testing section was completed in July, 1955.

The annual report for 1958–59 shows a substantial increase in the local manufacture of parts for the vehicle—engine, gearbox, transmission, axle, frame. The company claims that the product is in every respect comparable to the standards of Daimler-Benz in their German factories.

The popularity of the TMB vehicles, based on their strength and quality, created such an upsurge in demand that it was necessary to revise the production target to an annual output of 12,000 units, from the initial plan of 3,000 units. This increase has been approved by the government of India, and the facilities for the additional output are scheduled to be completed by January, 1961. In this revised scheme the "line-method" of production, which demands more initial capital, was substituted for the "group-method" previously followed for keeping the capital low. (The group-method relies on a number of jobs being done by the same machine; this involves frequent changes in tooling and setting and calls for higher skill and training in the operator; the result is proportionately higher production costs. The line-method provides for a single operation along the line by a particular machine; the individual's skill becomes less important but because of the high capital cost involved, the method cannot be adopted unless the output is large enough to compensate for the additional investment. It proves ultimately to be more economical than the group-method). Production is now in accordance with this revised scheme.

While the demand for TMB vehicles continues at a high level and far exceeds the available supplies, production progress has been impeded by foreign exchange difficulties and the slow growth of ancillary industries. Thus, import restrictions have been responsible for shortages in certain types of spare parts; as the company's own manufacturing program expands, the need for import of spare parts will progressively decrease.

MANAGEMENT

The Automobile Division is an integral part of Telco which is administered and managed by Tata Industries (Bombay), the managing agent of Telco. The division has a manager who works subject to the administrative control of the general manager of Telco.

There are some services utilized in common by the Automobile

Division and Telco, and these are under the administrative control of the general manager of Telco. These common services include personnel matters, accounts, plant maintenance, and civil engineering.

The administrative and managerial structure is designed to insure unity of command. Even the administration of the accounts section is under the control of the general manager. No formal delegations of power in any branch have been made. But the auto manager and his German subordinates apparently enjoy considerable autonomy in day-to-day administration and management, a result they have created by their devotion to duty and hard work.

Two of the directors of Telco are Germans, as stipulated in the agreement with Daimler-Benz, who visit India at least once a year. German managerial and technical personnel numbers 44. Included in this group are the manager, the chief superintendent, the assistant manager, and the planning engineer.

The Indian understudies, who are expected ultimately (within three years generally) to replace the German technicians, number 58, 8 of whom are being trained in Germany. The understudies belong to the categories of assistant engineer, foreman, and assistant foreman. It is the duty of the Germans assigned to the auto works to train their understudies, some being sent to Germany for advanced training with Daimler-Benz.

FINANCIAL RESULTS

Out of the total authorized share capital of Telco, amounting to rs70 million, ordinary share capital for rs20 million has been issued to meet a part of the capital requirements of the Automobile Division. Of this sum, rs8 million has been issued to Daimler-Benz and rs12 million to ordinary shareholders of Telco in proportion to their previous holdings of the capital equity. A sum of rs15 million has been raised through the issue of five percent debentures valued at rs1,000 each repayable in 1965 or earlier at the option of Telco. The company has a cash credit arrangement, for the benefit of the Automobile Division, with the Bank of India and Central Bank of India, for rs60 million a year. Daimler-Benz allows a credit of only two months from the date of dispatch of goods ex-factory.

The enterprise is allowed by the government to charge 10 percent over cost to the dealer, who in turn is allowed a margin of 7½ percent on his sales to the public. While prices of the company's products are higher than the comparable products in Germany, they are lower than in other countries where Daimler-Benz vehicles are produced. According to the annual report of the chairman of the company on August 19, 1959, the retail price of the TMB truck is about 27 percent higher than that of the same vehicle in Germany, but the comparable prices in Argentina, Brazil, and Australia are 87 percent, 59 percent, and 48 percent respectively, higher than in Germany.

The company made some profits in the first year of production and has since been consistently earning profits. For the financial year ended March 31, 1959, Telco distributed a 5 percent dividend on preference shares and 9 percent on ordinary shares.

The annual report of 1957–58 indicated that the directors, "in view of the satisfactory financial results," sanctioned the payment of a bonus amounting to two months' basic salary to all employees who had put in not less than a year's service and proportionate amounts to employees with less than a year's service. This was raised to two and a half months for the year ended March 31, 1959.

PERSONNEL

In addition to wages and salaries, other allowances are paid. These consist of cost-of-living allowance, food rebate, and marriage allowance. The minimum monthly wage combined with the allowances amounts to rs65.

Bonuses are categorized as production, maintenance, or service bonuses, and are paid differentially to employees in these categories. The maintenance bonus is allowed at the rate of ⅔ of the production bonus, and the service bonus is paid at the rate of ⅓ of the maintenance bonus to those earning rs200 or less a month. For determining the basic production bonus, the work in various shops is grouped and standard man-hours and machine-hours are prescribed, taking into consideration the ratio between German and Indian productivity. Those achieving productivity at the rate of 85 percent or more of the standard are entitled to a bonus payment.

In practice it has been found that average efficiency rates oscillate around 100 percent. As indicated the production bonus, computed as a percentage of wages, provides the basis for calculating the rates for the non-productive bonuses.

The employer contributes equally to the provident fund of the employee at the rate of 6½ percent of pay.

By 1954, 23 percent of the employees had been provided with housing accommodations. The percentage has now risen to 40 percent, and the management is conscious of the benefits of keeping workers contented in this manner. A first-class canteen provides vegetarian lunches at the subsidized rate of only five annas (the equivalent of about seven cents). Workers have the right to 15 days leave with pay once a year, and the monthly-rated staff is allowed a month's leave in addition to 7 days occasional leave. There are facilities for sports and medical care within the factory.

Promotion to superior posts is generally made on the basis of seniority and suitability. Suitability is determined by the head of the department. The Labor Union can intervene, but there is an understanding that it will not do so for the supervisory staff. The Apprentice Training School, taking 100 boys every year, gives preference to sons of employees.

In the area of workers' consultation, three committees (rates committee, works committee, and labor relations committee) operate at various levels. The labor relations committee considers matters of policy between representatives of the management and workers.

While, initially, cooperation between management and labor was very satisfactory, the year 1957 was disturbed by serious labor disputes. A violent strike organized by the Communist-led young Jamshedpur Mazdoor Union affected most of the industrial establishments in Jamshedpur, including Telco. Actual loss of work hours at Telco was small, and the management, after the strike, took disciplinary action against the principal leaders, on the ground that the strike was illegal since the matters at issue were being referred for adjudication to the Industrial Tribunal by the government of India. In an award made during 1959, the Tribunal decided the issues in favor of the company. Since then, labor-management relations have shown a substantial improvement.

EVALUATION

In evaluating the contribution of this enterprise to national development, first consideration must be given to the fine vehicle it has produced for the Indian roads. The vehicle is strong enough to negotiate bad roads and, therefore, suits Indian conditions. Its engine has a quick pick-up and high capacity to develop power. It provides an important contact between rural and urban areas, industrial centers, and consumer markets. The low operation cost of TMB vehicles has given economic incentives to transportation of goods and passengers, and tended to relieve pressure on the overworked railway system.

West German association seems to have created a love for hard work in Indian personnel. But the somewhat authoritarian methods of management of the Germans, and differences of temperament and background between supervisors and workers sometimes create problems. Indian workers, although quiet and peace loving by nature, occasionally find it difficult to accept all that the German supervisors ask them to do. The Germans often adhere almost fanatically to the principle of giving precedence to efficiency over length of service and this creates discontent in the senior workers. If the principle is unerringly followed, it could lead to labor troubles. But the Germans are apparently also learning to adjust themselves to the local conditions.

The training programs are giving India its own automotive experts.

The foreign exchange savings, as a result of the development of local manufacture, are likely to amount to rs150–200 million over a five-year period even if payments to Daimler-Benz, and the importation of foreign raw material components of manufactured parts are taken into consideration.

On the whole, the collaboration seems to have worked to the mutual advantage of the partners, and there is sufficient reason to believe that Indo-German collaboration is bound to increase in volume and variety in the years to come.

Tube Investments of India Ltd.

ORIGIN OF THE ENTERPRISE

The bicycle industry in India has established itself as one of the leading light engineering industries supplying the cheapest form of individual transport. Before 1947, there was only one bicycle manufacturing unit in the country producing complete cycles. The annual output in the best prewar year was about 50,000 bicycles. By 1951, at the beginning of the first Five-Year Plan, two more manufacturing units in collaboration with well-known British manufacturers came into production, and the output rose to 114,000. These two units had a great advantage due to the financial backing and technical knowledge of the foreign manufacturers associated with them, and they gave a decided impetus to the bicycle industry in India.

One of these two units started early in the post-independence period was T. I. Cycles of India Limited, which came into existence in September, 1949. In September, 1955, an associated company called Tube Products of India Limited was incorporated; in January, 1959, the two companies were merged, and in September of that year the name Tube Investments of India Limited was adopted.

The factory covers an area of about 56 acres, located 13 miles from Madras City at Ambattur.

CAPITAL STRUCTURE

The authorized capital of the concern was originally rs7 million, made up of 70,000 ordinary shares of rs100 each. The capital investment ratio between the Indian and British interests was 51 to 49. However, equal representation was given to both on the board of directors.

The main features of the original agreement, dated October 30, 1950, between T. I. Cycles of India, on the one hand, and Tube Investments, and the Hercules Cycle & Motor Co. of England, on the other, were as follows:

(i) Tube Investments Ltd. of England to be paid Rs. 1,000,000 in the form of 10,000 ordinary shares of Rs. 100 each in T. I. Cycles of India,

Ltd., in consideration of the right acquired by the latter to manufacture bicycles with the "Hercules" Trade Mark in India.

(ii) T. I. Cycles of India Ltd. to manufacture the bicycles as per the specifications prescribed by Tube Investments Ltd., the latter to have the right to inspect the manufacture.

(iii) T. I. Cycles of India Ltd. to use the Trade Mark "Hercules-India" on the bicycles manufactured by them and no other trademark.

(iv) The specifications of manufacture to be deemed confidential.

(v) The agreement to be terminated:

(a) if the original Indian group of T. I. Cycles of India Ltd. cease to be the beneficial holders of 25% of the issued ordinary share capital; or

(b) if the directors of T. I. Cycles of India Ltd. are unable to take the directions of Tube Investments Ltd.; or

(c) on breach or default of agreement which breach or default is not remedied within 30 days of the receipt of notice; or

(d) on liquidation of the company; or

(e) on cancellation of the Trade Mark by the Registrar.

After some years of successful operation, T. I. Cycles of India decided to increase the capacity of its factory. It obtained the sanction of the government of India, pursuant to the Industries Development and Regulation Act (1951) as amended. At the same time, the company had under consideration various proposals for taking up new lines of manufacture of certain components.

In September, 1955, as an adjunct to T. I. Cycles of India, Tube Products of India Ltd. was incorporated. It engaged in the manufacture of steel tubes and particularly steel tubing required for the manufacture of cycles. This company also hoped to supply components to other industries, such as the boiler and automobile industries, as well as supplying tubing to other cycle manufacturers.

The financial requirements necessary for increasing the capacity of the cycle factory were estimated at rs5 million, and those for the expansion of the tube products factory and for the establishment of a new cold rolling mill at rs12 million. The major share of the capital involved was in the form of foreign currency to finance the import of plant and machinery. The management of the two concerns and their foreign collaborators, after giving thoughtful consideration to the methods of providing the required finances, and in particular the foreign exchange, came to the conclusion that in order to achieve effectively and economically the expansion programs contemplated, it was necessary that the two companies be amalgamated by a merger. Accordingly, an agreement was entered into between the two companies on November 14, 1958, which became effective on January 22, 1959. Tube Products was absorbed by T. I. Cycles, and the name was changed to Tube Investments of India Limited on September 16, 1959.

The authorized capital of the company was raised to rs70 million. The management also came to the conclusion that the subscribed capital of the firm should be raised to rs25 million in the following way: rs7 million to be issued to the shareholders of T. I. Cycles of India for subscription at par, the company to allot thereafter rs5.96 million, being 59,600 shares of rs100 each, credited as fully paid up for consideration other than cash to the shareholders of Tube Products of India. A further capital of rs500 thousand, being 5,000 shares of rs100 each, was allotted to Tube Investments (United Kingdom) in consideration of their agreeing to grant their trade mark rights, patent licences, etc. The balance was to be allotted to all the shareholders, after the completion of the amalgamation, in such a way that the holding of Tube Investments (United Kingdom) was brought to 60 percent of the proposed subscribed capital and that of the others remained, as nearly as convenient, proportionate to their original holding. This arrangement included an understanding that the foreign capital investment would, at a later date, be brought down from 60 percent to 52.5 percent of the subscribed capital.

In addition to the increase in capital, the company also negotiated with their British associates, a loan of £1 million at six percent per annum, repayable in two equal installments at the end of five and ten years respectively from the date of issue.

ROLE IN THE ECONOMY

The development of the industry as a whole in India has not followed the same pattern as in more highly industrialized countries. The industrially advanced countries developed the subsidiary industries specializing in the manufacture of component parts common to the whole industry, and these parts were supplied to the major manufacturers, who thus saved the expense of putting up separate plants to manufacture sufficient quantities to meet their individual requirements. In India, the burden of component production has rested on the major manufacturers themselves. As a consequence, the anomaly arises that in a country which is comparatively retarded industrially, the major manufacturers of bicycles are producing 90 to 95 percent of the total component parts which make up the cycle.

Tube Investments of India is now making 17,500 bicycles per month. Nearly 95 percent of the components which go into the bicycle are either manufactured in the factory or locally bought. The remaining five percent is imported from abroad. There is every reason to hope that in the very near future the concern will be manufacturing bicycles with components wholly and completely made at its plant.

The bicycle industry was granted protection by the government on the recommendation of the Tariff Commission. The government decided to impose a specific duty of rs60 per cycle imported, as it was felt that only a high protective tariff wall could insure the smooth expansion of the indigenous industry. The policy of the government to make the bicycle industry in India self-sufficient has been ably and actively supported by the Indian manufacturers and this cooperation between the government and the manufacturers is evidenced by the fact that while the indigenous manufacturers were depending on an allowed import of components of the value of rs80 per pack in 1953, they are now managing with imported components worth rs7.50 only.

In addition to the Hercules bicycle, the company has started producing another well-known brand of bicycle, the Phillips, as well as Brampton fittings. A plant to produce both bicycle chains and industrial chains is being erected, and was scheduled to begin production toward the latter half of 1960.

FINANCIAL RESULTS

The progress of the concern can be judged from the following figures of profit and loss since 1950:

Year	*Loss*	*Profit*
	(*rupees*)	
1950	76,386	
1951	753,478	
1952		61,278
1953		792,240
1955		1,548,408
1956		1,586,605
1957		3,690,565

The profit in 1959 amounted to rs2,411,166, having declined from earlier levels as a result of increased costs of raw materials and labor with no corresponding increase in the price of bicycles, as well as because of shortages of raw materials supply.

MANAGEMENT AND PERSONNEL

The general control and direction of the company's management is vested in a board of directors which has at present a membership of eight. According to the articles of association, the company can have not more than ten and not less than four members on the board of directors. The day-to-day affairs of the company are carried on by two managing directors.

The factory employs 390 salaried employees and 1,060 hourly paid workers. Most of the employees reside in Madras City, but it is expected that as Ambattur gains industrial importance, they will settle near the factory site. In this connection, the company has recently started an industrial housing scheme, having acquired a large area for this purpose in a village adjoining Ambattur.

Indian engineers were sent by the concern to Birmingham, England, for technical training in the initial years of the enterprise. Three foreign technicians approved by the government of India are now guiding Indian personnel at the factory. Labor-management relations have been cordial.

EVALUATION

How the slightest improvement in per capita income and an increase in industrial output affect the need for various forms of personal transport can be seen from the fact that, against an import into India of 160,000 bicycles in peak and boom years in pre-independence days, today, in spite of the fact that the country is manufacturing nearly 700,000 bicycles per annum, the demand is still growing.

Tube Investments of India provides an example of a highly successful joint venture which has taken up the challenge of the ever-growing demand for bicycles in India. The British have provided both capital and technical assistance and have added a fund of good will which redounds to the benefit of the parent concern. The manufactures of Tube Investments of India Ltd. have fully established themselves in the market.

Financially, the company has been recording a satisfactory increase in profits since two years after its establishment. With the government's policy of protection, and a constantly increasing demand for the company's products, there is no doubt that it will grow in strength.

III. Middle East

E. R. Squibb & Sons Ilaclar A.O.

ORIGIN OF THE ENTERPRISE

E. R. Squibb & Sons Ilaclar A.O. was founded in Turkey about a decade ago. The firm, which is an affiliate of Olin Mathieson Chemical Corporation, was organized in 1951 and ground was broken the same year for the erection of a manufacturing laboratory at Istanbul. Two years later the facilities were completed. These included special rooms for the packaging of antibiotics under sterile conditions and testing laboratories for the examination of all products during manufacture and in final form before being placed on the market.

With the completion of production facilities, Squibb products prepared in Turkey were made available to the Turkish medical and pharmaceutical professions for the first time. Previously, they had been imported from the United States. The first group of products included some of the most important antibiotics available at that time.

Recognizing the need for a source of modern, high-quality pharmaceuticals, the Industrial Bank of Turkey encouraged the Squibb move by making available to Squibb Ilaclar Turkish funds from the Marshall Plan Private Enterprise Fund.

The primary objective of Squibb Ilaclar is to provide to the medical and pharmaceutical professions in Turkey modern drugs required for the practice of medicine. Because the latest production techniques used by Squibb in the United States are available to the Turkish organization, it is possible to duplicate exactly Squibb products manufactured in the United States and in other Squibb plants throughout the world. Through its close working relationship with the Squibb Institute for Medical Research, Squibb Ilaclar is also enabled to place new drugs on the market shortly after they have been tested and deemed valuable. In addition, the research and development facilities of Squibb in New York have made it possible for Squibb Ilaclar to market certain products designed exclusively for Turkey. The second objective is to accomplish all of this within the framework of the national economy. This aim is attained by manufacturing within Turkey, by employing Turkish nationals, and, since importation of these drugs is no longer necessary, by conserving urgently needed foreign exchange to some extent.

The pharmaceuticals manufactured and processed by Squibb in Turkey encompass a wide range of products and medical requirements. The present list comprises antibiotics, including recently developed antifungal preparations, and drugs for use in combating tuberculosis, hematinics, vitamins, tranquilizers and drugs to reduce high blood pressure, cardiac preparations, medications for treatment of ulcers and bronchial ailments, pediatric products, dermatological products and a recently discovered coricosteroid for the treatment of rheumatic disease, allergies and skin conditions.

CAPITAL STRUCTURE AND TECHNICAL ARRANGEMENTS

At the inception of the Turkish venture, a "know-how" agreement was signed between Squibb Ilaclar and Squibb in New York, by which the Squibb research organization is to keep the Turkish company constantly informed of the results of its research activities. In addition, the New York organization agreed to test materials provided by Turkey through its facilities in New York and London; to apply quality control tests to samples of pharmaceuticals manufactured by Squibb Ilaclar to assure their compliance with Squibb standards; to keep the Turkish staff informed about new equipment and machinery which might prove useful; and to install the accounting system of the company and to review it from time to time. For this "know-how," a royalty is paid by Squibb Ilaclar to Squibb in New York.

Technical and scientific personnel were provided from New York during the early stages of manufacturing for instruction, assistance and training of Turkish manufacturing, technical and scientific personnel. In addition, the New York organization periodically sends a quality control auditor to Turkey to inspect processing, tests, and controls. This is done to insure a final product which will fully meet the same high Squibb standards as those which apply to its pharmaceuticals produced in New York or in any of its other plants.

Squibb Ilaclar facilities represent an initial investment of over 2½ million TL (Turkish liras). Of the initial capital of 1,400,000 TL, equivalent at that time to about $500,000, 71 percent or $355,357 was contributed by E. R. Squibb & Sons, New York, in payment of 1,990 original shares. The remaining 29 percent was provided by Turkish investors. The balance of the funds required for the investment was acquired through a loan from the Industrial Development Bank of Turkey.

The Turkish equity investment was made in Turkish funds; the Squibb (New York) contribution in United States dollars ($355,357). At the same time, Squibb obtained licenses from the Turkish Ministry of Finance to import the necessary machinery and equipment.

Under the loan agreement dated December 8, 1951 between E. R. Squibb & Sons Ilaclar A.O. and the Industrial Development Bank of Turkey, Squibb Turkey borrowed 1,250,000 TL from the Marshall Plan Private Enterprise Fund, to be repaid in ten installments beginning June 6, 1955 and ending December 31, 1959.

The amount of capital has since been increased by reinvestment of earnings through stock dividends to 4,200,000 TL. This procedure was carried out in accordance with the latest (1954) Law for the Encouragement of Foreign Capital Investment in Turkey.

ROLE IN THE ECONOMY

Net sales for Squibb Ilaclar products have been as follows:

Year	*Sales in Turkish Liras* [a]
1953	1,738,000
1954	7,707,000
1955	16,192,000
1956	16,884,000 [b]
1957	11,292,000
1958	10,410,000

[a] Turkey has undergone a period of steady inflation since the end of World War II and all figures should be considered in this light.

[b] Sales increased until 1955 but 1956 sales remained almost stationary because of exchange shortages.

Net profits for Squibb Ilaclar for 1958 were 11.6 percent.

The growth and progress of the company may be seen in the growth of the staff. In 1953, the first year of production, Squibb employed 190 people; in May, 1959, the staff consisted of 309; 150 of this group are technicians. Another index of growth is the constant increase in the number of pharmaceuticals produced by Squibb Ilaclar, particularly the inclusion in its line of the latest medical discoveries. In 1953, Squibb placed on the market 28 products. This group comprised important antibiotics, hematinics, vitamins, including a special vitamin for children, and a product used for heart and bronchial conditions. In 1954, it added another 20 products. Among these were a new antihypertensive-tranquilizer, improved sulfa and penicillin compounds, a cardiac drug, B-12—a specific for pernicious anemia, an improved hematinic-vitamin combination, a muscle relaxant important in surgery and diagnosis, and antispasmodics. A new anti-tuberculosis drug, discovered at the Squibb Institute for Medical Research, which revolutionized the treatment of tuberculosis and its rate of cure, was marketed by Squibb Ilaclar during the next year. In 1956 the firm introduced streptomycin, also important in the treatment of tuberculosis and many other diseases. Two other medications were also added: a drug for treatment of severe high blood pressure, and a medication for ulcer treatment; and in 1957 another antihypertensive was introduced.

Still another Squibb Institute discovery, a dermatological preparation whose development opened up new horizons in pharmaceutical research, was incorporated into the Squibb line of products made in Turkey in 1958. A corticosteroid developed as a result of this research was added to the Turkish list in 1959. The product is used in the treatment of a wide range of disorders, particularly in rheumatic disease, allergies, and skin ailments. Other new products were the first antifungal antibiotic and the first antibacterial-antifungal agent (both made available through Squibb development processes). New tranquilizers were introduced, including a Squibb discovery with antiemetic properties which extends its range of use from psychiatry to surgery and obstetrics.

Currently, at full capacity, the Squibb Ilaclar laboratories can convert almost $2.4 million worth of raw materials into finished pharmaceuticals, about half the supply needed by Turkey.

Squibb Ilaclar has established a Squibb Encouragement Fund whose purpose is to encourage technical research in Turkey, to assist physicians in following special fields of interest, and to help keep physicians throughout the country posted on the latest medical advances. The fund is administered by a board composed of the deans of the three medical colleges: the University of Istanbul, the University of Ankara, and Izmir University, and professors of pharmacology from the University of Istanbul and Ankara University. This board meets annually to review applications and to decide on grants.

The fund provides money and other assistance in the following four areas:

1. Scholarships. Squibb of Turkey provides four scholarships, one in each of the medical schools in the University of Ankara, University of Istanbul and University of Izmir, and one in the School of Pharmacy in Istanbul.

2. Fellowships. The purpose of the fellowship is to enable young Turkish physicians to increase their knowledge and experience in a field of their interest in the United States. Recently a Turkish physician has been doing graduate work in rheumatic disease at New York University Medical College under the Squibb Fellowship.

3. Research Grants. Grants are provided annually to assist a qualified individual to carry on research in a specific medical field. A recent recipient of this grant, an assistant professor of the School of Pharmacy in Istanbul, has investigated a native plant, "ephedra major," for its ephedrine content and its possible content of khellin.

4. Symposia. Squibb recognizes the ever-accelerating pace of medical achievements and the constantly growing complexity of medical practice. At the same time, it is aware of the difficulties faced by the busy practitioner in keeping abreast of modern medicine. To overcome this difficulty in Turkey, Squibb has instituted a series of annual symposia to bring physicians not only the latest information on medical advances in a particular field but also an assessment and evaluation of such advances by practitioners who are experts in their fields. While the symposia are held under Squibb sponsorship and are made possible through Squibb financial as-

sistance, the choice of subject is determined independently by the board of the Squibb Encouragement Fund, which is composed entirely of faculty members of professional schools. All physicians in Turkey are invited to attend these symposia, which are conducted under the guidance of an outstanding medical leader or teacher. Lectures and panel discussions by experts in the subjects under consideration are presented at the symposia. Recent symposia have dealt with anemia and liver disease. The proceedings are then published and distributed by Squibb to all physicians in Turkey. This provides information to those unable to attend and serves as a record for those who participated.

In addition to the usual contribution to community organizations, such as the "Red Crescent" (counterpart of "Red Cross"), some of which provide educational facilities, Squibb Ilaclar in 1957 made a donation to Robert College for the foundation of a School of Business. This school is expected to produce professionally trained executives to serve the needs of Turkey's expanding industry.

MANAGEMENT AND PERSONNEL

E. R. Squibb & Sons Ilaclar A.O. is administered by a board of directors, composed of eight members, elected by company shareholders. Five of the board members are Americans, and three are Turks. The board of directors elects an executive director from among its own members. The executive director is the only resident American in the firm. The executive director is assisted by three assistant directors who are heads of the three divisions of the company, namely production, sales, and finance. These assistant directors are all Turks. The executive director and the three assistant directors constitute the administrative committee, and are responsible for the day-to-day administration of the company.

Squibb Ilaclar works closely with government health and research bureaus and makes its facilities available to such organizations. Squibb scientific personnel are available to the government for consultation as part of a continuing program of cooperation with the government to improve the health standards of the nation.

Labor relations at Squibb Ilaclar have been amicable and uneventful. Wages paid are slightly higher than for comparable work in similar type plants. Squibb believes that in this manner it attracts a higher type of worker, which it considers important because of its rigid standards in producing pharmaceuticals of uniformly high quality.

Staff training is for many individuals a continuous process. For example, the head of the Quality Control Laboratory was recently sent to the Squibb laboratory in Italy to learn the latest tests and controls to be applied to new products. The Production Department of Squibb in Turkey has a training system for talented workers, leading to better jobs at higher pay. As a result, a number of production workers have been promoted from the ranks to supervisory jobs. When a man joins the Squibb Ilaclar organization to become a detailman, i.e., a representative who visits pharmacies, physicians, hospitals and clinics to explain Squibb products, he is given a brief but intensive schooling in the technical aspects of Squibb products as well as in the administrative and commercial activities of the organization. After supervised experience in the field and additional training, the new representative is recalled to Istanbul for a formal training course. Here he is given intensive instruction in physiology, Squibb product information, Squibb services to the physician, selling instruction and "paper work." Lectures are delivered by top executives and professional men in the Turkish organization.

EVALUATION

The history of the past decade has proven the wisdom of Squibb's move in Turkey. Greater industrialization has led to higher standards of living and better education. The future promises an ever-increasing demand for high grade pharmaceuticals, which Squibb will continue to make available.

In the field of pharmaceutical manufacturing, Squibb has definitely left its mark. Since the establishment of Squibb Ilaclar, two of the most important local laboratories have built new plants. The Turkish government has passed regulations governing sanitary conditions in laboratories patterned on specifications of the Squibb Ilaclar Laboratory presented to the government at the time of its establishment. High Squibb standards of drug manufacturing have had a salutary effect on the Turkish concept of pharmaceutical processing.

The relationships of Squibb Ilaclar during its initial decade of existence with the various groups it deals with have been happy ones—with labor, the scientific professions, the financial community, the general public, and the Turkish government. The outlook seems auspicious for further strengthening of these relationships.

General Elektrik Turk A.O.

ORIGIN OF THE ENTERPRISE

In 1946, Vehbi Koc, a prominent Turkish businessman, approached the General Electric Company of the United States, and Is Bankasi, a well-known Turkish bank, with the idea of erecting a plant for the manufacture of electric light bulbs in Turkey. General Electric eventually accepted the proposal and in 1948 a corporation was established under the name of "General Elektrik Turk Anonim Ortakligi" (General Electric Turkish Corporation), pursuant to a decree of the council of ministers, which was then required since the Law for the Promotion of Foreign Capital Investments in Turkey had not yet been adopted. The aim of the corporation was to manufacture the electric light bulbs needed in the country and save a considerable amount of foreign exchange.

CAPITAL STRUCTURE

The capital of the corporation initially was 3 million TL, of which 1,800,000 liras (60 percent) were subscribed by General Electric; 750,000 liras (25 percent) were subscribed by the Is Bankasi; and the rest, i.e. 45,000 liras (15 percent) by Vehbi Koc.

In 1950, the capital was increased to 5 million TL, and the proportion was changed to 66 percent for General Electric, 25 percent for Is Bankasi and 9 percent for Vehbi Koc. The capital structure recently reverted to its original proportions, by virtue of a transaction in which Vehbi Koc acquired shares from General Electric to bring his interest back to 15 percent and to reduce the GE holdings to 60 percent. General Electric brought part of its share to Turkey in the form of machinery and equipment. The capital invested by

Vehbi Koc was actually provided by himself and his colleague, Mr. Fazil Ozis, and also by a company called Turk Tecim Anonim Sosyetesi.

The capital of the corporation is divided into 2,500 shares with a par value each of 2,000 TL.

MANAGEMENT AND PERSONNEL

The company has a board of directors consisting of seven members. Presently four of the members are representatives of the General Electric Company, and three of the other two groups. Three persons representing the General Electric capital are Americans, and the other four are Turks. The board meets in Istanbul with two members sitting as the representatives of the American group. The two other American members participate in the meetings of the board whenever they are present in Istanbul.

The managing director of the company is American. Under him there are the heads of the marketing, manufacturing, employee and community relations, finance, legal and corporate operations, and product and product engineering departments, all of whom are Turks.

There are about 20 administrative employees in the company. Of the total, 3 work in marketing, 6 in employee and community relations, 9 in finance, legal and corporate operations, and 2 in the product and product engineering department. In the manufacturing department, there are 137 persons, 79 of whom are direct laborers and 58 supporting personnel.

The factory was built by Turkish workers under an American engineer and following American plans.

In the early part of the operation of the factory, several foremen were brought to Turkey and they stayed until local workers were completely trained. Now, all the employees and workers of the company, except for the managing director, are Turkish citizens.

The company has a technical agreement with the parent company in the United States, according to the terms of which the United States company gives patent rights and all technical information to the company in Turkey, and in return gets royalties and service charges not exceeding five percent of the net sales in Turkey.

ROLE IN ECONOMY

The factory and the main office were established in Istanbul, on the highway to Tekirdag. The factory presently occupies 30,000 square meters of land out of the 70,000 square meter space allocated for this purpose. The following are the main reasons why this site was chosen for the establishment of the factory:

1. The place was allocated as an industrial zone by the municipal authorities.
2. It has advantages in finding workers easily.
3. The location has transportation facilities.
4. The land was very cheap at the time the company bought the lot; it was bought at 2 TL per square meter, and is now worth 100 liras per square meter.

The capacity of the plant, at two shifts daily, is 60 percent greater than the total demand of the entire country. Aside from this market factor, the main element limiting the volume of production in the past has been the lack of components due to exchange shortages. The factory is the sole producer in the country; no bulbs are imported from abroad.

The principal raw materials necessary for production are glass bulbs, brass bases, filaments, argon, nitrogen, and packing supplies.

At the beginning of operation of the factory, all raw materials were imported, and the Turkish government allocated the necessary foreign exchange to import them all.

Glass bulbs constitute 45 percent of the total raw materials necessary for the production of the electric bulbs. In 1953, the factory began to obtain glass bulbs from a local glass factory located on the Bosphorus. Packing supplies constitute 20 percent of the total raw materials. The factory began also in 1953 to procure them from the Thira paper mill of Izmit.

Thus, provision was made to obtain up to 65 percent of the raw materials locally. However, the company found that the local glass bulb production was not sufficient for its needs, and for this reason it built a plant, with the support of the Industrial Development Bank, to make exclusively glass bulbs of various specifications. This is the only installation that has been added to the factory since it was first established. The plant started production in November, 1959.

The company imports brass bases, filaments, argon, and nitrogen from European countries, especially from Holland and Germany, but from time to time since the early stage of operations there has been difficulty in securing foreign exchange to effect these imports.

The company distributes its goods through general distributors, associated with it by special contracts.

General Elektrik in Turkey manufactures electric bulbs of the Edison and General Electric brands, as well as other brands for other foreign manufacturers.

The company limits its production because of the size of the market as well as because of the difficulty in securing foreign exchange to import raw materials from Western Germany, Holland, and other countries. It therefore studies the needs of the market very closely and manufactures accordingly.

FINANCIAL RESULTS

General Elektrik Turk initiated operations in 1950, and, due to excessive competition from abroad, operated at a loss until the end of 1952. In 1953 the Turkish government recognized that, through increased use of locally produced materials, the company was contributing to an ever greater extent to the saving of foreign exchange, which was beginning to be in short supply in Turkey. As a consequence, the government concluded that the importation of bulbs of the types manufactured by General Elektrik Turk was not in the best interest of the country, and discontinued giving import permits for such bulbs.

Since 1954, the company has been able to increase its production and to make reasonable profits, except in 1957 when, due to the lack of foreign exchange, it operated well below capacity at too low a level of production.

Although the devaluation of the Turkish lira in mid-1958 has decreased the dollar earnings of the American shareholder and increased the company's requirements of operating funds, the company considers its operations a success, has confidence that it will continue to grow in line with the economic growth of the country, and it is planning expansion into new lines of business.

Mannesmann-Sümerbank Boru Endüstrisi T.A.S.

ORIGIN OF THE ENTERPRISE

In 1954, Sümerbank, a Turkish state economic enterprise, approached Mannesmann Aktiengesellschaft of Germany concerning its interest in building a plant for the manufacture of steel pipe in Turkey.

Sümerbank was established in Turkey in the year 1933 by a special law (statute no. 2252). Pursuant to this law, the bank engages in industrial banking transactions of various kinds. The law states the purposes of the bank as follows:

1. To operate the factories turned over to it by the State Industrial Office (Devlet Sanayi Ofisi), and to administer the participation shares of the State in private industrial establishments, in accordance with the provisions of the Code of Commerce.
2. To study projects for and the management problems of all industrial institutions which would be created with state capital, except the factories to be founded under powers given by special laws.
3. To participate in or to help within the limits of its own capital, industries, the establishment or management of which would be economically useful for the country.
4. To train specialists for industry and seek measures for the development of national industry.

The proposal of Sümerbank, which plays an important part in the industrial development of Turkey, was accepted by Mannesmann of Germany, and a joint venture was established under the name of "Mannesmann-Sümerbank Boru Endüstrisi TAS" (Mannesmann-Sümerbank Steel Pipe Manufacturing Corporation), in accordance with the Law for the Encouragement of Foreign Capital (statute 6224).

The aim of the corporation was to manufacture the steel pipe needed in the country and thus save a considerable amount of foreign exchange.

CAPITAL STRUCTURE

The Mannesmann-Sümerbank Steel Pipe Manufacturing Corporation is established as a stockholding company in accordance with the provisions of the Turkish Code of Commerce.

The capital of the corporation is 5,600,000 TL, of which 3,200,000 TL correspond to Mannesmann. Mannesmann brought this amount to Turkey in the form of machinery and equipment. Thus, 57 percent of the capital belongs to Mannesmann and 43 percent to Sümerbank. The capital of the corporation is divided into 560 shares, each with a value of 10,000 TL.

Actually, the capital subscribed by Mannesmann was equally provided by four different German firms, but they all come under the Mannesmann group; the capital provided by Sümerbank can similarly be divided as follows: 2 million TL by Sümerbank; 200,000 TL by Karabuk Iron and Steel Works; and 200,000 TL by Izmit Paper Mill, the last two being Sümerbank subsidiary enterprises.

The capital of the corporation is now being increased to TL 35 million, of which TL 20 million correspond to the Mannesmann group and TL 15 million to the Sümerbank group.

In addition to its capital contribution of 2,400,000 TL, Sümerbank has also opened a credit to the firm for working capital.

MANAGEMENT AND PERSONNEL

The company has a board of directors consisting of five members, elected by the general meeting of the shareholders. Presently three of the members are representatives of the Mannesmann group and two of the Sümerbank capital. Two of the persons representing the Mannesmann capital are Germans, and the third is a Turk, who is the permanent representative of the Mannesmann Company in Turkey.

The company has a Turkish manager appointed by the board, who is in charge of commercial affairs, and also a German manager cooperating with him, who is responsible for the technical side. Important decisions are resolved by the board.

The company also has a Turkish assistant-manager. Under him

there are the heads of the administrative, technical, accounting, sales, and social services divisions. There are 46 administrative employees, and 328 workers in the company. The German manager, the head of the technical division, and four foremen are Germans; the rest of the employees and workers are Turkish citizens.

The factory was built by Turkish workers with materials imported from Germany. The plans of the factory were entirely German.

ROLE IN THE ECONOMY AND FINANCIAL RESULTS

The factory was established outside the town of Izmit, which is situated on the Sea of Marmara and is about 100 kilometers from Istanbul. It is connected by a state highway system and a railroad to Istanbul and Ankara. The factory presently occupies 30,000 square meters out of the 50,000 square meters of land allocated for this purpose. The following are the main reasons for the establishment of the factory at this site:

1. The land belonged to Sümerbank and could thus be bought by the company at favorable terms.

2. There is access to a plentiful water supply, which is a very essential element in the manufacture of steel pipe.

3. The site has transportation facilities (sea, railway, and highway connections).

4. It has advantages in finding workers.

The one-shift capacity of pipe production of the factory is 15,000 tons. Approximately 10,000, 5,600, and 13,000 tons were manufactured in the years 1957, 1958, and 1959 respectively.

At present the factory is producing at a rate of about 25,000 tons per annum by working extra shifts.

The main element limiting the volume of production at present is the lack of raw materials. The raw materials necessary for the factory, i.e., the steel rolls, are imported from Germany. The capacity of the factory is being adapted to meet the needs of the country in sizes it manufactures. Thus, the capacity will be increased to about 60,000 tons in the near future and the present range of sizes of ½″ to 2½″ will be extended to 6″.

In order to secure the necessary foreign exchange to import raw materials from abroad, the company obtained a license to export a certain quantity of chrome and iron to foreign countries. The foreign exchange secured by these exports has been used to obtain the necessary raw materials. This procedure only applied to the period when sufficient foreign exchange for imports was not available in Turkey. Due to the new Turkish export and import regulations, such compensation transactions are no longer necessary. The Karabuk Iron and Steel Works are building a skelp mill. As soon as this new mill starts production, the company at Izmit will be almost independent of foreign exchange for imports of raw materials.

The company has agencies in 14 provinces, associated with it by special contracts. The agencies pay in advance 30 percent of the value of the goods they purchase, and 70 percent after the goods are sold. Transportation costs and 7 percent of profit added to the price offered by the company make up the final selling price.

Raw materials and equipment costs constitute 70 percent of the expenditures of the company. Wages of the workers and other personnel constitute 10 percent, and general expenses 20 percent of the overall expenses.

The company made a profit of 3,500,000 TL, 1,139,000 TL, and 6,367,000 TL respectively during the years 1957, 1958, and 1959, which it considers quite satisfactory in relation to the total equity of 5,600,000 liras.

The company has not had any difficulty in taking its profits out of the country, in accordance with the provisions of the Law for the Encouragement of Foreign Capital. Both the Turkish and the German managers are of the opinion that the Turkish government is doing its utmost to help the company in its operations. This reflects the nature of the Turkish participant in the company, and the importance of pipe manufacturing in Turkey.

Tamek Konservecilik Ltd. Sirketi

ORIGIN OF THE ENTERPRISE

The Tamek Canning Company was formed at Istanbul as a limited partnership in 1954, under the Turkish Foreign Investment Encouragement Law (statute no. 6224), between German and Turkish investors to engage in the production of canned and bottled foods. The German partner was a firm engaged in the production of machinery, and had had business dealings with the Turkish partner for some time. The Turkish partners are members of the Sipahioglu family, headed by Mehmet Sipahioglu, prominent as businessmen in foreign trading, and financial and other activities. The scheme for a canning plant was hit upon as a good prospect in the search by these interests for a profitable investment in which they might jointly engage in Turkey. The arrangement was set up with minority capital participation by the German partner, in the form of machinery for the enterprise, and with majority participation by the Turkish entrepreneurs, whose cash investment was used for the necessary local currency expenditures. The factory was built in the town of Bursa, about 200 miles southeast of Istanbul, located in an area where the fruits and vegetables for canning and bottling are produced in abundance. The factory was completed in time for the first canning season to be in 1956. The loss was great during that first year of operation, with a spoilage rate of 43 percent, probably the result of inadequate technical planning for the complex problems involved in this new branch of activity for Turkey.

In mid-1957, the German assets were acquired by an American investor, the British American and Eastern Company, Inc., a New York firm with much experience in business activities in Turkey.

The Tamek Canning Company continues as a limited liability company with four partners: the British American and Eastern Company, and three members of the Sipahioglu family, Mehmet, the father, and two sons, Semih and Melih. As a closely held limited company with fewer than five shareholders, all decisions of the company's board must be unanimous, pursuant to the Turkish Code of Commerce. The capital of the firm is nominally listed at 1.5 million TL. Actually, the net worth of the firm is estimated to be at least 6 million TL, with the present foreign partner having brought in machinery to complement the original installations. The distribution between the foreign and Turkish partners continues to be a minority for the former (40 percent) and a majority for the latter (60 percent). The firm also obtained a long-term loan at the time of its founding from the Turkish Industrial Development Bank, in the total amount of 872,000 TL (principal plus interest), repayable in eight equal semi-annual installments beginning in June, 1958.

There are no formal arrangements for foreign technical supervision. The foreign partner is very active in working with the firm in this respect, availing itself of its connections and access to sources of information abroad.

MANAGEMENT AND PERSONNEL

Since there are so few partners in the enterprise, all are represented on the board of directors, and all decisions of the board require the unanimous consent of its members. The manager of the firm, subject to election and dismissal by the shareholders, is Mr. Semih Sipahioglu, one of the shareholders. One of the members of the American participating firm, who resides in Europe, spends about a third of the year in Turkey working actively with the firm.

There have been several foreign technical supervisors. By mid-1959, there was only one, the production manager, a German. It was expected that he would leave the firm soon, and it then would have all Turkish personnel. There has been an active program of training of Turkish personnel to take over the positions of responsibility. This includes training of selected personnel in other countries. The total work force consists of about 400 at the peak of the canning season. Excellent relationships are maintained with Turkish labor unions.

FINANCIAL RESULTS

The firm's profits are limited by the 20 percent markup over production costs imposed by Turkish law for producers (the additional margin limits are 10 percent for wholesalers and 15 percent for retailers). Observance of this limit has led to some administrative problems for the firm, but it has been able to keep within the margin. Indeed, despite increasing costs as a result of the inflationary pressures in Turkey during recent years, the firm has been able to reduce the prices of its products by more efficient organization of its production, purchasing, sales, and advertising activities.

Profits for the most part have been left undistributed in the company. This was true of all but a small amount in 1957 and of the total profit made in 1958. The foreign partner was able to remit its portion of distributed profits for 1957 without any problem.

ROLE IN THE ECONOMY

Tamek Canning is the only modern canner and bottler in Turkey of fruits, vegetables, and prepared foods. It produces some 45 different items, of which the largest is tomato paste, and juice; other items include ketchup, peas, beans, okra, mixed vegetables, 8 types of marmalades and jams, 7 types of canned fruit, 3 types of pickles, 2 types of olives, sauerkraut, applesauce, and 14 types of Turkish prepared foods (for example, grape leaves stuffed with rice).

All raw material food items are, of course, domestic. Bottles are obtained from local plants, based on imported molds brought in by Tamek Canning. Cartons are also obtained from local producers. The firm itself produces its own cans from imported tinplate. An index of its increased volume is provided by the increasing number of cans it has produced: about 800,000 in 1957, 1.3 million in 1958, and an estimated 2.5 million in 1959. All these cans are made by hand processes; automatic can equipment cannot be used economically because of the relatively limited output, and the small numbers of cans of different sizes that are needed. For its main items of output, a total of 2,200 metric tons of tomatoes were processed in 1958.

The output of the firm is virtually all for domestic consumption. However, some token exports have been made to Cyprus, and it is hoped to expand these as well as to institute exports to Arab countries in the Middle East. The outlets for the firm's products are the main cities of western Turkey. No canned goods are imported into Turkey, and the firm has been selling all of its output each season.

The firm's products have been tested in the United States and accepted on the basis of the standards of the Pure Food and Drug Act. This reflects the great efforts that have been exerted for the rationalization of production, quality control, and standardization. In these connections, it is also significant that the spoilage rate has dropped to less than 0.1 percent.

PROBLEMS

The principal problems have related to the proper organization of production. Considering the fact that canned foods are a relatively new item of consumption in Turkey, there is a great variety of items to produce, each in limited quantities, in order to cultivate consumer tastes properly. There have also been supply problems resulting from the difficulties of contracting sufficiently far ahead with farmers, who are keyed primarily to developments in the markets for fresh fruit and vegetables. Assistance has been obtained in this respect from technicians of the United States government (International Cooperation Administration, or Point Four) working in Turkey to improve local agricultural techniques.

It has also been necessary to devise imaginative advertising techniques to develop consumers in the local market for these new products. Still another problem has been the need for high working capital requirements characteristic of the Turkish economy, and this has in recent years coincided with tight local credit conditions as a result of anti-inflationary policies adopted by the monetary authorities.

EVALUATION

After a false start, the joint venture has worked out very much to the satisfaction of both sets of partners since the acquisition of the foreign interest by the present foreign partner. Consideration is being given to new investments by the same partners in fish canning and in beer production.

The closely held nature of the organization, involving unanimous consent and active cooperation by all parties, has produced highly satisfactory results, and the question of whether the foreign or domestic partners hold a minority or majority, seems to have had little significant bearing on the results. The active role of both groups in the operation of the enterprise has made it possible to rescue a faltering investment, and to set it on the path of rapidly expanding development of locally produced, new consumption items for the Turkish market.

IV. Selected Investor Companies

Ente Nazionali Idrocarburi of Italy, with special reference to Société Irano-Italienne des Petroles (Sirip, a venture in Iran)

The Société Irano-Italienne des Petroles (Sirip) a joint Italo-Iranian company, was established on September 8, 1957. The capital of this company was subscribed in equal parts by the two partners, both government-owned corporations: Agip Mineraria on the Italian side, and the National Iranian Oil Company (Nioc) on the Iranian side. The object of this joint company is the exploration for and the production of liquid and gaseous hydrocarbons in three specific areas of Iran.

For a number of reasons, this case study is of particular interest: Sirip represents one of the most important Italian oil ventures abroad. It is a venture in a type of activity which has developed and is still developing in Italy largely with the help of capital and know-how from foreign countries and particularly from the United States. The agreement which resulted in the establishment of Sirip constitutes an innovation, if not a revolution, in the pattern of relationship between petroleum concession holders and host countries. The old system of concessions issued against a 50-50 split of the profits has given way here to the system of a joint company in which the host country is an equal partner in terms of financial contribution and representation on the board of directors, the profits being split 75-25 in favor of the host country. Both partners are wholly-owned government corporations. The Italian partner has received financial and technical (mostly financial) assistance from more highly industrialized countries (United States, Great Britain, and Germany), and has in turn become capable of supplying capital and technical assistance to less developed countries of North Africa and of the Middle East.

ENTE NAZIONALI IDROCARBURI

The Italian partner in Sirip, Agip Mineraria, is a corporation owned by the Ente Nazionali Idrocarburi (National Hydrocarbons Agency, hereafter referred to as Eni). Eni is a government entity established by a law of February 10, 1953, for the purpose of promoting and implementing projects of national interest in the following fields: 1) exploration for and production of hydrocarbons; 2) construction and operation of natural gas pipelines; 3) processing, conversion, use and marketing of hydrocarbons; and 4) nuclear power generation.

Eni has a capital endowment fund supplied by the Italian government in the amount of 36.9 billion lire, or approximately $60 million. It operates through controlled and affiliated companies; it may purchase stock in corporations, dispose of the assets it is not interested in retaining, and reorganize the controlled companies into homogeneous groups. The operating companies of Eni are separate corporations and are therefore subject to the provisions of the civil code and of other laws governing the activity of private enterprises. In a strictly legal sense, Eni is in the position of a majority stockholder, and therefore its influence on the operating companies is formally expressed through participation in the meetings for the election of the directors and auditors. Eni's intervention in the controlled and affiliated companies takes the form of a program of orientation and coordination of the group's investments by major sectors of activity.

While the Eni operating companies, as private corporations, do not enjoy any particular privilege as compared to normal private enterprises, their parent organization, as a public entity, does enjoy preferred treatment and certain tax benefits.

Eni was granted the exclusive right to explore for and produce hydrocarbons in the Po Valley (except for the territories of the

Provinces of Rovigo and Ferrara, but limited to the quaternary strata at depths not below 3,900 feet), without the obligation to pay royalties to the state. In the same area Eni has the exclusive right to build and operate oil and gas pipelines. In the non-exclusive area of continental Italy, the government may issue to Eni exploration permits for areas in excess of 300,000 hectares and production concessions for areas in excess of 80,000 hectares. Eni's bond issues are exempt from all taxes, present and future, while similar issues by private companies are subject to a tax on capital and a tax on returns. The price of other power sources is controlled by an interministerial price committee on the basis of production costs ascertained by the committee, but the price of the natural gas produced by Eni is pegged to that of fuel oil, including taxes. This enables Eni to realize a substantial profit on natural gas operations.

Eni's operating companies are grouped into five major sectors as follows: hydrocarbon mining, processing, transport, products distribution, and nuclear activities. In addition to these activities, Eni is also engaged in the construction of equipment for the oil industry, and in the design and construction of plants for the oil, chemical and allied industries.

The Eni group operates a complex of laboratories for scientific and technical research, located at San Donato Milanese near Milan. The Eni group comprises some 50 companies. Eni's statement and balance sheet as of April 30, 1958, showed stock holdings totaling 38,599,737,545 lire (slightly less than $62 million), plus loans to the same companies totaling 68,026,165,005 lire ($108 million).

In 1957 the sales of the whole Eni group totaled 296 billion lire ($473 million). The group employs 19,493 factory and office workers and executives.

While Eni was established in 1953, some of its controlled companies, and in particular the leading ones, had been in existence for a number of years earlier. However, it was only in 1953 that it was found desirable to establish a government entity to take over the various enterprises which the state had been creating or absorbing in past years in the sector of hydrocarbons.

The board of directors of Eni, including the chairman, is appointed by decree of the Prime Minister. The directors serve three year terms and may be reappointed. The economic policy of the agency, and consequently that of the controlled companies, is laid down by a special committee of ministers. The balance sheet of Eni must be approved by the ministers of finance, treasury, and industry and trade, and submitted to Parliament. A magistrate from the court of accounts must participate in the meetings of Eni's board of directors and board of auditors. The agency's net profits must be distributed in the following way: 20 percent to the ordinary reserve fund; 15 percent for the encouragement of scientific and technical research; and 65 percent to the state.

Agip Mineraria was established in Milan on May 30, 1953, as a joint stock company. It has a capital stock of 10 billion lire ($16 million), divided into 10,000-lire shares. The shares are not listed on the stock exchange. The stock is owned 99.75 percent by Eni.

Agip Mineraria carries on its activities throughout the country, and particularly in the Po Valley (the area in which Eni holds exclusive rights), in certain regions of south-central Italy, and in Sicily. Agip Mineraria is active in the field of exploration, prospecting, drilling, and production of gaseous and liquid hydrocarbons.

In 1958, the crude oil and natural gasoline produced by Agip Mineraria and its operating companies totaled 345,400 tons, or 20 percent of total Italian production. Agip also operates at Cortemaggiore near Parma, in the vicinity of a field discovered in 1949 (richer in natural gas than in oil), a refinery which processes both the natural gas and the crude oil from the field. The company employs a total of about 4,500 factory and office workers and executives. In the four years ending with 1957, the annual profits realized averaged about 2 billion lire or $3.2 million.

FOREIGN INVESTMENTS IN ENI COMPANIES

Among the companies affiliated with Eni, there are some in which foreign interests have substantial holdings. These are two oil refining companies (Irom and Stanic), one plastics company (Società Chimica Ravenna), and one chemical company (Phillips Carbon Black Italiana).

Industria Raffinazione Oli Minerali (Irom) is a company established in Rome in 1947 by Agip (the leading company in the sector of products distribution), and the Anglo-Iranian Oil Company, with the capital stock being subscribed 51 percent by Agip and 49 percent by British interests. The object of Irom is to operate its own plants for the industrial processing of the crude oil supplied by each of the partners and/or their associates, in proportion to their respective holdings of the company's stock. The present board of directors of Irom is composed of nine members—five Italians and four Britons. Article 22 of the by-laws provides that the chairman must be an Italian national.

Stanic Industria Petrolifera was established in 1949 in Milan by Anic (the leading company in the refining sector), and the Standard Oil Company of New Jersey, each holding 50 percent of the capital stock. The object of Stanic is the processing, marketing and transport of crude oil and its products. The present board of directors of Stanic is composed of six members, four Italians and two Americans. Under article 21 of the by-laws of Stanic, the chairman of the board must be an Italian national.

The Società Chimica Ravenna was established in January, 1958 by Anic and the German company Wacher Chemie of Munich (a limited liability company capitalized at 40 million DM, or about $10 million), with Anic subscribing 51 percent of the stock and Wacher Chemie 49 percent. The company is at present capitalized at 500 million lire, or about $800,000. The object of Società Chimica Ravenna is the production of vinyl chloride from the acetylene produced by Anic at Ravenna in a synthetic rubber and nitrogenous fertilizer plant. The Anic plant at Ravenna, now nearing completion, will have an annual production capacity of 60,000 tons of synthetic rubber and 750,000 tons of nitrogenous fertilizers. The vinyl chloride plant is now completed and is about to enter into operation. The board of directors of Società Chimica Ravenna consists of six members: three Italians and three Germans. Under article 14 of the by-laws, half of the directors, including the chairman, must be Italian nationals.

Phillips Carbon Black Italiana was established in Milan on November 10, 1959, by Anic and various foreign companies. The company has at present a capital stock of 100 million lire, owned 30 percent by Anic and 70 percent by the foreign groups. At Ravenna the company will start the production of carbon black from liquid hydrocarbons.

In addition to these joint investments, Eni has also entered into various agreements of technical cooperation, especially in the production of nuclear reactors.

ENI'S INDUSTRIAL ACTIVITIES ABROAD

In the past few years, the companies of the Eni group, taking advantage of the experience acquired in their manifold activities in Italy, have launched into ventures abroad, ranging from oil and gas exploration and production to the construction of refineries and pipelines, and to the distribution of oil products. Within the framework of its objectives, Eni has decided to turn to the exploration for oil resources abroad as a means of supplementing Italian resources.

The activities of the Eni companies are centered largely in a number of less developed countries of Africa (Morocco, Tunisia, Libya, Egypt, Somali Republic, Sudan), of the Middle East and Far East (Iran, Pakistan, Jordan, Lebanon, Saudi Arabia), and of Latin America (Argentina). Certain projects have recently been initiated in some European countries, such as Switzerland, Germany, Austria, and Spain.

Certain of these activities are carried out directly by Eni affiliates operating as contractors for third parties. The most interesting activities of this kind are those taking place in Spain and in Argentina. In Spain an Eni affiliate (Agip Mineraria) carries on exploration work for the account of the Empresa Nacional Adaro de Investigaciones Mineras. In Argentina, another Eni affiliate (the Saipem company) signed a contract on July 28, 1959 with the Argentine governmental agency Yacimientos Petrolíferos Fiscales (Y.P.F.) for the drilling of 300 oil and natural gas wells in the area of Comodoro Rivadavia by October 27, 1962.

In other cases the activities are carried out by joint business ventures in which Eni affiliates have substantial holdings. The principal joint business ventures abroad, with the participation of companies of the Eni group, based on the Eni balance sheet of April 30, 1960, are included in the following foreign ventures:

Germany. Sudpetrol A.G. was established on September 15, 1959 at Munich, with a capital stock of 1 million DM. It is owned 50 percent by the Italian Eni group (Oleodotti Internazionali) and 50 percent by German interests. The company is concerned with the transport and refining of oil in Germany.

Agip A.G. was established on February 25, 1960 at Munich, with a capital stock of 1 million DM, owned entirely by the Eni group (90 percent Agip and 10 percent Agip Mineraria). It is concerned with the distribution of oil products in Germany.

Austria. Agip A.G. was established on May 15, 1959 in Vienna, with a capital stock of 1 million Austrian shillings, owned entirely by the Eni group (90 percent Agip and 10 percent Agip Mineraria). The capital has been recently increased to 20 million Austrian shillings. It is concerned with the distribution of oil products in Austria.

Switzerland. Agip S.A. was established on September 23, 1959 at Lugano, with a capital stock of 1 million Swiss francs, owned entirely by the Eni group (90 percent Agip and 10 percent Agip Mineraria). The capital has been recently increased to 5 million Swiss francs. It is concerned with the distribution of oil products in Switzerland.

Greece. Olympiagas was established at Athens, with a capital stock of 1,250,000 drachma, 60 percent of which was subscribed by a hydrocarbon transport company of the Eni group (Agipgas Citta') and 40 percent by Greek interests. The company is concerned with the distribution of natural gas in Greece.

Morocco. Somip (Société Anonyme Marocaine-Italienne des Petroles) was established in 1958 in Rabat, as a 50-50 joint venture in which the partners are on the one side Agip Mineraria (45 percent) and other companies of the Eni group (5 percent), and on the other the Moroccan government (50 percent). The company's object is to explore for and produce hydrocarbons in a concession in the Tarfaya area covering some 11,500 square miles. Preliminary exploration activities were started in September, 1958, and geological and geophysical surveys are now in progress. In case deposits are found and worked, 75 percent of the profits of Somip will accrue to the Moroccan government. Somip has a capital stock of 60 million Moroccan francs.

Samir (Société Anonyme Marocaine-Italienne de Raffinage) was established in 1959 at Mohammadia, as a 50-50 joint venture in which the partners are on the one side Anic (45 percent) and other companies of the Eni group (5 percent), and on the other the Moroccan governmental agency Bepi (50 percent). The company's initial capital stock was set at 20 million Moroccan francs, but in March, 1960, the capital was increased to 1,220,000,000 Moroccan francs. This company's object is to build and operate a refinery capable of processing 1,250,000 tons per year. The Moroccan government has granted this company a monopoly on oil refining in Morocco.

Agip S.A. was established on October 9, 1959, at Casablanca, with a capital stock of 20 million Moroccan francs, owned entirely by the Eni group (90 percent Agip and 10 percent Agip Mineraria). The capital has been recently increased to 60 million Moroccan francs. It is concerned with the distribution of oil products in Morocco.

Tunisia. Agip S.A. was established on January 23, 1960 at Tunisi, with a capital stock of 20,000 Tunisian dinars, owned entirely by the Eni group (90 percent Agip and 10 percent Agip Mineraria). The capital has been recently increased to 40,000 Tunisian dinars. It is concerned with the distribution of oil products in Tunisia.

Libya. Asseil (Società Libica per il Petrolio) was established on October 16, 1957 at Tripoli, as a 50-50 joint business venture between a Libyan group and the Petrolibia Co. The latter is in turn a 50-50 Agip-Fiat joint venture. Petrolibia participated by contributing its Tripoli plants. The object of Asseil is to distribute Agip oil products in Libya. It is capitalized at 200,000 Libyan pounds.

Cori (Compagnia Richerche Idrocarburi) was established in Milan, Italy on July 31, 1959. It has at present a capital stock of 1.2 billion lire, owned entirely by the Eni group (90 percent Agip Mineraria and 10 percent Snam). It is concerned with exploration and production activities in the field of oil as well as natural gas. On November 19, 1959, Cori was granted a concession in Cyrenaica to carry out oil exploration in an area of about 12,000 square miles. Cori will pay to the Libyan government a royalty of 17 percent as well as 50 percent of its profits. Depending upon the amount of oil and natural gas that is found, the Libyan government will be entitled to enter into a joint venture with Cori to the extent of 30 percent.

Egypt. Ieoc (International Egyptian Oil Company) is a company established in 1953 with head offices in Panama and capitalized at $15,000,000, its stock being held 20.3 percent by Agip Mineraria and 79.7 percent by other interests. Ieoc in turn owns 51 percent of the stock of the Compagnie Orientale des Petroles d'Egypte (Cope), the remaining 49 percent being held by the Egyptian government. Cope has head offices at Cairo and is capitalized at one million Egyptian pounds. Cope is engaged in exploration and production activities in Egyptian territory, and particularly in the Sinai region, where production started a few years ago. In this activity of exploration and production, Cope depends largely on the services of Agip Mineraria, while for the erection of crude oil storage tanks and pipelines it employs another Eni affiliate, the Saipem company. Agip Mineraria purchases an appreciable portion of the oil produced by Cope: in 1958, 1,144,715 tons out of a total of 1,802,986 tons. As a result of the Egyptian government's holding of 49 percent of Cope's stock, almost 75 percent of this company's profits goes to the Egyptian government as is the case in Iran with Sirip and in Morocco with Somip.

Sudan. Agip Mineraria (Sudan) Ltd. was established on May 15, 1959 at Khartoum, with a capital stock of 500,000 Sudanese pounds. It is owned entirely by two companies of the Eni group (95 percent Agip Mineraria and 5 percent Agip). The company's object is to explore for and produce hydrocarbons in Sudan, along the Red Sea coasts, including the continental shelf. The company will carry on the exploration at its own expense and under its own responsibility. Once oil and natural gas are found, 50 percent of the company's profits will be paid to the Sudanese government as taxes and royalties; the Sudanese government will also be entitled to buy 50 percent of the company's capital stock.

Agip (Sudan) Ltd. was established on May 13, 1959, at Khartoum, with a capital stock of 150,000 Sudanese pounds, owned entirely by the Eni group (90 percent Agip and 10 percent Agip Mineraria). The capital has been recently increased to 300,000 Sudanese pounds. It is concerned with the distribution of oil products in Sudan.

Somali Republic. Mineraria Somala was established in Rome, with a capital stock of 100 million lire, owned entirely by the Eni group

(90 percent Mineraria and 10 percent Snam). Mineraria Somala is engaged in exploration and production activities in a large part of the territory of the Somali Republic.

Petrosomala was established at Mogadiscio, Somali Republic, with a capital stock of 3 million somali owned entirely by Agip. It is concerned with the distribution of oil products in the Somali Republic.

Lebanon. Gaz-Orient was established in January, 1956 at Beirut, with a capital stock of 300,000 Lebanese lire. It is owned 50 percent by two hydrocarbon transport companies of the Eni group (Agipgas Citta' 46.67 percent and Metano Citta' 3.33 percent) and 50 percent by the Lebanese government. The company is concerned with the distribution of natural gas in Lebanon.

Iran. Sirip (Société Irano-Italienne des Petroles) was established at Teheran on September 8, 1957, as a 50-50 partnership between Agip Mineraria and the National Iranian Oil Co. (Nioc), to explore for and produce hydrocarbons in certain regions of Iran. It is capitalized at 20 million rials.

NATIONAL IRANIAN OIL COMPANY

The National Iranian Oil Company (Nioc) is a company established in 1951 by the Iranian government.

The commercial exploitation of Iranian oilfields dates back to 1908. Until 1951, most of the development of this industry was effected by the Anglo-Iranian Oil Company. In 1951 the oil industry was nationalized and placed under the control of the National Iranian Oil Company. Oil activities in Iran are now regulated by the agreement signed in October, 1954 between the Iranian government and Nioc on the one hand, and a group of international oil companies referred to as "the Consortium" on the other. The members of the Consortium are the following:

Company	*Interest (%)*
British Petroleum Co. Ltd.	40
Royal Dutch-Shell Group	14
Standard Oil Co. (New Jersey)	7
Gulf Oil Corporation	7
Texas Company	7
Standard Oil Co. of California	7

Company	*Interest (%)*
Compagnie Française des Petroles	6
Socony Mobil Oil Co. Inc.	7
Group of 9 Companies (American Independent Oil Co., Atlantic Refining, Getty Oil Co., Hancock Oil Co., Richfield Oil Co., San Jacinto Petroleum Corp., Signal Oil & Gas Co., Standard Oil Co. of Ohio, Tidewater Oil Co.)	5
Total	100

Under this agreement, two operating companies were established: the Iranian Oil Exploration and Producing Company and the Iranian Oil Refining Company. The former conducts oil exploration and production activities in an area of southern Iran (Khuzistam and Fars), while the latter is responsible for oil refining activities at Abadan. The two operating companies purchase materials outside of Iran through Iran Oil Services Ltd. On the boards of directors of these companies sit two Iranian representatives out of a total of seven directors for each board. The marketing of both the crude oil and the products is reserved to the members of the Consortium. The existing plant and equipment are considered the property of Nioc. The agreement is valid for 25 years but can be extended 3 times for 5 years each time, subject, however, to a progressive reduction of the area given in concession.

Under the agreement of October, 1954, the Consortium turns over to the Iranian government 50 percent of the profits made from the sale of the oil produced. Profit is considered to be the difference between the "posted price" (FOB Persian Gulf) at which the oil handled by the members of the Consortium is offered for sale, and the crude oil production cost.

Nioc, in addition to its functions under the agreement with the international oil consortium, owns and operates a small refinery at Kermanshah and the nearby oil wells of Naft-i-Shah. This refinery has a production capacity of 250,000 tons a year.

Iran's own demand for petroleum is met in part with the products from Abadan and in part with those from Kermanshah. Nioc is directly responsible for the distribution of petroleum products in Iran. It also builds pipelines. It has completed one from Ahwaz to

Teheran, is building another from Aznah to Esfahan, and a third from Teheran to Resht. Moreover, Nioc, through its subsidiary the Iran Oil Company, holds oil exploration rights for the territory not assigned to the Consortium. In August, 1956, Iran Oil discovered a promising field at Qum.

In 1957, a new law was enacted in Iran, regulating the exploration for and production of hydrocarbons on the Iranian territory and continental shelf. This law is based on the principle of grading downwards the weight of the royalties and other costs, depending on whether the concession is attributed to enterprises:

(a) in which Nioc does not participate;
(b) in which Nioc participates with a holding of more than 30 percent and less than 50 percent; or
(c) in which Nioc participates with a holding of 50 percent or more.

The country has been divided into some twenty oil zones, and the Iranian government has announced that about two-thirds of them will be offered at auction. Since 1957, three concessions have been awarded to three joint companies, with Italian, United States, and Canadian participation. The Qum area is reserved for Nioc.

AGREEMENT BETWEEN AGIP MINERARIA AND NIOC

The agreement between Nioc and Agip Mineraria was signed in Teheran on August 3, 1957, by Mr. Abdullah Entezam, chairman of Nioc, and by Mr. Enrico Mattei, chairman of Agip Mineraria.

Article 1 of the agreement provides that:

> The Nioc and Agip Mineraria shall form within sixty days of the entry into force of this Agreement a joint stock company which, in their common interest, shall exercise activities in connection with the exploration for, and production of, crude oil and other natural hydrocarbons, the sale of the products obtained and any operations necessary or useful for the purpose of sale.

The activities of the new company may, by mutual agreement, extend to the processing (refining, chemical conversion, etc.) of said extracted products.

In the following paragraphs the salient features of the agreement, consisting of 47 articles, and subsequent provisions are discussed.

SIRIP'S CAPITAL STRUCTURE

The company's initial capital stock was set at 10 million rials, being the equivalent of $100,000, divided into 100 shares of the face value of 100,000 rials each. This capital was subscribed in equal parts by the two partners: 50 percent by Nioc and 50 percent by Agip Mineraria. The company's capital was later increased to 20 million rials.

Each share carries one vote. The shares are registered, and can be freely transferred to the companies controlled by either partner. The stockholder who wishes to dispose of all or part of his shares is required to offer to the other stockholders an option in proportion to their holding. If any stockholder does not avail himself of this offer, the stockholder who wishes to dispose of his shares is required to extend the offer to the other stockholders, until all shares have been sold to the old stockholders. The price of the shares thus offered must be agreed upon by the stockholders concerned; if they fail to reach an agreement, the price shall be set by the board of directors on the basis of the company's financial position, taking into account the last balance sheet published and the prospects of future developments. If the board fails to reach a decision, the matter shall be decided by arbitration.

In any event, where the option is not taken up, the seller may not transfer his share to third parties without the unanimous consent of the board of directors. In such case, the rights and liabilities arising from the agreement shall be conveyed to the third parties, without affecting in any way the liabilities assumed by the existing parties.

In the case of an increase in the capital stock, the new shares must be subscribed by the old stockholders in proportion to the respective holdings. The price of the new shares may not be lower than the face value.

If funds are required above the sums contributed by the parties in subscribing to the original capital and its subsequent increases, Sirip shall raise the required funds by borrowing. Should Sirip be unable to borrow the required sum, or should it be able to borrow it only at unfavorable terms, Nioc and Agip Mineraria shall be required each to provide half of the necessary funds. The rate of interest charged to Sirip by Agip Mineraria and Nioc shall be the same for both parties and shall in no case exceed seven percent.

According to article 15 of the agreement of August 3, 1957, monies and funds contributed by both parties shall be in the form of foreign exchange (cash) or in the form of plants, machinery and parts, equipment, patents, consulting and allied services and/or such other services as may be necessary or useful for the operations envisaged in the agreement. However, any contribution other than in cash shall be made only on the request of Sirip for the purposes of its work. Such contributions shall, in any case, conform to world prices and be competitive.

When making contributions other than in cash, Nioc or Agip shall indicate to Sirip the currency in which they wish their contributions to be entered. Sirip shall take this indication into account as one of the elements in determining whether the contribution is offered at competitive terms.

IMPORTED EQUIPMENT

The parties agree that preference shall be given to the Italian market and to Italian products for equipment and services, provided that prices and other terms are competitive.

Machinery, equipment, and other products not manufactured or available in Persia and required exclusively for Sirip and Agip operations may be imported free of customs duties, taxes, and other charges.

Agip and companies or enterprises working in Persia under contract to Sirip have the right to reexport any imported item without any licensing requirement and free of all taxes.

Without prejudice to the aforesaid rights, Agip and Sirip are required to give preference, with regard to the purchase of necessary materials and equipment, to goods manufactured in Persia, provided they can be purchased at the same conditions of quality, price, availability, and usefulness as foreign-made goods. When comparing prices of imported articles with those of Persian production, allowance must be made for freight costs and customs duties applicable to imported goods.

MANAGEMENT

Sirip is managed by a board of six directors who serve four-year terms. The parity of shareholding of both groups is reflected in the composition of the board; half of the directors are appointed by Nioc and half by Agip. The office of chairman of the board is to be filled by a director appointed by Nioc, and that of deputy chairman by a director appointed by Agip. The managing director, who is also general manager, is appointed by Agip.

The present board of directors of Sirip is composed of Messrs. Amir Gholi Azari, Houshang Farkhan, and Djafar Khamali (Nioc representatives); and Messrs. Attilio Jacoboni, Carlo Sarti, and Pietro Sette (Agip representatives). Amir Gholi Azari is chairman of the board; Attilio Jacoboni is deputy chairman; and Carlo Sarti is managing director and general manager.

The presence of at least five directors is required for the validity of board meetings. The approval of at least four directors is required for the validity of the board's decisions. Directors may not be partners in competing companies. Unless authorized to do so, directors may not accept positions as directors in competing companies in Italy or in Persia.

The technical managers of Sirip are appointed by the managing director from among personnel designated by Agip Mineraria. The board of auditors consists of three members: one is appointed by Nioc, one by Agip, and the third, who holds the position of chairman of the board of auditors, is appointed by a Swiss trust company or auditing agency, which shall appoint a person of neither Persian nor Italian nationality, completely unconnected with either party and having no interest in the oil industry. The directors, auditors, and heads of departments may be Persian or foreign nationals, with the exceptions noted.

EXPLORATION AND PRODUCTION AREA

Under the agreement of August 3, 1957, three areas of Persian territory have been exclusively leased to Sirip, namely:

1. An area of about 2,160 square miles of the continental shelf in the northern part of the Persian Gulf.

2. A continental area of about 4,300 square miles in a region east of Central Zagros.

3. An area of about 2,300 square miles of the coastal region of the Oman Sea extending to the continental shelf.

OBLIGATIONS OF AGIP MINERARIA

Agip has assumed the following obligations:

(a) to draw up exploration plans, at its expense and after consultation with Nioc;

(b) to carry out such plans, through its own efforts and means, either directly or indirectly; the expenditure involved in the preparation and implementation of such plans is inclusive of the cost of exploration work and of all expenditures in connection with the use of land;

(c) to submit to Sirip periodic and detailed progress reports and a detailed final report;

(d) to bear in full Nioc's share in the expenditure incurred in connection with exploration work in the event that exploration has proved unsuccessful;

(e) to act in the light of Persia's rights and interests in conducting exploration and development work;

(f) to advance on Sirip's account sums to cover expenses to be incurred in exploration work required to investigate the existence of other deposits after the discovery of the first deposit.

Geological or geophysical exploration must begin within six months of the date of entry into effect of the agreement. Drilling work must begin when judged expedient, but in any case within four years of the entry into effect of the agreement. Exploration work must be continued until all possibilities in areas leased to Sirip are exhausted. Such operations may not be carried out after twelve years from the entry into force of the agreement.

In the event that, at the end of the said twelve-year period, no commercial result shall be obtained, the agreement shall expire and Sirip shall be dissolved.

In order to insure the implementation of a concrete plan with respect to exploration work, it has been agreed that the sum to be spent by Agip Mineraria during the exploration period shall be not less than $22,000,000. Agip Mineraria shall, without prejudice to its full discretion or initiative in the technical field, prepare plans involving the expenditure of the equivalent of $6 million for the first four years of life of the agreement, and $16 million for the following eight years, at the rate of not less than $2 million a year. In the event that, on the expiration of the first four years and because of delays in carrying out work, such sum has not been spent in its entirety, the balance thereof shall be added to the minimum rate of expenditure envisaged for the following eight years. Any over-expenditure incurred in the course of the first four years shall be deducted from the amount envisaged for the following eight years. Also, any expenditure incurred over and above the minimum rate for each of the last eight years shall be deducted from the minimum rate for the succeeding years.

At the end of the first four years, and at the end of each of the following eight years, Agip may cease exploration work, after having notified Sirip, provided:

(a) that it show proof that, up to the date of the notice, work to be carried out under the plans had been actually done, and that expenditures to be incurred in the period preceding the date of the notice had actually been incurred; in the event of there being an unspent balance, half of it shall be turned over to Nioc for the account of the Persian Government;

(b) that it surrender all areas leased for exploration purposes. In this case, the limitations envisaged in article 26 of the agreement shall cease to take effect, the agreement having been completely rescinded. [Article 26 provides that on the expiration of the fifth year from the beginning of exploration, the total area leased shall be reduced by 25 percent; on the expiration of the ninth year it shall be further reduced by 25 percent of the original area.]

On the expiration of the 12th year, there shall be left to Sirip only the land on which there will have been discovered deposits commercially exploitable within the meaning of the agreement.

OBLIGATIONS OF SIRIP

Sirip shall be required to refund to Agip Mineraria the aforementioned expenditures and capital costs in connection therewith only in the event that exploration work has led to the ascertainment, on the basis of internationally recognized technical standards, of the existence of commercially recoverable oil reserves.

The yield of the deposit shall be deemed to warrant commercial operation under present market conditions where the recoverable quantity of oil, by any reasonable assumption, shall be such that delivery on board shall be possible on the basis of costs computed by taking production costs and adding thereto freight and loading costs and a sum equivalent to 12.5 percent of the posted price which shall be a minimum royalty payable to Persia as income tax and royalty, such cost, when subtracted from the posted price of oil of similar quality to leave a net profit allowing a reasonable return.

When the existence of an oil deposit sufficient to warrant commercial operation shall have been ascertained, Sirip shall bear any expenditure to be incurred thereafter for the purpose of developing and working the deposit.

Reimbursement operations shall be effected on the basis of the following procedure: Sirip shall credit Agip Mineraria with a sum equal to the amount of the exploration expenditure as of the day on which it has been incurred, on the basis of the expenditure accounts which Agip Mineraria shall submit to Sirip within two months of the end of each calendar quarter. Sirip shall be entitled to check and verify the accuracy of such accounts, and to require that evidence of expenditure be produced. On the expiration of one and a half months from the date of submission of such accounts, unless objections have been raised, no complaints shall be admissible.

The payment of the sum credited against exploration work shall be made by Sirip as promptly as possible and in any case through annual payments at the rate of not less than the equivalent of $0.10 per barrel of exported crude oil. Fifty percent of the amount credited to Agip Mineraria as refund for exploration work done shall be paid by Sirip to Nioc.

DIVISION OF PROFITS

Net profits (gross income less operating expenses in Persia and abroad including overhead, depreciation, and losses as provided under the Income Tax Act, 1949) shall be paid one-half to Persia as taxes and royalties and the other half to Agip Mineraria and Nioc in equal parts. Therefore, in effect 75 percent of Sirip profits goes to the Iranian government, whereas 25 percent goes to Agip Mineraria.

The foregoing provisions do not in any way preclude the liability to pay for any service rendered (water and electricity supplies, pilots' services in harbors, sewage, health services, etc.); in such cases, however, Sirip shall enjoy the most favorable treatment granted to other users. Depreciation is computed at an annual average of 14 percent.

SALES POLICY

Sirip shall use its best endeavors to raise its oil sales to the highest level, and to this end it shall develop the yield of each deposit by using every means of production known to the oil industry.

The annual production program shall be drawn up in advance, and shall be such as to cover:

(a) Nioc's demand for the purpose of meeting the requirements of the economic area of each deposit, provided such demand does not exceed five percent of the total output. The price payable by Nioc for said oil shall be cost price plus a commission at the rate of $0.14 per cubic meter [1 cu.mt = approx. 8.4 bbl];

(b) any undertakings and contracts for the sale of crude oil to be delivered to purchasers at export points;

(c) any other opportunities that Sirip may envisage after a market survey.

Sirip shall grant to Nioc and Agip Mineraria the right of "first refusal" on any quantity of petroleum available for sale. If neither Nioc nor Agip is prepared to purchase the oil at conditions acceptable to Sirip, then Sirip shall be free to sell it to other purchasers at conditions no less favorable to itself. Where no such purchasers are found, Sirip may make amended offers to Nioc and Agip.

Sirip shall publish and notify Nioc and Agip of "posted prices," these being the prices at which crude oil of given qualities and densities is generally offered for sale by Sirip to all buyers at each export point. Said posted prices shall be the current Persian Gulf area prices for products of similar qualities and densities. Where Sirip deems it necessary to grant rebates to buyers, such rebates shall be determined, on Sirip's proposal, by a panel including two Sirip directors, one of them chosen by Agip.

Under special conditions, Sirip shall be required to deliver to Nioc natural gas produced by Sirip and required by Nioc for consumption in Persia. At the same time, in no case shall Sirip and Agip Mineraria be liable for any payment to Nioc for the natural gas used by them. In the event that Sirip activities should extend to refining operations, Sirip shall have the right to use natural gas as fuel for such operations. In this case Sirip shall pay to Nioc for each 1,000 cubic meters of gas thus supplied five percent of the weighted average of the posted prices (in effect on the date of delivery) for one cubic meter of 37°–37.9° API crude oil of the Agha Jari grade, FOB Bandar Mashur.

All foreign currencies accruing to Sirip through its operations shall remain at its free disposal; it may use them without limit, restriction or charge for meeting its expenses, the payments of its debts and interest thereon, as well as the payment of Persian taxes and dividends to its shareholders.

Accounts shall be kept in United States dollars. Entries related to business transacted in Persian currency shall be expressed in rials. The conversion into dollars of any payment and receipt in Persian currency shall be made at the average commercial rate applied by the banks in the same month when Persian currency was bought against dollars by Sirip.

Any payment or receipt made in currencies other than United States dollars or rials, when such currencies are not quoted in Persia, shall be converted into dollars on the basis of the arithmetic means of the daily average rates ruling in New York during the month in which dollars were exchanged against the said currencies. In the case of currencies quoted in Persia, they shall first be converted into rials, and then into dollars at the monthly average commercial rate. At the end of each year, any differences shown in Sirip ledgers resulting from exchange rate variations shall be adjusted.

TRAINING OF STAFF

Sirip is required to limit the use of foreign personnel by seeing to it that, within reasonable limits, foreign personnel be recruited only to fill positions for which Sirip cannot hire Persian nationals possessing the required qualifications and experience.

Sirip shall, with the assistance of Nioc and Agip, draw up a plan and a program, and assist in its implementation, for the technical and industrial training of Persian personnel with a view to enabling them to replace, as soon as possible and within reasonable limit, the foreign personnel, and to offering to Persian individuals the possibility and opportunity to fill responsible positions in Sirip.

TERMINATION AND DISSOLUTION

The agreement shall remain in force for 25 years from the date on which the sale of petroleum has begun. Before the expiration of the 23d year, either party may give to the other notice of its intention to extend the agreement; in this case the agreement shall be extended *de jure* as from the expiration of the 25th year and for a further period of 5 years. Prior to the expiration of the latter period, either party may give to the other notice of its intention to extend the validity of the agreement by an additional 5 years, said extension being effected *de jure* as from the end of the 5th year of the first extension period. Finally, with the same procedure, either party may request and obtain a final 5-year extension.

With regard to the second and third extension, the following conditions shall apply:

Where, on Sirip's requesting an extension, other foreign oil companies associated with Nioc for the conduct of similar activities and having already achieved production results equal to or better than those achieved by Sirip, shall have signed agreements at terms and conditions generally more favorable to Persia than those provided for in the agreement with Agip Mineraria, any such conditions embodied in such agreements shall apply when an extension is requested by Sirip, provided said conditions have been notified within 3 months by the interested party to the other.

The parties understand that, for any given deposit, the stage of the "beginning of sales" shall be deemed to have been reached on completion of the installations required for the carriage and lading of oil, and when the first 20,000 tons of oil from the deposit have been sold.

Should events occur—such as wars, insurrections, popular uprisings, strikes, hurricanes, high tides, floods, epidemics, explosions, fires, lightning, earthquakes, etc.—beyond the control of the persons assuming obligations under the Agreement, preventing, hindering or delaying the fulfillment of such obligations, this non-fulfillment shall not be deemed a breach of the agreement. Any obstacle arising from the said causes, which shall be present for more than one year, shall be sufficient cause for a *de jure* extension of the agreement by a corresponding period.

On the expiration of the agreement, Sirip shall be dissolved. Sirip assets may then be sold or transferred to shareholders in proportion to their respective holdings. Fixed assets and lands shall be transferred to Nioc without charge, but taking write-offs into account.

SETTLEMENT OF DISPUTES

Any dispute may be submitted to a joint conciliation committee composed of four members, two for each party, to be responsible for seeking a mutually acceptable solution to the dispute. The conciliation committee, after hearing the parties or their representatives, shall render its decisions within three months of the date on which the dispute was referred to it. The committee's decision shall be binding on the parties only if it is unanimous.

Any dispute bearing on technical or accounting points may, by agreement between the parties, be submitted to a single referee, or to three referees, two appointed by the parties (one each), and the third by common agreement. Should the parties be unable to agree on the appointment of the single referee or third referee, either of them may request that such appointment be made by the director of the Zurich Polytechnical School in the case of a technical dispute, or in the case of an accounting dispute, by the president of the Swiss Chamber of Auditing at Zurich.

Any dispute on the interpretation, application, or execution of the agreement, including the validity of the conciliation clause, the competence of referees or the nullity of the agreement, shall be decided by an arbitration panel of three referees, two appointed by the parties (one each), and the third, who shall act as chairman, appointed by the first two referees. Should the latter fail to agree on the appointment of the third referee, the referee shall be designated, on the request of the most diligent party, by the chief justice of the Geneva Cantonal Tribunal. The referees shall be appointed from among the nationals of countries other than Italy and Persia; they may be appointed from among magistrates, university professors, and members of the Bar admitted to plead before supreme and appellate courts. The arbitration panel shall sit in Geneva. Procedural rules shall be laid down by the parties or, lacking action from the parties, by the law of the country where the arbitration takes place.

The parties are required to furnish the expert or experts, the single referee or the arbitration panel with any facility (including access to the area) as may be necessary to enable them to obtain any information required for the settlement of the dispute. The arbitration procedure may not be hindered or stopped at any stage by the absence or default of the party. The parties undertake to consider the arbitration decision as final, and to comply with it in good faith.

PRODUCTION PROGRESS

Sirip is still in an initial stage of activity, and no oil discovery has as yet been made.

Starting in October, 1957, Agip Mineraria undertook a preliminary reconnaissance in an area of the Zagros Mountains. In May, 1958, three teams started the geological survey, which was completed in this area by the end of the year. In the Mekran area, the geological survey work was started in February, 1958. In both the Zagros and Mekran areas, several structures have been located which appear to be of considerable interest.

In the area of the continental shelf in the Persian Gulf, the geophysical survey work was started in December, 1957, and an exploration well has been sited. Early in 1959, offshore drilling work was started.

EVALUATION

The initiative taken by Agip has been, both in Italy and abroad, the object of much heated debate and comment. In Italy, which is still suffering from an inadequate supply of capital for its own needs, doubts have been expressed as to the wisdom of the heavy financial effort Agip Mineraria has undertaken to make. Abroad, the circles most directly interested have raised as the main objection the fact that Agip Mineraria has offered to Iran conditions that are excessively favorable to that country, violating the 50-50 profit-split principle and endangering the traditional balance of the relations between oil countries and concessioned oil companies.

The responsible officials of Agip Mineraria have answered the Italian criticism by arguing that the principal benefit which Italy has derived from the agreement with Nioc lies in the possibility of participating in exploration activities in one of the world's most promising oil regions, and of obtaining direct sources of oil supply. The criticisms from international oil companies were countered by arguing that the conditions offered by Agip are in keeping with Iran's desire, as clearly reflected in its new oil law, to get away from the system of mere concessions to foreign companies and to enter into arrangements of active participation in the development of oil resources. The formula accepted for the first time by Agip Mineraria has been accepted in agreements subsequently signed by Nioc with two other oil companies, one American (the Pan American Petroleum Corporation), and one Canadian (Sapphire Petroleum).

In the light of these agreements, it may be inferred that the acceptance by North American companies of terms which are at least as onerous as those offered by Agip Mineraria, justifies the contention that the new formula remains advantageous to the oil companies concerned.

Snia Viscosa of Italy, with special reference to Sociedad Nacional Industria Aplicaciones Celulosa Española (Sniace, a venture in Spain)

Sniace was established in Spain in 1939 for the production of artificial textile fibers (rayon and short-staple fiber). The Italian partner contributed technical assistance and a minority of the capital, and the Spanish partner contributed the majority of the capital. The Italian partner is Snia Viscosa, Italy's largest producer of synthetic and artificial textile fibers, and one of the best known firms in this field. Sniace was Snia Viscosa's first foreign venture, and the experience gained from it provided the foundations for the other ventures established in more recent years in various less developed countries of Latin America and Africa.

The Italian partner (whose origins date back to 1917) has financial and technical relations with other European industrial concerns. A few years ago, Snia Viscosa established in Italy, with British financial and technical participation, a new company (Novaceta) for the production of acetate rayon. We are therefore dealing with an enterprise which, having received the technical and financial contribution of industrially more developed countries, has in turn assisted in the industrial development of economically less advanced countries.

SNIA VISCOSA

The origins of Snia actually have nothing to do with the production of artificial textile fibers. It was established in Turin on July 1, 1917, with the name Societa' di Navigazione Italo–Americana (hence the initials Snia), the object being the construction and operation of merchant vessels. The end of the First World War and the resulting availability of an excess of low-cost shipping forced Snia to find new directions in which its activities could be developed. In 1919 the company, while remaining active in the shipping business, began taking an interest in industrial activities, including in particular the production of artificial fibers. In November, 1922, Snia changed to its present name of Snia Viscosa—Società Nazionale Industria Applicazioni Viscosa.

Between 1920 and 1927, Snia Viscosa acquired a controlling interest in six Italian companies concerned with the production of artificial fibers, as well as in several smaller companies in complementary industries.

In 1927, two European companies of international fame in the sector of artificial textiles, Courtaulds Limited of London, and Vereinigte Glanzstoff Fabriken A.G. of Wuppertal-Elberfeld, Germany, acquired substantial interests in Snia Viscosa. Courtaulds Ltd. has a capital of £32 million. Vereinigte Glanzstoff Fabriken A.G. has a capital of 91.5 million DM. Late in 1925 the two companies established at Koln a joint venture named Glanzstoff-Courtaulds, for the production of artificial fibers. Through this venture, provision was made for both companies to acquire substantial quantities of Snia Viscosa stock.

Snia Viscosa thus achieved a position of considerable importance, and in 1928 it became a member of the international cartel formed to regulate prices and markets, together with Courtaulds Limited, Glanzstoff, Comptoir des Textiles Artificiels, and smaller Swiss and

Dutch companies. In that year, the four larger members of the cartel controlled 75 percent of the world's production of artificial fibers. In 1929, however, the great worldwide depression practically forced this cartel out of business.

The onset of the Great Depression of the late twenties and early thirties resulted in Snia Viscosa's being converted from purely a holding company into a real industrial concern engaging in manufacturing and research activities.

In 1931, Snia, whose productive activity had been concentrated on rayon, began to produce short-staple artificial fiber. In 1935, under Antonio Ferretti's patents, Snia went into the production of a new fiber obtained from casein, then called lanital and now merinova, license rights to which have been sold by Snia in several European and non-European countries.

To insure a supply of high-grade cellulose, the principal raw material for the production of almost all artificial fibers, Snia decided to undertake the large-scale growing of water reed (arunds donasc). To this end, Snia purchased in 1938 the stock of two agricultural enterprises (Bonifiche di Torre Zuino, and Bonifiche del Friuli), and merged them into a new company, called Saici-Societa' Agricola Industriale per la Cellulose Italiana. This company undertook at Torviscosa the growing of water reed, and later built a plant for the processing of the cane. This plant is now capable of producing approximately 80,000 tons a year of high-grade cellulose.

In 1939, Snia acquired financial control of Cisa Viscosa, another industrial group which, like Snia, had carried out pioneer activities in introducing artificial fibers into Italy. Through this transaction, Snia assumed a leading position, both nationally and internationally, in the field of production of both rayon and short-staple artificial fiber. This position was further strengthened by an agreement reached the same year between Snia and Cisa Viscosa on the one side, and the Chatillon Company (another Italian firm operating in the same sector), for the coordination of national and international sales of products. To this end, a trading company was created, with the name of Italviscosa. The Snia group has considerably expanded its traditional activities in the sector of artificial fibers, and has started the production of synthetic fibers.

The industrial center of Torviscosa, operated by Saici, has been substantially expanded to insure the integral utilization of all products obtainable from the cellulose processing cycle. The new plants built at Torviscosa include a plant for the extraction of the alcohol contained in the cane before it is processed into cellulose (the present capacity of this plant is approximately 296,000 gallons of pure alcohol); a plant for the electrolytic production of soda and chlorine and chlorine by-products (annual capacity 10,000 tons of soda, and 8,000 tons of chlorine); three power plants producing over 100 million kwh a year. Saici, which is now capitalized at 2 billion lire ($3.2 million), has transformed Torviscosa into a major industrial center.

The postwar development of production activities at Torviscosa increased the requirements for cellulose, which could no longer be met entirely by the processing of water reed. The decision was made to turn to a new raw material, eucalyptus, a fast-growing tree typical of the Mediterranean climate. Thus, two Saici affiliates were established, Terra Apuliae and Siace, for the purpose of establishing and operating eucalyptus plantations in southern Italy, in Puglia and Sicily. Snia Viscosa has introduced the use of eucalyptus in its foreign ventures in less developed countries. This has given to these countries an opportunity for developing their unused resources, as happened with the aforementioned underdeveloped regions of southern Italy, where areas suitable for the growing of eucalyptus trees were found. Furthermore, the discovery of the possibility of using this wood on an industrial scale for the production of high-grade cellulose has meant an innovation in modern processes, which are still largely based on the northern European tradition of using fir wood.

In order to insure regular outlets for certain of its products, Snia has also acquired control of two important cotton-mill companies, Cotonificio Vittorio Olcese and Cotonificio Veneziano.

Finally, faced with foreign developments in the field of production of synthetics, and particularly of polyammide fibers, which are the largest group, in 1952 Snia started the production of polyammide fibers with one which it is marketing under the brand name of lilion.

Subsequently, Snia started production of another polyammide

fiber called rilsan, the polymer of which is obtained from castor oil. The patent is of French origin, from the French chemical group of Pechiney, but Snia introduced refinements of its own in the production processes, and particularly in spinning, which have helped in making rilsan an outstandingly successful product.

Using lilion and rilsan, Snia then started the production of papertex. This involves a special patented process by which the two polyammide fibers are made to assume the appearance of paper, but with special characteristics which have attracted great interest in this product, both in Italy and abroad.

Snia Viscosa has also ventured into the field of exploration for hydrocarbons. Exploration work is in progress in southern Italy and Sicily. In 1955, agreements were signed with various United States companies specializing in well-drilling and oil field development work for the development of exploration permits held by Snia. In these arrangements, Snia retains a majority of the capital stock.

FOREIGN INVESTMENTS IN SNIA VISCOSA

Snia Viscosa, established in 1917 with a capital of 5 million lire ($675,000), by 1925 had increased it to 1 billion lire ($40 million). Since that time the company's capital has gone through many and complex changes, in connection with changing national and international conditions and as a result of the absorption of other companies in the same or in allied sectors.

Since the end of the Second World War, the capital has been increased on five occasions. The latest capital change was adopted on March 21, 1959: Snia Viscosa's capital stock now totals 27,450 million lire (slightly less than $44 million). It is divided into 22,875,000 shares with a face value of 1,200 each, of which 437,500 are preferred shares each carrying ten votes, and 22,437,500 are common shares, each of which carries one vote. Preferred shares are also subject to special provisions concerning their transfer.

In addition to the capital stock, there are a statutory reserve fund, a special reserve fund, and a frozen revaluation fund (which can be used for further free increases in capital stock). As of December 31, 1958, these three funds totaled approximately 24.5 billion lire ($40.8 million). The depreciation fund totaled approximately 51.8

billion lire (approximately $83 million), or 65 percent of the value of buildings, land, plant, and machinery, furniture, and furnishings as of the same date. The same balance sheet shows that, as of December 31, 1958, Snia Viscosa's stock holdings totaled 25.1 billion lire ($40 million), plus a security revaluation balance totaling about 11 billion lire (approximately $18 million).

European concerns of great importance in the field of artificial fiber production own comparatively important, though minority, holdings of Snia Viscosa stock. Since Snia Viscosa stock is listed on the stock exchange, the amount of foreign holdings cannot be estimated precisely. However, as can be deduced from the composition of the successive boards of directors, the principal foreign groups which own stock in Snia Viscosa are Courtaulds Ltd., and the Compagnie Industrielle de Textiles Artificiels et Synthetiques—C.T.A., a large French company capitalized at 5,450 million francs. While the financial relations with Courtaulds date back to 1927, those with the French group were established later. Until 1956 the French company which owned stock in Snia Viscosa was Comptoir des Textiles Artificiels. In 1956 Comptoir merged with another French company, Viscose Française, and the new company was named Compagnie Industrielle de Textiles Artificiels et Synthetiques —C.T.A.

MANAGEMENT

Snia Viscosa is managed by two separate bodies, a board of directors and an executive committee. The board is composed of a number of members—between 11 and 19—to be decided by the stockholders' meeting. Under article 14 of the present by-laws, at least half of the total membership of the board, including the chairman, must be made up of Italian nationals. The directors hold office for three years. The executive committee is made up of a number of directors—no less than three—to be decided by the board of directors, which also designates the committee members, except for the chairman who is, ex-officio, the chairman of the board of directors.

The present board of directors of Snia Viscosa is composed of 18 members—13 Italians and 5 foreigners. The present chairman of the board is Mr. Franco Marinotti, who has held this position since

1937, after having been general manager from 1929 to 1934 and managing director from 1934 to 1937. Mr. Marinotti is also managing director and general manager of the company. All the other top positions in the Snia Viscosa board of directors are also held by Italian nationals. Of the foreign directors, three are Englishmen, one Belgian, and one French. The executive committee is composed of five members—four Italians and one Belgian. The board of auditors consists of five members—all Italian nationals.

NOVACETA

Snia Viscosa's production activity had always been concentrated largely on the viscose process for the production of rayon and short-staple fiber. Another known process for the production of these fibers is the acetate process, which Snia had not been using because the costs involved are somewhat higher than with the viscose process. But in 1952 Snia decided to go into this type of production, using foreign capital and know-how. A new company was established, with head offices in Milan, and owned 50-50 by Snia Viscosa and Courtaulds Ltd. In addition to the capital participation, Courtaulds has also been supplying the know-how deriving from its long experience in this field of production.

The company, now named Novaceta–Nuova Filatura Acetato, was established with an initial capital of 250 million lire, which was subsequently increased to 1 billion lire ($1.6 million) without changing the proportion between the Italian and British shares of stock ownership. The present board of directors consists of six members —three Italians, two Englishmen, and one Belgian. The chairman is Mr. Luigi Crosti. In 1954, Novaceta established at Magenta, near Milan, a plant for the production of acetate rayon and short-staple fiber.

ROLE IN THE ITALIAN ECONOMY

The Snia Viscosa group (including Snia, Cisa Viscosa, Saici, Novaceta, Cotonificio Olcese, Cotonificio Veneziano and various smaller companies), now owns and operates 67 production and research facilities in Italy. The Snia group employs a total of 28,000 office and factory workers and technicians, all Italian nationals.

Italy is one of the world's major producers of artificial and synthetic textile fibers. In the two years 1957–58, Italy's annual production averaged 162,500 metric tons, or 6 percent of the average annual world production (2,772,500 tons). The Snia Viscosa group accounted for 62 percent of the Italian production, averaging in the same period 100,600 tons. Snia Viscosa reached its peak level of activity in 1941, when its plants turned out 155,000 tons of fibers, or 81 percent of the Italian production at that time (approximately 190,000 tons). This extremely high production level, which has not yet been equaled since the war, was due to the fact that at that time the Italian demand for textiles had to be met by domestically produced fibers, since the imports of natural fibers had been virtually eliminated.

Italy also occupies a notable position among countries exporting rayon, short-staple fiber, and fabrics and manufactures of artificial fibers. In the two years 1957–58 Italian exports averaged 68,100 tons a year, or about 12 percent of the average volume of the total export sales of all producing countries (582,100 tons). These exports are vitally important for Italy's textile trade balance, because they make it possible to reduce considerably the foreign exchange deficit in the trade in natural textile fibers. In 1957, for instance, foreign trade in cotton, wool, hemp, flax, and jute resulted in a deficit for Italy totaling 126 billion lire ($200 million). The foreign trade in artificial and synthetic fibers and cellulose resulted on the other hand in a surplus totaling 53.5 billion lire ($86 million). Taking into account the surplus registered in the trade in silk and garments ($19 million), the deficit in Italy's textile trade balance in the year indicated was thus reduced to 60.6 billion lire, or slightly less than $100 million.

The Snia Viscosa group participates in an important way in this flow of Italian exports, selling in foreign markets 65 to 70 percent of its total production. Snia Viscosa products are exported chiefly to east and southeast Asia, the United States, and the countries of the Soviet Bloc.

SNIA VISCOSA'S INDUSTRIAL ACTIVITIES ABROAD

In the last two decades (1939–59) Snia Viscosa has engaged in a number of ventures in the less developed countries of Europe, Latin

America, and Africa. The participation of the Italian enterprise has assumed chiefly the form of exports of machinery, of the assignment of patents, and technical assistance. Machinery supplied for the processing of textile fibers was produced in the mechanical plants owned by the Snia group; other machinery was produced by other Italian industries. There were also actual cash investments, in the form of either capital transfers or reinvestment of local profits. As a general rule, Snia has minority holdings in the ventures established abroad, as a matter of deliberate policy which reflects its appreciation of national sensibilities as well as confidence in Snia's technological and scientific lead.

Snia's principal ventures abroad are the following:

1. Sniace—Sociedad Nacional Industria Aplicaciones Celulosa Española, Snia's first venture abroad, was first organized at the end of 1939. It was established with the participation of Spanish interests, for the production of rayon and short-staple fiber. It has head offices in Madrid, and is capitalized at 524,081,500 pesetas. Snia Viscosa owns 25 percent of the stock.

2. Fibracolor S.A. was established in 1956 in Madrid as a joint venture by Sniace (70 percent), Snia Viscosa (8 percent), and other Spanish groups, for the finishing of artificial and mixed fabrics. Fibracolor is capitalized at 125 million pesetas.

3. Sniafa (Sociedad Nuevas Industrias Argentinas Fibras Artificiales) was established in 1948 in cooperation with Argentine interests. It has its own plant at Platanos (Buenos Aires) for the production of rayon and short-staple fiber. It has head offices in Buenos Aires and a capital stock of 300 million pesos, of which 200 million are paid in. Snia Viscosa owns 21 percent of the stock.

4. Fibra S.A. (Fiação Brasileira de Rayon Americana), with head offices at São Paulo, was established in partnership with Brazilian interests, for the production of rayon and short-staple fiber. It has recently started the construction of plants for producing cellulose from linters. It is capitalized at 460 million cruzeiros. Snia Viscosa owns 23 percent of the stock.

5. Cechisa (Celulosa de Chihuahua) was established in Mexico in cooperation with local interests. It uses local woods, particularly ponderosa pine, for the production of paper and high-grade cellulose for the production of textile fibers. It has head offices at Chihuahua,

and is capitalized at 150 million Mexican pesos. Snia Viscosa owns 18 percent of the stock.

6. Vischisa (Viscosa de Chihuahua) was established in 1955 at Chihuahua, Mexico in cooperation with the Mexican group interested in Cechisa. It has built a plant, inaugurated in November, 1957, for the production of short-staple fiber. It is capitalized at 35 million Mexican pesos. Snia Viscosa owns 50 percent of the stock.

7. Saic (South African Industrial Cellulose Corporation) was formed by Snia Viscosa, the British firm Courtaulds Ltd., and the Industrial Development Corporation of the South African government. Saic built a plant at Umkomaas, for the production of cellulose from eucalyptus wood (this tree being quite common in that area), which entered into operation in January, 1955. Snia Viscosa supplied the machinery as well as a large group of Italian technicians and workers, who settled in the country. Having completed its task of initial cooperation, Snia Viscosa sold its share in the venture to Courtaulds Ltd.

Other projects in other parts of the world are now under consideration.

SNIACE

The first attempt to produce artificial textile fibers in Spain dates back to 1901, but it was not until 1920 that a company was established for the introduction of that new industry, the Sociedad Española de Seda Artificial S.A. (Sesa).

This initiative was followed by Safa, which set up its own factory at Blanes (Province of Gerona), with the cooperation of Comptoir des Textiles Artificiels of France, and by Seda de Barcelona S.A., which established a plant in Barcelona with the cooperation of a Dutch group for the production of artificial silk. All of these were comparatively small enterprises, concerned only with the production of rayon, while Sniace, from its inception, engaged in the large-scale production of short-staple fiber and later of rayon and cellulose, in vertically integrated plants where wood is converted to cellulose, and cellulose into artificial fibers.

Sniace can trace its origin back to the industrial recovery program drafted by the Spanish government in 1938. This program called, among other things, for the establishment of plants for the production of artificial textile fibers to make up for the deficit of local production of natural textile fibers (cotton, wool, flax, and hemp). The task of implementing the program in this sector was assumed by a Spanish financial group, comprising a number of banks including the Banco Español de Crédito of Madrid and local private investors. The group decided to accept an offer made by Snia Viscosa. This decision made it possible to start production immediately without having to go through a costly experimental stage, and insured that in the future the Spanish plant would benefit by all improvements introduced by the Italian partner in its own Italian plants.

On December 1, 1939, Snia Viscosa and the group of Spanish bankers and investors formed a joint stock company called Sociedad Nacional Industrias Aplicaciones Celulosa Española S.A., commonly referred to by the initials Sniace. Sniace's capital stock, entirely paid in, now totals 524,081,500 pesetas ($12.5 million), divided into 500-peseta shares. The company's principal office is in Madrid.

Since the establishment of Sniace, Snia Viscosa has held 25 percent of its capital stock, the remaining 75 percent being in the hands of the Spanish financial group. This share represents the maximum which, at the time Sniace was established, Spanish law allowed foreigners to own in a Spanish company.

The capital, which was initially 90 million pesetas, has been increased several times during the two decades of life of Sniace, in connection with the enlargement of plants and in particular with the establishment of the cellulose plant. Under the by-laws, when capital is increased the new shares must be offered for subscription to the existing stockholders; those not subscribed are offered to the public. In practice the existing stockholders have taken up their option rights and therefore the respective shares of the Italian and Spanish groups have remained unchanged.

Snia Viscosa's capital contributions have consisted chiefly of the supply of machinery and the reinvestment of part of the dividends. Sniace's shares are bearer shares and are listed on the Madrid stock exchange. In addition to the capital stock of 524,081,500 pesetas, Sniace has statutory and voluntary reserve funds amounting at present to 300 million pesetas.

Sniace's present board of directors consists of 17 members, of whom 13 are Spaniards and 4 Italians. The chairman is Pablo de Garnica Echeverría, chairman of the Banco Español de Crédito of Madrid, a Spaniard as required by Spanish law. There are two deputy chairmen, one Spaniard and one Italian (the managing director of Snia Viscosa).

Under a special clause in the by-laws, as long as Snia Viscosa retains ownership of 25 percent of Sniace's capital, the company may not be dissolved or its by-laws amended without Snia's consent. Snia Viscosa is also given the right to freely appoint and replace one fourth of the directors of Sniace.

The company's duration is unlimited. Provision is made for the settlement of disputes through the arbitration of three persons, the first two designated by the parties and the third selected by the first two from among persons who are neither Italian nor Spanish nationals.

The cooperation agreement between Snia Viscosa and Sniace calls for the fullest supply of technical data and information on plants to be installed and on machinery to be used in production. In effect, Snia Viscosa agreed not only to install under its supervision a plant made up of the most modern and efficient components existent on the date of the contract, but also to make available to Sniace all future improvements and modifications to insure at all times the greatest possible efficiency of Sniace's installations. The contract explicitly provides that the two companies are mutually obligated to exchange information concerning all improvements introduced in production processes.

Specialized Italian technicians have been made available to Sniace, while employees of the latter have gone through training periods at various Snia Viscosa plants in Italy. Technical assistance services are included in the general financial arrangements, and therefore Sniace is not required to pay royalties for them to Snia.

As regards the purchase of plants for the Spanish company, Snia has not reserved the right to act as sole agent for Sniace. The latter does, however, consult Snia regarding the machines it needs or wishes to purchase in other countries to insure that they are suited to production requirements.

Sniace has not been explicitly granted exclusive rights of production in Spain or in any geographic area. No provision is made, however, for its production to be limited to domestic market requirements only. Each increase of Sniace's production above the limits agreed upon by contract requires concurrence by Snia. No specific provision was made for conditions of sale of products of Sniace to third countries.

Sniace is entitled to use only its own name in designating its products. But the name suggests that of Snia Viscosa, and implies the technical guarantees offered by its products as a result of the cooperation of the Italian firm.

ROLE IN THE SPANISH ECONOMY

Sniace laid the cornerstone of its plant on October 12, 1941, at Torrelavega near Santander. In 1944, the first Spanish short-staple fiber, produced from imported cellulose, made its appearance on the local market. This period coincided with the Second World War, which gives an idea of the difficulties that had to be overcome in moving 2,000 tons of machinery from Italy to Spain to equip the plant.

For the first decade Sniace utilized imported raw materials. The decision was then taken to utilize a national resource, eucalyptus wood, since Spain has regions ideally suited to the growing of this tree. Experts from Snia Viscosa and, more specifically, from Saici were sent to Spain to start the development of this raw material. Today, Sniace owns eucalyptus forests covering about 22,000 acres.

At the same time, construction was started, also with Snia Viscosa technical assistance, of the plant for the production of high-grade cellulose, which entered into operation in 1950. This plant is part of the Torrelavega plant, in which Sniace has concentrated its entire production cycle. In 1955, it was decided to enlarge this plant, and to this end Sniace's capital was further increased in 1956, with Snia Viscosa participating by making available new machinery. The enlargement was completed late in 1958; the production capacity of high-grade cellulose, originally 16,000 tons a year, has been increased to 36,000 tons a year.

In the last decade, Sniace's production of short-staple fiber has averaged about 11,000 tons a year, and the production of rayon about 2,000 tons, while cellulose production has registered a continuous increase, from 2,000 to 17,000 tons.

Sniace's output accounts for 35 percent of the short-staple fiber, 17 percent of the rayon, and 64 percent of the textile cellulose produced in Spain. Rayon and short-staple fiber are produced by the viscose process; cellulose by the bisulphate process.

Normal employment at the Torrelavega plant is 3,000, or 30 percent of the total employment in the Spanish artificial fiber industry. There is practically no employment of Italian labor, but the plants have been under continuous Italian technical management and specialized technicians from Snia Viscosa have been supplying technical advice and assistance. The relations between Italians and Spaniards at all levels have always been completely cordial, helped by the close affinity existing between the two peoples.

Sniace's exports have always been sporadic in nature and have usually been limited to the quantity required to compensate for the imports of cellulose or machinery. The saving in imports which Sniace's production has realized for the Spanish economy equals the entire amount of the fibers produced by Sniace. For 1958, this saving is estimated at $9 million. Sniace was able to distribute to its stockholders a 10 percent dividend in each of the years 1946, 1947, and 1948. Since that time, stockholders have received a uniform dividend annually of 15 percent.

FIBRACOLOR

The cooperation between Snia Viscosa and Sniace was extended through the establishment in 1956 of Fibracolor S.A., a company engaged in the finishing of artificial and mixed fabrics. The owners of this company are Sniace with a majority holding (70 percent of the capital stock), Snia with a modest holding (8 percent), and other Spanish artificial textile interests with minority holdings (22 percent).

Fibracolor now has a capital stock of 125 million pesetas, or $3 million. Its principal offices are in Madrid, and it has established a plant at Tordera in Catalonia, with the latest facilities for the processing of artificial and mixed fabrics. This plant processes fabrics made from the fibers produced not only by Sniace but also by the various Spanish interests associated in the company.

GOVERNMENT RELATIONS

Sniace plays a significant role in the Spanish economy, since it has provided for Spain internal sources of supply not only of artificial fibers but also of the basic raw materials from which such fibers are made.

The fact that the Spanish Civil War was almost immediately followed by the Second World War made it extremely difficult for Spain to purchase textile raw materials, and spinning and weaving mills were often forced to close down. In that critical period the existence of Sniace proved most useful in alleviating the effects of the wars on the Spanish textile economy.

The usefulness of the joint enterprise has been appreciated by the Spanish government, which from the very beginning has given Sniace the fullest support, and recognized its merits by awarding it the title of "model enterprise." A decree of the head of state, in addition to granting to Sniace the privileges reserved for industries of national importance, granted it in 1940 a number of special benefits, including a 50 percent tax exemption for fifteen years, not only on capital but also on dividends distributed to the stockholders, and special facilities for the purchase of machinery and other production equipment, as well as for the purchase of the land for the staple-fiber factory.

W. R. Grace & Company

GENERAL NATURE OF ACTIVITIES

W. R. Grace & Co., now a diversified company engaged principally in the chemical business in the United States, industry and commerce in Latin America, and intra-American shipping had its origin in a ship chandlery established in 1854 by William Russell Grace at Callao, the principal seaport of Peru. Success in this operation led to an expansion of activities into other Latin American countries, and later into the United States. This has brought the company to the present point where, although it continues to be heavily committed abroad, especially in South America, more than two-thirds of its earnings arise from the United States and United States-based chemical business, in which it has invested in the past ten years.

The company's activities also include miscellaneous business activities in the United States including banking and insurance, and a half interest with Pan American World Airways in an international aviation company (Panagra). Latin American activities include the production of paper, chemicals, textiles, sugar and other food products, and trading and ship agency activities.

The total Grace capital employed in all of these ventures, consisting of paid-in capital plus surplus reserves and long-term debt, amounted to $405 million at the end of 1959. Of this total, approximately $75 million, or 19 percent, was capital employed in the company's operations based abroad, mainly in Latin America and more specifically in South America, where the company first started.

FOREIGN INVESTMENTS AND JOINT VENTURES

Many of the company's overseas operations are wholly-owned, but ventures in association with local capital in the particular countries concerned nevertheless represent an appreciable part of the total. It is estimated that $18 million, or 24 percent of the total Grace capital employed overseas at the end of 1959, represented holdings in joint ventures. Most of the joint venture investments, amounting to some $15 million, were in enterprises in which Grace has active participation, and its holdings in these cases amounted to a majority of the total capital in the ventures. Only some $3 million of the total consisted of passive, minority holdings.

Of the $15 million in active joint ventures, about $7 million was in enterprises that produce textiles in South America. Approximately another 2 million dollars was in enterprises producing paint and chemicals, and the balance was distributed among various enterprises engaged in the production of paperboard containers, food products, and in trading and shipping activities.

Recent trends in company policy indicate that there is likely to be a changing emphasis in these fields of activity in the future. There is interest in moving away from the production of articles of prime necessity, such as textiles and food products, where Grace does not have any special technical competence, into fields such as chemicals and paper production, which meet the two criteria of being industries with greater growth prospects in Latin America and being fields where Grace has developed highly specialized experience both in the United States and abroad. The original reason for the investments in the consumer goods industries traditional to Latin America was, of course, largely the opportunity for profits, but there was also the desire for integration of Grace trading activities in the area. Pursuant to the recent changing emphasis, a substantial amount of investment in joint ventures in textiles, consisting of $5.1 million in an enterprise in Colombia, was sold during 1958. In that same year, Grace moved into two new joint ventures in Colombia in chemicals, with a total investment of some $450,000.

The Grace ventures that are wholly-owned amounted to about $57 million at the end of 1959 (total overseas investments of $75 million less investments in joint ventures of $18 million). The largest block of these wholly-owned enterprises, amounting to $23 million, was in the various Grace companies engaged in paper converting in Puerto Rico, Mexico, and Colombia. Another large block, amounting to close to $18 million, was in the large sugar and paper operations in Peru, the country where the Grace enterprise was first founded. This paper venture, involving the production of pulp from sugarcane bagasse, was the first such production development anywhere, and was the result of Grace research activities undertaken in Peru. Chemical enterprises in South America, Europe, and New Zealand accounted for about $8 million, and most of the balance of wholly-owned enterprises was in trading and shipping operations.

CHARACTERISTICS OF GRACE JOINT VENTURES

Grace participates actively in most of its joint ventures. Only a relatively small minority have consisted of passive investments, where the intention is eventually to become actively involved in the enterprise, or where the reason is to safeguard the interests of other Grace enterprises by assuring supplies of raw materials, by obtaining supplies for distribution, or by assuring distribution outlets for their products. In the cases where Grace participates actively, it generally prefers and has in fact acquired majority financial control.

There are several reasons for Grace's preference for majority control. One is its ability to consolidate the investments and earnings of its joint ventures into the parent company balance sheet. Under regulations of the United States Securities and Exchange Commission, it is not possible to consolidate earnings of minority subsidiaries, for the obvious reason that the minority shareholder cannot control the disposition of his earnings. The earnings in such subsidiaries must, therefore, be stated separately from consolidated earnings in company reports, and the judgment of the value of company shares on the exchanges is correspondingly affected.

Another reason for the preference for majority control is the desire to manage the enterprises. This is particularly the case in the new fields that Grace is now emphasizing abroad, such as chemicals and paper, where the company has highly specialized technical competence. Although this has been cited by the company as a general reason for the preference for majority control, Grace has, in fact, allowed competent minority interests to run the enterprises even where it has had majority financial control. The essence of the matter seems to be not so much management by Grace itself as the power to determine who shall manage the enterprises, whether Grace itself or some other interest that Grace may determine to be competent.

A third reason for the preference for majority control is the possible conflict of interests with local partners.

Usually, local minority investors are avoided at the "grassroots" stage of formation of a new enterprise, unless they have something special to contribute such as a raw materials resource or marketing channels. Otherwise, Grace has found it to be more desirable to buy into an existing enterprise, or to develop an enterprise itself and invite local capital participation at a later stage. It is felt that it is either difficult or undesirable to attempt to interest local capital in an idea before it has become a going concern. Where Grace has started in an enterprise simultaneously with local capital, it has been either a result of local initiative, that has sought Grace help for capital, know-how, or distribution facilities, or where Grace has sought the cooperation of local interests that have something special to contribute besides capital alone. One principle that Grace has studiously followed is that of never becoming involved in a joint venture with local governments.

In summary, it may be stated that Grace has not deliberately sought joint ventures for its foreign investments as a matter of general policy, but that its flexible policies in foreign investments have nevertheless resulted in a considerable number of joint ventures which constitute an appreciable minority of its total foreign holdings. Usually, Grace participation in the enterprise is active, and financial control is acquired. The company's far-flung foreign operations have, however, also led it into a variety of passive, minority holdings in local enterprises which are related to objectives of its own enterprises in the respective countries.

JOINT VENTURES BY PRINCIPAL COUNTRIES

In Peru, Grace is in three joint ventures on an active basis. The principal one is the textile enterprise Compañías Unidas. Grace owns 63 percent of this enterprise, and 37 percent is held by local investors. The Grace capital employed in the enterprise amounted to $1,670,000 at the end of 1959. The local people were brought in through the merging of mills they had controlled. It was felt to be particularly desirable for an enterprise in a field such as textiles to be closely identified with the country. Grace handles the distribution of much of the company's products.

The other two joint ventures are a candy and cracker factory, and a container factory. The candy and cracker enterprise is Arturo Field y Compañía. Grace holds a slight majority of 50.08 percent. The enterprise was for some time run by its former manager after Grace bought the majority, but, upon his retirement, Grace took over the management. Its purchase into the enterprise arose from the attraction of profit and from its distribution interests in the country. Grace capital employed amounted to $250,000 at the end of 1959.

The container enterprise, Envases San Martí, manufactures paperboard containers. Grace owns a majority of 79 percent, and the minority consists of local owners of a printing plant and bag-making plant. The Grace capital employed in the company amounted to $240,000 at the end of 1959. The local investors do not participate very actively in the management of the enterprise. The operation is an offshoot of Grace's wholly-owned Paramonga paper enterprise in the country.

Grace also has a number of passive, minority holdings in Peru in various types of enterprises. One is in a bank, the Banco Internacional del Perú; the amount of Grace capital involved is some $169,000. The original idea of this investment was that it might involve a profitable extension of the foreign activities of the Grace National Bank of the United States. Another important minority holding is in a fertilizer plant, Fertilizantes Sintéticos, S.A. (Grace holding of $250,000). There are also very small shares in the Volcan Mines Company (about $10,500), which arose from the provision of financial assistance to this company, some of whose products Grace distributes; and in Fibras Industriales (some $2,600), which supplies raw materials to Compañías Unidas.

Grace's other important interests in Peru, in the production of sugar and paper, and in shipping and distribution activities, are all wholly-owned enterprises. Outstanding among them is the Paramonga paper operation, which was a pioneer in developing the production of paper from bagasse, and which has served as a model for other similar enterprises elsewhere. A new chemicals project in Peru, Alcalis Peruanos, S.A., is being developed as a wholly-owned venture.

There are numerous Grace joint ventures in Chile. The principal, active ones are in textiles, various food products, and paints. The largest is the textile enterprise Tejidos Caupolicán. It is owned 70 percent by Grace. The Grace capital employed amounted to close to $5.3 million at the end of 1959. As in the case of the Peruvian Compañías Unidas, a minority of shares was sold to the general public in the country, primarily for public relations reasons.

The food products (vegetable oils, lard, and refined sugar), and paints are produced by one enterprise, which has two different plants, the Compañía de Industrias y Azúcar (Coia). Grace holds 67 percent (some $500,000 at the end of 1959), and the balance is held by local investors. Public offerings of shares in the company were made to bring Chilean capital into the venture. It is obvious that this has been a pattern in industries which produce articles considered to be of prime necessity in Latin America, such as textiles and food products.

Grace holds an important interest, although a minority, in a woolen cloth enterprise in Chile, the Fábrica de Paños Bellavista. The Grace investment in this enterprise amounted to $2 million as of June 30, 1959. This investment, made some years ago, may have been effected with the intention of acquiring a larger share in the enterprise at some future date, but the holding has not progressed beyond the minority position indicated.

Grace also holds minority positions in some other enterprises in Chile, which have had varying objectives. Some have at one time or another involved the intention of acquiring larger shares in the future, as in the case of Paños Bellavista. In this category are small investments in a container enterprise, the Compañía Manufacturera de Papeles y Cartones, and in a candy and cracker firm, Hucke Hermanos, S.A. Some other minority investments are related to the procurement of raw materials or the distribution interests of other Grace enterprises. This is the case with some four enterprises (Compradora de Maravilla, S.A.; Importadora de Azúcar, S.A.; Industrias Vinica "Patria," S.A.; and Nacional de Ventas de Azúcar, S.A.), related to the raw materials and distribution requirements of Coia.

In still another case, Grace entered into a joint venture together with General Electric and some local investors related to its distribution activities in the country. This is the Electromat, S.A. enterprise, which produces electric light bulbs. Grace had exclusive distribution rights in Chile for General Electric bulbs before they were produced in the country. When, in response to pressures to produce locally, General Electric decided to engage in manufacture in Chile, Grace joined in the investment, which is now owned one-third by GE, one-third by Grace, and one-third by local investors. The Grace capital employed amounted to approximately $200,000 as of December 31, 1958.

Grace is a party to four joint ventures in Colombia. During the last few years, it sold its interests in two other joint ventures in which it had also been involved. Two of the four present joint ventures are in the field of food processing, and the other two are in chemicals.

One of the food processing enterprises is the Compañía Colombiana de Conservas California, in which Grace holds a 51 percent interest. The total amount of capital employed by Grace in this venture was $119,000 at the end of 1959. The firm, engaged in the bottling and canning of food products, was started as a purely Colombian venture. The field had been little developed in Colombia, and Grace bought its 51 percent holding in 1956 because of the growth prospects of the enterprise as well as because of its complementary nature in relation to Grace's distribution activities in the country.

The Grace wholly-owned subsidiary which engages in distribution, as well as other activities, in Colombia is Grace y Compañía. It has exclusive distribution rights for the products of Conservas California. Although Grace holds the majority of the company, the Colombian former sole owner and now minority shareholder continues to run the enterprise. Grace's earnings in the company are not included in its consolidated earnings, despite its majority control, because of the fact that it does not manage the enterprise. Technical know-how in this field normally is obtained to an adequate extent from the suppliers of bottling and canning machinery, and Grace, therefore, feels that there is no need for any other special arrangements on the technical side.

The other food processing enterprise is the Trilladora Santa Rita, a plant which processes coffee for export. This is an old investment, in which Grace holds a 70 percent interest. Grace is an important factor in the exportation of coffee from Colombia, and originally entered into this venture with local coffee producers to insure a supply of the raw material for the plant. The investment is very small.

Grace bought into two existing chemicals plants in Colombia in 1958, in line with its general policy of moving into investments in this field in Latin America. One of these enterprises is Carboquímica, S.A., which was started about four years ago by enterprising European residents of Colombia. The firm produces basic solvent chemicals, such as benzol, toluol, and zylol, based on raw materials obtained from the coking of coal. In this latter connection, it has a contract to buy coal tar products from the only primary steel mill in the country, the government-owned Acerías Paz del Río. This is a new line of production in Colombia, and will undoubtedly expand substantially as the country's industrialization increases. The plant also supplies some solvents for a new paint plant in Colombia in which Grace is also involved. The Grace interest in Carboquímica is 51 percent, yet the plant is run by its former owners, as in the case of the California food enterprise. The amount of Grace capital employed in it was about $120,000 as of the end of 1959.

The other chemicals venture is Probst y Compañía, which produces resins for the leather and textile industries as well as for paints. This operation, together with Carboquímica and the Grace paint enterprise in Colombia, forms a nucleus for future expansion in chemicals in the country. Probst was originally formed about 20 years ago, also by resident Europeans in Colombia. Grace bought an 86 percent interest, but retained the local management. Grace capital in the venture was about $537,000 at the end of 1959.

Of the two joint ventures in which Grace has sold its interest, one was in paints and the other in textiles. The paint enterprise is Pinturas Colombianas (Pintuco). Pintuco was formed in 1945 with 49 percent Grace capital and 51 percent private Colombian capital. The Grace share was finally sold to the Colombian partners in 1955. Grace subsequently formed another paint enterprise since it believed this to be a promising growth field in Colombia, but this other enterprise (Ico) was set up as a joint venture not with Colombian partners but rather with the Glidden Company of the United States, a specialized paint company with which Grace has a technical know-how arrangement covering other paint operations as well.

The other joint venture in Colombia in which Grace sold its interest is the Tejidos el Cóndor (Tejicóndor) textile enterprise.

Tejicóndor, the third largest cotton cloth manufacturer in the country, was originally started in 1934 as a purely domestic enterprise. Grace first entered the company in 1940 with a 40 percent interest to help finance its expansion, and further stock purchases raised this participation to 50.12 percent in 1951. The Grace participation in this enterprise had been primarily financial, and it decided to move out of the textiles field to fields where it could make a contribution based on its specialized technical experience, as in the case of chemicals. The Grace share in Tejicóndor was sold in December, 1958 to various Colombian textile interests; it had amounted to $5.1 million, including a Tejicóndor holding in a synthetic fibers firm, Indurayón Consolidada, S.A.

With disposal of the investment in Pintuco, all Grace joint ventures in Colombia involve Grace majority financial participation, although in most cases, despite the financial control, active participation by the local partners continues in the management.

Its other enterprises in the country are either wholly-owned: the Grace y Compañía transport agency, coffee trading, and distribution company, and Comestibles La Rosa, a candy and cracker factory; or joint with other foreign interests: the Ico paint enterprise.

The earliest joint international business ventures in Bolivia are those in which W. R. Grace & Co. has been involved. Grace has several wholly-owned enterprises in the country engaged in shipping services, trading, and related activities, and its joint ventures are in mining and in manufacturing industries. It also has, indirectly, a small minority holding in a Bolivian aviation enterprise. The total combined net value, in dollar terms, of Grace investments in these joint ventures is very small, amounting only to slightly more than $30,000 at the end of 1959. This small value in dollar terms is a result of the tremendous depreciation of the Bolivian currency that has taken place over the years.

The mining joint venture is the International Mining Company. This is the only venture in an extractive industry (except for a petroleum exploration project in Libya) in which Grace is involved, and it was the first joint venture for the company as well as for the country. It had its origin during the First World War. A

Bolivian businessman had concluded a supply contract for wolfram with the United States government, but the suppliers on whom he had counted failed to come through. In order to be able to meet his commitment, he prospected for other sources of the mineral and came upon a valuable property. He approached Grace for capital and for the procurement of technical assistance from the United States, in order to be able to develop the enterprise. Grace purchased a 51 percent share in the mining property from the beginning and the percentage has been maintained to date. The original Bolivian promoter was made a vice-president of the Grace organization, and managed the property on behalf of Grace until his death. The enterprise now continues to be managed directly by Grace.

The joint ventures in manufacturing are in the fields of cement and flour milling. The cement enterprise is the Sociedad Boliviana de Cemento. This enterprise was started in 1925 by the Foundation Company, a United States construction company, together with other foreign companies operating in Bolivia, and Bolivian capital. Grace purchased a 52 percent interest in the enterprise in 1939 from Foundation and others, because of the promising prospects in the country of cement production itself as well as because of the possibility of utilizing the Grace trading setup to market this product. The Grace share has since been increased to the present level of 60 percent. The minority holdings in the firm are very widely distributed, and Grace actively manages the enterprise. This company has been the only important producer of cement in Bolivia. A second plant has been built by the government.

The flour milling enterprise, one of the two large millers in the country, is the Compañía Molinera Boliviana. The enterprise was formed in the early 1930s by Argentines. Later, the company ran into financial difficulties and Grace extended loans to it. At the same time, because of the favorable prospects of the business Grace started buying its stock and it soon held a majority, which now amounts to 53 percent. Grace had formerly been an important wheat importer in Bolivia. Important among the minority shareholders is a British-owned railroad in Bolivia, which holds about 15 percent of the enterprise.

The aviation enterprise is Lloyd Aéreo Boliviano, in which Pan

American Grace Airways (Panagra, held 50-50 by Grace and Pan American World Airways) holds a 20 percent interest. This enterprise had originally been set up in 1925 with a majority of Bolivian government capital and German participation. Early in the Second World War, the German interest was bought out by the Bolivian government, and for a period of five years starting in 1941, the company was managed by Panagra. Panagra was paid for this service by being given 20 percent of the total shares of the enterprise. Since 1946, although Panagra has rendered some technical assistance, the enterprise has been managed essentially by the Bolivian government. The Bolivian government holds close to 60 percent of the capital, Panagra has 20 percent, and the balance is held by private Bolivian investors.

Grace has two enterprises in Brazil, in chemicals and electronic components, but these are either wholly-owned (Produtos Quimicos "Darex" Ltda.) or joint with other foreign rather than with Brazilian interests (Eriez S.A. Produtos Magneticos e Metalurgicos, joint with precision foundry specialists from the United States).

Grace enterprises in other countries are for the most part wholly-owned. However, there are a few in Central America and one in Argentina which are joint investments. In El Salvador, the Agencia Salvadoreña, a port agency, is held 60 percent by Grace ($125,000 of Grace capital at the end of 1959). A similar enterprise in Guatemala, the Agencia Marítima, is 64 percent Grace owned ($47,000 at the end of 1959). These are all old investments, dating from the time when Grace interests in Latin America were mainly in trading. In Argentina, Dewey and Almy (Argentina) SAIC, an affiliate of the Dewey and Almy Chemical Company Division of Grace, is owned 70 percent by Grace.

Index

RENEWALS: 691-4574
DATE DUE